Writer's Choice

GRAMMAR and COMPOSITION

GRADE 8

ACKNOWLEDGMENTS

Grateful acknowledgment is given authors, publishers, photographers, museums, and agents for permission to reprint the following copyrighted material. Every effort has been made to determine copyright owners. In case of any omissions, the Publisher will be pleased to make suitable acknowledgments in future editions.

Cover (Anne Frank) Hulton Archive/Getty Images; (laptop) Masterfile; (fountain pen) C Squared Studios/Getty Images; (bkgd) © Gerry Charm/SuperStock **vi** Brand X Pictures/Punchstock; **vii viii** PhotoDisc, Inc; **ix** (t)PhotoDisc, Inc., (b)Allan Landau; **x** Hampton University Museum; **xi** Greg Probst/Allstock; **xii** (t)Art Wise, (b)Cathlyn Mellon/Getty Images; **xiii** (t)Historical Pictures/Stock Montage, (b)PhotoDisc, Inc; **xiv** Tom McCarthy/PhotoEdit; **xv** (l)courtesy Brookfield Zoo, (r)file photo; **xvi** (t)Art Wise, (b)PhotoDisc, Inc; **xvii** (t)PhotoDisc, Inc., (b)Phillip Everwood, *Lily and the Sparrow*, 1939. Oil on composition board, 30 x 24 in. (72.6 cm x 61cm). Collection of the Whitney Museum of American Art. Purchase 41.42; **xviii** Courtesy Nereyda Garcia-Ferraz; **xix** Artville; **xxi** Faith Ringgold; **xxii** PhotoDisc, Inc; **xxiii** (t)Art Wise, (b)Digital Stock; **xxiv** (t)PhotoDisc, Inc., (b)file photo; **xxv** Courtesy Anthony Ortega; **xxvii** Courtesy Bernice Steinbaum Gallery; **xxviii** R. Fukuhara/Westlight;

Acknowledgments continued on page 861.

TIME

The **Facing the Blank Page** feature in this book was prepared in collaboration with the writers and editors of *TIME*.

6+1 Trait® is a registered trademark of Northwest Regional Educational Laboratory, which does not endorse this product..

The **McGraw·Hill** Companies

McGraw Hill **Glencoe**

Send all inquiries to:
Macmillan/McGraw-Hill • Glencoe/McGraw-Hill
8787 Orion Place
Columbus, OH 43240-4027

ISBN: 978-0-07-888770-3
MHID: 0-07-888770-4

Printed in the United States of America.

3 4 5 6 7 8 9 10 071/043 12 11 10 09

PROGRAM CONSULTANTS

Mark Lester is Professor of English Emeritus at Eastern Washington University. He served as Chair of the Department of English at Eastern Washington University and Chair of the Department of English as a Second Language at the University of Hawaii. He is author of *Grammar and Usage in the Classroom* (Allyn & Bacon, 2000), co-author of *a Commonsense Guide to Usage* (Bedford/St. Martins, 2006) *Essential ESL Grammar* (McGraw-Hill, 2008), and numerous other professional books and articles.

Sharon O'Neal is Associate Professor at the College of Education, Texas State University–San Marcos, where she teaches courses in reading instruction. She formerly served as Director of Reading and Language Arts of the Texas Education Agency and has authored, and contributed to, numerous articles and books on reading instruction and teacher education.

Jacqueline Jones Royster is Professor of English and Executive Dean of the Colleges of Arts and Sciences at The Ohio State University. Her professional interests include the rhetorical history of women of African descent, the development of literacy, and contexts and processes related to the teaching of writing. In addition to her many years of teaching writing, directing writing programs and writing centers, and serving as a leader in several English professional organizations, she is also the author of numerous articles in literacy studies, and several books, among them: *Traces of a Stream: Literacy and Social Change Among African American Women*, *Critical Inquiries: Readings on Culture and Community*, and *Calling Cards: Theory and Practice in the Study of Race, Gender, and Culture.*

Jeffrey Wilhelm, a middle and high school English teacher for thirteen years, is currently Associate Professor of English Education at Boise State University, where he specializes in adolescent literacy, with research interests including gender and literacy, and assisting struggling readers and writers. He is the founding director of the Maine Writing Project and Boise State Writing Project. He has authored fifteen books on literacy and education and has won the top two research awards in English Education: the NCTE Promising Research Award for *You Gotta BE the Book* and the Russell Award for Distinguished Research for *Reading Don't Fix No Chevys.*

Denny Wolfe, a former high school English teacher and department chair, is Professor of English Education, Director of the Tidewater Virginia Writing Project, and Director of the Center for Urban Education at Old Dominion University in Norfolk, Virginia. Author of more than seventy-five articles and books on teaching English, Dr. Wolfe is a frequent consultant to schools and colleges on the teaching of English language arts.

Advisors

Student Advisory Board

The Student Advisory Board was formed in an effort to ensure student involvement in the development of *Writer's Choice*. The editors wish to thank members of the board for their enthusiasm and dedication to the project. The editors also wish to thank the many student writers whose models appear in this book.

BOOK OVERVIEW

Part 1 Composition

Part 2 Grammar, Usage, and Mechanics

Part 3 Resources and Skills

Reference Section

CONTENTS

Part 1 Composition

Part 2 Grammar, Usage, and Mechanics

UNIT 10   Verbs 400

Instruction and Practice

MAIN CLAUSE   SUBORDINATE CLAUSE

18 Diagraming Sentences 570

Instruction and Practice

19 Capitalization 582

Instruction and Practice

Grammar Review

Literature Model

from *Morning Star, Black Sun* by Brent Ashabranner

Writing Application

Part 3 Resources and Skills

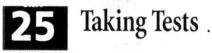

Quick Help

Reference Section *Fast answers to questions about writing, research, and language*

LITERATURE MODELS

Composition Models

Each literature selection is an extended example of the mode of writing taught in the unit.

Skill Models

Excerpts from outstanding works of fiction and nonfiction exemplify specific writing skills.

LITERATURE MODELS

Language Models

Each Grammar Review uses excerpts to link grammar, usage, or mechanics to literature.

FINE ART

Fine art—paintings, drawings, photos, and sculpture—is used to teach as well as to stimulate writing ideas.

GLENCOE
Writer's Choice
Grammar and Composition

Welcome to Writer's Choice!

Your writing and your choices are what this book is all about. Take a few minutes to get to know each of the book's four main parts: Composition; Grammar, Usage, and Mechanics; Resources and Skills; and the Writing and Research Handbook.

Part 1

Composition

How do you become a better writer? By writing! Four-page lessons give you the strategies you need to improve your writing skills. Each lesson focuses on a specific writing problem or task. The lessons offer clear instruction, show models of effective writing, and—most importantly—provide a variety of writing activities for you to practice what you've learned.

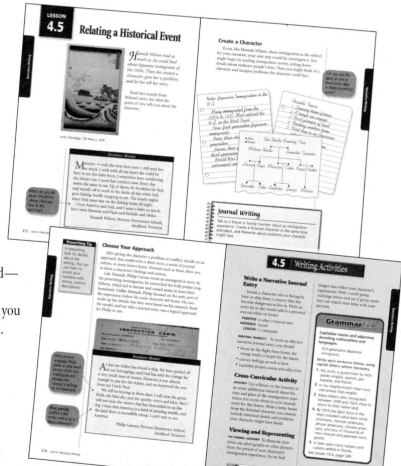

Part 2

Grammar, Usage, and Mechanics

Short focused lessons make learning grammar easy. Rules and definitions teach you the basics, while examples and literature models show you how the concepts are used in real-life writing.

Part 3

Resources and Skills

Would you like to improve your study skills, learn how to give a speech, or get better at taking tests? The lessons in this part give you the skills you need to do all these things and more. Each lesson is complete, concise, and easy to use.

WRITING AND RESEARCH HANDBOOK

This user-friendly handbook gives explanations, examples, and tips to help you write strong sentences, paragraphs, compositions, and research papers. Use it whenever you get stuck!

Helen Frankenthaler, Acres, 1959

*"I want to write, but more than that,
I want to bring out all kinds of things
that lie buried deep in my heart."*

—Anne Frank,
Anne Frank: The Diary of a Young Girl

PART 1

Composition

"*Warm skies and gulf blue streams are in my blood*"

—Margaret Walker,
"Sorrow Home"

UNIT 1

Personal Writing

Writing in the Real World

MEDIA
Memoir
Connection

The memoir—a recollection of a person's past—is a popular form of personal writing in the media. The following excerpt is from the memoir of Laurence Yep. In it, Yep recalls the grocery store his parents owned during his childhood in San Francisco.

from *The Lost Garden* by Laurence Yep

The one thing that ruled my family's lives was our grocery store. I can still smell it. Even today, if I smell old plaster, I feel almost as if I am back in our old storeroom where the plaster was crumbling off the wooden laths. Or if I smell the coppery odor of liver, I think of washing out the bloody pan in which we used to display that kind of meat. If I smell old dollar bills, I can imagine myself back in the dark, quiet store, helping my mother put away the day's receipts.

A small grocery store is like a big beast that must be continually fed and cared for. Cans, packages, and bottles have to be put on shelves to take the place of things sold, produce like greens and celery have to be nursed along to keep them fresh as long as possible, and there are hundreds of other details that the customers never notice—unless they aren't done. In a small, family-owned store, certain chores must be done at a specific time each day. There is no choice.

Our store had its own daily rhythms just like a farm would have. It began before eight in the morning when my mother would pick her way down the unlit back stairs and along the dark alleyway to the backdoor of the store. Balancing the box with the cash register money in the crook of her arm, she would find the keyhole by feel and let herself in. Then, going through the darkened store, she would put the money in the cash register drawer. There were no neat rolls of coins. Instead, she had them each in a small paper bag, from pennies to fifty-cent pieces, and also dollar bills and bigger denominations in separate sacks.

At about the same time of day, my father stumped down the front steps of the Pearl Apartments. He usually wore thick-soled shoes for his feet, tan work pants, a flannel shirt, and a felt hat. Though a former athlete, his legs were slowly going bad from having to stand on them constantly for twelve hours seven days a week. He obviously was carrying no money, so there would be no temptation to rob him.

aurence Yep, award-winning writer of fantasies, went in a totally new direction when he decided to write *The Lost Garden.* This personal story, or memoir, of growing up in San Francisco challenged him to piece together memories of his past. He began writing the book shortly after his father's death. "In a way, *The Lost Garden* was therapy," Yep explains. "It was my way to go back to these various places I used to go to with my father, and in some cases I tried to do it physically, but most of the time it was in my imagination and in my memory."

Memoir author
Laurence Yep

A Writer's Process

Prewriting
Gathering Memories

To help him recall memories, Yep used his senses, especially the sense of smell. "The layer of memory that is closest to the brain is not a layer of visual memories; it's the memory of smells. That's why a smell is more evocative than any visual detail," Yep explains.

Yep used memories of scents to help him mentally reconstruct his family's grocery store. The smell of crumbling plaster and wall materials brought back the hot summer afternoons he spent in a place that no longer exists. Smells brought back sights as one memory led to another. "From there I drew a map of the whole store, as best I could, and as I did that, I started remembering certain corners of the store," Yep recalls.

Photographs can also be helpful when gathering memories. During the writing of *The Lost Garden,* Yep kept several photographs of family members in front of him on his desk.

Memories provide rich background material for personal writing. Yet simply recalling past events isn't enough. The writer must understand them as well. What do the past events mean? What impact did they have?

"People think that, because they've lived something, they actually understand it, when that's not true," says Yep. "What they've done is experience it, but understanding is quite another matter—it's the next step."

Yep explains, "What it requires, to understand something, is actually to step away from that experience, so you can look at things more objectively, and that's also one of the steps in writing."

Writing in the Real World

Photos of the the family store in San Francisco helped Yep recall memories of his childhood.

Drafting
Fitting the Pieces Together

Simple memories provide rich details for personal writing. While drafting his memoir, Yep focused on writing about daily life. Yep says, "Really the best writing is bringing out the specialness of ordinary things."

Yep compares the drafting stage to solving a puzzle. The pieces of the puzzle are his collection of memories. While drafting, he has to find a way to fit all those pieces together. Like most puzzle solving, the process can be both fun and frustrating.

To help organize his draft, Yep makes an informal outline, which he uses as a guide. He accepts the fact that he may have to go back and start a scene again.

He says, "You realize that you've got to redesign the puzzle, that an outline is only a scaffolding inside of which you've got to build a ship. And sometimes you get the ship almost built, and you realize that this darned thing isn't going to float, and so you have to tear it down, and

Yep's memoir *The Lost Garden* includes many photos from his life.

bring it down to the keel, and begin again."

Yep doesn't get discouraged about starting over. He realizes that rewriting is an essential part of the writing process.

Revising
Testing the Fit

A chief quality that Yep looks for in his own work is *authenticity,* the characteristic of being real or true. He revises to make certain that he has described events as accurately as possible in his own voice, or unique style. He makes sure that the feelings behind the scenes have a ring of truth.

By asking friends or relatives for their feedback, a writer can see how well his or her point of view has been communicated. But, finally, the writing is whatever the writer wants it to be. Yep says, "You have to write for yourself."

He tells students, "Writing is a way of exploring other selves and other worlds inside yourself. I think it can be very satisfying, whether you get a good mark on it or not."

Analyzing the Media Connection

Discuss these questions about the article on page 4.

1. What are some sensory details in Yep's excerpt that appeal to the sense of smell?

2. In the second paragraph, to what does Yep compare a small grocery store? What are some details that he uses to support the comparison?

3. What detail does Yep use to help the reader visualize the darkness of the "unlit back-stairs" that his mother navigated each morning?

4. What other details does Yep use that appeal to the sense of sight?

5. What details help the reader understand that Yep's parents are hard-working shopkeepers?

Analyzing a Writer's Process

Discuss these questions about Laurence Yep's writing process.

1. How does Yep use various senses to recall locations and personal experiences?

2. What graphic aids does Yep look at or create to help him gather his memories?

3. During drafting, does Yep always follow his outline, or does he tend to try new ideas and approaches? Explain why.

4. What chief criteria does Yep use to evaluate his writing?

5. When revising, how can a writer test whether he or she has succeeded in communicating the intended point of view?

Grammar Link

Use appositives to make your writing clearer and more interesting.

An appositive is a noun or a noun phrase placed next to another noun to identify it or add information about it.

Laurence Yep, **award-winning writer of fantasies,** *went in a totally new direction. . . .*

Write each sentence, adding an appositive to each italicized noun.

1. In this photo are my *cousins.*
2. I clearly remember the *scene.*
3. We used to live in *Burton.*
4. These *items* helped me gather details.
5. The memory sparked two *feelings.*

See Lesson 9.6, pages 391–392.

Writing for Yourself

In personal writing you express your own thoughts and feelings. Sometimes you write to share with others. At other times, you write just for yourself.

You can't wait to tell someone. It's such great news. You grab the phone and call a friend. "I have a brand-new baby sister!" you brag. In a brief note you tell another friend how excited you are about your new sister. These are personal thoughts and feelings, and your note is an example of personal writing.

Get Personal

Notes to yourself or letters to friends and family are personal writing. A private journal—a book for your most personal thoughts and feelings—is one of the best places for personal writing. What you write there is only for you. A classroom journal is another place for personal writing. Classroom journals are a tool for recording ideas and information, and they are often shared with classmates or teachers. Your classroom journals can also be an excellent source of ideas for writing assignments.

You can include more than just your writing in a journal. You might add photographs, magazine clippings, drawings, or even doodles.

Letters are another form of personal writing. Lonnel wrote the following letter to his sister Tamika, and he included the photograph on the right. Read the letter to see what personal experience Lonnel wanted to share.

Dear Tamika,

It's a really nice day here at Bowen Lake. It's almost noon, and the woods and the lake are warm in the sun. I'm sitting on a rock on the top of a kind of hill—as much like a hill as anything they have around here. I haven't seen anyone for over an hour. Earlier two people in a canoe drifted by. They were far away, and I could hardly see them. I could hear their voices, though. It's quiet now. There's a kind of magic in being all alone with nature.

How's the family? Is Jason back from training camp? What's Mom's job like now that she's back at work? Send me news!

Your brother,

Lonnel

Journal Writing

Jot down the names of friends or family members to whom you might write a letter. Then list ideas of what to tell them. You can include both experiences and thoughts.

Keep a Journal

Writing in a journal can help you explore and remember your private thoughts without worrying about what anyone else thinks. Once you've begun your journal, you'll get more out of it if you write in it regularly. The following journal entry was written by author Louisa May Alcott as a girl.

Her writing here sounds like a conversation with a close friend.

Do you think this writing could appear in a letter to a friend? Why?

Literature Model

I am in the garret with my papers round me, and a pile of apples to eat while I write my journal, plan stories, and enjoy the patter of rain on the roof, in peace and quiet. . . . Being behind-hand, as usual, I'll make note of the main events up to date, for I don't waste ink in poetry and pages of rubbish now. I've begun to *live*, and have no time for sentimental musing. . . .

Norma Johnston, editor, *Louisa May: The World and Works of Louisa May Alcott*

Below are some journal entries and a postcard. The writer used a private journal to record thoughts and experiences. Some of them were shared in a postcard to a friend. Read both and see how alike and how different they are.

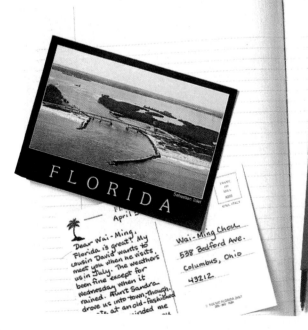

F L O R I D A

Dear Wai-Ming,
Florida is great! My cousin David wants to meet you when he visits us in July. The weather's been fine except for Wednesday when it rained. Aunt Sandra drove us into town, though. —Te at an old-fashioned —inded me

Wai-Ming Chou
538 Bedford Ave.
Columbus, Ohio
43212

April 3
I'm really enjoying our visit to Aunt Sandra's. My cousins have all changed—David is almost as tall as I am.
I didn't think it would be so different down here: palm trees, amazing plants and insects, blue-green ocean—and warm sand everywhere!
It's raining today, so Aunt Sandra drove us into town. We had lunch at an old-fashioned diner.

April 4
The sun's out again, and it's warm. Lee says they practically live on the beach when the weather is this nice. The rest of us have to go to school.
We rented bicycles today and rode up the coast. Along one stretch of beach there's a bike path for cyclists and joggers. Dave said he thought he saw dolphins, but no one else saw them.

April 5
Went back to the beach. David's friend Chris came with us, and we

Write a Letter

You can write to a friend who is distant or to one whom you see often. Write about some experience you have had recently or about anything that's on your mind. Write as though you're talking to your friend.

PURPOSE To write a personal letter
AUDIENCE A good friend
LENGTH 1 page

WRITING RUBRICS To write your letter effectively, you should

- express your thoughts and feelings.
- include a doodle or drawing.

Listening and Speaking

In a small group, discuss your thoughts about sending and receiving personal letters. Have one group member act as a discussion leader, asking questions such as: Do you write many personal letters? Do you receive many? What do you like most about writing or receiving personal letters? Why? What do you like least? Summarize your group's discussion for the class.

Cross-Curricular Activity

HISTORY The image on this page is from a wall painting found in the ruins of the ancient city of Pompeii. That city and its people were buried when Mount Vesuvius suddenly erupted in A.D. 79. Look at the young woman in this painting. Write the entry she might have written in her personal journal the day of the catastrophe. Remember, life was going on peacefully. What might she have done on that day?

Artist unknown, Pompeii, *Portrait of a Young Woman,* first century A.D.

GrammarLink

Use the possessive pronoun *its* and the contraction *it's* correctly.

The tree lost its leaves.
It's getting colder every week.

Complete each sentence with the correct word: *it's* or *its*.

1. It rained this morning, but _____ a beautiful afternoon.
2. My dog has injured _____ paw.
3. As I look at our house, I see _____ paint is cracking.
4. When _____ my turn to recite, I have to be ready.
5. Do you know _____ title?

See Lesson 11.4, pages 441–442.

Writing to Learn

A learning log is another type of journal. In it you can keep a record of new facts or ideas you have learned in a class, as well as your thoughts and reactions to what you've learned. The example below was written after a science class. Read the entry and notice the clippings the writer included with it.

Great moonrock! Ms. Alvarez got this photograph from NASA.

Earth Science   May 15

Constellations are groups of stars that are named after animals, characters in mythology, or familiar objects.

The constellation Canis Major looks like a dog.

It is the faithful companion of the hunter Orion, a nearby constellation.

Record Your Progress

A learning log is a form of personal writing. It's for you. Writing in a log is an opportunity to become more involved in your learning and more aware of the progress you're making. For example, after reading a passage in your textbook, you can record your questions and thoughts in your learning log. Perhaps you'll raise these questions during your next class discussion. The chart below shows the kinds of entries you might put in your log. The goal is to make the information you study make sense to you.

Summarizing Tip

Briefly state the main points in your own words. Focus on key details that support the points. Use key words and phrases.

Personal Writing

Keeping a Learning Log	
Purpose	**Entry**
Summarize content.	Very hot stars are blue-white; cooler stars are orange or red.
Identify main ideas.	Sunspots are dark areas on the sun's surface that are cooler than surrounding areas.
Define problems, and ask questions.	I'm still not clear why our sun is called an average star.
Evaluate schoolwork.	The information on planets seemed easier than that on stars (because of the unit review?).

Journal Writing

What questions do you have about something you're learning now? Begin a learning log by writing down one or two of these questions.

Write and Think

Below is an example of how a learning log can be used. A student took the notes on the left as she read a textbook chapter on exploration of Mars. Then she wrote in her learning log. After a class discussion of this topic, she reread the textbook passage and looked over her notes. Then she used her learning log to rewrite the passage in her own words.

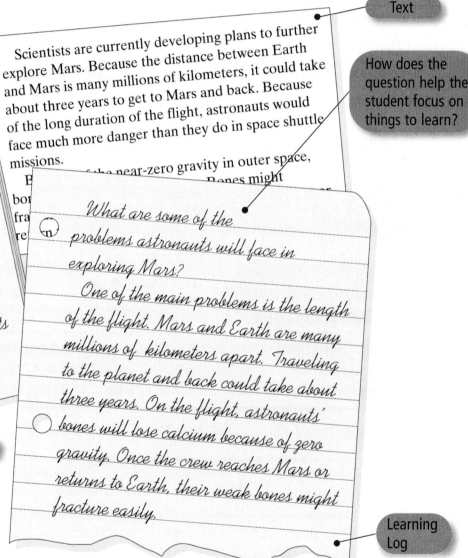

Text

How does the question help the student focus on things to learn?

Scientists are currently developing plans to further explore Mars. Because the distance between Earth and Mars is many millions of kilometers, it could take about three years to get to Mars and back. Because of the long duration of the flight, astronauts would face much more danger than they do in space shuttle missions.

...near-zero gravity in outer space, ...Bones might...

Notes

Distance to Mars—
many millions of
kilometers
Length of Mars trip—
maybe three years
Danger—lowered
calcium in bones due
to near-zero gravity;
weak bones might
break once astronauts
land on Mars or
return to Earth.

What are some of the problems astronauts will face in exploring Mars?

One of the main problems is the length of the flight. Mars and Earth are many millions of kilometers apart. Traveling to the planet and back could take about three years. On the flight, astronauts' bones will lose calcium because of zero gravity. Once the crew reaches Mars or returns to Earth, their weak bones might fracture easily.

Learning Log

Write a Learning Log Entry

Choose a difficult paragraph, page, or chapter from a homework assignment for another class. Then choose one of the options in the chart on page 13 and write a learning log entry.

PURPOSE To clarify a difficult section of a book
AUDIENCE Yourself
LENGTH 1 paragraph

WRITING RUBRICS To use your learning log entry effectively, you should

- use the entry you have created to make sense out of the information
- during the next class of the subject for which you wrote the learning log entry, ask any question raised by the assignment.

Using Computers

Try keeping your learning log on the computer. You can underline or boldface key ideas. You can also keep an index or glossary of important words or ideas.

Viewing and Representing

Choose three images you like from magazines. Describe in a paragraph why you find these images interesting or useful. What does a graphic image show that words alone cannot express? Would you use graphics in a learning log? Explain. Share your ideas with the class.

Grammar*Link*

Use the correct verb form when the subject of a sentence is an indefinite pronoun.

Some indefinite pronouns—*all, any, most, none,* and *some*—can be either singular or plural, depending on the phrase that follows.

*What **are some of the problems** astronauts will face? . . .*

Complete each sentence with the correct choice of verb.

1. All of the water (is, are) crucial.
2. None of the other planets (is, are) hospitable to human life.
3. Most of the problems (has, have) been anticipated.
4. Some of the constellations (is, are) difficult to spot.
5. Any of this (is, are) suitable.
6. None of it (is, are) complete.
7. Any of these questions (is, are) worthy of further research.
8. All of my notes (is, are) here.
9. Most of the work (requires, require) special skills.
10. Some of the confusion (is, are) due to the difficult terminology.

See Lesson 16.4, pages 547–548.

LESSON 1.3

Writing About Wishes and Dreams

If I had a photograph of myself ten years from now, this is what I'd see. I am a tall, sleepy-eyed medical student in a white coat. I'm studying to be a heart surgeon. My white coat is rumpled because I slept in it on my break. I'm at a patient's bedside listening to his heart. He had heart surgery yesterday, and I was there in the operating room. During the operation I was

*J*ournal writing is a good way to explore and record your wishes or dreams. Can you see yourself ten years from now? What will you look like? How will you have changed? What will you be doing? Where will you be? Read the journal entry at the left to see what one student wrote.

Look at Yourself

To imagine the future, it could be helpful to look at yourself as you are now. One way to do that is to use a cluster diagram like the one below. In your diagram you can record your interests, successes, failures, feelings, and reactions. You can even indicate how they relate to one another. Making connections may help you uncover interests you can combine as you begin to think about your future.

getting up early

music — dancing

What I Hate — Me — What I Love

long car rides — getting carsick

helping people — being with lots of people

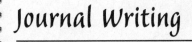

Journal Writing

In your journal make a *me* diagram—a cluster of magazine pictures that illustrates your interests. Below your diagram, write a paragraph entry explaining how the pictures show who you are.

Shape Your Future

You can explore your wishes and dreams in a number of ways. You could write a letter to a friend, relative, or favorite teacher. You could privately explore this topic in your journal. You might draw a picture of yourself as you want to be and include a few sentences describing your picture.

In the diary excerpt below, the poet Sylvia Plath reflects, at seventeen, on the future.

Literature Model

What is the best for me? What do I want? I do not know. I love freedom. I deplore constrictions and limitations. . . . I am not as wise as I have thought. I can see, as from a valley, the roads lying open for me, but I cannot see the end—the consequences. . . .

Oh, I love *now,* with all my fears and forebodings, for now I still am not completely molded. My life is still just beginning. I am strong. I long for a cause to devote my energies to. . . .

Sylvia Plath,
Letters Home

Write a Journal Entry

In your journal describe a childhood dream that has come true.

PURPOSE To describe a childhood dream
AUDIENCE Yourself
LENGTH 2 paragraphs

WRITING RUBRICS To write your journal entry effectively, you should

- give details to make images clear
- tell how you feel now and how you felt before
- explain what the fulfillment of this dream means to you

Cross-Curricular Activity

ART Suppose that someone were to photograph you in the future. Your appearance and an object you are holding will reflect the career dreams you have achieved. Write a paragraph in which you describe the photo and tell how it represents the future you.

Listening and Speaking

Think again about your future photo. Write a dialogue between the you of the photo and the you of today. What would you like to ask the future you? What answers might you get? Present the dialogue to a partner to get feedback on its effectiveness.

GrammarLink

Avoid sentence fragments in formal writing.

Sentence fragments are acceptable in your personal journal. When you write for others, however, use complete sentences.

I am a tall sleepy-eyed medical student in a white coat.

Revise each fragment below into a sentence by adding either a subject or a predicate.

1. My career in art.
2. Have enrolled in a pottery class.
3. Jennifer DuBerry, the instructor.
4. The wheel and the kiln.
5. Created an odd-looking vase.

See Lesson 8.2, pages 361–362.

LOG ON ► **Writing** Online | For more writing and grammar practice, go to **glencoe.com** and enter QuickPass code WC87703p1.

19

Writing One's Own Story

An autobiography is the story of a person's life written by that person. The passage below is autobiographical. Maya Angelou describes her first meeting with Martin Luther King Jr. Read it and see what her reaction was.

Literature Model

I walked into my office and a man sitting at my desk, with his back turned, spun around, stood up and smiled. Martin King said, "Good afternoon, Miss Angelou. You are right on time."

The surprise was so total that it took me a moment to react to his outstretched hand.

I had worked two months for the SCLC, sent out tens of thousands of letters and invitations signed by Rev. King, made hundreds of statements in his name, but I had never seen him up close. He was shorter than I expected and so young. He had an easy friendliness, which was unsettling. Looking at him in my office, alone, was like seeing a lion sitting down at my dining-room table eating a plate of mustard greens.

Maya Angelou,
The Heart of a Woman

Identify Turning Points

You have had important moments, turning points, in your own life. Some may have even changed the course of your life. The diagram below shows turning-point events in one student's life. Study the diagram and its entries. Make a similar map for yourself. Put the important events in chronological order, the order in which they happened. If you need help recalling either the event or the timing, ask someone in your family. Save your diagram to use as you plan your own autobiographical writing.

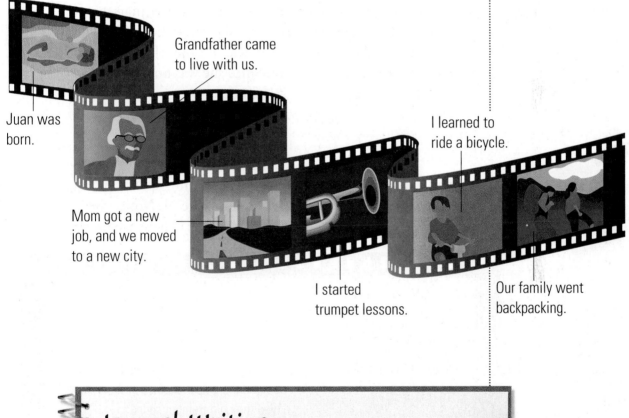

Grandfather came to live with us.

Juan was born.

I learned to ride a bicycle.

Mom got a new job, and we moved to a new city.

I started trumpet lessons.

Our family went backpacking.

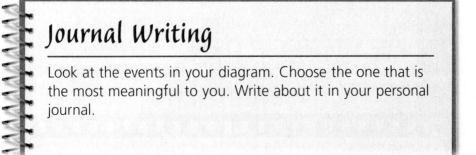

Journal Writing

Look at the events in your diagram. Choose the one that is the most meaningful to you. Write about it in your personal journal.

Write About Your Life

Choose a turning point in your life, and think about how you felt before and after that time. Consider which details would bring this event to life for someone else. A student wrote the journal entry below. Read it and notice the details he used to make clear how he felt.

> **Which details show that Rosenberg's life has changed for the better?**

Student Model

During cold, snowy days, I love to cuddle up with Shelly. As she lies against me, I feel as though I had just drunk a cup of hot chocolate. Whenever I walk into the room, her eyes light up brighter than the sun as she recognizes me. Then, she smiles her toothless grin and tries to say, "Barrwie." At those times, I love my little Shellster a lot. Since she was born, nothing has been the same; it's been better.

Barry Rosenberg, Southfield, Michigan
First appeared in *Stone Soup*

The chart below shows the steps in autobiographical writing. It uses a turning point from the map on page 21. Notice the kinds of details the student uses to bring the experience to life.

Writing About Turning Points

Steps in the Process	Examples
Choosing an event	start of trumpet lessons
Noting feelings about event	was happy about taking lessons admired the golden surface of the trumpet loved the bold trumpet sound
Writing about event	*Excited, I lifted the glittering trumpet to my lips. A thundering note marched out. I was sold on the trumpet for life.*

1.4 Writing Activities

Write About an Event

Choose an event from your life, and write an autobiographical composition. To plan and draft your composition, follow the steps outlined on page 22.

PURPOSE To describe a turning point in your life

AUDIENCE Your teacher and classmates

LENGTH 1 page

WRITING RUBRICS To write your autobiographical composition effectively, you should

- tell what happened
- explain how you felt before and after
- use details that make the event come to life for a reader

Viewing and Representing

You have often seen paintings or photographs of people that seemed to capture the subject's personality. What kind of picture would best represent you? Does such a picture exist? Describe a picture of yourself, whether it exists or may someday exist. Write your description. Share it with a partner or small group. If the picture exists, share it also.

Cross-Curricular Activity

HEALTH One way to feel good about yourself is to review events in your life that you feel positive about. In your journal complete the following sentence to help you identify these events: "I felt really proud of myself when. . . ." Write a one-page description of the incident or event.

Grammar*Link*

Use object pronouns—*me, us, him, her, them*—as the object of a verb or a preposition.

 . . . I had never seen **him** *up close.*
 Looking at **him** *in my office . . .*
 . . . at Jane and **him.**

Write each sentence correctly.

1. The gift from Jem and she is here.
2. Jarmila chose he.
3. The news about Su and I is false.
4. Rodrigo met they at school.
5. The boys were kind to we.
6. Tino walked she to the door.
7. Tara wrote a thank-you letter to he.
8. The storm woke I last night.
9. The test was easy for she.
10. Don't call they too early tomorrow.

See Lesson 11.1, pages 435–436, and Lesson 11.3, pages 439–440.

Personal Writing

LOG ON ▶ **Writing** Online | For more writing and grammar practice, go to **glencoe.com** and enter QuickPass code WC87703p1.

23

WRITING ABOUT LITERATURE
Responding in a Journal

Poems are often a form of personal writing, and people's reactions to poetry can be very personal. What is your response to the poem below?

Ray Vinella, *Aspen Grove,* 1960

Literature Model

The Clouds Pass

The clouds pass in a blue sky
Too white to be true
Before winter sets in
The trees are spending all their money

I lie in gold
Above a green valley
Gold falls on my chest
I am a rich man.

Richard Garcia

A journal is a good place for responding to literature. Which images did you see most clearly in the poem? Record these in your journal. Also tell how you liked the poem.

Respond to Literature

The way you react to a poem can take many forms. Your response may be a quiet smile, a hearty laugh, or a flood of memories. Compare the following journal responses to Richard Garcia's poem to your own response.

Student Model

In the poem "The Clouds Pass," Richard Garcia explains a great gift of nature. In autumn time nature gives the trees' leaves a beautiful golden color. Now these leaves are the money which the trees are dropping—spending.

Sarah Fisher, Solomon Schechter Day School,
Skokie, Illinois

This reader reacts to Garcia's poem with an explanation and with appreciation.

What aspects of the poem does this reader highlight?

An autumn afternoon. The air is crisp and cool, a hint of the frosty weather to come. But the sun is warm on my skin. Like the trees in Garcia's poem, I want to spend my "money" before winter arrives and sends me indoors. The warm, gold days of Indian summer make everyone feel rich. Garcia's poem celebrates Indian summer. It makes me feel lucky to be alive to enjoy this glorious time of year.

This reader responds to Garcia's poem with sensory descriptions.

What feelings does Garcia's poem raise for this reader?

Journal Writing

In your journal jot down the name of a poem that you've enjoyed. Close your eyes, and try to remember what you thought and felt as you read the poem. Record your answers in your journal.

Vary Your Responses

Writing is one way to respond to literature or to explore your reactions to what you've read. You can express your thoughts and feelings in many ways. You could create an illustration, research and write about a topic contained in your reading, or write what one character might say to another. Which way is best for you? Begin by asking questions about the literature and how you felt about it. Look at some of the questions below to help you get started.

Questions to Help You Get Started

1. What did the literature make you think about?

2. How did it make you feel?

3. Which words brought pictures to mind?

4. What would you change about it?

Forms of Response

Write about how the literature makes you feel.

Write a poem expressing your feelings about the work.

Draw a picture of an image from the work.

Write a letter to the author.

Rewrite a passage with your own changes.

Make a cartoon based on the work.

Create a magazine ad for the work.

If the work is a poem, set it to music.

Dramatize a scene from the work.

Write a Response to Literature

Read a poem of your choice, and write an entry about it in your journal.

PURPOSE To respond to a poem
AUDIENCE Yourself
LENGTH 2–3 paragraphs

WRITING RUBRICS To write your response effectively, you should

- explain what you like best about the poem in general: its subject, its sound, its setting, the pictures it created in your mind
- think about whether the poem tells you anything new or says something you haven't heard before

Using Computers

On the computer, write a poem of your own that responds to the one you chose or that is similar to it in form or subject. If you correspond with someone on e-mail, send that person your poem and ask for a response.

Listening and Speaking

Think about the difference between silent and oral reading of poems. With a partner, take turns selecting a poem and reading it aloud. Discuss the meaning of each poem. Then write your own journal response to both poems and to the experience of reading aloud and hearing a poem read aloud.

GrammarLink

Use vivid adjectives in your writing.

Vivid adjectives help crystallize images in your reader's mind and make your meaning very precise.

*The air is **crisp** and **cool**, a hint of the **frosty** weather to come.*

Revise the sentences below, replacing the underlined adjectives with stronger, more vivid ones.

"The Clouds Pass" praises the <u>yellow</u> leaves of fall. The color of the leaves makes the speaker feel <u>rich</u> and <u>happy</u>.

When I read the poem, I shared the speaker's <u>happy</u> emotions. At the same time, the falling leaves make me <u>sad</u>. The poem is a <u>good</u> one.

See Lesson 3.3, pages 122–125.

LOG ON ▶ **Writing** Online | For more writing and grammar practice, go to glencoe.com and enter QuickPass code WC87703p1.

27

Writing Process in Action

Personal Writing

In preceding lessons you've learned how to gather and organize your ideas to describe the events in an important personal experience. You've learned how to describe the feelings you had because of that experience. You've also had the chance to write journal entries about your personal experiences. Now, in this lesson you will write about an experience you shared with someone else.

Assignment

Context	You have decided to contribute to *America, America,* a publication of personal reflections and images from across the United States. Write about an experience you have shared with someone else.
Purpose	To share, in writing, a personal experience
Audience	A general audience of all ages
Length	2 paragraphs

LOG ON ▶ **Writing** Online

For prewriting, drafting, revising, editing and publishing tools, go to **glencoe.com** and enter QuickPass code WC87703p1.

Planning to Write

The following pages can help you plan and write your personal experience composition. Read through them, and then refer to them as you need to. But don't be tied down by them. You're in charge of your own writing process. Before you start, set a time frame for completing the assignment so that you can pace yourself as you move through each step of the writing process. Keep in mind the controlling idea: to write about an experience you shared with someone else.

Prewriting

To come up with possible topics for this assignment, try to recall shared experiences that taught you something about life, another person, or yourself. This may help you focus on the people who are close to you and whom you see every day.

The options graphic below offers ways to tap into memories for ideas. The notebook gives an example of freewriting to generate ideas.

Drafting

Exploring your ideas thoroughly during prewriting helps drafting go smoothly. As you review your notes, consider details that will help the reader understand what happened. Write down your ideas just as they come to you. You can polish the good ones later.

Your writing may be clearest if you time-order events. Notice how Gary Soto uses time transitions:

Option A
Review journal entries.

Option B
Brainstorm with a friend.

Option C
Freewrite for ideas.

Helped Mrs. Magnino paint lawn furniture; then she painted her kitchen—nothing could stop her. Both of us almost overcome by paint fumes. Opened the window and a bird flew in.

Literature Model

The next day I woke tired and started picking tired. The grapes rained into the pan, slowly filling like a belly, until I had my first tray and started my second. So it went all day, and the next, and all through the following week, so that by the end of the thirteen days the foreman counted out, in tens mostly, my pay of fifty-three dollars.

Gary Soto, *Living up the Street*

Writing Process in Action

Personal Writing

Drafting Tip

For more information about putting events in order, see Lesson 1.4, pages 20–23.

Remember to focus on the shared experience and your own feelings. At this stage, don't edit—just write. You may find it helpful to review pages 4–8 and 16–19.

Revising

To begin revising, read over your draft to make sure that what you've written fits your purpose and audience. Think about whether the writing reflects your voice—the values, beliefs, and attitudes that make you unique. Then have a **writing conference.** Read your draft to a partner or small group. Use your audience's reactions to help you evaluate your work.

Question A

Have I put events in time order?

Question B

Have I elaborated with interesting details?

Question C

Have I shared my feelings about the experience and done so in my own voice?

> Mrs. Magnino lived down the street from us for as many years as I could remember.
>
> Her husband died several years ago. I hardly ~~remember him.~~ her husband passed away. She's been alone ever since, and Now she 's ~~has~~ depended on neighbors for favors and help whenever possible. ~~My parents thought it would~~ One day she asked Mom if I could help with a few odd jobs around the yard. ~~be a good idea if I offered to help her around~~ Mom thought it was a good idea. ~~the house.~~
>
> We started by painting her lawn furniture.
>
> It hadn't been painted in years, but it was still in decent shape.

Editing/Proofreading

You must complete one more step before you share your writing with others. In the editing stage carefully look over every sentence and word. Don't make your readers struggle through incorrect grammar or misspellings. **Proofread** for these errors, and use the standard proofreading symbols.

Use the editing checklist on the right to help you edit your writing. If certain grammar or punctuation rules give you problems, add them to the checklist. Then read through your work several times, looking for only one or two kinds of errors each time.

Editing/Proofreading Checklist

1. Have I corrected any sentence fragments?
2. Do my verbs agree with their subjects?
3. Are all personal pronouns in the correct form?
4. Have I used standard spelling, capitalization, and punctuation?

Publishing/Presenting

Before you turn in your assignment, think of some suggestions you could give to the editors of *America, America* for the published version of your article. For example, you might suggest some footnotes to help readers with unfamiliar words or names. Maybe you have ideas for illustrations or photographs that could accompany your story. Turn your suggestions in with your writing.

Proofreading Tip

For proofreading symbols, see pages 79 and 863.

Journal Writing: Write to Learn

Reflect on your writing process experience. Answer these questions in your journal: What do you like best about your personal experience writing? What was the hardest part of writing it? What did you learn in your writing conference? What new things have you learned as a writer?

Literature Model

FROM

Living up the Street

by Gary Soto

In Living up the Street, *Gary Soto writes about his growing-up years in Fresno, California. In the excerpt below, Soto describes the experience and feelings he had on his first job, picking grapes along-side his mother. As you read, pay special attention to the details Soto uses to make his experiences and feelings clear. Then try the Linking Writing and Literature activities on page 38.*

I cut another bunch, then another, fighting the snap and whip of vines. After ten minutes of groping for grapes, my first pan brimmed with bunches. I poured them on the paper tray, which was bordered by a wooden frame that kept the grapes from rolling off, and they spilled like jewels from a pirate's chest. The tray was only half filled, so I hurried to jump under the vines and begin groping, cutting, and tugging at the

Susan Moore, *With No Visible Sign*, 1988

grapes again. I emptied the pan, raked the grapes with my hands to make them look like they filled the tray, and jumped back under the vine on my knees. I tried to cut faster because Mother, in the next row, was slowly moving ahead. I peeked into her row and saw five trays gleaming in the early morning. I cut, pulled hard, and stopped to gather the grapes that missed the pan; already bored, I spat on a few to wash them before tossing them like popcorn into my mouth.

> *I had to daydream and keep my mind busy because boredom was a terror almost as awful as the work itself.*

So it went. Two pans equaled one tray—or six cents. By lunchtime I had a trail of thirty-seven trays behind me while Mother had sixty or more. We met about halfway from our last trays, and I sat down with a grunt, knees wet from kneeling on dropped grapes. I washed my hands with the water from the jug, drying them on the inside of my shirt sleeve before I opened the paper bag for the first sandwich, which I gave to Mother. I dipped my hand in again to unwrap a sandwich without looking at it. I took a first bite and chewed it slowly for the tang of mustard. Eating in silence I looked straight ahead at the vines, and only when we were finished with cookies did we talk.

"Are you tired?" she asked.

"No, but I got a sliver from the frame," I told her. I showed her the web of skin between my thumb and index finger. She wrinkled her forehead but said it was nothing.

"How many trays did you do?"

I looked straight ahead, not answering at first. I recounted in my mind the whole morning of bend, cut, pour again and again, before answering a feeble "thirty-seven." No elaboration,[1] no detail. Without looking at me she told me how she had done field work in Texas and Michigan as a child. But I had a difficult time listening to her stories. I played with my grape knife, stabbing it into the ground, but stopped when Mother reminded me that I had better not lose it. I left the knife sticking up like a small, leafless plant. She then talked about school, the junior high I would be going to that fall, and then about Rick and Debra, how sorry they would be that they hadn't come out to pick grapes because they'd have no new clothes for the school year. She stopped talking when she peeked at her watch, a bandless one she kept in her pocket. She got up with an *"Ay, Dios,"* and told me that we'd work until three,

---

1 elaboration (i lab′ ə rā′ sh ən) giving more details

Personal Writing

Anthony Ortega, *Farmworkers de Califas,* 1990

leaving me cutting figures in the sand with my knife and dreading the return to work.

Finally I rose and walked slowly back to where I had left off, again kneeling under the vine and fixing the pan under bunches of grapes. By that time, 11:30, the sun was over my shoulder and made me squint and think of the pool at the Y.M.C.A. where I was a summer member. I saw myself diving face first into the water and loving it. I saw myself gleaming like something new, at the edge of the pool. I had to daydream and keep my mind busy because boredom was a terror almost as awful as the work itself. My mind went dumb with stupid things, and I had to keep it moving with dreams of baseball and would-be girlfriends. I even sang, however softly, to keep my mind moving, my hands moving.

I worked less hurriedly and with less vision. I no longer saw that copper pot sitting squat[2] on our stove or Mother waiting for it to whistle. The wardrobe that I imagined, crisp and bright in the closet, numbered only one pair of jeans and two shirts because, in half a day, six cents times thirty-seven trays was two dollars and twenty-two cents. It became clear to me. If I worked eight hours, I might make four dollars. I'd take this, even gladly, and walk downtown to look into store windows on the mall and long for bright madras[3] shirts from Walter Smith or Coffee's, but settling for two imitation ones from Penney's.

> *If I worked eight hours,*
> *I might make four dollars.*

That first day I laid down seventy-three trays while Mother had a hundred and twenty behind her. On the back of an old envelope, she wrote out our numbers and hours. We washed at the pump behind the farm house and walked slowly back to our car for the drive back to town in the afternoon heat. That evening after dinner I sat in a lawn chair listening to music from a transistor radio while Rick and David King played catch. I joined them in a game of pickle, but there was little joy in trying to avoid their tags because I couldn't get the fields out of my mind: I saw myself dropping on my knees under a vine to tug at a branch that wouldn't come off. In bed, when I closed my eyes, I saw the fields, yellow with kicked up dust, and a crooked trail of trays rotting behind me.

The next day I woke tired and started picking tired. The grapes rained into the pan, slowly filling like a belly, until I had my first tray and started my second. So it went all day, and the next, and all through the following week, so that by the end of thirteen days the foreman counted out, in tens mostly, my pay of fifty-three dollars. Mother earned one hundred and forty-eight dollars. She wrote this on her envelope, with a message I didn't bother to ask her about.

The next day I walked with my friend Scott to the downtown mall where we drooled over the clothes behind fancy windows, bought popcorn, and sat at a tier of outside fountains to talk about

---

2 squat (skwot) short and thick; low and broad
3 madras (mad′ rəs) a fine, striped or plaid cotton cloth

girls. Finally we went into Penney's for more popcorn, which we ate walking around, before we returned home without buying anything. It wasn't until a few days before school that I let my fifty-three dollars slip quietly from my hands, buying a pair of pants, two shirts, and a maroon T-shirt, the kind that was in style. At home I tried them on while Rick looked on enviously; later, the day before school started, I tried them on again wondering not so much if they were worth it as who would see me first in those clothes.

Linking Writing and Literature

◆ Learning to Learn

Jot down some notes that explain why Soto is working in the vineyard with his mother. In your notes, tell how his experience is similar to or different from ways you prepare for the school year. Then jot down what else you learn about the author's childhood from this excerpt.

◆ Talk About Reading

Discuss with your classmates the excerpt from *Living up the Street.* Choose one person to lead the discussion and another person to take notes. Use the following questions to guide your discussion.

1. **Connect to Your Life** In what ways are you and young Gary Soto alike? What traits, feelings, and opinions do you share?

2. **Critical Thinking: Evaluate** What kind of person is the narrator's mother? Mention some specific details from the excerpt that support your answer.

3. **6+1 Trait®: Word Choice** How would you describe Gary Soto's use of language? Give examples to support your description.

4. **Connect to Your Writing** *Living up the Street* is a memoir, a retelling of some part of the author's life. Why would you want to read someone's memoir? List what you think are the traits of a successful memoir.

5. **Active Reading Strategies: Summarize** In your own words, briefly summarize the main idea of this excerpt.

◆ Write About Reading

Memoir Write a brief memoir that retells an experience that added to your understanding of yourself or your world. Try to model your own memoir after *Living up the Street.* As you write, remember what you and your classmates decided makes a memoir interesting and successful.

Focus on Word Choice Try to choose rich, colorful, precise language that will make places, people, feelings, and situations seem real. Include strong action verbs, vivid modifiers, and literary devices such as metaphors, similes, and alliteration.

For more information on word choice and the 6+1Trait® model, see **Writing and Research Handbook,** pages 838–840.

6+1 Trait® is a registered trademark of Northwest Regional Educational Laboratory, which does not endorse this product.

Personal Writing

Reflecting on the Unit: Summarize What You Learned

Focus on the following questions to help summarize what you learned in this unit.

❶ What is personal writing?

❷ Why is a journal a good place to develop your writing voice?

❸ What is a learning log?

❹ How can you explore the future through personal writing?

❺ What kinds of events might you describe or explore in an autobiography?

❻ In what ways can you respond to a piece of literature?

Adding to Your Portfolio

CHOOSE A SELECTION FOR YOUR PORTFOLIO Look over the writing you did for this unit. Select a piece of writing for your portfolio. The piece you choose should reflect your unique voice. It should be about one or more of the following:

- your personal experiences: ideas, thoughts, feelings, activities, and memories
- discoveries you have made about yourself and the world in which you live
- your wishes or dreams for the future
- important events or turning points that have changed the direction of your life
- a personal response to a poem or other piece of literature

REFLECT ON YOUR CHOICE Attach a note to the piece you chose, explaining why you chose it and what you learned from writing it.

SET GOALS How can you improve your writing? What will you focus on the next time you write?

Writing Across the Curriculum

MAKE A SCIENCE CONNECTION Select a personal experience that happened in the natural world. To think of ideas, list places where you have contact with nature. Then write a journal entry describing an experience. Use sensory details to create a picture of the setting.

"The night had warmed and the rain had stopped, leaving puddles at the curbs."

—Walter Dean Myers,
The Treasure of Lemon Brown

The Writing Process

Writing in the Real World

The process of producing a documentary involves steps similar to those used in the process of writing: research, drafting a script, and editing the film. The following is a script written for a TV documentary. Bill Kurtis, award-winning journalist, produced the show.

from "Rock 'n' Roll Physics"
produced by Bill Kurtis

VISUALS	SOUND
Fade up on professor and bored kids in classroom	(Bring up Dave's music, then sound of "professor" droning on) (Prof.: Now let's continue with our review of Isaac Newton's theories concerning universal gravitation and we'll begin on the second paragraph of page 252. What property of the earth determines how large 4 or pie square in case sub b of the sun. Now Newton certainly suspected that the inverse square log attraction to light an object, not only to the earth and moon but also to the planet's moon. Alright, class, now we're getting to the most important part of our lesson on universal gravitation. What property of a body determines it's gravitational . . .)
Bill on camera in classroom.	(BILL OC[2]: This is no way to teach physics!)
Diz[1] to Bill on camera in roller coaster.	(BILL OC: *This* is the way to teach physics!) Bring up nat sound of rollercoaster, riders, then bring up Dave's music. BILL VO[3]: **Two men on an impossible mission: teaching physics you can actually understand.**

BILL VO: **Their names are Chris Cheviarina and Jim Hicks, but to their high school physics classes, they are Mr. C and Uncle Jim and they are leading a teaching revolution.**

Underwriter credits

(JIM: "You see how the wave kind of gets very narrow?")

(CHRIS: "Hang on, Stacey! Here we go!")

Montage Jim & Chris teaching

(JIM: "Now if you were into reading flames, you could tell what frequency they were. . .")

(CHRIS: "Keep pushing at 50! Good, good.")

¹ Diz: dissolve
² OC: on camera
³ VO: voice-over

A Writer's Process

Bill Kurtis often travels when filming *The New Explorers*. His filming location might be the Amazon or an amusement park.

Prewriting
Gathering Information

One night back in 1987, TV journalist Bill Kurtis was filming a zoologist who was searching for a new species of bird in Peru. Kurtis said that suddenly "a light went on. In a flash I saw a series of stories following scientists into the field."

His idea developed into a television series called *The New Explorers* produced by Kurtis himself. Each program in the series profiles a scientist—a hero to Kurtis. One episode featured Chris Cheviarina and Jim Hicks—Mr. C and Uncle Jim. They're high school science teachers "on a mission to teach physics you can actually understand."

To tell their story, Kurtis wanted to combine graphics, action, and kids. So Kurtis's staff went after more information. "We may go to the library," Kurtis explained. "We may do interviews. Ultimately, we have to go out and shoot film or video."

In this case, shooting takes place before the script for the show is written. The film visuals guide the writing of the scenes.

The first step in shooting "Rock 'n' Roll Physics" was to catch the teachers in action. Kurtis sent a camera crew to Barrington High School outside Chicago. "I said, just follow the teachers and shoot everything they do," Kurtis explained.

Drafting/Revising
Creating a Rough Cut

Kurtis wanted to show the teachers bringing physics to life. So the producer pulled the best moments from the interviews. Based on these moments, a script was drafted with a clear opener, a beginning, a middle, and an end.

Next the script called for Kurtis to explain the show's subject and to introduce the heroes—the new explorers. "This is my getting-to-know-you section," Kurtis said. "I want viewers to get to know the heroes and their work." High-energy scenes would then take viewers from class to pool to parking lot to roller coaster. "I like to change the pace often to keep the viewer's attention," Kurtis emphasized.

The ending would showcase students discussing the class and their teachers. Who could explain better why Uncle Jim and Mr. C's unusual teaching style works?

Revising/Editing
Fine-Tuning the Show

The draft of the script was revised. The film editor cut fifty hours of video down to four using only the images that best fit the script.

The editor then created a rough cut of the show. A "rough cut" is the first rough cutting together of film or video images. Little details—such as background music or exactly how long a shot lasts—will be decided later, in the final version, or fine cut.

Now it was time for Kurtis and his team to revise. "I'll tell you," he said, "on 'Rock 'n' Roll Physics' we looked at the rough cut and said 'We need to do some work here.' Frankly, I wasn't understanding the science." The team re-edited the video. After nearly eight weeks of work, "Rock 'n' Roll Physics" was ready to go.

Presenting
Broadcasting the Show

Unlike most other kinds of writing, TV writing doesn't end in a written script. Kurtis's final presentation was the documentary itself, which was broadcast on television.

Examining Writing in the Real World

Analyzing the Media Connection

Discuss these questions about the script on pages 42–43

1. What two things does Kurtis compare and contrast in the script? Why do you think he opens this way?

2. Why do you think Kurtis chose to dissolve from the image of bored kids to a roller coaster? Describe the impact the roller coaster images might have on a viewer.

3. How does Kurtis describe what Mr. C and Uncle Jim are doing? Why did he choose the phrase *impossible mission?*

4. Kurtis presents a strong point of view about his subject. How would the script be more or less effective if Kurtis had used an impartial point of view?

5. Kurtis's purpose is to get viewers excited about a new way of teaching physics. How well does this excerpt fulfill his purpose? Explain.

Analyzing a Writer's Process

Discuss these questions about Bill Kurtis's writing process.

1. What are the steps that Kurtis follows to put a program on the air? Compare and contrast these steps with the ones you use in your writing process.

2. Where did Kurtis get the idea for the series? Do you think it's a good idea? Why or why not?

3. Why do you think Kurtis begins by shooting film rather than by creating script? What problems might arise if the script came first and the shooting second?

4. What is the difference between a rough cut and a fine cut? Why are both stages necessary?

GrammarLink

Use vivid, specific verbs to add liveliness and interest to your writing.

> The train **zoomed** along.

Revise each sentence below by replacing the italicized verb with a more specific verb.

1. The class *looked* at the roller coaster demonstration.
2. Mr. C *said*, "Watch out!"
3. I really *like* this class.
4. Bored kids *sat* at their desks.
5. I *walked* out of the room, ready to make my own video.

See Lesson 3.3, pages 122–125.

Working with the Writing Process

*W*hen the Camera Club members decided to build a
*darkroom in the basement of their school, they made
a plan. First they scouted for a location; then they made a
few sketches and lists.*

Go Through a Process

Just as building doesn't begin with a hammer, writing doesn't
begin with a pen. Both activities involve several stages—from
the first idea to a finished product.

PREWRITING   The prewriting stage begins with selecting and
exploring a topic. One useful technique is to search your memory for experiences you'd like to share. Begin by looking at old
photos of yourself and your friends, jotting down
ideas as you go. Think about which ideas you'd
enjoy writing about and which might interest others. Decide how to organize these ideas.

DRAFTING   When you draft, you turn your
prewriting notes into sentences and paragraphs.

This writer
made several
prewriting notes
before finding an
idea she wanted
to explore.

Making the soccer team

Working on the science
project

Trying out for the play

Tutoring the third graders

Starting the newcomers
club

Being a new student

I felt nervous
Strangers, but friendly
Ms. Osaka broke the ice

You arrange your ideas in the order you chose in prewriting. New ideas will continue to come. Write them all down. Some will work, and some won't. Your draft may look messy, but don't worry. You can fix it later.

REVISING Step back and look over what you've written. Read it aloud to peer reviewers, and answer questions like the following: Are your ideas clear? Do they fit together? What other details might help your readers understand and enjoy what you've written?

EDITING/PROOFREADING In the editing/proofreading stage, you examine each word, phrase, and sentence in your writing. This is the time to find and correct any errors in grammar, spelling, and punctuation. Your goal is to make a neat, error-free copy for others to read and enjoy.

PUBLISHING/PRESENTING In the publishing/presenting stage, you share your writing. You can read a report aloud in class. You can work with others to publish a class poetry book. You can write a letter to the editor of the school newspaper. What other ways can you think of to share your work?

Drafting

I felt nervous walking in that first morning. The halls were crowded. People seemed happy to ... new year. They

Revising

~to Carver Junior High School
I felt nervous walking in that

first morning. The halls were
                    Friends greeted each other,
crowded. ~~People seemed~~ happy to
                              together
be starting a new year. They

didn't seem to need to know a new
                    especially
person, ~~and~~ one from ~~another~~
faraway Japan ⊙
~~country at that.~~

Journal Writing

Create your own chart to summarize the writing process and to help you remember it. Refer to it as you complete your writing assignments.

Be Flexible

Writing is a messy process. Ideas rarely flow in an orderly way. Novelist James A. Michener once said, "I have never thought of myself as a good writer. Anyone who wants reassurance of that should read one of my first drafts. But I'm one of the world's great rewriters."

At any stage in the writing process, a writer can think of new ideas to include and better ways to say something. Feel free to move backward and forward in the writing process. For example, if you get stuck while writing your draft, go back to prewriting and add to your notes. In editing, if a sentence doesn't say what you mean, return to drafting. If you have a new idea, insert it. One of this writer's best ideas about a small world came during a revision.

Revising

How wrong I was! The ~~first surprise~~ icebreaker came when I met ~~the school librarian~~ Ms. Osaka. I couldn't believe that she'd moved here just a year ago from Kushiro, my native city in Japan. Immediately, I understood the meaning of the term "small world."

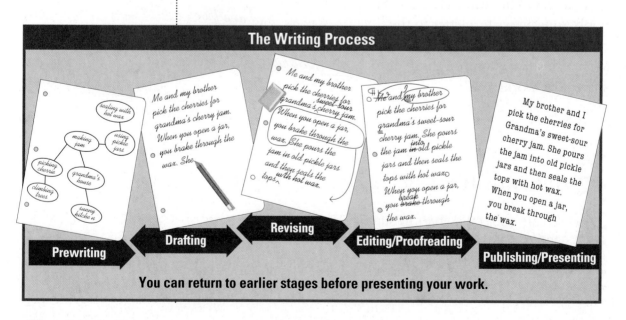

The Writing Process

Prewriting **Drafting** **Revising** **Editing/Proofreading** **Publishing/Presenting**

You can return to earlier stages before presenting your work.

2.1 Writing Activities

Write a Paragraph

Are the stages of creating a sculpture like the stages of creating a piece of writing? Make some notes to yourself about the process Oldenburg may have used to create his toothbrush sculpture. How is it like the writing process? Write a paragraph comparing the two processes.

PURPOSE To compare two creative processes
AUDIENCE Your classmates
LENGTH 1 paragraph

WRITING RUBRICS To write a compare-and-contrast paragraph, you should

- think about each process you are comparing
- list ways they are alike; then list ways they are different
- use your lists to write your comparison

Claes Oldenburg, *Notebook Page: Cross-section of Toothbrush in Glass, 'sun dial,'* 1980

Claes Oldenburg, *Cross-section of a Toothbrush with Paste, in a Cup, on a Sink: Portrait of Coosje's Thinking,* 1983

Viewing and Representing

Imagine you are planning a video presentation. You will show Oldenburg's sculpture to a television audience. What camera angles will you use? Create a storyboard for each view of the sculpture you will show. Write a caption for each storyboard.

Cross-Curricular Activity

MATH The sketches in Oldenburg's notebook lead one to ask whether the toothbrush sculpture might have been planned as a sundial. Could the sculpture have been a sundial? Research to find out how sundials work. Then write a paragraph for or against using the sculpture in a sundial, giving reasons for your views.

Grammar*Link*

Use subject pronouns—*I, we, she, he, they*—in the subject of a sentence.

*My brother and **I** pick cherries.*

Write each sentence, correcting errors in the use of pronouns.

¹ Me and her take piano lessons.
² Us often play duets. ³ Me and you can sing this song. ⁴⁻⁵ In fact, me and Maria can play while you and him sing.

See Lesson 11.1, page 435, and Lesson 11.3, page 439.

LOG ON ▶ **Writing** Online For more writing and grammar practice, go to glencoe.com and enter QuickPass code WC87703p1.

49

The Writing Process

Prewriting: Determining Audience and Purpose

*T*he tools of a writer are words. The words must be chosen to suit the writer's purpose and audience.

The eighth-graders at Carver Junior High School did many different kinds of writing. For example, they wrote an article about the Foods-of-the-World Festival. They wrote postcards during their class trip to Washington, D.C. They wrote a program for the talent show. They created posters advertising the craft fair. Finally, they made a memory book—a kind of yearbook—about their eighth-grade activities. Jot down one or two possible audiences for each of these pieces of writing.

CARVER EIGHTH-GRADE CRAFT FAIR

TIE-DYE SHIRTS
FRIENDSHIP BRACELETS
POTTERY
JEWELRY
TOYS
AND MUCH MORE

BROUGHT TO YOU BY
CREATIVE CARVER KIDS
CARVER JUNIOR HIGH SCHOOL

MAY 8 AND 9

Un- **This forgettable Year**

In the Spotlight
Talent Show

By Eighth-Graders at
Carver Junior High School

Write for Your Readers

When writers know who their readers are, they can tailor their writing to their readers. How does the writer of the first article below signal that the audience is young readers?

Literature Model

Hollis Conway has always had long, skinny legs. When he was growing up in Shreveport, Louisiana, his minister called him Linky Legs.

Little did anyone know that those slender legs would one day launch Hollis over a high-jump bar set nearly eight feet off the ground! Hollis, now 24, is one of the best high jumpers in history.

Sports Illustrated for Kids

> What words and ideas make this opening right for young readers?

Literature Model

Low, smoky clouds rolled in off the Wasatch Mountains above Provo, Utah, last Saturday night as high jumper Hollis Conway prepared for his second attempt at an American record 7′ 9$\frac{3}{4}$″.

Merrell Noden, *Sports Illustrated*

> What audience do you think this writer had in mind?

Journal Writing

Find two magazines with similar content, one for children and one for adults. Examine some articles in each. Write notes in your journal about how the words and ideas in each magazine reflect its audience.

Know Your Purpose

The purpose of both passages about high jumping was to inform. The selection below has a different purpose—to narrate, or tell a story. Read this narrative about an exciting event in the writer's life. To consider two more purposes for writing, consult the chart below.

Student Model

Finally, it was my turn. . . . I ran as fast as I could, and approaching the first hurdle, I made it over but bumped my toe slightly. I was embarrassed. I ran on, afraid that I would repeat my error on the next hurdle. Perspiration rolled down my face.

I leaped over the second hurdle with the grace of an antelope; I felt as if my feet had wings. My classmates cheered. I heard comments like "Boy, that kid's good!" and "Wow, look at him go!"

I then flew over the third hurdle like an eagle and raced to the finish line. The gym teacher looked at his stopwatch in disbelief. "You got the highest score in the class, Ken!" he said. I felt good that I had done something better than everybody else.

Ken Priebe, Grosse Pointe Woods, Michigan
First appeared in *Cricket*

What purpose and audience do you think Ken had in mind? How does his writing reflect both?

Purposes for Writing

To describe	Although short and thin, Ken was a fast runner.
To narrate	Finally, Ken leaped over the last hurdle.
To inform	Ken finished in first place because of his great efforts.
To persuade	Your contribution will help support the track team.

Collect Topic Ideas

Choose a topic for the piece you will develop through the stages of the writing process.

PURPOSE To list topic ideas, to identify purpose and audience

AUDIENCE Yourself

LENGTH 1 page

WRITING RUBRICS To plan your writing, you should

- decide on your purpose. Do you want to give information? Tell a story? Describe? Persuade?
- brainstorm for topic ideas
- identify the audience for each of your topic ideas

Listening and Speaking

Brainstorm in a small group for writing ideas. Spin off ideas from the painting on this page. List two ideas for each purpose listed in the chart on page 52. Here are some ideas to get started.

- a story set in the past (narrate)
- what people should eat (persuade)

Viewing and Representing

ANALYZING COLOR What is happening in the scene in *Humble Ménage?* Does the scene show a happy or a serious moment? How can you tell? How do the colors help you understand the painting's meaning? Share your ideas with a partner.

Grammar*Link*

Avoid run-on sentences.

One way to correct a run-on sentence is to use a semicolon between the two main clauses to combine them.

I leaped over the second hurdle with the grace of an antelope; I felt as if my feet had wings.

Write five compound sentences that are punctuated with a semicolon.

See Lesson 14.1, page 505.

Elizabeth Nourse, *Humble Ménage*, 1897

The Writing Process

LOG ON ▶ **Writing** Online   For more writing and grammar practice, go to **glencoe.com** and enter QuickPass code WC87703p1.

53

Prewriting: Investigating a Topic

Once you have chosen your topic and decided on your purpose and your audience, you need to explore ideas about your topic. What will you include? What will you leave out?

The eighth-graders had decided to make a memory book about their last year at Carver Junior High. Which activities should they include? Miguel said, "Let's brainstorm." In brainstorming, one idea sparked others, so the class listed all of them. Later they decided which ideas to include in their memory book.

Opening football game

Skit for after-school program

Art museum trip

Explore Your Topic

Once you have chosen a topic, you can explore it by brainstorming, freewriting, clustering, or listing. To freewrite, set a time limit—say, ten minutes—and write everything that comes to mind about the topic.

Don't let the pen stop moving. If you can't think of anything, keep writing the same word again and again. Often your best ideas—or at least the seed of them—will pop out.

Clustering and listing are also helpful techniques. Some students used clustering to explore ideas for the memory book. Kelly listed details for the class mural project. No matter which method you use, keep every idea for now.

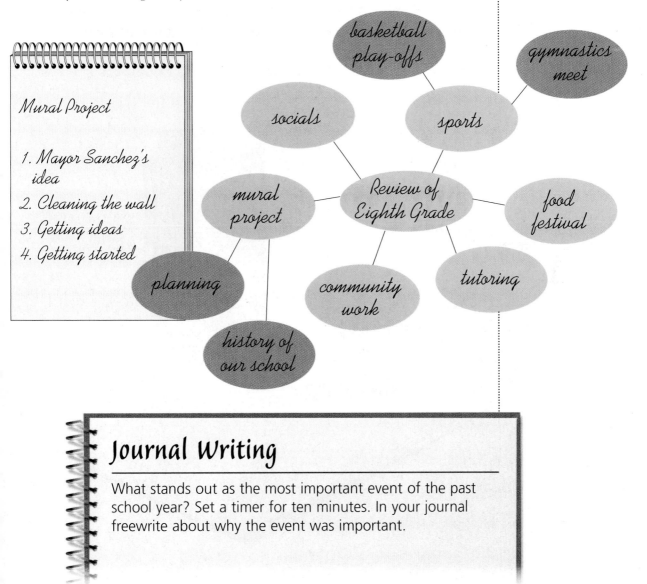

Mural Project

1. Mayor Sanchez's idea
2. Cleaning the wall
3. Getting ideas
4. Getting started

Journal Writing

What stands out as the most important event of the past school year? Set a timer for ten minutes. In your journal freewrite about why the event was important.

Gather Facts and Details

Writers start with what they know, but they often need more information to help them shape their ideas. To find it, they tap a wide range of sources, such as books, magazines, and newspapers. Sometimes the best sources are people with special knowledge of the topic. For example, Ayako wondered, "Why was our class chosen to work on the mural? What do people think of it?" To find out, she interviewed the mayor.

To conduct a successful interview, come prepared with good open-ended questions, such as the ones Ayako listed. Listen well, and take notes carefully. With the interviewee's permission, you can use a tape recorder as well. Don't interrupt or rush ahead to the next question. Allow the person time to answer. Ask follow-up questions: "That's interesting. Can you say more about it?" After the interview reread your notes, and jot down what you learned.

Investigate Your Topic

Choose two of your best topic ideas to explore and investigate. For each topic idea, do one of the activities listed under the Writing Rubrics heading.

PURPOSE To create a set of prewriting notes about your topic

AUDIENCE Yourself

LENGTH 1–2 pages

WRITING RUBRICS To explore your topic ideas, you can

- brainstorm for ideas about the topic
- freewrite about the topic
- list ideas about the topic
- cluster to explore the topic
- interview someone about your topic

Using Computers

A computer allows you to do "invisible writing," which is an excellent freewriting technique. Choose a topic and set a timer for ten minutes. Dim the screen and begin to freewrite about your topic. Since you cannot see what you are writing, you will be able to let your ideas flow without interrupting your thoughts to make corrections.

GrammarLink

Use correct verb forms.

Write each sentence, using the past tense or past participle of the verb in parentheses.

1. Dylan had (rise) to his feet.
2. He (take) notes on our ideas.
3. All of us have (draw) on many sources.
4. We (seek) out new sources too.
5. We had (speak) to many people.
6. Books and articles (give) us additional facts.
7. Then we (make) use of all that information.
8. We have (begin) to discover a unifying thread.

See Lesson 10.11, page 421, and Lesson 10.12, page 423.

Viewing and Representing

COOPERATIVE LEARNING In a small group, view a videotape of a TV interview with a famous or newsworthy person. Then read an interview of a similar figure in the newspaper. Do you learn more from watching or from reading an interview? Why? Take notes as you discuss your ideas. Then share ideas with another group.

The Writing Process

LOG ON ▶ **Writing** Online | For more writing and grammar practice, go to **glencoe.com** and enter QuickPass code WC87703p1.

57

Prewriting: Organizing Ideas

*O*rganizing ideas involves several steps—weeding out what doesn't belong, organizing the remaining ideas in a sensible way, and filling in missing details.

Rafael prepared to organize his ideas for the introduction to the class memory book. He gathered his notes and found resources, such as back issues of the school newspaper, to help him fill in missing details.

Weed Out What Doesn't Belong

Not all the ideas you gather on a topic belong in your writing. You have to decide what to keep and what to take out. First, think about what you want to say about your topic and express that central idea in one sentence. Then list the details and cross out any that don't belong. Rafael asked himself which activities really helped to support his idea about "the activities our class did together." Notice how he weeded out some ideas.

Listing ideas   Topic

The activities our class did together made eighth grade a year to remember.

talent show — April

mural project — October

~~tutoring~~   not a group activity

craft fair — May

Olympic Day — June

~~parents' night~~   more for the parents

Foods-of-the-World Festival — December

class trip — March

~~visiting author~~   she talked, we listened

Journal Writing

Write a sentence expressing your opinion about a school activity. List details about the activity. Then ask yourself: Which details support my opinion or the central idea? Which do not? Cross out the "weeds."

Organize Your Ideas

Now you need to organize your ideas in a way that makes sense. How you do that depends on your purpose: are you going to describe, narrate, inform, or persuade?

To describe something, you sometimes arrange the details in order of location, or **spatial order.** You might begin with what you see first; then move from left to right or from near to far. To narrate a story, you'd usually arrange the events in the order in which they happened, or **chronological order.** To explain, you could **compare and contrast ideas** or use chronological order to tell when events happened. If you plan to persuade, you might give reasons for an opinion **in order of importance.** You'd begin with your most important reason and then work toward your least important, or you could begin with your least important reason and build up to your most important reason. Which order did Rafael choose?

> Could Rafael have chosen another order for these events? Explain your answer.

Organizing ideas

The activities our class did together made eighth grade a year to remember.

④ *talent show—April*

① *mural project—October*

tutoring

⑤ *craft fair—May*

⑥ *Olympic Day—June*

parents' night

② *Foods-of-the-World Festival—December*

③ *class trip—March*

visiting author

The Writing Process

Organize Your Ideas

Look back at your prewriting notes. Now choose the topic you want to write about—you can always change your mind later.

PURPOSE To organize your ideas
AUDIENCE Yourself
LENGTH 1–2 pages

WRITING RUBRICS To organize your ideas, you should

- state your central idea in a topic sentence
- circle supporting ideas in your prewriting notes
- add any new ideas you have
- plan how you will organize your writing

Listening and Speaking

COOPERATIVE LEARNING In a small group, brainstorm to create a list of jobs you might like to have someday. Each group member should copy the completed list. Individually each member should cross out the jobs that seem less attractive and number the remaining jobs in order of importance, with number one as the favorite. Discuss reasons for your choices.

GrammarLink

Capitalize the names of people, places, institutions, events, months, and days.

*C*arver *J*unior *H*igh *S*chool
*O*lympic *D*ay

Write the paragraph below, using capital letters correctly.

¹One of my favorite relatives is uncle joe. ²A veteran of the vietnam war, he is now principal of kennedy high school in hawaii. ³I visited him last july. ⁴One saturday and sunday we spent in oahu. ⁵The pacific regatta was being held there. ⁶The crew from the university of hawaii came in first.

See Lesson 19.2, page 585; Lesson 19.3, page 587; and Lesson 19.4, page 589.

Using Computers

Use a word processing program to list all your prewriting notes. Highlight the notes you think you'll use for this writing project, using boldface type. Move any prewriting notes that aren't needed into a new file; you may want to refer to them for another writing project.

LOG ON ▶ **Writing** Online — For more writing and grammar practice, go to **glencoe.com** and enter QuickPass code WC87703p1.

61

Drafting: Writing It Down

Drafting is putting your notes into sentences and paragraphs that work together to make an effective piece of writing.

This mural artist used sketches to help her decide what to include and how to arrange and rearrange all the mural parts. Rafael is at a similar point in the writing process. His next step is drafting. He'll turn his prewriting notes into the sentences and paragraphs that will work together to introduce the class memory book.

Start Your Draft

One place to begin drafting is at the beginning, with an introduction. Leads, or openings, are important. A writer must create interest and make readers want to keep reading. Try out some techniques that professionals use in writing leads. You could ask a question, present an unusual detail, or use a dramatic quotation. Be sure to state the central idea clearly and explain what will follow. Here's a first draft that Rafael wrote as an introduction to the memory book.

Was it worth the wait? Turn the pages to see for yourself. Remember how hard it was to decide what to include in our memory book? We finally picked the great activities our eighth-grade class did together. Join us as we relive the mural project, the Foods-of-the-World Festival, the D.C. trip, the talent show, the craft fair, and the Olympic Day.

What does Rafael accomplish in his first and last sentences?

Notice that Rafael lists the series of activities in parallel structure—all are nouns modified by adjectives.

Not all writers begin at the beginning. Some start in the middle, on a part that seems easier to write. Others tackle their conclusion first. Drafting means trying options and taking chances. You may get stuck. To get unstuck, try one of these strategies.

Ways to Get Unstuck

Draw a picture about your topic.	Have a healthful snack.	Freewrite in your journal.	Take a walk, or ride your bike.

Journal Writing

What strategies have helped you start drafting or get unstuck? What new strategies could you try? In your journal make a list to refer to when you're stuck.

Let It Flow

As you draft, use your prewriting notes. They'll remind you of your purpose, audience, and plan of organization. Let your ideas flow freely. Don't interrupt the flow of ideas by thinking about grammar or spelling or even about writing in paragraphs. You'll have a chance to make changes later.

~~How can we forget~~ The mural project began the year. The idea was to capture the spirit of our school and community in paint strokes. Barb and Deji led us in forming comitees, and then we all got into the act. Four paint-soaked months later our beautiful mural was done, ready for all to see.

> Later, the writer will correct spelling errors in this line. When the ideas are flowing, keep going!

Write a Draft

Use your prewriting notes to help you draft your piece. To leave room for changes, double space if you are using a computer. Skip every other line if you are using pen and paper. Don't worry about correctness at this stage.

PURPOSE To create a draft
AUDIENCE Yourself
LENGTH 1–2 pages

WRITING RUBRICS To create a draft, you should

- decide where to start—with the lead or in the middle
- let your ideas flow

Diego Rivera, *Allegory of California,* 1931

Cross-Curricular Activity

MUSIC Draft song lyrics to go with the mural on this page. Begin with notes about what your purpose is and what parts of the mural you want to write about.

GrammarLink

Use various kinds of sentences: declarative, interrogative, imperative, and exclamatory.

Write a paragraph, following the directions below.

1. Write an imperative sentence. Tell readers to create a committee.
2. Write a declarative sentence. Explain the committee's job.
3. Write an exclamatory sentence. Warn the committee of what's ahead.
4. Write an interrogative sentence. Ask about an event.

See Lesson 8.1, page 359.

Viewing and Representing

The mural on this page is about California. What would you show on a mural of your state? Work in a small group. Research to learn about your state. List the ideas to include on a state mural. Then sketch and create the mural on poster board.

The Writing Process

LOG ON ▶ **Writing** Online | For more writing and grammar practice, go to glencoe.com and enter QuickPass code WC87703p1.

65

Revising: Taking a Fresh Look

*W*hen you revise, *you take a fresh look at your writing and refine it. After you've finished your first draft, put it aside for a time—at least a day, if possible. When you read your draft again, you'll have a better idea about how your writing will sound to readers.*

Revise for Clarity and Sense

Begin by reading aloud. Ask yourself, Is this clear? Does it make sense? Have I chosen the right words? The revising stage is a good time to consider whether you've used the best words. You can use a thesaurus—in book form or on a computer—to find words that say exactly what you mean. Examine the suggested revisions on the facing page. Then study the chart to help you revise.

Revising Tip

Elaboration

As you revise, consider whether you have provided enough supporting details and information. Elaborate where necessary.

After some recipe revisions suggested by his family, Ben's contribution to the Foods-of-the-World Festival was just right.

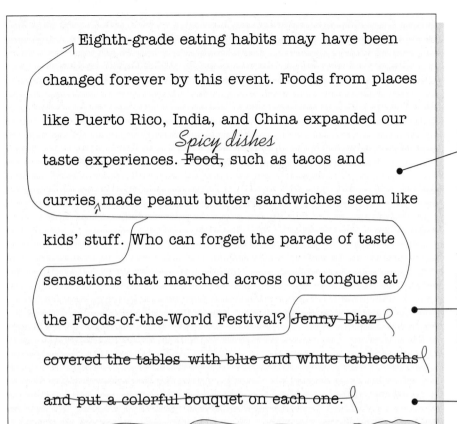

Eighth-grade eating habits may have been changed forever by this event. Foods from places like Puerto Rico, India, and China expanded our taste experiences. *Spicy dishes* ~~Food,~~ such as tacos and curries, made peanut butter sandwiches seem like kids' stuff. Who can forget the parade of taste sensations that marched across our tongues at the Foods-of-the-World Festival? ~~Jenny Diaz covered the tables with blue and white tablecoths and put a colorful bouquet on each one.~~

How did the writer improve the paragraph by changing "food" to "spicy dishes"?

Moving this topic sentence to the beginning will help the writer focus on the main idea.

The writer has deleted this sentence because it does not support the main idea of the paragraph.

Questions for Revising

1. Is my writing clear? Does it make sense?
2. What is my purpose, and do I accomplish it?
3. Have I chosen the best, most precise words to meet the needs of my audience?
4. Do I say enough about my idea?
5. Have I maintained a consistent focus on my central idea?
6. Where can I elaborate, adding details that will make my ideas clearer?

Revising Tip

For help with revising, see **Writing and Research Handbook,** pages 833–840.

Journal Writing

Review your journal for entries about recent events in your life. Choose one entry that interests you. To strengthen it, make at least two major revisions. Refer to the list above for ideas.

Ask a Peer to Review Your Work

One way to identify trouble spots in your work is to read it to others and ask for their comments. These peer reviewers will help you see your writing from the point of view of your audience. You can return the favor by listening to their work. As a peer reviewer, comment first on what is successful about the piece—in other words, say what works well for you. Then suggest any changes you think would help readers understand better. Read the paragraph below, comparing the peer reviewer's comments with the writer's revisions.

You made the food festival sound like fun.

Maybe you should list the ingredients.

Does the sentence about learning to cook belong?

I am confused by the last sentence.

~~We sampled delicious treats from several countries, but~~ among the highlights *of the festival* were the pot stickers from the kitchen of Ms. Yu, our teacher. Ms. Yu used *an old family recipe* ~~a way~~ that had been passed down to her from her mother. ~~Her mother taught her how to cook.~~ Ms. Yu offered everyone a fortune cookie. Reading our fortunes aloud added a touch of humor to the event. Our greatest fortune came *when Ms. Yu gave us* ~~with~~ the recipe for those yummy pot stickers.

You can follow all or some or none of your peer reviewer's suggestions. Notice that the writer of the paragraph above made two of the three suggested changes. A peer reviewer's comments can help you decide what changes to make, but the final decisions are up to you. As the writer, you're in charge.

Revise Your Draft

Look again at the draft you have written. Make sure some time has gone by—at least a day—before you begin to revise it.

PURPOSE To revise your draft, to have a writing conference

AUDIENCE Yourself, your peer reviewers

LENGTH 1 page of comments

WRITING RUBRICS To revise your draft, you should

- put yourself in the place of your audience and read over your draft, using the questions on page 67
- have a writing conference
- make changes to your paper

Listening and Speaking

COOPERATIVE LEARNING In a small group, discuss the ways peer reviewers can help writers improve their writing. (For example, peer reviewers may suggest new ideas about the topic.) Discuss the kinds of comments from peer reviewers that are most helpful.

Using Computers

Revising on a computer allows you to move text around and to try out different words and phrases. Save versions of your drafts and go back to a previous version if you think you've lost track of your original ideas.

Grammar*Link*

Use specific nouns in your writing.

*Spicy **dishes**, such as **tacos** and **curries**, made peanut butter **sandwiches** seem like **kids' stuff**.*

Rewrite the sentences below, replacing each italicized noun with a more specific noun.

1. Other *people* and I went shopping yesterday.
2. All of us found just what we needed at the *store*.
3. Jenny bought a *tool* for her father's birthday.
4. George bought a *book* and immediately sat down to read it.
5. A lovely little *plant* charmed Kathleen.
6. The twins were drawn to a display of *clothes*.
7. The *pets* in the window snagged Jemal's attention.
8. As for me, I bought *footwear*.
9. The *employees* rang up our purchases.
10. After shopping, we treated ourselves to *food*.

Revising: Writing Unified Paragraphs

As a writer, you want to make sure that each paragraph has a single, clear focus and that the sentences work together.

Alicia wanted to write about the class visit to the Washington Monument. When she looked at photos of the class trip, she found two of the monument. Which photo do you think best illustrates the focus of her subject? Why?

Check for Unity

A paragraph is unified if all its sentences work together to express one main idea. That main idea is usually expressed in a topic sentence, which may appear at the beginning or the end or even in the middle of the paragraph. In revising, decide whether the main idea would be clearer if you added or revised a topic sentence. Make sure that all the details support the main idea. What unifies the paragraphs below?

Literature Model

There are two levels on which to enjoy a tour through black history in the nation's capital: Visit those neighborhoods that stand now and those monuments erected in memory of past struggles and accomplishments. Then, as you drive or walk around the city, try to imagine what once was.

Since 1790, when Congress ordered that a federal city be built on the Potomac River, blacks have made rich and varied contributions. Benjamin Banneker, a black surveyor, assisted Pierre L'Enfant, the city's designer, in laying out the new capital. When the temperamental L'Enfant was dismissed, taking his design notes with him, Banneker's memory was invaluable.

Patrice Gaines-Carter,
"Washington as a Mecca of Black History"

The details explain the "two levels" introduced in the topic sentence.

Why does the writer begin a new paragraph here?

Journal Writing

List ten or more ideas about what you think is special about your town or city. Review your list, and write topic sentences for paragraphs that could include two or more of the ideas.

Connect Ideas

The ideas in a paragraph must relate in clearly understandable ways. Writers connect their ideas, using words and phrases called *transitions.* Notice the transitions in the following passage.

Transitions		
Time		
after	before	finally
first	next	at once
Place		
above	across	beside
below	next to	near
Cause and Effect		
as a result		because
since		therefore

Using Transition Words

After our long bus ride, we were glad to reach our hotel in downtown Washington, D.C. The next morning found us revived and ready for our tour. The first stop was the Washington Monument. After waiting in line for an hour, we took the minute-long elevator ride to the top. When we got there, we looked out across the city. How awesome it was!

Our next stop was the Lincoln Memorial. Since Lincoln is one of my heroes, I took some photos of the seated statue. The statue's huge size reminded me of what a great president Lincoln was.

You don't think about transitions as you draft. When you revise, however, be sure that you've made smooth connections between ideas. In descriptive writing you may use spatial transitions, such as *nearby* and *on one side.* In narrative writing you may arrange ideas chronologically and use time transitions, such as *first* and *then.* When writing to explain, you can use cause-and-effect transitions, such as *therefore* and *as a result.*

Check for Unified Paragraphs

Take another look at your draft. Are there ways you can make it even clearer for your audience? For help with writing unified paragraphs and linking ideas with transition words, see **Writing and Research Handbook,** pages 835–836.

PURPOSE To revise your draft for unity
AUDIENCE Yourself
LENGTH Necessary changes on your draft

WRITING RUBRICS To revise your draft for unity, check that

- each paragraph focuses on one main idea
- all the sentences in each paragraph support the main idea
- you have used transition words to link ideas

Monika Steinhoff, *La Plazuela, La Fonda (Hotel)— Santa Fe, New Mexico,* 1984

Viewing and Representing

Examine the painting on this page. Is the artist inviting you into the scene or closing it off from you? Write a paragraph giving your interpretation. Use examples from the painting to support your ideas.

Cross-Curricular Activity

ART Notice the patterns surrounding the doors in Steinhoff's painting. As a group project, create similar designs. Together, experiment with placing the designs in an order that will create a unified look. Discuss reasons for moving and rearranging the designs.

GrammarLink

Use commas to set off introductory elements and word groups that interrupt the sentence.

Write each sentence, adding commas where necessary.

1. Rudely awakened by the alarm clock I slowly opened my eyes.
2. Mario you see had set it an hour early.
3. With a sudden burst of energy I jumped out of bed.

See Lesson 20.2, page 601, and Lesson 20.3, page 603.

Revising: Creating Sentence Fluency

A good writer tries to produce a pleasing rhythm, or fluency, in his or her sentences. Varying the length and the structure of sentences gives writing this rhythm.

Kim and Emily arranged the acts for a class talent show. Rather than opening with three vocal solos in a row, they inserted a comedy act and a dance routine between two singers' solos. The variety gave a pleasing rhythm to the show.

In much the same way, a writer strives to produce a pleasing rhythm in his or her sentences. When you revise, read your sentences aloud, and listen to them. What will they sound like to your readers? Do they seem to plod along like three vocal solos in a row? Or do they flow smoothly, with the rhythm of a well-planned talent show?

Vary Sentence Structure

One way to give your writing a pleasing rhythm is to vary your sentence structure. Instead of always beginning with a subject, start some sentences with an adverb, a prepositional phrase, a participial phrase, or a subordinate clause. Rafael realized that he'd used the same basic pattern—a subject followed by a predicate—over and over again. Notice how he achieved a better rhythm by combining some sentences and varying his sentence beginnings.

Revising Tip

For help with varying the structure of sentences, see **Writing and Research Handbook,** page 833.

To open the show,
~~*The opening act was*~~ *Maria. She sang the song "Memory" from the musical Cats. Everyone was surprised at the emotion Maria put into her song.*
Since
She's usually so quiet, Raoul performed next. His comedy act drew peals of laughter from the audience. We weren't surprised by that.
Raoul is funny even when he's not on stage.
and Kim
For the next act Shanti performed a dance routine to rap music. ~~*Kim danced with her.*~~

How did Rafael change his first sentence?

What else did Rafael do to vary his sentences so his writing would have fluency, or a pleasing rhythm?

Journal Writing

Read several paragraphs of your writing aloud. How do the paragraphs sound? Examine the sentence patterns. Look especially at your sentence beginnings. If necessary, revise your work to vary the structure and the patterns of sentences so your writing will have fluency.

The Writing Process

Vary Sentence Length

Good writers avoid monotony. They do not string long sentences together. They avoid the choppiness that results from too many short sentences in a row. The narrator of the passage below is a young boy traveling by train from Mexico to California. Notice the sentence rhythm. Then study the graphic to see how you can improve the rhythm of your writing by combining short sentences or by breaking long sentences into shorter ones.

Which sentences vary widely in length? How does this variety affect the rhythm, or fluency, of the writing?

Literature Model

During the afternoon dark clouds had piled up over us, rolling over the desert from the mountains. At sunset the first drops fell on our canvas roof. The rain picked up and the train slowed down. It was pouring when we began to pass the adobe huts of a town. We passed another train standing on a siding, the deck of our flatcar flooded and the awnings above us sagging with rainwater and leaking. It was night.

Ernesto Galarza, *Barrio Boy*

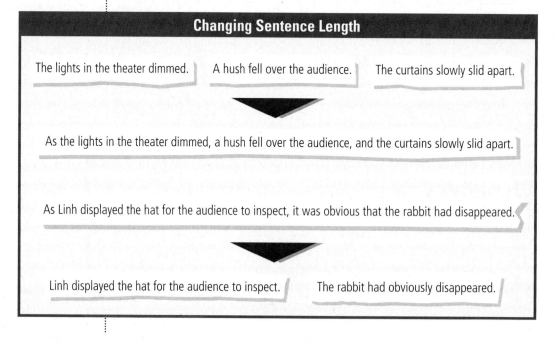

Changing Sentence Length

The lights in the theater dimmed.   A hush fell over the audience.   The curtains slowly slid apart.

As the lights in the theater dimmed, a hush fell over the audience, and the curtains slowly slid apart.

As Linh displayed the hat for the audience to inspect, it was obvious that the rabbit had disappeared.

Linh displayed the hat for the audience to inspect.   The rabbit had obviously disappeared.

Revise for Fluency

Now look at your sentences. Are there ways you can make them more varied?

PURPOSE To revise for sentence fluency
AUDIENCE Yourself
LENGTH Changes on the draft

WRITING RUBRICS To revise your draft for sentence fluency, check for

- a mixture of long and short sentences
- variety in the order of words and phrases
- sentences that can be combined to express ideas more clearly

Listening and Speaking

Tape-record yourself as you read your draft. Then listen to the recording. Is there a pleasing rhythm to your work, or does it drone on? Are your sentences too much alike? How can you change them? Take notes as you listen and use your notes to revise for fluency.

Using Computers

Word processing programs include an editing feature that allows you to cut and paste easily. This is especially useful when combining two or three short sentences into one long one or when breaking a long sentence into two or three shorter ones.

Grammar*Link*

Use adverb clauses to achieve sentence fluency.

You can often combine the ideas in two simple sentences into one sentence. One effective method is to state the idea in one of the sentences in an adverb clause.

Even when he's not on stage, Raoul is funny.

When the adverb clause comes first in a sentence, use a comma after it.

Combine each of the pairs of sentences below by turning one of the sentences into an adverb clause. Use commas where necessary.

1. Sophia called. I went to meet her.
2. There was a sale. We walked to the mall.
3. It was raining. We took our umbrellas.
4. The prices were low. We did not buy anything.
5. We spotted the bus at the bus stop. We climbed aboard.

See Lesson 14.5, page 513; Lesson 20.3, page 603; and Lesson 21.4, page 635.

LOG ON ▶ **Writing** Online | For more writing and grammar practice, go to **glencoe.com** and enter QuickPass code WC87703p1.

77

LESSON 2.9

Editing/Proofreading: Fine-tuning Your Work

During the editing stage, the goal is to get your writing ready to share with others. You want your finished product to be as nearly perfect as possible.

After all that hard work on the memory book, the first thing people see shouldn't be a misspelled word on the cover. Correcting spelling may seem like a little thing, but it's important to do before the book reaches its audience. To begin the editing process, ask a peer reviewer to look over your piece of writing. A fresh pair of eyes will often catch mistakes you have overlooked.

Check Your Sentences for Errors

Your first step is editing your sentences. Read them over carefully to check word choice and to identify any sentence fragments or run-on sentences. Examine the following edited paragraph. The writer has identified errors and marked them with proofreading symbols.

Proofreading Symbols			
Symbol	**Meaning**	**Symbol**	**Meaning**
∧	Insert	⊙	Period
℉	Delete	⌃	Comma
∽	Reverse	≡	Capital letter
¶	New paragraph	/	Lower-case letter

Lydia displayed
At the craft fair ∧ Several items of jewelry

made from ordinary office supplies. One of the

most beautiful pieces was a pin in the shape of a

skyscraper ⊙ ∧ it was made out of neon-colored
≡

paper clips, gold staples, and by adding on the

cap from a portable pencil sharpener.

> The writer has broken the sentence into two shorter ones. Is there another way to correct this run-on sentence?

> The writer has improved the fluency of the sentence by removing a phrase. This makes the structure of the list parallel.

Journal Writing

In your journal freewrite for five minutes about any topic that interests you. Let your work sit for a few hours. When you return to it, fix the errors that you find.

Proofread for Mechanics and Grammar

After editing for sentence structure, proofread for errors in mechanics—spelling, capitalization, and punctuation—and in grammar. Once you've proofread your draft, prepare a clean, legible final copy. Read your work over one more time. If you find a small mistake, correct it neatly.

> Why did the writer circle "staggerd" and "principle"?

> What is the meaning of each proofreading mark used in this paragraph?

¶ After the minimarathon had ended and the last

few runners had (staggerd) into the schoolyard,

the closing ceremonies for Olympic Day began.

Justin, our star musician, had composed a song

just for this day. The words reflected the spirit of

the events. With the winning athletes leading the

parade, we marched into the School auditorium,

singing Justin's song. Ms. tsao, our (principle)

handed out ribbons as we all cheered.

Some writers proofread as they draft and revise. Most writers, however, concentrate on getting their ideas down during these stages and leave proofreading for a later stage.

Notice the proofreading symbols this writer uses to correct this paper. You can find these symbols on pages 79 and 864 of this book.

Edit Your Writing

After revising the draft of your paper, you should be satisfied that your draft says what you want it to in the best possible way. Now you are ready for the editing stage of the writing process. During this stage, you will proofread your paper, checking carefully for errors.

PURPOSE To edit for corrections
AUDIENCE Yourself
LENGTH Changes on the draft

WRITING RUBRICS To edit your paper, you should

- check your paper word-by-word to see that you have followed the conventions of written language —correct spelling, grammar, usage, and punctuation
- look for one kind of error at a time
- use proofreading symbols to mark your paper

Using Computers

The ability of your word processing program to check spelling can be useful, but do not leave all the proofreading up to the computer. Your program probably won't alert you if you've written *form* instead of *from* or *their* instead of *there*. After using your computer to find obvious misspellings, proofread your work again.

Grammar*Link*

Use proofreading symbols to edit your writing.

As you edit, correct run-on sentences and sentence fragments. Fix errors in capitalization and punctuation. Add missing words and delete extra words.

Ms. tsao, our principle, handed out ribbons as we all cheered.

First, copy the passage below just as it is written. Then use proofreading symbols to edit it.

[1]Sean took also a booth at the craft fair, this was a chance for him to display his pottery. [2]Including several vases. [3]He was thrilled when he sold three Pieces, a vase a pot with a lid and a bowl bowl. [4]Sean been practicing with irish designs in his work. [5]The bowl he sold is a copy of an ancient Ceremonial piece.

See Lessons 7.1–7.9, pages 308–331.

You may wish to include a visual with your work. Create an illustration, draw a cartoon, sketch a diagram, or find another way to represent an idea in your paper.

LESSON 2.10

Publishing/Presenting: Sharing Your Writing

Now that you've invested so much time, energy, and talent in your writing, you'll want to share it. Who will want to read it? What is the best way to present it to them?

These pages of pictures are from the eighth-grade memory book, *This Unforgettable Year.* Who in Carver Junior High School will probably want a copy? What audience might the memory book have outside the school?

This Unforgettable Year in Pictures

Everybody helped us with the Foods of the World Festival. The result was a feast fit for a king or queen of any nation.

Mrs. Talerico waited with us patiently to visit the United States Capitol.

The talent show gave everyone a chance to perform. Sylvia Lin practiced her solo for hours before going on stage.

Present Your Writing at School

Some of the best audiences you'll ever find are at school. Here are ways to share your writing. Submit a piece to the school newspaper. Write the text for a bulletin-board display, or create a poster to promote an activity. Some classes exchange letters with students in other countries. Others publish an anthology of poems and stories, a memory book, or a yearbook.

This is the final revision of a page from *This Unforgettable Year.*

Who can forget the parade of taste sensations that marched across our tongues at the Foods-of-the-World Festival? This event may have changed eighth-grade eating habits forever. Foods from places such as Puerto Rico, India, and China expanded our taste experiences. Spicy dishes, such as tacos and curries, made peanut butter sandwiches seem like kids' stuff.

Among the highlights of the festival were the pot stickers from the kitchen of Ms. Yu, our teacher. Ms. Yu used an old family recipe passed down to her from her mother. These traditional treats tickled our taste buds and made us all want to travel to China. To add to our pleasure, Ms. Yu offered everyone a fortune cookie. Reading our fortunes aloud added a touch of humor. Our greatest fortune came when Ms. Yu gave us the recipe for those yummy pot stickers.

Journal Writing

In your journal list opportunities for presenting your writing in your school. Choose two you would like to try. Find out where and how to submit your work.

Presenting Tip

For help with deciding how the words and the design elements in your writing should look on the page, see **Writing and Research Handbook,** page 839.

Present Your Writing to Others

How can you "publish" your writing outside school? One of the best ways is to write letters to friends and family members. If you have ideas about a local problem, write a letter to the editor. If you are interested in a hobby or sport, find a specialty magazine, and exchange ideas with fellow enthusiasts. Two excellent magazines, *Merlyn's Pen* and *Stone Soup,* publish stories, poems, and other writing by students your age.

Contests offer still another opportunity for presenting your writing. The National Council of Teachers of English and other local and national organizations sponsor writing contests for young people. Your teacher or librarian may know about local groups, such as civic and veterans organizations, that sponsor essay contests. You can find other ideas in the collage below.

Present Your Writing

You have taken your writing through prewriting, drafting, revising, and editing, and now it's time for the payoff—presenting, publishing, or sharing your writing!

PURPOSE To present your finished work

AUDIENCE Your chosen audience

LENGTH Whatever is appropriate for your purpose

WRITING RUBRICS To present your finished work, you should

- prepare your work in the format that is best for your audience and purpose
- make your paper as neat and attractive as you can

Viewing and Representing

COLLABORATIVE WRITING In a small group, plan a class newsletter. Brainstorm for ideas for articles and stories related to school activities and events. Have one member of the group record your ideas. Once the group has decided what activities and events to include, each member should choose a writing assignment. When all members have completed their writing, come together to revise and edit each piece. Then work together to lay out the newsletter. If possible, duplicate a copy for each class member or present your completed newsletter as part of a classroom bulletin-board display.

Grammar*Link*

Make subjects and verbs agree.

Occasionally the subject of a sentence comes after the verb, but subject and verb must still agree.

Among the highlights of the festival were the **pot stickers** *from the kitchen of Ms. Yu, our teacher.*

Write each sentence, underlining the subject and using the correct form of the verb in parentheses.

1. There (is, are) many unusual sights on this camping trip—too many for Soraya.
2. Outside our tent (sits, sit) two fat raccoons, begging for a handout.
3. At the crossroads (stands, stand) a huge bull moose, watching us unconcernedly.
4. Here (comes, come) three baby porcupines and their mother.

See Lesson 16.2, page 543.

Using Computers

Write an e-mail to a friend. Describe the writing process you just finished. Share the problems you solved and tell what you are most proud of about your work.

Writing Process in Action

The Writing Process

In preceding lessons you've learned about the stages of the writing process and how writers go back and forth between stages before they present their writing in final form. You've also practiced what you've learned about the writing stages. In this lesson you're invited to relive an exciting event you've experienced by writing about it.

Assignment

Context	The theme of your school newspaper's writing contest is "And You Were There." You must portray an exciting event you experienced.
Purpose	To involve readers with your account of an exciting event
Audience	Readers of your school newspaper
Length	2 paragraphs

Writing Online

For prewriting, drafting, revising, editing and publishing tools, go to **glencoe.com** and enter QuickPass code WC87703p1.

Planning to Write

The following pages can help you plan and write an account of an experience. Read through them, and then refer to them as you need to. But don't be tied down by them. You're in charge of your own writing process. Give yourself a time frame for completing the assignment. It will help you pace yourself as you write. Keep in mind the controlling idea of the writing assignment: to communicate an exciting event that you've experienced.

Prewriting

What have you done recently that was exciting? Did you compete in a race or a chess match? Did you attend a concert or a pep rally? Did you have your artwork shown at an exhibit?

Use one of the options below, or an idea of your own, to begin thinking about a topic. Once you have decided on a topic, develop your ideas by listing, brainstorming, or interviewing.

Drafting

You can make an account of an event exciting by creating suspense. One way to create suspense is to emphasize time pressures. For example, in the brainstorming example on the right, the writer focused on guests fighting the snow to get to a wedding on time. In the example below, the author uses time pressures to create suspense throughout his account of a basketball game.

Prewriting Tip

Look at pages 54–57 for suggestions on using prewriting techniques to develop a topic.

Prewriting Tip

Pages 58–61 tell you how to use lists to make sure your supporting details fit your main idea.

Option A

Look at old programs and photos.

Option B

Read through your journal.

Option C

Brainstorm for ideas.

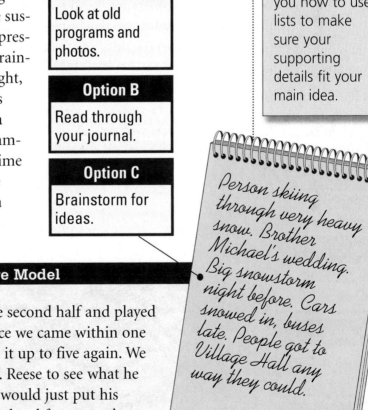

Person skiing through very heavy snow. Brother Michael's wedding. Big snowstorm night before. Cars snowed in, buses late. People got to Village Hall any way they could.

Literature Model

We came out in the second half and played it pretty cool. Once we came within one point, but then they ran it up to five again. We kept looking over to Mr. Reese to see what he wanted us to do and he would just put his palms down and nod his head for us to play cool. There were six minutes to go when Mr. Reese put me and another guy named Turk in.

Walter Dean Myers, "The Game"

Writing Process in Action

Drafting Tip

For more information about using transitions to show the passage of time, see Lesson 2.7, page 70.

Revising Tip

Read your writing aloud to check its fluency. For more help, see Lesson 2.8, pages 74–77, and **Writing and Research Handbook,** pages 833, 834, and 839.

Question A

Is my account clear?

Question B

Have I varied my sentences?

Question C

Have I written unified paragraphs?

As you write your draft, think about ways to emphasize the time element to create suspense. For example, in a movie, a hero needs to defuse a bomb. Suspense is created by repeatedly showing the bomb's timer ticking away the seconds.

Remember, in the drafting stage you need to let your writing flow to get your ideas down. You can make changes later. See pages 62–65 for more help with drafting.

Revising

To begin revising, read over your draft to make sure that what you have written fits your purpose and your audience. Then have a writing conference. Read your draft to a partner or small group. Use your audience's reactions to evaluate your work so far. The questions on the next page can help you and your listeners.

> "I can't imagine where she is," Michael said into counted the eighth ring of his call to Anika's. the receiver as he paced back and forth.
> and the wedding was scheduled for noon. It was eleven thirty. I wanted to ask if they'd had
> , knowing that she was probably stuck in the snow, a fight, but I kept my mouth shut.
> from the front door of the Village Hall, Just then I heard Kenny yell, "Hey, everyone, As I reached the door, you've got to see this!" I couldn't believe my eyes.
>
> It was Anika in her wedding dress, skiing down the street to the hall. It was 11:45. The guests who had made it to the hall applauded when Anika came inside, shaking the snow from her dress.

Editing/Proofreading

A careful editing job shows your readers that you care about your work and that you don't want errors to distract them from your ideas. The Editing/ Proofreading Checklist will help you catch errors. Usually writers **proofread** for only one kind of error at a time. If you do the same, you will probably do a better job of finding your mistakes. Use a dictionary and the Grammar, Usage, and Mechanics part of this book to help you with your editing.

Editing/Proofreading Checklist

1. Have I used the correct form of each pronoun?
2. Have I used irregular verbs correctly?
3. Have I capitalized all proper nouns?
4. Have I used commas and semicolons correctly?
5. Is every word spelled correctly?

Publishing/Presenting

Make sure your account of an exciting event is neatly written or typed on clean white paper before you submit it to "And You Were There."

As an alternative way of presenting your writing, you might like to give an oral presentation. Let the excitement of the event come through in your voice, facial expressions, and gestures. You might want to include recorded background noise or music for your presentation. For example, you might want to record the sound of a crowd cheering or booing if your account is of a sports event.

Proofreading Tip

For proofreading symbols, see pages 79 and 863. If you composed on the computer, use the spelling-checking feature.

Journal Writing: Write to Learn

Reflect on your writing process experience. Answer these questions in your journal: What do I like best about my article? What was the hardest part of writing it? What did I learn in my writing conference? What new things have I learned as a writer?

Literature Model

THE GAME

by Walter Dean Myers

With New York City's 116th Street as the setting, Walter Dean Myers's narrator, Stuff, reports the play-by-play action at the year's most important neighborhood basketball game in this chapter from Fast Sam, Cool Clyde, and Stuff. *As you read, pay special attention to how the author gets you interested in the story. Then try the activities in Linking Writing and Literature on page 95.*

We had practiced and practiced until it ran out of our ears. Every guy on the team knew every play. We were ready. It meant the championship. Everybody was there. I never saw so many people at the center at one time. We had never seen the other team play but Sam said that he knew some of the players and that they were good. Mr. Reese told us to go out and play as hard as we could every moment we were on the floor. We all shook hands in the locker room and then went out. Mostly we tried to ignore them warming up at the other end of the court but we couldn't help but look a few times. They were doing exactly what we were doing, just shooting a few lay-ups and waiting for the game to begin.

They got the first tap and started passing the ball around. I mean they really started passing the ball around faster than anything I had ever seen. Zip! Zip! Zip! Two points! I didn't even know how they could see the ball, let alone get it inside to their big man. We brought the ball down and one of their players stole the ball from Sam. We got back on defense but they weren't in a hurry. The same old thing. Zip! Zip! Zip! Two points! They could pass the ball better than anybody I ever saw. Then we brought the ball down again and Chalky missed a jump shot. He missed the backboard, the rim, everything. One of their players caught the ball and then brought it down and a few seconds later the score was 6–0. We couldn't even get close enough to foul them. Chalky brought the ball down again, passed to Sam cutting across the lane, and then walked. They brought the ball down and it was 8–0.

They were really enjoying the game. You could see. Every time they scored they'd slap hands and carry on. Also, they had some cheerleaders. They had about five girls with little pink skirts on and white sweaters cheering for them.

Clyde brought the ball down this time, passed into our center, a guy named Leon, and Leon turned and missed a hook. They got the rebound and came down, and Chalky missed a steal and fouled his man. That's when Mr. Reese called time out.

"Okay, now, just trade basket for basket. They make a basket, you take your time and you make a basket—don't rush it." Mr. Reese looked at his starting five. "Okay, now, every once in a while take a look over at me and I'll let you know when I want you to make your move. If I put my hands palm down, just keep on playing cool. If I stand up and put my

Red Grooms, *Fast Break,* 1983–1984

hands up like this"—he put both hands up near his face—"that means to make your move. You understand that?"

Everyone said that they understood. When the ball was back in play Chalky and Sam and Leon started setting picks from the outside and then passed to Clyde for our first two points. They got the ball and started passing around again. Zip! Zip! Zip! But this time we were just waiting for that pass underneath and they knew it. Finally they tried a shot from outside and Chalky slapped it away to Sam on the break. We came down real quick and scored. On

the way back Mr. Reese showed everybody that his palms were down. To keep playing cool.

They missed their next shot and fouled Chalky. They called time out and, much to my surprise, Mr. Reese put me in. My heart was beating so fast I thought I was going to have a heart attack. Chalky missed the foul shot but Leon slapped the ball out to Clyde, who passed it to me. I dribbled about two steps and threw it back to Leon in the bucket. Then I didn't know what to do so I did what Mr. Reese always told us. If you don't know what to do then, just move around. I started moving toward the corner and then I ran quickly toward the basket. I saw Sam coming at me from the other direction and it was a play. Two guards cutting past and one of the defensive men gets picked off. I ran as close as I could to Sam, and his man got picked off. Chalky threw the ball into him for an easy lay-up. They came down and missed again but one of their men got the rebound in. We brought the ball down and Sam went along the base line for a jump shot, but their center knocked the ball away. I caught it just before it went out at the corner and shot the ball. I remembered what Mr. Reese had said about following your shot in, and I started in after the ball but it went right in. It didn't touch the rim or any-thing. Swish!

One of their players said to watch out for 17—that was me. I played about two minutes more, then Mr. Reese took me out. But I had scored another basket on a lay-up. We were coming back. Chalky and Sam were knocking away just about anything their guards were throwing up, and Leon, Chalky, and Sam controlled the defensive backboard. Mr. Reese brought in Cap, and Cap got fouled two times in two plays. At the end of the half, when I thought we were doing pretty well, I found out the score was 36–29. They were beating us by seven points. Mr. Reese didn't seem worried, though.

"Okay, everybody, stay cool. No sweat. Just keep it nice and easy."

We came out in the second half and played it pretty cool. Once we came within one point, but then they ran it up to five again. We kept looking over to Mr. Reese to see what he wanted us to do and he would just put his palms down and nod his head for us to play cool. There were six minutes to go when Mr. Reese put me and another guy named Turk in. Now I didn't really understand why he did this because I know I'm not the best basketball player in the world, although I'm not bad, and I know Turk is worse than me. Also, he took out both Sam and Chalky, our two best players. We were still losing by five points, too. And they weren't doing any-thing wrong. There was a jump ball between Leon and their center when all of a sudden this big cheer goes up and everybody looks over to the sidelines. Well, there was Gloria, BB, Maria, Sharon, Kitty, and about four other girls, all dressed in white blouses and black skirts and with big T's on their blouses and they were our cheerleaders. One of their players said something stu-pid about them but I liked them. They looked real good to me. We controlled the jump and Turk drove right down the lane and made a lay-up. Turk actu-ally made the lay-up. Turk once missed seven lay-ups in a row in practice and no one was even guarding him. But this one he made. Then one of their men double-dribbled and we got the ball and I passed it to Leon, who threw up a shot and got fouled. The shot went in and when he made the foul shot it added up to a three-point play. They started down court and Mr. Reese started yelling for us to give a foul.

"Foul him! Foul him!" he yelled from the sidelines.

Now this was something we had worked on in practice and that Mr. Reese had told us would only work once in a game. Anybody who plays basketball knows that if you're fouled while shooting the ball you get two foul shots and if you're fouled while not shooting the ball you only get one. So when a guy knows you're going to foul him he'll try to get off a quick shot. At least that's what we hoped. When their guard came across the mid-court line, I ran at him as if I was going to foul him. Then, just as I was going to touch him, I stopped short and moved around him without touching him. Sure enough, he threw the ball wildly toward the basket. It went over the base line and it was our ball. Mr. Reese took me out and Turk and put Sam and Chalky back in. And the game was just about over.

We hadn't realized it but in the two minutes that me and Turk played the score had been tied. When Sam and Chalky came back in they outscored the other team by four points in the last four minutes. We were the champs. We got the first-place trophies and we were so happy we were all jumping around and slapping each other on the back. Gloria and the other girls were just as happy as we were, and when we found that we had an extra trophy we gave it to them. Then Mr. Reese took us all in the locker room and shook each guy's hand and then went out and invited the parents and the girls in. He made a little speech about how he was proud of us and all, and not just because we won tonight but because we had worked so hard to win. When he finished everybody started clapping for us and, as usual, I started boo-hooing. But it wasn't so bad this time because Leon starting boo-hooing worse than me.

You know what high is? We felt so good the next couple of days that it was ridiculous. We'd see someone in the street and we'd just walk up and be happy. Really.

Linking Writing and Literature

Learning to Learn

Throughout the game, Coach Reese signals to his players to keep "playing cool." What do you think "playing cool" means? Does "play cool" seem like good advice for parts of life other than sports? Write your thoughts about that in your journal.

Talk About Reading

Hold a group discussion with your classmates about this chapter from *Fast Sam, Cool Clyde, and Stuff*. The following questions will help focus your discussion.

1. **Connect to Your Life** Basketball is a competitive game. Think about how you compete in sports and in other parts of your life. In what ways are you like the players in "The Game"? In what ways are you different?

2. **Critical Thinking: Infer** Stuff wonders about the way Coach Reese shuffles players in and out of the game. What do you think is the purpose of the coach's actions?

3. **6+1 Trait®: Sentence Fluency** How does Walter Dean Myers use sentence structure to suggest the rapid, back-and-forth pace of the game? Point to some examples in the chapter.

4. **Connect to Your Writing** "The Game" is filled with suspense. Think about suspenseful writing you have read. Then create a list of techniques writers can use to build and maintain suspense.

Write About Reading

Personal Narrative: Write a personal narrative that describes a time when you had to "play cool" to achieve an important goal. Describe the incident as it really happened. Try to incorporate suspense in your narrative by using some of the techniques you listed in question 4 above.

Focus on Sentence Fluency As you write, use a variety of sentence structures and transitional words and phrases to reflect your ideas, add suspense, and help your writing flow smoothly.

For more information on sentence fluency and the 6+1 Trait® model, see **Writing and Research Handbook,** pages 838–840.

6+1 Trait® is a registered trademark of Northwest Regional Educational Laboratory, which does not endorse this product.

Reflecting on the Unit: Summarize What You Learned

Focus on the following questions to help you summarize what you have learned in this unit.

1. What are the stages of the writing process?
2. Why should the writing process be flexible?
3. What is involved in the prewriting stage?
4. What does drafting mean?
5. What does revising a piece of writing involve?
6. What kinds of errors are corrected in the editing stage?
7. What does presenting mean?

Adding to Your Portfolio

CHOOSE A SELECTION FOR YOUR PORTFOLIO Look over the writing you did for this unit. Choose a piece of writing to put into your portfolio. The piece you choose should show one or more of the following:

- connections to ideas found and explored in prewriting
- words and ideas that reflect a specific audience and purpose
- an opening that interests readers and explains what will follow
- revisions that you made after you and a peer had reviewed it
- a pleasing sentence rhythm
- editing for sentence structure, grammar, and mechanics

REFLECT ON YOUR CHOICE Attach a note to the piece you have chosen, explaining briefly why you chose it and what you learned from writing it.

SET GOALS How can you improve your writing? What skill will you focus on the next time you write?

Writing Across the Curriculum

MAKE A SCIENCE CONNECTION Think about an important scientific invention or discovery that interests you. Write a paragraph about the event as if you had been there working with the scientists. Try to help readers sense your scientific team's excitement about the event or discovery.

TIME

Facing the Blank Page

Inside the writing process with TIME writers and editors

THE CENTURY'S GREATEST MINDS

TIME

100

The fourth in our series on the 100 most influential people of the century looks at Scientists & Thinkers

CARSON

KEYNES

Writing for TIME

The stories published each week in TIME are the work of experienced professionals who research, write, and edit for a living. The writing is clear; the facts are accurate; and the grammar, spelling, and punctuation are as error-free as possible.

Behind the scenes, however, another story emerges. TIME staffers face many of the same challenges that students do in the messy, trial-and-error process that is writing. Just like you, they must find a topic, conduct research, get organized, write a draft, and then revise, revise, and revise again. In these pages, they tell you how they do it.

What is the secret to the quality of writing in TIME? Beyond experience and hard work, the key is collaboration. As the chart below illustrates, TIME stories are created through a form of "group journalism" that has become the magazine's hallmark. The writers and editors teach and learn from each other every week. You can do the same. Try out the writing and collaboration strategies in "Facing the Blank Page" to discover what works for you.

PREWRITING

Editor   Writer   Correspondent

Story idea is born

Writer takes assignment, refines topic, asks researchers and reporters for help

Research begins

Correspondents investigate, conduct interviews

Researchers gather material from reliable sources: "clips" from articles, studies, statistics

DRAFTING

Correspondents send their reporting or "files" to writer

Researchers compile and submit research files

Writer reads and organizes information, drafts the story

REVISING

Editor reads draft, suggests revisions

Correspondents
check interpretation,
make suggestions ◄┄┄┄┄► **Writer revises, sends draft to members of the team for comments** ◄┄┄┄┄► **Researchers**
check accuracy,
details

Writer and editor revise again, "green" (edit for length)

EDITING AND PROOFREADING

Checks for conformity to TIME
style and conventions ◄┄┄┄┄► **Copy Desk** ◄┄┄┄┄► Checks and corrects grammar,
mechanics, spelling

PUBLISHING AND PRESENTING

Managing Editor chooses to print, hold, or "kill" (omit) story

Circulation of TIME
rises or falls ◄┄┄┄┄► **Readers respond to published story** ◄┄┄┄┄► E-mail and letters
to the editor

Prewriting

Reading to Write

TIME writers know that the most important preparation for writing is reading. They read extensively to gather background material. Reading also helps generate story ideas.

Assistant Managing Editor Howard Chua-Eoan explains how the process works at TIME:

❝Before a TIME writer begins drafting, he or she has to read through and organize the information that has been gathered by correspondents and researchers. If you have the luxury of time, you should read all the material;

JAY COLTON FOR TIME

Howard Chua-Eoan: Reading paves the way for writing.

at the least, you should skim everything. That will help you decide what's important. What is the story you have to tell? What's the best way to tell it? Is the best way to open the story with a discussion of the issue, or to start with an anecdote, or to begin with a quote? You'll have all the material you need at hand, and you'll figure out what the best way is to deploy it throughout the story.❞

TIME staffers need to read to have a general background for their writing too. Andrea Sachs writes about books, authors, and book trends for TIME. Like all journalists, she has to stay on top of the news.

Senior Reporter Andrea Sachs:

❝I'm a big newspaper reader. If you want to be a news reporter, you have to do a lot of reading. I read a couple of newspapers a day, and I read a lot of magazines. I'm not a big reader online, however. I much prefer paper. But I do monitor TV news in my office. I have to know every 15 minutes what is going on! I can't get enough news.❞

LEARNING FROM THE WRITERS

TALK ABOUT IT

1. What role does reading play in Howard Chua-Eoan's and Andrea Sachs's lives? How does reading help them do their jobs better?

2. Recall a piece of your writing that required extensive reading first. What did you need to read? How did the reading shape or influence what you wrote?

3. What sources do you find most useful in preparing to write a report? For types of sources and for tips on taking notes properly, read Get the Facts and Take Notes in Lesson 5.7. For tips on how to use sources well, read Lessons 24.1 and 24.2, "Using Book Features," and "Skimming, Scanning, and Careful Reading."

Background Reading: Using the Web

Andrea Sachs covers the publishing industry for TIME. Though she prefers not to read newspapers online, she knows the value of the Internet in researching her stories. As a TIME reporter, she has access to special Internet periodical search services, but she also uses Web sites to lead her to the information she needs.

Senior Reporter Andrea Sachs:

"We have some fancy bells and whistles here to pull clips, or articles, on any subject, but there are periodical search services on the Web, too. To learn what's new in publishing, I visit booksellers' Web sites. They have all the book listings; that's free to anyone with a computer. When I'm looking for a particular company, that's how I locate it. There are a lot of small publishing companies with their own Web sites that I couldn't find otherwise.**"**

TIME has its own Web site, located at *www.time.com*

Some of the resources TIME's writers and researchers gather to write articles for the magazine become material for the Web site. A special section called Newsfiles serves as an excellent resource for information related to current stories. It includes time lines, references to other articles, and background material.

LEARNING FROM THE WRITER

TALK ABOUT IT
What magazines, newspapers, or other periodicals do you read on the Web? In print? With the class, develop a list of publications that you read regularly, online or off. How can reading them help you as a writer?

TRY IT OUT
1. Explore a Web site. Visit a news Web site to read the top stories. Find out more about a story that interests you by following the links on the site.
2. Search the Web. Go to a newspaper or magazine Web site. In the "search" space, type the word for a topic that you would like to write about. Are the results useful? Surprising? Try another topic.

Drafting

Writing as Thinking

Writing freely, whether in a journal, diary, or as a first step in drafting, can help you discover what you want to say and enable you to say it better. Writing gives shape to your thoughts; by writing on a daily basis, you can develop the discipline required for clear thinking. Early, exploratory drafts help you shape your ideas.

Editor Barrett Seaman reflects on the value of keeping a journal:

❝Anytime you sit down to gather your thoughts, whatever the subject, there is a crystallizing effect. Some things that you allow to be mushy in your mind as you mull them over cannot be mushy when you put them down on paper.

That was one of the first things I learned in keeping a daily diary. First of all, there is discipline in doing so, and second, that crystallizing effect takes place when you have to say, 'All right, this is what I think. No more messing around here.' If you have a debate that you can't resolve in your mind, then you crystallize the points of the debate, identifying what exactly are the areas of dispute. That is a terrific discipline for anyone to go through.❞

KEITH BEDFORD

**Lance Morrow:
Thinking on paper.**

Staff Writer James Poniewozik has also found that writing clarifies his thinking:

❝In the process of writing, you really learn more about what you think about your subject. Writing itself is an exercise through which you are setting ideas in opposition to each other, exploring tangents, and teasing out the implications of what you've already learned. The process of writing can stimulate you to go down different alleys.

Some people argue that before you begin to write, you should know exactly what you're going to say, and I think the opposite is true. There's a famous quote from the writer E.M. Forster: 'How do I know what I think until I see what I say?' Writing is not just getting down a completely formed thought that you have in your head. Writing is actually a process of thinking in itself.❞

Essayist Lance Morrow agrees:

❝Writing is a way of thinking on paper. I can't think unless I do it on paper or on a computer. I have to test my ideas with language and with an architecture of language and propositions: 'If this, then what about this?' My thinking then becomes coherent.❞

In its January 1, 2000, issue, TIME published an essay by Roger Rosenblatt. Written as a letter to America in the future, it is an informal and reflective piece in which the reader can hear the writer "thinking on paper."

A Letter to the Year 2100

Dear America,

Are you wearing pajamas? I do not mean to begin this letter by getting personal. I was just wondering if you people leave the house anymore—something that seems to be increasingly unnecessary these days, a hundred years ago. Not that leaving the house is always a good idea. Outside lies the wide and brittle world of wars, scandal, disease, superstition, willful ignorance, envy, and pettiness. In your perfected age, all such things undoubtedly have been eradicated. (How I wish I could hear your laughter.) Are you six-feet-six? Are you fly-fishing on Mars? Are you talking on a cell phone? We are, usually.

As lovers leaving lovers say, By the time you read this, I'll be gone. Or possibly I won't. Given the way life is being prolonged these days, I could write this letter in my century and pick it up in yours. No thanks. It is enough to be able to send these words across the years to tell something of who we are. We are members of a storytelling species, you and I—two eras connected by a story that changes just enough to keep it interesting.

As long as I am on the subject of language, do the following have any meaning for you: "like"; "you know"; "what's up with that?"; "like, you know, what's up with that?"? You have no idea what I am talking about? Good. How about "yada yada yada": "fuhgeddaboutit"; "pumped"; "zine"; "you're history"? (*We're* history.)

—**Roger Rosenblatt**

Revising

The Role of the Editor

At TIME, writers submit their completed drafts to editors who read them and suggest changes. The process is remarkably similar to the one used in student writing conferences. TIME's writers agree that, in the end, editors help them refine their thoughts and convey their ideas in clear, concise, and convincing language.

Staff Writer James Poniewozik:

❝You need to have someone look over your piece and give you the devil's advocate argument, to test your piece and make it stronger. I think it can be collaborative, too. I've often had editors rewrite or reorganize sections of my stuff, and I'll think, 'Wow, they just said what I was trying to say better and in half the space and more coherently than I did.' If you're a good writer, you probably have some sort of natural resistance to having your work tampered with. But it's necessary and good to have another set of eyes going over your work. **❞**

Assistant Managing Editor Howard Chua-Eoan explains how a good editor can help writers revise:

❝Even the best writers need an editor. For example, sometimes you think you've figured everything out, but you've slid over an essential step in reasoning a story. An editor will say: 'I know what you're trying to do and I agree with you, but you missed a step explaining how you got from this point to that point.' **❞**

WRITING TIP

Listening to Editors

"Editors are helpful; they serve as the first reader of the story. They might find something confusing and want it clarified, or they might want one more example. When the editor is good, it can be so useful. But it's scary, too. People are sensitive about having their writing changed." —**Andrea Sachs**

LEARNING FROM THE WRITERS

TALK ABOUT IT
1. In what specific ways do Poniewozik and Chua-Eoan think an editor can help improve a piece of writing? Why can having work edited be difficult?
2. What is the "devil's advocate argument" that Poniewozik mentions?
3. Who edits your work? Explain how you feel about criticism of your writing.

TRY IT OUT
Revise, revise revise. James Poniewozik argues, "Writers don't revise enough." Look at the first draft of your letter. Reorganize and rewrite it for clarity and sense. Have your friends or family help revise it further. Does their advice improve your letter?

LOOK IT OVER
1. As a writer, how do you feel about having your work edited? If you have edited another person's work, describe the process. Was it a collaborative effort? How was it the same as or different from the process at TIME?
2. If you have never edited another person's work, exchange papers with a classmate. Use the tips for peer review in Lesson 2.6 as you edit each other's work.

Tightening: Editing for Space

Writers' drafts are typically too long. It is the editor's job to "green" or shorten the piece to fit the allotted space, making sure that each printed word carries its weight.

Read these two drafts of "Kinder Grind" by TIME columnist Amy Dickinson.

FIRST DRAFT

Today's typical kindergartner is a kid anywhere between 4 to 6 years old, with an increasing number of parents (especially affluent ones) deciding to delay the start of school to give their children (usually boys) an extra year of pre-school. This trend—known as "redshirting," after the practice of holding back freshman college athletes—is widening the developmental and age gaps among the students chronologically and developmentally. Younger students generally go to kindergarten with little or no pre-schooling, while older children may have been in nursery school for up to three years. Add to that the naturally wide variation in the developmental range of young children, and a "typical" kindergarten class now contains some students who barely know their letters, while others may be fairly fluent readers. Sue Bredekamp, editor of "Developmentally Appropriate Practice in Early Childhood Programs," a guide for teachers published by the National Association for the Education of Young Children, says she wonders how more rigid instruction will serve children well. "What teachers tell us is that expectations for kindergartners have become more standardized, while the pool of kids in kindergarten has become more diverse."

FINAL DRAFT

More parents (especially affluent ones) are delaying the start of school to give their children an extra year of pre-school. This trend—known as "redshirting," after the practice of holding back freshman college athletes—is widening the developmental and age gaps among students. A "typical" kindergarten class contains kids ages 4 to 6 whose level of development varies widely. Some barely know their letters, while others are fairly fluent readers. Sue Bredekamp, editor of a widely used guide for teachers of young children, says, "What teachers tell us is that expectations for kindergartners have become more standardized, while the pool of kids in kindergarten has become more diverse."

TALK ABOUT IT

1. What is the difference in line count between the unedited and final versions of this excerpt about kindergarten from TIME?

2. Identify one passage that the editor cut or "greened." If you were the writer, would you object to this revision?

3. What tips for tightening a piece of writing can you draw from this example? List them as a class.

TRY IT OUT

Strive for conciseness. Take a sample paragraph from a recent piece of writing and count its lines. Rewrite the paragraph to fit in a space or line count 25% smaller. What can you cut? What can you rephrase, rewrite, and tighten?

Editing and Proofreading

Clichés: No Laughing Matter

Copy editors at TIME work to ensure that every article, caption, and headline in the magazine is correct. They catch and change errors in grammar, usage, and spelling. Copy editors also strive to make every story as clean and readable as possible. Sometimes this means spotting and getting rid of clichés, expressions that were once original but have been so overused that they've lost their impact. See "As Stale as Day-old Bread" on page 670 for more on clichés.

Henry Muller, a former Managing Editor at TIME, sent this memo to the TIME staff:

❝ In our ongoing search-and-destroy mission to ferret out journalistic clichés in all ways, shapes and forms, I have resolved with grim determination to compile a list of these offenses, which are anathema to all true believers in our craft. I invite you to hold your feet to the fire, keep your nose to the grindstone and go through your copy with a fine-tooth comb, excising badly splintered parties, stunning upsets, stern warnings, yawning deficits, rumbling tanks, rattling machine guns and other frequent offenders. ❞

Below are a few of the words and phrases that made Muller's list. This compilation is but the tip of the iceberg (to use yet another tired expression!). Some of these are certified clichés, while others threaten to become so. All of them need a rest.

at the end of the day
awesome ■ big break
brief stint ■ fast lane
force to be reckoned with
lifestyle ■ no easy answers
no laughing matter
not to worry ■ stay tuned
running on empty
up for grabs

LEARNING FROM THE EDITORS

DISCUSSION
1. What is a cliché? Think of a common example. Why do writers try to avoid them?
2. Analyze the memo from Henry Muller. List the clichés he uses. What do you think he was trying to impress upon his staff, and why did he choose this way to do it?

TRY IT OUT
Campaign against clichés. Write a memo modeled on Muller's. Use a variety of clichés to persuade your classmates not to use such worn-out terms in their own writing. Then rewrite the memo without using a single cliché.

LOOK IT OVER
Look through your writing portfolio, journal, and old papers to find clichés. Add them to a class cliché list. Do you see a pattern of worn-out expressions? Rewrite three of your sentences by replacing the worn-out expressions in them with creative phrases.

Publishing and Presenting

Why I Write

Journalism is not just a job for TIME writers and editors. For many, it is a calling, the expression of their lifelong love of language and storytelling. Assistant Managing Editor Howard Chua-Eoan calls writing his passion; Senior Reporter Andrea Sachs describes journalism as "the best profession there is."

Howard Chua-Eoan:

❝ The thing that I'm passionate about, and what I have always been passionate about, is writing. I love working with words. I like seeing what words can do and what words can convey. The journalism part is something that I fell in love with as I worked more and more with it. Journalism is about conveying what's out there in as vibrant, powerful, and yet as accurate a way as possible. The other side of writing, of course, is fiction and poetry and everything else. But in newswriting, you have the most powerful sort of structure of all: the truth. How do you convey that, how do you perceive that, and how do you make other people see that? ❞

Andrea Sachs recalls why, working as a lawyer in Washington, D.C., she changed paths to become a journalist:

❝ The day President Reagan was shot, I went down the street to George Washington University Hospital, and I watched the reporters work. There must have been 1000 people out there, and I got interviewed as a 'person on the street.' I watched television reporter Sam Donaldson do his report. My heart was pounding: 'This is what I want to do!' I knew it. I never questioned that, and I went back to journalism school. That's why I became a writer. It's the best profession there is. It's so exciting to be tapped into the news and to get paid for learning things. I've never been disappointed. I've been doing this for 15 years now, and I love it. ❞

LEARNING FROM THE WRITERS

TALK ABOUT IT
1. Do you agree with Chua-Eoan's thoughts on what journalism is? How would you define *journalism*? For Sachs, what are the benefits of being a journalist?
2. Chua-Eoan distinguishes between journalism and "the other side of writing"—fiction and poetry and everything else. He says that journalists use the most powerful structure of all: the truth. Do you agree with his statement? Why? What might poets and novelists say in response to his statement? Do imaginative forms of writing like poems and short stories convey the truth? If so, how?

TRY IT OUT
1. Identify a passion.
Write a paragraph similar to Howard Chua-Eoan's with this opening line: "The thing that I'm passionate about is . . ."
2. Recall a defining moment.
Like Andrea Sachs, have you had an experience in which you discovered "This is what I want to do!"? Write about it. Tell whether what you want to do is linked to what you are passionate about.

" *A drowsy, dreamy influence seems to hang over the land.* **"**

—Washington Irving,
The Legend of Sleepy Hollow

Descriptive Writing

Writing in the Real World

In the following passage from *How the García Girls Lost Their Accents,* Alvarez describes the mother through the eyes of her young daughter Sandi.

**From *How the García Girls Lost Their Accents*
by Julia Alvarez**

Sandi leaned her elbows on the vanity and watched her mother comb her dark hair in the mirror. Tonight Mami was turning back into the beauty she had been back home. Her face was pale and tragic in the lamplight; her bright eyes shone like amber held up to the light. She wore a black dress with a scoop back and wide shoulders so her long neck had the appearance of a swan gliding on a lake. Around her neck sparkled her good necklace that had real diamonds. "If things get really bad," Mami sometimes joked grimly, "I'll sell the necklace and earrings Papito gave me." Papi always scowled and told her not to speak such nonsense.

Novelist
Julia Alvarez

A Writer's Process

❝ Entering the world of the imagination, that's a portable homeland. . . . I can take out my pad of paper in the Dominican Republic, here in Vermont, in California, in Turkey—and it's the same blank page. It's the same sense of creating a world, of making meaning, wherever you go. ❞

—Julia Alvarez

Prewriting
Playing with Words

"Much of writing is playfulness with words. It's trying things out," Alvarez says. "You're not probably going to get it right the first time. So just let yourself get *some* of it right."

Learning to create vivid description takes time and practice for every writer. The writer must learn to notice the things of the world and to describe those things in fresh ways. To help herself do this, Alvarez plays a word game. In her journal she'll describe what she sees in daily life. She might look at the sheep grazing near her house and think of different images to describe them, such as powder puffs and cumulus clouds.

She explains the benefits of this practice: "What's great is that maybe two weeks down the line—maybe two years down the line—wouldn't you know it, but I'll have a character looking at a sheep farm!"

Drafting
Discovering Details

People often say that something important is "beyond words." Yet Julia Alvarez finds the words to describe complicated experiences and feelings. She does so by keeping things simple. "I think when somebody says that they can't describe something, they're trying for the big thing, instead of the little details that, of course, they can describe," she says.

Alvarez creates large effects with small details. She notices the intimate details that bring a reader close to a character or experience. The detail might be the feel of sun shining on top of a character's head. Or it might be the look of Mrs. García's neck while she is combing her hair. When writing the description of Mrs. García shown in the excerpt on page 110, Alvarez wanted to give a picture of what the mother looked like. Alvarez says, "I was trying to get a sense of the glamour and beauty of the mother, as seen from a little girl's eyes. I wanted to show that there was something beautiful and mysterious about the mother."

Revising
Seeing What Works

As Alvarez writes a draft, she often discovers new images and ideas. "That's part of the fun—when it all falls into place," she says. "You know I'll discover something, and then all of a sudden, I'll have to go back and redo the beginning."

Alvarez sometimes reads her work out loud after she writes a few sentences. If it doesn't sound right, she makes the necessary changes. In this way she does some revising as she goes along.

When she finishes a draft, she does more revising. She may add details to a description to make it more clear, precise, or interesting. Alvarez says, "As you revise and revise, you happen upon things that you see are working. Then you polish them, or bring in new things to enhance them."

Sometimes Alvarez invites others to read her descriptions aloud. That makes it easier for her to hear what needs revising. "What you write gets coated with your voice," Alvarez explains. "Having somebody else read out loud to you, you hear all the places that it's really off, in a way you can't hear it when you're writing."

The revision process requires writers to think from their readers' point of view. Will readers understand what a character is feeling? Will they pick up on the mood or tone of a description? Alvarez revises her work until she is confident that her ideas have been communicated clearly to the readers. Sometimes, communicating ideas clearly requires many rewrites. Alvarez says, "I know it's a process! And that certain things that get you started in a description later have to go."

How the García Girls Lost Their Accents

A major family sequence

CONTEMPORARY FICTION

Examining Writing in the Real World

Analyzing the Media Connection

Discuss these questions about the excerpt on page 110.

1. Who is described in the passage? From whose point of view is the description narrated?

2. Is the mood of this description quiet and nostalgic or lively and spirited? What words and images help establish the mood?

3. A simile is a comparison using the word *like* or *as*. What simile does Alvarez use to describe Mami's eyes? Why is this image effective?

4. Why do you think Alvarez uses the image of a swan to describe Mami's appearance?

5. How can you tell that the diamond necklace is worth more to Mami and Papi than the jewels inside it?

Analyzing A Writer's Process

Discuss these questions about Julia Alvarez's writing process.

1. How does Alvarez's journal contribute to her descriptive writing?

2. What would Alvarez advise you to do if you were struggling with describing a breathtaking scene?

3. When does Alvarez read her work out loud? Why does she do this?

4. Why does she sometimes ask others to read her work aloud?

5. Do you agree with Alvarez that the process of revision can be fun? Why or why not?

GrammarLink

Use adjective clauses to describe a noun or a pronoun.

An adjective clause often begins with a relative pronoun—*who, whom, whose, which,* or *that.*

> Around her neck sparkled her good necklace **that had real diamonds.**

Incorporate each adjective clause below into a sentence. Start by thinking of a noun or a pronoun for each to modify.

1. who was shouting
2. which had been lost
3. whose hands were like ice
4. that won the game
5. that they liked the best

See Lesson 14.3, page 509, and Lesson 21.3, page 633.

Writing Descriptions

A good description re-creates sights, sounds, and other impressions. Read the passage below, and share a hot summer night with Lorraine Hansberry.

Pat Thomas, *Picnic in Washington Park*, 1975

Lorraine Hansberry recalls the sights, sounds, smells, and feelings from her Chicago childhood. The reader can hear doors slamming and can sniff freshly cut lemons in the steamy night air.

In this excerpt, we glimpse Hansberry's personality. It is revealed by her word choice, sentence structure, fluency, and attitude toward her subject— her voice. What kind of person do you think Hansberry is?

Literature Model

Evenings were spent mainly on the back porches where screen doors slammed in the darkness with those really very special summertime sounds. And, sometimes, when Chicago nights got too steamy, the whole family got into the car and went to the park and slept out in the open on blankets. Those were, of course, the best times of all because the grownups were invariably reminded of having been children in rural parts of the country and told the best stories then. And it was also cool and sweet to be on the grass and there was usually the scent of freshly cut lemons or melons in the air. And Daddy would lie on his back, as fathers must, and explain about how men thought the stars above us came to be and how far away they were.

Lorraine Hansberry, "On Summer"

Descriptive Writing

Observe Details

Descriptive writing often starts with a memory or an observation—something that catches your attention. The details that make someone or something stay in your mind become the raw material for creating a description. Notice how writer Nicholasa Mohr brings to life details about Puerto Rico through the observation of one of her characters.

Literature Model

She saw the morning mist settling like puffs of smoke scattered over the range of mountains that surrounded the entire countryside. Sharp mountainous peaks and curves covered with many shades of green foliage that changed constantly from light to dark, intense or soft tones, depending on the time of day and the direction of the rays of the brilliant tropical sun. Ah, the path, she smiled, following the road that led to her village. Lali inhaled the sweet and spicy fragrance of the flower gardens that sprinkled the countryside in abundance.

Nicholasa Mohr, *In Nueva York*

What words does the writer use to help you see the changing mountains?

Mohr draws you into her memories with a walk along the path.

Journal Writing

Think about how Nicholasa Mohr brings her village to life. List at least five words that the author uses to describe it. Then choose a memory of your own. Write at least five specific details.

Notice Descriptive Writing

Good descriptive writing involves using your senses to observe, selecting precise details, and organizing your ideas. You probably read descriptions more often than you realize. The chart below shows some examples of descriptive writing. In the model that follows the chart, Michael Lim describes an unusual fish.

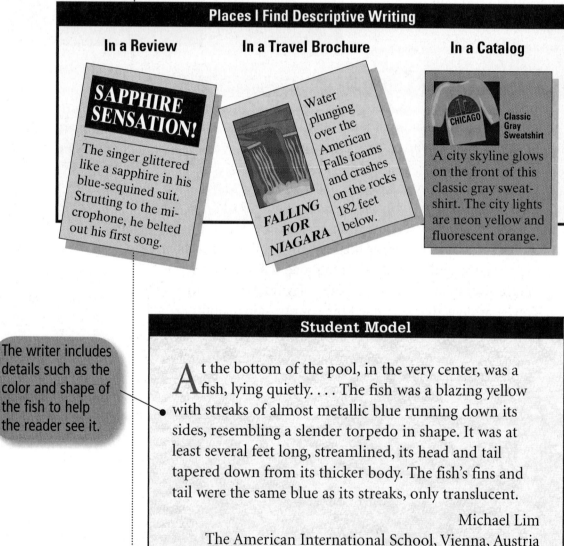

Places I Find Descriptive Writing

In a Review

SAPPHIRE SENSATION!

The singer glittered like a sapphire in his blue-sequined suit. Strutting to the microphone, he belted out his first song.

In a Travel Brochure

Water plunging over the American Falls foams and crashes on the rocks 182 feet below.

FALLING FOR NIAGARA

In a Catalog

CHICAGO

Classic Gray Sweatshirt

A city skyline glows on the front of this classic gray sweatshirt. The city lights are neon yellow and fluorescent orange.

Student Model

At the bottom of the pool, in the very center, was a fish, lying quietly. . . . The fish was a blazing yellow with streaks of almost metallic blue running down its sides, resembling a slender torpedo in shape. It was at least several feet long, streamlined, its head and tail tapered down from its thicker body. The fish's fins and tail were the same blue as its streaks, only translucent.

Michael Lim
The American International School, Vienna, Austria
First appeared in *Merlyn's Pen*

The writer includes details such as the color and shape of the fish to help the reader see it.

Describe a Person

Picture in your mind a person with whom you enjoy spending time. List words or phrases that capture the person's appearance and personality. Use these details in a written description.

PURPOSE To describe a person by using details

AUDIENCE Yourself

LENGTH 1–2 paragraphs

WRITING RUBRICS To describe by using details, you should

- choose details that will bring life to your description
- use your senses to help you choose details

Artist unknown, Mughal, *Fantastic Birds*, c. 1590

Cross-Curricular Activity

ART Imagine you saw one of the birds in the painting on your way to school. Write to a friend and describe what you saw. Include as many precise details as possible about the bird to help your friend picture it.

Listening and Speaking

COOPERATIVE LEARNING Describe to a small group a favorite memory or special place. Make notes on what you will say and include several precise details. As you speak, change the loudness and tone of your voice to fit what you are saying. Use your voice to help bring your description to life for your listeners.

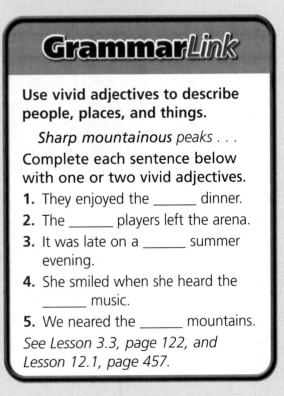

GrammarLink

Use vivid adjectives to describe people, places, and things.

Sharp mountainous peaks . . .

Complete each sentence below with one or two vivid adjectives.

1. They enjoyed the _____ dinner.
2. The _____ players left the arena.
3. It was late on a _____ summer evening.
4. She smiled when she heard the _____ music.
5. We neared the _____ mountains.

See Lesson 3.3, page 122, and Lesson 12.1, page 457.

Collecting Sensory Details

We use our sight, hearing, smell, touch, and taste to experience the world. These sensory details help bring a description to life.

Imagine that you've stepped into the painting below. What do you see, hear, feel, smell, and taste?

Thomas Hart Benton, *Cradling Wheat*, 1938

Use Sensory Detail

Artists use color, shape, and pattern to pull you into a painting. Writers do the same thing with sensory language—language that appeals to the senses. Sensory language describes how something looks, sounds, feels, smells, or tastes. In the following passage, Beverly Cleary's word choice helps engage our senses.

These walks, with the sound of cowbells tinkling in the woods by the river, and bobwhites, like fat little hens, calling their names, filled me with joy as I searched for flowers whose names Mother taught me: shy kitten's ears with grayish white, soft-haired pointed petals which grew flat to the ground and which I stroked, pretending they really were kitten's ears; buttercups and Johnny-jump-ups to be gathered by the handful; stalks of fox-gloves with pink bell-shaped flowers which I picked and fitted over my fingers, pretending I was a fox wearing gloves; robin's eggs, speckled and shaped like a broken eggshell, which had such a strong odor Mother tactfully placed my bouquet in a mason jar on the back porch "so they will look pretty when Daddy comes in."

Beverly Cleary, *A Girl from Yamhill*

Prewriting Tip

Before you take notes for a description, close your eyes and concentrate on the senses of taste, touch, hearing, and smell.

What words does Cleary use to appeal to different senses?

Cleary, like all good writers, tries to engage her reader's senses when she writes a description. You can hear the tinkling cowbells and see grayish white kitten's ears. You can feel the velvet touch of petals and smell the nasty odor of robin's-eggs flowers. The writer takes you with her by telling exactly what she experienced.

Journal Writing

In your journal, list words and phrases describing a meal you remember: the food you ate and the people you were with. Use words and phrases from all five senses.

Use Observations to Write Descriptions

Writing a good description begins with careful observation. This first step may be difficult if you are not used to looking at things closely. The chart shows how you can move from observing details to writing descriptions. In the model Jessica Griffiths uses details she observed to describe a familiar day.

From Observing to Writing	
Impressions	**Description**
Relaxed smile **New (short) haircut**	Mr. Marshall greets students with a relaxed smile. His thick black hair, which was rather long last year, is clipped neatly above his ears.
Slamming lockers **Squeaky new shoes**	As the hallways fill with students, locker doors slam with a staccato beat. New shoes squeak as they skid across the freshly polished floor.
Shiny pencil sharpener **Smelly pencil shavings**	On the first day of school, the shiny pencil sharpener doesn't get a rest. It grinds pencils to a sharp point. The strong smell of shavings fills the air.

Student Model

What sounds of the first day of school does the writer describe?

The writer combines sounds and scents to create this description.

The first day of school is always exciting and a bit scary. Students greet old friends, and teachers chat in the hallways. The squeak of new shoes and the scuffling of sneakers on the linoleum floor mingle with the girls' giggling. Slamming lockers echo in the long corridors. The scent of bubble gum contrasts with the sharp smell of erasers and lead shavings. Pencil sharpeners grinding are a reminder that class has started. Late students hurry to their classrooms. A new school year has begun.

Jessica Griffiths, Springman Junior High School
Glenview, Illinois

Write a Description of a Walk

Think of a walk you take often. It could be down the hall of your school or through a park. List sensory details from your walk.

Use the details to write a paragraph describing your walk. Have a friend read and comment on your description. Take into account your friend's comments as you revise your writing.

PURPOSE To describe a familiar walk using sensory details

AUDIENCE A friend

LENGTH 1 paragraph

WRITING RUBRICS To use sensory details in a description, you should

- observe or recall the details of your experience
- take notes on what you see, hear, smell, touch, and taste
- use your notes to write your description

Listening and Speaking

COOPERATIVE LEARNING In a group, list names of characters from television or books. Select characters familiar to everyone in the group. List details that describe each character. Then choose a character to describe. Share your description and challenge the group to identify the character you described.

Viewing and Representing

Choose an advertisement from a magazine. The advertisement should picture an item that appeals to the senses, such as a pile of dried leaves or a freshly baked pizza. Write a one-paragraph description to go with the picture. Be sure to use sensory details. Share your description with a partner.

GrammarLink

Use apostrophes correctly in possessive nouns.

Use an apostrophe plus *s* to form the possessive of a singular noun and of a plural noun that does not end in *s*. Use an apostrophe alone to form the possessive of a plural noun that ends in *s*.

Some examples are *a **kitten's** paws, the **mice's** tails, the **girls'** friends.*

Write each sentence, using apostrophes where necessary.

1. The childrens tears were salty on their tongues.
2. The suns rays warmed my skin.
3. When Al opened the carton, both boys noses wrinkled in disgust.
4. Not a ripple disturbed the lakes placid surface.

See Lesson 20.7, page 611.

LOG ON ▶ **Writing** Online   For more writing and grammar practice, go to glencoe.com and enter QuickPass code WC87703p1.

121

LESSON
3.3

Using Precise Language

*P*recise language is exact language; it says what the writer means and creates an image in the reader's mind. On a poster for a lost dog, precise language gets results.

LOST
During Storm

Small dog, smooth coat.
Some black marks.
Funny-looking tail.
Please call 555-3454
if you see our dog.

Harry the beagle is
LOST

Mixed brown, black,
and white coat.
Pink nose
with small black marks.
All-black ears.
Tail bent slightly.
Please call 555-3454.

Choose Precise Nouns and Adjectives

A good description includes specific nouns and exact adjectives. A precise noun, *beagle* or *Harry*, is more informative than a general noun, *dog*. The adjectives *brown, black,* and *white* describe the dog's coat more precisely than the vague adjective *smooth.* The difference between a general and a precise description is like the difference between the dogs in the pictures on the next page. Notice the precise words that Sarah Burch used in the next model.

From General to Specific

Dog | Golden Retriever | Jake

Student Model

As the sound of thunder rumbles through the foggy November rain, you sit next to the roaring fire in your cozy living room. Waiting patiently for the wicked storm to pass, you notice clouds of varying shapes and textures highlighted by zig-zags of lightning. Branches plunge to the ground as winds gust violently. Rain forms muddy puddles along the rutty driveway. The crackling birch in the fireplace and the constant glow of the embers comfort you throughout the ferocious storm.

Sarah Burch, Springman Junior High School
Glenview, Illinois

> What adjectives does the writer use to contrast the scenes inside and outside the house?

Journal Writing

Imagine that you have lost an object that is important to you. Make a list of precise words that describe the lost object. Then use the words to write a notice asking for help in locating the object.

Before reading your finished writing aloud, use a dictionary to check the pronunciation of any words you are not sure how to pronounce.

Choose Precise Verbs and Adverbs

Just as precise nouns and adjectives help create a vivid description, precise verbs and adverbs energize descriptive writing. Your choice of words will depend on the impression you want to make. For example, you might decide on the verb *devour* or *gobble*, rather than *eat*, to describe the action of eating hungrily.

Notice how the writer concentrated on finding more precise verbs and more vivid adverbs as she revised her description of her guinea pig.

Find examples of precise, well-chosen adverbs.

Why does "whirls" create a clearer picture of Attila than "circles"?

"Stalks" is more exact than "walks."

Attila is a guinea pig with an attitude. From his tiny white ears to his short black legs, Attila wages war mercilessly. Mealtime is his battlefield. At dinnertime he fixes his beady eyes on me as he ~~eats~~ *devours* his well-prepared guinea pig salad. Then his plump, black-and-white body tenses. He waits impatiently for the main course. Attila ~~scratches angrily~~ *claws fiercely* at the cage. He ~~circles~~ *whirls* around the cage. All night long Attila ~~walks~~ *stalks* restlessly near his plate. The next morning the battle begins again.

Describe from an Animal's Point of View

Using precise words, write a description of an object from an animal's point of view. Choose your own topic or one of these: a canoe as it might seem to a whale; a pizza slice as it appears to an ant; a ball of yarn from the point of view of a cat playing with it.

PURPOSE To use precise words to create vivid and energetic descriptions

AUDIENCE Your classmates

LENGTH 1–2 paragraphs

WRITING RUBRICS To write a vivid description, you should

- use specific nouns and adjectives
- use precise verbs and adverbs

Collaborative Writing

In a small group, revise a piece of writing found in a newspaper or magazine. One person in the group should list precise nouns. The second should list vivid adjectives. The third should list strong verbs. The fourth should list intense adverbs. The group should work together to complete the revision. Finally, one member of the group should make a final copy that includes all the changes and read the revised article aloud to the group.

Viewing and Representing

Make up a sales brochure—for clothing, hobbies, music, or another kind of product. Draw illustrations of your product or clip them from magazines. Arrange the pictures on paper that has been folded in thirds, like a letter. Then write two or three sentences of vivid, precise description beneath each illustration.

Grammar*Link*

Use vivid adverbs to describe verbs, adjectives, and other adverbs.

Attila wages war **mercilessly.**
Attila claws **fiercely** *at the cage.*

For each sentence below, list three different adverbs that could be used to complete it.

1. The horse trotted _____ around the paddock.
2. Jamila approached the foul line _____ tentatively.
3. Quentin searched _____ for his lost notebook.
4. The _____ graceful dancers moved to the beat of the music.
5. The car traveled _____ down the street.

See Lesson 3.3, page 122, and 12.5, page 465.

LOG ON ▶ **Writing** Online For more writing and grammar practice, go to **glencoe.com** and enter QuickPass code WC87703p1.

125

LESSON 3.4

Using Spatial Order

A painter arranges details so that the viewer sees an ordered picture. A writer describes details so that the reader imagines a scene clearly.

The Flemish painter Jan Vermeer arranged the details in this image so that the viewer's eye moves from behind the artist to the scene he is painting. Writers, like painters, arrange the details of a scene in a certain order and for a particular reason.

Jan Vermeer, *Allegory of the Art of Painting*, c. 1665–1670

Order Details Logically

Writers can order details in several ways, depending on the point in space that seems a logical starting place. Details can be ordered from top to bottom, from near to far, or from left to right. When looking at a building, for example, you might first see a nearby detail such as a decorative door frame. Then, farther up the front of the building, you notice decorative stone faces above the windows. To describe this building, you could order these details from near to far.

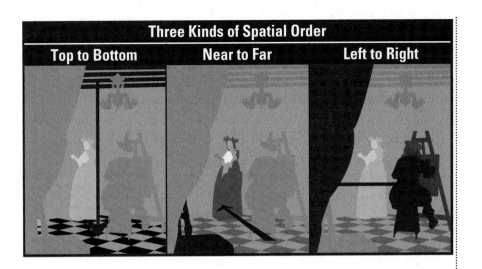

Three Kinds of Spatial Order

Top to Bottom	Near to Far	Left to Right

Sometimes a scene lends itself to a particular kind of spatial order. Notice how Laurence Yep uses top-to-bottom spatial order to describe a Chinese playground.

Literature Model

In those days, it consisted of levels. The first level near the alley that became known as Hang Ah Alley was a volleyball and a tennis court. Down the steps was the next level with a sandbox (which was usually full of fleas), a small director's building, a Ping-Pong table, an area covered by tan bark that housed a slide, a set of bars, and a set of swings and other simple equipment.

Laurence Yep, *The Lost Garden*

> Which words in the description identify the spatial order as top to bottom?

Journal Writing

Imagine that you are at a place you remember well. Choose one type of spatial order to describe the details of the place. In your journal write your description in that order.

Editing Tip

As you edit, punctuate prepositional phrases correctly. For more information see Lesson 20.2, page 601.

Link the Details

When you use spatial order, you must give your audience a way to picture the scene as you move from one detail to the next. Transition words, such as *under, to the right,* and *behind,* help to link details so that readers can follow the path you have created. Notice how transition words act as directional sign posts in Sarah Fisher's description of a room and in the diagram based on her description.

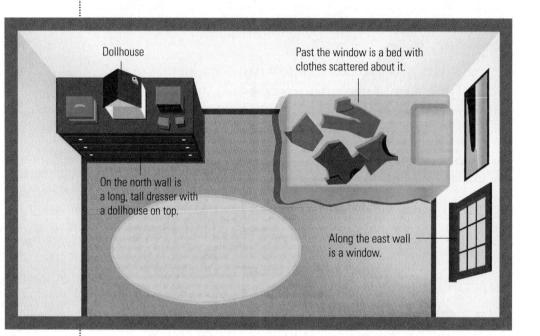

Dollhouse

Past the window is a bed with clothes scattered about it.

On the north wall is a long, tall dresser with a dollhouse on top.

Along the east wall is a window.

Notice how Sarah uses phrases like "on the north wall" to help you find your way around the room.

Sarah's use of parallelism unifies the paragraph. How do the sentences begin?

Student Model

Along the east wall is a window. Past the window is a bed with clothes scattered about it. On the north wall is a long, tall dresser with a dollhouse on top. To the right of the dollhouse are three jewelry boxes, one big and two small. To the left of the dollhouse is a purple box with a pink handle. This box holds my hair accessories and small gift boxes.

Sarah Fisher, Solomon Schechter Day School
Skokie, Illinois

Use Spatial Order

Use spatial order to write a one-paragraph description. Choose your own topic or one of these: a person's face from top to bottom or a ballpark from home plate to left field. For help with using spatial order in describing details, see **Writing and Research Handbook,** page 836.

PURPOSE   To describe, using spatial order
AUDIENCE   Your teacher
LENGTH   1 paragraph

WRITING RUBRICS   To describe using spatial order, you should

- decide how you will describe—from top to bottom, near to far, or left to right
- use transition words to help readers follow your spatial description

Carolyn Brady, *Sky Blue and Peach,* 1989

Cross-Curricular Activity

ART   Write a one-paragraph description of Carolyn Brady's painting, using one kind of spatial order. Show your description to a friend, and ask if he or she can identify the type of order you have used.

Grammar*Link*

Use prepositional phrases in spatial descriptions.

  Down the steps *was the next level . . .*

Incorporate each prepositional phrase below into a sentence of spatial description.

1. through the swinging doors
2. across the street
3. between the two paintings
4. on top of the crates
5. against the opposite wall

See Lesson 13.1, page 481, and Lesson 21.1, page 629.

Listening and Speaking

Write a one-paragraph spatial description of a real or imagined place. Read your description to a partner. Your partner should sketch the place according to the details you have provided. Use the drawing to evaluate whether your description was precise. Then trade roles.

Describing a Thing

Describing a thing involves creating a clear image of that particular thing in the reader's mind. The reader can picture the object's size and shape; more importantly, the reader knows what makes it special.

A packed suitcase bulges before you. You're in a new place, about to unpack and start a new life. Your thoughts turn to the things you couldn't bring with you. You picture some of the treasures you left behind. How can you describe something that is important to you? In the student model below, notice how Amanda Morgan describes a well-loved bear.

Student Model

Teddy is no placid-looking bear. He is stubborn looking. He is very well loved (as bears often get), and he is beginning to come apart at the seams. Mom tried to fix this tragic problem by sewing him up with bright red-and-blue yarn. The yarn is faded and looking a bit tattered itself, for the surgery was done about nine years ago.

Amanda Morgan, Neskowin, Oregon
First appeared in *Treasures: Stories and Art by Students in Oregon*

Choose the Details

The process of writing a good description begins with choosing an object that has meaning for you. It may be right in front of your eyes, or it may be stored in your memory. Once you decide on your subject, note details that will help you describe it. If you're looking at the object, jot down the details you observe. If you're remembering something, list details that make it memorable for you.

Asking yourself questions can help you choose details. For example, you might ask how something appears at different times of the day, what senses you use to observe it, or to what you might compare it. The questions below, although linked to a specific object, may help you think of other questions you can ask yourself to remember descriptive details.

1. How old is my bike?
   My brother bought it new three years ago.
2. What condition is it in?
   worn but well cared for; cracked seat
3. What color is my bike?
   mostly metallic blue with gray tires
4. What memories about my bike come to mind?
   the first time I rode it down our street after moving here; riding in the rain with Chris

Journal Writing

Write three or four questions about the appearance of something that is important to you. Answer your questions in your journal, making sure to record specific details.

Revising Tip

As you revise a description, be sure that the details you have included follow the grouping you are using.

Prewriting Tip

For help with organizing details that describe a thing, see **Writing and Research Handbook,** page 836.

Organize the Details

As you list the important details that describe a thing, consider ways to group these details. The thing itself may suggest a certain kind of grouping. The chart below shows three principles you can use to group details.

Grouping Details by Different Principles	
Principle	**Examples**
Shape/Color	Baggy blue-gray sweater, ankle-length denim skirt
Appearance/Function	Porch chair, rusted and bent, but still comfortable
Whole/Parts	Broken checkerboard, a bag of dominoes

Make the Details Interesting

Notice how Leslie Marmon Silko groups her details around the color of the sandstone. Like Silko, you can make your writing interesting by using vivid sensory details—details that appeal to the senses. Comparisons in the form of similes and metaphors also work to bring your subject to life. Remember to use precise language and include transitions.

What precise adjectives does the writer use?

Literature Model

But this time there was something about the colors of the sandstone. The reddish pink and orange yellow looked as if they had been taken from the center of the sky as the sun went down. She had never seen such intense color in sandstone. She had always remembered it being shades of pale yellow or peppered white—colors for walls and fences. But these rocks looked as if rain had just fallen on them.

Leslie Marmon Silko, "Private Property"

Write a Description of a Childhood Treasure

Think of something that was important to you in your childhood, such as a book or a stuffed animal. Write a description of it to share with a friend.

PURPOSE To write an effective description of an object

AUDIENCE A friend

LENGTH 1–2 paragraphs

WRITING RUBRICS To write an effective description, you should

- list details
- group the details in a logical order, such as by shape/color, appearance/function, or whole/parts

Cross-Curricular Activity

SOCIAL STUDIES One common childhood treasure is the teddy bear. How did teddy bears come to be? What president is the bear named after, and why? Find out the history of teddy bears. Write a paragraph and share your findings with the class.

Using Computers

Create a computer vocabulary file listing words that describe or name sensory details related to your childhood treasure. Use your computer's thesaurus to find adjectives that precisely describe colors, shapes, textures, smells, and sizes. Refer to the list as you draft a description.

Grammar*Link*

Be sure that each pronoun clearly refers to its antecedent.

The antecedent is the word or group of words to which a pronoun refers. A pronoun must agree with its antecedent in number and gender.

*But these **rocks** looked as if rain had just fallen on **them.***

Complete the sentences below with appropriate pronouns.

1. When Sam's mother asked to see his report, ____ showed ____ to ____.
2. The principal posted the announcements so that we could read ____.
3. The students weren't expecting the fire drill buzzer, so ____ were startled when ____ heard ____.
4. Since my younger sister knows I'm good in math, ____ asked ____ to help ____ with the word problems.
5. Sarah said that ____ does not know who will be at the party.

See Lesson 11.1, page 435, and Lesson 11.2, page 437.

LOG ON ▶ **Writing** Online | For more writing and grammar practice, go to **glencoe.com** and enter QuickPass code WC87703p1.

133

WRITING ABOUT LITERATURE
Describing the Subject of a Biography

In a biography a writer, or biographer, tells the true story of a person's life. In the following passage, Lisa Aldred creates a verbal snapshot of the young boy who would later become Supreme Court Justice Thurgood Marshall.

Literature Model

He "was a jolly boy who always had something to say." But, she added, Thurgood showed a serious side as well. "I can still see him coming down Division Street every Sunday afternoon about one o'clock," she said. "He'd be wearing knee pants with both hands dug way into his pockets and be kicking a stone in front of him as he crossed over to Dolphin Street to visit his grandparents at their big grocery store on the corner. He was in a deep study, that boy, and it was plain something was going on inside him."

Lisa Aldred, *Thurgood Marshall*

A biographer's purpose is to make the subject of the biography come to life on the page. In this model biographer Lisa Aldred uses the words of a family friend, Odell Payne, to give us a vivid glimpse of the serious side of young Thurgood Marshall (pictured in the center)—future Supreme Court Justice.

Form Strong Impressions

By telling what a person did and said, a biographer can bring the person to life on the pages. Descriptions of the subject's physical appearance and personality help the reader form impressions of the person. Here are some students' reactions to young Thurgood Marshall.

The description of the boy reminds me of my cousin Wilma. She used to spend hours skipping stones at the pond. I once crept up behind her. She didn't even notice me. Like Thurgood, Wilma was always "in a deep study." Sometimes that annoyed me, though!

How is Thurgood like this student's cousin Wilma?

I just read a book my grandfather should read. It tells about the early life of Thurgood Marshall, who was a Supreme Court justice. Grandfather's always telling me to pay attention. If he reads the book, he'll know I'm just "in a deep study."

This student has a good impression of Thurgood because he sees some of his own traits in the famous man.

Journal Writing

Describe someone you know well doing something he or she does often. Concentrate on using this action to illustrate your subject's personality.

Editing Tip

As you edit, be sure that you have correct subject-verb agreement in your sentences. For more information, see Lessons 16.1–16.5, pages 541–550.

Focus on the Subject

A good biography paints a portrait of the subject, including his or her appearance, personality, and attitudes. With precise language, sensory details, clear organization, and strong transitions, the subject of a biography comes into sharp focus. After reading Jean Fritz's *The Great Little Madison,* Andrea Gaines wrote the imaginary letter below. Notice how she uses details that paint a portrait of the young Madison.

Student Model

October 16, 1769

Dear Aunt Winnefred,

How are you?

Sorry I haven't written you lately, but I've been busy here at Princeton. This is only my first year here, but I feel as though I have a number of friends already. One of them is a quiet sophomore, James Madison. He's kind of short and thin, and has a very low voice. His handsome face glows with energy. He throws himself into everything he does, whether it's reading books, protesting British taxes, or joining student fun.

I must run to class. I'll write to you later about my other friends.

Your loving niece,
Susan

Andrea Gaines,
Martha M. Ruggles
Elementary School,
Chicago, Illinois

What details of Madison's appearance does Andrea provide?

What details of Madison's personality does Andrea point out?

Eighteenth-century Princeton University

Write a Descriptive Response

Respond to a biography about a political figure. You may use the excerpt from *Thurgood Marshall* or choose another biography that interests you. Think of creative ways to respond, as Andrea Gaines does on the previous page. Include your own description of the subject, as you see him or her.

PURPOSE To write a descriptive response
AUDIENCE Your teacher and classmates
LENGTH 2 paragraphs

WRITING RUBRICS To write a descriptive response, you should

- use vivid details and precise language to describe your impressions
- make sure your description brings the subject to life

Viewing and Representing

Locate images of the subject you have chosen for your response. View photographs, portraits, political cartoons, and even film footage, if available. What does each image show of the personality of your subject? List your reactions and discuss them with a partner.

GrammarLink

Use quotation marks and other punctuation correctly in direct quotations.

"A painting, as well as a book, can be a biography," said the art teacher.

Write each sentence, adding quotation marks and other punctuation where necessary.

1. The student asked Did Joan Brown really swim to Alcatraz?
2. She tried said the teacher but she did not make it to the island.
3. A ship passed by her and the wake nearly caused her to drown explained the teacher.
4. The teacher explained She created a painting after she attempted to swim to the island.

See Lesson 20.6, page 609.

Using Computers

Using a software drawing program, create a graphic organizer, such as a web. Organize details about your subject in the graphic organizer. Add precise words that will help you describe. Then use your web to develop your descriptive response.

Descriptive Writing

Writing Process in Action

Descriptive Writing

In preceding lessons you've learned about using memories and observations in descriptive writing. You've learned about sensory details, precise language, and order of details. You've written a variety of descriptions. Now, in this lesson, you'll have a chance to describe the people, places, and things that are part of something you enjoy doing.

Assignment

Context	You are writing an article for the magazine *Popular Hobbies*. This magazine contains descriptions of the people, places, and things associated with various student hobbies.
Purpose	To describe people, places, and things related to your favorite hobby
Audience	Student readers of *Popular Hobbies*
Length	1 page

Planning to Write

The following pages can help you plan and write your descriptions. Read through them, and then refer to them as you need to. But don't be tied down by them. You're in charge of your own writing process. Be sure to set a time frame for completing this assignment. It will help you to manage your time wisely. Keep in mind the controlling idea: to describe people, places, and things related to your hobby.

Writing Online

For prewriting, drafting, revising, editing and publishing tools, go to **glencoe.com** and enter QuickPass code WC87703p1.

Prewriting

Start by thinking about the people, places, and things that go with your favorite hobby. To explore your answers, you might use one or all the options at the right. Perhaps you'll observe and take notes, use your journal to recall details, or freewrite.

Option A
Observe and take notes on details.

Option B
Review your journal.

Option C
Explore your ideas through freewriting.

I zoom along the smooth path by the park. People picnic, play radios, and eat things like fried chicken. I remember my bike rides by the songs I hear and food that I smell.

Drafting

Look over your prewriting, and think about ways of organizing your material into clear images. You might start with the most important details or with the details closest to you. Just use the order that makes the most sense to you, and let the writing flow. Notice how David Weitzman sets the scene at an old-time

Literature Model

It was like the Fourth of July. Kids clambered up and slid down the hay stacks, played tag and skip-to-my-lou. Some of the men were pitching horseshoes and you could hear the thump of shoes fallen too short and the solid clank of a ringer. The women looked after all the little kids and put out lunches on big tables—heaps of potato salad, sandwiches, cakes and cookies, and frosty pitchers of iced tea.

David Weitzman, *Thrashin' Time*

Drafting Tip

For more information about using sensory details, see Lessons 3.1 and 3.2, pages 114–121.

harvest. A description rich in detail and sensory language can give your readers a clear picture of the world of your hobby.

Writing Process in Action

Revising Tip

Check to see that your word choice makes sense. For more information, see Lesson 3.2, page 18.

Revising

Begin by rereading the assignment. Have you written what's been asked for? As soon as you're satisfied that you have, you can move on.

Now it's time to look at your draft and make it better. But first put your draft aside for a day, if possible. During this time, you might go back and review pages 66–77.

To begin revising, read over your draft to make sure that what you have written fits your purpose and your audience. Then have a writing conference. Read your draft to a partner or small group. Use your audience's reactions to help you evaluate your work.

Look at the revision below and use questions like the ones shown to guide your own revisions. Remember, revising is where many great writers do their best work, so work with care.

Question A

Have I used all my senses?

Question B

Are my images crisp and clear?

Question C

Are my details specific and linked with transitions?

Biking by the park is a great hobby because of
all the picnics you wiz past. On weekends you
zoom   blasting and smell the barbecues
can go by and hear radios. You pass by all the
on soft blankets
people sitting or throwing Frisbees. And
see
sometimes when you sea people you know, you
can stop and talk to them or share a glass of
sweet pink
lemonade. Alongside you all the sights, sounds,
and smells blur together.

Editing/Proofreading

Edit your description to correct any mistakes. Read it several times, using the questions in this checklist. Ask a different question each time through. For example, you might **proofread** for capitalization and punctuation on your first pass and spelling on your second pass. Afterward, have someone else review your work. Other people can often see your mistakes better than you can.

Publishing/Presenting

Make a clean copy of your description. If possible, use a computer or word processor to give your work a professional look. Now you are ready to send your work to *Popular Hobbies*. You may want to include a drawing or photograph to illustrate your description. Do not feel that you have to include an illustration, though. Even without a picture, your description should be detailed enough so that your readers should be able to imagine the people, places, and things related to the hobby you have chosen.

Editing/Proofreading Checklist

1. Have I correctly used apostrophes in possessive nouns?
2. Do my pronouns have clear antecedents?
3. Have I correctly punctuated quotations?
4. Have I spelled every word correctly?

Proofreading Tip

For proofreading symbols, see pages 79 and 863. If you have composed on the computer, use the spelling and grammar checkers to help with proofreading.

Journal Writing: Write to Learn

Reflect on your writing process experience. Answer these questions in your journal: What did you like best about your description? What was the hardest part of writing it? What did you learn in your writing conference? What new things have you learned as a writer?

Literature Model

FROM

Thrashin' Time

by David Weitzman

In Thrashin' Time: Harvest Days in the Dakotas, *David Weitzman describes farm life in 1912 North Dakota through the eyes of young Peter Anders. As you read the following passage, pay special attention to the way Peter describes an autumn day when the whole neighborhood gathers to see a steam traction engine for the first time. Then try the activities in Linking Writing and Literature on page 148.*

Anna and I began pestering Pa to take us over to see the new engine. But it didn't take much doing. I could tell he wanted to go as much as we did. Pa glanced again at the smoke billowing into the sky. "Ya, sure, we can go. I'll finish up a bit here. Peter, you go hitch the horses up to the wagon. Maggie, if you and Anna put up a picnic, we'll go have us a look at that steam engine."

We got there to find that a lot of folks had come in wagons and buggies to gather 'round and watch the thrashin'.[1] Steam engines were still

---

1 thrashin' (thrash′ ən) [or threshing (thresh′ ing)] separating grain or seeds from a plant

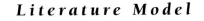

new in these parts. And there it was, the engine with its dark blue boiler, shiny brass whistle, red wheels all decorated with yellow stripes, gears spinning and rods going back and forth, rocking gently in time to the puffs of smoke from the stack—*tucka-tucka-tucka-tucka-tucka*. The sounds, that's what I liked. *Tucka-tucka-tucka-tucka* and the little steam engine going *ss—ss—ss—ss—ss—ss—ss*. The engine was quieter than I thought it would be. It was almost alive like the horses working everywhere 'round it. And the horses. Why, I'll betcha there were sixty head, big horses—Belgians and Percherons[2]—coming and going that afternoon. Teams pulled bundle wagons heaped tall with sheaves of wheat in from the fields, pulled wagons of yellow grain away from the separator to the silo. Another team hauled the water wagon, and another wagon brought loads of cord wood to keep the engine running sunup to sundown.

It was like the Fourth of July. Kids clambered up and slid down the hay stacks, played tag and skip-to-my-lou. Some of the men were pitching horseshoes and you could hear the thump of shoes

David Weitzman, from *Thrashin' Time*, 1991

---

2 Belgians (Bel′ jǝnz) **and Percherons** (Pur′ chǝ ronz′) large, powerful horses used to drag heavy loads

fallen too short and the solid clank of a ringer. The women looked after all the little kids and put out lunches on big tables—heaps of potato salad, sandwiches, cakes and cookies and frosty pitchers of iced tea. Dogs napped in the dark cool under the wagons, not paying any mind to the puppies tumbling all over them. The older boys stood around together, pretending they were chewing plugs of tobacco, hawking and spitting, like the thrashermen, only theirs wouldn't come brown. The men stood around the engine and the separator, puffing on their pipes, thumbs hooked under their suspenders. They inspected every part of that machine, pointing to this and that, looked up and down the belt stretching between the engine and the separator in a long figure eight. Most of them had never seen a steam traction engine before.

> ❝ *You know, Peter, that's a wonderful thing, the steam engine. You're witnessin' the beginnin's of real scientific farmin'.* ❞

Some of the older folks didn't like the new machine. "The old ways is the best ways," one of them said, tug-ging on his whiskers. "All this talk about steam engines is just a bunch of gibble-gabble," agreed another, "I'll stick to my oxen and horses." Others told of hearing all about engines exploding, killing and maiming[3] the thrashin' crews, of careless engineers starting fires that burned up the farmer's whole crop and his barn besides. "Horses live off the land," Mr. Bauer said, "and don't need wood or coal. No, nothin' but some hay and oats and we don't have to buy that! What's more they give you foals." He reached over and rubbed his hand down the neck of a stout gray Percheron mare hitched to a grain wagon. "All you get from steam engines is debt." Mr. Bjork agreed, "and what would we do for fertilizer? Steam engines don't make much manure, you know." Everyone laughed. "More trouble than they're worth. Why, last year Silas McGregor had to come borrow my oxen to pull his engine out of the mud. Wouldn't have one of those smoke-snortin' strawburners on my place," old Mr. Erstad scoffed, turning and waving away the scene.

---

3 maiming (mām′ ing) causing an injury so as to cripple or cause the loss of some part of the body

Thomas Hart Benton, *July Hay,* 1943

But Mr. Torgrimson, now I could tell he was enjoying it. We were looking at the steam engine there up on the boiler, the connecting rod whizzing back and forth and the flywheel spinning so that the spokes were just a red blur. He was smiling and his eyes just twinkled. Then he pointed the stem of his pipe at the engine, squinted in a thoughtful way and rocked back and forth on his heels. "You know, Peter, that's a wonderful thing, the steam engine. You're witnessin' the beginnin's of real scientific farmin'." He couldn't take his eyes off that engine. "I read about a steam outfit—over Casselton way it was—that thrashed more than six thousand bushels in one day! Imagine that, six thousand bushels in just one day! Why you and your Ma and Pa all workin' together couldn't do more'n twenty or thirty in the same time."

Mr. Torgrimson was the one who told me all about bonanza farming, where a bunch of engines would start out together, side-by-side, before daybreak, each pulling a fourteen-bottom plow almost as wide as our house. "They go all day, Peter, breakin' up thousands of acres of prairie grasslands before they rest at night—some even have head lamps so they can just keep going all night. The holdin's are so big, young fellow, that they go on 'n on for days like that 'fore they reach their line and turn 'round and plow back to where they started. Day after day, week after week they go up and back. Then they sowed all that land to wheat and thrashed one hundred and sixty-two thousand—here, I'll just write that number in the dust so you can see how big it is—162,000 bushels of wheat that season."

> **They go all day, Peter, breakin' up thousands of acres of prairie grasslands before they rest at night**

I could tell Pa liked the engine too. He got up on the wagon and pitched bundles for a while, and then stood on the engine platform talking to the engineer, Mr. Parker. When he got down, he came over and put his hand on my shoulder, all the time looking at the engine, shaking his head like he couldn't believe his eyes. "Parker's got some machine there, by jippers, quite an outfit. What do you think about all this, Peter, steam power instead of horse power?"

I wasn't sure. "If the engine took the place of the horses, I think I'd miss Annie and Lulu and Quinn. Wouldn't you, Pa?"

"I would, but, you know, horse-power thrashin' is awful hard on them, son. Sure, I'd miss them, but we work them hard all year plowin' and diskin',[4] and seedin' and mowin'.

> **If the engine took the place of the horses, I think I'd miss Annie and Lulu and Quinn. Wouldn't you, Pa?**

Then just when they're so tuckered out, about to drop and needin' a good rest, we put them to thrashin'.

You and I both have seen too many good horses broken, seen them drop, die of the heat and tiredness right there in the traces. And for all their work we might get a hundred bushels, maybe two in a day. I don't know, Peter, maybe steam power is a better thing. I just don't know." Pa chuckled and his eyes got all crinkled and wrinkled with laugh lines the way they do. "I do know one thing though. If you asked the horses, I betcha they wouldn't be against this new steam power the way some folks 'round here are."

---

4 diskin' (disk´ən) breaking up soil with a disk-shaped tool

Linking Writing and Literature

◆ Learning to Learn

Think about the main idea of *Thrashin' Time*. Write briefly in your journal about the effects of new technologies in your life. Do you usually accept new technology readily, or are you sometimes resistant? Explain.

◆ Talk About Reading

Discuss with your classmates the issues raised in *Thrashin' Time*. Select one classmate to lead the discussion and another to take notes. The following questions will help focus your discussion.

1. **Connect to Your Life** In this story, it is clear that the steam engine is going to change life on North Dakota farms. Think about one exciting new technology that you have experienced. How has it changed your life?

2. **Critical Thinking: Evaluate** The characters in this story express a number of opinions about the new steam engine. Which of these opinions do you most agree with? Why?

3. **6+1 Trait®: Ideas** What is the main idea of *Thrashin' Time*? What technique does David Weitzman use to express that main idea in his writing? In other words, how do you know what the main idea is?

4. **Connect to Your Writing** Think about how David Weitzman describes the steam engine. Make a list of the details he includes to bring the steam engine to life for his readers.

◆ Write About Reading

Persuasive Essay Write a persuasive essay in which you argue for or against some new technology you have seen or read about. Begin with a vivid description of the technology. Then explain why you find this technology either exciting or troublesome. Be sure to state your position clearly and support it with solid arguments. Once you have supported your position, restate your main idea in the conclusion.

Focus on Ideas The ideas of your persuasive essay are the arguments you use to support your position. As you develop these arguments, ask yourself what those who disagree with you might say. In the end, your ideas will be stronger if you have thought about opposing views.

For more information on ideas and the 6+1 Trait® model, see **Writing and Research Handbook,** pages 838–840.

6+1 Trait® is a registered trademark of Northwest Regional Educational Laboratory, which does not endorse this product.

Personal Writing

Reflecting on the Unit: Summarize What You Learned

Focus on the following questions to help you summarize what you have learned in this unit.

❶ How does descriptive writing begin?
❷ How do sensory details improve descriptive writing?
❸ What does describing an object involve?
❹ What kind of language improves a description?
❺ Why is clear spatial order important to descriptive writing?
❻ How can a biographer bring a person to life?

Adding to Your Portfolio

CHOOSE A SELECTION FOR YOUR PORTFOLIO Look over the writing you did for this unit. Choose a piece of writing for your portfolio. The writing you choose should show one or more of the following:

- personal memories or observations
- vivid word pictures
- sensory details that appeal to more than one of the five senses
- precise language
- details in a clear spatial order
- an effective choice of details

REFLECT ON YOUR CHOICE Attach a note to the piece you chose, explaining briefly why you chose it and what you learned from writing it.

SET GOALS How can you improve your writing? What skill will you focus on the next time you write?

Writing Across the Curriculum

MAKE A HISTORY CONNECTION Think about your favorite hobby, and imagine that you are living before electricity was used in homes. How would living then affect the people, places, or things that are part of your hobby? Would your hobby exist? If not, what hobby might you have instead? Write a paragraph explaining how you might have spent your time.

> **"You are the prettiest girl here, will you dance . . . and we are dancing. . . . "**
>
> —Sandra Cisneros,
> "Chanclas"

Narrative Writing

Writing in the Real World

MEDIA
Monologue
Connection

A narrative is writing or speech that tells a story. Since history abounds with compelling stories about real people, it is fertile ground for narrative writing. Arthur Johnson is an interpreter of African American history for Colonial Williamsburg, a "village" that recreates life in the 1700s. Johnson attempts to take on the personality, mannerisms, and character of the historical figure he portrays—Matthew Ashby.

Matthew Ashby of Colonial Williamsburg, Monologue performed by Arthur Johnson

"I'll never forget when I got married. For me it was a great, great day. You see, that night the preacher had come around. His name was Gowan. It seemed like all of my friends were around, such as Adam, who gave me a bucket.

"Gowan said a few words to Ann and me. And it seemed like when he told us to jump over that broom—and we jumped—Ann let me jump the farthest, to let me know that she would be with me no matter what."

History interpreter
Arthur Johnson

A Writer's Process

Prewriting
Researching Matthew Ashby

Many narrative writers invent the characters in their stories, so they need only consult their imaginations before beginning to write. Arthur Johnson, however, was writing about a historical figure. Before he could write his narrative, he needed to unearth facts and events of Matthew Ashby's life.

Johnson learned that Matthew Ashby was one of the African Americans who made up half of Williamsburg's population in the 1700s. He was a carter by trade, which meant he transported goods by cart or wagon. "Ashby was born free sometime in the 1720s," Johnson says. "As a teenager, he worked with a slave by the name of Joe, who took care of horses and carted his master's property. Ashby learned his work from Joe."

Johnson also learned that Matthew Ashby met his wife, Ann, when she was a slave. The couple married in 1762. The marriage ceremony involved the tradition of jumping over a broom (see the opening excerpt). After his marriage, Ashby worked hard as a carter, earned a good reputation in Williamsburg, and won freedom for Ann and his two children in 1769.

How did Johnson uncover these facts about Matthew Ashby? Johnson studied historical records that had survived the Revolutionary War. Ashby's will, for example, listed his belongings, including carpenter's tools, a harness for two horses, and a cart. As Johnson read these documents, he took careful notes that would become part of his presentation.

Drafting
Creating the Character

While more was known about Matthew Ashby than about most free African Americans of the 1700s, the historical records were far from complete. How did Johnson flesh out Matthew Ashby's character? He built on the information he found. For example, historians know that a free-black community once existed outside Williamsburg, so Johnson felt safe assuming that Matthew Ashby and his family had lived there. "With a skeleton of facts, we can add meat to a character, based on what we know about the period," Johnson explains.

Like any narrative writer, Johnson needed to find ways

Arthur Johnson prepares for his role as Matthew Ashby. ▼

In character as Ashby, Johnson performs Ashby's daily tasks as a carter. ▼

to make his character believable. Johnson realized that one of Ashby's strengths was perseverance. "I feel I can relate to Matthew Ashby because Ashby would be a survivor whether he was in the eighteenth century or the twentieth century," Johnson says.

Day by day, Johnson developed his narrative. Since he would be enacting the role of Ashby for an audience, a lot of his preparation involved speaking practice. Working in front of a mirror, Johnson practiced speaking with words and mannerisms that he thought Matthew Ashby might have used. Later, Johnson rehearsed the narrative in front of his wife. She listened, commented, and encouraged Johnson. Finally, Johnson was confident that he had developed an accurate, realistic monologue for his character.

Revising/Editing
Keeping in Character

Narrative writers need to maintain their characters' point of view. Johnson reviewed his monologue to make sure he was staying "in character." During a performance, Johnson always thinks of what Ashby would do or say. "Matthew wouldn't say a word like *cool*," for example, Johnson explains. Nor would Ashby recognize

modern electronic items. What does Johnson do if a visitor asks to take his picture? "In the eighteenth century there were no cameras," Johnson explains. "So Matthew would say, 'Sir, I don't know what you're talking about. And whatever that is you're holding up to your eye, please, you might want to take it down.'"

Publishing/Presenting
The Narrative Is Shared

As carriages slowly creak past old brick buildings at Colonial Williamsburg, visitors come upon Johnson spinning the story of Matthew Ashby. To draw an audience, the six-foot, five-inch bearded giant in colonial work clothes calls to visitors strolling by. "Good day! . . .We need some help on the wagon. . . ."

He might also say, "I'm getting some runners and putting them up and getting these barrels on the cart here. You see, Mr. Prentis has given me some credit for taking these barrels and boxes down to Queen Anne's Port. That's what I do. I'm a carter, a carter by trade. I take anything, anywhere, anytime."

When his work is done, the character of Ashby relaxes and takes questions from the audience. Johnson answers as completely as he can. He uses his narrative to give visitors to Colonial Williamsburg a valuable glimpse into one facet of America's past.

Examining Writing in the Real World

Analyzing the Media Connection

Discuss these questions about the excerpt on page 152.

1. What is the main impression Johnson wants visitors to take away from his narrative? Do you think he accomplishes his aim? Why or why not?

2. What historical details does Johnson use to make his narrative authentic?

3. How does Arthur Johnson help visitors become engaged with Matthew Ashby's life?

4. Why do you think Johnson mentions specific names, such as "Gowan," "Adam," and "Ann"?

5. Why do you think Arthur Johnson selected Matthew Ashby as the subject of his narrative?

Analyzing a Writer's Process

Discuss these questions about Arthur Johnson's writing process.

1. What historical documents did Johnson research as he was interpreting Matthew Ashby's life and character?

2. After researching historical documents, how did Johnson further round out Ashby's character?

3. Who helped Johnson refine his narrative and performance? Why might it be helpful to have someone edit your writing?

4. Why is it so important for Johnson to stay in the character of Ashby when performing for visitors to Colonial Williamsburg?

5. What lessons does Johnson teach as he presents his narrative?

Grammar*Link*

Use an appositive to identify a noun. Use commas to set off an appositive that adds nonessential information to a sentence.

Arthur Johnson, **an interpreter of African American history at Colonial Williamsburg,** *makes the past come alive.*

Use an appositive to combine the following pairs of sentences.

1. Matthew Ashby was a free African American. He worked in Colonial Williamsburg.

2. Ashby learned his trade from Joe. Joe was a local carter.

3. Ashby was employed at Prentis & Company. It was a Williamsburg business.

4. He married his wife in 1762. Her name was Ann.

See Lesson 9.6, pages 391-392.

LESSON

4.1

Writing the Stories of History

Jacob Lawrence, *Frederick Douglass Series, No. 21, The Fugitive*, 1938–1939

A narrative is a story or account of an event. A historical narrative is a story about people and events in history.

In any time period you can find exciting stories of real people who changed the world. The 1800s, for example, gave us the great antislavery fighter Frederick Douglass. Like a story, Jacob Lawrence's painting presents one event in Douglass's life. A person, a place, an event—the basic elements of a story are all here.

Find Your Inspiration

Some writers get their ideas for historical narrative from an event; others, from a person. Writer Victoria Ortiz was inspired by a woman from the 1800s. Ortiz was a civil rights worker in Mississippi when she became interested in Sojourner Truth. In the biography she wrote, Ortiz tells how Sojourner spoke strongly for the abolition of slavery and for women's rights. An uneducated former slave, Sojourner lectured with wit and power. On the next page is a paragraph from Victoria Ortiz's book. Read it to see how she showed the character of Sojourner Truth.

Literature Model

One of the first times Sojourner was present at a Woman's Rights Convention was in October, 1850, in Worcester, Massachusetts. As she later retold the experience to Harriet Beecher Stowe, Sojourner sat for a long time listening to Frederick Douglass, Lucy Stone, Wendell Phillips, William Lloyd Garrison, and Ernestine Rose speak about women's rights. She soon became intrigued, and when called upon to speak she presented her position quite concisely: "Sisters, I aren't clear what you be after. If women want any rights more than they got, why don't they just take them and not be talking about it?" For Sojourner, it was obvious that action was more effective than words.

Victoria Ortiz, *Sojourner Truth: A Self-Made Woman*

Note that Sojourner Truth was a real person involved in a real event in history.

Why do you think some of the same people were advocates of both abolition and women's rights?

To find a topic for a historical narrative, think about people, places, times, and events in history that interest you. A person, a setting, an event—any one of these can spark an idea for a historical narrative.

Once you have an idea, explore and narrow it. Focusing on one point allows you to explore a topic in depth. For example, if you decide to write about a person, you may need to narrow your topic to a single event in his or her life. It is the details, such as Sojourner's statement on women's rights, that bring history to life.

Activist Sojourner Truth

Journal Writing

Create a chart entitled Story Ideas from History. Make three columns, headed Person, Event, and Setting. Skim your history textbook for ideas for historical narratives. List each idea under the appropriate heading.

Vocabulary Drafting Tip

As you draft, remember that concrete nouns and colorful adjectives strengthen the descriptions of people and settings, bringing history to life.

Hook Your Readers

Realistic details are especially important in writing about a historical event. Often writers uncover valuable details through research. Sometimes, however, a writer also needs to make up likely details to keep a narrative realistic and exciting. When you're ready to draft your historical narrative, you can use realistic details in your introduction to interest your reader immediately.

A good introduction often presents a person, a setting, and an event. One writer chose the persons and event below for a historical narrative. Read the paragraph that introduces the narrative, and think about the question in the box.

What question does this introduction raise? How does this question make readers want to keep on reading?

> It's a bright August morning in 1962. Many of the major grape growers of southern California have come to Delano City Hall to hear a man named Cesar Chávez. He has come to talk with the people who have the power to improve the lives of his followers. The outcome will have a serious effect on the farm workers' future.

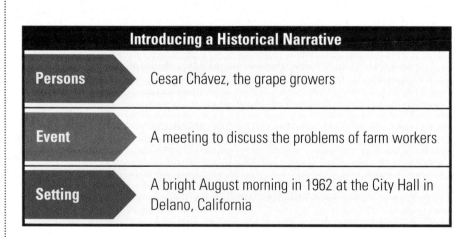

Introducing a Historical Narrative	
Persons	Cesar Chávez, the grape growers
Event	A meeting to discuss the problems of farm workers
Setting	A bright August morning in 1962 at the City Hall in Delano, California

4.1 Writing Activities

Write an Introduction

Consult the Story Ideas from History chart in your journal, and plan a historical narrative for younger students to read.

PURPOSE To introduce a historical narrative
AUDIENCE Fifth-grade students
LENGTH 1–2 paragraphs

WRITING RUBRICS To write an effective introduction for a historical narrative, you should

- make prewriting notes based on your chart
- use specific details about the person or setting to get your readers' attention
- write legibly in cursive or print for your young readers

Cross-Curricular Activity

HISTORY In a group, brainstorm historical periods that have exciting stories. Pick a historical period, and brainstorm story ideas. Each member should list persons, settings, and events, including problems the persons faced. Each member should then write a narrative introduction to the event, trying to create interest and excitement.

Listening and Speaking

COOPERATIVE LEARNING In your group, read your introduction aloud, using your voice to make your introduction dramatic. Compare and contrast the introductions written by group members. Use feedback from the group to make your introduction more effective.

Use complete sentences for clarity.

Your notes for a historical piece will often be in the form of sentence fragments, but use complete sentences in your narrative.

For Sojourner, it was obvious that action was more effective than words.

Revise the fragments below into paragraphs about scientist Robert Goddard. Use complete sentences.

1. As boy, read H. G. Wells, dreamed of space flight.
2. Wrote article on rocketry in 1919—largely ignored.
3. Launched first liquid propellant rocket in 1926—tiny.
4. Flight of two and a half seconds.
5. Vision of lunar landing ridiculed.
6. When real lunar landing—gained wider recognition.
7. Also predicted orbiting space station and probe to Mars.
8. Goddard ahead of time.
9. Speculated about journeys to distant solar systems.
10. Some day true?

See Lesson 8.2, page 361.

Writing Online   For more writing and grammar practice, go to **glencoe.com** and enter QuickPass code WC87703p1.

159

Using Chronological Order

Any story makes better sense if the writer thinks about time order, or chronology. A story is in chronological order when the events are presented in the time order in which they occurred.

Movies, television, and videotapes allow us to tell stories in words and images. Suppose you use pictures alone or pictures with words to tell a story—in a comic strip, a slide series, a videotape, or even a photo album. In what order would you arrange your pictures to tell a story?

Choose a Time Frame

When you write a narrative, you have to decide on a time frame—when your story will begin and end. The chart on the next page shows that time spans for narratives vary widely. Some narratives cover decades, even centuries. A short narrative may cover days, hours, or even minutes.

In *Homesick: My Own Story,* Jean Fritz tells about her childhood in China and her teen years in the United States. Fritz presents realistic pictures of life in China and America in the early 1900s. The following excerpt tells about a time just before Fritz began eighth grade in her first American school. As you read it, notice how she relates some of one day's events in chronological order. What details suggest that the setting is long ago?

Literature Model

The next day Aunt Margaret took me to Caldwell's store on Main Street and bought me a red-and-black-plaid gingham [cotton] dress with a white collar and narrow black patent leather belt that went around my hips. She took me to a beauty parlor and I had my hair shingled [a close-cut style].

When I got home, I tried on my dress. "How do I look?" I asked my grandmother.

"As if you'd just stepped out of a bandbox [a box for hats and collars; means 'perfectly groomed']."

I wasn't sure that was the look I was aiming for. "But do I look like a regular eighth grader?"

"As regular as they come," she assured me.

Jean Fritz, *Homesick: My Own Story*

> What words used here would not be used today in describing a well-dressed eighth grader?

Time Spans for Historical Narratives

A Day

One Lifetime

Two Centuries

Journal Writing

Freewrite about two time periods, one that covers one recent day and one that covers two days. Include details and events that you would include in a narrative.

Prewriting Tip

When you are organizing your notes, be sure to put them in an order that would make sense to your reader.

Make Time Order Clear

Ben Aylesworth researched the history of Wheaton, Illinois, a city near his home. He visited the Wheaton History Center and the Wheaton Public Library, where he read about his topic. He also interviewed his grandmother. Finally, Ben decided to focus on one event in the city's history and to relate the stages of that event in chronological order.

As he drafted, Ben used good transitions, such as *later* and *afterward,* to clarify the order of events. In writing a narrative, vary your transitions. If you always use *first, next,* and *finally,* your writing may sound dull. Find the transitions in the model below.

Lester Schrader, *Theft of the Records,* mid- to late-nineteenth century

Student Model

How would you feel if citizens of a rival town stole your town's records, forever changing its history? In 1838 Naperville held the county records of the new DuPage County. Naperville and nearby Wheaton were fierce rivals. Both wanted the county seat. In an 1867 referendum Wheaton narrowly won the county seat, but the records stayed in Naperville.

Late one night that year, some young Wheaton men broke into the Naperville courthouse and stole the county records. An alarm sounded, and they dropped some of the papers. Later, fearing another raid, Naperville officials moved the remaining records to Chicago for safekeeping. But these were destroyed in the Great Chicago Fire of 1871. Wheaton has been the county seat ever since that famous midnight raid.

Ben Aylesworth, Hadley Junior High School, Glen Ellyn, Illinois

What transitions does Ben use to make the chronological order clear?

4.2 Writing Activities

Write a Narrative

A future historian will want to know about special events in your school and community. Plan and write a narrative about one annual event, such as a concert, a game or tournament, or a holiday parade and picnic. For help with organizing your narrative in chronological order, see **Writing and Research Handbook,** page 836.

PURPOSE To narrate the story of a school or community event

AUDIENCE Future historians

LENGTH 1–2 paragraphs

WRITING RUBRICS To write an effective narrative, you should

- choose an event, and list its stages
- arrange the stages in chronological order
- in drafting and revising, use appropriate transitions
- use appropriate verb forms

Cross-Curricular Activity

HISTORY In a small group, brainstorm to discover what you all know about the history of your town or city. Choose one important event from that history and work together to write a narrative of that event. Arrange the details, or stages, of that event in chronological order. Include transitions to make the order of the events clear.

GrammarLink

Use the correct verb—singular or plural—when the subject is an indefinite pronoun.

Some indefinite pronouns (like *one* and *each*) are singular and require a singular verb. Some (like *both* and *many*) are plural and take a plural verb.

Both want the county seat.

Choose the correct verb to complete each sentence.

1. Many of the families (has, have) lived in Park Cities for several generations.
2. Everyone in the community (knows, know) the brilliantly lit pecan tree on Armstrong Parkway.
3. Each of the other old pecan trees in Park Cities (was, were) damaged or destroyed by an ice storm in 1965.
4. Only one of the trees (was, were) left standing.
5. Ever since, few in the town of Park Cities (has, have) taken pecan trees for granted.

See Lesson 16.4, page 547.

Viewing and Representing

CREATING A COMMUNITY COLLAGE Use your town library and other local sources to find pictures of the historical event you wrote about. Arrange copies of the pictures into a collage.

LOG ON ▶ **Writing** Online | For more writing and grammar practice, go to glencoe.com and enter QuickPass code WC87703p1.

163

LESSON 4.3

Establishing Point of View

In narratives the point of view is important. Some stories are told by a main character in the first person—using "I" or "we." Others are told by an observer in the third person—using "he," "she," or "they."

In the story below, Justin Hoest speaks in the voice of a fictional grandfather in the early 2000s, telling his grandson about the 1960s civil rights movement.

Student Model

Let me start in the beginning. I was born in Birmingham, Alabama, in 1952. Back then, in southern states, it was segregated. There were separate water fountains, waiting rooms, stores, schools. Everywhere, some people were trying to keep segregation, and others were trying to stop it. The times were troubled.

Martin Luther King Jr. came to Birmingham when I was ten. I met him some years later during the Selma marches. He helped organize demonstrations. There were sit-ins like in Nashville, and adults would picket up and down the streets. We'd go to the meeting house in the evening. We would sing all night, or so it seemed. Everyone would dress in nice clothes, and the church smelled so good with the fresh candles burning.

> Note that although the story is fictional, it is set in a real time and place.

Song filled the place:

> I'm so glad; I'm fightin' for my rights;
> I'm so glad; I'm fightin' for my rights;
> Glory, Hallelujah!

Finally my day came. We were clapping and singing. Some of us were carrying signs. The day was bright, but there was a menacing dark cloud lingering in the sky. We weren't scared, only nervous. Our feet on the hard pavement made a sound that represented the whole movement.

Justin Hoest, Maplewood Middle School,
Menasha, Wisconsin

Why do you think Justin chose to have the grandfather tell his own story?

Presenting Tip

When you present your narrative, you can accompany your writing with photos or recordings.

Use the First Person

In telling his story, Justin has chosen a first-person point of view. That is, he lets the grandfather tell the story using the pronouns *I* and *me*. First-person narratives describe just what the narrator witnesses and thinks. The reader sees all the events through the narrator's eyes and views them as the narrator views them.

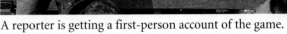

A reporter is getting a first-person account of the game.

Journal Writing

Make column headings that name three important events in American history. In ten minutes create as many fictional characters as you can think of under each heading. They may be participants, like the grandfather, or just observers.

Grammar Editing Tip

In editing your narrative, check to make sure you've used subject and object pronouns correctly. For more on using pronouns, see page 439.

Try the Third Person

Many short stories and other narratives are told from the third-person point of view. That is, the author uses the pronouns *he*, *she*, *it*, and *they*. In the following narrative poem, the poet uses the pronoun *she* because the main characters are the Island Queen and her daughter. From what you know about the history of the American Revolution, you may be able to figure out who these characters are.

Literature Model

There was an old lady lived over the sea
And she was an Island Queen.
Her daughter lived off in a new country,
With an ocean of water between;
The old lady's pockets were full of gold
But never contented was she,
So she called on her daughter to pay her a tax
Of three pence a pound on her tea.

The tea was conveyed to the daughter's door,
All down by the ocean's side;
And the bouncing girl pour'd out every pound
In the dark and boiling tide;
And then she called out to the Island Queen,
"O mother, dear mother," quoth she,
"Your tea you may have when 'tis steep'd enough
But never a tax from me."

Traditional

What point of view would you choose for a narrative? You may write a short story, an imaginary journal or letter, a song, or a narrative poem from the first-person point of view. The main character is then the *I* of the story. Or you may write it from the third person point of view. The main character will be *he* or *she*. Most writers decide on their point of view in prewriting. Then they use their imaginations to bring their narratives to life.

Formats

Journal

Ballad

Letters

Write a Narrative Paragraph

Choose one of the fictional characters you created in your journal entry for this lesson. Write a narrative paragraph from the point of view of that character. Describe the historical event the character observed or took part in. Don't identify yourself specifically in the writing. See if your classmates can tell exactly what event you are describing and how your character related to the event.

PURPOSE To use the first-person point of view
AUDIENCE Classmates
LENGTH 1 paragraph

WRITING RUBRICS To write an effective first-person narrative paragraph, you should

- use first-person pronouns correctly
- make clear your character's relationship to the event
- use specific details from the event
- proofread to make sure pronouns and verb tenses are consistent and correct

Viewing and Representing

ILLUSTRATING HISTORY Create a poster to illustrate the historical event you have written about. The poster should project the viewpoint of the character you have created. In a small group, share your posters and see whether you can connect the posters with the written narratives.

Using Computers

To enhance your understanding of the historical event you have chosen, use the Internet to learn more about the event. In addition to general facts and information, look for details that your character might use in his or her narrative—details about the event that are not common knowledge.

Grammar*Link*

Make subjects and verbs agree in sentences beginning with *there*.

> There **was** an old *lady*. . . .
> There **were** sit-ins. . . .

Complete each sentence below with the correct verb: *was* or *were*.

[1]There _____ more than four thousand people killed in a 1995 earthquake in Kobe, Japan. [2]There _____ also massive property damage. [3]There _____ little looting, though goods lay everywhere. [4]There _____ many people who helped care for others.

See Lesson 16.1, page 541.

LOG ON ▶ **Writing** Online | For more writing and grammar practice, go to glencoe.com and enter QuickPass code WC87703p1.

167

Writing Realistic Dialogue

Dialogue can make a story come to life—or fall flat on its face.

Study the picture below. What do you think the two figures might be saying? How do you think they might be saying it? Jot down your ideas.

Anthony Ortega, *Two Little Old Men*, 1984

Now read two openers that were written for a story. Which one would be more likely to catch your interest? Why?

Jenny said she saw Joseph walking home.

Jenny burst in shouting, "Hey, everybody, Joseph's come home!"

Let Characters Speak for Themselves

Dialogue—direct quotations of spoken words or conversations—is a way of revealing character. What does the following conversation reveal about Hideyo and his mother?

Literature Model

Mother opened her mouth and could not close it for several seconds.

"Most of my classmates have enlisted," said Hideyo, serious for once. "I have decided to go to help our country."

"You cannot go, Hideyo!" Mother told him. "You must talk with Father. You just cannot make such a decision alone."

"Mother, I have already sent in my application," said Hideyo. "I will take the written and physical examinations!"

"How could you?" Mother moaned. "Why didn't you tell me?"

"I am eighteen. Big enough to make my own decision."

Yoko Kawashima Watkins, *So Far from the Bamboo Grove*

> The mother's words tell you she loves her son and fears for his life.

> What does the dialogue reveal about Hideyo?

Letting characters speak for themselves is easy when you write about someone you know well. Ask yourself, "What would this person say here?" After you draft some dialogue, it helps to put it aside for a day or so. Then, when you reread it, you can ask yourself if it sounds authentic. If it does not, see how to improve it.

Grammar Editing Tip

As you edit your dialogue, check your punctuation, capitalization, and paragraphing. For more about writing dialogue, see Lesson 20.6, page 609.

Journal Writing

Listen to the speech of others, and jot down bits of conversation you hear. Next to each quotation identify the speaker—a bus driver, for instance, or a relative.

Make Conversation

Your dialogue will sound natural if your characters talk the way real people do. Below is a natural-sounding dialogue between a brother and sister. What did the writer do to make this conversation sound realistic?

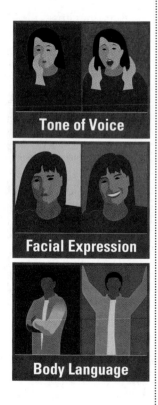

Tone of Voice

Facial Expression

Body Language

> "I can too run!" Antonio glared at her, arms locked stubbornly over his chest.
>
> "I didn't say you can't run, 'Tonio," Gina retorted. "I just said I can run faster than you!"
>
> "Yeah, well, I can run farther!"
>
> Gina rolled her eyes. "In your dreams, <u>fratello</u>!" she crowed. "You can't even run without tripping on something!"
>
> "Can too!"
>
> "Think about it, 'Tonio! Remember last year's Fourth of July picnic? Who wanted to run barefoot and then stepped on a wasp four seconds into the race? Not me!" Gina roared.

Did you notice the slang, sentence fragments, contractions, and descriptions of facial expressions and body language? Without these, the conversation would sound stiff and unnatural. Suppose the writer had Gina say this: "I am sorry, but you are badly mistaken, brother. You cannot run without falling down." Even Gina's use of the Italian term *fratello*, which means "brother," adds interest.

4.4 Writing Activities

Write a Dialogue

What's happening in the painting on this page? Where is the man? What is he doing there? Write a dialogue between two students trying to make sense of the picture.

PURPOSE To create a realistic dialogue
AUDIENCE Your teacher and classmates
LENGTH 1–2 short paragraphs

WRITING RUBRICS To write an effective dialogue, you should

- list some words or phrases you might use to react to the painting
- make your dialogue sound natural
- punctuate and indent correctly

Hughie Lee-Smith, *Man Standing on His Head*, 1969

Using Computers

Use a computer to prepare scripts. Your word processing program allows you to indent actors' parts so that each character's name is clearly visible in the left margin.

Listening and Speaking

COOPERATIVE LEARNING In a small group, present oral readings of your dialogue. Discuss the similarities and differences in the opinions and interpretations of the characters you and your group members created.

GrammarLink

In dialogue, use quotation marks and other punctuation correctly.

"Most of my classmates are going," said Hideyo. . . .

"You cannot go, Hideyo!" Mother told him.

Write each sentence below, using quotation marks and other punctuation where necessary.

1. You're not leaving this house in that outfit Mrs. Curphy announced.
2. But Mom! All the kids are wearing pants like these Patty whined.
3. I don't care what the other kids are doing, Mrs. Curphy declared.
4. Mom! Patty moaned.
5. No daughter of mine is leaving my house looking that way, said Mrs. Curphy, and that's final.

See Lesson 20.6, page 609.

LOG ON ▶ **Writing** Online | For more writing and grammar practice, go to glencoe.com and enter QuickPass code WC87703p1.

171

LESSON 4.5
Relating a Historical Event

Andō Hiroshige, *The Wave*, c. 1850

*H*annah Wilson read as much as she could find about Japanese immigrants of the 1920s. Then she created a character, gave her a problem, and let her tell her story.

Read this excerpt from Wilson's story. See what the point of view tells you about the character.

Student Model

*M*amma—I wish she were here now. I still miss her so much. I wish with all my heart she could be here to see this baby born. I remember how comforting she always was. I need that comfort now. Every day seems the same to me. Up at dawn, fix breakfast for Seiji and myself, off to work in the fields all day while Seiji goes fishing, hardly stopping to eat. The lonely nights when Seiji must stay on the fishing boats all night.

I love America and Seiji, and I want a baby so much, but I miss Mamma and Papa and Sachiko and Akiko.

Hannah Wilson, Newton Elementary School,
Strafford, Vermont

> What can you tell about the person whose voice you hear in this narrative?

Create a Character

If you, like Hannah Wilson, chose immigration as the subject for your narrative, your next step would be investigation. You might begin by reading immigration stories, jotting down details about ordinary people's lives. Then you might think of a character and imagine problems the character could face.

Can you see the germ of one or more story ideas in these prewriting notes?

Notes—Japanese Immigration to the U. S.

Many immigrated from the 1890s to 1920. Most entered the U. S. on the West Coast.
Issei: first-generation Japanese immigrants
Nisei: their chi... generation
Sensei: their g... third generation
World War I...
internment ca...

Possible Topics
1. Leaving home forever
2. A rough sea voyage
3. First glimpse of land
4. Finding another home
5. First day in an American school

The Ikeda Family Tree
● Male
■ Female

Mitsuo Ikeda   Sumiko Tanaka

Haruo Kiyo Masaru Eiko Kenji Reiko

Yasuko Eiko Sadako Genzo Mitsuo

Journal Writing

Talk to a friend or family member about an immigration experience. Create a fictional character in the same time and place, and freewrite about problems your character might face.

Prewriting Tip

In prewriting look for details about the setting. You can use them to enrich your narrative with strong, colorful descriptions.

Choose Your Approach

After giving the character a problem or conflict, decide on an approach. You could write a short story, a series of journal entries, or some letters home. Formats such as these allow you to show a character's feelings and actions.

Like Hannah, Philip Garran wrote an immigration story. In his prewriting investigation, he researched the Irish potato crop failures, which led to famine and caused many to leave their homeland. Unlike Hannah, Philip focused on the early part of the experience, before his main character left home. He, too, made up the details, but they were based on his research. Read the model, and see why a journal entry was a logical approach for Philip to use.

Contract Ticket No. ....

INSPECTION CARD.
(Immigrants and Steerage Passengers.)

Port of Departure, LIVERPOOL.   Date of Departure,

Name of Ship "MEGANTIC,"   Jan. 8th 1921.

Name of Immigrant   Delany Lillie

Last Residence   Ireland

Student Model

Using sensory language, Philip paints a vivid word picture of the Irish countryside and conveys the narrator's feelings for his homeland.

At last my father has found a ship. We have packed all of our belongings, and Dad has sold the cottage for a very small sum of money. However, it was almost enough to pay for the tickets, and we borrowed the rest from my Uncle Paul.

We will be leaving in three days. I will miss the green fields, the blue sky, and the sparkly rivers and lakes. But I will not miss the misery that has descended on us like fog. I hear that America is a land of amazing wealth, and the land there is incredibly cheap. I can't wait to see America.

What possible conflict is the writer setting up in these sentences?

Philip Garran, Newton Elementary School,
Strafford, Vermont

Write a Narrative Journal Entry

Invent a character who is fleeing by boat or ship from a country that has become dangerous to live in. Write an entry he or she would add to a personal journal while on board.

PURPOSE To reflect a historical event
AUDIENCE Yourself
LENGTH 1–2 paragraphs

WRITING RUBRICS   To write an effective narrative journal entry, you should

- focus on the flight from home, the voyage itself, or hopes for the future
- convey feelings as well as facts
- capitalize proper nouns and adjectives

Cross-Curricular Activity

HISTORY Use a library or the Internet to do some additional research about the time and place of the immigration experience you wrote about in your journal entry for this lesson. Write a letter home from the fictional character you created. Include historical details and problems your character might have faced.

Viewing and Representing

PICTURING HISTORY To illustrate your letter, use photographs or other pictures from the period of your character's immigration experience. Try to find images that reflect your character's experiences. With a small group, exchange letters and see if group members can match your letter with your pictures.

GrammarLink

Capitalize nouns and adjectives denoting nationalities and languages.

first-generation Japanese immigrants

Write each sentence below, using capital letters where necessary.

1. My uncle, a guatemalan by birth, speaks english, spanish, portuguese, and french.
2. In my neighborhood I hear more vietnamese than english.
3. Many italians who immigrated between 1899 and 1924 chose to return to their native land.
4. By 1910 the labor force in the West included native-born white americans, mexican americans, african americans, chinese americans, and tens of thousands of new mexican and japanese immigrants.
5. In later years many haitians and cubans settled in Florida.

See Lesson 19.4, page 589.

LOG ON ▶ **Writing** Online | For more writing and grammar practice, go to **glencoe.com** and enter QuickPass code WC87703p1.

175

LESSON 4.6

Writing a News Story

News stories, which record history as it happens, can become a resource for future historians. Strong news stories, such as the one below, answer these questions: What happened? When? Where? Who was involved? How did it happen? Why was the event important?

Collaborating on Computers

Computer Museum consults Martin Luther King Jr. Middle School students in developing new exhibit

By Teresa A. Martin
SPECIAL TO THE GLOBE

When the Computer Museum designed its new 3,600-square-foot, $1 million personal computer exhibit, it looked for inspiration in many places, including an eighth-grade class at the Martin Luther King Jr. Middle School in Dorchester, Massachusetts.

The collaboration was so successful that the museum is making such arrangements part of the development of all future exhibits.

"One of the things you often see is lip service to consulting with schools," said Greg Welch, director of exhibits at the museum. "But for us this was a concerted effort to find out their needs."

The exhibit in question, which opened last month and will be permanent, is called "Tools and Toys: The Amazing Personal Computer."

Tell the Five Ws and an H

News writers try to answer all or most of these questions—*who? what? when? where? why?* and *how?*—in their lead, or opening. How many of the basic questions—five Ws and an H—are answered in each lead below?

FLORIDA BRACES FOR HURRICANE ANDREW
Associated Press

MIAMI–Hurricane Andrew surged relentlessly toward southern Florida Sunday, and forecasters warned it would be the most powerful storm to hit the United States in decades. More than 1 million residents were told to flee.

A SUMMER SEARCH
BY MARK FERENCHIK
Repository staff writer

LAKE TWP.–What did teacher Pete Esterle do for his summer vacation? He went slogging through a south Florida swamp, in search of an airplane wreck apparently undisturbed for about 50 years. Esterle, an art teacher at Lake High School, and his brother found it earlier this month.

RUNAWAY CHIMP FINDS UNWILLING PLAYMATE
NewYork Times News Service

INMAN, S.C.–A 78-year-old woman hanging sheets on a clothesline Monday became the unsuspecting playmate of a rambunctious chimpanzee that, along with two companions, escaped from nearby Hollywild Animal Park.

Some leads present only the basic facts; the details come later in the story. Other leads open with a question or an intriguing detail designed to get readers' attention. Which of the leads above opens with an attention grabber?

Journal Writing

Many things happen in a school day. Think about what happened yesterday, and choose one newsworthy event. Write answers to the five Ws and an H.

Grammar Revising Tip

When you revise, use possessive pronouns where appropriate. For more information about possessive pronouns, see Lesson 11.4, page 441.

Go into Detail

In investigating a topic for a story, news reporters gather all the information they can. Then, after writing the lead, they bring their story to life with details they have gathered. Read the opening section of this news story.

Literature Model

The national anthems played most often four years ago in Seoul—those of the USSR and the German Democratic Republic (GDR)—will be noticeably missing during the 25th Olympic Games that begin today. Now, the USSR and GDR no longer exist, and neither does the intense East-West rivalry that has marked the Games during the Cold War era.

This will be the first Olympics in decades with no "good guys" or "bad guys," and that could make these Games the most refreshing in recent memory— approaching the Olympic ideal of spectators cheering for the best athletes regardless of the country they represent.

Bud Greenspan, "Parade"

According to Bud Greenspan, why are there no "good guys" or "bad guys" in this Olympics?

Be sure to include details in your news story. Cover all sides of the story. Save your opinions for a letter to the editor. Finally, check the accuracy of your facts and the spelling of names.

If you were in this audience, how could you exemplify the "Olympic ideal"?

Write a News Story

Write a news story about a recent event at your school. Cover the five Ws and an H in a lively lead. Write two paragraphs for the story. Include important details about the event.

PURPOSE To create a lead and details for a news story

AUDIENCE Readers of your school newspaper

LENGTH 2–3 paragraphs

WRITING RUBRICS To write an effective news story, you should

- use vivid language and sharp details
- cover all aspects of the event
- base your story on fact, not opinion
- leave your readers well informed

Using Computers

Most word-processing software allows you to print text in parallel columns as in a newspaper. Find out how to set up the format line for this option, and print out your story in newspaper format.

Viewing and Representing

MAKE AN ILLUSTRATION Draw a cartoon (funny or serious) that captures a key moment in the event you have written about. In a small group, critique each other's news articles and illustrations.

GrammarLink

Avoid double comparisons.

To form the comparative and superlative degrees of modifiers that have one syllable and of some that have two syllables, add the suffixes -er and -est. For most modifiers of two or more syllables, use the words more and most. Never use both a suffix and more or most.

*Esterle . . . and his brother found it **earlier** this month.*

*. . . forecasters warned it would be the **most powerful** storm. . . .*

Write each sentence below, eliminating double comparisons.

1. Charlie Spradley was the most fastest sprinter in school.
2. He captured a more greater number of all-state titles than his brother.
3. Kate Shoemaker played more better tennis than ever before.
4. Nonetheless, she lost the match in straight sets to Shalewa Bigham, the most youngest player on the other team.
5. The audience applauded Kate's performance more longer than Shalewa's.

See Lesson 12.3, page 461, and Lesson 12.6, page 467.

LOG ON ▶ **Writing** Online | For more writing and grammar practice, go to **glencoe.com** and enter QuickPass code WC87703p1.

179

WRITING ABOUT LITERATURE

Responding to a Historical Narrative

The excerpt below was written by a young Jewish girl who was hiding from the Nazis during World War II.

Anne Frank was born to a German Jewish family in 1929. The family went to the Netherlands to escape the Nazis but later went into hiding, when Anne was thirteen. In a secret room of an Amsterdam building, Anne wrote letters in a diary that she addressed as a friend named Kitty. In 1944, the Nazis found the Frank family; Anne died in a concentration camp in early 1945.

Literature Model

Wednesday, 29 March, 1944

Dear Kitty,

Bolkestein, an M.P. [Member of Parliament], was speaking on the Dutch News from London, and he said that they ought to make a collection of diaries and letters after the war. Of course, they all [Anne's family and the others in hiding with them] made a rush at my diary immediately. Just imagine how interesting it would be if I were to publish a romance of the "Secret Annexe." The title alone would be enough to make people think it was a detective story.

But, seriously, it would seem quite funny ten years after the war if we Jews were to tell how we lived and what we ate and talked about here. Although I tell you a lot, still, even so, you only know very little of our lives.

Anne Frank, *The Diary of a Young Girl*

Respond to Historical Events

Anne Frank's diary offers stark glimpses into wartime reality. Johanna Yngvason responded to Anne's diary by describing the terror of living in hiding. She focused on how historic events affected ordinary people, such as Anne Frank and her family.

Student Model

Hide! Hide! The Nazis are invading!" This was a terrifying sound heard by many Jews, many times, and caused them to go into hiding. A small closet became a bedroom, an attic became a home. . . . The Jews were rounded up like cattle and shipped off to concentration camps such as Auschwitz and Bergen-Belsen, where the majority of them died.

Such a fate befell young Anne Frank. . . . The only surviving member of the party, Anne's beloved father, returned to the dusty attic after the war. There in the rubble was the diary, which he later published. . . . Although Anne didn't survive the Holocaust, her thoughts and memories live on.

Johanna Yngvason, Canyon Park Junior High School, Bothell, Washington

> Johanna reflects Anne's dread when she uses the word *terrifying*.

> What does this sentence reveal about Johanna's feelings?

Follow Johanna's example when you respond in writing to a nonfiction narrative. Tell what happened, but add your own thoughts and feelings.

Journal Writing

Take a few moments to think about a narrative story that moved you. How did it make you feel? Write some words and phrases that best express your feelings.

Vocabulary Revising Tip

As you revise, a thesaurus can help you locate just the right words to express your thoughts and feelings about a nonfiction historical narrative.

Respond to People Behind the Events

Amy Groat read, and wrote about, *Farewell to Manzanar*. This nonfiction narrative tells the story of Jeanne Wakatsuki, interned with her family in a wartime relocation camp for Asian Americans. Read it and see how Amy sympathizes with Jeanne.

Amy shows how important the book was to her by suggesting that all eighth-graders in the district should read it.

Which words and expressions reveal Amy's sympathy for Jeanne Wakatsuki?

Student Model

Farewell to Manzanar deals with a mixture of problems that bombarded the internees in the camp Manzanar. The minorities of today deal with the same discrimination but in a subtler form. By reading and discussing this book, eighth-graders in our district will have a better understanding of the events and traumas that rocked Japanese Americans during World War II. . . .

When the Wakatsuki family reentered the "real world," Jeanne faced a cultural gap between herself and her classmates. She wanted desperately to fit in but was discriminated against because of her ethnic background. She eventually was able to blend in with her classmates by joining after-school activities, but she was never able to deal with the generation gap in her family.

Amy Groat, Oak Creek Ranch School,
Cornville, Arizona

One way of responding to a historical narrative—fiction or nonfiction—is to show how a character is like you. In reading *Farewell to Manzanar*, Amy discovered how the people from another time and place were like her.

Responding to a Spoken Narrative

One type of narration is storytelling. Talk to a person who has survived a war. Have him or her describe fears, thoughts, and emotions of that time.

Write a one-page response. Tell how the survival story made you feel.

PURPOSE To respond to a spoken narrative
AUDIENCE Your teacher and classmates
LENGTH 1 page

WRITING RUBRICS To write an effective response to a spoken narrative, you should

- use precise language to describe your feelings about the story
- provide enough detail to suggest a basis for your feelings
- show how the event affected the narrator's life

Cross-Curricular Activity

HISTORY After you have heard the story of the war survivor, find out more about the war that affected the survivor. Use the library and the Internet to obtain more facts and information. Compile lists or create graphs and charts that reflect the general scope and impact of the war.

GrammarLink

Use commas to set off nonessential adjective clauses but not clauses that are essential to the meaning of the sentence.

There in the rubble was the diary, **which he later published***. . . .*

. . . the problems **that bombarded the internees in the camp Manzanar.**

Write the paragraph, using commas as needed.

In *The Road from Home* David Kherdian tells the story of his mother who grew up in the Armenian quarter of a Turkish town. Conflict raged in Turkey which was part of the Ottoman Empire. The Armenians who were often targeted by the Turks suffered terribly. Kherdian re-creates the tension that mounted in 1914 and 1915.

See Lesson 20.3, page 603.

Listening and Speaking

COOPERATIVE LEARNING In a small group, take turns reporting on the research you have done on the specific war. Then take turns summarizing the responses you wrote to the survivor's story. Discuss how the personal accounts reinforced, expanded, or contradicted what you learned about the war from the print and electronic sources.

LOG ON ▶ **Writing** Online   For more writing and grammar practice, go to glencoe.com and enter QuickPass code WC87703p1.

183

Writing Process in Action

Narrative Writing

In preceding lessons you've learned how time order, point of view, realistic details, and dialogue can make a historical narrative come to life. You've also had a chance to write narratives about people, places, and events in history. Now, in this lesson, you're invited to write a historical narrative about one of your ancestors or someone else whose life interests you.

Assignment

Context	You are going to write a historical narrative about an ancestor or someone else whose life is important to you. Although you may find facts about this person, you'll have to invent some likely—and lively—details about speech, actions, and attitudes.
Purpose	To make the past come alive in a historical narrative
Audience	Your family or friends
Length	4–5 paragraphs

Planning to Write

The following pages can help you plan and write your historical narrative. Read through the pages, and then refer to them as you need to. Don't be tied down by them, however. You're in charge of your own writing process. Set a time frame for completing this assignment. Keep in mind the controlling idea: to write a historical narrative about one of your ancestors or someone else you find important.

LOG ON ▶ **Writing** Online

For prewriting, drafting, revising, editing and publishing tools, go to **glencoe.com** and enter QuickPass code WC87703p1.

Prewriting

Is there a person in history whose life fascinates you? Would you like to know more about how an ancestor came to this country?

- Begin exploring ideas about an ancestor's life by interviewing relatives.
- Refer to old photo albums for pictures of where people lived, played, and worked. Look for letters, diaries, and family records. Jot down notes and ideas in your journal. Begin thinking about where you might begin and end your narrative. Make a list of events, or simply begin writing where it feels right.

Prewriting Tip

For more on interviewing, see Lesson 26.2, pages 760–763.

Option A

Interview people, look at photos, read letters.

Option B

Read about the period.

Option C

Jot down notes about a turning point in the story.

Drafting

As you draft your historical narrative, include details to make the life of your subject real. Notice the details Katherine Paterson uses to portray a nineteenth-century factory.

Krista given money on her eighteenth birthday. Not much—the farm in Denmark was too poor. Older children used money to move to the city to find work. Krista wanted to go to America.

Literature Model

Within five minutes, her head felt like a log being split to splinters. She kept shaking it, as though she could rid it of the noise, or at least the pain, but both only seemed to grow more intense. If that weren't trial enough, a few hours of standing in her proud new boots and her feet had swollen so that the laces cut into her flesh.

Katherine Paterson, *Lyddie*

Drafting Tip

For a reminder about chronological order, review pages 160–163.

When drafting your historical narrative, use details that put your readers in the subject's shoes by making them feel part of the events and surroundings. Instead of simply saying, "the factory was noisy," or "Lyddie's feet hurt," Paterson takes her readers back to the mill to see her character and to feel her pain.

If you get stuck while drafting, look again at your prewriting notes for fresh ideas.

Revising

To begin revising, read over your draft to make sure that what you've written fits your purpose and audience. Then have a writing conference. Read your draft to a partner or small group. Use your audience's reactions to help you evaluate your work so far. The following questions can help you and your listeners.

Question A

Does every sentence contribute to my narrative?

Question B

Have I used specific details?

Question C

Have I established a clear point of view?

> Krista's feet were bleeding by the time she walked the nine miles from the station to the farm where she was to work. She wished she had
> ~~brought old shoes instead of her best shoes, with~~ heavy boots, instead of her Sunday
> to America.
> her, This farm was bigger than the one she had left behind in Denmark. As she thought of the
> scrubbing, mending, and cooking
> hours of ~~hard work~~ that faced her, ~~she became~~ her heart sank.
> ~~sad.~~

Editing/Proofreading

You've worked hard to figure out what you want to say and how to say it well. Since you'll be sharing this with your family or friends, you'll want them to pay attention to the story, not to any errors you might have made. During the editing stage, you'll want to **proofread** your work and eliminate mistakes that might detract from the ideas and feelings you want to share.

This checklist will help you catch errors you might otherwise overlook.

Publishing/Presenting

You may wish to include a photograph or a drawing of your subject in your historical narrative. Pictures of a house or the city your subject lived in and of clothing or vehicles from your subject's era will also add interest to your narrative. If your computer software prints some old-fashioned type styles, they can also add a feeling of historical accuracy to your narrative.

Editing/Proofreading Checklist

1. Have I correctly punctuated appositives and adjective clauses?

2. Have I eliminated any double comparisons?

3. Do my verbs agree with their subjects?

4. Have I used standard spelling and capitalization?

5. Is my cursive or printed handwriting clear?

Proofreading Tip

For proofreading symbols, see pages 79 and 863.

Journal Writing: Write to Learn

Reflect on your writing experience. Answer these questions in your journal: What do you like best about your narrative writing? What was the hardest part of writing it? What did you learn in your writing conference? What new things have you learned as a writer?

FROM

LYDDIE

by Katherine Paterson

In the mid-1800s the hope for a better life prompted many to join the ranks of factory laborers. Katherine Paterson's historical narrative relates how thirteen-year-old Lydia Worthen travels to Lowell, Massachusetts, seeking mill work and the chance for a new life. As you read, pay special attention to how Paterson tells Lydia's story. Then try the activities in Linking Writing and Literature on page 194.

The four-thirty bell clanged the house awake. From every direction, Lyddie could hear the shrill voices of girls calling to one another, even singing. Someone on another floor was imitating a rooster. From the other side of the bed Betsy groaned and turned over, but Lyddie was up, dressing quickly in the dark as she had always done in the windowless attic of the inn.

Her stomach rumbled, but she ignored it. There would be no breakfast until seven, and that was two and a half hours away. By five the girls had crowded through the main gate, jostled their way up the outside staircase on the far end of the mill, cleaned their machines, and stood waiting for the workday to begin.

"Not too tired this morning?" Diana asked by way of greeting.

Constantin Meunier, *In the Black Country*, c. 1860–80

Lyddie shook her head. Her feet were sore, but she'd felt tireder after a day behind the plow.

"Good. Today will be something more strenuous, I fear. We'll work all three looms together, all right? Until you feel quite sure of everything."

Lyddie felt a bit as though the older girls were whispering in church. It seemed almost that quiet in the great loom room. The only real noise was the creaking from the ceiling of the leather belts that connected the wheels in the weaving room to the gigantic waterwheel in the basement.

The overseer came in, nodded good morning, and pushed a low wooden stool under a cord dangling from the assembly of wheels and belts above his head. His little red mouth pursed, he stepped up on the stool and pulled out his pocket watch. At the same moment, the bell in the tower above the roof began to ring. He yanked the

Narrative Writing

cord, the wide leather belt above him shifted from a loose to a tight pulley, and suddenly all the hundred or so silent looms, in raucous[1] concert, shuddered and groaned into fearsome life. Lyddie's first full day as a factory girl had begun.

Within five minutes, her head felt like a log being split to splinters. She kept shaking it, as though she could rid it of the noise, or at least the pain, but both only seemed to grow more intense. If that weren't trial enough, a few hours of standing in her proud new boots and her feet had swollen so that the laces cut into her flesh. She bent down quickly to loosen them, and when she found the right lace was knotted, she nearly burst into tears. Or perhaps the tears were caused by the swirling dust and lint.

Now that she thought of it, she could hardly breathe, the air was so laden with moisture and debris.[2] She snatched a moment to run to the window. She had to get air, but the window was nailed shut against the April morning. She leaned her forehead against it; even the glass seemed hot. Her apron brushed the pots of red geraniums crowding the wide sill. They were flourishing in this hot house. She coughed, trying to free her throat and lungs for breath.

Then she felt, rather than saw, Diana. "Mr. Marsden has his eye on you," the older girl said gently, and put her arm on Lyddie's shoulder to turn her back toward the looms. She pointed to the stalled loom and the broken warp[3] thread that must be tied. Even though Diana had stopped the loom, Lyddie stood rubbing the powder into her fingertips, hesitating to plunge her hands into the bowels of the machine. Diana urged her with a light touch.

I stared down a black bear, Lyddie reminded herself. She took a deep breath, fished out the broken ends, and began to tie the weaver's knot that Diana had shown her over and over again the afternoon before. Finally, Lyddie managed to make a clumsy knot, and Diana pulled the lever, and the loom shuddered to life once more.

How could she ever get accustomed to this inferno?[4] Even when the girls were set free at 7:00, it was to push and shove their way across the bridge and down the street to their boardinghouses, bolt down their hearty breakfast, and rush back, stomachs still churning, for "ring in" at 7:35. Nearly half the mealtime was spent simply going up and down the staircase, across the mill yard and bridge, down the row of houses— just getting to and from the meal. And

---

1 **raucous** (rô′kəs) hoarse; rough-sounding
2 **debris** (də brē′) bits of rubbish; litter
3 **warp** (wôrp) threads running lengthwise in a loom
4 **inferno** (in fur′nō) hell or any place suggesting hell

Eyre Crowe, *The Dinner Hour, Wigan*, 1874

the din[5] in the dining room was nearly as loud as the racket in the mill—thirty young women chewing and calling at the same time, reaching for the platters of flapjacks and pitchers of syrup, ignoring cries from the other end of the table to pass anything.

Her quiet meals in the corner of the kitchen with Triphena, even her meager bowls of bark soup in the cabin with the seldom talkative Charlie, seemed like feasts compared to the huge, rushed, noisy affairs in Mrs. Bedlow's house. The

half hour at noonday dinner with more food than she had ever had set before her at one time was worse than breakfast.

At last the evening bell rang, and Mr. Marsden pulled the cord to end the day. Diana walked with her to the place by the door where the girls hung their bonnets and shawls, and handed Lyddie hers. "Let's forget about studying those regulations tonight," she said. "It's been too long a day already."

Lyddie nodded. Yesterday seemed years in the past. She couldn't even remember why she'd thought the regulations important enough to bother with.

---

5 din (din) a loud, continuous noise

She had lost all appetite. The very smell of supper made her nauseous[6]—beans heavy with pork fat and brown injun bread with orange cheese, fried potatoes, of course, and flapjacks with apple sauce, baked Indian pudding with cream and plum cake for dessert. Lyddie nibbled at the brown bread and washed it down with a little scalding tea. How could the others eat so heartily and with such a clatter of dishes and shrieks of conversation? She longed only to get to the room, take off her boots, massage her abused feet, and lay down her aching head. While the other girls pulled their chairs from the table and scraped them about to form little circles in the parlor area, Lyddie dragged herself from the table and up the stairs.

Betsy was already there before her, her current novel in her hand. She laughed at the sight of Lyddie. "The first full day! And up to now you thought yourself a strapping country farm girl who could do anything, didn't you?"

Lyddie did not try to answer back. She simply sank to her side of the double bed and took off the offending shoes and began to rub her swollen feet.

"If you've got an older pair"—Betsy's voice was almost gentle—"more stretched and softer . . ."

Lyddie nodded. Tomorrow she'd wear Triphena's without the stuffing. They were still stiff from the trip and she'd be awkward rushing back and forth to meals, but at least there'd be room for her feet to swell.

She undressed, slipped on her shabby night shift, and slid under the quilt. Betsy glanced over at her. "To bed so soon?"

Lyddie could only nod again. It was as though she could not possibly squeeze a word through her lips. Betsy smiled again. She ain't laughing at me, Lyddie realized. She's remembering how it was.

"Shall I read to you?" Betsy asked.

Lyddie nodded gratefully and closed her eyes and turned her back against the candlelight.

Betsy did not give any explanation of the novel she was reading, simply commenced to read aloud where she had broken off reading to herself. Even though Lyddie's head was still choked with lint and battered with noise, she struggled to get the sense of the story.

The child was in some kind of poorhouse, it seemed, and he was hungry. Lyddie knew about hungry children. Rachel, Agnes, Charlie—they had all been hungry that winter of the bear. The hungry little boy in the story had held up his bowl to the poorhouse overseer and said:

"Please sir, I want some more."

And for this the overseer—she could see his little rosebud mouth rounded in

---

6 nauseous (nô′shəs) feeling sickness in the stomach

horror—for this the overseer had screamed out at the child. In her mind's eye little Oliver Twist looked exactly like a younger Charlie. The cruel overseer had screamed and hauled the boy before a sort of agent. And for what crime? For the monstrous crime of wanting more to eat.

"That boy will be hung," the agent had prophesied. "I know that boy will be hung."

She fought sleep, ravenous[7] for every word. She had not had any appetite for the bountiful meal downstairs, but now she was feeling a hunger she knew nothing about. She had to know what would happen to little Oliver. Would he indeed be hanged just because he wanted more gruel?

She opened her eyes and turned to watch Betsy, who was absorbed in her reading. Then Betsy sensed her watching, and looked up from the book. "It's a marvelous story, isn't it? I saw the author once—Mr. Charles Dickens. He visited our factory. Let me see—I was already in the spinning room—it must have been in—"

But Lyddie cared nothing for authors or dates. "Don't stop reading the story, please," she croaked out.

"Never fear, little Lyddie. No more interruptions," Betsy promised, and read on, though her voice grew raspy with fatigue, until the bell rang for curfew. She stuck a hair ribbon in the place. "Till tomorrow night," she whispered as the feet of an army of girls could be heard thundering up the staircase.

---

7 **ravenous** (rav′ə nəs) greedy

Literature Model

Linking Writing and Literature

◆ Learning to Learn

What is your reaction to Lyddie's first day at the mill? In your journal, reflect on the challenges of factory work facing a thirteen-year-old girl in the mid-1800s. Would you be willing to endure difficulties like those that Lyddie goes through in hope of finding a better life?

◆ Talk About Reading

With a group of classmates, discuss Lyddie's first day at the mill. Choose one classmate to lead the discussion and another to take notes. Use the following questions to guide the group's discussion.

1. **Connect to Your Life** Lyddie is exhausted at the end of the day. Think about a typical day in your life. Is it packed with activities? Do you ever wish things would slow down some? Are you ever exhausted at night? Explain.

2. **Critical Thinking: Evaluate** "I stared down a black bear, Lyddie reminded herself." Lyddie remembers this as she faces a challenge at the mill. What does this line tell you about Lyddie's character?

3. **6+1 Trait®: Organization** How has Katherine Patterson organized the events in *Lyddie*? How does that organization help you understand the story?

4. **Connect to Your Writing** When you describe events in the order in which they happened, provide your readers with clues that keep the organization clear. Make a list of words and phrases that can signal when an event takes place.

◆ Write About Reading

E-mail Write an e-mail to a friend describing things you did on a recent day, from rising in the morning to going to bed at night. Include important, interesting, and surprising events from that day. To prevent your e-mail from being just a list of events, offer comments on the events of the day.

Focus on Organization Clear organization will enable your reader to follow along with you as you describe your day. Tell about the events of your day in chronological order—the order in which they happened. Remember to use words and phrases that signal when events took place.

For more information on organization and the 6+1Trait® model, see **Writing and Research Handbook,** pages 838–840.

6+1 Trait® is a registered trademark of Northwest Regional Educational Laboratory, which does not endorse this product.

Reflecting on the Unit: Summarize What You Learned

Focus on the following questions to help you summarize what you learned in this unit.

❶ What is a narrative?
❷ Where can you get ideas for historical narratives?
❸ Why is the use of chronological order helpful?
❹ From what points of view can a narrative be told?
❺ How does dialogue help to enrich a narrative?
❻ On what facts do news stories focus?

Adding to Your Portfolio

CHOOSE A SELECTION FOR YOUR PORTFOLIO Look over the narrative writing you did for this unit. Choose a piece of writing for your portfolio. The writing you choose should show one or more of the following:

• a realistic portrayal of a person, event, or setting from history
• an opening that introduces a person, event, or setting and that draws readers into the story
• lively dialogue that shows what the characters are like
• fictional but true-to-life characters to portray a historical era or event
• a lead that tells most or all of the five *W*s and an *H*

REFLECT ON YOUR CHOICE Attach a note to the piece you chose, explaining briefly why you chose it and what you learned from writing it.

SET GOALS How can you improve your writing? What skill will you focus on the next time you write?

Writing Across the Curriculum

MAKE A HISTORY CONNECTION Think of a historical event that took place during the lifetime of the character about whom you wrote your narrative. Write a paragraph telling some of the effects that event had on your character's life.

*All the pages had let loose at the seams
and were flapping free into the gutters. . .*

—Naomi Shihab Nye,
"Thank You in Arabic"

UNIT 5

Expository Writing

Writing in the Real World

Expository writing invites readers to enter real worlds and meet actual people. Gary McLain, Choctaw-Irish author and artist, wanted to invite non-Indian travelers into his world. So he wrote a guide called *Indian America*, a traveler's guide to Native American peoples in the continental United States. Part of the guide, such as the following excerpt, provides basic facts to help readers locate and identify individual groups.

from *Indian America*
by Gary McLain
"Eagle/Walking Turtle"

Nett Lake Reservation
Business Committee
(Bois Fort)
Nett Lake, MN 55772
(218) 757-3261

Ojibwa (to roast till puckered up)

Location: The location of the powwow grounds can be obtained by calling the tribal office.

Public Ceremony or Powwow Dates: The first weekend in June is powwow time with traditional dancing and drum groups. Call the tribal office for dates and times.

Art Forms: Arts and crafts are sold at the powwow. The work will include paintings, feather work, leather work, and beadwork.

Visitor Information: The Bois Fort Wild Rice Company is doing well. For interesting information on wild rice, see the general history of the Ojibwa at the beginning of this section.

Ni-Mi-Win
Spirit Mountain Sky Facility
Duluth, MN
(218) 897-1251

Ojibwa (to roast till puckered up)

Location: Call the number above for the location of the powwow.

Public Ceremony or Powwow Dates: The third weekend in August is the Ni-Mi-Win celebration. It is the greatest joint Ojibwa celebration, and its goal is to bring everyone together. Traditional and intertribal dances are performed.

Art Forms: You will find black ash basket making along with leather work, beadwork, birch bark baskets, and all kinds of arts and crafts.

Visitor Information: If you like to powwow, don't miss this one.

A Writer's Process

Prewriting
Collecting and Organizing the Facts

When McLain decided to write *Indian America,* he already knew a great deal about many Native American groups. Even so, he needed to gather more information.

Using his knowledge and a list from the Bureau of Indian Affairs, McLain mailed five hundred letters to tribal offices around the country. Three hundred tribal offices responded with information that would be helpful to travelers. Information included the group's name, address, and tribal office phone number and location, as well as its public ceremonies and art forms. Some groups even responded with histories written by tribal historians. Before long McLain had a stack of material three feet high.

With the facts in hand, McLain next decided on the parts and organization of his guide. He says, "I divided the country into nine regions based mostly on how Indian people live."

McLain planned to open the guidebook with information on Indian beliefs. The guide to the tribes would follow, organized by region. To help travelers picture locations, McLain decided to include regional maps.

Drafting
Writing the Book

With his book plan in mind, McLain started writing, a job that would take him three months. For days at a time, he wrote from sunup to midmorning, from mid-afternoon until 10:00 P.M.

As McLain worked with his material, he found that he needed two writing styles to present the different types of information. In the introduction to each region, he wrote in conversational prose. For example, in his introduction to the Great Plains, McLain explained how people were bound together in a great sacred hoop.

McLain used a much different writing style for his guide to each group. Here he wrote in short, pertinent sentences for travelers on the go. He organized the copy for this part of the guide under a

The Great Plains

The Great Plains

set of heads that were easy to scan: tribal name, location, ceremony or powwow dates, art forms, and visitor information.

In the visitor-information section, McLain provided travelers with useful and intriguing facts. For the Taos Pueblo in New Mexico, he focused on photography rules for visitors. For the Cherokee in North Carolina, he described a restored Cherokee village, a museum, and various tourist activities. By contrast, his section on the Comanche in Oklahoma discussed the tribe's history, not its modern life. The

reason? "There are no more reservations in Oklahoma," McLain explains. "The Comanche live in white frame houses that don't look much different from those in Ohio or Indiana. Yet the Comanche were hunters who lived up and down the central plains. They were great horsemen and great warriors and had much ceremony in their lives. I thought a little more attention to the history of the tribe could help visitors feel connected to these people."

Revising
Making the Story Complete

Once McLain had his book on paper, he revised sections to make them clearer and more engaging. His editor suggested some of the changes. For example, McLain's editor asked him to expand his section on sweetgrass and sage, healing plants used by Medicine People in Plains ceremonies. In his first draft, McLain had done little more than mention the plants. He revised his brief comment to read: "The Medicine People use sage, cedar, and sweetgrass, and the sweet smell carries the healing forward from the past into the future . . . in the sacred dances of our people across the land."

8 / Great Plains

buckskins. And dances and songs and chants developed entertainment and spiritual appreciation of the creation ing things.

Medicines for the body and spirit evolved with time al cedar, and sweetgrass were used in the sacred ceremon ple. The Creator provided the knowled

Examining Writing in the Real World

Analyzing the Media Connection

Discuss these questions about the model on page 198.

1. When might you use the information in Gary McLain's guide?

2. What key words do you notice in the excerpt? What calls your attention to them?

3. McLain uses typographical features, such as italics. What other kinds of typographical features and formatting can help clarify information in your expository reports?

4. What information would be helpful to you if you were shopping for Indian jewelry? What information would help you find the dates for tribal ceremonies?

5. If you were traveling to Nett Lake Reservation, what information from the excerpt might you jot down in your personal travel journal?

Analyzing a Writer's Process

Discuss these questions about Gary McLain's writing process.

1. What audience did McLain choose for his book *Indian America?*

2. Why do you think McLain chose the topic for his book? What made him well qualified to write the book?

3. What sources of information did McLain use to collect his material?

4. How did he organize the material? Why was it important for McLain to choose a pattern of organization before he began to write?

5. Explain the two different writing styles McLain used in his guidebook. How did each style match a specific kind of information?

GrammarLink

When proofreading, professional writers make sure that their verbs agree with their subjects.

*The first **weekend** in June **is** pow-wow time.*

On your own paper, write the correct verb for each sentence.

1. The Bois Fort Wild Rice Company are doing well.

2. If you likes to powwow, don't miss this one.

3. The Comanches lives in white frame houses.

4. They was great horsemen.

5. We says that America is the great melting pot of the world.

See Lesson 16.1, pages 541–542.

Join

LESSON 5.1

Conveying Information

Expository writing informs and explains. In the model below, the writer uses expository writing to convey information about a traditional Inuit game, the blanket toss.

Literature Model

Members of the community grabbed hold of the edge of an animal skin. When everyone pulled at once, the center snapped up, propelling the person who sat or stood in the center of the skin into the air, just as if he or she were on a trampoline. The leader of the most successful whaling crew was often rewarded with the place on the skin; it was then a matter of pride to remain standing throughout the vigorous tossing.

Kevin Osborn, *The Peoples of the Arctic*

Write to Inform

The most familiar form of expository writing is the essay. An essay consists of an introduction, a body, and a conclusion. The **introduction** usually contains a **thesis statement**—a sentence that states the main or the central idea of the essay. The **body** is made up of one or more paragraphs that include details supporting the thesis statement. The **conclusion** draws the essay to a close. It may restate what has been said or suggest a different way of looking at the material. Notice in the model below how Michele Casey begins her essay on sharks.

Student Model

Although shark attacks do occur, they are not so frequent that swimmers must arm themselves with shark repellents. Survivors of airplane or ship disasters, though, need an effective shark repellent, since they have practically no defenses. The most promising advances are sound/electronic barriers. All other methods have major drawbacks.

Michele Casey, Glen Crest Junior High School, Glen Ellyn, Illinois

What is the thesis statement in Michele's essay?

The body of Michele's essay goes on to discuss various shark repellents. Her conclusion states, "Shark repellents of today and the future will help prevent further disaster for survivors at sea."

Journal Writing

Imagine that a friend has asked you how to play a game you know well. Write a thesis statement explaining the main objective of the game.

Prewriting Tip

While prewriting, brainstorm a list of questions your essay should answer. Then answer the questions in your draft.

Choose an Approach

The goal of expository writing is to explain or inform. The model on page 215 explains by describing the steps of a process. Expository writing can take other forms. The chart below explains four approaches to expository writing. These approaches can be used alone or combined in any expository piece. To explain about dolphins, the writer of the sample below chose the cause-and-effect approach.

Approaches to Expository Writing	
Approach	**Sample Writing**
Definition	Sivuquad, a name for St. Lawrence Island, means squeezed dry. The islanders believed that a giant had made the island from dried mud.
Compare-Contrast	The boats in a coastal fishing fleet often stay at sea for days or weeks. Long-range fishing fleet vessels can remain at sea for months.
Process	To breathe, a whale surfaces in a forward rolling motion. For two seconds, it blows out and breathes in as much as 2,100 quarts of air.
Cause-Effect	The discovery of oil and gas in Alaska in 1968 led to widespread development in that region of the world.

According to the writer, why has the dolphin been protected?

For centuries dolphins have fascinated people. Stories about dolphins that guided ships and rescued swimmers have led some people to idealize these creatures. Further, traditional respect and increasing public concern have resulted in measures intended to protect the dolphin.

Write an Informative Essay

A television program called *What in the World?* challenges viewers to send in answers to questions, such as "What is a solar eclipse?" or "How are a whale and a dolphin alike?" Choose one of these two questions, do some research, and write a brief essay that answers it.

PURPOSE To convey information
AUDIENCE Television viewers (your classmates)
LENGTH 2–3 paragraphs

WRITING RUBRICS To write an informative essay, you should

- choose an appropriate approach from the chart on the previous page
- elaborate, giving sufficient details and examples to support your answer
- include an introduction, a body, and a conclusion

Listening and Speaking

AS SEEN ON TV Work in a small group to prepare your essay as a presentation on *What in the World?* All group members should be prepared to both give feedback about each person's presentation and to receive feedback about their own. If possible, videotape your presentation and review the tape to make sure you speak clearly.

GrammarLink

Avoid using pronouns without clear antecedents.

To avoid confusion when using pronouns, you must be sure that the noun or group of words to which the pronoun refers—the antecedent—is clear.

> *Stories about dolphins that guided ships and rescued swimmers have led some people to idealize* **these creatures.**

If this sentence ended "to idealize *them,*" readers would not know if *them* referred to *dolphins, ships,* or *swimmers.*

Revise the paragraph below to eliminate confusing pronouns.

[1]Heather is helping Jen in the garden; Chad, Mike, and she are planting tomatoes. [2]They are proud of the garden. [3]Then Chad and Mike will weed his garden and the Wongs' garden.

See Lesson 11.2, pages 437–438.

Viewing and Representing

USING IMAGES TO EXPLAIN Assemble photos, drawings, and other visual aids to help make your TV talk more lively and interesting. Use the aids at appropriate times to illustrate your talk.

LOG ON ▶ **Writing** Online For more writing and grammar practice, go to **glencoe.com** and enter QuickPass code WC87703p1.

5.1 Conveying Information **205**

Structuring an Explanation

Choosing and arranging details to support a statement are the foundations of expository writing. Notice how the writer of the model below uses supporting details to explain how computers tackle mountains of information in a flash.

Literature Model

Printed circuit boards are the heart of the computer. On them are mounted the transistors, capacitors, chips, and other electrical marvels that create a computer. Their undersides have ribbons of solder, through which electricity flows. It is not necessary for you to have the foggiest idea how all this works. But do consider how small, lightweight, and portable the printed circuit boards are. Each board has a special function: some provide memory for the computer; others provide the processing and arithmetic logic functions; still others convert the power supply to and from the required voltages.

Carol W. Brown, *The Minicomputer Simplified*

Elaborate with Details

Supporting details are the heart of expository writing. They support the **thesis statement,** or central idea, in the introduction of your essay. The details you select will depend on your approach to expository writing. If you are writing a cause-and-effect essay, you might use reasons as supporting details. In the model Carol W. Brown uses facts to define circuit boards. You can also use statistics, examples, or incidents to support what you say. Note the examples of the types of details listed in the chart below.

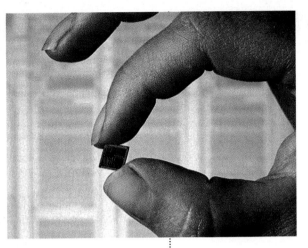

Details in Expository Writing	
Type	**Example**
Facts	Momenta International of California introduced a computer that can recognize and interpret printed handwriting.
Statistics	The processor inside a typical computer can carry out one million additions in only a second.
Examples/ Incidents	The optical processor is an example of a computer that uses light beams to process information.
Reasons	Computer manufacturers are developing smaller computers because businesspeople demand them for use when they travel.

Prewriting Tip

For help with planning strong paragraphs to introduce your thesis statement, support it with details, and sum it up, see **Writing and Research Handbook,** pages 833–840.

Journal Writing

Think about something you would like to explain to a friend. Write your thesis statement and list the details you would include, trying to use all four types of details.

Grammar Tip

When editing an essay that uses time order, be sure the verb tenses reflect the order. For more on tenses, refer to Lessons 10.5–10.9, pages 409–417.

Arrange the Details

Once you've selected supporting details for your explanation, you're ready to organize them. Ask yourself what you're trying to do in your essay. For example, are you going to show the cause and effect of a tidal wave? Are you going to use a comparison-contrast essay to point out the similarities and differences between two comedians? Questions such as these can help you organize your ideas—the supporting details—logically.

You might choose a number of ways to arrange information and supporting details. If you're defining something, you might arrange features from most to least significant. If you're writing about a process, then chronological order, or time order, might be more logical. In the model below, notice the kinds of details that Emilie Baltz uses and how she arranges them.

Student Model

What types of details are in the writing?

What kind of organization does the writer use?

Thomas Edison's invention of the electric light bulb in 1879 came about only after a long, hard process. Finding the right material for the tiny filament inside the light bulb had been difficult. Edison tested 1,600 materials before finally using a piece of burned thread. Because it contained no air, the thread did not burn quickly inside the bulb. This invention would eventually bring light into the world.

Emilie Baltz, Hufford Junior High School,
Joliet, Illinois

5.2 | Writing Activities

Write an Explanation

Imagine that a person from the 1800s has come to visit you. He is curious about some modern invention, such as a computer or a blender. Write a simple explanation of how the device works and what it can be used for.

PURPOSE To use supporting details to explain how a device works and what it can be used for

AUDIENCE A person from the 1800s

LENGTH 2–3 paragraphs

WRITING RUBRICS To explain the device, you should

- describe the major purposes of the device
- make clear how the device is used
- arrange the details in an organized, logical way
- make the explanation clear and legible for the audience.

Using Computers

You can use a computer to illustrate your explanation with pictures, graphs, charts, and diagrams. To make your explanation easier to understand, use the computer's formatting features to boldface words, change font sizes and styles, and make bulleted lists.

GrammarLink

Form the plurals of compound nouns correctly.

Add -s or -es to the end of one-word compound nouns and to the most important part of other compound nouns.

undersides

printed circuit boards

Use the plural form of each compound noun below in a sentence.

1. bookend
2. halfback
3. father-in-law
4. showcase
5. great-aunt
6. runner-up
7. storybook
8. basketball
9. pot of gold
10. paper plate
11. vice president
12. editor in chief
13. suitcase
14. brother-in-law
15. windowsill
16. nosebleed
17. groundhog
18. toothpaste
19. sunbeam
20. ice rink

See Lesson 9.2, pages 383–384.

Listening and Speaking

COOPERATIVE LEARNING In a small group, read your explanation aloud. Have group members pay special attention to word choices, making sure that any technical terms are explained or defined. Edit your explanation on the basis of the feedback you get.

Writing to Compare and Contrast

*W*hen you compare two things, you explain how they're similar. When you contrast two things, you explain how they're different. Comparing and contrasting two items can be a useful way of explaining them.

Tanya enjoys country and western music. Classmate Ben prefers Latin American music. These two kinds of music are different in some ways and alike in others. Think about two types of music. Jot down two or three things about them that are similar and two or three things that are different.

Identify Similarities and Differences

By looking carefully at two things, you see their similarities and differences. This close look often helps you understand each thing better. Comparing and contrasting requires an analytical approach.

Before you write a compare-and-contrast essay, you need to identify similarities and differences in your subjects. A Venn diagram, such as the one below, may help you. Be sure that your subjects are related, as two kinds of music are. Also, compare and contrast the same set of features, such as cultural sources and sound, that relate to the subjects.

Vocabulary Tip

When drafting an opening sentence for a compare-and-contrast essay, choose words that will grab your reader's attention.

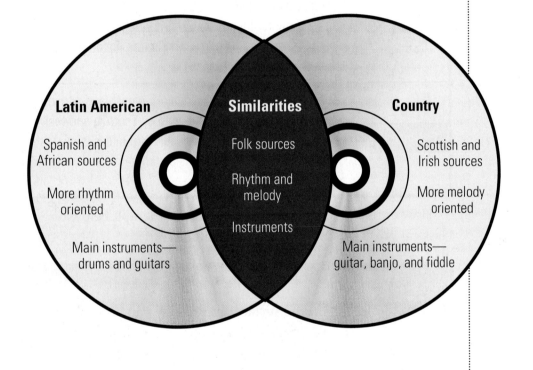

Latin American

Spanish and African sources

More rhythm oriented

Main instruments— drums and guitars

Similarities

Folk sources

Rhythm and melody

Instruments

Country

Scottish and Irish sources

More melody oriented

Main instruments— guitar, banjo, and fiddle

Journal Writing

Think of two musical artists or groups that are related in some way. In your journal make a Venn diagram. Use the diagram to compare and contrast the musicians in terms of the same features.

Organize by Subject or by Feature

You can organize compare-and-contrast writing either by subject or by feature. In organizing by subject, you discuss all the features of one subject and then the features of the other. For example, you might explain the sources and sound of Latin music and then discuss the contrasting sources and sound of country music. When organizing by feature, you discuss one feature at a time for both subjects. See the chart below.

Organizing by Subject or Feature	
Subject	Latin American music sources are Spanish and African. The beat of the music is strong and rhythmic. The main instruments used in Latin American music are drums and guitars. Country music, on the other hand, is influenced by Scottish and Irish sources. It is more melody oriented than Latin American music.
Feature	Latin American music sources are Spanish and African, while country music is influenced by Scottish and Irish sources. The sound of the two kinds of music is also different. Latin American music is rhythmic and country music is melodic.

How did Michael Shapiro organize the paragraph below on classical musicians Yo-Yo Ma and Emanuel Ax?

Does the writer organize his contrast by feature or by subject?

How are Yo-Yo Ma and Emanuel Ax different?

Literature Model

They seem, on the surface, an unlikely pair, as is often the case with friends who never seem to lose the rhythm of their relationship. Ma was the child wonder who came of age musically in the warm embrace of such mentors as Isaac Stern and Leonard Rose. Ax grew up never knowing whether he would be able to become a concert pianist. For Ma playing the cello has always come easily. For Ax the musician's life is one for which he feels forever grateful.

Michael Shapiro, *"Yo-Yo and Manny"*

Write a Compare-and-Contrast Essay

Write an essay about two people, places, or things that you are studying in school, such as two characters from a book or two cities.

PURPOSE To compare and contrast items
AUDIENCE Your teacher or classmates
LENGTH 2–4 paragraphs

WRITING RUBRICS To write an effective compare-and-contrast essay, you should

- use a Venn diagram to identify similarities and differences
- organize by subject or by feature

Cross-Curricular Activity

HEALTH AND PHYSICAL EDUCATION
Choose two sports that are popular in your school. In a brief essay, compare and contrast the two by explaining how they are alike or different in terms of factors such as cost, health benefits, danger, and strategy. Conclude by expressing an opinion about which of the two you believe is more deserving of school and community support. Base your opinion on the details you used in your essay.

Grammar*Link*

Make the verb agree with the closer subject when the parts of a compound subject are joined by *or* or *nor*.

Compound subjects are common in compare-and-contrast writing:

> *Neither Ma nor Ax hides* his talent.

Write the correct verb for each sentence.

1. Neither Mozart nor Haydn are very popular at my house.
2. Either the Beatles or the Grateful Dead were Mom's favorite.
3. Neither Nirvana nor Green Day appeal to my parents.
4. Either my uncles or my dad rave about the Rolling Stones.

See Lesson 16.5, pages 549–550.

Listening and Speaking

ADDRESSING THE ISSUE In a small group, deliver your sports paper as if you were presenting it to a meeting of the school board. Adjust your tone, volume, and vocabulary for that audience. Ask the "school board" to respond to your presentation. As a group, compare and contrast the various opinions about sports that are presented.

Writing Online For more writing and grammar practice, go to **glencoe.com** and enter QuickPass code WC87703p1.

213

Writing About a Process

Everyday life is full of step-by-step processes. In this lesson you will learn to explain an everyday process so that others can understand how to complete it.

Making pizza dough may look difficult, but it isn't. There are, however, some basic steps that you need to follow. You also need a recipe, of course. In the photos below, the basic steps in making dough are broken down.

Making Pizza Dough in Four Steps

| Mix Ingredients | Knead Dough | Let Dough Rise | Shape Dough |

Have a Clear Purpose

Knowing how to do something does not guarantee that you can easily share that knowledge with others. Some people find it more difficult to explain a step-by-step process than to actually do it. The instructions in the model on the next page use clear and simple language to explain a rather complicated process: handling hot chilies.

Literature Model

Wearing rubber gloves is a wise precaution, especially when you are handling fresh hot chilies. Be careful not to touch your face or eyes while working with them.

To prepare chilies, first rinse them clean in cold water. (Hot water may make fumes rise from dried chilies, and even the fumes might irritate your nose and eyes.) Working under cold running water, pull out the stem of each chili and break or cut the chilies in half. Brush out the seeds with your fingers. In most cases the ribs inside are tiny, and can be left intact, but if they seem fleshy, cut them out with a small, sharp knife. Dried chilies should be torn into small pieces, covered with boiling water and soaked for at least 30 minutes before they are used. Fresh chilies may be used at once, or soaked in cold, salted water for an hour to remove some of the hotness.

Recipes: Latin American Cooking

The word "first" helps identify what step to begin with.

What are the steps in preparing fresh chilies?

Grammar Tip

As you edit your essay, notice that some of your transitions can appear in adverb clauses. For information see Lesson 14.5, pages 513–514.

To explain a process, choose a topic that you understand well or can research if necessary. Then identify your audience and what they may already know. Locate terms they'll understand and those you'll have to explain. Be clear about your purpose. You may be helping readers make or do something themselves, such as making tacos. On the other hand, you may be explaining how something works or happens, such as how a Mexican chef makes tacos.

Journal Writing

In your journal use a cluster map to explore topics for a process explanation. You might choose a hobby or another activity you enjoy. Circle your three best ideas.

Make the Order Clear

Before you write about a process, gather information through research, observation, or interviews. List the steps of the process in chronological order. Then write your draft. Use transition words, such as *first, next,* and *later,* to connect the steps. The chart shows a plan one student followed to write the explanation that appears below.

Relating a Process	
Organizing Your Writing	**Example**
Topic	How to make a pizza
Audience	Friends
What the audience needs to know	The steps in making the pizza
Gathering information	Watch the video I taped. Read a pizza cookbook.
Listing steps	1. Spread dough. 2. Spread cheese. 3. Add vegetables. 4. Top with fresh tomatoes.

Student Model

The writer lists the four steps in chronological order.

What transition words does the writer use in the explanation?

First, spread the dough so that you have an inch-wide rim around the sides. The rim keeps the filling from leaking out while the pizza's cooking. Now it's time to put in the fillings. Place the cheese on the dough to keep it from getting soggy. Then add peppers, onions, or other vegetables that could burn if they were on top. Place fresh chopped tomatoes over the vegetables. Your pizza's oven-ready.

Luke Lapenta Proskine, Wilmette Junior High School, Wilmette, Illinois

Write a Step-by-Step Guide

Select an ordinary task, such as how to tie your shoes or how to find a library book. Write a step-by-step explanation for someone who knows little or nothing about the task.

PURPOSE To explain how to perform a simple task

AUDIENCE Someone who does not know how to perform the task

LENGTH 1/2 page

WRITING RUBRICS To write an effective step-by-step explanation, you should

• explain terms the reader may not know

• write the steps in chronological order

• use appropriate transition words

• use precise verbs to make your explanation clear

Listening and Speaking

COOPERATIVE LEARNING In a small group, brainstorm different kinds of foods that you know how to cook. Choose a food from the list, and draft a brief but clear step-by-step explanation of how to cook the food. If you need to do any research, individual students can take responsibility. Read your draft explanation in the group, and discuss how to revise the steps to make them clearer or more informative. Assemble your final explanation into a cookbook with other groups.

Grammar Link

Use precise verbs to clarify explanations.

Precise verbs tell your readers exactly what you mean.

. . . *pull* out the stem of each chili and *break* or *cut* the chilies in half.

Revise each sentence below, replacing general verbs with more specific ones.

1. To make sugar cookies, first put oil on a shiny cookie sheet.
2. After making the dough, get it to cool down for several hours in the refrigerator.
3. Cook the cookies at 350° for 10 minutes.
4. Enjoy the cookies with a glass of milk, but do not eat all of them at one time.
5. Be sure to clean up the counters afterward.

See Lesson 3.3, page 122, and Lesson 10.1, page 401.

Viewing and Representing

CREATING VISUAL AIDS Create a series of four or five drawings that illustrate your step-by-step explanation. In your small group, be sure group members can connect your drawings with your essay. Attach the drawings to the essays for a "How to. . ." booklet.

LOG ON ▶ **Writing** Online | For more writing and grammar practice, go to **glencoe.com** and enter QuickPass code WC87703p1.

217

Explaining Connections Between Events

Sometimes events are connected—one event or situation causes another, and so on. The cause always comes before the effect, or result.

The skyscraper reflects billowing clouds. You ask yourself, What would cause an architect to use reflective glass in a skyscraper's windows? James Cross Giblin answers this question.

Literature Model

The energy crisis of the 1970s presented yet another threat to the windows in homes, schools, and office buildings. The all-glass architectural styles of the post-war years had depended on a steady supply of inexpensive fuel for heating and air-conditioning. Now there was a danger that that supply might be cut off, or drastically reduced.

To conserve energy and meet the demand for even better climate control in buildings, manufacturers developed an improved window covering—reflective glass. Reflective glass was coated with a thin, transparent metallic film. This mirrorlike coating reflected the sun's rays away from the glass and lowered heat gain within the building much more than mere tinted glass could.

James Cross Giblin, *Let There Be Light*

Be Clear About Cause and Effect

Giblin uses cause and effect to explain the origins of mirror-like skyscraper windows. The cause (the energy crisis) led to an effect (the development of reflective-glass windows). A cause-and-effect explanation may show one cause and one effect. Or it may explain a series of effects resulting from a single cause. It can also present multiple causes and multiple effects.

Make sure that your topic describes true cause and effect. Because one event follows another doesn't mean that the first caused the second. Suppose you close a window, and then the phone rings. Shutting the window didn't make the phone ring. Nick Poole linked cause and effect correctly in the paragraph below.

Expository Writing

Student Model

During the nineteenth century, Americans were part of a tremendous expansion westward. These pioneering Americans left their homes back east for at least three reasons. Some were seeking fertile soil for farming. Many were looking for economic development. Trade was one way of making money. The pioneers traded with Native Americans, especially for furs. Various goods were also available from Mexicans. Finally, other Americans just went west for the adventure.

Nick Poole, Wilmette Junior High School,
Wilmette, Illinois

What three causes of westward expansion does Nick identify?

Journal Writing

Select a recent event that held some particular meaning for you. Identify the causes or effects of the event. In your journal list each cause or effect.

When revising, use transitions such as the following to help you make cause-and-effect relationships clear: *so, if, then, since, because, therefore, as a result.*

Choose an Organizational Pattern

The chart below shows steps you can take to organize a cause-and-effect essay. First, select a topic, and ask yourself if a clear cause-and-effect relationship exists. Next, explore the types of cause-and-effect relationships present. Is there one cause for several effects? Are there several causes leading to a single effect? Or are there multiple causes with multiple effects?

Finally, choose a pattern of organization for your writing. You can organize your cause-and-effect draft in one of two ways. One method involves identifying a cause and then explaining its effects. The other method involves stating an effect and then discussing its cause or causes. After you've completed your draft, review it to be sure the cause-and-effect relationships are clear.

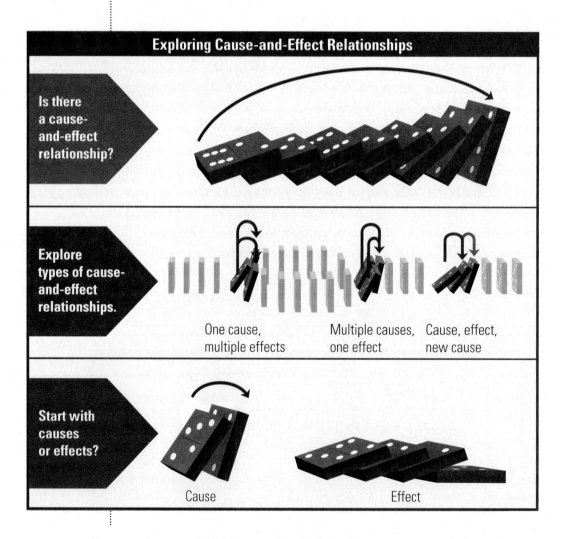

Exploring Cause-and-Effect Relationships

Is there a cause-and-effect relationship?

Explore types of cause-and-effect relationships.

One cause, multiple effects

Multiple causes, one effect

Cause, effect, new cause

Start with causes or effects?

Cause

Effect

Write a Cause-and-Effect Letter

You are concerned about the poor condition of the town's swimming pool and basketball courts. Write a letter to a town government official. Explain what could result if no action is taken. Present some solutions.

PURPOSE To present a cause-and-effect explanation
AUDIENCE Town government official
LENGTH 3–4 paragraphs

WRITING RUBRICS To write an effective cause-and-effect letter, you should

- establish a cause-and-effect connection between the conditions and possible outcomes
- explain possible multiple effects
- include facts and examples to support your case

Cross-Curricular Activity

SCIENCE Think of a natural process that involves a cause-and-effect relationship, such as the way a plant or a storm develops. Use your science book or other resources, including the Internet, to find information on the process. Then write a brief essay, aimed at fourth graders, designed to explain the cause-and-effect process. Be sure to explain or define any technical terms you use.

Grammar*Link*

Watch out for confusing word pairs.

Be sure to choose the correct word in pairs like *than* and *then*.

> . . . *lowered heat gain . . . much more **than** mere tinted glass could.*

Complete each sentence with the correct word.

I was [1](laying, lying) down; [2](than, then) my sister's friends arrived for her party. I had to [3](raise, rise)—no more [4](quiet, quite) for me. I could [5](accept, except) that because Ann would [6](leave, let) me join the party. To help out, I [7](sat, set) the table; [8](all together, altogether) there were ten of us. Each would [9](choose, chose) food from a buffet. [10](Beside, Besides) sandwiches, we were offering Chinese dishes.

See Lessons 17.1–17.3, pages 559–564.

Listening and Speaking

COOPERATIVE LEARNING In a small group, deliver your science essay as an oral presentation. Ask for feedback to help you make your presentation more suitable for younger students. If possible, arrange to present your science essay to a fourth-grade class.

LOG ON ▶ **Writing** Online For more writing and grammar practice, go to **glencoe.com** and enter QuickPass code WC87703p1.

221

LESSON 5.6 Answering an Essay Question

How did the invention of the automobile change daily life in the United States?

Essay questions on tests call for explanations. Understanding what the question calls for will help you improve your answers.

Writing a good answer to an essay question takes some planning. First, read the question carefully. Then decide roughly how many minutes you'll spend on each of the following tasks: (1) underlining key words and jotting down key ideas to include in the answer; (2) developing a thesis statement and a brief outline; (3) drafting your answer; and (4) revising and editing as time permits.

Begin planning your answer. Look at the question for clue words that can help you compose your answer. Then identify key ideas you'll want to discuss. You might explore them by using a cluster diagram or organize them by renumbering. The facing page shows how a student organized some key ideas to answer the test question at the top of this page. The chart below the student model gives examples of clue words.

Revising Tip

When you revise your answer, cross out any unnecessary details. Insert details that will make your answer more complete.

People

Farmers are no longer isolated. Places

Places like motels, drive-ins, and large

shopping malls are a part of daily life.

People within cities can travel to jobs many

miles from their homes.

People can drive many miles on short or

long vacations.

> The items in the list have been grouped as they will be discussed in the draft.

Clue Words in Essay Questions

Clue Word	Action to take	Example
Describe	Use precise details to paint a picture of something.	Describe the appearance of the first Model T Ford.
Explain	Use facts, examples, or reasons to tell why or how.	Explain how the car was developed.
Compare	Tell how two or more subjects are alike.	Compare the steam car and the electric car.
Contrast	Tell how two or more subjects are different.	Contrast the Model T with a car of today.
Summarize	State main points in brief form.	Summarize how a four-cycle engine works.

Journal Writing

Use one clue word from the chart to write a question. Choose a topic that intrigues you. Take the notes you would need to answer the question.

Write Your Answer

Your answer should be a well-organized essay. The introduction to your essay should contain a statement of the main ideas in your answer. One effective way to begin is by restating the question.

Follow your introductory statement with the body of your answer. Include information from your notes as you write your supporting details. Then write a conclusion that restates your beginning statement and summarizes your answer. When you've finished your draft, see whether your content words match the content words of the question. Content words are the key words that relate to the subject matter. Finally, revise and edit your draft. Notice how one writer drafted an answer to the question on page 222.

page 222.

> The invention of the automobile has changed daily life in the United States in two important ways. First, Americans are constantly on the move. City people can drive to jobs far from their homes. Farmers can travel to stores and offices miles away. Vacationers can drive to faraway places. Second, American businesses now provide services to go. Motels, drive-ins, and malls suit the needs of Americans on the run. Automobiles have changed America into a nation on wheels.

The first sentence of the answer restates the question.

What details does the writer use in the body to show the change in Americans' daily life?

The conclusion restates the introductory statement.

Expository Writing

Write a Question and Its Answer

Write an essay question and answer dealing with the issue of energy use and conservation in your community. The question should enable you to use facts and information that are generally known.

PURPOSE To answer an essay question
AUDIENCE Your history teacher
LENGTH 2 paragraphs

WRITING RUBRICS To write an effective essay question and answer, you should

- develop a question that is challenging but realistic
- plan an answer that connects to the key words of the question
- organize your answer with an introduction, a body, and a conclusion

Listening and Speaking

COOPERATIVE LEARNING With a small group look through another textbook for a single essay question for everyone to answer. Take twenty minutes to answer the question. Then share your answers. Talk about the best parts of the organization and content of each essay. Discuss possible improvements.

GrammarLink

Use commas to separate items in a series.

Motels, drive-ins, and malls. . . .

Write each sentence, adding commas where necessary.

1. Sound heat and light are all forms of energy.
2. Water wind and geothermal energy are used to generate electricity.
3. Environmentalists policymakers and consumers do not always agree on energy issues.
4. Ski resorts office buildings and airplanes all require large amounts of energy to operate.

See Lesson 20.2, pages 601–602.

Cross-Curricular Activity

ART In a small group, select an interesting piece of artwork from this book. Together, develop an essay question that requires the writer to interpret and explain the meaning of the artwork. Individually, write answers to the group's question. Compare and contrast answers to see how much agreement or disagreement there was about the meaning of the artwork.

LOG ON ▶ **Writing** Online | For more writing and grammar practice, go to **glencoe.com** and enter QuickPass code WC87703p1.

225

Expository Writing

Reports: Researching a Topic

Finding and narrowing a topic are the first tasks in preparing a research report.

On television you see a man flying an airplane, leading a flock of Canada geese. The man has raised these orphaned geese. Because they have not been able to learn to fly on their own, the pilot is teaching them. Why do the geese follow the airplane? When were they ready to learn to fly? Where will they go in the winter?

Find a Research Topic

When you prepare to write a research report, think about things that you would like to know more about. Read your journal for thoughts, questions, and possible topics. Make a list of questions about subjects that you would like to explore.

How and when do birds learn to fly?
Do geese use all their feathers to help them fly?
Why do birds migrate?
How do they find their way? Do they use landmarks or the position of the sun, moon, and stars?

After making a list of questions, consider the length of your report. Are you writing a two-page report or a twelve-page report? The length of your report will determine how broad your topic can be.

The list of questions on page 226 is about birds, but the general topic of North American birds is too large for one report. The topic of types of Canada goose feathers is probably too narrow. The topic of Canada goose migration is probably just the right size for a two-page report.

Next, consider your purpose and your audience. What do you want to explain? What information do you want to share? Decide who your readers will be and how much they already know about your topic. Can you provide all the necessary background information and facts?

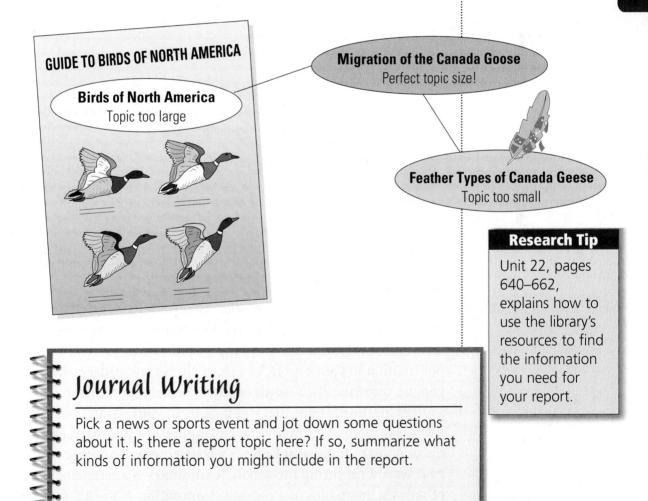

GUIDE TO BIRDS OF NORTH AMERICA

Birds of North America
Topic too large

Migration of the Canada Goose
Perfect topic size!

Feather Types of Canada Geese
Topic too small

Research Tip

Unit 22, pages 640–662, explains how to use the library's resources to find the information you need for your report.

Journal Writing

Pick a news or sports event and jot down some questions about it. Is there a report topic here? If so, summarize what kinds of information you might include in the report.

Research Tip

For help with preparing your list of works cited, see **Writing and Research Handbook,** pages 843–846.

Get the Facts

Begin by looking for sources of information on your topic. For example, you might find books, articles, Web sites, CD-ROMs, or videocassettes about your topic. The chart below includes examples of sources you might use. It also illustrates how to format the bibliography or works-cited list at the end of your report.

Source Types and Works Cited		
Sources	**Example**	**Works Cited**
Books	*Bird Migration*	Mead, Chris. *Bird Migration.* New York: Facts on File, 1983.
Magazines & newspapers	*Petersen's Photographic Magazine*	Warden, J. W. "Migration! The Great Spring Event." *Petersen's Photographic Magazine* April 1992: 22-25.
Encyclopedias	*World Book Encyclopedia*	"Canada Goose." *World Book Encyclopedia.* 1999.
Video materials	*Audubon Society's Video-Guides to Birds of North America: Volume 1*	*Audubon Society's VideoGuides to Birds of North America* 1. Godfrey-Stadin Productions, 1985.
Online references	*Canadian Wildlife Service Hinterland's Who's Who*	"Canada Goose." *Canadian Wildlife Service Hinterland's Who's Who.* 15 May 2002. Environment Canada. 23 Oct. 2003 <http://www.cws-scf.ec.gc.ca/index_e.cfm>.

Take Notes

As you gather information, take notes on index cards. Use one card for each piece of information. Name the source on each card so that you can give proper credit when you use the information in your report. You must always tell readers when you use someone else's words or ideas. Remember to name sources for illustrations that you include in your report.

In your notes, you may write a paraphrase, a summary, or a direct quotation. A **paraphrase** is a restatement of a passage in your words, capturing the details. A **summary** is a restatement of only the main idea of a passage. A **quotation** is a word-for-word copy of a passage.

Drafting Tip

If your teacher wants you to use parenthetical documentation in the text of your report, see **Writing and Research Handbook,** page 843, for guidance.

Choose a Topic and Begin Your Research

Write down a few topics that you would like to research. Decide which topic you would most enjoy writing about. Write your topic at the top of a piece of paper. List the headings *Books, Magazines and Newspapers, People, Technology, Illustrations, Other Sources.* Beside each one, note specific research sources. Use the library to get more ideas for sources and begin taking notes.

PURPOSE To gather information for a report
AUDIENCE Yourself
LENGTH 1 page of source ideas; at least 15 note cards

WRITING RUBRICS To begin, you should

- choose a topic you would enjoy learning more about
- narrow the topic so you can cover it thoroughly
- ask questions about your topic and use your sources to find answers
- write notes from your research on note cards, identifying the source of the information on each card
- keep a separate list of sources and the information about them that you will need for a works-cited list

Listening and Speaking

COOPERATIVE LEARNING Work with a small group of classmates to narrow your topics and find sources.

GrammarLink

Punctuate and capitalize titles correctly.

"Migration! The Great Spring Event"
The World Book Encyclopedia

Write each title, adding capital letters, quotation marks, and italics (underlining) as needed.

1. following in sherman's footsteps (magazine article)
2. minneapolis star tribune (newspaper)
3. robert m. stuart's guide to civil war battlegrounds (video)
4. the red badge of courage (book)
5. the journal of the civil war (magazine)
6. gettysburg as theme park? (newspaper article)
7. the battle hymn of the republic (song)
8. the battle of bull run (book chapter)

See Lesson 19.4, pages 589–590, and Lesson 20.6, pages 609–610.

Using Computers

Check to see whether your library's card catalog is online. If it is, ask a librarian to show you how to search it for books and magazine articles about your topic.

LOG ON ▶ **Writing** Online | For more writing and grammar practice, go to **glencoe.com** and enter QuickPass code WC87703p1.

229

Reports: Writing a Business Letter to Request Information

Writing a business letter can help you get answers to questions that other sources can't answer. As the model below shows, you can write a business letter to request information or to ask someone for an interview.

1565 Shadyside Road
Dover, DE 19809
January 10, 20--

Ms. Maria Washington, Director
Sellar's Island
National Wildlife Refuge
Route 3
Tyler, DE 19968

Dear Ms. Washington:

I am an eighth-grade student at Dover Junior High School in Dover, Delaware, and I am working on a report on the migration of the Canada goose. I am writing to you to ask for information on the Canada geese that spend the winter at Sellar's Island. I'd appreciate it very much if you would answer these questions for me.

1. What features at Sellar's Island attract the large flock of geese?

2. What is the estimate for the actual number of geese that pass through each winter?

3. Have you done any leg banding to try to find out whether the same geese return each year?

The answers to these questions, and any other information that you can provide, will be very helpful to me in my report.

I live only about thirty miles from Sellar's Island. Would it be convenient for me to visit you for a brief interview and a tour of the refuge? I could arrange to come any weekday after school in the next two weeks.

Thank you for your help. I look forward to hearing from you and learning more about the Canada goose.

Yours truly,

Roberto Estevado

Roberto Estevado

POCKET NATIONAL PARKS GUIDE

GUID TO TH NATIO PAF AR EAS ST

Know Why You're Writing a Business Letter

When you write a business letter, you should have a clear reason for writing. If you're writing a business letter to request information, state your questions clearly. Make your request specific and reasonable and make sure you're asking for information you can't get anywhere else. If you're requesting an interview, explain what you want to discuss. Suggest some dates and times. Business letters have other uses, such as placing an order or lodging a complaint. A letter to the editor is a business letter written to express an opinion.

Grammar Tip

When editing, check your use of pronouns and antecedents. For more information on pronouns, see Lessons 11.1–11.7, pages 435–448.

Expository Writing

Guidelines for Writing Business Letters

1. Use correct business-letter form. Some dictionaries and typing manuals outline different forms of business letters.
2. Be courteous and use standard American English.
3. Be brief and to the point. Explain why you need the information.
4. Use clean white or off-white paper. Make a neat presentation.
5. Be considerate. Request only information you can't get another way.
6. When requesting an interview, suggest a few dates so that the interviewee may be able to arrange a meeting with you.

Don't hesitate to write business letters to request information. Many people will be happy to tell what they know.

Journal Writing

Look in your journal for ideas for a report topic. Make a list of possible sources of information—other than the library—on this topic and think about how to contact those sources.

Get Down to Business

Readers expect business letters to be clear and to follow certain rules. At the beginning of your letter, introduce yourself and your purpose for writing. Use the paragraphs that follow to support your purpose with details. Conclude by stating clearly exactly what you want from the reader. Are you requesting an interview? Are you asking for answers to specific questions? Show your draft to a peer reviewer and ask whether your message is clear. When readers notice the care you took in writing to them, they will be more likely to respond to you.

The heading gives the writer's address and the date on separate lines.

The inside address gives the name, title, and address of the person to whom the letter is being sent.

The introductory paragraph states the purpose for writing.

The body presents supporting details—reasons and facts.

Use *Sincerely* or *Yours truly* (followed by a comma) for the closing.

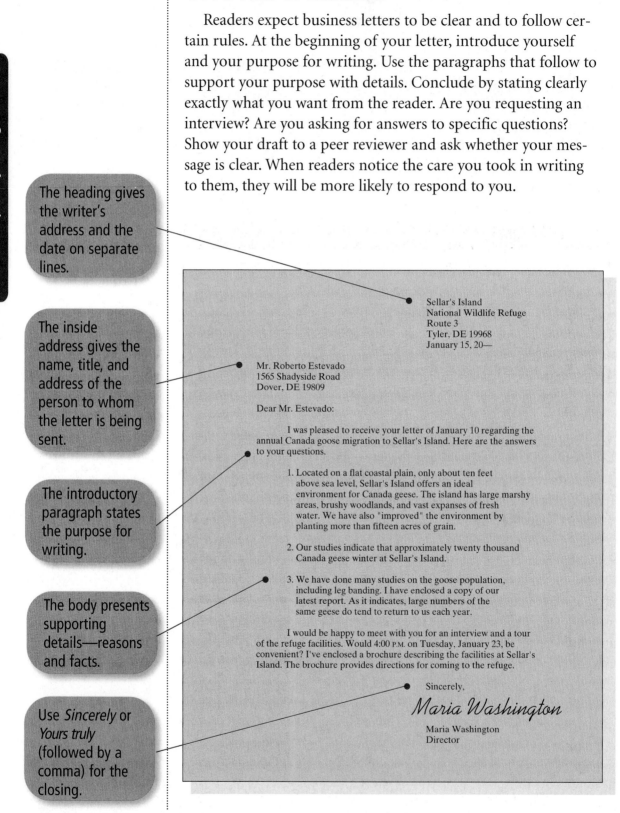

Sellar's Island
National Wildlife Refuge
Route 3
Tyler, DE 19968
January 15, 20—

Mr. Roberto Estevado
1565 Shadyside Road
Dover, DE 19809

Dear Mr. Estevado:

I was pleased to receive your letter of January 10 regarding the annual Canada goose migration to Sellar's Island. Here are the answers to your questions.

1. Located on a flat coastal plain, only about ten feet above sea level, Sellar's Island offers an ideal environment for Canada geese. The island has large marshy areas, brushy woodlands, and vast expanses of fresh water. We have also "improved" the environment by planting more than fifteen acres of grain.

2. Our studies indicate that approximately twenty thousand Canada geese winter at Sellar's Island.

3. We have done many studies on the goose population, including leg banding. I have enclosed a copy of our latest report. As it indicates, large numbers of the same geese do tend to return to us each year.

I would be happy to meet with you for an interview and a tour of the refuge facilities. Would 4:00 P.M. on Tuesday, January 23, be convenient? I've enclosed a brochure describing the facilities at Sellar's Island. The brochure provides directions for coming to the refuge.

Sincerely,

Maria Washington

Maria Washington
Director

Write a Business Letter

Look again at the topic you chose in the Journal Writing activity on page 231. Somewhere there is an expert on that subject who can give you information you can use in a report. Ask your local librarian to help you locate an expert. If the person lives in your area, use a letter to request an interview. Then prepare and carry out the interview. If your expert does not live near you, use a letter to ask the questions you would ask in an interview. For help with writing a business letter, see Business Letters, pages 333–337.

PURPOSE To gain information from an expert for a report

AUDIENCE Your interviewer; yourself

LENGTH 1-page letter; 1–2 pages of notes from the interview

WRITING RUBRICS To write an effective business letter, you should

- be clear about what you want
- be brief and considerate
- use correct form
- proofread to correct errors in the conventions of grammar, usage, spelling, and punctuation

Listening and Speaking

COOPERATIVE LEARNING In a small group, read your letters aloud to one another. Be prepared to both give and receive feedback about ways to improve the letters.

Grammar*Link*

Use correct punctuation in a business letter.

Write the business letter below, using the sample letter on page 232 as a guide.

> 4464 Rheims Place
> Dallas TX 75205
> January 20 20–

Dr. Cheryl Anne White
33 Parker Street
Cambridge MA 02138

Dear Dr. White

    I heard you speak in Austin Texas on November 10 20– and was impressed with your advice on feeding birds. Please send me information about how I can order copies of your brochure "Winter Feeding Stations."

    Thank you for your assistance.

Yours truly

Aaron Jacobs

See Lesson 20.4, pages 605–606, and Lesson 20.5, pages 607–608.

Using Computers

Proofread your business letter carefully—even after your computer checks for spelling errors. Most programs can't find errors caused by homophones, such as *to, too,* and *two.*

Reports: Planning and Drafting

In this lesson, as you use research notes to begin planning and drafting, you will pull together all that you have learned about reports.

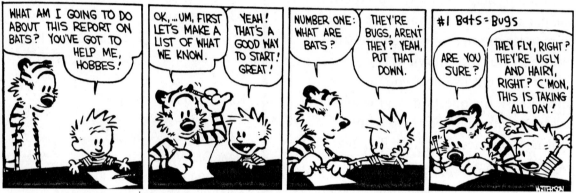

© Watterson 1992. Universal Press Syndicate

Like Calvin, you have decided on a topic for your report. Unlike Calvin, however, you have done your research. Now that you have collected a lot of valuable information, it's time to learn a few strategies to help you begin your report.

Develop a Plan of Action

Before you begin planning and drafting a report, make sure you have a clear idea of your purpose for writing and of your audience. Knowing this information will help you focus your planning and drafting.

Review your notes, looking for a focus or a central idea that you can express in a sentence or two. Draft a **thesis statement** based on this central idea. Although your thesis statement may change as you continue researching or begin drafting, it can guide you as you write your outline.

After determining your thesis statement, you need to decide what main ideas you will cover in your report and draft an outline. Begin by looking through your note cards and grouping them according to topics. Each group of note cards can then become a main heading in your outline. The facts and details on the cards can become subtopics. The beginning of Roberto's outline appears below.

The Canada goose's migration pattern has dramatically changed in recent years.

I. Characteristics of the Canada goose
  A. What the Canada goose looks and sounds like as it flies overhead
  B. What its traditional migration pattern used to be
  C. How the pattern has changed

II. Basic needs of the Canada goose, and how they relate to migration
  A. Food
  B. Water
  C. Protection

III. Why and where the Canada goose used to migrate

The thesis statement identifies the topic and the central idea of the report.

The major outline heads state the main ideas of the paragraphs. Subheads note supporting facts and details.

Like all wildlife, Canada geese have a few basic requirements for

Source: John Terborgh, Where Have All the Birds Gone? ... Princeton

...rld War I, corn harvested by ...er harvested by machine—leaves up ...nt of crop in field. This will feed ... birds. Therefore "the winter ...pacity for Canada geese ...ly been raised many fold."

Journal Writing

Read a newspaper or magazine article. In your journal, jot down the headline or title and the article's central idea or thesis. Then, on the basis of the article, create an outline of the article's main ideas and subtopics.

Drafting Tip

When drafting, refer to your outline and thesis statement to make sure you have included all your main ideas.

Drafting Tip

For more about drafting the introduction, body, and conclusion, see **Writing and Research Handbook,** page 837.

Put the Plan into Action

After you get your ideas organized, use your notes and outline to draft the three main parts of your report. The **introduction** presents your topic and your thesis statement. It offers a chance to engage your readers and should grab their attention. Consider including a thought-provoking quotation, fact, statement, eyewitness account, or anecdote. The **body** supports your thesis statement with reasons and facts. The **conclusion** may reflect your thesis statement by summarizing the report's main points. It should bring the report to a logical and graceful end. If your paper raises any new issues or questions, try including them in the conclusion.

Follow the process shown below in drafting a report from notes and an outline. You will correct grammar and spelling errors later.

Diet: grains, such as corn and wheat
—insects and water plants

Migration: families of Canada geese have flown as far south as northern Florida and northern Mexico

The Canada goose's migration pattern has dramatically changed in recent years.
I. Characteristics of the Canada goose
  A. What the Cana... goose looks and

Drafting

Like all wildlife, Canada geese have a few basic requirements for survival. They need food, and their favorite foods is grains. They need water. They migrate in order to find areas that will provide a rich supply of there basic requirments. They need safety. The main enemy of the Canada goose is the human.

The Canada geese always used to fly to warm, southern areas in the fall. However scientists who study

To leave room for corrections, double-space if you are drafting on a word processor; skip every other line if you are drafting by hand.

5.9 Writing Activities

Outline and Draft

You have done your research and made your note cards. You are ready to develop a plan of action and then to write the draft of your report. Now is the time to finalize the focus of your report. Be sure your main ideas all relate to your thesis statement. Group the notes you have taken into similar topics and then create an outline from the notes. Use your notes and your outline to draft the three main parts of your report—introduction, body, and conclusion. Do not worry about spelling and grammar; you will correct errors in these later.

PURPOSE To outline and draft a report
AUDIENCE Peer reviewers
LENGTH 2–3 pages

WRITING RUBRICS To plan and begin your draft, you should

- write a clear thesis statement
- use your note cards to create an outline
- use your outline to help you develop your draft

Collaborative Writing

Work in a small group and share your outlines with each other. Check to make sure the main ideas make sense and relate clearly to the thesis, or central idea, of the paper. Use the feedback to revise your outlines before beginning your draft.

GrammarLink

Use an apostrophe to form possessive nouns.

Canada goose's migration
To make the singular noun goose possessive, add *'s*. To make the plural noun *geese* possessive, also add *'s*: *geese's*. If a plural noun already ends in *-s*, add just an apostrophe: *birds'*.

Write each possessive phrase below, adding apostrophes where necessary.

1. the childrens playground
2. their parents voices
3. mices eating habits
4. a dogs life cycle
5. several students reports
6. the womens decision
7. my bosss orders
8. the planets orbits
9. universities research grants
10. peoples attitudes

See Lesson 20.7, pages 611–612.

Using Computers

Check to see whether your word processing program has an Outlining feature to help you create an outline. Use it to organize your report.

 Writing Online For more writing and grammar practice, go to glencoe.com and enter QuickPass code WC87703p1.

237

Reports: Revising, Editing, and Presenting

Revising and editing are crucial steps in presenting your topic clearly and effectively.

Sometimes you become so involved in researching and writing your report that you are too close to evaluate your work objectively. You need to read your report as if you were reading the information for the first time.

Read Between the Lines

After you have finished the first draft of your report, put the draft aside for a while so you can return to it with a fresh eye. Then you can begin revising. Start by reading for sense. Are your main ideas clear? Have you supported your ideas with strong facts, statistics, examples, incidents, and reasons? Have you used transitions to help your readers move from one main idea to the next? Put yourself in your readers' place. If they know little or nothing about the topic, imagine that you don't either. Read carefully. The hints in the following chart may help you.

Revising Checklist

Question	Example
Do the main ideas in the paper support the thesis statement?	Summarize the main idea of each paragraph in the paper's body. Be sure that each main idea supports the thesis statement.
Do the main ideas appear in a logical sequence that builds to the conclusion?	List the main ideas in the order in which they appear. Is there a better order?
Does the conclusion sum up the main ideas and reflect the report's purpose?	Summarize the conclusion and compare it with the thesis statement. The thesis statement should lead logically to the conclusion.

Like all wildlife, Canada geese have a few basic requirements for survival. They need *an ample supply of* food, and their favorite foods is grains. They need water. They migrate to find areas that will provide a rich *suply* of *there* basic *requirments*. They need safety. *also protection from their predators.* The main enemy of the Canada goose is the human. *predator*

The Canada geese always used to fly to warm, Southern areas in the fall. However scientists who study these birds have discovered a change.

> Moving this sentence connects two important thoughts.

Journal Writing

Review some of your earliest journal writing. How would you revise your writing now? Jot down some notes or revise a passage. Notice the difference a fresh eye can make.

Cross the t's and Dot the i's

When you edit your report, you proofread for any errors in the conventions of grammar, spelling, mechanics, and usage. For more information, review pages 78–81. For help with a particular problem, see the **Troubleshooter** Table of Contents on page 309. You may find it easier to proofread for one type of error at a time. Some word processing programs will help you check for spelling errors. Remember, however, to read your draft for missing words and for words that are easily confused, such as *their* and *there*.

Follow your teacher's directions for formatting the final draft or use the guidelines recommended by the Modern Language Association on page 843. If you include a bibliography—a works-cited list—follow the examples on page 228 and in **Writing and Research Handbook,** pages 844–846.

Presenting Tip

For guidelines for preparing your final draft, see **Writing and Research Handbook,** pages 843–846.

Spelling errors are corrected.

Errors in subject-verb agreement are corrected.

Double-space between lines of text in your report, including the works-cited list.

Presenting Tip

Study a student model of a research report, including a works-cited list, in **Writing and Research Handbook,** pages 847–848.

Like all wildlife, Canada geese have a few basic requirements for survival. They migrate to find areas that will provide a rich su~~p~~ply of ~~there~~ *their* basic requir*e*ments. They need an ample supply of food. Their favorite food*s* is grain*s*. They need water. They also need protection from their predators. The main predator of the Canada goose is the human.

Canada geese always used to fly to warm, Southern areas in the fall. However, scientists who study these birds have discovered a change. Over the past few years, more and more Canada geese have remained in northern areas during the winter.

Migration Habits of Canada Geese
*Roberto Estevado
February 28, 20—*

Revise, Edit, and Share Your Report

Now revise and edit your report, making sure that it says what you want it to say. Does it support your thesis statement? Will it interest your readers?

PURPOSE To finish and share a research report
AUDIENCE Classmates, teacher, family
LENGTH 2–3 pages

WRITING RUBRICS To refine and present your report, you should

- revise your report to make it clear, organized, and interesting
- proofread to correct errors in grammar, usage, spelling, and mechanics
- prepare a list of works cited, including the sources of illustrations and other graphics, using the guidelines in **Writing and Research Handbook,** pages 844–846
- make a neat, legible final copy

Listening and Speaking

COOPERATIVE LEARNING In a small group, take turns reading your drafts aloud. Are the sentence patterns varied? Do the thoughts flow smoothly and clearly from sentence to sentence? Exchange papers with a partner and write suggestions for varying the sentences to improve fluency. Discuss the suggested changes. Make only the changes that you agree with. Exchange papers again and edit for errors in conventions of grammar, usage, spelling, and mechanics.

Viewing and Representing

CREATING COVER ART Find or create a picture or drawing that would prepare a reader for your report. Reproduce or draw the image to use on the cover of your report.

GrammarLink

Use a comma after introductory words or phrases.

However, scientists who study these birds discovered a change.
Like all wildlife, Canada geese have a few basic requirements. . . .

Write each sentence, adding commas where necessary.

1. Indeed a family that adopts a dog takes on new responsibilities.
2. Unlike wild dogs domestic dogs depend on people to provide food and shelter.
3. Because of their long relationship with humans domestic dogs require human contact to thrive.
4. Originally bred to work most domestic dogs today are nonworking dogs and thus need regular exercise.
5. In return for all this care domestic dogs give their owners companionship and fun.

See Lesson 20.2, pages 601–602.

LOG ON ▶ **Writing** Online | For more writing and grammar practice, go to **glencoe.com** and enter QuickPass code WC87703p1.

241

WRITING ABOUT LITERATURE
Comparing Two Poems

Expository writing can be used to describe a piece of literature, answer an essay question about it, or compare and contrast two selections.

These two poems describe one part of fall—migration. As you read the poems, jot down some of your reactions.

Literature Model

Fall

The geese flying south
In a row long and V-shaped
Pulling in winter.

Sally Andresen

Something Told the Wild Geese

Something told the wild geese
     It was time to go.
Though the fields lay golden
     Something whispered,—"Snow."
Leaves were green and stirring,
     Berries luster-glossed,
But beneath warm feathers
     Something cautioned,—"Frost."
All the sagging orchards
     Steamed with amber spice,
But each wild breast stiffened
     At remembered ice.
Something told the wild geese
     It was time to fly,—
Summer sun was on their wings,
     Winter in their cry.

Rachel Field

Write a Personal Reaction

Reading a poem is like listening to a song. It may create a picture in your mind, stir up feelings, or bring back a memory. Think about the pictures that come to your mind as you read the two poems on the previous page. Then jot down your responses to the following questions.

Grammar Tip

When editing your comparison-contrast essay, be sure you have used comparative and superlative adjectives correctly. For more information see Lesson 12.3, pages 461–462.

Expository Writing

Questions About the Poems

1. In which poem do you see the geese from a distance? In which close up? Compare and contrast these views.

2. What sensory details does each poet use to describe the change of seasons from fall to winter?

3. How would you summarize the poems?

4. How would you compare their forms?

One student's answer to the second question appears below.

> In "Fall" I look at a _V_ of geese straining in the sky. They seem to be pulling in winter. In "Something Told the Wild Geese" I see the geese with summer sun on their wings. Below them I notice golden fields, shiny, sparkling berries, and orchards full of ripened fruit.

Journal Writing

Find two poems about the same topic. In your journal, note any details that interest you. Which poem do you like better? Why? Write your impressions.

Drafting Tip

For more information about compare and contrast writing, review Lesson 5.3, pages 210–213.

Compare and Contrast

To compare or contrast two poems in an essay, you might like to begin with a Venn diagram such as the one below. Decide how to arrange your essay. You can write about the features of one poem and then write about the same kind of features in another. Or you can compare and contrast the poems one feature at a time.

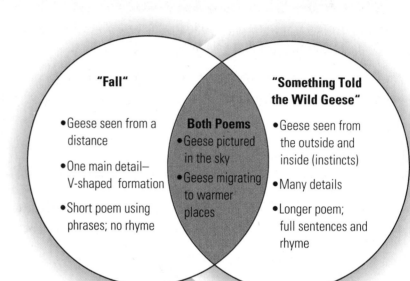

"Fall"

- Geese seen from a distance
- One main detail—V-shaped formation
- Short poem using phrases; no rhyme

Both Poems
- Geese pictured in the sky
- Geese migrating to warmer places

"Something Told the Wild Geese"

- Geese seen from the outside and inside (instincts)
- Many details
- Longer poem; full sentences and rhyme

Student Model

The introduction identifies the two poems and states the thesis.

What method of organization did this student use to compare and contrast the two poems?

"Fall" and "Something Told the Wild Geese" are two very different poems about geese. "Something Told the Wild Geese" is a sixteen-line poem that rhymes. Using descriptive words, the poet paints pictures of geese, fields, and orchards. "Fall," however, is a haiku, which does not rhyme. This poem shows geese flying, pulling in a different season. Reading the two poems is like looking at two different snapshots of geese.

John Moore, Wilmette Junior High School, Wilmette, Illinois

Writing About Similarities and Differences

Create a Venn diagram to compare and contrast the following poem with another poem about the sun. Then write an essay telling how the two poems are alike and different.

Sunset

The sun spun like
a tossed coin.
It whirled on the azure sky,
it clattered into the horizon,
it clicked in the slot,
and neon-lights popped
and blinked "Time expired,"
as on a parking meter.

Oswald Mbuyiseni Mtshali

PURPOSE Compare two poems
AUDIENCE Yourself
LENGTH 3–4 paragraphs

WRITING RUBRICS To write an effective compare-and-contrast essay, you should

- use a Venn diagram to organize your ideas
- choose a way to arrange your essay—selection-by-selection or feature-by-feature
- include similarities and differences

Listening and Speaking

READING POETRY In a small group, take turns reading the poems you found about the sun. Rehearse your presentation so that the rate, volume, pitch, tone, and

Grammar Link

Use participial phrases to modify nouns or pronouns.

In "Fall" I look at a V of geese straining in the sky.

Use each participial phrase below as an adjective in a sentence.

1. compared to our old house
2. staring at the ground
3. recommended by my brother
4. hidden in the grass

See Lesson 15.1, pages 527–528.

diction you use in your reading will help listeners understand the poem. After each person reads his or her poem, the group should read or listen to that person's compare-and-contrast essay. Group members should discuss their interpretations and opinions of the poems and essays.

Cross-Curricular Activity

ART Find copies of two paintings of dogs, horses, or other animals. In one or two paragraphs, compare and contrast the two paintings. Do the artists share the same view of the animal? Do the settings help suggest the artists' views? Are the moods alike or different?

LOG ON ▶ **Writing** Online | For more writing and grammar practice, go to **glencoe.com** and enter QuickPass code WC87703p1.

245

Writing Process in Action

Expository Writing

In preceding lessons, you've learned about writing essays and about using details to support various purposes, such as writing reports or answering test questions. You've also had the chance to write about a topic of interest to you. In this lesson, you're invited to apply what you know to research and write information for a guidebook for travelers in your state.

Assignment

Context	You have been asked to write about how a certain statue, memorial, or commemorative building came to be built in your neighborhood, city, or state. Your writing will be published in a guidebook for travelers.
Purpose	To inform travelers about the development and construction of a landmark
Audience	Visitors to your neighborhood, city, or state
Length	1 page

Planning to Write

The following pages can help you plan and write your essay. Read the pages. Refer to them as you need to, but don't be tied down by them. You're in charge of your own writing process. Give yourself a time frame for completing this assignment. That way, you will be able to allow the right amount of time for each step in the writing process. Keep in mind the controlling idea: to write information for a guidebook for travelers.

Writing Online

For prewriting, drafting, revising, editing and publishing tools, go to **glencoe.com** and enter QuickPass code WC87703p1.

Prewriting

You might begin prewriting by listing your own first impressions of landmarks in your neighborhood, city, or state or by thinking about where you'd take friends or relatives from out of town. What places and details would most fascinate them?

Use the options at the right to help you. If you need more facts, do research at a library, historical society, or travel agency.

Option A

Make a cluster diagram of local places of interest.

Option B

List five or six of your favorite places.

Option C

Do some small-group brain-storming.

Freedom House, on Hamilton Pike—historic home, Underground Railroad, museum about slavery in America. Just celebrated its twentieth anniversary as official landmark. Others in area: Strauss Hall?

Drafting

Once you've gathered all your facts, begin drafting. First, decide which facts would be the most interesting and useful to your audience. Next, decide how to organize your writing. In the passage below, notice how the author organizes his writing around the steps for choosing a design for the Vietnam War Memorial in Washington, D.C.

Literature Model

A total of 2,573 individuals and teams registered for the competition. They were sent photographs of the memorial site, maps of the area around the site and of the entire Mall, and other technical design information. The competitors had three months to prepare their designs, which had to be received by March 31, 1981.

Of the 2,573 registrants, 1,421 submitted designs, a record number for such a design competition. When the designs were spread out for jury selection, they filled a large airplane hangar.

Brent Ashabranner, *Always to Remember*

Drafting Tip

For more information about handling the details in an essay, see Lesson 5.2, pages 206–209.

The purpose of the drafting stage is to get your thoughts and ideas on paper. If your writing contains many statistics, wait to check your facts later as part of the revising process. Do not worry about spelling, grammar, or punctuation at this point—just let the words flow. You will correct your errors in the revising and editing stages.

Revising

To begin revising, read over your draft to make sure that what you've written fits your purpose and audience. Then have a **writing conference.** Read your draft to a partner or small group. Use your audience's reactions to help you evaluate your work.

Question A

Will my introduction command attention?

Question B

Are details clear and accurate?

Question C

Does my conclusion reflect the main idea?

You can explore our history at
Freedom House is half a mile west of town
one-
on Hamilton Pike. It once was the home of

Jeremiah and Abigail Hamilton, the young
from Boston   1843
couple who moved here in 1842. As tensions

over slavery grew, the Hamiltons stood with

the abolitionists. They learned about people

who opened their homes to escaping slaves as

part of the Underground Railroad.

Editing/Proofreading

At this point you've put a lot of time and effort into the assignment. Don't let a few editing mistakes spoil the effect of an otherwise good piece of writing. When you **proofread** your revised draft, ask yourself questions like those listed on the right. If any part of the draft doesn't sound quite right, you may want to get additional advice from a teacher or friend.

Publishing/Presenting

Before you present your finished work, con-

sider having someone at your chamber of commerce or local historical society read your report. That person might be able to give you some little-known details that you could add to the paper. Also, you might consider attaching copies of authentic photographs such as of people who inspired the memorial, a building being renovated, or a statue being installed.

Editing/Proofreading Checklist

1. Do all my subjects and verbs agree?
2. Do all my pronouns have clear antecedents?
3. Have I used commas correctly?
4. Have I used apostrophes correctly in possessive nouns?
5. Have I spelled every word correctly?

Proofreading Tip

For proofreading symbols, see pages 79 and 863.

Journal Writing: Write to Learn

Reflect on your writing process experience. Answer these questions in your journal: What do you like best about your expository writing? What was the hardest part of writing it? What did you learn in your writing conference? What new things have you learned as a writer?

Literature Model

FROM

Always to Remember

by Brent Ashabranner

In 1980 Vietnam War veteran Jan Scruggs and lawyers Roberet Doubeck and John Wheeler persuaded Congress to approve the building of a Vietnam War memorial in Washington, D.C. They hoped that the memorial would help to heal the bitter feelings that still existed because of this country's involvement in that war, even though it had ended in 1973. Brent Ashabranner tells the story of the national competition to design the war memorial. As you read his essay, notice what he does to capture and hold your attention. Then try the activities in Linking Writing and Literature on page 258.

The memorial had been authorized by Congress "in honor and recognition of the men and women of the Armed Forces of the United States who served in the Vietnam War." The law, however, said not a word about what the memorial should be or what it should look like. That was left up to the Vietnam Veterans Memorial Fund, but the law did state that the memorial design and plans would

A section of the Vietnam Veterans Memorial

have to be approved by the Secretary of the Interior, the Commission of Fine Arts, and the National Capital Planning Commission.

What would the memorial be? What should it look like? Who would design it? Scruggs, Doubek, and Wheeler didn't know, but they were determined that the memorial should help bring closer together a nation still bitterly divided by the Vietnam War. It couldn't be something like the Marine Corps Memorial showing American troops planting a flag on enemy soil at Iwo Jima. It couldn't be a giant dove with an olive branch of peace in its beak. It had to soothe passions, not stir them up. But there was one thing Jan Scruggs insisted on: the memorial, whatever it turned out to be, would have to show the name of every man and woman killed or missing in the war.

But there was one thing Jan Scruggs insisted on: the memorial, whatever it turned out to be, would have to show the name of every man and woman killed or missing in the war.

The answer, they decided, was to hold a national design competition open to all Americans. The winning design would receive a prize of $20,000, but the real prize would be the winner's knowledge that the memorial would become a part of American history on the Mall in Washington, D.C. Although fund raising was only well started at this point, the choosing of a memorial design could not be delayed if the memorial was to be built by Veteran's Day, 1982. H. Ross Perot contributed the $160,000 necessary to hold the competition, and a panel of distinguished architects, landscape architects, sculptors, and design specialists was chosen to decide the winner.

Announcement of the competition in October, 1980, brought an astonishing response. The Vietnam Veterans Memorial Fund received over five thousand inquiries. They came from every state in the nation and from every field of design; as expected, architects and sculptors were particularly interested. Everyone who inquired received a booklet explaining the criteria.[1] Among the most important: the memorial could not make a political statement about the war; it must contain the names of all persons killed or missing in action in the war; it must be in harmony with its location on the Mall.

A total of 2,573 individuals and teams registered for the competition. They were sent photographs of the memorial site, maps of the area around the site and of the entire Mall, and other technical design information. The competitors had three months to prepare their designs, which had to be received by March 31, 1981.

---

1 criteria (krī tēr′ ē ə) standards, rules, or tests by which something is judged

Of the 2,573 registrants, 1,421 submitted designs, a record number for such a design competition. When the designs were spread out for jury selection, they filled a large airplane hangar.[2] The jury's task was to select the design which, in their judgment, was the best in meeting these criteria:

- a design that honored the memory of those Americans who served and died in the Vietnam War.
- a design of high artistic merit.
- a design which would be harmonious with its site, including visual harmony with the Lincoln Memorial and the Washington Monument.

All who come here can find it a place of healing. This will be a quiet memorial . . .

- a design that could take its place in the "historic continuity" of America's national art.
- a design that would be buildable, durable, and not too hard to maintain.

The designs were displayed without any indication of the designer's name so that they could be judged anonymously, on their design merits alone. The jury spent one week reviewing all the designs in the airplane hangar. On May 1 it made its report to the Vietnam Veterans Memorial Fund; the experts declared Entry Number 1,026 the winner. The report called it "the finest and most appropriate" of all submitted and said it was "superbly harmonious" with the site on the Mall. Remarking upon the "simple and forthright" materials needed to build the winning entry, the report concludes:

This memorial, with its wall of names, becomes a place of quiet reflection, and a tribute to those who served their nation in difficult times.

All who come here can find it a place of healing. This will be a quiet memorial, one that achieves an excellent relationship with both the Lincoln Memorial or Washington Monument, and relates the visitor to them. It is uniquely horizontal, entering the earth rather than piercing the sky.

This is very much a memorial of our own times, one that could not

---

2 **hangar** (hang′ ər) a building or shed to store airplanes in

have been achieved in another time and place. The designer has created an eloquent[3] place where the simple meeting of earth, sky and remembered names contain messages for all who will know this place.

The eight jurors signed their names to the report, a unanimous decision.

How could this be? How could an undergraduate student win one of the most important design competitions ever held?

When the name of the winner was revealed, the art and architecture worlds were stunned. It was not the name of a nationally famous architect or sculptor, as most people had been sure it would be. The creator of Entry Number 1,026 was a twenty-one-year-old student at Yale University. Her name—unknown as yet in any field of art or architecture—was Maya Ying Lin.

How could this be? How could an undergraduate student win one of the most important design competitions ever held? How could she beat out some of the top names in American art and architecture? Who was Maya Ying Lin?

The answer to that question provided some of the other answers, at least in part. Maya Lin, reporters soon discovered, was a Chinese-American girl who had been born and raised in the small midwestern city of Athens, Ohio. Her father, Henry Huan Lin, was a ceramicist[4] of considerable reputation and dean of fine arts at Ohio University in Athens. Her mother, Julia C. Lin, was a poet and professor of Oriental and English literature. Maya Lin's parents were born to culturally prominent families in China. When the Communists came to power in China in the 1940s, Henry and Julia Lin left the country and in time made their way to the United States.

Maya Lin grew up in an environment of art and literature. She was interested in sculpture and made both small and large sculptural figures, one cast in bronze. She learned silversmithing and made jewelry. She was surrounded by books and read a great deal, especially fantasies such as *The Hobbit* and *Lord of the Rings*.

---

3 eloquent (el′ ə kwənt) having a strong effect on people's ideas and feelings
4 ceramicist (sə ram′ ə sist) an expert in making pottery

The Vietnam Veterans Memorial in Constitution Gardens, Washington, D.C.

But she also found time to work at McDonald's. "It was about the only way to make money in the summer," she said.

A covaledictorian[5] at high school graduation, Maya Lin went to Yale without a clear notion of what she wanted to study and eventually decided to major in Yale's undergraduate program in architecture. During her junior year she studied in Europe and found herself increasingly interested in cemetery architecture. "In Europe there's very little space, so graveyards are used as parks," she said. "Cemeteries are cities of the dead in European countries, but they are also living gardens."

---

5 **covaledictorian** (kō′ val ə dik tôr′ ē ən) one who shares the position of the highest-ranking student in a class, who delivers the farewell address at graduation

In France, Maya Lin was deeply moved by the war memorial to those who died in the Somme offensive in 1916 during World War I. The great arch by architect Sir Edwin Lutyens is considered one of the world's most outstanding war memorials.

Back at Yale for her senior year, Maya Lin enrolled in Professor Andrus Burr's course in funerary (burial) architecture. The Vietnam Veterans Memorial competition had recently been announced, and although the memorial would be a cenotaph—a monument in honor of persons buried someplace else— Professor Burr thought that having his students prepare a design of the memorial would be a worthwhile course assignment.

Surely, no classroom exercise ever had such spectacular results.

After receiving the assignment, Maya Lin and two of her classmates decided to make the day's journey from New Haven, Connecticut, to Washington to look at the site where the memorial would be built. On the day of their visit, Maya Lin remembers, Constitution Gardens was awash with a late November sun; the park was full of light, alive with joggers and people walking beside the lake.

It just popped into my head. . . . It was a beautiful park. I didn't want to destroy a living park.

"It was while I was at the site that I designed it," Maya Lin said later in an interview about the memorial with *Washington Post* writer Phil McCombs. "I just sort of visualized it. It just popped into my head. Some people were playing Frisbee. It was a beautiful park. I didn't want to destroy a living park. You use the landscape. You don't fight with it. You absorb the landscape . . . When I looked at the site I just knew I wanted something horizontal that took you in, that made you feel safe within the park, yet at the same time reminding

Expository Writing

you of the dead. So I just imagined opening up the earth. . . ."

When Maya Lin returned to Yale, she made a clay model of the vision that had come to her in Constitution Gardens. She showed it to Professor Burr; he liked her conception and encouraged her to enter the memorial competition. She put her design on paper, a task that took six weeks, and mailed it to Washington barely in time to meet the March 31 deadline.

A month and a day later, Maya Lin was attending class. Her roommate slipped into the classroom and handed her a note. Washington was calling and would call back in fifteen minutes. Maya Lin hurried to her room. The call came. She had won the memorial competition.

Linking Writing and Literature

◆ Learning to Learn

Look back to page 253 to review the criteria, or requirements, for the Vietnam Veterans Memorial. What criteria do *you* think are important for a memorial to people who lost their lives in war or in some other tragedy? Make some notes about criteria that you would include.

◆ Talk About Reading

Talk with a group of classmates about the excerpt from *Always to Remember.* Select one classmate to lead the group discussion and another to take notes. Use the following questions to direct your group's discussion.

1. **Connect to Your Life** The author notes that Scruggs, Doubeck, and Wheeler hoped the Vietnam Veterans Memorial "would help to heal the bitter feelings that still existed because of this country's involvement in that war." What role do you think memorials, such as the Holocaust Memorial in Washington, D.C., play in people's lives?

2. **Critical Thinking: Analyze** How does Ashabranner organize the facts and details in his essay? Why is this type of organization effective?

3. **6+1 Trait®: Conventions** On page 253, what punctuation does the author use to introduce the bulleted criteria for the memorial? What should you do as a reader when you encounter this punctuation?

4. **Connect to Your Writing** What draws you into Ashabranner's essay and makes you want to continue reading?

◆ Write About Reading

Reflective Essay Write an essay about memorials titled "Why It's Important to Remember." Think about your group discussion of Ashabranner's essay. Remember that this topic has no right or wrong answers. Your essay should be your personal reflections about the purpose and importance of memorials.

Focus on Conventions Pay special attention to the conventions of writing. Use correct grammar, usage, and mechanics such as spelling and punctuation.

For more information on conventions and the 6+1 Trait® model, see **Writing and Research Handbook,** pages 838–840.

6+1 Trait® is a registered trademark of Northwest Regional Educational Laboratory, which does not endorse this product.

Reflecting on the Unit: Summarize What You Learned

Focus on the following questions to summarize what you have learned in this unit.

❶ What are the parts of an essay?

❷ Name four types of expository writing.

❸ How can you get your message across clearly?

❹ How should you answer an essay question?

❺ What are the stages in writing a report?

❻ What is one way to respond to poetry?

Adding to Your Portfolio

CHOOSE A SELECTION FOR YOUR PORTFOLIO Look over the expository writing you did for this unit. Choose a piece of writing for your portfolio. The writing you choose should show one or more of the following:

- an introduction, body, and conclusion
- facts, statistics, examples, or reasons
- a strong organization and smooth transitions

REFLECT ON YOUR CHOICE Attach a note to the piece you chose, explaining briefly why you chose it and what you learned from writing it.

SET GOALS How can you improve your writing? What skill will you focus on the next time you write?

Writing Across the Curriculum

MAKE A MUSIC CONNECTION Choose two songs or other compositions by musicians with whom you are familiar. Write a one-page essay to compare and contrast the two compositions. Include information about the lyrics, rhythm, and melody, as well as your personal response to the two pieces. To review ways to organize information in comparison-contrast essays, see Lesson 5.3, pages 210–213, and Lesson 5.11, pages 242–245.

" *Now is the time to make real the promises of democracy. . .* **"**

—Martin Luther King, Jr.,
"I Have a Dream"

Persuasive Writing

Not-for-profit groups sometimes give money to support worthwhile projects. In order to receive funding support, interested people need to submit proposals. By definition, every proposal is an example of persuasive writing. Besides explaining their projects, the writers must convince the funding group that their projects are worth being supported. Many artists, like Indira Freitas Johnson, write proposals to get funding. This effort casts them in the dual role of artist and writer. The excerpt that follows is from Johnson's proposal.

From "Joint Venture"
by Indira Freitas Johnson

Joint Venture

Working title for a collaborative exhibition between SHARE (Support the Handicapped Rehabilitation Effort) and Indira Freitas Johnson.

Cloth and fiber arts have linked women all over the world for thousands of years. "Joint Venture" will be one more link, as it proposes to combine the drawings of an Indian-born American woman, Indira Freitas Johnson, and the hand work of SHARE, a Bombay-based group of women and handicapped persons.

A true collaboration means equal sharing. As such, while the drawings are done by Indira, they are interpreted totally by the various workers at SHARE. Hence, we see a unique blend of the trained and the untrained eye, the simple flow of a line drawing translated into the complexity of a pieced surface using miles upon miles of stitches.

Indira's work documents the feelings she experiences living between two vastly different cultures. She uses the philosophy and imagery of India to illustrate her experience of living in contemporary America. There is a surreal quality to much of her work, and the random choices of color, texture, and pattern used by SHARE employees sometimes enhance this surreal quality. . . .

Persuasive Writing

A Writer's Process

Prewriting
Getting Started

For some writers, getting started is the hardest part. Indira Johnson agrees. Johnson says, "I sometimes think that getting started is very difficult. You have all these ideas. I think that's when you just need to start [writing]."

At this early stage, when she is trying to describe her ideas for a project, Johnson uses a form of freewriting: she simply gets words down onto paper. She tries to explain her project ideas as clearly as possible. But she doesn't worry that her prose isn't perfect or that her ideas aren't yet totally coherent. "I think from that initial writing you can say, 'This part is good' or 'This part needs reworking' or 'Juggle it around.'"

Johnson also does research during the prewriting stage, not just to gather information but also to help develop ideas. "Very often," she says, "I'll go to the library and just read up on various aspects of a particular project that I want to do. For example, I'll ask myself, 'Has it been done before?'"

Drafting
Writing to the Audience

A successful proposal addresses the concerns and interests of a specific audience. Johnson carefully considers her audience as she writes. "Who am I asking for support?" she asks herself. If her readers are professionals in the art world, she stresses the artistic advantages of her project. If the audience is interested in social service or cultural issues, Johnson emphasizes those points in the proposal.

Adapting a proposal to an audience

The ideas that Johnson generates in her drawings eventually appear in details of the quilts made by SHARE.

Writing in the Real World

may also influence a writer's point of view. In her "Joint Venture" proposal, Johnson wrote about herself in the third person instead of using the pronoun *I*. She wanted to stress that she was a member of a group effort and that this was not just her personal project.

Revising/Editing
Getting Feedback

Johnson knows the stage of revising well. "When I was writing in school, my father always said that there was no way to write a good paper the first time. You have to rewrite," she recalls.

For Johnson rewriting sometimes means "reseeing". As Johnson explains, "What happens very often is you become too close to a particular subject. You may have the sense that you're explaining it very clearly. But,

because you know all the details, you could be skipping over important facts." Johnson likes to ask someone outside the project, often her son or the owner of the gallery that shows her work, to read her proposal in order to see if it makes sense.

Response from a reader helps Johnson bring clarity to her writing. "I have a tendency to write something that has beautiful words and sounds really nice, but is it really pinpointing the meaning?" After getting reader response, Johnson revises one more time, incorporating the feedback into her finished piece.

In this proposal Indira Johnson emphasized the group effort for the project.

Analyzing the Media Connection

Discuss these questions about the proposal excerpt on page 262.

1. Why did Indira Johnson write the proposal "Joint Venture"?

2. What do you think Johnson is emphasizing in this particular excerpt?

3. Is Johnson writing to an audience who is more interested in the fine arts or in the social benefits of collaborating with an Indian group? How can you tell?

4. What support does Johnson provide to show that her project is one of "true collaboration"?

5. Why does Johnson speak of herself in the third person throughout the excerpt?

Analyzing A Writer's Process

Discuss these questions about Indira Johnson's writing process.

1. What does Johnson say is the best thing to do when you have difficulty getting your writing started? When and how could you adapt her methods in getting started to your own writing process?

2. What kinds of research does Johnson conduct?

3. How does researching contribute to Johnson's writing?

4. What key question does Johnson ask herself to keep her persuasive writing on target?

5. How and why does Johnson use feedback from readers during revision?

GrammarLink

Capitalize proper nouns and proper adjectives.

Indira Freitas Johnson is an Indian-born American woman.

Write each sentence, using capital letters where necessary.

1. A new exhibit is opening at the garcia gallery on friday.

2. It will feature native american, european, hispanic, and asian art.

3. This area was first settled by the navajo, then by germans, then by mexicans and laotians.

4. Gallery owner jose garcia calls the show "visions of home."

5. It will truly be an all-american exhibit.

See Lessons 19.2–19.4, pages 585–590.

LESSON 6.1 Writing Persuasively

*W*hen you write to persuade, you try to convince your audience to think or act in a particular way. Often an image can be a powerful form of persuasion. This poster helped convince many Americans to enlist during World War I.

I WANT YOU
FOR U.S. ARMY
NEAREST RECRUITING STATION

Drafting Tip

For help with writing and elaborating on topic sentences that state an opinion or urge an action, see **Writing and Research Handbook,** page 835.

State Your Case

In most persuasive writing, the writer states an opinion or urges an action and then offers reasons why readers should accept the opinion or support the action. Reasons are often supported by facts, examples, or stories. What kinds of support does the writer of the model on the next page use to back up her opinion?

Student Model

One of the most disturbing trends I see is the draining of wetlands. Thousand-year-old swamps are being destroyed in just days to build skyscrapers and shopping malls or to plant crops. Where are ducks, geese, and other wildfowl going to raise their families or find food and rest when migrating? The answer is simple: each species will slowly die. These animals' habitats are being taken from *all* of us. It is sad, it truly is, to know the birds I love are moving closer to extinction.

April Barnes, Decatur, Alabama
First appeared in *Merlyn's Pen*

April wants her readers to take the problem personally, as she does. How does she appeal to their emotions?

Your world is full of topics for persuasive writing. What changes would you like to see in your school and community and in the larger world? By exploring the following sources, you can discover some issues you care about.

Look for Issues in Your Reading

Look for Issues in Other Media

Look for Issues in Conversations

Journal Writing

List some changes you'd like to see, using the sources above for ideas. As you study this unit, add to your list, and use the ideas in your persuasive writing.

Revising Tip

Even as you draft and revise, continue to look for information on your topic. Strengthen your case by adding any additional proof.

Back It Up

Research is an important step in persuasive writing. Your opinions will carry weight only if you can back them up. To gather support, investigate your topic by reading, observing, and discussing, and sometimes by interviewing experts—those with special knowledge about the issue. Patrick MacRoy felt strongly about a local issue: an electric company's plan to run wires along a nature trail. He wrote the following article for his school paper.

Student Model

The Prairie Path is one of the last areas around here in which to enjoy nature. It is used by cyclists, hikers, horseback riders, and even schools as a site for nature classes. It was even recognized by the U.S. government as a national recreation trail. Groups like Friends of the Illinois Prairie Path are working hard [to save] the trail by circulating petitions and holding public meetings. Citizen groups say there are alternate routes for the power lines, if [the electric company] is willing to find them.

If you want to help save the path, there will be a petition to sign in the lunchroom for the next few days. Thanks for your help.

Patrick MacRoy, Glen Ellyn, Illinois
First appeared in *Call of the Wildcat*

What information does Patrick include to show the usefulness of the path?

Notice that Patrick supports his opinion by referring to expert sources.

Write a Persuasive Paragraph

Think of an environmental issue that affects your school or community. You might see an appropriate issue on the list you created for this lesson's Journal Writing activity. Research the issue and discuss it with others. Make prewriting notes.

PURPOSE To state and support a position
AUDIENCE Classmates; city council
LENGTH 1–2 paragraphs

WRITING RUBRICS To write an effective persuasive paragraph, you should

- state your position clearly
- use facts to back up your position

Cross-Curricular Activity

ART Your city council intends to install the sculpture shown on this page in a park near your home. State your opinion in writing. Offer reasons that will persuade the city council to install or not to install the art.

Mariam Schapiro, *Anna and David*, 1987

Viewing and Representing

MAKE A POSTER In a magazine, find a picture of a sculpture, painting, or other work of art. Cut the picture out and paste it to a piece of poster board or cardboard. Surround the picture with persuasive comments—both favorable and unfavorable—about the art.

GrammarLink

Make sure the verb agrees with the subject, not with a word in an intervening phrase.

One of the most disturbing trends I see is the draining of wetlands.

Complete each sentence with the correct choice of verb.

1. The home of my ancestors (is, are) not for sale.
2. A classroom for small children (require, requires) toys.
3. Boys of my father's generation (was, were) routinely drafted at age eighteen.
4. A path through the woods (offers, offer) many small pleasures.

See Lesson 16.2, page 543.

 Writing Online | For more writing and grammar practice, go to **glencoe.com** and enter QuickPass code WC87703p1.

269

LESSON
6.2

Determining a Position

If you've visited a zoo, you've seen people of all ages looking at and learning about animals from around the world. Some people, however, claim that animals belong only in the wild, not in captivity. Other people defend zoos as humane, well-designed environments that preserve endangered species and educate visitors.

Take a Stand

Once you take a stand on an issue, you must find support for it. At the same time, you should also consider arguments your opponents might make against your position. During the prewriting step, list both *pros* (points that can be used to support your argument) and *cons* (points that might be used against it). Look at the example on page 271.

Pro

1. Zoos protect endangered species.
2. Modern zoo environments resemble habitats.
3. Zoos educate public about conservation.
4. Zoos are run by professionals.

Con

1. Zoos are animal prisons.
2. Captivity changes animals' behavior.
3. Animals should not be entertainment.
4. Capture/confinement can hurt animals.

Student Model

Zoos today are important to the survival of many species. They do not abuse the animals, but instead they offer a safe and healthy environment. At the same time they provide an enjoyable viewing experience for people of all ages. This gives us an opportunity to better appreciate animals and learn more about their preservation. As stated in the *Utne Reader* [a general-interest magazine about ideas and issues], zoos are "institutions we should see not as abusers of the world's animals, but as vital forces saving animals from extinction."

Jacqueline Parks, Springman Junior High School
Glenview, Illinois

According to Jacqueline, how do zoos benefit both animals and people?

Grammar Tip

In editing, check for a comma before a coordinating conjunction, such as *and, but, or,* or *nor,* when it joins the two main clauses of a compound sentence. For more on compound sentences, see Lesson 14.1, page 505, and Lesson 20.3, page 603.

Journal Writing

Think of an issue on which someone disagrees with you. Create pro and con lists like the ones above. Try to include strong points on both sides.

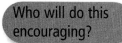

Consider Your Audience

Your audience is important in persuasive writing. When your goal is to influence opinions, you need to know who your readers are and how they think. Study the models below. The first, from the foreword of a book for children, is written to their parents. The second speaks to educators.

Literature Model

What criticism of video games is Berry answering?

It isn't that video games in and of themselves are harmful. Problems arise instead when the attitudes, priorities, or habits of their users are out of line. That's why children must be encouraged to view video games in a balanced, reasonable way and to take responsibility for their proper use.

Who will do this encouraging?

> Joy Wilt Berry, *What to Do When Your Mom or Dad Says . . ."Don't Overdo with Video Games!"*

Literature Model

What criticism of video games is Turkle answering?

There is nothing mindless about mastering a video game. The game demands skills that are complex and differentiated . . . and when one game is mastered, there is thinking about how to generalize strategies to other games. There is learning how to learn.

Why would this appeal to teachers?

> Dr. Sherry Turkle
> *The Second Self: Computers and Human Spirit*

Both writers defend video games but for different readers. Berry reassures worried parents and explains that attitudes and not video games are the problem. Turkle addresses educators and speaks about thinking skills.

Write a Position Paper

Think of a controversial issue on which you have not yet formed an opinion. Develop an argument for each side. Decide which side is stronger and defend it in a persuasive piece directed at others who are still undecided.

PURPOSE To defend a position

AUDIENCE Your classmates, readers of a newspaper

LENGTH 1 page

WRITING RUBRICS To write an effective position paper, you should

- state your position clearly

- use facts and language that are targeted to your audience

Cross-Curricular Activity

HEALTH You've traveled back in time to the nineteenth century. You're aboard an English sailing ship docked in a Caribbean harbor. The sailors tell you that for months they've eaten nothing but hard biscuits and salt pork, with no fresh fruits or vegetables. Now their gums are bleeding. They've heard from other sailors that oranges will help the condition, but on this island, there are only limes. Write a conversation between yourself and a sailor, trying to persuade him to eat the limes.

GrammarLink

Use a comma before a conjunction that links two main clauses.

They do not abuse the animals, but instead they offer a safe and healthy environment.

Write each sentence, adding commas where necessary.

1. Young people like the challenge of video games and that challenge can stimulate learning.
2. Some games are designed to be educational but even purely recreational games can spark the imagination.
3. Both young people and their parents should exercise good judgment for not all video games are appropriate for all ages.

See Lesson 14.1, page 505, and Lesson 20.3, page 603.

Listening and Speaking

PRESENT A DRAMATIC DIALOGUE With a partner, present your persuasive conversation from the Cross-Curricular Activity on this page as a dramatic dialogue for your classmates. As you rehearse, consider your audience and the setting. Use effective rate, volume, pitch, tone, diction, and gestures. Ask the class to evaluate your dialogue for content and presentation.

LESSON 6.3

Evaluating Evidence

*A*dvertisers and others who want to sell you products or services also use the techniques of persuasion. Even a cereal box can be a persuasive tool.

Nutrition information per one-ounce serving:

Calories	90
Protein	4 g
Carbohydrates	20 g
Fat	0 g
Cholesterol	0 mg
Sodium	0 mg
Potassium	105 mg

YOUR GOOD-HEALTH GAME PLAN

SUPER BOWL

"DELICIOUS"

FITNESS FLAKES

Research Tip

For help with evaluating the credibility of sources of information, see **Writing and Research Handbook,** pages 841–842.

Your grocery list says "healthful cereal," so you hurry past Sugary Chunks and Sweet Treats. You spot an unfamiliar brand, Super Bowl Fitness Flakes. Read the labels on the box. What is the real difference between Fitness Flakes and Sweet Treats? When it's time to make your choice, will the box front or the labels be more helpful? Why?

Support Opinions with Evidence

The information on the cereal box illustrates two kinds of evidence—facts and opinions. Facts can be proved—the cereal could be tested for the number of calories per one-ounce serving. Opinions, such as "delicious," are personal judgments. They

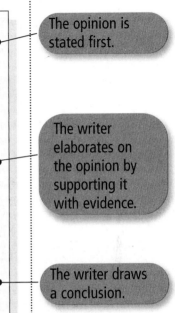

can't be proved. When you state an opinion, elaborate on it. Back it up with evidence: facts, statistics, and examples.

Read the following paragraph, and notice the facts, opinions, and other kinds of evidence it contains. Then study the chart that follows.

Many Americans hate their bodies. "We have declared war on our bodies," charges Andrew Kimbrell, the author of <u>The Human Body Shop</u>. This war includes 34 percent of all men and 38 percent of all women. They spent $33 billion on diets in 1990. A preteen boy guzzles protein drinks, hoping to increase his size and strength, while a fifty-five-year-old woman gets a face-lift. Technology and social pressure are causing us to make extreme changes.

The opinion is stated first.

The writer elaborates on the opinion by supporting it with evidence.

The writer draws a conclusion.

Evidence in Persuasive Writing	
Kinds	**Examples**
Fact	Americans spent $33 billion on diet products in 1990.
Statistic	Thirty-four percent of men and 38 percent of women spent $33 billion on diets in 1990.
Example	A fifty-five-year-old woman gets a face-lift.

Journal Writing

Jot down the evidence that persuaded you to change your mind about something or someone. Label each piece of evidence as one or more of the three kinds shown above.

Presenting Tip

When you present your persuasive writing, remember that charts, graphs, and other images can clarify your evidence and bring it to life.

Select Strong Evidence

Not all pieces of evidence are equally strong. Some "facts" are really opinions in disguise. When you write persuasively, check your facts, and make sure that they back up your point. In the model below, nutritionist Jane Brody says that choosing soft drinks over water "presents a . . . serious threat to good nutritional health." Does she persuade you? Why or why not?

Literature Model

No beverage in America gives water greater competition than flavored soft drinks. And probably no other choice presents a more serious threat to good nutritional health. Soft drinks are the epitome [ideal example] of empty calories. They contain water (with or without carbon dioxide), artificial colorings and flavorings, and sugar—as many as *6 teaspoons of sugar in one 8-ounce serving!* Nothing else. Some noncarbonated drinks add vitamin C, and "fruit" or "fruit-flavored" drinks may even contain some real fruit juice. But for the most part, they are just wet, sweet calories.

Jane Brody, *Jane Brody's Nutrition Book*

What kind of evidence does this sentence contain, facts or opinions?

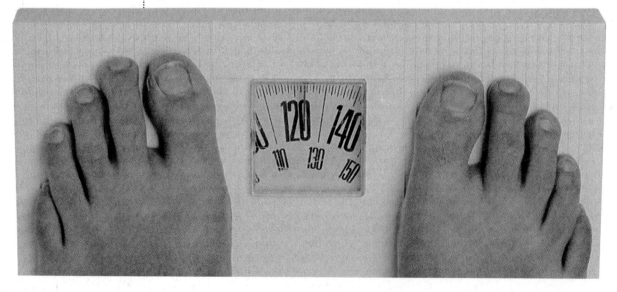

Write a Persuasive Essay

Usually you look for evidence supporting a position you already hold. Sometimes, however, the reverse happens. A fact "grabs" you, and you want to learn enough to develop a position on the issue. Find a piece of evidence, such as the fact that some fast-food chains use polystyrene containers rather than paper.

Try to connect this piece of evidence with what you already know. Develop a one page persuasive essay for an audience of your choice.

PURPOSE To persuade someone about an issue

AUDIENCE Your choice

LENGTH 1 page

WRITING RUBRICS To write an effective persuasive essay, you should

• include facts, statistics, examples, and reasons as evidence

• examine your evidence critically to be sure that facts are correct and that they support your argument

Listening and Speaking

PANEL DISCUSSION Has the world become warmer because of excess carbon dioxide and other gases? Are recent extreme temperatures simply normal climatic variations?

With two or three classmates, research the existence and possible causes of the greenhouse effect. Prepare and present a short panel discussion for the class. Afterwards, discuss the presentation's strengths and weaknesses.

GrammarLink

Use a plural verb with a compound subject joined by *and*.

Technology and social pressure are causing us to make extreme changes.

Write each sentence, correcting errors in subject-verb agreement.

1. At the end of this hilarious book, Perry's dog and his luggage ends up in China.
2. A sensible diet and an exercise program contributes to good health.
3. Three facts and one example supports the writer's opinion.
4. A sincere apology and a full refund has been sent to each angry customer.
5. Strong evidence and good organization makes your case more convincing.

See Lesson 16.5, page 549.

Viewing and Representing

In a science magazine or on the Internet, find some pictures relating to recent environmental changes due to temperature variations. Use the pictures to support the evidence you present in your panel discussion.

LOG ON ▶ **Writing** Online   For more writing and grammar practice, go to glencoe.com and enter QuickPass code WC87703p1.

277

LESSON 6.4

Developing a Strategy

As Calvin demonstrates in the cartoon below, even a reluctant audience can be reached with the right attention-grabbing strategy. The first step in persuasion is to get the attention of your reader. Newspapers, magazines, television, and radio all compete for attention. You must find ways to make your message stand out from all the rest.

MOMMMM! I'M THIRSTY! WHAT'S THIS? JUST WATER?

© Watterson 1992. Universal Press Syndicate

Prewriting Tip

For help with planning an introductory paragraph that will capture your readers' interest and present your message in an imaginative way, see **Writing and Research Handbook,** page 837.

Get Attention

How can you capture your readers' attention? As many writers have discovered, a playful imagination can work wonders. The following student model brings an everyday object to life in a humorous, imaginative way; her serious purpose, however, is to draw attention to an important issue.

Student Model

As one of the many cheap, unreliable, plastic department store bags, I'd like to speak out. Even though humans think of us as worthless, I wish they wouldn't throw us out their car windows, leaving us to fight for our lives on busy, treacherous highways. Wind gusts from cars going sixty miles an hour blow our flimsy bodies everywhere. Sometimes we land on windshields and cause accidents. Even worse, humans often leave us to baby-sit their small children. Don't get me wrong— we like kids, but not when they put us over their heads or in their mouths and begin to choke, turn blue, and die. . . .

So please, be careful when you dispose of us. Don't throw us out car windows or give us to babies. We like humans and definitely would not want to have them angry at us for wrecking their cars and killing their kids.

Dina Morrison, Pittsburgh, Pennsylvania
First appeared in *Merlyn's Pen*

> The surprise of a talking plastic bag attracts the reader's attention and arouses interest.

> What problems does the writer identify, and how does she suggest that people solve them?

Some lively formats for persuasive writing include real-life stories, fables, parables, ballads, and letters to people from the past or future. You might also use visuals, such as pictures, charts, and graphs, to call attention to the issue.

Journal Writing

Poet Robert Frost said that if there is no surprise for the writer, there will be no surprise for the reader. List some elements that have drawn your attention to persuasive messages. Analyze why they caught your attention.

Organize Your Argument

Your case, or argument, consists of a statement of your position and supporting evidence arranged in an orderly manner. Notice how this writer includes an answer to an opposing idea.

> On quiet nights the sound of a distant train reminds me of a time when railroads provided our most reliable passenger transportation. Rail passenger service, vital to America's past, can be even more important to its future. But, you say, trains are slow. True, but with today's crowded airports and new "bullet-train" technology, rail service can compete with the airlines in speed as well as cost. Trains use less fuel per passenger-mile than planes, cars, or buses do. Most important, trains' fuel efficiency conserves oil and decreases air pollution.

This is the topic sentence, since it expresses the main idea. What is the main idea?

The writer says this idea is the most important. Do you agree? Why might the writer have saved it for last?

First, the paragraph grabs attention with a nostalgic image involving trains. Then it presents its main point, answers opposition, and provides additional supporting evidence. The following chart summarizes what you should include in most arguments.

Grammar Tip

In editing make sure you use past and present tense correctly. For more information on verb tense, see Lesson 10.5, page 409.

How to Build Your Case

1. State your position clearly.

2. Present sound, relevant evidence.

3. Anticipate and answer the opposition.

4. Begin or end with your strongest point.

Write a Presentation

Your school district is considering ending athletic contests between schools. Supporters of this view argue that the athletic program wastes money and takes time away from education. Write a presentation to your school board supporting your view of interscholastic athletics.

PURPOSE To persuade readers about school athletic contests
AUDIENCE Your school board
LENGTH 2–3 paragraphs

WRITING RUBRICS To write an effective persuasive presentation, you should

- choose a strategy to gain attention and interest
- grab your readers' attention
- state your position and evidence
- begin or end with your strongest point
- answer the opposition

Listening and Speaking

ORGANIZE A FUND RAISER With a group of classmates, make a list of charitable projects you might support (for example, meals for homeless families). Debate the merits of each project and choose one. Meet with the class to consider other groups' ideas. Then decide on a fund raiser, such as a car wash, special athletic event, or bake sale. Create a flyer to urge families to support the project. Decide on the content of the flyer, and divide the tasks necessary to prepare it.

GrammarLink

Use commas to set off words that interrupt the flow of the sentence.

But, you say, trains are slow.

Rewrite the following, adding commas where necessary.

1. One way to reduce trash obviously is to reduce usage. Buying fewer objects you know means fewer discards.
2. Another way of course is to recycle materials. Organic materials even kitchen garbage can go to a compost heap. Some materials like glass and aluminum are easily reused.
3. Plastics and old tires on the other hand pose a challenge. Recycled plastic for example may be used in rugs.
4. Unrecycled materials for the most part end up in landfills or incinerators.

See Lesson 20.2, page 601.

Using Computers

To add a picture to a document, open the document, pull down the Insert menu, and select Picture. Browse through the picture file and select the one you want. Insert by clicking on the Insert button.

LOG ON ▶ **Writing** Online   For more writing and grammar practice, go to glencoe.com and enter QuickPass code WC87703p1.

281

LESSON

6.5

Strengthening Your Argument

*W*riting persuasively is a challenge. You can strengthen your argument by revising your work and filling in the gaps.

Just as the acrobats at the left must have sturdy equipment, your position must have strong support. And just as the acrobats have to synchronize their movements, you must organize your ideas so that they all work together to make your point.

Take Another Look

The word *revising* means "seeing again." To revise persuasive writing, set it aside for a time, and return to it later. You often have assignments that are due on a certain date, so you can't wait days or weeks to finish a piece of writing. However, if you begin your assignment several days before it is due, you will allow time for revision. Professional writers agree that setting your work aside, even if only for a day, will give you a fresh, new perspective. You may find that your best ideas will come during revision.

Peer reviewing is another helpful technique. Before you revise, ask a classmate to listen to your draft to help you identify any problems. To see how peer reviewing works, read the following draft. Then read the peer reviewer's comments, and decide whether you agree with them.

Paragraph 1:
I like your opening paragraph. It grabs my attention. Are the slang words OK here?

Paragraph 2:
Good ideas, but you provide little evidence. Do you have any facts and examples?

Paragraph 3:
Is summer employment a reason why you don't want year-round school? Can you make this paragraph clearer?

I have something to say to those adults who want to keep schools open all year long. Give me a break! Please don't do anything so drastic!

Eliminating summer vacation will cause enormous stress for everyone. Teachers will burn out faster. Nobody will pay attention in class in the middle of July, and the air-conditioning bills will be enormous. Also, additional salaries for teachers and janitors will be astronomical!

Year-round school will not help education, but it may reduce learning because many students take summer jobs to save for college tuition.

Notice that this peer review contains questions and suggestions—not commands. After peer review, it's up to you to read over the comments, decide which ones you agree with, and make those changes.

Vocabulary Tip

When drafting, remember that slang is inappropriate for any but the most informal writing, such as a personal note or friendly letter.

Journal Writing

Describe one good and one unsatisfactory experience you've had with a peer reviewer. In your opinion what are the characteristics of a good peer reviewer?

Fill in the Gaps

Holes, or gaps, in the argument weaken a persuasive appeal. The questions that follow will help you check your argument for adequate support.

Revising Persuasive Writing

1. Do I make my position clear?

2. Do I present enough evidence?

3. Is the evidence strong? Is it relevant?

4. Do I keep my audience in mind?

5. Are my ideas organized effectively?

Revision is far more than simply changing a word here and there. You may need to add, delete, or move whole sentences and paragraphs. During the revising stage, you must read, ask yourself questions, experiment, and revise some more. You may even need to do more research. The paragraph below works well because David Levine supports his point with strong evidence.

Literature Model

What position does Levine state in the first sentence?

Staying in school and graduating extends the range of options of what you can do with your life. It's also a fact that the consequences of dropping out are severe and the prospects for dropouts are bleak. According to the National Dropout Prevention Center, less than 50 percent of dropouts find jobs when they leave school.

Levine's evidence is powerful, solid, and relevant to his audience.

When they do, they earn 60 percent less than high school graduates (over a lifetime that adds up to $250,000).

David Levine, "I'm Outta Here"
First appeared in *Seventeen*

Revise a Persuasive Piece

Take another look at a writing assignment that you completed earlier in this unit. Consider the five questions on the chart on the preceding page. Then revise the piece.

PURPOSE To review and revise an earlier piece of persuasive writing

AUDIENCE Yourself

LENGTH 3–4 paragraphs

WRITING RUBRICS To effectively revise a persuasive piece, you should

- look at your piece with a new perspective
- ask yourself the five questions on the chart on page 284
- make sure there are no gaps in your argument
- add or change words and sentences as necessary

Using Computers

Sometimes writers prefer to revise at their computer terminals. Having a revision checklist right on the screen, along with the piece of writing you want to revise, is helpful. Develop a list of ten or twelve items for the checklist, and use a split screen to keep the list available as you revise.

GrammarLink

Use subject pronouns as the subject of a sentence and object pronouns as the object of a verb or preposition.

I have something to say. . . .
Give me a break!

Be especially careful with compound elements: *Sue and I saw Joe and him.*

Write each sentence, correcting errors in pronoun usage.

1. Rachel and me support the proposed art curriculum.
2. However, Rachel can better explain it to you and he.
3. Ginny was always available to help Ralph and she.
4. Here is a gift from Trudy and I.
5. Tell Martin and she the news.

See Lesson 11.1, page 435, and Lesson 11.3, page 439.

Listening and Speaking

EVALUATE YOUR REVISION With a small group, take turns reading aloud your original persuasive pieces and your revisions. Read your piece with appropriate volume, pitch, rate, tone, and diction. After each presentation, discuss the ways in which each revision improved the original work.

LOG ON ▶ **Writing** Online For more writing and grammar practice, go to **glencoe.com** and enter QuickPass code WC87703p1.

285

Creating an Ad

*Y*ou find advertising almost everywhere you look. Ads try to sell products, places, candidates, and ideas. Advertising agencies use many approaches in their efforts to persuade.

At what audience is this ad aimed? Does the ad make you want to visit Brookfield Zoo? Jot down your reaction and some reasons for it. Consider why the ad works or doesn't work for you.

Isn't it time you set your kids straight on tomato frogs?

Visit Brookfield Zoo, and your kids can see how nature's creatures *really* look, instead of jumping to conclusions. To find out more, call us at 708-485-0263. We're closer than you think. **BROOKFIELD ZOO** Where Imagination Runs Wild

Write to Sell

All those catchy commercial slogans that pop up in ads—and in your memory—come from the minds of ad writers. Persuasive writing is their business.

In advertising audience is of the utmost importance. Ads are not aimed at the world in general but rather at particular groups. Market research provides ad writers with information about a group of potential buyers—their needs, their desires, and how they will probably spend their money.

Once the audience is defined, or targeted, the writing begins. Ad writing demands a lively imagination and a good feel for language. Getting the point across in as few words as possible is essential.

Writers in advertising are constantly reminded that ads should attract Attention, arouse Interest, create Desire, and cause Action (AIDA). How well does the "tomato frogs" ad meet these standards?

AIDA in Action

Attention	"Tomato frogs! What an unusual name for an animal!"
Interest	"*Where imagination runs wild.* I certainly want to help my kids develop their imaginations."
Desire	"I want my kids to learn about many things, including tomato frogs. Let's visit the zoo."
Action	"I'll call this number to find out what the zoo's hours are, what the cost is, and what's the best way to get there."

Journal Writing: Persuasive Techniques

Find a magazine or newspaper ad that you consider persuasive. Decide whether it uses one of the following persuasive techniques: emotional appeal, celebrity endorsement, or glittering generalities. Identify its audience, and analyze it with an AIDA chart.

The slogan appeals to the consumer's desire for athletic and personal confidence.

How do the words and images in this ad work to persuade consumers to buy Power Pumps?

Distinguish the Truthful from the Tricky

Advertising is tricky. As the AIDA chart shows, an ad can turn facts into feelings. It is a fact that children can see tomato frogs at the zoo, but the ad appeals to feelings of curiosity and parental concern. Ad writers know that consumers base decisions about what to buy on feelings more than on facts. Ads may appeal to either positive feelings (hope, love, duty) or negative feelings (guilt, fear, envy).

Sometimes ads use language more for the way it sounds than for what it means. Words may sound scientific, for example, but actually say nothing except "buy this product." What does "high-tech design" mean? Advertisers must maintain certain standards of truth, but measuring "truth" is a complicated task.

Now look at the Power Pumps ad again. What evidence does it use to persuade you to buy? What feelings does it appeal to? Do you think this ad would work?

Write an Ad

An exhibit of works by artist Faith Ringgold will be shown at a local community center. Write a half-page newspaper ad to announce this exhibition. What can you say about the artist on the basis of the story quilt below? Notice how Ringgold combines quilting and painting, figures and words. What can you say to persuade people to come to this exhibit?

PURPOSE To persuade people to visit an exhibit

AUDIENCE Your choice

LENGTH 1/2 page

WRITING RUBRICS To write an effective ad, you should

- select your audience
- check that your ad draws attention, arouses interest, creates desire, and causes action
- appeal to people's feelings, but be truthful

Faith Ringgold, *Dream Two: King and the Sisterhood*, 1988

Grammar Link

Do not use apostrophes in possessive pronouns.

Put Pride in Your Stride!

Write each sentence, correcting any errors in possessive pronouns.

1. Notice it's quality.
2. If she takes our advice, the world is her's!
3. Travel with us—our's is a better way to go.
4. Compare and see—we can match theirs' any day, for less!
5. Remember, you're wish is our command.

See Lesson 11.4, page 441.

Listening and Speaking

CREATE A RADIO AD Working with a small group, create a radio ad for a particular product or event. Use literary devices (such as suspense, dialogue, or figurative language) as a way to persuade. Perform your ad aloud for the group or for the whole class.

Cross-Curricular Activity

SCIENCE Your class is having a science fair. Create a poster to promote the event. Be sure your text and visuals are attractive and interesting. Be persuasive.

LOG ON ▶ **Writing** Online | For more writing and grammar practice, go to **glencoe.com** and enter QuickPass code WC87703p1.

6.6 Creating an Ad **289**

Writing a Letter to the Editor

You may not be old enough to vote, but you can have a voice in public decision making. One of the most influential public arenas is the editorial page, and it's open to everyone.

Most newspapers and magazines invite letters from their readers. The following letter appeared in a popular magazine for young readers. Often in persuasive writing, the main idea comes at or near the beginning. This letter writer, however, has saved his main idea for the end. Why do you think he did that?

Dear Editor:

In the fall of 1989, I fractured one of my vertebrae playing football. I remained inactive for several months, wearing a full-body plastic jacket. The injury means no more football, no more soccer, no more baseball, or anything! As you may have noticed, my injury has a big effect on my life. Now I just go and watch my friends play.

I am not telling everybody to stop playing football. I'm just telling them to wear the right equipment.

Jon Good, Summit, New Jersey

First appeared in Sports Illustrated for Kids

Make and Support Your Point

A letter to the editor is really a letter to the readers of the newspaper or magazine. Like other persuasive writing, letters to the editor state a position and offer support for it. In the letter on the preceding page, Jon uses his own experience to support his argument that football players should use the right equipment. In the letter below, what does the writer want readers to think? What support does he offer?

Dear Editor:

I would like to tell readers that gymnastics is not only a sport for girls, but that it's also a sport for boys! Many people make fun of boys in this sport, but gymnastics is hard work, and all that hard work pays off when you get older. If you look at the men in the Olympics, you will see that they are fairly strong. So all you boys out there, don't tease us. Try gymnastics and see for yourselves: It's fun!

Philip Trevino, Gilroy, California
First appeared in Sports Illustrated for Kids

> What is the writer's opinion, and what evidence does he use to support it?

Journal Writing

In a newspaper or magazine find a letter to the editor that persuades you to think or act as the writer wishes. Paste it in your journal. Make notes about what persuades you.

When you write a letter to the editor, you are far more likely to see it in print if you use the correct business-letter form. For an example see Lesson 5.8, pages 230–233.

Think About Your Tone

Frustration and anger have inspired many a letter to the editor. To make your letter persuasive, however, you need to keep uncontrolled emotion from weakening your message. Editors reject angry outbursts. The following letter expresses strong emotions but supports the writer's point in a calm, controlled way. Remember that there are usually at least two sides to an issue. You should express *your* viewpoint reasonably; if you do, your letter will be much more persuasive.

Susan St...
St. Louis

Letters To The Editor
Address letters to St. Louis Magazine, Letters to St. Louis Magazine, Suite 2120, 211 North Broadway, ...i, 63102-2733. Fax number ...de address and daytime ...ay be edited for

Student Model

Dear Editor,

I am a thirteen-year-old native St. Louisan who lives in North County. I was extremely hurt when an article appeared in your April issue about plush and desirable places to live. To my surprise North County never appeared in the article. Why? North County is a beautiful place to live, filled with friendly faces. This to me, and probably many people, is extremely desirable.

The homes and subdivisions of this area are just as nice as the [ones] in the counties you featured. If you are *St. Louis Magazine*, then you should make a conscientious effort to represent *all* of the Metropolitan St. Louis area.

Kelinda Peaples, Florissant, Missouri
First appeared in *St. Louis Magazine*

How might referring to the magazine's purpose make Kelinda's letter more persuasive?

Write a Letter to the Editor

Select an organization in your community that serves an important role or offers fine service but rarely receives public attention. Write a letter to the editor of the local newspaper in which you praise this organization and its service. Persuade the public to pay more attention to the organization and to support it.

PURPOSE Support a worthwhile organization
AUDIENCE Your community, especially adults
LENGTH 3–5 paragraphs

WRITING RUBRICS To write an effective letter to the editor, you should

- state your main idea at the beginning or end—wherever it will be most effective
- support your views
- keep your tone reasonable

Listening and Speaking

DEBATE AN ISSUE In small groups, brainstorm about issues appropriate for letters to the editor of your school newspaper. Choose an issue that you have differing opinions about. Divide the group so that members can debate on the side of the issue with which they agree. Have each side support its opinion with evidence: facts, statistics, and examples. Then write letters to the editor. Read the letters aloud and evaluate constructively how well each letter succeeded in presenting a strong argument in a calm, reasonable manner.

GrammarLink

Avoid double negatives.

The injury means no more football, no more soccer, no more baseball, or anything!

Revise each sentence below to eliminate double negatives.

1. Sometimes football players don't have no protective equipment.
2. How people dress isn't none of your business.
3. He didn't have no reason to be so negative about everything.
4. Hardly nobody knows nothing about that.
5. I won't say nothing to him.

See Lesson 12.8, page 471.

Viewing and Representing

MAKE AN EDITORIAL DISPLAY Look in local newspapers for letters to the editor or for editorial columns written from a variety of ethnic and community perspectives. Clip the pieces and arrange them on the bulletin board. Identify and discuss the issues that concern and affect people across cultural and geographic boundaries.

LESSON 6.8

WRITING ABOUT LITERATURE
Writing a Book Review

*B*ook reviews—you have probably written dozens. *Book reviews can be persuasive. They help you decide what to read.*

Literature Model

My own grandma, AnadaAki, was born in a tipi during the eighteen eighties. She has come a long way to her present place in life, which includes being the family elder as well as being a devoted fan of the TV serial "As the World Turns." If you heard her British-accented voice calling out for someone to turn on the TV, you would not imagine that she was raised in the household of one of the last great medicine men among the Bloods.

Beverly Hungry Wolf, *The Ways of My Grandmothers*

Beverly Hungry Wolf's grandmother has something to give you—stories of a past you may know nothing about. She speaks in the pages of the book *The Ways of My Grandmothers*. But how will readers find out about her and hear her wonderful stories? Sometimes people tell others about a book they liked, and the word spreads. Often, though, the best way to learn about new books is through book reviews.

Know Your Audience

Book reviews can help readers in two ways. The reviews summarize a book's contents and in that way answer every reader's first question: What's it about? Reviews also evaluate the book, telling whether, in the reviewer's opinion, the book is worth reading:

Literature Model

It is a compilation of history, social life and customs. . . . There are stories . . . about the lives of her mother and grandmother, and others of her Elders, as well as accounts of some of her own experiences in learning how to live in the traditional [Blackfoot] manner. . . . Apart from its content, which is extremely valuable, one special quality of this work is its depiction of Native [American] people living a happy, normal and fulfilling existence— here are *anybody's* grandmothers, yours, mine, human beings. . . .

 Beverly Hungry Wolf is a very good writer. Her book is interesting, moving, and, here and there, pretty funny.

Doris Seale, review of *The Ways of My Grandmothers*
First appeared in *Interracial Books for Children Bulletin*

> Here the reviewer summarizes the book's contents, explaining what it is about.

> Here she evaluates the book. What does she consider its strengths?

Different people look for different qualities in books. Some enjoy drama and suspense, while others read mainly for information. Some respond to the quality of the writing itself. Many look for new books by their favorite authors. When you review a book you've liked, you may have too much to say about it. Knowing your audience and their interests can help you decide what to include and what to leave out.

Journal Writing

Think of a book that you feel strongly about. List reasons why you like it or don't like it. Then list some people you could try to persuade to read—or not read—this book. Explain how you would persuade your audience.

Grammar Tip

When editing a book review, be sure to underscore the book title. Use italics if your word-processing program allows you to. See Lesson 20.6, page 609.

What particular part of the main character's experience interested Melinda? Why?

Personalize Your Review

Some reviewers respond to books in a personal way. For example, *The China Year* tells of experiences similar to the reviewer's, so Melinda Eldridge also tells readers something about herself. Notice how Melinda's use of the first-person point of view makes her review all the more personal.

Student Model

The best parts of the book . . . are the friendships that evolved during Henrietta's year in China. I know first-hand how much fun it is to have friends from another culture, but I also know how much more painful it is to leave them because you don't know if you'll ever see them again.

The *China Year* is an excellent book for people of all types and from all walks of life. It stands as great testimony to the wonderful adventures one can have by living outside one's own culture.

Melinda Eldridge,
Arlington, Texas
First published in
Stone Soup

As a book reviewer, you have a wide range of options. You can compare the book to others by the same author or to others of the same type. You can comment on whether the book holds your interest. You can suggest certain types of readers who would enjoy the book. You can relate the book to events in your own experience, as Melinda did. The choice is yours.

Persuasive Writing

Write a Book Review

Think of a book you've read in the past that meant something special to you. Think especially of books in which you were able to identify with a character whose experiences were something like yours. Write a review, recommending the book to other readers your own age.

PURPOSE To review your favorite book
AUDIENCE Your classmates
LENGTH 1 page

WRITING RUBRICS To write an effective book review, you should

- tell what the story is about
- explain whether the book is worth reading
- keep your audience in mind

Carol Soatikee, *Students*, 1969

GrammarLink

Use the correct forms of the adjectives *good* and *bad*.

Rewrite each sentence below, correcting errors in the use of adjectives.

1. Of the two stories, the writing in LeGuin's is more good.
2. The plot is totally unbelievable, the worstest I've ever read.
3. The dialogue is most good when it's most natural.
4. The descriptions are badder than the action scenes.

See Lesson 12.3, page 461.

Cross-Curricular Activity

ART Study the painting on this page. Do the figures seem to be together or apart? How do colors and shapes create a mood? Write a review for a student art forum. Describe the painting's content and give your opinion. Include your reasons.

Listening and Speaking

PRESENT A REVIEW Taking turns with a partner, read aloud your book reviews from the writing activity on this page. Act as peer reviewers for one another's work. Evaluate the reviews, based on an adequate plot summary and a well-supported argument.

LOG ON ▶ **Writing** Online | For more writing and grammar practice, go to **glencoe.com** and enter QuickPass code WC87703p1.

297

Writing Process in Action

Persuasive Writing

In the preceding lessons you've learned how to state and support your opinions. You have had the opportunity to write a letter and a book review. Now, in this lesson, you're invited to write persuasively about how an important current issue might affect the future.

Assignment

Context	Your class has decided to publish *Our Future,* a magazine that deals exclusively with how what people do today may affect the future.
Purpose	To persuade people to behave today in ways that will improve the future
Audience	Your classmates and the readers of your magazine
Length	1 page

Planning to Write

The following pages can help you plan and write your persuasive article. Read through them, and then refer to them as you need to. But don't be tied down by them. You're in charge of your own writing process. Start by setting a time frame for this assignment. As you write, keep in mind the controlling idea: to persuade people to behave today in ways that will improve the future.

LOG ON **Writing** Online

For prewriting, drafting, revising, editing and publishing tools, go to **glencoe.com** and enter QuickPass code WC87703p1.

Prewriting

One of the best ways to find a topic about the future is to look around you today. What if pollution continues at the current rate? Ask yourself *what if* questions until you hit on a topic. The chart below suggests more ways to find a topic.

Your next task is to research your topic to learn exactly how it might influence the future.

Consider your audience; would it be best to write a letter, a short essay, or perhaps a short story?

Drafting

Once you have gathered facts concerning your topic, you will need to organize them in a way that has a strong impact on the reader. Your goal is to change people's behavior. In order to do this, you must use specific, vivid language.

Notice how Rachel Carson focuses on the negative events that have happened, using words such as *misfortunes* and *disasters*. These present realities influenced her fictional description of the world of tomorrow.

Option A

Explore your journal.

Option B

Brainstorm with a friend.

Option C

Freewrite for ideas.

> Watching the cars and trucks pour in all day carrying their bottles, papers, and cans for recycling—You can't convince me that this doesn't help people and the environment. We just need to keep it up!

Literature Model

I know of no community that has experienced all the misfortunes I describe. Yet every one of these disasters has actually happened somewhere, and many real communities have already suffered a substantial number of them.

Rachel Carson, *Silent Spring*

Drafting Tip

For more information about effectively making your case, see Lesson 6.4, pages 278–281.

Once you have all you need in order to write, think about the order in which you will present your ideas, facts, and examples. Then, using your notes, begin writing. At this stage just write steadily, and let your ideas flow.

Revising

To begin revising, read over your draft to make sure that what you have written fits your purpose and your audience. Then have a **writing conference.** Read your draft to a partner or a small group. Use your audience's reactions to help you evaluate your work so far. The questions below can help you and your listeners.

Question A

What is my purpose?

Question B

Do I consider my audience?

Question C

Have I captured my readers' attention?

Nuclear man probably recycled some materials. Scholars have not determined, however, if Nuclear man had any system for recycling. It may be that recycling was a haphazard occurrence in the life of Nuclear man. The fact that Nuclear man seemed obsessed with the word garbage suggests that Nuclear man had only the slightest notion of resource management and allocation. —a complex term with many meanings but thought to refer to unrecycled material—

[margin corrections: "organized" above "any system"; "is likely" above "It may be"]

Editing/Proofreading

Careful editing is essential to persuasive writing. Why? Some readers will dismiss your argument because of a misspelling or a grammatical error. Use your dictionary. Check your sentences and **proofread** for mechanics. Be sure you write legibly and in cursive if you aren't using a word processor. Check for only one kind of error at a time.

Publishing/Presenting

Once you've edited your composition, you are ready to submit your work to *Our Future*. Think about and discuss with your class what the cover of your magazine should look like.

Editing/Proofreading Checklist

1. Do my verbs agree with their subjects?

2. Have I used subject and object pronouns correctly?

3. Have I used possessive pronouns correctly?

4. Have I eliminated any double negatives?

5. Have I checked spelling and capitalization?

Proofreading Tip

For proofreading symbols, see pages 79 and 863.

Journal Writing: Write to Learn

Reflect on your writing process experience. Answer these questions in your journal: What do you like best about your persuasive writing? What was the hardest part? What did you learn in your writing conference? What new things have you learned as a writer?

Literature Model

FROM

Silent Spring

by Rachel Carson

Written more than thirty years ago by scientist Rachel Carson, Silent Spring *begins with this fable that shows humanity's carelessness and irresponsibility. As you read, think about how the fable affects your view of current environmental problems. Then try the activities in Linking Writing and Literature on page 306.*

There was once a town in the heart of America where all life seemed to live in harmony with its surroundings. The town lay in the midst of a checkerboard of prosperous farms, with fields of grain and hillsides of orchards where, in spring, white clouds of bloom drifted above the green fields. In autumn, oak and maple and birch set up a blaze of color that flamed and flickered across a backdrop of pines. Then foxes barked in the hills and deer silently crossed the fields, half hidden in the mists of the fall mornings.

> *Even in winter the roadsides were places of beauty.*

Along the roads, laurel, viburnum and alder, great ferns and wildflowers delighted the traveler's eye through much of the year. Even in winter the roadsides were places of beauty, where countless birds came to feed on the berries and on the seed heads of the dried weeds rising above the snow. The countryside was, in fact, famous for the abundance and variety of its bird life, and

Leonard Koscianski, *Whirlwind*, 1992

when the flood of migrants was pouring through in spring and fall people traveled from great distances to observe them. Others came to fish the streams, which flowed clear and cold out of the hills and contained shady pools where trout lay. So it had been from the days many years ago when the first settlers raised their houses, sank their wells, and built their barns.

On the mornings that had once throbbed with the dawn chorus of robins, catbirds, doves, jays, wrens, and scores of other bird voices there was now no sound . . .

Then a strange blight crept over the area and everything began to change. Some evil spell had settled on the community: mysterious maladies swept the flocks of chickens; the cattle and sheep sickened and died. Everywhere was a shadow of death. The farmers spoke of much illness among their families. In the town the doctors had become more and more puzzled by new kinds of sickness appearing among their patients. There had been several sudden and unexplained deaths, not only among adults but even among children, who would be stricken suddenly while at play and die within a few hours.

There was a strange stillness. The birds, for example—where had they gone? Many people spoke of them, puzzled and disturbed. The feeding stations in the backyards were deserted. The few birds seen anywhere were moribund; they trembled violently and could not fly. It was a spring without voices. On the mornings that had once throbbed with the dawn chorus of robins, catbirds, doves, jays, wrens, and scores of other bird voices there was now no sound; only silence lay over the fields and woods and marsh.

On the farms the hens brooded, but no chicks hatched. The farmers complained that they were unable to raise any pigs—the litters were small and the young survived only a few days. The apple trees were coming into bloom but no bees droned among the blossoms, so there was no pollination and there would be no fruit.

The roadsides, once so attractive, were now lined with browned and withered vegetation as though swept by fire. These, too, were silent, deserted by all living things. Even the streams were now lifeless. Anglers no longer visited them, for all the fish had died.

The roadsides, once so attractive, were now lined with browned and withered vegetation as though swept by fire.

In the gutters under the eaves and between the shingles of the roofs, a white granular powder still showed a few patches; some weeks before it had fallen like snow upon the roofs and the lawns, the fields and streams.

No witchcraft, no enemy action had silenced the rebirth of new life in this stricken world. The people had done it themselves.

This town does not actually exist, but it might easily have a thousand counterparts in America or elsewhere in the world. I know of no community that has experienced all the misfortunes I describe. Yet every one of these disasters has actually happened somewhere, and many real communities have already suffered a substantial number of them. A grim specter has crept upon us almost unnoticed, and this imagined tragedy may easily become a stark reality we all shall know.

Linking Writing and Literature

◆ Learning to Learn

Make some notes in your journal about the natural environment in your part of the country. What is the environment like? Are there mountains, forests, deserts, or lakes? What animals might someone see on a ride through your area? Also note environmental problems you have heard about in your area and tell how people are working to solve these problems.

◆ Talk About Reading

Discuss this excerpt from *Silent Spring* with a group of classmates. Select one person to lead the discussion and another to take notes. Use the following questions to guide the discussion.

1. **Connect to Your Life** In this fable, did you learn anything surprising or shocking about the effects of environmental pollution? Explain.

2. **Critical Thinking: Draw Conclusions** Why do you think Carson chose to begin her book with a fable rather than with dramatic examples of the misuse of dangerous chemicals in the environment?

3. **6+1 Trait®: Voice** How would you describe Carson's voice in *Silent Spring*? The author's *voice* includes her tone, her style, and the way she expresses her ideas. Where does the author's voice seem to change in this excerpt?

4. **Connect to Your Writing** After reading the selection, explain why the fable is a good introduction to the main idea of Carson's book.

◆ Write About Reading

Expository Essay Write an expository essay in which you explain what steps you, your family and friends, or your community are (or should be) taking to preserve and protect the environment. Steps may include everything from recycling to supporting national environmental organizations.

Focus on Voice Try to write in a voice appropriate to your feelings on the subject. If, for example, you feel passionately about the subject, your voice should convey that commitment.

For more information on voice and the 6+1 Trait® model, see **Writing and Research Handbook,** pages 838–840.

6+1 Trait® is a registered trademark of Northwest Regional Educational Laboratory, which does not endorse this product.

Reflecting on the Unit: Summarize What You Learned

Focus on the following questions to help you summarize what you have learned in this unit.

❶ How does persuasive writing effect change?

❷ What kinds of evidence can you use to support your position?

❸ What do you need to keep in mind in order to write persuasively?

❹ What kinds of activities go into developing a strategy?

❺ What should you focus on when revising your persuasive writing?

Adding to Your Portfolio

CHOOSE A SELECTION FOR YOUR PORTFOLIO Look over the writing you did for this unit. Choose a piece of writing for your portfolio. The writing you choose should show one or more of the following:

- an unusual or a surprising way of addressing a problem or an issue
- an opinion about a change you consider especially important
- words and ideas appropriate to a specific audience
- strong evidence gathered from at least two sources

REFLECT ON YOUR CHOICE Attach a note to the piece you chose, explaining briefly why you chose it and what you learned from writing it.

SET GOALS How can you improve your writing? What skill will you focus on the next time you write?

Writing Across the Curriculum

MAKE A SCIENCE CONNECTION Think of a current environmental problem, such as ozone deterioration or destruction of the rain forest, that you have learned about in science class. Write a persuasive composition that states and supports your opinion about what we should do to remedy the problem.

" 'You know, honey, we gotta figure a way'... "

—Gary Soto,
"Mother and Daughter"

308

Troubleshooter

Use Troubleshooter to help you correct common errors in your writing.

7.1 Sentence Fragment

Problem 1

Fragment that lacks a subject

frag Sol went to the airport. (Wanted to leave today.)

frag Dora jogged to school. (Was late for class.)

frag My car broke down today. (Couldn't start it.)

SOLUTION Add a subject to the fragment to make a complete sentence.

Sol went to the airport. He wanted to leave today.

Dora jogged to school. She was late for class.

My car broke down today. I couldn't start it.

Problem 2

Fragment that lacks a predicate

frag Jo caught a plane yesterday. (The plane at noon.)

frag Colin baked a cake today. (The cake in the oven.)

frag Tatiana likes that court. (The tennis court in the park.)

SOLUTION   Add a predicate to make the sentence complete.

Jo caught a plane yesterday. The plane left at noon.

Colin baked a cake today. The cake is in the oven.

Tatiana likes that court. The tennis court in the park is the one she likes.

Problem 3

Fragment that lacks both a subject and a predicate

frag   Sylvia played the violin. In the symphony orchestra.

frag   My cousin rode his bike. To the store today.

frag   Alex bought new skis. From the sports store.

SOLUTION   Combine the fragment with another sentence.

Sylvia played the violin in the symphony orchestra.

My cousin rode his bike to the store today.

Alex bought new skis from the sports store.

If you need more help avoiding sentence fragments, turn to Lesson 8.2, pages 361–362.

Run-on Sentence

Problem 1

Two main clauses separated by only a comma

run-on Barb went water-skiing, she skied behind the boat.

run-on I stopped reading, my eyes were tired.

run-on I worked hard on this chapter, I did well on my test.

SOLUTION A Replace the comma with a period or another end mark, and begin the new sentence with a capital letter.

Barb went water-skiing. She skied behind the boat.

SOLUTION B Replace the comma between the main clauses with a semicolon.

I stopped reading; my eyes were tired.

SOLUTION C Insert a coordinating conjunction after the comma.

I worked hard on this chapter, and I did well on my test.

Problem 2

Two main clauses with no punctuation between them

run-on My dog has fleas he scratches behind his ears.

run-on Husam bought that book he read it last week.

SOLUTION A   Separate the main clauses with a period or another end mark, and begin the second sentence with a capital letter.

My dog has fleas. He scratches behind his ears.

SOLUTION B   Insert a comma and a coordinating conjunction between the main clauses.

Husam bought that book, and he read it last week.

Problem 3

Two main clauses with no comma before the coordinating conjunction

run-on Samantha went home and she went to bed early.

run-on I can go to Roberta's party but I can't stay long.

SOLUTION   Insert a comma before the coordinating conjunction.

Samantha went home, and she went to bed early.

I can go to Roberta's party, but I can't stay long.

If you need more help in avoiding run-on sentences, turn to Lesson 8.6, pages 369–370.

Lack of Subject-Verb Agreement

Problem 1

A subject that is separated from the verb by an intervening prepositional phrase

agr   *One of the radios are broken.*

agr   *The boys in the class is singing.*

> **SOLUTION**   Ignore a prepositional phrase that comes between a subject and a verb. Make sure that the verb agrees with the subject of the sentence. The subject is never the object of the preposition.
>
> **One of the radios is broken.**
>
> **The boys in the class are singing.**

Problem 2

A sentence that begins with *here* or *there*

agr   *There go the local train.*

agr   *Here is the students who will write the report.*

agr   *There is oil paintings in the art gallery.*

SOLUTION The subject is never *here* or *there*. In sentences that begin with *here* or *there*, look for the subject *after* the verb. The verb must agree with the subject.

There goes the local train.

Here are the students who will write the report.

There are oil paintings in the art gallery.

Problem 3

An indefinite pronoun as the subject

agr Neither of the girls (have) their umbrella.

agr Many of the books (is) old.

agr All of my pleading (were) in vain.

Some indefinite pronouns are singular, some are plural, and some can be either singular or plural, depending upon the noun they refer to.

SOLUTION Determine whether the indefinite pronoun is singular or plural and make the verb agree.

Neither of the girls has her umbrella.

Many of the books are old.

All of my pleading was in vain.

Problem 4

A compound subject that is joined by *and*

agr   *Posters and balloons (was) strewn around the gym.*

agr   *The star and team leader (are) Rico.*

SOLUTION A If the parts of the compound subject do not belong to one unit or if they refer to different persons or things, use a plural verb.

Posters and balloons were strewn around the gym.

SOLUTION B If the parts of the compound subject belong to one unit or if both parts refer to the same person or thing, use a singular verb.

The star and team leader is Rico.

Problem 5

A compound subject that is joined by *or* or *nor*

agr   *Either the actor or the actress (appear) onstage.*

agr   *Neither the tomato nor the bananas (looks) ripe.*

agr   *Either Mom or Dad (are) driving us to the movie.*

agr   *Neither my brother nor my uncles (likes) trains.*

SOLUTION   Make the verb agree with the subject that is closer to it.

Either the actor or the actress appears onstage.

Neither the tomato nor the bananas look ripe.

Either Mom or Dad is driving us to the movie.

Neither my brother nor my uncles like trains.

Problem 6

A compound subject that is preceded by *many a*, *every*, or *each*

agr   Every nook and cranny (were) searched.

agr   Each boy and girl (smile) brightly.

SOLUTION Use a singular verb when *many a*, *each*, or *every* precedes a compound subject.

Every nook and cranny was searched.

Each boy and girl smiles brightly.

If you need more help with subject-verb agreement, turn to Lessons 16.1–16.5, pages 541–550.

Incorrect Verb Tense or Form

Problem 1

An incorrect or missing verb ending

tense   Have you (reach) all your goals?

tense   Last month we (visit) Yosemite National Park.

tense   The train (depart) an hour ago.

SOLUTION   Add *-ed* to a regular verb to form the past tense and the past participle.

Have you reached all your goals?

Last month we visited Yosemite National Park.

The train departed an hour ago.

Problem 2

An improperly formed irregular verb

tense   The wind (blowed) the rain from the roof.

tense   The loud thunder (shaked) the house.

tense   Sophia (bringed) the horse back to the barn.

Troubleshooter

The past and past participle forms of irregular verbs vary. Memorize these forms, or look them up.

> **SOLUTION**   Use the correct past or past participle form of an irregular verb.
>
> **The wind blew the rain from the roof.**
>
> **The loud thunder shook the house.**
>
> **Sophia brought the horse back to the barn.**

Problem 3

Confusion between the past form and the past participle

tense Mimi ⟨has rode⟩ the horse home from school.

> **SOLUTION**   Use the past participle form of an irregular verb, not the past form, when you use the auxiliary verb *have*.
>
> **Mimi has ridden the horse home from school.**

If you need more help with correct verb forms, turn to Lessons 10.1–10.12, pages 401–424.

7.5 Incorrect Use of Pronouns

Troubleshooter

Problem 1

A pronoun that could refer to more than one antecedent

pro *Sonia jogs with Yma, but she is more athletic.*

pro *After the dogs barked at the cats, they ran away.*

pro *When Sal called out to Joe, he didn't smile.*

SOLUTION Rewrite the sentence, substituting a noun for the pronoun.

Sonia jogs with Yma, but Yma is more athletic.

After the dogs barked at the cats, the cats ran away.

When Sal called out to Joe, Joe didn't smile.

Problem 2

Personal pronouns as subjects

pro *Vanessa and me like to camp in the mountains.*

pro *Georgianne and them drove to the beach.*

pro *Her and Mark flew to London.*

SOLUTION Use a subject pronoun as the subject of a sentence.

Vanessa and I like to camp in the mountains.

Georgianne and they drove to the beach.

She and Mark flew to London.

Problem 3

Personal pronouns as objects

pro Joel is coming with Manny and she.

pro Please drive Rose and I to the store.

pro The dog brought the stick to Chandra and I.

SOLUTION Use an object pronoun as the object of a verb or a preposition.

Joel is coming with Manny and her.

Please drive Rose and me to the store.

The dog brought the stick to Chandra and me.

If you need more help with the correct use of pronouns, turn to Lessons 11.1–11.7, pages 435–448.

7.6 Incorrect Use of Adjectives

Problem 1

Incorrect use of *good, better, best*

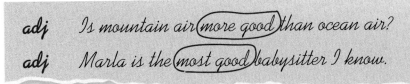

adj   Is mountain air more good than ocean air?

adj   Marla is the most good babysitter I know.

SOLUTION   The comparative and superlative forms of *good* are *better* and *best*. Do not use *more* or *most* before irregular forms of comparative and superlative adjectives.

Is mountain air better than ocean air?

Marla is the best babysitter I know.

Problem 2

Incorrect use of *bad, worse, worst*

adj   Mandy's cold is the baddest cold I've ever seen.

SOLUTION   The comparative and superlative forms of *bad* are *worse* and *worst*. Do not use *-er* or *-est* for irregular forms of comparative and superlative adjectives.

Mandy's cold is the worst cold I've ever seen.

Problem 3

Incorrect use of comparative adjectives

adj   *Twine is (more stronger) than thread.*

> **SOLUTION**   Do not use both *-er* and *more* at the same time.
>
> **Twine is stronger than thread.**

Problem 4

Incorrect use of superlative adjectives

adj   *This is the (most hardest) test I've ever taken.*

> **SOLUTION**   Do not use both *-est* and *most* at the same time.
>
> **This is the hardest test I've ever taken.**

If you need more help with the incorrect use of adjectives, turn to Lesson 12.3, pages 461–462.

 Incorrect Use of Commas

Problem 1

Missing commas in a series of three or more items

com	We had fish o vegetables o and bread for dinner.
com	Help me make the beds o sweep the floor o and wash the windows.

> **SOLUTION** When there are three or more items in a series, use a comma after each one, including the item that precedes the conjunction.
>
> **We had fish, vegetables, and bread for dinner.**
>
> **Help me make the beds, sweep the floor, and wash the windows.**

Problem 2

Missing commas with direct quotations

com	"The concert o " said Dora o "was loud and boring."
com	"Tomorrow o " said Burton o "I will read that book."

SOLUTION   The first part of an interrupted quotation ends with a comma followed by quotation marks. The interrupting words are also followed by a comma.

"The concert," said Dora, "was loud and boring."

"Tomorrow," said Burton, "I will read that book."

Problem 3

Missing commas with nonessential appositives

> com   Mr. Unser our English teacher was born in England.
>
> com   Ms. Charo my mother's supervisor is taking us to dinner.

SOLUTION   Determine whether the appositive is truly not essential to the meaning of the sentence. If it is not essential, set off the appositive with commas.

Mr. Unser, our English teacher, was born in England.

Ms. Charo, my mother's supervisor, is taking us to dinner.

Problem 4

Missing commas with nonessential adjective clauses

com   Devin, who arose early, smelled the eggs and bacon.

SOLUTION   Determine whether the clause is truly essential to the meaning of the sentence. If it is not essential, set off the clause with commas.

Devin, who arose early, smelled the eggs and bacon.

Problem 5

Missing commas with introductory adverb clauses

com   When the whistle blows, the workday is over.

SOLUTION   Place a comma after an introductory adverbial clause.

When the whistle blows, the workday is over.

If you need more help with commas, turn to Lessons 20.2–20.4, pages 601–606.

Incorrect Use of Apostrophes

Problem 1

Singular possesive nouns

> apos ⟨Beths⟩ dress is from France.
>
> apos My ⟨boss⟩ report is on ⟨Angelas⟩ desk.
>
> apos ⟨My gerbils⟩ fur is brown and white.

SOLUTION Use an apostrophe and an *s* to form the possessive of a singular noun, even one that ends in *s*.

Beth's dress is from France.

My boss's report is on Angela's desk.

My gerbil's fur is brown and white.

Problem 2

Plural possessive nouns ending in *s*.

> apos The ⟨boys⟩ shirts are too big for them.
>
> apos My ⟨horses⟩ manes are long and thick.
>
> apos My ⟨parents⟩ friends joined them for dinner.

SOLUTION Use an apostrophe alone to form the possessive of a plural noun that ends in *s*.

The boys' shirts are too big for them.

My horses' manes are long and thick.

My parents' friends joined them for dinner.

Problem 3

Plural possessive nouns not ending in *s*

apos   *The ⟨childrens⟩ books are in the library.*

apos   *The ⟨womens⟩ meetings are in this building.*

SOLUTION   Use an apostrophe and an *s* to form the possessive of a plural noun that does not end in *s*.

The children's books are in the library.

The women's meetings are in this building.

Problem 4

Possessive personal pronouns

apos   *This new tape is ⟨her's⟩ but the CD is ⟨their's⟩*

SOLUTION   Do not use an apostrophe with any of the possessive personal pronouns.

This new tape is hers, but the CD is theirs.

Confusion between *its* and *it's*

apos The bird built (it's) nest in the oak tree.

apos I want to know if (its) going to be sunny today.

SOLUTION Do not use an apostrophe to form the possessive of *it*. Use an apostrophe to form the contraction of *it is*.

The bird built its nest in the oak tree.

I want to know if it's going to be sunny today.

If you need more help with apostrophes and possessives, turn to Lesson 20.7, pages 611–612.

Troubleshooter

7.9 Incorrect Capitalization

Problem 1

Words referring to ethnic groups, nationalities, and languages

 cap Many (canadian) citizens speak (french.)

> **SOLUTION** Capitalize proper nouns and adjectives that refer to ethnic groups, nationalities, and languages.
>
> **Many Canadian citizens speak French.**

Problem 2

The first word of a direct quotation

cap Devon said, ("the) new highway runs through town."

> **SOLUTION** Capitalize the first word in a direct quotation that is a complete sentence.
>
> **Devon said, "The new highway will run through town."**

Problem 3

Words that show family relationships

 *cap* Dennis asked (aunt) Silvie to drive him to school.

> **SOLUTION** Capitalize words that show family relationships when used as titles or as substitutes for people's names.
>
> **Dennis asked Aunt Silvie to drive him to school.**

 If you need more help in capitalizing, turn to Lessons 19.1–19.4, pages 583–590.

7.10 Lack of Parallelism

Problem 1

Failure to include articles before all the items in a series.

> *You should have fun at the beach with the dolphins, fish, **all those** seagulls, and the sand.*

SOLUTION   Apply articles to all the items in a series, or to only the first item in the series.

You should have fun at the beach with the dolphins, the fish, the seagulls, and the sand.

You should have fun at the beach with the dolphins, fish, seagulls, and sand.

Problem 2

Failure to apply pronouns to all items in a series

> *I defeated Bob, a chess champion, Jenny, **who was** the fastest kid in school, and Michael, the football coach.*

SOLUTION   Apply pronouns to all the items in a series or only to the first item in a series.

I defeated Bob, who was a chess champion; Jenny, who was the fastest kid in school; and Michael, who was the football coach.

I defeated Bob, who was a chess champion; Jenny, the fastest kid in the school; and Michael, the football coach.

If you need more help with parallelism, see pages 63, 79, 128, 367, and 834.

Business and Technical Writing

Contents

We encounter a number of business and technical documents in every day life. These types of documents are forms of expository writing because they inform or tell us how to do something. Among these types of documents are business letters, memos, work plans and contracts, public service announcements (PSAs), newsletters, and multimedia presentations.

Business Letters

A business letter is a formal letter written to a person who can grant a request, satisfy a complaint, or give information.

The following business letter is written to express a complaint. Note how the writer follows the tips suggested in the chart on the following page.

440 Mountain Rd.
Pickett, Idaho 67098
August 15, 20--

Mr. David Payne, Manager
The Sport Shop
2786 Aspen Avenue
Pickett, Idaho 67098

Dear Mr. Payne:

On August 13, I purchased a pair of in-line skates at the Sport Shop. That same day, I discovered that one of the wheels on the left skate is permanently stuck and won't roll.

On August 14, I took the skates back, and a customer service representative, Mr. Greely, said the skates couldn't be returned because they were bought on sale. Then he showed me a sign that said, "No Returns or Exchanges on Sale Items." I explained that the skates were unusable because of a defect, but Mr. Greely just pointed at the sign and helped the next person.

I understand that the skates were on sale and are not returnable, but I feel that your store should either replace the defective skate or refund my money. I am enclosing a copy of my receipt.

I also feel that it was wrong of Mr. Greely to ignore my complaint. My family has been shopping at the Sport Shop for years, and nothing like this has happened before. Thank you for taking care of this problem.

Sincerely yours,

Rachel Goldstein

> The letter is addressed to a specific person.

> The writer explains her complaint in the first paragraph.

> The writer tells the story of what happened.

> The writer tells how she thinks the complaint should be resolved.

> The writer gives additional information.

Business Letters

Types of Business Letters

Business letters are a direct and effective way to communicate on many topics.

Use a business letter when you want to inquire, make a request, state an opinion, or voice a complaint. Keep the tone of your business letter formal and polite. Use standard American English, not slang or clichés (worn out expressions). Keep the language simple. "Thank you for taking care of this problem" is better than "I would appreciate it if you would look into this situation at your earliest convenience and take appropriate action."

When you write a business letter, remember that the person receiving it is probably very busy, so a short letter is more likely to be read than a long wordy one. Keep business letters to one page or less. Include only necessary information in a logical sequence.

When you write a business letter, use persuasive writing. If you are writing to complain about a problem with a product or service, you want to convince the person to correct the problem. When you write a letter of opinion, you want to persuade someone to agree with you and take action. Use a letter of application to convince someone to hire you for a job or consider you for membership or an award. Use a letter of inquiry when you want someone to give you information.

Knowing how to write an effective business letter is a skill you will use often.

TYPES OF BUSINESS LETTERS

COMPLAINT LETTER	REQUEST LETTER	OPINION LETTER	APPLICATION LETTER
Identify the product or service clearly.	Be brief.	State your opinion in the first sentence or two.	Write to a specific person.
Describe the problem accurately.	State your request clearly.	Support your opinion with reasons, facts, and examples.	Describe the job or program for which you are applying.
Request a specific solution.	Include all necessary information.	Summarize your main points and offer a solution if possible.	List your qualifications.
Be polite.	Make your request specific and reasonable.		Tell why you're the best person for the job or award.
Keep a copy of your letter until your complaint has been resolved.	Include your phone number or a stamped self-addressed envelope.		Request an application form or an interview.

Style

Business letters are usually written in one of two forms: block style or modified block style.

Block Style In the block style, all lines begin at the left margin. Paragraphs are not indented; they are separated by a line space. The letter on page 333 is typed in the block style.

Modified Block Style In the modified block style, the heading, the closing, your signature, and your typed name begin in the center of the line. The paragraphs may be indented—five spaces on a typewriter or half an inch on a computer—or not indented. The letter below is in the modified block style with paragraphs indented.

Heading

455 Pleasant Street
Moran, California 78987
May 3, 20--

Mr. Kevin Kulakowski, Manager
Moran Movie Theater
304 South Main Street   **Inside Address**
Moran, California 78987

Dear Mr. Kulakowski: **Salutation**

On Saturday, May 1, I went to a movie at your theater. During the movie, I stood up to go to the concession stand and almost fell over because my feet had stuck to the floor! I know you can't clean up every single spill after every movie, but the sticky mess was so thick that it must have been there for a long time. When I moved to sit in a different part of the theater, the floor there was just as sticky.

The men's restroom was very messy. Paper towels were strewn all over, and there were bugs around the floor drain.

Body

Please let me know when these problems have been corrected, so that my friends and I can come back to your theater and enjoy the movies again.

Closing   Sincerely,

Name and signature   Kurt Brady

The Parts of a Business Letter

A business letter has six parts.

The Heading   There are three lines in the heading.
- your street address
- your city, state, and ZIP code
- the date

The Inside Address   The inside address has four or more lines.
- the name of the person to whom you're writing (with or without a courtesy title such as *Ms., Mr.,* or *Dr.*)
- the title of the person to whom you're writing (Place a short title on the same line with the person's name. A long title requires a separate line.)
- the name of the business or organization
- the street address of the business or organization
- the city, state, and ZIP code

The Salutation or Greeting   The salutation should include a courtesy title, such as *Dear Mrs. Biedermeyer* or *Dear Mr. Bogden.* If you don't know the name of the person, begin with Dear and the person's title: *Dear Customer Service Representative* or *Dear Manager.* The salutation of a business letter is followed by a colon.

The Body   The body tells your message.

The Closing   The closing is a final word or phrase, such as *Sincerely* or *Yours truly.* The closing is followed by a comma.

Name and Signature   Type your name four lines below the closing. Then sign your name in the space between the closing and your typed name.

Neatness Counts

Your reader will pay more attention to your opinion if your letter is neat.
- Type your letter or use a computer.
- Use unlined white paper.
- Leave a two-inch margin at the top and at least a one-inch margin at the left, right, and bottom of the page.
- Single-space the heading. Allow one or more blank lines between the heading and the inside address, depending on the length of your letter.
- Single-space the remaining parts of the letter, leaving an extra line between the parts and between the paragraphs in the body.

Friendly Letters

A personal, or friendly, letter differs from a business letter in purpose, tone, and length. The tone of a letter depends on the closeness of your relationship with the receiver. A friendly letter may be short (a thank-you note) or long (a detailed account of an interesting experience). Contrast the following friendly thank-you letter with the business letters on pages 333 and 335.

The familiar greeting is followed by a comma.

24 Hardcastle Lane
Pickett, Idaho 67098
August 10, 20——

Dear Aunt Elsie,

Thank you for the beautiful card and the generous birthday check. You never forget my special day!

Now I'll be able to buy the in-line skates I've had my eye on for months. Whenever I go skating, I promise I'll think of you.

Mom and Dad send their best. We're looking forward to seeing you for Thanksgiving. Thanks again for remembering me.

Your loving niece,

Rachel

The tone is informal and friendly. The letter may be typed or handwritten.

The closing is informal. Even if the letter is typed, the signature is handwritten.

Activity

Imagine that your family traveled a long way to get to a vacation spot where you had reservations at a motel. When you arrived, your rooms had been given to someone else and the motel was full. Write a letter of complaint to the motel manager. Use either the block or the modified block format.

PURPOSE   To write a letter of complaint

AUDIENCE   Classmates

LENGTH   One page

WRITING RUBRICS To write an effective letter of complaint, you should

- state your complaint in the first paragraph of your letter
- tell what you think is a fair solution and why

Technology Tip

You can set up a template for one or both of the business letter formats. Select **Page Setup** in the **File** menu to set the margins. Next, use the ruler to set any tabs or paragraph indentations you need. Then type in a made-up letter, format it with the size and style of type you want, and save the letter as a template. When you need to write a business letter, open the template, rename it (so that the original remains unchanged), and replace the made-up copy with your new letter. Some word processing programs have built-in templates or offer free downloads of templates at their Web sites.

Memos

A memo is a brief business note that gives the reader important information on a topic. Memos are written in formal language but have a friendly tone. Memos are usually written to people you know or work with.

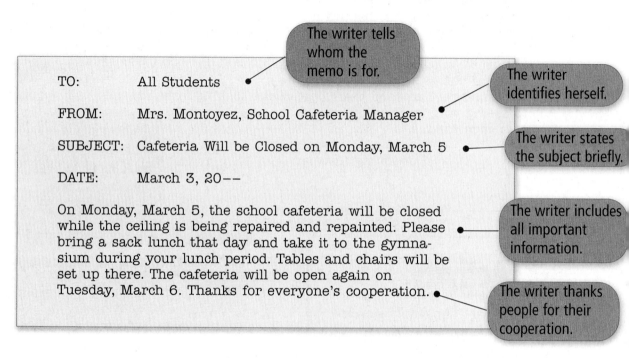

TO: All Students

FROM: Mrs. Montoyez, School Cafeteria Manager

SUBJECT: Cafeteria Will be Closed on Monday, March 5

DATE: March 3, 20--

On Monday, March 5, the school cafeteria will be closed while the ceiling is being repaired and repainted. Please bring a sack lunch that day and take it to the gymnasium during your lunch period. Tables and chairs will be set up there. The cafeteria will be open again on Tuesday, March 6. Thanks for everyone's cooperation.

The writer tells whom the memo is for.

The writer identifies herself.

The writer states the subject briefly.

The writer includes all important information.

The writer thanks people for their cooperation.

Types of Memos

Memos can be used to convey many kinds of important messages. You can write a memo to make an announcement, ask or answer a question, or make an assignment. A grocery store manager might write a memo to all cashiers about how to redeem a new store coupon. A church pastor might write a memo to the ushers, thanking them for volunteering and inviting them to a special dinner.

When you write a memo to make an announcement, include the most important details in one or two paragraphs. If you are using a memo to make a request, tell your reader exactly what you want him or her to do. For example, you might say, "Please see me on Tuesday at 1:30 P.M. to discuss this." Use a memo when you want to remind people of an upcoming event they may have known about but forgotten or to remind them to do something. When you write a memo to assign a task, describe the task and include the date when it must be finished.

Always keep memos brief—one page or less. Don't include any extra information. Use formal language, but keep the tone friendly.

Memos

TYPES OF MEMOS

ANNOUNCEMENT	REQUEST	REMINDER	ASSIGN A TASK
Headline your announcement in a few words on the subject line.	State your request briefly on the subject line.	Begin the message with words such as, "I'd like to remind you to . . ."	Name the task in the subject line.
Make the announcement in one or two short sentences in the first paragraph.	Make your request clear in the first sentence.	Give the most important information in the first sentence.	In the first sentence, use language such as, "Your job is to . . ." or "This assignment includes . . ."
Give details in a second paragraph.	Tell how people can respond to your request.	Include necessary details like dates, times, and phone numbers.	Give a brief description of the task.
Include dates and times.	Thank the readers for their help.		Give a date by which the task must be completed.

Business & Technical Writing

Style

Memos are written in the block style. Each heading and paragraph starts at the left margin. Memo headings are printed in capital letters and followed by a colon. The words following the colon are capitalized like a title. Memos can include simple charts or a bulleted list if needed.

Words after headings align at the left.

Headings

TO: All Members of the Student Photography Club

FROM: Mr. Lee

SUBJECT: Pinhole Camera Project

DATE: September 9, 20-- **Date**

Message The activity during our September 20 meeting will be to make a pinhole camera. You will need the following supplies:
- cereal box
- sewing needle
- 1 sheet of wax paper **Bulleted list**
- rubber band
- pair of scissors

Please bring all materials to the meeting with you.

Memos

The Parts of a Memo

Headings A memo heading is a title word in capital letters followed by a colon. Most memos have four headings: TO, FROM, SUBJECT, and DATE, followed by the corresponding information.

Message The message is written in one or more paragraphs. Sentences are usually short—not longer than about twenty words. Some memos may include a bulleted or numbered list.

Neatness Counts

Create memos on a typewriter or computer. If you must handwrite a memo, neatly print in black ink.

- Use unlined white paper.
- Leave a two-inch margin at the top and one-inch margins at the sides and bottom of the page.
- Double-space each heading line.
- Use a double space between the headings and the message and between paragraphs.
- Single-space the lines of each paragraph.

Activity

Write a memo to your classmates about an event at a place you know. Include directions from your school to the place. Write the memo on a computer and revise it to make sure it is concise and flows logically. Proofread it for grammar and usage, spelling, and word choice. Post it in your classroom.

PURPOSE	To write clear directions
AUDIENCE	Classmates
LENGTH	One page or less

WRITING RUBRICS To write an effective memo, you should

- state the topic clearly in the subject heading
- include all important information
- be brief

 Technology Tip

Use a computer's word processing functions to help create a neat memo. Your software may contain one or more templates for memos. You can also create your own memo design. Experiment with typefaces and styles and sizes of type, but don't get too fancy. A memo's appearance, like its message, should be simple and to the point.

Work Plans and Contracts

Work plans are documents that describe the details of a project and show the progression of the work. The following work plan shows assigned tasks and the completion dates. A contract often accompanies a work plan.

The writer identifies the plan in a title.

The writer organizes information into columns.

Cady School Newsletter Work Plan
March 20—— Issue

Student	Assignment	Due Date
Ali Ziad	writing article on school election distributing newsletter to all classrooms	2/5 3/3
Matt Abrams	writing school calendar column	2/9
Tracy Everett	compiling sports schedule	2/9
Eiko Sanjo	editing election articles editing school calendar & sports schedule editing newsletter draft	2/9 2/15 2/28
Enrique Salinas	taking photos developing film	2/15 2/20
Greta Anderson	typing all articles into computer layout taking final copy to printer picking up copies from printer	2/23 3/3 3/5
Reema Johnson	adding graphics and scanning in photos	2/25

The writer lists each assignment and its due date.

Types of Work Plans

Work plans can be written to describe a project, list dates and times when work will be completed, and show who is assigned to each task. Contracts usually accompany work plans and must include the parties involved, the work to be done, the payment terms, and the time of performance.

When you describe a project, start by listing its objectives (goals). Then list all tasks to be completed. Describe in detail how each one is to be done.

Create a schedule to show when each task must be completed. List each task under its deadline date.

The schedule should show the responsibilities of each person working on the project. You could organize this schedule in three columns, showing the person's name, his or her tasks, and the due date of each assignment, as in the model on this page.

Some work plans need a budget column that shows the expected costs of a project. To make a simple budget, list all the materials and other expenses involved.

Work Plans and Contracts

Then, next to each item, list the estimated cost. Leave a blank column to show the actual cost as money is spent.

Work plans make clear to everyone involved what his or her responsibilities are and when the work must be finished. A well thought out work plan can keep people working smoothly together to finish a project on time.

TYPES OF WORK PLANS			
PROJECT SCHEDULE	**ASSIGNMENT SCHEDULE**	**PROCESS OUTLINE**	**BUDGET**
Use a title to show what the schedule is for.	Name tasks briefly.	Use an outline or a series of numbered steps to explain a process (how a task should be done).	Include a list of all of the costs involved in the project.
List every task to be done.	Make a graphic organizer to show who does what and when it is due.		Estimate each cost.
Give the date each task is to be completed.		List the steps of a process in the order in which they must be completed.	Record actual expenses as they are paid.
Organize the information in a table or columns so that it will be easy to understand.	Include every person involved and every task that must get done.	Be brief.	
	Include a due date for each task.	Include only necessary steps.	

Style

Work plans may include some sections written in paragraph form. Do not indent paragraphs. Instead, leave a line of space between paragraphs. Begin each line at the left margin.

If your work plan includes an outline, use Roman numerals for each item and capital letters to list details under each item.

Tables should be centered on the page if they are narrower than the width of your type block.

The Parts of a Work Plan

Title Work plans are titled to show the project or job they are for.

Objectives Work plans begin by stating the goals of the project.

Body The body can but does not need to include task descriptions and assignments, dates, schedules, an outline, and a budget.

Organization Counts

A badly organized work plan will confuse people and delay the completion of the project. Before writing a work plan, make lists of pertinent information; then experiment with the organization of your plan. Use a computer to create and revise your plan.

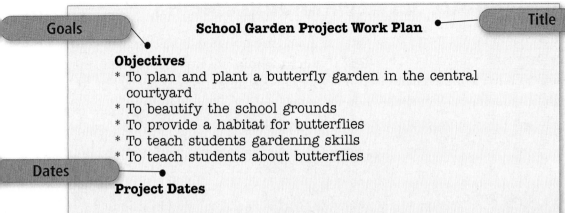

Goals

Title

School Garden Project Work Plan

Objectives

* To plan and plant a butterfly garden in the central courtyard
* To beautify the school grounds
* To provide a habitat for butterflies
* To teach students gardening skills
* To teach students about butterflies

Dates

Project Dates

The project will begin on February 1, 2010, and will be completed by June 15, 20--.

Work schedule

Task Listing

Work Schedule

	February	March	April	May	June
Tasks	Research flowers and shrubs Make final plant and tree selection Study seed catalogues	Draw land-scape plan Order Seeds	Lay out garden Dig beds Start seeds in trays indoors	Plant trees and flowering shrubs Install bird-bath	Transfer seedlings to garden Purchase annuals and plant them Make mulch beds

Activity

Brainstorm a list of projects for solving a technical problem or for providing a service. Choose one and create a work plan to show the progression of the project. Use the models on pages 341 and 343 to help you organize your plan.

Trade plans with a partner and discuss how the plans could be made clearer.

After you have finished revising your plan, make a final clean copy to display in the classroom.

PURPOSE To write a work plan
AUDIENCE Classmates
LENGTH One page

WRITING RUBRICS In order to write an effective work plan, you should
• write clear objectives
• list each task separately
• set realistic due dates
• organize the information in a clear, easy-to-read format

Public Service Announcements

A public service announcement or ad carries a message for a good cause. These ads are created by advertising agencies free of charge at the request of government agencies and nonprofit organizations. The ads are often published at no charge by media such as radio, TV, newspapers, and magazines. The model below is a script for a thirty-second radio spot created for the state police.

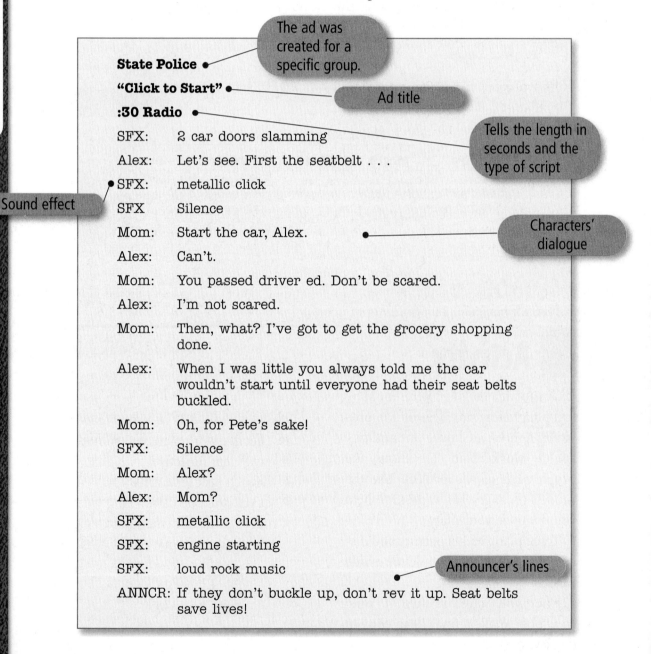

The ad was created for a specific group.

Ad title

Tells the length in seconds and the type of script

Sound effect

Characters' dialogue

Announcer's lines

State Police

"Click to Start"

:30 Radio

SFX:	2 car doors slamming
Alex:	Let's see. First the seatbelt . . .
SFX:	metallic click
SFX	Silence
Mom:	Start the car, Alex.
Alex:	Can't.
Mom:	You passed driver ed. Don't be scared.
Alex:	I'm not scared.
Mom:	Then, what? I've got to get the grocery shopping done.
Alex:	When I was little you always told me the car wouldn't start until everyone had their seat belts buckled.
Mom:	Oh, for Pete's sake!
SFX:	Silence
Mom:	Alex?
Alex:	Mom?
SFX:	metallic click
SFX:	engine starting
SFX:	loud rock music
ANNCR:	If they don't buckle up, don't rev it up. Seat belts save lives!

Types of Public Service Announcements

Public service announcements are written for a wide range of causes. Writers of these announcements use persuasive writing to make their messages convincing. The following are examples of public service messages: adopt a pet from the humane society; exercise for good health; stop smoking; don't do drugs.

There are three types of public service ads.

Broadcast ads include TV and radio commercials and announcements. TV ads rely on sights (visuals) and sounds. TV commercials are made up of action scenes to catch and hold the viewer's attention. Radio commercials rely on spoken dialogue and sound effects.

Outdoor ads are created for billboards, posters, and the sides of buildings. Billboards are only seen at a glance as people drive past, so the message uses large, eye-catching visuals and few words.

Print ads are found in magazines and newspapers. A headline catches the viewer's attention and a visual holds it. Print ads include a few lines of copy (text) to explain the message and to give other information the audience may need such as a phone number or location.

When you create a public service ad, you should always limit it to a single idea. Make that idea clear at first glance. Make your ad tell a story, as in the radio spot on page 344. Use persuasive writing to convince your audience to change an opinion or take action. You can persuade by example, as in the model radio script, or by including reasons to do something, as in the model print ad on page 346. Sometimes public service announcements are factual and serious in tone. For example, an announcement might show the effects of a car accident caused by a drunk driver. Other public service announcements use humor to deliver the message.

TYPES OF PUBLIC SERVICE ANNOUNCEMENTS

BROADCAST (TV AND RADIO)	OUTDOOR (BILLBOARDS AND POSTERS)	PRINT (NEWSPAPERS AND MAGAZINES)
Limit ad to fifteen or thirty seconds for TV, thirty or sixty seconds for radio.	Use colorful visuals.	Use a clever headline to get the audience's attention.
Check the timing of an ad by reading it aloud several times.	Let the picture tell the story at a glance.	Include pictures and copy.
Use persuasive writing to support a cause.	Keep the copy to a very few words.	Keep the copy brief and persuasive.
		Include information on how people can take action.

Public Service Announcements

Style

TV and radio commercials are written in script form, as shown in the model on page 344. Billboards, posters, and print ads are created as art to fit the size of the finished ad. Print ads are published in standard sizes, such as a full page, half page, and quarter page. The space you have for an ad will help you determine how many details and how much copy you can include.

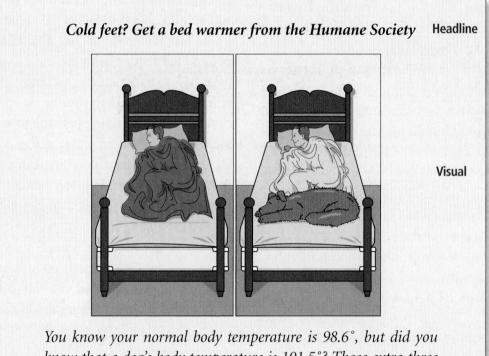

Cold feet? Get a bed warmer from the Humane Society **Headline**

Visual

You know your normal body temperature is 98.6°, but did you know that a dog's body temperature is 101.5°? Those extra three degrees are the reason the Inuits brought a dog or two into the igloo on frigid arctic nights. **Copy**

Now you can get your own personal igloo warmer (OOPS!) bed warmer from the Humane Society. The best friend bit is a bonus.

The Humane Society has three locations in Rock Creek. **Information on where to go and what to do**

Call 1-800-DOG-GONE

The Parts of a Public Service Ad

Public service ads have some or many of the following parts, depending on the medium used.

Headline A headline is a short, catchy statement designed to get attention. Both print and outdoor ads use headlines, but headlines on outdoor ads are even shorter than those on print ads.

Message The purpose of an ad is to carry a message to an audience. Each of the following parts helps to convey the message of an ad:

- headline
- copy (the written text in a print ad)
- visuals (any part of an ad that appeals to sight, such as pictures, artwork, movies, or animation)
- sound effects (in radio and TV ads)
- contact information (where to send a donation, what phone number to call, travel directions to a place)

Presentation Counts

In an ad, presentation is everything. If you are writing a TV or radio commercial, your story must unfold in a logical sequence to keep your audience watching or listening. In outdoor ads, your billboards must be eye-catching and deliver the message at a glance. In print advertising, your ad must first catch the audience's eye and then keep its interest with clever copy.

Activity

Work in a small group to choose a good cause for which you will create a public service announcement. Your ad may be a print ad, a poster, or a radio or television commercial. Decide which form is best for your announcement.

If you choose to create a print ad or a poster, you will want to start by making a sketch that shows the location of the headline, visual, and copy. When your ad is ready for publication, display it in the classroom.

If you choose to create a radio or television commercial, first write a script and read it aloud while timing it. It should fit a thirty- or sixty-second time slot. When your commercial is ready to be aired, play the final recording for the class.

PURPOSE	To create a public service ad
AUDIENCE	Teachers and students
LENGTH	Thirty- or sixty-second commercial, one-page print ad, or one poster

WRITING RUBRICS To create an effective public service announcement, you should

- keep your copy short and to the point
- include contact information
- use visuals that work well with your copy
- use precise wording
- proofread carefully

Newsletters

A newsletter is a publication that reports on topics of interest to a specific group. Newsletters are collections of articles and are often formatted in columns. The model below is from a newsletter sent to residents of a particular neighborhood.

The newsletter is for a specific group.

The articles report on items of interest to the group.

Walnut Acres Newsletter

A Newsletter for Residents of Walnut Acres

Volume 1, No. 3   October 20– –

Board Meeting Schedule

Following is the schedule for board meetings for the last three months of 2001. All meetings will be held at the community room in the public library from 7 P.M. to 10 P.M. Every homeowner is welcome to attend.

Monday, October 8
Tuesday, November 6
Monday, December 3

Snow Plow Contract Awarded

The board of directors has awarded a contract to Snowbusters, Inc., to plow our streets after each snowfall throughout the winter.

Walnut Acres Teenager to the Rescue!

Thirteen-year-old Demetra Koufalis of Hazelnut Street was walking by the north Walnut Acres entrance when a truck, eastbound on Hickory Road, veered out of control and demolished the entrance sign. The driver was not hurt, but he backed up over the sign and drove away.

Demetra memorized the license number of the truck and later identified the driver to the police.

Because of Demetra's great memory and quick thinking, the board was able to collect $534.98 from the driver to replace the sign. Thanks, Demetra!

President's Message

At the September meeting, the board of directors set the following goals for 2002:

- Establishing a garden committee to develop and maintain flowerbeds for the south and west entrances to Walnut Acres. Anyone who is interested in serving on this committee should call Janelle Whitmore at 987-0876.

- Purchasing and installing new playground equipment in the west park. To help with this project, call Josh Bernard at 987-4356.

- Hiring a lawn-cutting service for the park areas. Neighborhood teens are welcome to bid for this job. Call Steve Harms at 987-6545 for a complete job description and information on how to submit a bid.

The writer gives specific information, such as times and dates.

The writer includes contact information.

Types of Newsletters

Newsletters can be used to communicate information of interest to different audiences. Newsletters are published at regular intervals, such as weekly, monthly, or quarterly. How often a newsletter is published and how it is distributed depends on its purpose. A newsletter to keep employees aware of work progress might be published weekly and distributed by putting out a pile of copies in the room where workers take their breaks. A newsletter for stamp collectors might be published once a month and mailed to members' homes. A newsletter whose purpose is to give information on an annual event, such as an art fair, might only be published once a year and mailed to people who attended previous fairs.

You might regularly receive more than one newsletter, depending on what your interests and hobbies are.

When you create a newsletter, include factual information such as dates, times, and locations of meetings and events. Also include articles on topics of interest to your audience. Keep newsletter articles short and to the point. You can include graphics to illustrate articles.

TYPES OF NEWSLETTERS		
CLUB OR SPECIAL INTEREST GROUP	**EMPLOYEE**	**CUSTOMER**
Give the newsletter a name that reflects the purpose of the group, such as *Bits and Bytes* for a computer group.	Include dates, times, and details on events for employees, such as the company picnic.	Publish as a form of advertising for a business.
Publish the newsletter on a regular schedule.	Report news about employees, such as promotions, awards earned, retirement dinners, and new people in the company.	Send to customers or potential customers.
Include a calendar of club meetings and special events of interest to members.	Include photographs if possible.	Include information about special sales or store events.
Include a summary of the last group meeting.	Employees may be encouraged to produce the newsletter themselves.	Include a column of information useful to customers, such as household hints or safety tips.

Style

Newsletters are written as a series of articles. The articles can be laid out in columns, like a newspaper, or in a single column the width of the page. Headings are used to separate articles. Some newsletters are more formal than others. A newsletter published by a large corporation might be printed on glossy white paper, written in formal language, and be several pages long. A club newsletter might have a catchy name, be printed on brightly colored paper, and be written in a conversational tone.

A newsletter keeps the same style and organization of articles from issue to issue. For example, the masthead (box with the newsletter name) is always printed in the same style so that readers will recognize the newsletter on sight. The main column on the front page might always be a message from the club president, and the lower right corner of the front page might always be used for the meeting schedule.

Masthead

Trail Talk

The Newsletter of the Fresh Air Hiking Club for Teens

Volume and issue numbers

Volume 3, No. 4

Date of this issue *April 20--*

On the Trail
by Byron Brock

Articles

Last month five members of the Coventry Chapter walked the five-day route of the Painted Rock Trail through the Coventry Wilderness Area. The first day was very slow going because the trail was muddy from recent rains. On the second day, as we climbed higher, the trail became dry and views of the canyon below were spectacular. On the third day, we saw two black bears and a moose. In spite of the mud, I recommend this trail to experienced hikers.

Upcoming Club Hikes

The following backpack trips are open to all members. For more information or to sign up, call Tanya Smith at (877) 876-3939.

Trail	Dates
Redmond	April 6-8
Cling Peak	April 20-21
Black Creek	May 11-13

May Meeting Features Slide Show

Our May meeting will be held at 5:00 P.M. on May 27 in the Grange Hall at 594 Forest Street in Coventry. Andrew Lim, who hiked part of the Appalachian Trail last summer, will present a slide show entitled "Scenes of Appalachia." This meeting includes a potluck dinner. Bring your favorite trail dish and copies of the recipe.

Classified

Coleman Dual Fuel Backpack Lantern for sale. Good condition. Call Jeff at (734) 555-7477.

Lightweight tent for sale. Two-person dome with fly. Only used once. Best offer. Call Murph at (734) 555-8897.

Business & Technical Writing

The Parts of a Newsletter

The Masthead The masthead includes the following information:
- title of the newsletter
- volume number (The volume number represents a period of publication, such as one year. All newsletters published in the first year would be Volume 1. All newsletters published the next year would be Volume 2, and so on. A school newsletter might start a new volume when the school year begins in September.)
- issue number (Issues are numbered in order throughout a volume. The first issue of each volume would be number 1.)
- date

Articles Newsletters are divided into articles on different topics. Some topics appear regularly, such as a meeting schedule or a classified ad section.

Organization Counts

Your newsletter is more likely to be read if it looks interesting and is well organized. Some tips:
- Create your newsletter on a computer.
- Give each article a title.
- Use graphics or illustrations to add interest.
- For a one- or two-page newsletter, use a single sheet of 8½-by-11-inch paper.
- Jazz up your newsletter with colored paper.

Activity

Class Project: Create and publish a class or school newsletter.
- Divide the following jobs among teams and individuals: design a masthead, decide on a title, brainstorm for article ideas, interview subjects, write articles, edit articles, design graphics and illustrations, lay out the newsletter on a computer.
- Some things you might include in your newsletter are coming events, school news, cafeteria menus, lost and found items, and student essays.
- Edit and proofread your newsletter, publish it, and distribute it to students, parents, and teachers.

PURPOSE To create and publish a newsletter

AUDIENCE People interested in your school

LENGTH One page

WRITING RUBRICS In order to create an effective newsletter, you should
- give your newsletter an appropriate title
- create a layout that is both attractive and easy to read
- use visuals to enhance the messages of articles and features

Multimedia Presentations

In multimedia presentations multiple kinds of media are used to present a topic. A television commercial might be described as multimedia because it has both sights and sounds.

Types of Media

In a multimedia presentation, you use multiple sight and sound media to give your audience information on your topic. You can use such media as photos, slides, posters, diagrams, charts, videos, handouts, CDs, and audio cassettes. If presentation software is available, you can combine text, various graphics, and sounds on a computer "slide show."

Multimedia presentations can be used for many kinds of reports. You can make a multimedia presentation to inform your audience about a subject, to persuade an audience to take some action, or even to sell a product. The chart below gives examples of different kinds of media you might use. Begin by thinking of possible subjects. Think about each subject and how it could be presented with different types of media. What facts could be made into graphic organizers? What sounds are associated with the subject? Do research at the library or on the Internet to learn more about each possible subject. Search for facts, statistics, and expert opinions.

Once you choose a topic, you can contact experts on the subject by fax or e-mail. Experts can answer your questions and also give you quotations you can use to make your presentation stronger.

When making a sales presentation, you want to make your product as appealing as possible. For example, if you are trying

TYPES OF MEDIA		
VISUALS (SIGHTS)	**SOUND**	**OTHER OPTIONS**
Use a photograph or slide to make your subject clear.	Play a cassette or CD—of a bird's song or sounds of the ocean, for example—to help your audience hear your subject.	Appeal to your audience's sense of touch by having individuals handle an object such as a seashell or a snake's shed skin.
Give a demonstration of how something works.	Use background music to help create a mood.	If you are selling a food product, pass out samples to taste.
Make a video to show action and appeal to your audience's sense of hearing.	Add sound effects to a slide show.	
Use a series of slides to show a process.		
Make handouts of information you want your audience to have.		

to promote your new lawn-mowing service, you might make a series of slides that tell why your mowing service is better than your competitors' services. You could even add the sound of a lawn mower as a sound effect every time you change slides. You could conclude your presentation by giving the audience a handout showing your rates and information on how to contact you.

Style

- Keep each visual simple.
- Use large type for visuals. Experiment with type sizes in the room where you will present. See which type sizes would be visible from the back of the room.
- Do not crowd your visuals. Two type-faces and three colors are sufficient.
- Use the same border and background color on all your visuals to tie them together.

The Parts of a Multimedia Presentation

All multimedia presentations have three parts.

Introduction   Introduce your topic in a way that will attract your audience's attention by using sound or a visual, or both.

- Introduce yourself by saying something like, "I'm Mario, and my presentation will show you why you should use my mowing service to keep your yard looking its best."

- Use a transparency or a slide to show your thesis in headline form while you introduce yourself orally.
- Use music to set the mood; then introduce yourself and your thesis.
- Give a demonstration of a product while explaining who you are and what you are doing.

The Body   The body is the longest and most important part of your presentation. You explain your topic and support it with facts gathered from reliable sources, such as experts on the subject and encyclopedias and other reference books. Use media to present your facts and arguments in interesting ways. You can make sure your audience gets your message by allowing time for questions. You should try to think of possible questions in advance so that you can have extra facts and statistics ready to answer them.

Conclusion   Use the final few moments of your presentation to restate your thesis and sum up the most important points. Keep your conclusion brief. Thank your audience for their attention.

Presentation Counts

If you were Mario, you could begin by playing a short recording of a lawn mower and then saying, "That's the sound of your grass being mowed down to size by Mario's Mowing Service." Or you could present a video commercial showing your service in action.

Experiment with the order of your presentation on your family and friends until you find the most successful combination. Use humor when possible.

When it comes time to give your presentation, be enthusiastic, and your audience will be enthusiastic too.

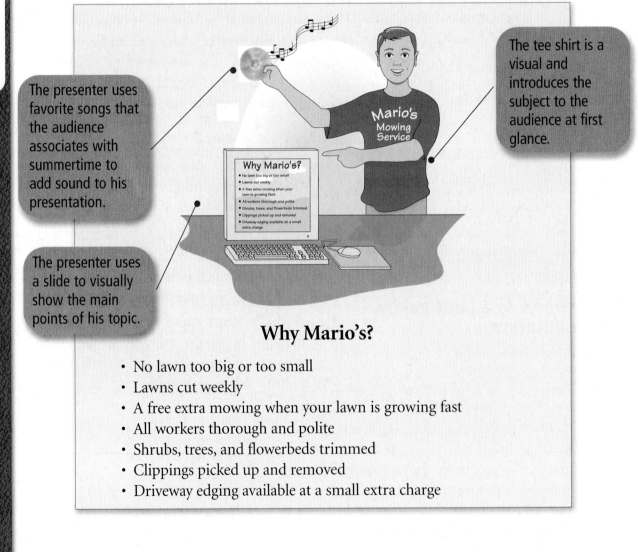

The presenter uses favorite songs that the audience associates with summertime to add sound to his presentation.

The tee shirt is a visual and introduces the subject to the audience at first glance.

The presenter uses a slide to visually show the main points of his topic.

Why Mario's?

- No lawn too big or too small
- Lawns cut weekly
- A free extra mowing when your lawn is growing fast
- All workers thorough and polite
- Shrubs, trees, and flowerbeds trimmed
- Clippings picked up and removed
- Driveway edging available at a small extra charge

Activity

As a class, use a video camera to make a multimedia commercial to sell a product or a service. Present your finished commercial to another class.

- Divide the class into working groups. Researchers can identify a product or a service, writers can write the script, and actors can star in the commercial. Other specialty jobs include set designers, prop persons, camera operators, and director.

- Include a description of all scenes in the script. You can find screenplay scripts in a library to show you how to do this. Specify how your commercial will include visuals and sounds.

- You may want to do a storyboard of your presentation. A storyboard includes rough sketches that show each shot of your movie as the shot should look on camera. You can combine storyboard and script into a single document that will vividly summarize your commercial.

- Before filming the commercial, review the script with your classmates. Discuss ways to rearrange the material to make the commercial more effective.

PURPOSE   To make a multimedia video commercial

AUDIENCE   Another class

LENGTH   Three minutes

WRITING RUBRICS In order to create an effective multimedia commercial, you should

- write an engaging script that will persuade the audience
- create and use visuals that will strengthen the message
- use reference materials as needed

Technology Tip

Presentation software allows you to combine text with sounds and graphics into a single production that can be shown on a computer monitor. Programs include a Help function that will help you create a presentation.

Tilly Willis, Sun Sea and Sand, 2003

"During the day the glass sun shimmered a beautiful yellow, the blue a much better color than the sky outside: deeper, like night."

—Alma Luz Villanueva,
"Golden Glass"

PART 2

Grammar, Usage, and Mechanics

UNIT
8

Subjects, Predicates, and Sentences

8.1 Kinds of Sentences

■ A **sentence** is a group of words that expresses a complete thought.

Different kinds of sentences have different purposes. A sentence can make a statement, ask a question, give a command, or express strong feeling. All sentences begin with a capital letter and end with a punctuation mark. The punctuation mark at the end of the sentence is determined by the purpose of that sentence.

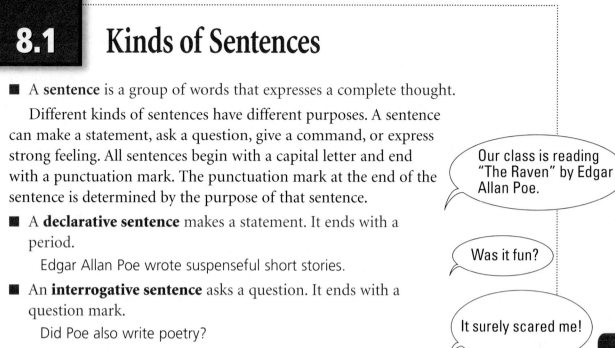

Our class is reading "The Raven" by Edgar Allan Poe.

■ A **declarative sentence** makes a statement. It ends with a period.

Edgar Allan Poe wrote suspenseful short stories.

Was it fun?

■ An **interrogative sentence** asks a question. It ends with a question mark.

Did Poe also write poetry?

It surely scared me!

■ An **exclamatory sentence** expresses strong feeling. It ends with an exclamation point.

What a great writer Poe was!

Read some of his other poems.

■ An **imperative sentence** gives a command or makes a request. It ends with a period.

Read "The Pit and the Pendulum."

Édouard Manet, Illustration to Poe's "The Raven," c. 1875

Subjects, Predicates, amd Semtences

Exercise 1   **Identifying Kinds of Sentences**

Write whether each sentence is *declarative, interrogative, exclamatory,* or *imperative.*

1. Edgar Allan Poe was born in Boston in 1809.
2. Did you know that Poe lost his parents at a very early age?
3. How awful that must have been!
4. The boy lived with his foster parents.
5. Wasn't his foster father a wealthy merchant?
6. Poe was raised in Richmond, Virginia.
7. He attended college briefly.
8. Did he enlist in the army?
9. I can't believe that he went to West Point!
10. Read a biography of Poe.
11. Didn't he also edit magazines?
12. What impressive writing Poe produced!
13. Poe was a master of the short story.
14. How greatly he influenced other writers!
15. Tell me what you think about his writing.
16. Poe died at the age of forty.
17. Isn't that very young?
18. How sad that his life was so short!
19. What a tragedy!
20. Find out more about Poe.

Exercise 2   **Capitalizing and Punctuating Sentences**

Write each sentence, adding capital letters and punctuation marks where needed.

1. is it true that Edgar Allan Poe wrote the first detective story
2. is private detective C. Auguste Dupin in one of Poe's tales
3. tell me if you have read Poe's famous poem about the raven
4. what a harrowing ending this poem has
5. Poe's writings are very popular in Europe
6. Did the young man go to college in Virginia
7. poe is also highly regarded for his literary criticism
8. he lived in Philadelphia during a part of his career
9. His writing includes mystery, suspense, fantasy, and humor
10. What a great adventure story "The Narrative of A. Gordon Pym" is

Sentences and Sentence Fragments

Every sentence has two parts: a subject and a predicate.

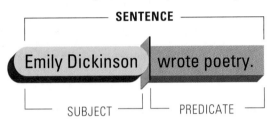

- The **subject part** of a sentence names whom or what the sentence is about.
- The **predicate part** of the sentence tells what the subject does or has. It can also describe what the subject is or is like.

A sentence must have both a subject and a predicate. It must also express a complete thought.

- A **sentence fragment** does not express a complete thought. It may also be missing a subject, a predicate, or both.

You often use fragments when talking with friends or writing personal letters. Some writers use sentence fragments to produce special effects. You should use complete sentences, however, in anything you write for school or business.

Correcting Sentence Fragments		
Fragment	**Problem**	**Sentence**
Her sister.	The fragment lacks a predicate. *What did her sister do?*	Her sister discovered the poems in her bureau.
Wrote about her emotions.	The fragment lacks a subject. *Who wrote about her emotions?*	This gifted poet wrote about her emotions.
Of meaning.	The fragment lacks both a subject and a predicate.	Her poems contain many layers of meaning.

Exercise 3   Identifying Sentences and Sentence Fragments

Write each sentence, underlining the subject part once and the predicate part twice. If it is a fragment, write *fragment* and explain why it is a fragment.

1. Emily Dickinson lived in Amherst, Massachusetts.
2. At her parents' home.
3. Few of her poems were published during her lifetime.
4. Considered one of the greatest American poets.
5. You should study her poems carefully.
6. Dickinson's sister collected her poems.
7. This famous poet.
8. Insisted on complete privacy.
9. Her poems reflect her intensely emotional nature.
10. Many readers are attracted to her highly original style.
11. Dickinson's poetry comments on all matters of life.
12. Wrote about love and beauty.
13. Dickinson analyzes her emotions poetically.
14. So much fine work.
15. Found a world of her own.
16. With clear, precise observation.
17. Her writing style gives every word weight.
18. Her poetry uses sharp phrases and rich imagery.
19. Most of her poems include original insights.
20. To every possible human concern.

Exercise 4   Correcting Sentence Fragments

Rewrite each sentence fragment to make it a complete sentence. Add a subject or a predicate or both.

1. Emily Dickinson author.
2. Lived from 1830 to 1886.
3. With clarity and style.
4. Began to retreat into herself at the age of twenty-three.
5. Moved quietly about the house.
6. Caught only glimpses of her.
7. In the nineteenth century.
8. Biographies of Dickinson.
9. Dickinson's poetry.
10. Observed the world and wrote about it.

8.3 Subjects and Predicates

A sentence consists of a subject and a predicate that together express a complete thought. Both a subject and a predicate may consist of more than one word.

Complete Subject	Complete Predicate
Dickens's **novels**	**are** still popular today.
My English **teacher**	**wrote** an article on Dickens.

- The **complete subject** includes all of the words in the subject of a sentence.
- The **complete predicate** includes all of the words in the predicate of a sentence.

Not all of the words in the subject or the predicate are of equal importance.

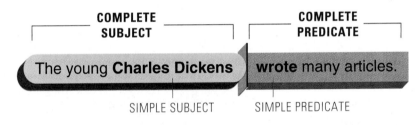

- The **simple subject** is the main or most important word or group of words in the complete subject.

The simple subject is usually a noun or a pronoun. A **noun** is a word that names a person, a place, a thing, or an idea. A **pronoun** is a word that takes the place of one or more nouns.

- The **simple predicate** is the main word or group of words in the complete predicate.

The simple predicate is always a verb. A **verb** is a word that expresses an action or a state of being.

Sometimes the simple subject is also the complete subject. Similarly, the simple predicate may also be the complete predicate.

Identifying Subjects and Predicates

Write each sentence. Draw a line between the complete subject and the complete predicate.

1. Charles Dickens's first works consisted of articles about life in London.
2. These early works appeared under the name of Boz.
3. Their popularity led to publication of *Pickwick Papers*.
4. That first novel was highly successful.
5. Dickens wrote for the rest of his life.
6. Dickens's early experiences influenced much of his writing.
7. His only historical novel is *A Tale of Two Cities*.
8. *David Copperfield* is one of his most popular books.
9. The novel *Martin Chuzzlewit* reflects Dickens's trip to America.
10. The author gave dramatic readings of his works.

Exercise 6   **Identifying Subjects and Predicates**

Write each item. Draw a vertical line between the complete subject and complete predicate. Underline the simple subject once and the simple predicate twice.

1. Charles Dickens wrote many great novels during his lifetime.
2. The English novelist remains a very popular writer.
3. He created memorable characters.
4. This very popular writer lived in poverty as a child.
5. Dickens lived with his family in London.
6. The youngster labored in a shoe polish factory at an early age.
7. The English courts sent Dickens's father to debtors' prison.
8. His family needed money then.
9. The young Dickens found work for a short while as a court stenographer.
10. He took notes at court for two years.
11. Dickens reported news for a local newspaper too.
12. He published short articles on life in London.
13. His writing appeared first under a different name.
14. The best early articles appeared in *Sketches by Boz*.
15. His first novel was *Pickwick Papers*.
16. Most Dickens novels appeared in installments in periodicals.
17. People waited eagerly for each new chapter.
18. Dickens edited two periodicals.
19. My favorite Dickens novel is *Hard Times*.
20. Dickens's own favorite novel was *David Copperfield*.

8.4 Identifying Subjects and Predicates

In most sentences, the subject comes before the predicate.

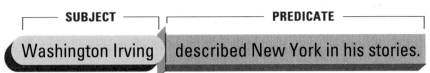

Other kinds of sentences, such as questions, begin with part or all of the predicate. The subject comes next, followed by the rest of the predicate.

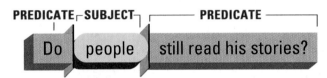

To locate the subject of a question, rearrange the words to form a statement.

Predicate	Subject	Predicate
Did	Irving	write many funny stories?
	Irving	did write many funny stories.

The predicate also precedes the subject in sentences with inverted word order and in declarative sentences that begin with *Here is, Here are, There is,* or *There are.*

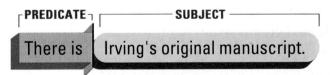

In requests and commands, the subject is usually not stated. The predicate is the entire sentence. The word *you* is understood to be the subject.

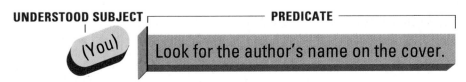

Subjects, Predicates, and Sentences

Exercise 7   **Identifying the Subject in Sentences**

Write the complete subject in each sentence. If the sentence is a command, write *(You)*.

1. Did Washington Irving achieve international fame?
2. Name two stories about Irving's childhood in New York.
3. There is a Washington Irving story with roots in German folklore.
4. Did Washington Irving live from 1783 to 1859?
5. Does Irving use a particular writing style in this tale?
6. Read Irving's satire on New York.
7. Examine Irving's humorous sketches of New York society first.
8. Did he write during his stay in England?
9. Did Irving devote himself completely to literature?
10. Has the class discussed his short story "The Legend of Sleepy Hollow"?
11. Here are Irving's two books on Columbus.
12. There are four books about his travels in Spain.
13. Study his style of writing.
14. Did Irving's *The Sketch Book* bring new importance to the short story?
15. Here is *The Sketch Book of Geoffrey Crayon.*
16. Do critics regard his short stories as his best achievement?
17. Discuss Irving's influence on other writers.
18. Here is a collection of his short stories.
19. There lies Irving's biography.
20. Did you read all of Irving's stories?

Exercise 8   **Identifying the Subjects and Predicates in Sentences**

Write each sentence. If the sentence is a command, write *(You)* before it. In each sentence, underline the complete subject once and the complete predicate twice.

1. Learn more about Washington Irving.
2. Was his life interesting?
3. Did Irving use the pen name Diedrich Knickerbocker?
4. There was *A History of New York* published under that name.
5. Find out the origin of his pen name.
6. Irving lived in Spain twice.
7. Was he interested in Spanish culture?
8. Did Irving represent the U.S. in Spain?
9. Tell about Irving's travels in the West.
10. Did Irving read his works to frontier audiences?

8.5 Compound Subjects and Compound Predicates

A sentence may have more than one simple subject or simple predicate.

■ A **compound subject** is two or more simple subjects that have the same predicate. The subjects are joined by *and, both . . . and, or, either . . . or, neither . . . nor,* or *but.*

COMPOUND SUBJECT

Charlotte Brontë and **Emily Brontë** were sisters.

When the two simple subjects are joined by *and* or by *both . . . and,* the compound subject is plural. Use the plural form of the verb to agree with this plural compound subject.

When the two simple subjects are joined by *or, either . . . or,* or *neither . . . nor,* however, the compound subject may be singular or plural. The verb must agree with the nearer simple subject.

> Either **Charlotte** or **Emily is** my favorite author.
> Neither **Charlotte** nor her **sisters were** outgoing.

In the first sentence, *Emily* is the nearer subject, and so the singular form of the verb is used. In the second sentence, *sisters* is the nearer subject, and so the plural form is used.

■ A **compound predicate** is two or more simple predicates, or verbs, that have the same subject. The verbs are connected by *and, both . . . and, or, either . . . or, neither . . . nor,* or *but.*

COMPOUND PREDICATE

Many students **read** the novel *Jane Eyre* and **enjoy** it.

The compound predicate in this sentence consists of *read* and *enjoy.* Both verbs agree with the plural subject. Notice the balanced, parallel structure of the verbs *read* and *enjoy.*

Exercise 9   **Identifying Compound Subjects and Predicates**

Write whether each sentence has a *compound subject* or a *compound predicate.*

 1. Either Charlotte or Emily Brontë will be the subject of my research paper entitled "A Great Nineteenth-century Novelist."
 2. Neither Anne nor Emily is as well known as Charlotte.
 3. Many readers have read and enjoyed their books.
 4. Some scholars buy or sell rare editions of their books.
 5. Neither the Brontë sisters nor their brother was long-lived.
 6. The Brontë sisters lived and wrote in Yorkshire, England.
 7. Charlotte's mother and sisters died early.
 8. Anne Brontë both wrote novels and worked as a governess.
 9. Scholars study and discuss the Brontës' novels.
10. Either *Wuthering Heights* or *Jane Eyre* is my favorite Brontë novel.

Exercise 10   **Making Subjects and Verbs Agree**

Write the correct form of the verb in parentheses.

 1. Neither Emily Brontë's poems nor her one novel (deserve, deserves) to be forgotten.
 2. Either *Wuthering Heights* or her poetic works (draw, draws) praise from critics everywhere.
 3. Her writing (show, shows) an understanding of people and (reveal, reveals) her love of England.
 4. Critics and other readers (discuss, discusses) and (praise, praises) her single novel.
 5. Critics or other readers (pay, pays) more attention to Charlotte Brontë's works.
 6. Charlotte's novel *Shirley* (paint, paints) a portrait of Emily and (show, shows) her feelings for her sister.
 7. Charlotte's novels (reflect, reflects) her life experiences and (reveal, reveals) her dreams.
 8. Both Anne Brontë's novel *Agnes Grey* and Charlotte's *The Professor* (tell, tells) love stories.
 9. Charlotte's novels *Shirley* and *Villette* (receive, receives) less attention today.
10. Neither Anne's *The Tenant of Wildfell Hall* nor Charlotte's *Shirley* (attract, attracts) many readers today.

Simple and Compound Sentences

■ A **simple sentence** has one subject and one predicate.

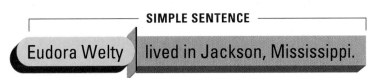

SIMPLE SENTENCE

Eudora Welty lived in Jackson, Mississippi.

A simple sentence may have a compound subject, a compound predicate, or both, as in the following example.

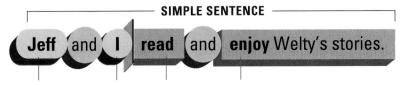

SIMPLE SENTENCE

Jeff and I read and enjoy Welty's stories.

COMPOUND SUBJECT   COMPOUND PREDICATE

■ A **compound sentence** is a sentence that contains two or more simple sentences joined by a comma and a coordinating conjunction or by a semicolon.

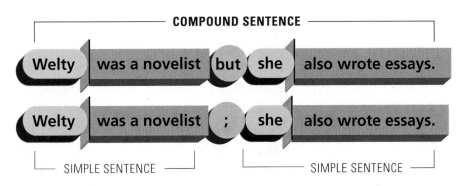

COMPOUND SENTENCE

Welty was a novelist but she also wrote essays.

Welty was a novelist ; she also wrote essays.

SIMPLE SENTENCE   SIMPLE SENTENCE

A run-on sentence is two or more sentences incorrectly written as one sentence. To correct a run-on, write separate sentences or combine the sentences as shown below.

Correcting Run-on Sentences	
Run-on	**Correct**
Welty wrote novels she wrote essays.	Welty wrote novels. **S**he wrote essays.
Welty wrote novels, she wrote essays.	Welty wrote novels, **and** she wrote essays.
	Welty wrote novels; she wrote essays.

Exercise 11   Identifying Simple and Compound Sentences

Write whether each sentence is *simple* or *compound*.

1. Elizabeth Barrett Browning and Robert Browning were poets.
2. They were famous for their poetry and their love.
3. Browning liked Elizabeth Barrett's poetry, and he wrote to her.
4. Elizabeth and Robert wrote hundreds of letters to each other.
5. Scholars and other people read and study these letters.
6. Elizabeth wanted to marry Robert, but her father forbade this.
7. The couple got married anyway, and they moved to Italy.
8. Her father never forgave her; he returned her letters unopened.
9. Elizabeth wrote love poems, and Robert wrote dramatic poems.
10. People still read and enjoy the couple's poems and letters.

Exercise 12   Identifying Simple, Compound, and Run-on Sentences

Write whether each sentence is *simple, compound,* or *run-on.* If it is a run-on sentence, rewrite it correctly.

1. Percy Bysshe Shelley lived and wrote in the nineteenth century.
2. He was a Romantic poet his wife, Mary Shelley, was a novelist.
3. Three of his poems are "Ozymandias," "Ode to a Skylark," and "Adonais."
4. *Frankenstein* was Mary Shelley's most famous novel.
5. Percy Shelley traveled in Europe and visited friends.
6. Shelley made friends with other poets; John Keats was Shelley's friend.
7. William Godwin was another friend, Shelley liked his daughter.
8. Mary Godwin and Percy Shelley met and fell in love.
9. Mary's father was a philosopher, her mother worked for women's rights.
10. Percy respected Mary's father and visited him often.
11. Percy and Mary married and went to continental Europe.
12. Mary and Percy were friendly with the poet Lord Byron.
13. Byron wrote long, beautiful poems; some of them are almost epic in scope.
14. Byron was one of the greatest Romantic poets students still study his work.
15. Byron, Keats, and Shelley were ranked together as great Romantic poets.
16. Poetry lovers and scholars read and discuss the men's poems.
17. I love Byron's lyrical poems, but some people prefer his satirical work.
18. *Childe Harold's Pilgrimage* and *Don Juan* are Byron's masterpieces.
19. Byron loved Greece, he traveled there.
20. He fell ill in Greece, and he died there.

Grammar Review

SUBJECTS, PREDICATES, AND SENTENCES

Russell Baker wrote about his early life in the memoir *Growing Up*. In this excerpt, he describes his reaction to having his work read publicly for the first time. The passage has been annotated to show some examples of the kinds of subjects, predicates, and sentences covered in this unit. Notice how he uses fragments for special effect.

Literature Model

from **Growing Up**
by Russell Baker

"Now boys," he said, "I want to read you an essay. This is titled 'The Art of Eating Spaghetti.'"
And he started to read. My words! He was reading *my words* out loud to the entire class. What's more, the entire class was listening. Listening attentively. Then somebody laughed, then the entire class was laughing, and not in contempt and ridicule, but with openhearted enjoyment. Even Mr. Fleagle stopped two or three times to repress a small prim smile. . . .
For the first time, light shone on a possibility. It wasn't a very heartening possibility, to be sure. Writing couldn't lead to a job after high school, and it was hardly honest work, but Mr Fleagle had opened a door for me. . . .
My mother was almost as delighted as I when I showed her Mr. Fleagle's A-Plus and described my triumph. Hadn't she always said I had a talent for writing?

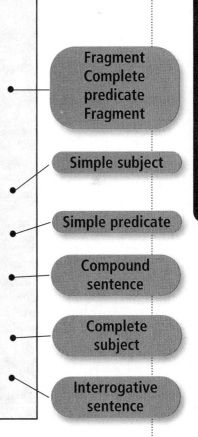

Fragment
Complete
predicate
Fragment

Simple subject

Simple predicate

Compound
sentence

Complete
subject

Interrogative
sentence

Grammar Review

Review: Exercise 1 **Identifying Sentences and Sentence Fragments**

Write each sentence and draw a line between the complete subject and the complete predicate. If it is a fragment, write *fragment,* and explain why it is a fragment.

SAMPLE Said he could write.
ANSWER fragment; no subject

1. Baker wrote an essay about eating spaghetti.
2. Mr. Fleagle read the essay out loud.
3. The entire class.
4. Laughed with genuine and honest good humor.
5. The author ranked Mr. Fleagle as one of the finest teachers.
6. He showed his mother the A-Plus on his paper.
7. Baker's proud mother.
8. Didn't think writing would lead to a job after high school.
9. This experience opened a door for him.
10. Baker's newspaper column is read by millions of people.

Review: Exercise 2 **Identifying Complete Subjects and Complete Predicates**

Write each sentence. Underline the complete subject once and the complete predicate twice.

SAMPLE The class studied English with Mr. Fleagle.
ANSWER <u>The class</u> <u>studied English with Mr. Fleagle.</u>

1. Mr. Fleagle assigned the class an informal essay.
2. This form of writing seemed dull to Russell Baker.
3. A homework sheet listed a choice of topics.
4. Russell Baker chose "The Art of Eating Spaghetti."
5. That title brought up memories.
6. The young boy remembered a spaghetti dinner.
7. Not many people ate spaghetti in those days.
8. The family talked about this exotic dish.
9. Everyone had a good time that night.
10. Russell wrote about their funny arguments.

Review: Exercise 3   **Identifying Simple Subjects and Simple Predicates**

Write the simple subject and the simple predicate for each sentence.

SAMPLE   Russell Baker wanted a career in newspapers.
ANSWER   Russell Baker wanted

1. The author began his career in journalism in 1947.
2. The *Baltimore Sun* hired the young journalist.
3. He joined the *New York Times* in 1954.
4. The new *Times* reporter covered the White House and Congress.
5. Baker started his "Observer" column in 1962.
6. The award winner received the Pulitzer Prize in 1979.
7. His columns appear in several collections.
8. Baker's humor entertains millions of people.
9. The writer became a television host.
10. Watchers of *Masterpiece Theater* enjoy Baker's introductions to the show.

Review: Exercise 4   **Identifying Subjects and Predicates in Questions**

Rewrite each question to form a statement. Then underline each complete subject once and each complete predicate twice.

SAMPLE   Was the story about spaghetti?
ANSWER   The story was about spaghetti.

1. Had Baker's mother encouraged his writing skills?
2. Did Baker's teacher like his essay?
3. Did the class enjoy the essay?
4. Was the class laughing at Baker's story?
5. Did everyone like the essay?
6. Did Baker get an A-Plus on his paper?
7. Did this experience give Baker ideas about a career?
8. Had Mr. Fleagle opened a door for Baker?
9. Was Mr. Fleagle one of the finest teachers in Baker's school?
10. Was Baker's mother pleased with her son?

Grammar Review

Review: Exercise 5   **Identifying Subjects and Predicates**

Write the simple subject and the simple predicate in each sentence. If the sentence is a command, write *(You)*.

SAMPLE   Was Russell Baker born in Virginia?
ANSWER   Russell Baker   was born

1. Find out about Baker's early life.
2. Was Baker's father a stonemason?
3. Did his mother teach school?
4. Was Baker's sister named Doris?
5. Here is a picture of Baker's family.
6. Point to Baker in the picture.
7. Did Baker win a college scholarship?
8. Tell the name of his college.
9. There are many books by Russell Baker.
10. Read *Growing Up.*

Review: Exercise 6   **Identifying Compound Subjects and Compound Predicates**

Write whether the sentence has a *compound subject* or a *compound predicate*.

SAMPLE   The cook boils spaghetti and adds sauce.
ANSWER   compound predicate

1. Russell Baker and his family ate spaghetti one night.
2. They enjoyed the food and argued about technique.
3. Both children and adults like spaghetti.
4. People all over the world prepare and eat pasta.
5. The Italians created and named dozens of different types of pasta.
6. The Chinese and the Japanese use noodles in many dishes.
7. My family and I eat ziti often.
8. Mom boils the ziti and covers it with sauce.
9. She adds cheese and bakes the ziti.
10. My sister and I wait with our forks ready!

Review: Exercise 7 **Making Compound Subjects and Verbs Agree**

Write the correct form of the verb in parentheses.

1. Russell Baker's wisdom or his humor (attract, attracts) readers.
2. Critics and other readers (praise, praises) his autobiography.
3. *Growing Up* or his other books (earn, earns) him fame.
4. Baker's childhood memories and stories (create, creates) a picture of his family.
5. His family and his life (interest, interests) readers.
6. His words and his voice (affect, affects) and (delight, delights) people.
7. His newspaper columns or his television appearances (win, wins) praise.
8. Critics or other viewers (enjoy, enjoys) his commentaries.
9. His columns and poems (appear, appears) regularly and (sell, sells) well.
10. The George Polk Award or the Pulitzer Prize (prove, proves) his worth.

Review: Exercise 8 **Identifying Simple and Compound Sentences**

Write whether each sentence is *simple* or *compound*.

1. Russell Baker began his journalism career at the age of eight; his mother got him a job.
2. He and his mother met and talked to a man from Curtis Publishing Company.
3. The man liked Russell, and he hired the boy.
4. Russell began his career at the bottom; he sold the *Saturday Evening Post.*
5. Russell placed the magazines in a bag and walked to a busy intersection.
6. He stood on a corner and waited for customers.
7. Russell waited for hours, but no one bought a single magazine.
8. Russell's mother was upset by this, and she taught Russell about salesmanship.
9. Russell's uncle felt sorry for the boy and bought a magazine.
10. Russell handed him a magazine, and Uncle Allen paid Russell a nickel.

| Review: Exercise 9 | Identifying Compound Sentences and Run-on Sentences |

Write whether each sentence is *compound* or *run-on.* If it is a run-on sentence, rewrite it correctly.

1. Russell Baker's mother wanted him to do well, and she encouraged him to study.
2. She didn't have much money, but she bought books and literary magazines for Russell.
3. Russell wasn't interested in literature he never read the books.
4. The magazines didn't appeal to him, he didn't read them either.
5. Russell's friend Charlie applied to Johns Hopkins University; he encouraged Russell to apply also.
6. Russell's family couldn't afford college, but Charlie told him about scholarships.
7. Russell applied for a scholarship to Johns Hopkins he didn't expect to get it.
8. Many students wanted scholarships they had to pass an exam.
9. The exam lasted four hours, and Russell worried about passing it.
10. Two weeks later a letter came from Johns Hopkins, Russell had won the scholarship.

| Review: Exercise 10 | Writing Compound Sentences |

Combine each pair of simple sentences to form a compound sentence. Use the coordinating conjunction *and, but,* or *or.*

1. Russell Baker grew up in Baltimore. His first job was with a Baltimore newspaper.
2. Baker dreaded Mr. Fleagle's reaction. Mr. Fleagle liked Baker's story very much.
3. Mr. Fleagle read Baker's story to the class. The class enjoyed it.
4. Baker could have covered his ears. He could have left the room.
5. Baker needed a real job. He loved to write anyway.

Review: Exercise 11

Proofreading

The following passage is about American artist Joseph Raffael, whose work appears below. Rewrite the passage, correcting the errors in spelling, capitalization, grammar, and usage. Add any missing punctuation. There are ten errors.

Joseph Raffael, *Joseph and Reuben,* 1984

Joseph Raffael

¹Joseph Raffael is an american artist known for his brightly colored paintings of landscapes, fish, flowers, and birds. ²In the painting on the previous page, however, Raffael has took a different approach. ³Its a portrait of the artist and his son, who appear as if they were posing. ⁴For a photograph

⁵The strong contrast between light and dark in the painting add to the effect and give it the accidental quality of a snapshot. ⁶Raffael is experimanting with the different qualities of light and color. ⁷The colors—from the warm yellow to the deep purple—are as much the subject of the painting as the artist and his' son. ⁸What a dramatic portrait this is

---

Review: Exercise 12

Mixed Review

Identify the underlined words as *complete* or *simple subjects* or *complete* or *simple predicates*. Write *C* beside any compound subjects or predicates.

1. Russell Baker <u>showed his talent in high school.</u>
2. His English <u>teacher</u> assigned the class an essay.
3. <u>Baker and the other students</u> had a choice of topics.
4. Baker <u>chose and wrote about the topic "The Art of Eating Spaghetti."</u>
5. <u>Another title for Baker's essay</u> might have been "How Not to Eat Spaghetti."
6. Baker's <u>teacher</u> returned everyone's paper but Baker's.
7. Mr. Fleagle <u>read</u> Baker's essay to the class.
8. <u>Mr. Fleagle's encouragement and support</u> gave Baker food for thought.
9. <u>The young writer</u> liked to make people laugh.
10. He <u>thought</u> about journalism as a career.
11. Journalism <u>couldn't lead to a job and wasn't honest work.</u>
12. Many people <u>write for a career.</u>
13. <u>Both magazines and newspapers</u> use many writers.
14. Newspaper reporters <u>gather information and write articles.</u>
15. <u>Columnists such as Russell Baker</u> present their opinions and ideas to the readers.
16. <u>Writers</u> for magazines write articles on a wide variety of topics.
17. Other writers <u>create</u> books of fiction and nonfiction.
18. Some writers <u>combine words with photography and create photo essays.</u>
19. <u>All these possibilities</u> are open to a young writer.
20. Russell Baker <u>finally realized his luck.</u>

Writing Application

TIME

For more about the writing process, see **TIME Facing the Blank Page,** pp. 97-107.

Sentence Patterns in Writing

Maya Angelou varies both the length and the organization of her sentences in this passage from *The Heart of a Woman.* Pay particular attention to the sentence structure.

> I had worked two months for the SCLC, sent out tens of thousands of letters and invitations signed by Rev. King, made hundreds of statements in his name, but I had never seen him up close. He was shorter than I expected and so young. He had an easy friendliness, which was unsettling. Looking at him in my office, alone, was like seeing a lion sitting down at my dining-room table. . . .

Techniques with Sentence Patterns

Try to apply some of Maya Angelou's techniques when you write and revise your own work.

❶ Mix short and long sentences to create variety. Compare the following:

REPETITIVE SENTENCE PATTERN
He had an easy friendliness. It was unsettling. I looked at him in my office. It was like seeing a lion sitting down at my dining-room table.

IMPROVED VERSION He had an easy friendliness, which was unsettling. Looking at him in my office, alone, was like seeing a lion sitting down at my dining-room table. . . .

❷ Combine two simple sentences into one compound sentence to communicate related ideas:

CHOPPY VERSION I had made hundreds of statements in his name. I had never seen him up close.

IMPROVED VERSION I had made hundreds of statements in his name, but I had never seen him up close.

Subjects, Predicates, and Sentences

Practice Revise the following passage on a separate sheet of paper. Pay particular attention to the underlined words.

Last year my dad made some shelves for my rock collection. <u>I watched as he cut the wood. Then he sanded it.</u> Perched on top of some old boxes, <u>I could feel the vibrations of the saw. I watched it slice through each length of wood.</u> Buzzing filled the room. Sawdust piled up like blonde snow. <u>The sawdust was under the workbench. I wanted to help. Dad said why didn't I just keep him company.</u> So I told him stories <u>about my rocks. I described</u> where they came from. It was a special time together.

Writing Online | For more grammar practice, go to **glencoe.com** and enter QuickPass code WC87703p2.

Writing Application **379**

UNIT 9

Nouns

9.1 Kinds of Nouns

Look at the incomplete sentence below. Decide which of the words in the box that follows can complete the sentence.

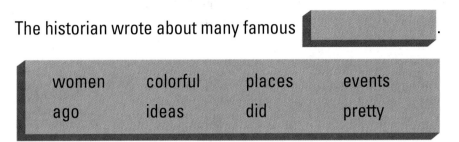

The words *women, ideas, places,* and *events* can complete the sentence. These words are called nouns.

■ A **noun** is a word that names a person, place, thing, or idea.

There are two basic kinds of nouns: proper nouns and common nouns.

■ A **proper noun** names a *specific* person, place, thing, or idea.

■ A **common noun** names *any* person, place, thing, or idea.

The first word and all other important words in proper nouns are capitalized.

Common nouns can be either concrete or abstract.

■ **Concrete nouns** name things that you can see or touch.

■ **Abstract nouns** name ideas, qualities, or feelings that cannot be seen or touched.

Kinds of Nouns		
Proper	**Common**	
	Concrete	**Abstract**
Supreme Court	document	truth
Queen Victoria	crown	courage
December	snow	time
Museum of Anthropology	museum	history
Native American	buffalo	heritage

Exercise 1 **Identifying Common and Proper Nouns**

Write each noun that appears in the following sentences. Indicate whether each is a *common noun* or a *proper noun*. Remember to capitalize each proper noun.

1. A baby named isabella began life in slavery in the united states.
2. Slavery was allowed in the united states before the civil war.
3. Isabella worked very hard as a child.
4. The slaveholder chose a husband for isabella.
5. Isabella had thirteen children.
6. Isabella later became a free person.
7. Then isabella took the name sojourner truth.
8. This brave crusader worked for the freedom of women and african americans.
9. Sojourner truth traveled around the country.
10. Sojourner talked about the evils of slavery.
11. The brave woman spoke to large numbers of people in many states.
12. The speaker faced danger on many occasions.
13. Sojourner truth became famous as a result of her many speeches.
14. Sojourner met with president abraham lincoln at the white house.
15. After her visit with the president, sojourner stayed in washington, d.c.
16. She worked to improve conditions for african americans in the city.
17. She helped find work for other people who had once been enslaved and had come to washington.
18. Like sojouner truth, harriet tubman was also born in slavery in maryland.
19. Harriet tubman led her people to freedom on the underground railroad.
20. Sojourner truth and harriet tubman were important women in history.

Exercise 2 **Identifying Concrete and Abstract Nouns**

Write *abstract* or *concrete* for each underlined noun.

1. Born in <u>slavery</u>, Frederick Douglass escaped and fled to Massachusetts.
2. In 1841 he addressed a meeting and talked about <u>freedom</u>.
3. After he spoke, he was hired to talk to other <u>groups</u>.
4. It took <u>courage</u> for him to speak out as he did.
5. After his <u>autobiography</u> was published in 1845, he went to England.
6. When he returned, he continued to talk about his <u>beliefs</u>.
7. He helped <u>men, women,</u> and <u>children</u> flee to Canada.
8. Frederick Douglass is honored by many <u>people</u> in this <u>country</u>.
9. Douglass's books are appreciated for their <u>honesty</u>.
10. He was an important <u>person</u> in the <u>history</u> of the United States.

9.2 Compound Nouns

The noun *storybook* is made up of two words: *story* and *book*. Such a noun is called a compound noun.

■ **Compound nouns** are nouns made of two or more words.

A compound noun can be one word, like *storybook*; more than one word, like *ice cream*; or joined by hyphens, like *runner-up*.

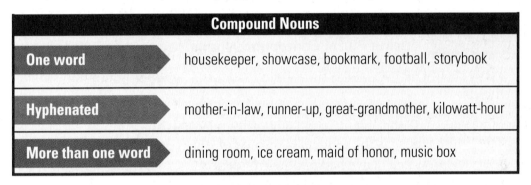

Compound Nouns	
One word	housekeeper, showcase, bookmark, football, storybook
Hyphenated	mother-in-law, runner-up, great-grandmother, kilowatt-hour
More than one word	dining room, ice cream, maid of honor, music box

To form the plural of compound nouns written as one word, add *-s* or *-es*. To form the plural of compound nouns that are hyphenated or written as more than one word, make the most important part of the compound noun plural.

Forming Plural Compound Nouns		
	Singular	**Plural**
One word	Add **-s** to most words. Add **-es** to words that end in **ch, sh, s,** or **x.** Exception:	football**s**, headlight**s** strongbox**es**, rosebush**es** passer**s**by
Hyphenated	Make the most important part of the compound noun plural.	great-grandmother**s**, runner**s**-up, mother**s**-in-law
More than one word	Make the most important part of the compound noun plural.	maid**s** of honor, music box**es**

Whether the compound noun is singular or plural, the verb must agree with it.

My sister-in-law **writes** books. My sisters-in-law **write** books.

Exercise 3 — Making Compound Nouns Plural

Write the plural form of each compound noun below.

1. lifeguard
2. vice-principal
3. golf club
4. master-at-arms
5. sweet potato
6. father-in-law
7. sheepskin
8. window sash
9. president-elect
10. clubhouse
11. textbook
12. police station
13. passerby
14. roller skate
15. headache
16. music box
17. flight deck
18. great-grandson
19. driving range
20. drugstore

Exercise 4 — Using Plural Compound Nouns

Write each sentence, using the plural form of the compound noun in parentheses.

1. Voters go to (ballot box) to determine who is president.
2. The White House is the residence for each of our (commander in chief).
3. All (vice president) have had another residence.
4. Many (sergeant-at-arms) guard the White House.
5. John Adams was the first of the (chief executive) to live there.
6. (Sightseer) flock to the White House.
7. (Editor in chief) of newspapers must show passes to enter the White House.
8. President Franklin D. Roosevelt had small (swimming pool) added to the residence.
9. Under President John F. Kennedy, (guidebook) to the building's history were published.
10. Presidents can have daily (workout) in the gymnasium.
11. (Grandparent) sometimes visit the White House.
12. Overnight visitors sleep in (guest room) on the second floor.
13. In 1908 a meeting on the conservation of (natural resource) was held in the White House.
14. Many of the visitors to the White House are (jobholder).
15. In the West Wing are (workplace) for the president's staff.
16. Once a week the Cabinet, a group of (policymaker), gathers for a meeting.
17. Some presidents asked their daughters or (daughter-in-law) to serve as hostesses.
18. A meeting of (mapmaker) was held in the map room, a private area.
19. At the White House, no (shortcut) are taken where security is concerned.
20. (Political scientist) study how the White House operates.

9.3 Possessive Nouns

A noun can be singular, naming only one person, place, thing, or idea; or it can be plural, naming two or more. A noun can also show ownership or possession of things or qualities. This kind of noun is called a possessive noun.

■ A **possessive noun** names who or what owns or has something.

Possessive nouns can be common nouns or proper nouns. They can also be singular or plural. Notice the possessive nouns in the following sentences:

Rita has a book on history.
Rita's book is new.

Read the **books**.
Note the **books'** major themes.

Possessive nouns are formed in one of two ways. To form the possessive of most nouns, you add an apostrophe and *-s ('s)*. This is true for all singular nouns and for plural nouns not ending in *-s*. To form the possessive of plural nouns already ending in *-s*, you add only an apostrophe. These rules are summarized in the chart below.

Forming Possessive Nouns		
Nouns	**To Form Possessive**	**Examples**
Most singular nouns	Add an apostrophe and **-s** (**'s**).	a girl—a girl**'s** name a country—a country**'s** products
Singular nouns ending in **-s**	Add an apostrophe and **-s** (**'s**).	Lewis—Lewis**'s** explorations Chris—Chris**'s** homework
Plural nouns ending in **-s**	Add an apostrophe (**'**).	animals—animals**'** habits the Joneses—the Joneses**'** car
Plural nouns not ending in **-s**	Add an apostrophe and **-s** (**'s**).	women—women**'s** history children—children**'s** history

Nouns

Forming Possessive Nouns

Write the possessive form of each underlined word or group of words.

1. <u>Queen Elizabeth</u> reign
2. <u>documents</u> pages
3. <u>Arizona</u> landscape
4. <u>citizens</u> rights
5. <u>Dickens</u> work
6. <u>people</u> choice
7. <u>King Charles</u> laws
8. <u>women</u> rights
9. <u>city</u> law
10. <u>children</u> books
11. <u>artists</u> works
12. <u>birds</u> nests
13. <u>car</u> engine
14. <u>New England</u> weather
15. <u>democracy</u> benefits
16. <u>whales</u> bones
17. <u>Cape Cod</u> bicycle trails
18. <u>song</u> refrain
19. <u>book</u> theme
20. <u>Andy Warhol</u> soup cans

Exercise 6 **Using Possessive Nouns**

For each sentence, write the correct possessive form of the noun in parentheses.

1. Meriwether Lewis was one of (Virginia) famous people.
2. He shared many (children) love of exploring.
3. Lewis served as President (Jefferson) personal secretary.
4. Jefferson guided (Lewis) preparations for an expedition.
5. Lewis and William Clark explored the (nation) uncharted territory.
6. Lewis depended on (Clark) skill at map making.
7. The (expedition) route ran through the Louisiana Territory and the Oregon region.
8. With the (Native Americans) help, they were able to cross the Rocky Mountains.
9. The team spent more than two (years) time in the Northwest.
10. They followed the Columbia (River) waters to the Pacific Ocean.
11. The (explorers) friends in St. Louis thought they had died on their trek.
12. The (men) bravery won great praise.
13. Later John Charles Frémont followed in Lewis and (Clark) footsteps.
14. (Frémont) explorations took him to Oregon, Nevada, and California.
15. He inspired Americans to oppose (Mexico) control of California.
16. He served as (California) U.S. Senator from 1850–1851.
17. In 1856 he became the Republican (Party) first candidate for president.
18. In the Civil War, he commanded one of the Union (Army) departments.
19. Strongly antislavery, he took over (slaveholders) lands in Missouri.
20. Frémont was married to (Thomas Hart Benton) daughter.

Distinguishing Plurals, Possessives, and Contractions

Most plural nouns, most possessive nouns, and certain contractions end with the letter -s. As a result, they sound alike and can be easily confused. Their spellings and meanings are different, however.

Noun Forms and Contraction		
	Example	**Meaning**
Plural Noun	The **students** wrote a play.	more than one student
Plural Possessive Noun	The **students'** play is good.	the play of the students
Singular Possessive Noun	I saw the **student's** play.	the play of one student
Contraction	The **student's** the author.	The student is the author.

■ A **contraction** is a word made by combining two words into one and leaving out one or more letters. An apostrophe shows where the letters have been omitted.

In the sentence *Naomi's participating in the science fair,* the word *Naomi's* is a contraction. It is made by combining the singular proper noun *Naomi* and the verb *is.* The apostrophe takes the place of the letter *i.* The contraction *Naomi's* sounds the same and is spelled the same as the singular possessive form of the proper noun *Naomi.*

Possessive Nouns and Contractions		
	Example	**Meaning**
Possessive	**Naomi's** exhibit is about bone fractures.	the exhibit prepared by Naomi
Contraction	**Naomi's** participating in the science fair.	Naomi is participating.

Forming Possessives and Contractions

Write each sentence, adding apostrophes to the possessive nouns and the contractions.

1. Woodrow Wilson was Americas twenty-eighth president.
2. As a student at Princeton, he joined the schools debating society.
3. Before becoming president, he served as Princeton Universitys president.
4. Wilsons regarded today as an educational and political reformer.
5. He was elected New Jerseys governor in 1910.
6. His success in New Jersey brought him to the Democrats attention.
7. Wilsons first term of office as president began in 1913.
8. The wars outbreak in Europe kept his attention on foreign affairs.
9. During his second term, he helped make the peace among Europes powers.
10. He had a stroke and was not able to fight for the peace treatys acceptance.

Exercise 8   **Using Plurals, Possessives, and Contractions**

Write the word in parentheses that correctly completes each sentence.

1. Herman (Melville's, Melvilles) a great American writer.
2. Herman (Melville's, Melvilles) life was full of adventure.
3. Melville traveled on sailing (ships, ship's) as a young man.
4. The (sailor's, sailors') lives were full of challenges.
5. Did Melville keep a record of his (experience's, experiences)?
6. Melville began his (adventures', adventures) as a cabin boy in 1837.
7. The young (man's, mans') destination was Liverpool.
8. (Liverpool's, Liverpools') an important city in Great Britain.
9. Special ships hunted (whales', whales) at this time.
10. These whaling (ships', ships) crews searched the world for whales.
11. (Whales, Whales') blubber provided many products.
12. (Nantucket's, Nantuckets) wealth depended on trade in whale products.
13. You can still visit the whaling (captains, captains') beautiful homes there.
14. Melville joined a whaling (ships, ship's) crew in 1841.
15. He visited the beautiful (islands, islands') of the Pacific Ocean.
16. Melville wrote (books', books) about his experience.
17. The public enjoyed this (writers', writer's) work.
18. In his masterpiece, *Moby Dick,* (sailors, sailors') hunt a great white whale.
19. The book describes the (dangers, dangers') of life aboard a whaling ship.
20. At the time, few people appreciated the (books, book's) power.

9.5 Collective Nouns

■ A **collective noun** names a group that is made up of individuals.

Collective Nouns			
committee family flock	audience team class	swarm crowd jury	club orchestra herd

Nouns and verbs always must show agreement in sentences. Collective nouns, however, present special agreement problems. Every collective noun can have either a singular meaning or a plural meaning. If you speak about the group as a unit, then the noun has a singular meaning. If you want to refer to the individual members of the group, then the noun has a plural meaning.

> The **crowd cheers** the passing parade. [refers to group as a unit, singular]
>
> The **crowd move** to their favorite spots along the parade route. [individual members, plural]

When you are thinking of the group as a unit, use a collective noun and the form of the verb that agrees with a singular noun. When you want to refer to the individual members of the group, use the collective noun and the form of the verb that agrees with a plural noun.

To help you determine whether a collective noun in a sentence is singular or plural, substitute the word *it* for the collective noun and any words used to describe it. If the sentence still makes sense, the collective noun is singular. If you can substitute they, the collective noun is plural.

> The **team** works on its project. [it, singular]
>
> The **team** work on their separate projects. [they, plural]

The **crowd move** to their favorite spots.

The **crowd cheers.**

Exercise 9 — Identifying Singular and Plural Collective Nouns

For each sentence, write the collective noun. Write *singular* or *plural* to describe it.

1. The group received first place in the competition.
2. The crowd in the club danced the entire night.
3. The gaggle of geese made a tremendous racket.
4. The students were given a range of choices on the test.
5. After the program, the band played an encore.
6. The family received a memento of the event.
7. The jury returned to their seats.
8. Company came to dinner last night.
9. A majority of the players voted to cancel the game.
10. The infantry fought from a dangerous position.

Exercise 10 — Using Collective Nouns

For each sentence, write the collective noun. Then write the correct form of the verb in parentheses.

1. The class of seventh-graders (describes, describe) their vacations.
2. The entire class (meets, meet) at 2:00 p.m. every day.
3. The family (takes/take) their biggest towels with them to the beach.
4. The film club (devours/devour) its popcorn in the darkened theater.
5. Girl Scout Troop 39 (presents, present) a tribute to athletes.
6. The committee (argues, argue) among themselves over the suggestion.
7. The audience (cheers, cheer) its favorite contestants.
8. The orchestra (performs, perform) my favorite symphony.
9. The football team (eats/eat) its pregame meal in silence.
10. The herd (returns, return) to the same meadow each year.
11. The crowd of students (claps, clap) their hands to the music.
12. The public (supports, support) its local basketball team.
13. The whole wolf pack (roams, roam) the countryside.
14. The audience (shows/show) its approval by clapping and whistling.
15. The jury (reaches, reach) its verdict.
16. The battalion (marches, march) five miles each day.
17. The majority of stockholders (demands/demand) their ballots.
18. That family (takes, take) their responsibilities very seriously.
19. The whole litter (is, are) being given away to another family.
20. The flock of geese (grooms/groom) their feathers after the rain.

9.6 Appositives

■ An **appositive** is a noun that is placed next to another noun to identify it or add information about it.

> James Madison's wife **Dolley** was a famous first lady.

The noun *Dolley* adds information about the noun *wife* by giving the wife's name. *Dolley* in this sentence is an appositive.

■ An **appositive phrase** is a group of words that includes an appositive and other words that describe the appositive.

> Madison, **our fourth president**, held many other offices.

The words *our fourth* describe the appositive *president.* The phrase *our fourth president* is an appositive phrase. It adds information about the noun *Madison.*

An appositive or appositive phrase must appear next to the noun that it identifies.

> **Our fourth president**, Madison held many other offices.
>
> Many historians have studied the life of Madison, **our fourth president**.

An appositive phrase is usually set off from the rest of the sentence with one or more commas. If, however, the appositive is needed to identify the noun or if it is a single word, you do not use commas.

> Madison's friend **Thomas Jefferson** was president before him.
>
> Madison's father, **James Madison**, was a plantation owner.

Since Madison had more than one friend, the name *Thomas Jefferson* is needed to identify this particular friend. No commas are needed. Since Madison had only one father, however, the father's name is not needed to identify him. Then commas are used.

Exercise 11   **Identifying Appositive Phrases**

Write each sentence. Underline each appositive noun or phrase and draw an arrow to the noun it identifies. Add commas where they are needed.

1. Madison and his friend Jefferson formed a new political party.
2. This party the Democratic-Republican party was the forerunner of the present Democratic party.
3. Thomas Jefferson the author of the Declaration of Independence was the third president.
4. Jefferson appointed his friend James Madison as secretary of state.
5. The Louisiana Purchase one of Madison's most significant achievements took place in 1803.
6. Madison and his vice president George Clinton were elected in 1809.
7. Dolley Madison a vivacious and very pleasant hostess was known for her extravagant parties.
8. Britain and France two major powers were engaged in a trade war.
9. In 1812 the United States declared war on Great Britain a much stronger nation.
10. American forces tried to take Canada a British territory but they were unsuccessful.

Exercise 12   **Using Appositives**

Write each sentence, using commas around appositives where needed.

1. James Madison grew up on Montpelier a plantation.
2. He attended Princeton a college in New Jersey.
3. Madison a dedicated student completed college in two years.
4. He first held office in his home colony Virginia.
5. In 1776 Thomas Jefferson another young politician served in the first state assembly with Madison.
6. Madison a devoted patriot served in the Continental Congress.
7. He also represented his home state Virginia at the Constitutional Convention of 1787.
8. Madison a believer in strong government played an active role at the convention.
9. He wrote *The Federalist* with his colleagues Hamilton and Jay.
10. A series of letters to newspapers *The Federalist* still offers the best explanation of the Constitution.

NOUNS

Barbara Jordan, by James Haskins, is a biography of the first African American woman from Texas to serve in the United States Congress. The following passage contains an excerpt from Jordan's keynote speech at the 1976 Democratic National Convention. The passage has been annotated to show some of the kinds of nouns covered in this unit.

Nouns *(sidebar)*

Literature Model

from **Barbara Jordan**
by *James Haskins*

"One hundred and forty-four years ago, members of the Democratic Party first met in convention to select a presidential candidate. Since that time Democrats have continued to convene once every four years and draft a party platform and nominate a presidential candidate. . . .

"But there is something different about tonight. There is something special about tonight. What is different? What is special? I, Barbara Jordan, am a keynote speaker."

She was interrupted by wild applause and cheering, and she would be interrupted again and again as she spoke of the problems of the country and her hopes for America. . . . The overwhelming response was one of pride, not just from women because she was a woman, not just from blacks because she was black, not just from Democrats or from Texans, but from all segments of the population, because she was an American.

Annotations: Common noun • Concrete noun • Appositive • Singular noun • Plural noun • Proper noun • Abstract noun

---

Grammar Review

Review: Exercise 1 **Identifying Kinds of Nouns**

Write each noun that appears in the following sentences. Indicate whether each is a *common noun* or a *proper noun*. (Remember to capitalize each proper noun.)

SAMPLE As keynote speaker, barbara jordan had an important role.
ANSWER speaker, common; Barbara Jordan, proper; role, common

1. Texas is the birthplace of barbara jordan.
2. It gained independence from mexico in the last century.
3. It is bordered by the states of oklahoma, arkansas, and louisiana.
4. The rio grande forms the southern border.
5. Texas has many artificial lakes formed from dams on rivers.
6. The weather is usually very hot.
7. Some places average 48 inches of precipitation a year.
8. Oil fields produce many gallons of petroleum.
9. The arkansas national wildlife refuge is home to some rare birds.
10. Major cities include dallas, houston, and san antonio.

Review: Exercise 2 **Using Possessive Nouns**

For each sentence, write the correct possessive form of the singular or plural noun in parentheses.

SAMPLE Washington, D.C., is our (nation) capital.
ANSWER nation's

1. It is the (committee) decision to report out the bill.
2. Here is the minority (party) report on the bill.
3. Hearings will be held in a (month) time.
4. This new law will affect the (nation) postal system.
5. Senator (Jones) bill goes to the floor of the Senate tomorrow.
6. Not everyone agrees with the (bill) provisions.
7. Both (sides) opinions have to be taken into consideration.
8. The (members) votes were tallied by computer.
9. The House will now debate the (Senate) version of the bill.
10. The bill still requires the (president) signature.

Review: Exercise 3   Using Plurals, Possessives, and Contractions

The following sentences are based on the passage from *Barbara Jordan*. Write the word in parentheses that correctly completes the sentence.

SAMPLE   The audience cheered (Jordans, Jordan's) speech.
ANSWER   Jordan's

1. Barbara Jordan described the Democratic (Parties, Party's) first meeting.
2. She was welcomed by listeners at the (Democrats, Democrats') convention.
3. There is something special about being the (conventions, convention's) keynote speaker.
4. A (conventions, convention's) an important part of choosing a presidential candidate.
5. (Styles, Style's) an important aspect of public speaking.
6. The applause and cheers expressed the (Democrats, Democrats') pride in the congresswoman from Texas.
7. A better (Americas, America's) everyone's hope for the future, including Jordan's.
8. Jordan also talked about (womens, women's) rights.
9. This country's (populations, population's) impressed by speeches like Jordan's.
10. (Jordans, Jordan's) remembered as a notable force in American politics.

Review: Exercise 4   Using Collective Nouns

Each sentence contains a collective noun. Write the form of the verb in parentheses that agrees with the noun.

SAMPLE   The audience (roars, roar) its approval during the keynote speech.
ANSWER   roars

1. A committee (chooses, choose) the convention city.
2. The group (meets, meet) to draft its party's policies.
3. Then the committee (states, state) their opinions.
4. During the convention, the party (nominates, nominate) its candidates for president and vice president.
5. After both candidates have been nominated, the team (delivers, deliver) their speeches.

Grammar Review

The following sentences are about Barbara Jordan. Write each sentence, adding the appositive or appositive phrase. Add a comma or commas where needed. In some cases, more than one answer may be possible.

SAMPLE   Barbara Jordan received her law degree from Boston University. (a lawyer)

ANSWER   Barbara Jordan, a lawyer, received her law degree from Boston University. **OR**
A lawyer, Barbara Jordan received her law degree from Boston University.

1. When Jordan was born, Texas was segregated by race. (her home state)
2. In high school, Jordan did well in debating. (the art of formal discussion)
3. Her university had only African American teachers and students. (Texas Southern)
4. Jordan studied law at an integrated school. (Boston University)
5. After returning to Houston, Jordan became involved in local politics. (a lawyer with her own practice)
6. In 1960 Jordan campaigned for John F. Kennedy. (the Democratic nominee)
7. Kennedy's running mate was a Texan like Jordan. (Lyndon Johnson)
8. Jordan was asked to run for office in Texas. (a strong organizer and speaker)
9. Jordan was elected to the Texas State Senate in 1966. (a good campaigner)
10. The senate awarded her the Outstanding Senator Award her first year. (a body of thirty-one members)
11. Lyndon Johnson invited Jordan to a conference. (the vice president)
12. The participants discussed fair-housing proposals. (civil rights leaders)
13. Jordan served in the House of Representatives. (a Texas Democrat)
14. She sat on the House Judiciary Committee. (a very important assignment)
15. Jordan took a firm stand to impeach Richard Nixon. (the president)
16. She said no one should lie to the American people. (freedom's champion)
17. Jordan worked to promote the good of the country. (a role model)
18. She worked to pass legislation banning discrimination and dealing with another important issue. (the environment)
19. Jordan was also asked to address the Democratic National Convention in 1992. (a powerful speaker)
20. The audience's response to Jordan's speech was a tribute to a notable American. (a standing ovation)

Review: Exercise 6

Proofreading

The following passage is about the artist Henri Matisse, whose work appears below. Rewrite the passage, correcting the errors in spelling, grammar, and usage. Add any missing punctuation. There are ten errors.

Henri Matisse

[1]Henri Matisse a French artist, was the leader of the Fauves. [2]This group of painters began one of the twentieth centurys important art movements. [3]These painter's bright colors and simple designs was one of their trademarks.

[4]Matisse made no atempt to represent reality in his colorful paintings or in the compositions he made from paper cutouts. [5]Many of Matisses cutouts represents dancers. [6]In one cutout, for example, the vivid colors and bold shape's suggest an enormous energy. [7]A dancer stands proud and tall among the birds' and flowers. [8]Shes full of strength and dignity.

Henri Matisse, *La Négresse*, 1952

Nouns

Review: Exercise 7

Mixed Review

Identify the underlined nouns as *common, proper, collective,* or *possessive.* More than one label may apply to a single noun.

Franklin Delano Roosevelt

¹<u>Franklin Delano Roosevelt</u> inspired ²<u>Americans</u> with his speeches, as well as with his actions. He became ³<u>president</u> in 1933, when the country was in the depths of the ⁴<u>Great Depression</u>. The ⁵<u>public</u> was suffering, and many people were starving. His inaugural ⁶<u>address's</u> words gave Americans ⁷<u>courage</u> and confidence. His ⁸<u>words</u> "The only thing we have to fear is fear itself" called for faith in our ⁹<u>country</u>.

Born into a wealthy ¹⁰<u>family</u>, he believed in public service. At the age of thirty-nine, Roosevelt was stricken with polio. His ¹¹<u>legs</u> were paralyzed, and he was unable to stand without help. Eleven years later he was elected president of the United States, following ¹²<u>President Herbert Hoover</u>.

In ¹³"<u>The Hundred Days</u>" after he first took office, Roosevelt launched his ¹⁴<u>New Deal</u>. The laws that he introduced and that Congress passed helped farmers, ¹⁵<u>industry</u>, the unemployed, and the common worker.

Though the Great Depression continued, Roosevelt won ordinary ¹⁶<u>citizens'</u> admiration and affection. He was elected president four times—a ¹⁷<u>record</u> unmatched by any other president.

Roosevelt knew how to reach voters. He used the radio effectively to speak to the American ¹⁸<u>people</u>. He often addressed the ¹⁹<u>nation</u> in radio talks that were called "fireside chats." The public liked the sound of his ²⁰<u>voice</u> and gained ²¹<u>confidence</u> in him and in the ²²<u>ideals</u> that he represented.

At the time of ²³<u>Japan's</u> attack on Pearl Harbor, Roosevelt, in his address before Congress, called December 7 "a date that will live in infamy." ²⁴<u>Roosevelt's</u> ringing words inspired Americans and helped prepare them for the long and very difficult ²⁵<u>war</u> that lay ahead. Roosevelt met many times during the war with Winston Churchill, the prime minister of ²⁶<u>England</u>, and with ²⁷<u>Joseph Stalin</u>, the premier of Russia.

Roosevelt died in April 1945, just before the end of the war. A huge ²⁸<u>crowd</u> gathered at the ²⁹<u>White House</u> as word of his death spread. He was deeply mourned by millions of people all over the ³⁰<u>world</u>.

Writing Application

TIME

For more about the writing process, see **TIME Facing the Blank Page,** pp. 97-107.

Nouns in Writing

In this passage from *Thrashin' Time,* David Weiztman uses nouns to capture the excitement and details of an early twentieth-century farming event. Read the passage carefully, noting the italicized nouns.

> The *engine* was quieter than I thought it would be. It was almost alive like the horses working everywhere round it. And the horses. Why, I'll betcha there were sixty *head,* big *horses*—*Belgians* and *Percherons*—coming and going that *afternoon. Teams* pulled *bundle wagons* heaped tall with *sheaves* of *wheat* from the *fields,* pulled *wagons* of yellow *grain* away from the *separator* to the *silo.* Another team hauled the water *wagon,* and another *wagon* brought loads of cord *wood* to keep the *engine* running sunup to sundown.

Techniques with Nouns

Try to apply some of David Weiztman's techniques when you write and revise your own work.

❶ When appropriate, use proper nouns to make your writing more exact:

COMMON NOUNS there were sixty head, big horses coming and going

WEIZTMAN'S VERSION there were sixty head, big horses—*Belgians* and *Percherons*—coming and going

❷ Make your writing more vivid by replacing general or abstract words with concrete specific nouns. Compare the following:

GENERAL WORDS heaped tall with *crops*

WEIZTMAN'S VERSION heaped tall with *sheaves* of *wheat* in from the *fields*

Nouns

Practice Practice these techniques as you revise the following passage on a separate piece of paper. Instead of the underlined words, use proper nouns and more specific nouns to make the passage more vivid.

Today I saw <u>an ocean</u> for the first time. <u>Birds</u> dove and soared above the hills lining the <u>coast of the land</u>. Waves curled and crashed onto the beaches below. Out on the water, <u>pieces</u> of white <u>wave</u> spread like lace across a huge blue <u>piece of fabric</u>. Amongst the people gathered at the edge of the road, I could see people wearing <u>city</u> T-shirts, <u>people</u> struggling to read the <u>signs in another language</u>, and <u>people</u> holding eager children away from the <u>side</u>.

Writing Online | For more grammar practice, go to **glencoe.com** and enter QuickPass code WC87703p2.

Verbs

UNIT 10

10.1 Action Verbs

You may have heard of the movie director's call for "lights, camera, *action!*" The actions in movies and plays can be named by verbs. If a word expresses action and tells what a subject does, it is an action verb.

■ An **action verb** is a word that names an action. An action verb may contain more than one word.

ACTION VERB

Notice the action verbs in the following sentences.

The director **shouts** at the members of the cast.

The lights **are flashing** above the stage.

The audience **arrives** in time for the performance.

Several singers **have memorized** the lyrics of a song.

Action verbs can express physical actions, such as *shout* and *arrive*. They can also express mental activities, such as *memorize* and *forget*.

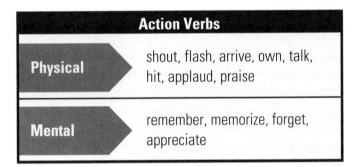

Action Verbs	
Physical	shout, flash, arrive, own, talk, hit, applaud, praise
Mental	remember, memorize, forget, appreciate

Have, has, and *had* are action verbs too when they name what the subject owns or holds.

The actors in this play already **have** their uniforms.

The director **has** a script in her back pocket.

The theater **has** a trapdoor.

Rosa **had** a theater program from 1959.

She **acted** as if . . .

. . . she **remembered** her lines.

Exercise 1   Identifying Action Verbs

Write each action verb and then write whether it expresses a *physical* or a *mental* action.

1. Eugene O'Neill's father, an actor, toured the country.
2. O'Neill learned about the theater from his father.
3. O'Neill's father sent him to Princeton University.
4. Soon O'Neill developed an interest in the sea.
5. He left home for two years of travel.
6. Later, a drama teacher at Harvard University inspired O'Neill.
7. O'Neill knew the value of his own work.
8. He journeyed to Cape Cod for the summer.
9. A group of friends admired this new playwright.
10. They used a stage in their town for theatrical productions.
11. O'Neill also wrote many plays while in Connecticut.
12. He joined a group of performers and writers.
13. The young O'Neill worked long hours.
14. On some days, O'Neill walked along the wharves.
15. Sometimes he met friends along the way.
16. The playwright considered ideas for new plays.
17. In 1936 he received the Nobel Prize for literature.
18. Many theater groups perform his plays each year.
19. Audiences like the dramatic situations.
20. Most of the plays express dark moods.

Exercise 2   Using Action Verbs

Write an appropriate action verb for each sentence. Answers will vary.

1. Our drama and history teachers _____ a joint project for our class.
2. First, our history teacher _____ us into four small groups.
3. Then he _____ the new assignment in detail.
4. The whole class _____ to the library every day for a week.
5. In our small groups, we _____ everyday life in colonial times.
6. Then the drama coach _____ us the next part of the assignment.
7. Each group _____ a one-act play set in the colonial period.
8. The coach _____ our plays for an acting workshop.
9. All of us _____ our lines and movements over the weekend.
10. Finally, we _____ our plays for the class and in a competition.

10.2 Transitive and Intransitive Verbs

In some sentences, the predicate consists of only a verb.

The actor **remembered.**

Usually sentences provide more information. The predicate often names who or what received the action of the verb.

The actor remembered **lines** from the play.

DIRECT OBJECT

In the sentence above, *lines* tells what was remembered. It is the direct object.

■ A **direct object** receives the action of a verb. It answers the question *whom?* or *what?* after an action verb.

Some sentences have a compound direct object. That is, a sentence may have more than one direct object.

We saw **Maurice** and **Inez** in the audience.

When an action verb transfers action to a direct object, it is transitive. When an action verb has no direct object, it is intransitive.

■ A **transitive verb** has a direct object.

■ An **intransitive verb** does not have a direct object.

Many action verbs can be transitive or intransitive. Such verbs can be labeled transitive or intransitive only by examining their use in a particular sentence.

The audience **applauds** the actors. [transitive]
The audience **applauds** loudly. [intransitive]

Exercise 3   **Identifying Transitive Verbs**

For each sentence, write the action verb. If the verb is transitive, write the direct object.

1. Japanese kabuki theaters present popular scenes from dramas and dances.
2. Kabuki performers often wear very elaborate costumes.
3. Male actors perform all the female roles.
4. Characters make entrances and exits along the "flower way" aisle.
5. Instrumentalists behind a screen on stage provide the music.

Exercise 4   **Distinguishing Transitive and Intransitive Verbs**

For each sentence, write the action verb. If the verb has a direct object, write *T*. If it does not, write *I*.

1. The director remembered this fine old theater from past performances.
2. He loved its air of history and elegance.
3. Day after day, week after week, the cast rehearsed.
4. Finally, the day of the first performance arrived.
5. The director inspected the scenery, costumes, and lights.
6. Many people bought tickets to the new play.
7. The almost-silent audience watched.
8. Nearly all the people liked the music and the drama.
9. At the end of the play, everyone clapped wildly.
10. Some enthusiastic spectators even cheered.
11. The majority of the critics enjoyed the performance.
12. They wrote favorable reviews.
13. The musical show succeeded.
14. In fact, the director won an award for it from a theater guild.
15. At the awards ceremony, the director spoke.
16. The cast and their guests listened carefully.
17. The director thanked the producers.
18. A newspaper reporter asked some questions.
19. The director complimented the stage crew for the scenery.
20. He praised the actors for their performances.

10.3 Verbs with Indirect Objects

Words that answer the question *whom?* or *what?* after an action verb are called direct objects.

Amalia wears a **costume.**

Sometimes both a direct object and an indirect object follow an action verb.

■ An **indirect object** answers the question *to whom?* or *for whom?* an action is done.

Friends sent the **actors** flowers.

to whom?

INDIRECT OBJECT

The direct object in the sentence above is *flowers.* The indirect object is *actors. Actors* answers the question *to whom?* after the action verb *sent.*

Some sentences have a compound indirect object.

The audience gave the **cast** and the **orchestra** an ovation.

An indirect object appears only in a sentence that has a direct object. Two easy clues can help you recognize an indirect object. First, an indirect object always comes before a direct object. Second, you can add the preposition *to* or *for* before the indirect object and change its position. The sentence will still make sense, although there will no longer be an indirect object.

Friends sent the **actors flowers.**
[*Actors* is an indirect object.]
Friends sent flowers **to the actors.**
[*Actors* is not an indirect object.]

You know that in the first sentence *actors* is the indirect object because it comes before the direct object and because it can be placed after the preposition *to,* as in the second sentence.

Exercise 5   Distinguishing Direct and Indirect Objects

For each sentence, write the direct object. If the sentence contains an indirect object, write it and underline it.

1. None of the musicians know the composition.
2. The orchestra leader brings the musicians the music.
3. For several days, the orchestra leader teaches the orchestra a song.
4. The sopranos learn their part first.
5. The audience loves the musical comedy.
6. That famous director frequently gives performers drama lessons.
7. She also gives children lessons in the afternoon.
8. She wrote plays and operas for many years.
9. Now she shows her students her special techniques.
10. The theater offers young people many opportunities.
11. Students ask actors and directors questions about different roles.
12. The expert director and producers bring the show success.
13. The director offers her students advice about their careers.
14. The actors memorize scripts.
15. One young writer sold a producer and a director his screenplay.
16. The theater club offers subscribers a discount.
17. The theater also sends subscribers performance information.
18. Subscribers often buy extra tickets for their friends.
19. Generous patrons give the theater large donations.
20. The theater usually gives generous patrons free tickets.

Exercise 6   Using Indirect Objects

Rewrite each sentence, changing each prepositional phrase into an indirect object.

SAMPLE   The cast members gave interviews to the press.
ANSWER   The cast members gave the press interviews.

1. The playwright gave a special tribute to her mother.
2. The youngest cast member handed a dozen roses to the star.
3. Cast members made a comical top hat for the director.
4. The audience offered thunderous applause to the entire cast.
5. The play's producer sent fifteen photographs of the event to the local newspaper.

10.4 Linking Verbs and Predicate Words

■ A **linking verb** connects the subject of a sentence with a noun or adjective in the predicate.

Bess Powell **was** the director.

LINKING VERB

LINKING
VERB

The verb *was* is a form of the verb *be*. It links the word *director* to the subject, telling what the subject is.

■ A **predicate noun** is a noun that follows a linking verb. It defines the subject by telling what it is.

■ A **predicate adjective** is an adjective that follows a linking verb. It describes the subject by telling what it is like.

A sentence may contain a compound predicate noun or a compound predicate adjective.

> The set designer was a **carpenter** and **electrician.** [compound predicate noun]
>
> He is **stern** but **kind.** [compound predicate adjective]

Some of the more common linking verbs are listed below.

Common Linking Verbs			
be	appear	turn	smell
become	look	taste	sound
seem	grow	feel	

Many of these verbs can be used as action verbs also.

> The director grew angry. [linking verb]
>
> The director grew a beard. [action verb]

　　　Identifying Action and Linking Verbs

Write each verb. Then write whether it is an *action* verb or a *linking* verb.

1. Lorraine Hansberry became the first African American woman with a play on Broadway.
2. *A Raisin in the Sun* is the title of that play.
3. Hansberry used a line from a Langston Hughes poem for the title.
4. The play tells the story of an African American Chicago family and the dreams of the different family members.
5. In the course of the play, the family grows stronger and closer.

Exercise 8　　　**Identifying Linking Verbs and Predicate Nouns and Adjectives**

Write each verb and label it *action* or *linking*. If it is a linking verb, write the predicate word or words and add the label *predicate noun* or *predicate adjective.*

1. William Shakespeare was a great playwright and poet.
2. In fact, he is a giant in world literature.
3. Characters in Shakespeare's plays seem universal.
4. Some of the characters were actually historical figures.
5. Some costumes in Shakespeare's plays look odd.
6. The styles of earlier times appear strange today.
7. Shakespeare's language puzzles some modern listeners.
8. In time, however, that language becomes very clear and understandable.
9. Many of Shakespeare's plots sound exaggerated.
10. His stories thrill audiences all over the world with their power, beauty, and truth.
11. Some of the characters are more popular than others.
12. In *Romeo and Juliet* a character drinks poison.
13. In *Othello* the main character grows jealous.
14. In *The Merchant of Venice* a clever young woman teaches other characters about justice and mercy.
15. Some members of Shakespeare's original casts were children.
16. The children played women's roles.
17. Films of Shakespeare's plays are plentiful and popular.
18. Great actors and actresses perform complex roles.
19. Laurence Olivier and John Barrymore were great Hamlets.
20. More recently Mel Gibson and Kenneth Branagh have played Hamlet.

Verbs

10.5 | Present and Past Tenses

The verb in a sentence tells what action takes place. It also tells when the action takes place. The form of a verb that shows the time of the action is called the **tense** of the verb.

■ The **present tense** of a verb names an action that is occurring now or that occurs regularly. It can also express a general truth.

A great actor **wins** awards.

In the present tense, the base form of a verb is used with all subjects except singular nouns and the words *he, she,* and *it.* When the subject is a singular noun or *he, she,* or *it, -s* is usually added to the verb. Remember that a verb in a sentence must agree in number with its subject.

Present Tense Forms	
Singular	**Plural**
I **walk.**	We **walk.**
You **walk.**	You **walk.**
He, she, *or* it **walks.**	They **walk.**

■ The **past tense** of a verb names an action that already happened.

The past tense of many verbs is formed by adding *-ed* to the verb.

The actors **practiced** their lines.

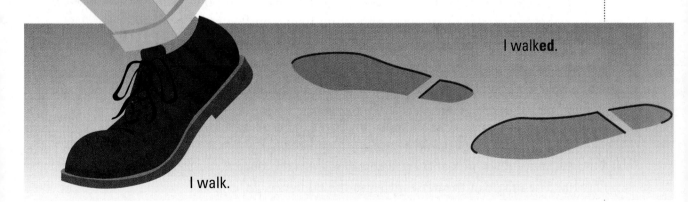

I walk**ed**.

I walk.

Exercise 9   **Distinguishing Present and Past**

Write the correct form of the verb that is in parentheses. Then write whether it is in the *present tense* or *past tense.*

1. A month ago, our music teacher (introduce) my sister and me to opera.
2. Opera is a form that (combine) music and drama into one production.
3. That combination (suit) my sister and me perfectly.
4. Last week we (attend) a light opera by Gilbert and Sullivan.
5. Every day that week, the show (start) precisely on time.
6. However, we (arrive) late because of bus delays.
7. After the show, we always (purchase) tickets for tomorrow's opera.
8. Yesterday a reviewer (compare) the lead performer with Caruso.
9. Enrico Caruso (live) at the beginning of the twentieth century.
10. In his lifetime, he (appear) in many operas throughout the world.
11. Caruso (arrive) in America in 1903.
12. Sometimes he (pass) out free tickets to poor people.
13. Caruso (earn) more money than any other singer at the time.
14. He always (maintain) a warm affection for his many fans.
15. Caruso often (play) tricks on his fellow performers.
16. He (possess) a dynamic personality.
17. Today singers still (talk) about his wonderful voice.
18. Now some people (listen) to his original recordings.
19. Some modern singers (copy) the great singer's style and technique.
20. That great Italian tenor (inspire) singers even today.

Exercise 10   **Using Past Tense**

For each sentence, write the present tense verb. Then write its past tense form.

1. People in the audience chat with one another before the performance.
2. Several classes of students almost fill the second balcony.
3. The lights blink on and off—once, twice, three times.
4. Members of the audience settle into their seats.
5. Darkness descends on the theater except for the glow of safety lights.
6. Not a sound disturbs the silence.
7. Then a spotlight focuses on the heavy red curtain across the stage.
8. The curtains part and reveal a city street.
9. Suddenly actors and actresses appear on the stage.
10. The magic of theater captivates the audience.

Main Verbs and Helping Verbs

Verbs have four principal parts that are used to form all tenses. Notice how the principal parts of a verb are formed.

Principal Parts of Verbs			
Base Form	**Present Participle**	**Past Form**	**Past Participle**
act	acting	acted	acted

You can use the base form itself and the past form alone to form the present and past tenses. The present and past participles can be combined with helping verbs to form other tenses.

■ A **helping verb** helps the main verb tell about an action or make a statement.

■ A **verb phrase** consists of one or more helping verbs followed by a main verb.

   They **are acting** in another play right now.

In the sentence above, the word *are* is the helping verb, and the present participle *acting* is the main verb. Together they form a verb phrase.

The most common helping verbs are *be, have,* and *do.* Forms of the helping verb *be* include *am, is,* and *are* in the present and *was* and *were* in the past. They combine with the present participle of the main verb.

Forms of the helping verb *have* include *has* in the present and *had* in the past. They combine with the past participle form of a verb.

Have, Has, Had, and the Past Participle			
Singular	**Plural**	**Singular**	**Plural**
I **have** acted.	We **have** acted.	I **had** acted.	We **had** acted.
You **have** acted.	You **have** acted.	You **had** acted.	You **had** acted.
She **has** acted.	They **have** acted.	She **had** acted.	They **had** acted.

Exercise 11   **Identifying Helping Verbs and Participles in Verb Phrases**

For each sentence, write each verb phrase. Then circle the helping verbs.

1. Stagehands are preparing the scenery.
2. They had started their work before dawn.
3. One young woman is checking on the correct placement of all the props.
4. Earlier she had inspected all the backstage props and equipment.
5. The director had joined the crew later in the day, and now he is conducting his own last-minute check.
6. The star of the show has earned her fame by a number of huge successes.
7. The press and the public are expecting an excellent performance from this famous cast.
8. Theater has remained a popular form of entertainment.
9. People are buying tickets to many different shows.
10. Theater companies are staging plays, musicals, and revivals of older shows.

Exercise 12   **Using Helping Verbs and Present and Past Participles**

For each sentence, choose and write the correct helping verb that is in parentheses. Then write the participle and label it *present participle* or *past participle.*

1. Now groups (are, have) performing dramas on television.
2. As a result, people (are, have) developing a taste for theater.
3. Television audiences (are, had) watching great performances, both comedies and tragedies.
4. Many of these productions (are, have) attracted huge numbers of viewers from all over the country.
5. The best of them (are, have) achieved very high ratings and rave reviews from critics and viewers alike.
6. Emmy awards (are, have) announced each year in the category for drama-comedy specials.
7. The number and success of these productions (are, have) awakened substantial interest in drama.
8. Producers and advertisers (are, have) responding to people's interest in high-quality television programs.
9. Live theater (is, has) experienced a surge in interest.
10. Both professional companies and community theater groups (are, have) welcoming a new generation of theatergoers.

Verbs

10.7 | Progressive Forms

You know that the present tense of a verb names an action that occurs repeatedly. To describe an action that is taking place at the present time, you use the present progressive form of the verb.

■ The **present progressive** form of a verb names an action or condition that is continuing in the present.

Althea **is finishing** her song.

The present progressive form of a verb consists of the present participle of the main verb and a form of *be,* such as *am, are,* or *is.*

Present Progressive Form	
Singular	**Plural**
I **am leaving**.	We **are leaving**.
You **are leaving**.	You **are leaving**.
He, she, *or* it **is leaving**.	They **are leaving**.

The past progressive form names an action that was continuing at some point in the past.

■ The **past progressive** form of a verb names an action or condition that continued for some time in the past.

The plot **was becoming** scary.

The past progressive form of a verb consists of the present participle and the helping verb *was* or *were.*

Past Progressive Form	
Singular	**Plural**
I **was following**.	We **were following**.
You **were following**.	You **were following**.
He, she, *or* it **was following**.	They **were following**.

Exercise 13   Using Present and Past Progressive Forms

For each sentence, write the present progressive or past progressive form of the verb that is in parentheses.

1. This next semester my music class (go) to an opera production every week.
2. We (examine) the difference between nineteenth- and twentieth-century operas.
3. We (compare) German, French, Italian, and American operas.
4. The schedule (tire) for some students.
5. They (fall) behind in their schoolwork.
6. Our teacher (plan) a big party for us later.
7. She (praise) us yesterday for our patience and diligence.
8. At the end of this semester, we (expect) a period of relaxation.
9. Last month we (attend) two productions a week.
10. Together with our other responsibilities, that schedule (overwhelm).
11. Our parents said they (worry) about our lack of time for anything else.
12. Last year we (study) the comic operas of Gilbert and Sullivan.
13. From 1875 to 1895, the two men (collaborate) on a number of light operas.
14. William Gilbert (work) as a lawyer and a journalist.
15. Arthur Sullivan (write) music for various productions of Shakespeare.
16. Even today many theater groups (present) Gilbert and Sullivan.
17. Time and again, new audiences (discover) the joys of these lively comedies.
18. Last year the city (prepare) a plan for a Gilbert and Sullivan festival.
19. As part of that festival, next spring we (stage) *The Pirates of Penzance.*
20. Many of us in the music class (hope) for good roles in that production.

Exercise 14   Using Progressive Forms

In each sentence, if the verb is in the present tense, change it to the present progressive form. If the verb is in the past tense, change it to the past progressive form.

1. The new theater season begins soon.
2. Local playwrights submitted their entries over a two-week period.
3. A committee reads the scripts.
4. Committee members hoped for a play with a large cast.
5. Last season this company attracted large audiences to its productions.
6. This year the members dream of an equally successful season.
7. One new play caused much excitement among the entries.
8. In this play, a brother and sister investigate the story of a treasure.
9. Meanwhile, the children's parents organize a search for them.
10. Near the end of the play, everyone rushes to the same hilltop.

10.8 Perfect Tenses

■ The **present perfect tense** of a verb names an action that happened at an indefinite time in the past. It also tells about an action that happened in the past and is still happening now.

> The actor **has rehearsed** for many hours.
>
> Nick and Maria **have seen** *Guys and Dolls* five times.
>
> He **has played** in the band for three years.

The present perfect tense consists of the helping verb *have* or *has* and the past participle of the main verb.

Present Perfect Tense	
Singular	**Plural**
I **have performed**.	We **have performed**.
You **have performed**.	You **have performed**.
He, she, *or* it **has performed**.	They **have performed**.

■ The **past perfect tense** of a verb names an action that took place before another action or event in the past.

The past perfect tense is often used in sentences that contain a past tense verb in another part of the sentence.

> We **had** just **arrived** when the play **began.**
>
> The play **had been rewritten** several times before it **opened.**

The past perfect tense of a verb consists of the helping verb *had* and the past participle of the main verb.

Past Perfect Tense	
Singular	**Plural**
I **had started**.	We **had started**.
You **had started**.	You **had started**.
He, she, *or* it **had started**.	They **had started**.

Verbs

Identifying Present Perfect and Past Perfect Tenses

For each sentence, write the verb phrase. Then write whether it is in the *present perfect* or the *past perfect* tense.

1. My favorite television show has earned six Emmy nominations this year.
2. Before this year, it had collected three major Emmies: for best drama, best actor, and best actress.
3. The actress had appeared in several other shows before this one.
4. All of her shows have challenged the boundaries of television.
5. This new one, however, has proved itself the best of all.

Exercise 16 **Using Present Perfect Tense**

For each sentence, write the present perfect tense of the verb that is in parentheses.

1. That actress (perform) in several award-winning plays.
2. Her drama coach (help) her a great deal.
3. The cast (learn) discipline and craft.
4. Our drama club (wait) for the opening of the opera season.
5. The members (plan) weekly theater parties.
6. Some new students (join) the club this year.
7. The club (elect) Tanya president.
8. She (appear) in most of our club's productions.
9. She (contribute) time and energy to every one of them.
10. All of us (benefit) from her work and good nature.

Exercise 17 **Using the Past Perfect Tense**

For each sentence, write the past perfect tense of the verb that is in parentheses.

1. Before the show began, the cast (rehearse) for weeks.
2. Artists (create) the scenery before the opening.
3. The costume designers (locate) boxes and boxes of Roaring Twenties clothes.
4. Before the first rehearsal, our teacher (talk) to us.
5. She (warn) us of the hard work ahead.
6. Also, however, she (predict) an enjoyable, worthwhile activity for us.
7. Before opening night, the cast (suffer) from stage fright.
8. We (present) only one show before last year.
9. Until last week, every member of the cast (attend) every rehearsal.
10. The director (demonstrate) many valuable techniques.

Verbs

10.9 Expressing Future Time

The future tense of a verb is formed by using the helping verb *will* before the main verb. The helping verb *shall* is sometimes used when the subject is *I* or *we* (or with *you* or *they* to express determination).

There are other ways to show that an action will happen in the future. *Tomorrow, next year,* and *later* are all words that express a future time. These words are called **time words,** and they are used with the present tense to express future time. Read the sentences below.

> Our show **opens next week.**
>
> **Tomorrow** we **design** scenery and rehearse.

The present progressive form can also be used with time words to express future actions.

> **Next Friday** our show **is opening.**
>
> **Soon** we **are ending** rehearsals.

Another way to talk about the future is with the future perfect tense.

- The **future perfect tense** of a verb names an action that will be completed before another future event begins.

The future perfect tense is formed by adding *will have* or *shall have* before the past participle of the verb.

> Thursday I **shall have performed** six times.
>
> By next week the production **will have closed.**

| **Exercise 18** | **Using the Perfect Tense** |

For each sentence, change the underlined verb to the future perfect tense.

1. Until the show, we <u>shall practice</u> every day.
2. Tomorrow I <u>will learn</u> my part by heart.
3. I <u>give</u> my first performance next Saturday.
4. By the time the show closes, I <u>shall perform</u> "Some Enchanted Evening" fifteen times.
5. My presence on stage <u>will startle</u> many skeptical people.

| **Exercise 19** | **Identifying Verb Tenses** |

For each sentence, write the verb or verb phrase, and write whether it is in the *present, future, present progressive,* or *future perfect* tense.

1. All the dancers are practicing tomorrow morning.
2. That afternoon we will have our final dress rehearsal.
3. Tomorrow evening we are giving our first benefit performance for senior citizens.
4. By then Adam will have organized the ticket booth.
5. The O'Leary twins go today for another make-up lesson.
6. Tomorrow they demonstrate their techniques on the rest of us.
7. The day after tomorrow, my new costume arrives.
8. Until then I am wearing a costume from last year's production.
9. Our official first night will come on Saturday.
10. By then we will have ironed out all the problems.
11. In the next few weeks, we will stage six performances of our show.
12. Then, next month, we are going to the state drama competition.
13. At the state competition, we present our play in front of a panel of expert judges.
14. They will have observed four other clubs before us.
15. Judges will score us on the basis of action, dialogue, and pace.
16. On the last day, we shall learn the names of the winners.
17. We will cross our fingers very tightly.
18. After the competition, we are changing our schedule completely.
19. Next year we are focusing on musical theater.
20. We will have gained considerable stage experience by then.

10.10 Active and Passive Voice

■ A sentence is in the **active voice** when the subject performs the action of the verb.

> George Bernard Shaw **wrote** that play.

■ A sentence is in the **passive voice** when the subject receives the action of the verb.

> That play **was written** by George Bernard Shaw.

In the first sentence above, the author, George Bernard Shaw, seems more important because *George Bernard Shaw* is the subject of the sentence. In the second sentence, *play* seems more important than the name of the author because *play* is the subject of the sentence.

Notice that verbs in the passive voice consist of a form of *be* with the past participle. Often a phrase beginning with *by* follows the verb in passive voice construction.

> Plays are performed **by actors.**

The active voice is usually a stronger, more direct way of expressing ideas. Use the passive voice only if you want to emphasize the receiver of the action or to de-emphasize the performer of the action or if you do not know who the performer is.

The curtain **was drawn** to reveal an empty stage.

The Tempest **was performed.** [You may want to emphasize the play.]

The curtain **was drawn.** [You may not want to say who did it.]

The theater **was burned.** [You may not know who did it.]

For each sentence, write whether the sentence is in the *active* or *passive voice*. For passive voice sentences, write the word that names the receiver of the action.

1. *Pygmalion* was written by George Bernard Shaw.
2. Shaw's play is based on an ancient Greek myth.
3. Many people saw the play at the theater.
4. A show at the playhouse was criticized by many in the audience.
5. Critics gave it poor reviews in the newspapers.
6. The script was written by a brilliant playwright.
7. She created strange and unusual characters.
8. The director did his very best with the material.
9. The director was praised by several critics.
10. The scenery was designed by the playwright's relatives.
11. Costumes were created by the cast members.
12. The show was produced by members of a local drama club.
13. Most people predicted a short run for the show.
14. The public was surprised by the show's long run.
15. The cast used the criticism as a source for improvement.
16. Many people liked the show.
17. They told their friends about it.
18. Critics reconsidered their reviews.
19. The show was awarded a prize.
20. Now it is performed everywhere.

Exercise 21   **Using Active Voice**

Rewrite each sentence, changing the verb from the passive to the active voice. Some modifiers can be placed in more than one position.

1. In 1861 a church in Washington, D.C., was leased by John T. Ford.
2. The building was managed by Ford as a music hall.
3. It was destroyed by fire in 1862.
4. An architectural gem was built on the site by Ford.
5. On April 14, 1865, the theater was attended by President Abraham Lincoln.
6. That night *Our American Cousin* was performed by the theater company.
7. During the performance, Lincoln was assassinated by John Wilkes Booth.
8. In 1866 the building was bought by the federal government for office space.
9. It was restored to its original function by the government in 1968.
10. Today Ford's Theater and its museum are visited by many tourists.

Verbs

10.11 Irregular Verbs

Irregular Verbs			
Pattern	Base Form	Past Form	Past Participle (have, had)
One vowel changes to form the past and the past participle.	begin	began	begun
	drink	drank	drunk
	ring	rang	rung
	shrink	shrank *or* shrunk	shrunk *or* shrunken
	sing	sang	sung
	spring	sprang *or* sprung	sprung
	swim	swam	swum
The past form and past participle are the same.	bring	brought	brought
	buy	bought	bought
	catch	caught	caught
	creep	crept	crept
	feel	felt	felt
	get	got	got *or* gotten
	keep	kept	kept
	lay	laid	laid
	lead	led	led
	leave	left	left
	lend	lent	lent
	lie	lay	lain
	lose	lost	lost
	make	made	made
	pay	paid	paid
	say	said	said
	seek	sought	sought
	sell	sold	sold
	sit	sat	sat
	sleep	slept	slept
	swing	swung	swung
	teach	taught	taught
	think	thought	thought
	win	won	won

Verbs

Identifying the Past and Past Participle of Irregular Verbs

For each sentence, write the verb or verb phrase. Then write whether it uses the *past form* or the *past participle.*

1. We had thought the old theater a good home for our production.
2. However, problems began with our first rehearsal there.
3. We had paid good money for renovation of the curtains.
4. Somehow, in the process, they shrank.
5. A number of us caught the habit of carelessness too.
6. Before, we had kept our props and costumes in a member's barn.
7. A week after our arrival at the old theater, however, someone lost them.
8. We had made an examination of the electrical system some time ago.
9. We had sought out every possible problem.
10. Then bells in the sound system rang at odd moments.

Exercise 23   **Using the Past and Past Participle of Irregular Verbs**

Write the correct form (either *past form* or *past participle*) of the verb that is in parentheses.

1. Earlier the first performance had (begin).
2. I had (lose) my way to the new theater.
3. The star had (sing) two songs before my arrival.
4. I already had (pay), but I could not find the ticket.
5. I have (sit) in the theater for a long time.
6. Unfortunately the manager (leave) for a few minutes.
7. He has (keep) me waiting for ten minutes.
8. Luckily I (bring) a book with me.
9. I finally have (catch) my breath by sitting quietly.
10. One of my friends (bring) me a copy of the program.
11. Finally I (get) in.
12. I (think) the show was superb.
13. A famous teacher had (teach) the performers well.
14. At the show's end, the members of the audience (spring) to their feet.
15. The leading actor had (win) our hearts.
16. I (feel) happy and sad at the same time.
17. After the performance, we (seek) autographs.
18. The shy star (shrink) from the crowd.
19. At last she (creep) away.
20. She (say) she wanted to rest.

Verbs

10.12 More Irregular Verbs

Irregular Verbs			
Pattern	**Base Form**	**Past Form**	**Past Participle**
The base form and the past participle forms are the same.	become come run	became came ran	become come run
The past form ends in *-ew*, and the past participle ends in *-wn*.	blow draw fly grow know throw	blew drew flew grew knew threw	blown drawn flown grown known thrown
The past participle ends in *-en*.	bite break choose drive eat fall give ride rise see speak steal take write	bit broke chose drove ate fell gave rode rose saw spoke stole took wrote	bitten broken chosen driven eaten fallen given ridden risen seen spoken stolen taken written
The past form and the past participle do not follow any pattern.	am, are, is do go tear wear	was, were did went tore wore	been done gone torn worn
The base form, past form, and past participle are the same.	cut let put	cut let put	cut let put

Verbs

Identifying the Past and Past Participles of Irregular Verbs

For each sentence, write the verb or verb phrase. Then write whether it uses the *past* form or the *past participle*.

1. Our class went on a field trip to Broadway in New York City.
2. For a long time, Broadway has been a symbol of American theater.
3. The name came from the Dutch *Brede Weg,* broad way.
4. The midtown section of the street is known as the Great White Way.
5. The many theaters in the area have run thousands of productions over the years.
6. The winds of fortune blew one way and then another over these theaters.
7. Over the years, some have fallen into disrepair.
8. Others rose to glory, elegance, and prominence.
9. Through Broadway's influence, the theater bug has bitten many young people.
10. Broadway has done a great deal for theater professionals and audiences.

Exercise 25 **Using the Past and Past Participle of Irregular Verbs**

Write the correct form (*past* or *past participle*) of the verb in parentheses.

1. A prominent actress has (write) about her experiences with stage fright.
2. One night onstage she (become) immobile.
3. Before her appearance on stage, she had (know) her lines by heart.
4. She (take) several slow, deep breaths.
5. She regained her confidence and (throw) herself into the part.
6. Her drama coach had (give) her good advice about stage fright.
7. The actress eventually (come) through with a fine performance.
8. She (draw) on her knowledge of the character's personality.
9. The actress (grow) into the part.
10. She (see) through her character's eyes.
11. She even (wear) similar clothes.
12. By the end of the play, the actress (speak) her lines flawlessly.
13. A majority of theater critics have (choose) her for an award.
14. They say she has (steal) the show.
15. She has (grow) more confident.
16. Awareness of her experiences has (drive) me to try again.
17. I have (let) the director assign me to a speaking role.
18. Before that I had (draw) away from any public performance.
19. I had (run) away from opportunities for personal growth.
20. Now with this new determination, I have (break) away from the old me.

UNIT 10 Grammar Review

VERBS

The play *Our Town* by Thornton Wilder focuses on the fictional New England town of Grover's Corners, New Hampshire. The play consists of three acts, each with a single theme. These themes are a typical day in the town, love and marriage, and death. Each act is introduced by the stage manager, who also breaks into the action now and then to explain something about the town or its inhabitants. In the excerpt presented here, the stage manager sets the stage for the second act. The passage has been annotated to show examples of the kinds of verbs covered in this unit.

Literature Model

from Our Town
by Thornton Wilder

STAGE MANAGER: Three years have gone by. Yes, the sun's come up over a thousand times. Summers and winters have cracked the mountains a little bit more and the rains have brought down some of the dirt. Some babies that weren't even born before have begun talking regular sentences already; and a number of people who thought they were right young and spry have noticed that they can't bound up a flight of stairs like they used to, without their heart fluttering a little. All that can happen in a thousand days. Nature's been pushing and contriving in other ways, too: a number of young people fell in love and got married. Yes, the mountain got bit away a few fractions of an inch; millions of gallons of water went by the mill; and here and there a new home was set up under one roof.

Present perfect tense of an irregular verb

Action verb followed by a direct object

Past tense of an irregular verb

Passive voice

Verbs

Grammar Review

Review: Exercise 1   Identifying Action Verbs and Direct Objects

For each sentence, write the action verb. Then write and circle each direct object.

SAMPLE   This semester we read Thornton Wilder's play.
ANSWER   read (play)

1. Thornton Wilder used unconventional forms in his plays.
2. For example, any production of *Our Town* requires very few props.
3. Wilder's words and the audience's imagination provide the scenery.
4. This technique emphasizes the characters in the play.
5. The Henry Miller Theater hosted the first New York performance in 1938.
6. Thornton Wilder won the Pulitzer Prize for drama that year.
7. He wrote other successful plays and novels, too.
8. In 1965 he received the first National Medal for literature.
9. Both critics and ordinary people enjoy his books.
10. Thornton Wilder truly deserves his high position in American literature.

Review: Exercise 2   Distinguishing Transitive and Intransitive Verbs

For each sentence, write the action verb. Then write any direct objects. Write whether the verb is *transitive* or *intransitive*.

SAMPLE   This edition of the play gives stage directions in italics.
ANSWER   gives, directions — transitive

1. Thornton Wilder includes few stage directions in the script of *Our Town*.
2. The audience arrives to a stage with nothing on it.
3. The stage manager brings tables, chairs, and a bench on stage.
4. Then he leans against a pillar on the left of the stage.
5. At that moment the theater darkens.
6. Now the stage manager speaks into the darkness.
7. He provides a verbal map of Grover's Corners.
8. He also introduces the major characters to the audience.
9. The tables and chairs remain on stage for act 2.
10. In this act the stage manager talks about the passage of time.

Review: Exercise 3   Distinguishing Direct and Indirect Objects

For each sentence, write the direct object. If the sentence contains an indirect object, write it and then underline it.

1. In the first scene of *Our Town,* the audience sees morning activities.
2. Young Joe Crowell hands Dr. Gibbs a newspaper.
3. The stage manager shows the audience Joe's future.
4. Mrs. Webb serves her family a hearty breakfast.
5. Mrs. Webb and Mrs. Gibbs both scold their children for their misbehavior.
6. George Gibbs asks his mother for a larger allowance.
7. Mrs. Gibbs sends Rebecca's teacher her congratulations.
8. Mrs. Gibbs and Mrs. Webb discuss antiques and beans.
9. The stage manager tells the audience the history of Grover's Corners.
10. A woman in the balcony asks Mr. Webb a question.

Review: Exercise 4   Identifying Action Verbs and Linking Verbs

For each sentence, write each verb and write whether it is an *action verb* or a *linking verb.* Then write whether each underlined word is a *predicate noun, predicate adjective, direct object,* or *indirect object.*

SAMPLE   Organist Simon Stimson directs the church <u>choir.</u>
ANSWER   directs, action verb; direct object

1. Joe Crowell's knee predicts the day's <u>weather.</u>
2. Howie Newsome delivers <u>milk</u> to local families.
3. Banker Cartwright is very <u>wealthy.</u>
4. Rebecca Gibbs loves <u>money</u> most of all.
5. A second-hand furniture man offers <u>Mrs. Gibbs</u> money for her highboy.
6. Long ago Mrs. Gibbs promised <u>herself</u> a trip to Paris, France.
7. Professor Willard became an <u>expert</u> on the history of Grover's Corners.
8. Charles Webb edits the local <u>newspaper,</u> the *Sentinel.*
9. In Mr. Webb's opinion, Grover's Corners seems very <u>ordinary.</u>
10. Emily Webb and George Gibbs are very good <u>friends.</u>

Verbs

Grammar Review

Review: Exercise 5 **Distinguishing Past and Present Tenses**

Write the correct form of the verb in parentheses. Then write whether it is in the *present* or *past tense.*

SAMPLE For eight years in childhood, Thornton Wilder (live) in China.
ANSWER lived, past

1. Thornton Wilder was born in 1897 and (die) in 1975.
2. At the announcement of a new Wilder novel, buyers (line) up at bookstores.
3. Critics today still (applaud) Wilder's emphasis on ordinary people.
4. That emphasis (make) his work very appealing to us today.
5. Many new readers (comment) on Wilder's compassion.
6. Probably his most famous novel (remain) *The Bridge of San Luis Rey.*
7. He (publish) this book in 1927.
8. This story (explore) the lives of five people who die in a bridge collapse.
9. In 1944 Hollywood (release) a film version of *The Bridge of San Luis Rey.*
10. This movie (fail) at the box office.

Review: Exercise 6 **Using Present and Past Progressive Forms**

For each sentence, write the verb form indicated in italics.

SAMPLE I (join) the community theater. *present progressive*
ANSWER am joining

1. Our theater (consider) a production of *Our Town. present progressive*
2. Committee members (debate) between that play and *The Glass Menagerie* by Tennessee Williams. *present progressive*
3. At first they (lean) toward a musical production. *past progressive*
4. Then they (worry) about the cost of a musical. *past progressive*
5. Now they (look) for a regular drama. *present progressive*
6. I (hope) that they choose *Our Town. present progressive*
7. If so, I (try) out for the role of Emily. *present progressive*
8. My sister (tell) me about her experiences with the play. *past progressive*
9. Last year she and her friends (aim) for a production. *past progressive*
10. That project, however, (interfere) with other plans. *past progressive*

Review: Exercise 7   Identifying Future Tenses

For each sentence, write the verb and whether it is in the *future* or *future perfect* tense.

SAMPLE   By act 2, we will have met the important characters.
ANSWER   will have met, future perfect

1. Mr. Cartwright will buy the first automobile in Grover's Corners in 1906.
2. By 6:00 A.M., Shorty Hawkins will have flagged the train to Boston.
3. Folks in town will wake up shortly.
4. Miss Foster will marry a man from Concord sometime soon.
5. According to the stage manager, Joe Crowell will earn a scholarship.
6. By the time of his college graduation, a world war will have broken out.
7. By ten o'clock, Wally will have his head full of information about Canada.
8. Because of her sore throat, Mrs. Webb will skip choir this evening.
9. Mrs. Webb will have canned forty quarts of beans over the next few weeks.
10. In her dreams, Mrs. Gibbs will travel to Paris, France, someday.

Review: Exercise 8   Using Active Voice

Rewrite each sentence, changing the sentence from the passive voice to the active voice.

SAMPLE   The factory is owned by Banker Cartwright.
ANSWER   Banker Cartwright owns the factory.

1. *Our Town* was written by Thornton Wilder.
2. Each act is introduced by the stage manager.
3. The baby was delivered by Doc Gibbs.
4. The newspaper is published by Charles Webb.
5. The choir is directed by Simon Stimson.
6. The dead are remembered by the living.
7. The kitchen stove is filled with wood by Mrs. Webb.
8. Part of her allowance was saved by Rebecca Gibbs.
9. Fossils were found by archaeologists in Silas Peckham's cow pasture.
10. A hundred years ago, the area of Grover's Corners was settled by the English.

Verbs

Grammar Review

Review: Exercise 9   **Using the Past and Past Participle of Irregular Verbs**

For each sentence, write the appropriate form of the verb in parentheses.

1. Grover's Corners has (see) the comings and goings of many generations.
2. Not many young people (leave) Grover's Corners after graduation.
3. The stage manager has not (know) any remarkable people to come out of Grover's Corners.
4. Dr. Gibbs (bring) the Goruslawksi twins into the world—and most of the other babies in town too.
5. The folks in town (sleep) later in the morning than those out on the farms.
6. The residents of Grover's Corners had (begin) their morning routine.
7. Rebecca Gibbs (wear) her blue gingham dress to school.
8. George Gibbs (eat) his breakfast with his geography book on the table.
9. Before her marriage, Miss Foster (teach) Joe Crowell's grade-school class.
10. Mrs. Webb has (grow) enough beans to feed her family for the winter.
11. She (bite) into one to see whether it was sweet and ripe.
12. That day Emily had (spoke) to her class about the Louisiana Purchase.
13. Despite criticism, George has again (throw) his ball into the air.
14. George had (break) one of his father's rules.
15. Dr. Gibbs had (take) his biannual trip to the Civil War battlefields.
16. By now he has (seek) out almost all of them.
17. The church bell (ring) out over the town of Grover's Corners.
18. Despite her poor voice, Mrs. Gibbs (sing) in the church choir.
19. According to the ladies in the choir, Mr. Stimson had (drink) too much before practice.
20. Dr. Gibbs worried that Mrs. Gibbs had (catch) cold on her way home from choir practice.
21. The Cartwright family has just (lay) the foundation for a new bank in Grover's Corners.
22. From her window, Emily (give) George hints about his algebra homework.
23. Professor Willard had (come) over from the university for his lecture on the history of Grover's Corners.
24. As editor of the town newspaper, Mr. Webb had (become) the town's unofficial spokesperson.
25. A woman in the balcony had (rise) to her feet to ask Mr. Webb a question.

Verbs

Proofreading

The following passage is about artist Roger Brown, whose work appears below. Rewrite the passage, correcting the errors in spelling, grammar, and usage. Add any missing punctuation. There are ten errors.

Roger Brown

¹The painting below was did by Chicago artist Roger Brown. ²This work show a row of houses backed by sand dunes and palm trees. ³The ocean and the setting sun lies beyond the dunes and trees. ⁴The dunes rigid mounds of sand, seem to be carved out of stone.

⁵The characters in this work have shrank to silhouettes. ⁶They are either sitting seperately in their homes or walking alone along the sidewalk. ⁷The walkers are moving fast; perhaps they will think they are late. ⁸They are the only things moveing in the picture. ⁹The ocean looks as if no one has ever swam there. ¹⁰Even the sun, cutted in half by the horizon, looks motionless.

Roger Brown, *Coast of California*, 1987

Verbs

Grammar Review

Review: Exercise 11

Mixed Review

For each numbered item, write the appropriate form of the word requested. Be sure that your completed sentences make sense.

The title of the play *Our Town* [1](*action verb, present tense*) a strong clue to the story's theme. Even though the action [2](*keep—present tense, passive voice*) in one small New Hampshire town, author Thornton Wilder is really giving [3](*indirect object*) the whole world. Other clues [4](*linking verb, present tense*) obvious too. In act 1, Rebecca notices that the same moon [5](*intransitive verb, present tense*) down on other countries. Later in the act, she [6](*tell—future tense*) her brother the story of a letter addressed to Jane Crofut, Grover's Corners, the Universe.

Wilder once wrote that he deliberately [7](*emphasize—past tense*) big numbers such as *thousands* and *millions.* By doing so he [8](*suggest—present progressive tense*) that the big and the small [9](*linking verb, present tense*) one. The stage manager is one [10](*predicate noun*) who comments on the big picture and the small.

Many universal events [11](*intransitive verb, present tense*). In act 1, twin babies [12](*deliver—present tense, passive voice*) by Dr. Webb. In act 2, Emily Webb and George Gibbs [13](*get—present progressive tense*) married, just as millions of people [14](*do—present perfect tense*) in the past and millions [15](*do—future tense*) in the future. Some characters in the play [16](*intransitive verb, present tense*) and are buried in the town cemetery.

Many scenes in the play emphasize ordinary [17](*direct object*). Families [18](*transitive verb, present tense*) meals together in every act. Children [19](*intransitive verb, present tense*) to school, and adults do chores. Wilder also stresses small daily [20](*direct object*), such as the sound of birds, the scent of flowers, the smell of food, or the feel of newly ironed clothes. These joys, he suggests, are the real [21](*predicate noun*) of life. In act 3, Emily [22](*learn—present tense*) anew to appreciate such joys. Dead people in the cemetery give [23](*indirect object*) advice about achieving peace and harmony. She [24](*learn—present perfect tense*) not to take life for granted.

By the end of the play, the audience [25](*catch—future perfect tense*) a glimpse of their own lives.

Verbs

Writing Application

TIME

For more about the writing process, see **TIME Facing the Blank Page**, pp. 97-107.

Verbs in Writing

As you read this passage from *Lyddie*, notice Katherine Paterson's precise verbs and how verb forms convey the sounds and actions of Lyddie's first day in the factory. Study the passage, focusing on the italicized words.

His little red mouth *pursed*, he *stepped* up on a stool and *pulled* out his pocket watch. At the same moment, the bell in the tower above the roof *began* to *ring*. He *yanked* the cord, the wide leather belt above *shifted* from a loose to a tight pulley, and suddenly all the hundred or so silent looms, in raucous concert, *shuddered* and *groaned* into fearsome life. Lyddie's first full day as a factory girl *had begun*.

Techniques with Verbs

Try to apply some of Katherine Paterson's writing techniques when you write and revise your own work.

❶ Whenever possible, replace vague and common verbs with vivid and specific verbs. Compare the following:

VAGUE COMMON VERBS *moved* into fearsome life

PATERSON'S VERSION *shuddered* and *groaned* into fearsome life

❷ Keep the timing of your characters' actions clear by correctly forming the tenses of irregular verbs:

INCORRECT VERB TENSE Lyddie's first full day as a factory girl *had began.*

PATERSON'S VERSION Lyddie's first full day as a factory girl *had begun.*

Practice   Practice these techniques by revising the following passage, using a separate sheet of paper. Pay particular attention to the underlined words.

Park and Noah <u>walked</u> slowly along the sidewalk, deep in conversation. They took no notice of their surroundings, <u>not noticing</u> the hustle and bustle of busy commuters and the noise of cars <u>driving</u> by on the street. An occasional pedestrian <u>made</u> a glance at the two friends, but neither boy <u>noticed.</u> After several blocks, Park finally <u>touched</u> Noah's shoulder and <u>turned</u> him towards a small coffee shop. "Let's <u>take</u> a bite. I haven't eaten since breakfast!" Then they <u>started</u> their conversation <u>again,</u> heads close together.

Pronouns

11.1 Personal Pronouns

- A **pronoun** is a word that takes the place of one or more nouns and the words that describe those nouns.

- Pronouns that are used to refer to people or things are called **personal pronouns**.

Personal pronouns are singular or plural. Some personal pronouns are used as the subjects of sentences. Others are used as the objects of verbs or prepositions.

- A **subject pronoun** is a pronoun in the nominative case used as the subject of a sentence.

  Rita likes books. **She** particularly likes novels.

In the example above, the pronoun *She* replaces the noun *Rita* as the subject of the sentence.

- An **object pronoun** is a pronoun in the objective case used as the object of a verb or a preposition.

  The novel amuses Rita. The novel amuses **her.** [direct object of the verb *amuses*]

  For Raul's birthday Rita gave **him** a novel. [indirect object of the verb *gave*]

  Rita presented a biography of Mark Twain to **us.** [object of the preposition *to*]

Personal Pronouns		
	Singular	**Plural**
Used as Subjects	I	we
	you	you
	he, she, it	they
Used as Objects	me	us
	you	you
	him, her, it	them

Identifying Personal Pronouns

Write each pronoun and identify it as a *subject* pronoun in the nominative case or an *object* pronoun in the objective case.

1. Gwendolyn Brooks wrote poems; they are about everyday life.
2. Slang and the rhythms of jazz and the blues were important to her.
3. She was born in Topeka, Kansas, but grew up in Chicago.
4. The poet Langston Hughes gave her literary advice.
5. Brooks always loved poetry; she wrote it from the age of seven.
6. Brooks taught poetry to students; she was a role model for them.
7. In 1949 she wrote a poetry collection called *Annie Allen*.
8. It made Brooks the first black poet to receive a Pulitzer Prize.
9. I have read the book, and the poems fascinate me.
10. The combination of street talk and American verse will amuse you.

Exercise 2 **Using Personal Pronouns**

Write the pronoun you could use in place of each underlined word or words.

1. Sarah Orne Jewett was an American writer of the nineteenth century.
2. The *Atlantic Monthly* first published Jewett.
3. This author wrote the stories at age nineteen.
4. These stories are about history and tradition.
5. The Jewetts lived amid Maine's many villages.
6. Sarah's father was a doctor with an interest in books and people.
7. Sarah studied books and people with her father.
8. Young Sarah observed people's ways of life.
9. She described the people in her stories.
10. She wrote stories about her experiences.
11. Readers learned about life in New England.
12. Bob wrote a research report on Sarah Jewett.
13. "A White Heron" is Sarah Jewett's best-known story.
14. The heron catches a young girl's attention.
15. The young girl approaches the nest.
16. The wild bird avoids the young girl.
17. "A White Heron" appeals to Robert.
18. Our class had difficulty with the story.
19. Luisa pointed out the theme to our class.
20. Rosa said, "Let Rosa help you."

11.2 Pronouns and Antecedents

Read the following sentences. Can you tell to whom the pronoun *She* refers?

> Louisa May Alcott wrote a novel about a young woman. **She** has three sisters.

The sentence is not clear because *She* could refer either to the *young woman* or to *Louisa May Alcott.* Sometimes you must repeat a noun or rewrite a sentence to avoid confusion.

> Louisa May Alcott wrote a novel about a young woman. **The young woman** has three sisters.

■ The noun or group of words that a pronoun refers to is called its **antecedent.**

When you use a pronoun, you should be sure that it refers to its antecedent clearly. Be especially careful when you use the pronoun *they.* Notice this pronoun in the following sentence.

> **WRONG:** **They** have two books by Alcott at the school library.

To whom does *They* refer? Its meaning is unclear. The sentence might be corrected in the following way.

> **RIGHT:** The school library has two books by Alcott.

Be sure every pronoun agrees with its antecedent in number (singular or plural) and gender. The gender of a noun or pronoun may be masculine, feminine, or neuter (referring to things). Notice the pronoun-antecedent agreement below.

> The Marches must face a death in their family. **They** face **it** with courage.

Write the correct pronoun for the second sentence in each pair. Then write the antecedent the pronoun refers to.

1. Louisa May Alcott lived near Boston, Massachusetts. _____ had many famous neighbors.
2. Alcott came from a poor family. _____ wanted to help earn money.
3. Alcott worked as a teacher. Students learned history from _____.
4. But that job was not enough. _____ did not pay well.
5. Alcott also made dresses. Women paid Alcott money for _____.
6. The writer also tried housekeeping. That job didn't suit _____.
7. Alcott then tried writing. Finally _____ had found a career!
8. Alcott's first book contained stories for young children. _____ was called *Flower Fables.*
9. Two more books by Alcott appeared quickly. _____ describe her hospital work and her teaching days.
10. An editor asked Alcott to write a book for girls. The editor finally persuaded _____.
11. In 1868 Alcott published the first part of *Little Women.* _____ was a success.
12. The full-length edition of *Little Women* was very popular. _____ changed people's ideas about women's role in society.
13. In the novel, Jo March is the main character. _____ eventually becomes a writer.
14. The father is a chaplain in the Civil War. _____ is away.
15. The girls and mother have little money. Life is hard for _____.
16. The March sisters attend school. _____ also earn money for their family.
17. Women had difficulty finding suitable work. _____ were not paid well.
18. Jo has an independent spirit. _____ is the most independent girl.
19. Jo turns down marriage to the boy next door. Jo says no to _____.
20. She tells her sisters. _____ are shocked.
21. Then Jo meets Fritz Bhaer. She ultimately falls in love with _____.
22. Beth is a musician. _____ dies of a terrible illness.
23. Alcott relied on incidents from her own childhood. _____ seem realistic.
24. At the library, I found Alcott's *An Old-Fashioned Girl.* _____ was published in 1870.
25. We have *Little Men* and *Jo's Boys.* I have read _____.

Pronouns

11.3 Using Pronouns Correctly

Subject pronouns in the nominative case are used in compound subjects, and object pronouns in the objective case are used in compound objects.

SUBJECT

Tina and Sam recently read *Heidi*. **She** and **he** recently read *Heidi*. [*She* and *he* form the compound subject.]

Heidi appealed to Sam and Tina. *Heidi* appealed to **him** and **her**. [*Him* and *her* form the compound object.]

Tina and Sam

she   he

Whenever the subject pronoun *I* or the object pronoun *me* is part of the compound subject or object, *I* or *me* should come last.

Tina and **I** liked the book. [not *I and Tina*]

Sometimes a pronoun and a noun are used together for emphasis. The form of the pronoun depends on its function in the sentence.

We students read the book. [*We* is the subject.]
The book delighted **us** readers. [*Us* is the direct object.]

read
about

Some sentences make incomplete comparisons. The form of the pronoun can affect the meaning of such sentences. In any incomplete comparison, use the pronoun that would be correct if the comparison were complete.

Heidi liked Peter more than **she** [did]. [Heidi and Klara liked Peter, but Heidi liked him more than Klara did.]

Heidi liked Peter more than [she liked] **her**. [Heidi liked Peter and Klara, but Heidi liked Peter more than she liked Klara.]

him   her

Peter and Heidi.

OBJECT

In formal writing, use a subject pronoun after a linking verb.

Heidi's closest friend is **he.**

Pronouns

Identifying Pronouns in the Nominative and Objective Cases

Write the correct pronoun for each underlined noun. Then write whether each one is a *subject* pronoun in the nominative case or an *object* pronoun in the objective case.

1. Eudora Welty and <u>William Faulkner</u> are famous writers from Mississippi.
2. Works by <u>Welty</u> and Faulkner are intimately connected to the atmosphere of the South.
3. Faulkner wrote in a more serious tone than <u>Welty</u>.
4. <u>Faulkner</u> demands much of us readers.
5. Important prizes were awarded to both Welty and <u>Faulkner</u>.

Exercise 5 **Using Pronouns in the Nominative and Objective Cases Correctly**

Write the correct word or words in parentheses. Then write whether each pronoun is a *subject* pronoun in the nominative case or an *object* pronoun in the objective case.

1. *Heidi* entertained (we, us) readers.
2. Steffi and (me, I) read the story last weekend.
3. Heidi is an orphan; Grandfather takes care of (she, her).
4. (She, Her) and Grandfather live in the Swiss Alps.
5. Heidi and (he, him) tend goats together.
6. Peter and (her, she) love the mountains.
7. Peter becomes a friend to Heidi's grandfather and (she, her).
8. Grandfather is stern, although no one is kinder than (he, him).
9. (We, Us) readers grow fond of Grandfather.
10. My favorite character is (he, him).
11. Grandfather became almost real to (Juan and I, Juan and me).
12. (She, Her) and Peter tend goats.
13. Heidi says good-bye to (Peter and he, Peter and him).
14. (We, Us) readers feel very sympathetic toward Heidi.
15. In fact, I felt almost as sad as (she, her).
16. Between Peter and (she, her), they help Klara toward recovery.
17. Klara and (she, her) become friends in the city.
18. Heidi's dearest friends are Grandfather and (he, him).
19. Klara cannot walk, so Heidi aids the family and (she, her).
20. (Tom and I, Me and Tom) guessed the ending.

Possessive Pronouns

You often use pronouns to replace nouns that are subjects and nouns that are objects in sentences. You can use pronouns in place of possessive nouns too.

■ A **possessive pronoun** is a pronoun in the possessive case. It shows who or what has something. A possessive pronoun may take the place of a possessive noun.

Read the following sentences. Notice the possessive nouns and the possessive pronouns that replace them.

> Lisa's class put on a play. **Her** class put on a play.
> The idea was Lisa's. The idea was **hers.**

Possessive pronouns have two forms. One form is used before a noun. The other form is used alone. The chart below shows the two forms of possessive pronouns.

Possessive Pronouns		
	Singular	**Plural**
Used Before Nouns	my your her, his, its	our your their
Used Alone	mine yours hers, his, its	ours yours theirs

Unlike possessive nouns, such as *Mei's* or *cats'*, possessive pronouns do not contain an apostrophe.

Do not confuse the possessive pronoun *its* with the word *it's*. *It's* is a contraction, or shortened form, of the words *it is*.

> **Its** subject is William Shakespeare. [possessive pronoun]
> **It's** a famous play by Shakespeare. [contraction of *it is*]

Identifying Possessive Pronouns

Write each possessive pronoun. Then write *N* if the pronoun *comes before a noun* or *A* if it *stands alone*.

1. Our class is putting on a play by Shakespeare.
2. He wrote centuries ago, but his plays still thrill audiences.
3. *Hamlet* is Lian's favorite, but *Romeo and Juliet* is mine.
4. Have you seen your favorite play yet?
5. Gina was in *Hamlet,* but it's not a favorite of hers.
6. I know my part in the play, but some students have trouble with theirs.
7. The language of Shakespeare sounds strange to their ears.
8. To Shakespeare our English would seem like a foreign language.
9. Some of his words look odd in print; the spellings are unfamiliar.
10. The spoken words of Shakespeare are more eloquent than mine.

Exercise 7   **Using Pronouns in the Possessive Case**

Write the correct possessive pronoun for each underlined word or group of words.

1. The play's setting is the city of Verona.
2. Romeo was an uninvited guest at the feast of Romeo's enemy.
3. When Romeo and Juliet meet, Romeo and Juliet's love story begins.
4. Later Romeo sees Juliet and hears Juliet's confession of love for him.
5. A friar performs Romeo and Juliet's secret marriage the next day.
6. Mercutio, a friend of the bridegroom's, meets Tybalt, an enemy of Mercutio's.
7. Mercutio and Tybalt fight; Romeo stops Mercutio and Tybalt's fight.
8. Romeo draws his sword and kills Romeo's friend's murderer.
9. Romeo's sentence is banishment.
10. Romeo visits Juliet secretly; the meeting was Romeo and Juliet's alone.
11. Juliet refuses to marry Count Paris, but Juliet's father insists.
12. The night before the wedding, Juliet drinks a sleeping potion of Juliet's.
13. The potion's effects will render her apparently lifeless for forty hours.
14. The friar's message to Romeo is, "Rescue Romeo's wife; she is awake."
15. The friar's message gets mixed up; Romeo hears that Juliet is dead.
16. Romeo buys poison, goes to Juliet, and says, "Death is Romeo and Juliet's."
17. Thinking that Juliet is dead, Romeo drinks Romeo's poison and dies.
18. Juliet awakes and finds Romeo's body and the cup by her side.
19. Juliet guesses what has happened; she stabs Juliet's chest.
20. This story is a favorite of our class's.

Indefinite Pronouns

■ An **indefinite pronoun** is a pronoun that does not refer to a particular person, place, or thing.

Each thinks about the plot.

Most indefinite pronouns are either singular or plural.

Some Indefinite Pronouns			
Singular			**Plural**
another	everybody	no one	both
anybody	everyone	nothing	few
anyone	everything	one	many
anything	much	somebody	others
each	neither	someone	several
either	nobody	something	

In addition, the indefinite pronouns *all, any, most, none,* and *some* are singular or plural, depending on the phrase that follows.

When an indefinite pronoun is used as the subject of a sentence, the verb must agree with it in number.

Everyone reads part of the novel. [singular]
Several enjoy it very much. [plural]
Most of the story **takes** place in England. [singular]
Most of the characters **are** memorable. [plural]

Possessive pronouns often have indefinite pronouns as their antecedents. In such cases, the pronouns must agree in number. Note that the intervening prepositional phrase does not affect the agreement.

Several are presenting **their** interpretations of the novel.
Each of the students has **his** or **her** ideas about its meaning.

Pronouns

Exercise 8   **Choosing Indefinite Pronouns**

Write the indefinite pronoun that agrees with the verb or possessive pronoun.

1. (Neither, All) of Robert Frost's poems are enjoyed by their readers.
2. (One, Many) of the poems have New England as their setting.
3. (Much, Many) of their narrators are people living close to nature.
4. (Much, Others) of the poetry has rhythm, and its lines rhyme.
5. (Both, Each) of these poems has its own rhyme.
6. (Somebody, Several) in this poem narrates his or her own tale.
7. (Most, Everyone) have their own interpretations of Frost's metaphors.
8. (All, One) of the guests have read their poems at the bookstore.
9. (Both, One) of the guests has read her own poem about Frost.
10. (Each, Several) of the readers of Frost's poems has his or her favorite.

Exercise 9   **Using Indefinite Pronouns**

Write each sentence, using the correct verb or possessive pronoun in parentheses. Then underline the indefinite pronoun and write whether the pronoun is *singular* or *plural.*

1. Everyone studies (his or her, their) *Alice's Adventures in Wonderland.*
2. Most of the characters (is, are) animals.
3. Some of them (attends, attend) a comical tea party.
4. Nothing (makes, make) sense in Wonderland.
5. Everything in Wonderland (confuses, confuse) Alice.
6. No one (answers, answer) her questions.
7. Many of the characters (talks, talk) peculiarly.
8. Some of them even (speaks, speak) in riddles.
9. The Cheshire cat disappears; nothing (is, are) left but its smile.
10. Few really (believes, believe) in disappearing cats.
11. None of the characters (looks, look) more bizarre than the Mock Turtle.
12. Several offer Alice (his or her, their) advice.
13. Each has (their, his or her) point of view.
14. Nothing predictable (happens, happen) in Wonderland.
15. Most of the story (occurs, occur) down a rabbit hole.
16. Everyone (know, knows) the story's author—British writer Lewis Carroll.
17. Much (has, have) been written about *Alice's Adventures in Wonderland.*
18. All of the critics (praises, praise) it.
19. None of them (gives, give) a bad review.
20. Everyone in class enjoys (his or her, their) reading the book.

11.6 Reflexive and Intensive Pronouns

Reflexive and intensive pronouns are formed by adding *-self* or *-selves* to certain personal and possessive pronouns.

Reflexive and Intensive Pronouns	
Singular	**Plural**
myself	ourselves
yourself	yourselves
himself, herself, itself	themselves

Sometimes *hisself* is mistakenly used for *himself* and *theirselves* for *themselves.* Avoid using *hisself* and *theirselves.*

■ A **reflexive pronoun** refers to a noun or another pronoun and indicates that the same person or thing is involved.

The woman bought **herself** a book by Horatio Alger.

REFLEXIVE PRONOUN

■ An **intensive pronoun** is a pronoun that adds emphasis to a noun or pronoun already named.

Horatio Alger **himself** wrote more than one hundred books.

I **myself** have never read his books.

Reflexive and intensive pronouns have special uses. They should never be used as the subject of a sentence or as the object of a verb or preposition.

Yolanda and **I** read *Sink or Swim*. [not *Yolanda and myself*]

It pleased Yolanda and **me**. [not *Yolanda and myself*]

REFLEXIVE PRONOUN

Exercise 10   Identifying Reflexive and Intensive Pronouns

Write each reflexive and intensive pronoun and identify it as a *reflexive pronoun* or an *intensive pronoun.*

1. You should occupy yourselves by reading one of Edgar Allan Poe's tales.
2. His first three books of poetry were themselves not successful.
3. Poe did not think himself a writer of inferior material.
4. Poe himself had a high opinion of his abilities.
5. One of his first tales was superb; the tale itself won a $100 prize.
6. One of the contest judges himself got Poe a job as a magazine editor.
7. Edgar Allan Poe has endeared himself to readers of the macabre.
8. I myself would not read any of his short stories at night.
9. Poe may not be the author for you; only you yourself can decide.
10. You can get yourself a book of his stories and poems from the library.

Exercise 11   Using Reflexive and Intensive Pronouns

Write the correct pronoun in parentheses. Write whether the pronoun is a *reflexive, intensive, subject,* or *object* pronoun.

1. I (me, myself) wrote a review of a book by Horatio Alger.
2. I found (me, myself) inspired by the characters' adventures.
3. Read a story (yours, yourself) about making hard work into a fortune.
4. Alger's life (it, itself) seems like one of his success stories.
5. Harvard Divinity School was near his home; Alger attended (it, itself).
6. His church congregation thought (themselves, theirselves) lucky.
7. Alger thought (hisself, himself) ambitious and moved to New York.
8. He helped the homeless; (they, themself) became characters in his stories.
9. The characters improve (them, themselves) through work and luck.
10. Yusuf and Tony (themselves, theirselves) were impressed by Alger's books.
11. Horatio Alger (he, himself) lived from 1832 to 1899.
12. Alger's birthplace (it, itself) attracts visitors.
13. We enjoyed (us, ourselves) during a visit to his home.
14. Alger's stories (them, themselves) usually take place in large cities.
15. A friend and (I, myself) have read ten of Alger's books.
16. Alger's style seems warm and light to (me, myself).
17. For Alger, ambition (it, itself) can bring about success.
18. According to (him, himself), any child could become a success.
19. (He or she, Themselves) just has to be intelligent, hard-working, and honest.
20. Alger's books became symbols of success (theirselves, themselves).

11.7 Interrogative and Demonstrative Pronouns

■ An **interrogative pronoun** is a pronoun used to introduce an interrogative sentence.

The interrogative pronouns *who* and *whom* both refer to people. *Who* is used when the interrogative pronoun is the subject of the sentence. *Whom* is used when the interrogative pronoun is the object of a verb or a preposition.

> **Who** borrowed the book? [subject]
>
> **Whom** did the librarian call? [direct object]
>
> For **whom** did you borrow the book? [object of preposition]

Which and *what* are used to refer to things and ideas.

> **What** interests you?   **Which** is it?

Whose shows that someone possesses something.

> I found a copy of *Great Expectations*. **Whose** is it?

When writing, be careful not to confuse *whose* with *who's*. *Who's* is the contraction of *who is*.

■ A **demonstrative pronoun** is a pronoun that points out something.

The demonstrative pronouns are *this, that, these,* and *those. This* (singular) and *these* (plural) refer to something nearby. *That* (singular) and *those* (plural) refer to something at a distance.

> **This** is an interesting book. [singular, nearby]
>
> **These** are interesting books. [plural, nearby]
>
> **That** is a long book. [singular, at a distance]
>
> **Those** are long books. [plural, at a distance]

that

this

Exercise 12   **Using Interrogative and Demonstrative Pronouns**

Write the correct word given in parentheses.

1. (These, This) is Arturo's favorite book.
2. From (who, whom) did you get that copy?
3. (That, Those) is the small orphan named Pip.
4. (That, Those) are Pip's books.
5. (Who, Whom) taught Pip about books?
6. With (who, whom) does Pip live?
7. (This, These) are Pip's sister and her husband.
8. (Who, Whom) does Pip meet?
9. (What, Who) does the stranger want?
10. (This, These) is food for the stranger.

Exercise 13   **Distinguishing Between Pronouns and Contractions**

Write the correct word given in parentheses. Then write *I* if your choice is an *interrogative* pronoun, *D* if it is a *demonstrative* pronoun, or *C* if it is a *contraction.*

1. (Whose, Who's) Joe?
2. To (who, whom) was Joe married?
3. (Who's, Whose) Miss Havisham?
4. (This, These) is the mansion of Miss Havisham.
5. (That, These) was the time on the clocks.
6. (This, Those) are her bridal robes.
7. (Who, Whom) did Miss Havisham see?
8. (This, These) was the girl at Miss Havisham's home.
9. To (who, whom) did Estella get married?
10. (This, What) are Pip's great expectations?
11. (Who, Whom) becomes Pip's guardian?
12. (That, These) is a mystery.
13. (Who's, Which) of the schools does Pip attend?
14. To (who, whom) does Pip turn for help?
15. (What, Who) did Lawyer Jaggers give Pip?
16. (Who, Whom) paid Lawyer Jaggers?
17. (This, These) are the payments from the stranger.
18. (What, Who) became of the stranger?
19. (What, Who's) helping Pip now?
20. (Whose, Who's) the author of this novel?

Grammar Review

PRONOUNS

The following passage is from a biography of Emily Dickinson by Bonita Thayer. In addition to writing nearly eighteen hundred poems, Dickinson wrote many letters to friends. These letters reveal much about her thinking at different periods of her life. In the passage below, Thayer quotes from Dickinson's letters to Colonel Higginson, a writer and abolitionist (someone who opposed slavery). The passage has been annotated to show examples of the kinds of pronouns covered in this unit.

Literature Model

from Emily Dickinson
by Bonita E. Thayer

Some of Emily's letters to Higginson reveal her feelings about the public in general. "Truth is such a rare thing, it is delightful to tell it," she says in one note. Later she asks him, "How do most people live without any thoughts? There are many people in the world—you must have noticed them in the street—how do they live? How do they get strength to put on their clothes in the morning?"

She seemed satisfied with her life as she was living it. Her own thoughts filled her mind and were joined with the thoughts of others whose writings she studied.

"There is no frigate like a book to take us lands away," she wrote. She felt that she could travel the world and meet all the people she wanted to through books. She never had to leave her own home, which she considered to be the best and safest place for her.

> Indefinite Pronoun

> Subject Pronoun agrees with its antecedent, *Emily*

> Object pronoun agrees with its antecedent, *many people*

> Possessive Pronoun

Pronouns

Grammar Review

Review: Exercise 1   Using Subject, Object, and Possessive Pronouns

Write each sentence, replacing the underlined word or words with the correct pronoun. Write whether the pronoun you used is a *subject* pronoun, an *object* pronoun, or a *possessive* pronoun.

1. <u>Emily Dickinson</u> avoided having <u>Dickinson's</u> picture taken.
2. <u>Dickinson</u> had <u>one photograph</u> taken at about age sixteen.
3. <u>The author</u> craved biographies and portraits about <u>literary favorites.</u>
4. Dickinson started writing poetry in <u>Dickinson's</u> early twenties.
5. <u>The thought of publishing her poems</u> was abhorrent to <u>Dickinson</u>.

Review: Exercise 2   Using Pronouns and Antecedents

Write the second sentence in each of the following pairs, using the correct pronoun in each blank. Then write the antecedent of the pronoun with its number (singular or plural) and gender (masculine, feminine, or neuter).

SAMPLE   After their mother's death, Emily and her sister, Lavinia, became recluses. Emily and _____ never left home.

ANSWER   Emily and she never left home. Lavinia, singular, feminine

1. Emily Dickinson was born in Amherst, Massachusetts, in 1830. _____ was the daughter of Edward and Emily.
2. Dickinson's father was a Renaissance man. _____ was a lawyer, a politician, and a college treasurer.
3. The poet's brother, named William Austin, was always called Austin. _____ was the oldest child and only son.
4. The mother's job was care of the family. _____ was an important task.
5. Austin became treasurer at the same college as the father. Eventually Austin succeeded _____ father.
6. Austin married Susan Gilbert. The father built _____ a house next door.
7. Dickinson and her sister, Lavinia, never married. _____ lived at home all their lives.
8. After the father died, the mother became paralyzed. _____ was confined to bed.
9. Emily and Lavinia shared the task of caring for the mother. Both took good care of _____.
10. The three children were close in age. _____ were devoted to one another.

Review: Exercise 3   **Using Subject and Object Pronouns Correctly**

Write the correct pronoun in parentheses. Then write whether each pronoun is a *subject* pronoun or an *object* pronoun.

1. Emily and (she, her) were sisters and friends.
2. (She, Her) and Charles Wadsworth were friends and correspondents.
3. Dickinson and (he, him) were friends and companions.
4. The poet and a friend corresponded with Thomas Higginson and (he, him).
5. (She, Her) and other poets wrote poems and letters.
6. (They, Them) and others are published in English and other languages.
7. Emily's poems and letters amused those students and (we, us).
8. An editor and (her, she) gave the poems numbers but no titles.
9. (Me and Surya, Surya and I) read poem 812 and poem 1017 today.
10. Poem 173 and poem 188 made Akim and (me, I) smile.

Review: Exercise 4   **Using Indefinite Pronouns**

Write each sentence, using the correct verb in parentheses. Then underline the indefinite pronoun and write whether it is *singular* or *plural*.

SAMPLE   Some of her poetry (is, are) deceptively simple.
ANSWER   <u>Some</u> of her poetry is deceptively simple. *Singular*

1. Many (consider, considers) Dickinson one of the best American poets of the nineteenth century.
2. Few of her poems (was, were) published during her lifetime, perhaps only seven.
3. Most of her poems (is, are) very brief.
4. All of her work (is, are) interesting.
5. Some of her poems (was, were) circulated among her close friends.
6. Everything in her poems (reveal, reveals) her love of nature.
7. Everyone (like, likes) the spoofing fun of her valentines.
8. Much (has, have) been written about how she never left home.
9. Several of us (enjoy, enjoys) her work.
10. Something about her poetry (capture, captures) the reader's imagination.

Grammar Review

Review: Exercise 5 **Using Subject, Object, Reflexive, and Intensive Pronouns**

Write the correct pronoun given in parentheses. Write whether the pronoun is a *reflexive, intensive, subject,* or *object* pronoun.

1. Dickinson (she, herself) knew that her words could attract readers.
2. But she did not want the readers (theirselves, themselves) at her door.
3. In midlife she rarely left the Dickinson property (it, itself).
4. Within the homestead, (she, herself) had an active life.
5. The poet had many friends and wrote many letters to (them, themselves).
6. Friends and neighbors brought the outside world to (her, herself).
7. The garden needed tending in summer; she did that (itself, herself).
8. The cause of her reclusiveness (it, itself) is not fully understood.
9. She may have made the choice (her, herself) to remain in seclusion.
10. Emily Dickinson was devoted to her parents and took care of (them, themselves) until they died.

Review: Exercise 6 **Using Interrogative and Demonstrative Pronouns**

Write the correct word given in parentheses.

SAMPLE (Who, Whom) was the most important influence on her poetry?
ANSWER Who

1. To (who, whom) did Dickinson send the first samples of her poetry?
2. (This, These) are the first four poems she showed him.
3. (What, Whose) was his opinion of the poems?
4. (This, What) were the questions he asked of the poet?
5. (Which, Whom) are the three poems she sent in reply?
6. (What, Which) did writer Helen Hunt Jackson think of the poetry?
7. (Who's, Whose) poetry did Jackson praise?
8. (This, These) is the poetry Dickinson's niece brought to the publisher.
9. (Whose, Who's) idea was it to publish only some of them?
10. (That, Those) were the last of her poems to be published.

Review: Exercise 7

Proofreading

The following passage is about the artist Paul Sierra, whose work appears below. Rewrite the passage, correcting the errors in spelling, grammar, and usage. Add any missing punctuation. There are ten errors.

Paul Sierra

¹Paul Sierra was born in Havana the capital of Cuba. ²His parents wanted himself to become a doctor, but he wanted to be a painter. ³When Sierra was sixteen, him and his family immigrated to the United States and settled in Chicago.

⁴Sierra began his formal training as a painter in 1963 and he later went to work as a commercial layout artist. ⁵He still works in advertizing as a creative director. ⁶Because he does not have to rely on sales of paintings for his' livelihood, he is free to paint whatever he wants.

Paul Sierra, *Degas' Studio*, 1990

Pronouns

⁷Sierra's unusual use of color is saw in the painting on the previous page. ⁸The images theirselves, however, are drawn from the paintings of Edgar Degas. ⁹The woman's head, for instance, is taken from a famous portrait done by he. ¹⁰The horse and jockey reflects Degas's fascination with the sport of racing.

Review: Exercise 8

Mixed Review

After each sentence number, list in order the pronouns that appear in the sentence. Identify each pronoun as *personal, possessive, indefinite, reflexive, intensive, interrogative,* or *demonstrative.*

¹Emily Dickinson drew her last breath on May 15, 1886. ²She left a legacy of nearly eighteen hundred poems and a thousand remarkable letters. ³These were not published in their entirety until 1958.

⁴In the late 1850s, Dickinson herself had copied dozens of finished poems into booklets. ⁵Dickinson had made them by sewing folded notepaper into sheaves. ⁶This was a way to organize the bits of scrap paper containing the drafts. ⁷What became of the booklets? ⁸Who found them?

⁹After Dickinson's death, Lavinia discovered the booklets; she persuaded Higginson and one of Austin's friends to edit a volume of the poetry. ¹⁰Reviews of the book were discouraging, but the public demand for it was heartening. ¹¹In 1945 the last of Dickinson's poetry was published, and virtually all of Dickinson's poems were finally in print, sixty years after her death!

¹²Dickinson's poetry itself is concise and intense. ¹³Most of the poems are brief. ¹⁴They usually are about nature and the themes of love, death, and immortality. ¹⁵She introduced new rhymes and rhythms, often within a single poem. ¹⁶Both give her poems originality and add richness. ¹⁷The phrases are themselves quite simple. ¹⁸Her diction is stripped to the fewest words. ¹⁹She delighted herself with paradox; the concrete and the abstract, the serious and the funny, the usual and the unusual exist side by side in Dickinson's work. ²⁰The style is easily recognized as hers.

Pronouns

Writing Application

TIME

For more about the writing process, see **TIME Facing the Blank Page,** pp. 97-107.

Pronouns in Writing

This passage from *The Game* includes references to many characters. Writer Walter Dean Myers uses different pronouns to lend variety to his prose and make the references to his characters clear. Review the passage below, noticing the italicized pronouns.

> *We* controlled the jump and Turk drove right down the lane and made a lay-up. Turk actually made the lay-up. Turk once missed seven lay-ups in a row in practice and *no one* was even guarding *him.* But this one *he* made. Then one of *their* men double-dribbled and *we* got the ball and *I* passed *it* to Leon, *who* threw up a shot and got fouled. The shot went in and when *he* made the foul shot *it* added up to a three-point play.

Techniques with Pronouns

Try to apply some of Walter Dean Myers's writing techniques when you write and revise your own work.

❶ When appropriate, use possessive pronouns to make your writing more concise. Compare the following:

WORDY VERSION Then one of *the men on the other team* double-dribbled

MYERS'S VERSION Then one of *their* men double-dribbled

❷ Avoid confusing your readers. Be sure to choose correctly between subject and object pronouns.

INCORRECT PRONOUN CHOICE But this one *him* made.

MYERS'S VERSION But this one *he* made.

Practice Apply these techniques as you revise the following passage. On a separate sheet of paper, complete the sentences by adding appropriate pronouns.

When the phone rang, Kay jumped up quickly to answer it. "It's for _____," _____ yelled. Just then Mrs. Oliver entered the room, carrying Willy, the baby, on _____ left hip and _____ briefcase in _____ right hand.

"Good thing _____ were here to answer the phone, Kay. _____ might have dropped _____ trying to reach _____ ," _____ said.

As _____ mother spoke, Kay waved _____ away and quickly finished the phone call.

Pronouns

UNIT
12

Adjectives and Adverbs

12.1 Adjectives

An adjective describes a person, place, thing, or idea. An adjective provides information about the size, shape, color, texture, feeling, sound, smell, number, or condition of a noun or a pronoun.

The **eager, large** crowd of visitors examines the

huge painting.

In the sentence above, the adjectives *eager* and *large* describe the noun *crowd*, and the adjective *huge* describes the noun *painting*.

■ An **adjective** is a word that modifies, or describes, a noun or a pronoun.

Most adjectives come before the nouns they modify. However, an adjective can be in the predicate and modify the noun or pronoun that is the subject of the sentence.

The painting is **realistic** and **timeless.**

In the sentence above, the adjectives *realistic* and *timeless* follow the linking verb *is* and modify the subject, *painting.* They are called predicate adjectives.

■ A **predicate adjective** follows a linking verb and modifies the subject of the sentence.

The present participle and past participle forms of verbs may be used as adjectives and predicate adjectives.

Christina's World is a **haunting** painting. [present participle]

Christina's World is **inspired.** [past participle]

Exercise 1   Identifying Adjectives

For each sentence below, write each adjective and the noun or pronoun it modifies. If any adjective is a participle form, circle it.

1. Georgia O'Keeffe is a major artist.
2. Her permanent residence was in the Southwest.
3. O'Keeffe's works hang in numerous museums.
4. The dry desert provided her with interesting material.
5. Georgia O'Keeffe spent several years in Wisconsin.
6. She studied art at a large school in Chicago in the early 1900s.
7. She lived for a short time in bustling New York City.
8. As a young woman, O'Keeffe had not yet found the right subjects.
9. In 1912 she became aware of the interesting scenery in Texas.
10. She made an enlightening journey to Amarillo, Texas.
11. The bright flowers and whitened bones of the desert inspired her.
12. The endless landscape seemed filled with strange objects and ghostly figures.
13. Her unique style combined abstract design with realistic scenery.
14. O'Keeffe's best paintings were based on nature.
15. She might pick up an interesting shell on a sandy beach.
16. At first she made realistic paintings of what she found.
17. She would paint the white shape of the shell alongside a gray shingle.
18. Perhaps she would add two large green leaves to the objects.
19. She kept a large collection of shells under a glass tabletop.
20. O'Keeffe was recognized by leading museums as a major artist.

Exercise 2   Identifying Predicate Adjectives

Write each predicate adjective. Then write the noun or pronoun it modifies in parentheses.

1. The day was young.
2. The beach was deserted except for one lone walker.
3. The others were still asleep.
4. Even the waves were distant and respectful.
5. That silent woman was aware of everything around her.
6. She was curious about all she saw.
7. Everything around her was radiant in the morning light.
8. The colors were true and clear.
9. A piece of red coral was especially eye-catching.
10. Such a simple thing was wonderful to her.

Articles and Proper Adjectives

The words *a, an,* and *the* make up a special group of adjectives called **articles.** *A* and *an* are called **indefinite articles** because they refer to one of a general group of people, places, things, or ideas. *A* is used before words beginning with a consonant sound, and *an* before words beginning with a vowel sound. Don't confuse sounds with spellings. When speaking, you would say *a university* but *an uncle.*

> **a** unit   **a** painting   **an** etching   **an** hour

The is called a **definite article** because it identifies specific people, places, things, or ideas.

> **The** valuable statue is **the** only one of its kind.

■ **Proper adjectives** are formed from proper nouns. A proper adjective always begins with a capital letter.

> The **Italian** statue is on exhibit in the **Houston** museum.
> The **February** exhibit follows a show of **French** paintings.

Although most proper adjectives are formed from proper nouns by adding one of the endings listed below, some are formed differently. Check the spellings in a dictionary.

Common Endings for Proper Adjectives				
-an	Mexico Mexic**an**	Morocco Morocc**an**	Alaska Alask**an**	Guatemala Guatemal**an**
-ese	China Chin**ese**	Bali Balin**ese**	Sudan Sudan**ese**	Japan Japan**ese**
-ian	Canada Canad**ian**	Italy Ital**ian**	Nigeria Niger**ian**	Asia As**ian**
-ish	Spain Span**ish**	Ireland Ir**ish**	Turkey Turk**ish**	England Engl**ish**

Using *A* and *An*

Write the correct indefinite article that would come before each word or group of words.

1. satellite
2. electrical storm
3. transmitter
4. vehicle
5. howling wind
6. expedition
7. unicorn
8. unique event
9. anonymous writer
10. unexplored part
11. unknown rock
12. typical day
13. masterpiece
14. awkward age
15. instrument
16. high-wire act
17. explanation
18. hourly report
19. honest effort
20. activity

Exercise 4 **Forming Proper Adjectives**

Rewrite each sentence, changing the proper noun into a proper adjective. You may have to change the article and eliminate other words.

1. The first exhibit included a drum from Africa.
2. One of my classmates was wearing a bracelet from Mexico.
3. Our class included an exchange student from China.
4. We braved a snowstorm in January to come to the show.
5. An artist from Poland was listening to an audio tape.
6. One painting represented a wedding in April.
7. A class favorite featured a bobsled from Alaska.
8. One parent arrived late in a car from Japan.
9. A snowy scene reminded the teacher of a winter in Minnesota.
10. A writer from Ireland introduced himself to the tour guide.
11. The furniture display included a clock from Taiwan.
12. Some of us chatted with a visitor from Italy.
13. Two people were copying a portrait of a dancer from Mexico.
14. I heard an art critic from Germany talking about the exhibit.
15. What he said puzzled a sailor from France.
16. A tourist from Egypt listened to her with interest.
17. At the museum restaurant, the waitress offered us tea from Australia.
18. A flag from Nigeria was displayed in the museum gift shop.
19. One postcard there showed a celebration in July.
20. The jewelry counter had a copy of a ring from Bolivia.

12.3 Comparative and Superlative Adjectives

■ The **comparative form** of an adjective compares two things or people.

■ The **superlative form** of an adjective compares more than two things or people.

For most adjectives of one syllable and some of two syllables, -*er* and -*est* are added to form the comparative and superlative.

Comparative and Superlative Forms	
Comparative ▶	She is **younger** than the other painter.
Superlative ▶	She is the **youngest** painter in the entire group.

For most adjectives with two or more syllables, the comparative or superlative is formed by adding *more* or *most* before the adjective.

Comparative and Superlative Forms of Longer Adjectives	
Comparative ▶	The one next to it is **more colorful.**
Superlative ▶	The painting in the next room is the **most colorful.**

Never use *more* or *most* with adjectives that already end with -*er* or -*est*. This is called a double comparison.

Some adjectives have irregular comparative and superlative forms.

Irregular Comparative and Superlative Forms		
Adjective	**Comparative**	**Superlative**
good, well	better	best
bad	worse	worst
many, much	more	most
little	less	least

Exercise 5   Identifying Correct Comparative and Superlative Forms

Rewrite each sentence, correcting the comparative or superlative form of the adjective.

1. You can't really say that my taste is worser than yours.
2. If someone has good taste in art, how can there be gooder taste?
3. You just don't like my favoritest painter.
4. Does that mean that the one you like is more good?
5. First of all, my favorite is more young than your favorite.
6. As she gets more older, her work improves.
7. Her bestest work has been done in the last ten years.
8. I know that critics have attacked her most early works.
9. The more large her paintings get, the more exciting they are.
10. The later paintings all sell for much more high prices.

Exercise 6   Using Comparative and Superlative Adjectives

Write the correct comparative or superlative form of the adjective in parentheses.

1. Michelangelo was one of the (great) artists of all time.
2. He was also the (famous) artist of his own time.
3. Are his statues (good) than his paintings?
4. Which is the (fine) statue, *David* or the *Pietà?*
5. Michelangelo's figures were (large) than life.
6. Few paintings are (beautiful) than the one on the ceiling of the Sistine Chapel.
7. His buildings may be (famous) than his renowned statues and paintings.
8. Pablo Picasso may be the (great) painter of our century.
9. His early paintings are (realistic) than his later work.
10. His (early) works were really quite traditional.
11. The work of Picasso's Blue Period included some of his (dark) views of life.
12. Picasso's (bleak) mood of all came during World War II.
13. During his Rose Period, though, his paintings were much (cheerful).
14. For Picasso painting was the (important) thing in his life.
15. His cubist works are probably the (famous) of all.
16. Cubism may have been the (original) of Picasso's many styles.
17. Critics argue over the question of his (good) style of all.
18. They also disagree on his (bad) style.
19. Few artists completed (many) paintings than he did.
20. Of all artists, he showed the (quick) response to change.

The words *this, that, these,* and *those* are called demonstratives. They "demonstrate," or point out, people, places, or things. *This* and *these* point out people or things near to you, and *that* and *those* point out people or things at a distance from you. *This* and *that* describe singular nouns, and *these* and *those* describe plural nouns.

This, that, these, and *those* are called demonstrative adjectives when they describe nouns.

■ **Demonstrative adjectives** point out something and describe nouns by answering the questions *which one?* or *which ones?*

The words *this, that, these,* and *those* can also be used as demonstrative pronouns. They take the place of nouns and call attention to, or demonstrate, something that is not named.

Notice the demonstratives in the following sentences.

That gallery has modern art.

This gallery contains Impressionist works.

Demonstrative Words	
Demonstrative Adjectives	**Demonstrative Pronouns**
This painting is my favorite.	**This** is my favorite painting.
I like **these** kinds of paintings.	**These** are the paintings I like.
That portrait is well known.	**That** was the first stage.
He draws **those** sorts of pictures.	**Those** are from his Cubist phase.

The words *here* and *there* should not be used with demonstrative adjectives. The words *this, these, that,* and *those* already point out the locations *here* and *there.*

> **This** painting is by Matisse. [not *This here painting*]

The object pronoun *them* should not be used in place of the demonstrative adjective *those.*

> I saw **those** pictures. [not *them pictures*]

Adjectives and Adverbs

Exercise 7   Identifying Demonstrative Adjectives and Pronouns

Write the demonstrative from each sentence. Then write *adjective* or *pronoun* to tell what kind it is.

1. You can tell that this artist admired Cézanne's work.
2. All of these pictures show, in some way, Cézanne's influence.
3. This doesn't mean that the artist copied Cézanne's work.
4. Can you see how he uses these colors the same way?
5. Doesn't it remind you of those paintings of Cézanne's we just saw?
6. On the other hand, this one reminds me more of Van Gogh's work.
7. Now, this is a painting I could look at every day.
8. All of those paintings by the Impressionists appeal to me.
9. I'm also interested in those abstract paintings in the next room.
10. This was a good day for seeing a wide variety of styles.

Exercise 8   Using Demonstratives

Write the correct word or words from the parentheses.

1. The artist saw (that, those) things in a new way.
2. (This, This here) painting shows her imaginative style.
3. This (kinds of, kind of) painting has become famous.
4. (This, That) painting over there shows an acrobat.
5. Usually (those, them) colors together would clash.
6. (This, These) are her brushes and palette.
7. (That there, That) painting by Paul Cézanne is influential.
8. (This, This here) is an early work.
9. Cézanne breaks up the dimensions of (this, these) objects.
10. Then he rearranges (these, these here) fragments.
11. This (kind of, kinds of) painting shows his technique.
12. (These, These here) are explorations of space.
13. The angles in (this, this here) picture seem to overlap.
14. These (kinds of, kind of) angles do form solids.
15. The *Pietà* is not (that, that there) kind of sculpture.
16. (This, These) is a fine example of abstract art.
17. Many are familiar with (that, that there) artist.
18. One artist produced all (this, these) works.
19. (Those, Them) paintings are older than his.
20. (These, These here) pieces are by an unknown artist.

12.5 Adverbs

■ An **adverb** is a word that modifies, or describes, a verb, an adjective, or another adverb.

What Adverbs Modify	
Verbs	People handle old violins **carefully.**
Adjectives	**Very** old violins are valuable.
Adverbs	Some violins are played **extremely** rarely.

Some adverbs tell *to what extent* a quality exists. These adverbs are sometimes called **intensifiers.** *Very, quite,* and *almost* are intensifiers.

An adverb may tell *when, where,* or *how* about a verb. The adverbs in the sentences below all modify the verb *play.*

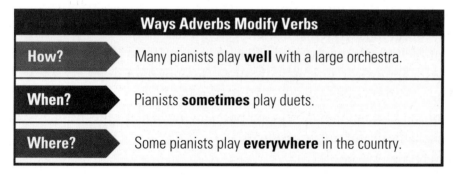

Ways Adverbs Modify Verbs	
How?	Many pianists play **well** with a large orchestra.
When?	Pianists **sometimes** play duets.
Where?	Some pianists play **everywhere** in the country.

When modifying an adjective or another adverb, an adverb usually comes before the word. However, when modifying a verb, an adverb can occupy different positions in a sentence.

Many adverbs are formed by adding *-ly* to adjectives. However, not all words that end in *-ly* are adverbs. The words *friendly, lively, kindly,* and *lonely* are usually adjectives. Similarly, not all adverbs end in *-ly.*

Adverbs Not Ending in *-ly*			
afterward	often	there	hard
sometimes	soon	everywhere	long
later	here	fast	straight

Exercise 9   Identifying the Purpose of Adverbs

Write each adverb, and write whether it tells *how, when,* or *where.*

1. Our chorus finally has enough basses.
2. Unlike in previous years, our conductor can comfortably assign the parts.
3. Becky sometimes had to find choral arrangements with three parts.
4. Now she heads straight for the four-part works.
5. We've moved to another room because we have more space there.
6. She's arranged the seating differently, too.
7. Now each part sits in a wedge-shaped section.
8. That will give us better balance anywhere we sing.
9. She conducts us well, so we are happy.
10. We sing enthusiastically.

Exercise 10   Identifying Adverbs

Write each adverb and write the word it describes in parentheses.

1. The early Greeks studied music thoroughly.
2. To the Greeks, music and mathematics were very similar.
3. Pythagoras strongly believed in the enormous power of music.
4. His ideas about music were certainly important.
5. People sang choral music often at ancient ceremonies.
6. The notes of each singer were exactly alike.
7. These choruses almost surely sang without accompaniment.
8. Composers later wrote separate parts for different voices.
9. Musicians of the Middle Ages developed part singing rather quickly.
10. Some unusually beautiful music resulted.
11. The parts were highly complex.
12. Modern choruses are very professional groups of singers.
13. These choruses perform everywhere.
14. Many choral singers are totally dedicated to their work.
15. People often overlook this kind of music.
16. Some people await major choral concerts eagerly.
17. Chorus singers are sometimes called choristers.
18. They generally sing pieces for four parts, or voices.
19. Tenors are sometimes female singers.
20. Some conductors always insist on male tenors.

Comparative and Superlative Adverbs

- The **comparative form** of an adverb compares two actions.
- The **superlative form** of an adverb compares more than two actions.

Long adverbs require the use of *more* or *most*.

Comparing Adverbs of More than One Syllable	
Comparative	The audience listened **more attentively** last night than tonight.
Superlative	Last Sunday's audience responded **most enthusiastically** of all.

Shorter adverbs need *-er* or *-est* as an ending.

Comparing One-Syllable Adverbs	
Comparative	Did the pianist play **louder** than the cellist?
Superlative	Did the drummer play the **loudest** of all?

Here are some irregular adverbs.

Irregular Comparative and Superlative Forms		
Adverb	**Comparative**	**Superlative**
well	better	best
badly	worse	worst
little (amount)	less	least

The words *less* and *least* are used before some short and long adverbs to form the negative comparative and the negative superlative.

I play **less well.** I play **least accurately.**

Adjectives and Adverbs

Forming the Comparative and Superlative

Write the comparative and superlative forms of each of the following adverbs.

1. tenderly
2. fast
3. little
4. easily
5. violently
6. rapidly
7. close
8. gently
9. awkwardly
10. loud
11. soon
12. well
13. harshly
14. eerily
15. hard
16. effectively
17. late
18. openly
19. negatively
20. often
21. gracefully
22. slow
23. frequently
24. effortlessly
25. long

Using Comparative and Superlative Adverb Forms

For each sentence, write the correct comparative or superlative form of the adverb in parentheses.

1. The performance began (late) tonight than last night.
2. My sister sat (far) from the stage than we did.
3. Several backup singers rehearsed (long) than the piano player.
4. The lead singer sang (badly) last year than this year.
5. The guitarists sang (little) during this concert than during their last one.
6. The drummer played (forcefully) during her solo than before.
7. We heard the first song (clearly) of all the songs.
8. The band played (energetically) of all at the end.
9. I clapped (loudly) during the second half than during the first.
10. I understand the band played (badly) at rehearsals than they ever had before.
11. (Often) than not, Miss Elly had to say, "Now, James, now!"
12. She expected (good) of him but couldn't be sure of it.
13. The night of the dress rehearsal came (quickly) than seemed possible.
14. There sat James in the percussion section as the music grew (fast).
15. He was staring even (blankly) into space than before.
16. "Now, James, now!" Miss Elly cried (desperately) than ever.
17. The entire band turned around and shouted even (loudly)than Miss Elly, "Now, James, now!"
18. The actual performance, however, went (well) than anyone expected.
19. James hit that triangle the (hard) he ever had, right on time.
20. The evening ended (soon) than expected.

Adjectives and Adverbs

12.7 Using Adverbs and Adjectives

Adverbs and adjectives are often confused, especially when they appear after verbs. A predicate adjective follows a linking verb.

> The musicians are **professional.**

In the sentence above, the predicate adjective *professional* describes *musicians.*

In the sentence below, the adverb *professionally* describes the action verb *behaved.*

> The musicians behaved **professionally.**

People also sometimes confuse the words *bad, badly, good,* and *well. Bad* and *good* are both adjectives. They are used after linking verbs. *Badly* is an adverb. It is used after an action verb. *Well* can be either. When used to describe an adjective or verb, *well* is an adverb. When used after a linking verb to describe a person's health or appearance, *well* is an adjective.

Louis Armstrong was a **real** innovator in jazz.

His music was **really** popular.

Distinguishing Adjective from Adverb	
Adjective	**Adverb**
The sound is **bad**.	The actor sang **badly**.
The band sounds **good**.	The band played **well**.
The soloist seems **well**.	

People also confuse *real, really; sure, surely;* and *most, almost. Real, sure,* and *most* are adjectives. *Really, surely,* and *almost* are adverbs.

Distinguishing Adjective from Adverb	
Adjective	**Adverb**
Music is a **real** art.	Music is **really** popular.
A pianist needs **sure** hands.	Piano music is **surely** popular.
Most pianos have eighty-eight keys.	Piano strings **almost** never break.

Exercise 13   Using *bad, badly, good,* and *well*

For each sentence, write the correct adjective or adverb given in parentheses.

1. The big bands did very (good, well) during the 1930s and 1940s.
2. As (good, well) as they were, they needed national radio to succeed.
3. Even (bad, badly) bands took advantage of the interest in this music.
4. The big bands' era is over, but their records still sell (good, well).
5. If you listen really (good, well), you'll still hear bands with that sound.

Exercise 14   Identifying Adjectives and Adverbs

Write each sentence, and underline each verb. Circle the adverb or adjective that follows it, and draw an arrow to the word it modifies. Label each adjective or adverb.

1. Louis Armstrong was famous as a jazz trumpeter.
2. Armstrong began his music career early in the 1900s.
3. He played the trumpet well during his teens in New Orleans.
4. Armstrong listened carefully to other musicians' styles.
5. He seemed enthusiastic about a new singing style called "scat."
6. Scat was rhythmic in its use of syllables instead of words.
7. He seemed ready for a new career as an actor in motion pictures.
8. Big bands played everywhere.
9. They were popular in the 1930s.
10. Louis Armstrong traveled widely and made a number of hit records.
11. Both the soloists and the conductors of the big bands became widely known.
12. The Dorsey brothers were extremely successful as popular musicians.
13. They worked steadily throughout the 1940s.
14. Dinah Shore sang often with big bands.
15. Dinah became very popular as a solo artist.
16. The Spike Jones band is still popular with some people.
17. Spike's versions of some well-known songs were hilarious.
18. In some songs a fire whistle screamed wildly.
19. Meanwhile, the poor tenor sang unconcernedly in the background.
20. The Spike Jones band played well but sounded bad.

12.8 Avoiding Double Negatives

The adverb *not* is a **negative word,** expressing the idea of "no." *Not* often appears in a shortened form as part of a contraction. Study the words and contracted forms below.

Contractions with *Not*		
is not = isn't	cannot = can't	have not = haven't
was not = wasn't	could not = couldn't	had not = hadn't
were not = weren't	do not = don't	would not = wouldn't
will not = won't	did not = didn't	should not = shouldn't

The apostrophe replaces the *o* in *not* in all but two words. In *can't* both the letter *n* and the letter *o* are dropped. *Will not* becomes *won't.*

Other negative words are listed below. Each negative word has several opposites. These are **affirmative words,** or words that show the idea of "yes."

Negative and Affirmative Words	
Negative	**Affirmative**
never	ever, always
nobody	anybody, somebody
none	one, all, some, any
no one	everyone, someone, anyone
nothing	something, anything
nowhere	somewhere, anywhere

Be careful to avoid using two negative words in the same sentence. This is called a **double negative.** You can correct a double negative by removing one of the negative words or by replacing one with an affirmative word.

Incorrect:	The clarinet **isn't no** new instrument.
Correct:	The clarinet **isn't a** new instrument.
Correct:	The clarinet is **no** new instrument.

| Exercise 15 | Correcting Double Negatives |

Rewrite each sentence, avoiding any double negatives.

1. My older brother doesn't take no piano lessons.
2. He plays the piano, but he can't hardly read music.
3. He plays by ear, but I haven't never been able to do that.
4. If we both want to play, we don't never agree who'll get the piano.
5. Sometimes I get there first, and he can't never stand it.
6. He hangs around, as though he doesn't have nothing to do.
7. Then he acts like he hasn't never wanted to play, just to sing.
8. But he starts singing so badly, I can't stand it no more.
9. I start laughing, and there isn't nothing can stop me.
10. Anyone laughing that hard can't hardly play the piano very well.

| Exercise 16 | Using Negative Words |

Write the correct word or words given in parentheses.

1. Didn't (anyone, no one) play pipe organs before Roman times?
2. We (would, wouldn't) hardly recognize the Roman pipe organ today.
3. Aren't there (no, any) old Roman pipe organs still in existence?
4. The pipe organ (was, wasn't) scarcely used outside of churches.
5. Scarcely (no, any) ancient civilizations were without musical instruments.
6. The Egyptians (weren't, were) no exception.
7. Hardly (any, none) of their paintings leave out cymbals and drums.
8. The harp and flute weren't seen (nowhere, anywhere) until centuries later.
9. The zither (was, wasn't) heard nowhere before it was developed in China.
10. Hardly (no, any) ancient lyres are on public display.
11. If you haven't (ever, never) seen a lyre, try an art museum.
12. Some museums have instruments that are rarely played (anymore, no more).
13. They have instruments that can't be seen (nowhere, anywhere) else.
14. No one (should, shouldn't) have trouble understanding how music is made.
15. Didn't you (never, ever) learn that sounds come from making the air move?
16. Early stringed instruments weren't (ever, never) rubbed, only plucked.
17. Only later did (nobody, somebody) think of striking a string with a hammer.
18. Not all woodwind instruments (aren't, are) made of wood.
19. The brass instruments don't have (no, any) reeds at all.
20. Older percussion instruments aren't too different from ours (either, neither).

Grammar Review

ADJECTIVES AND ADVERBS

During the 1600s, Juan de Pareja became enslaved to the great Spanish painter Diego Velázquez. *I, Juan de Pareja,* by Elizabeth Borton de Treviño, tells how Juan became the artist's friend and assistant. In this passage, de Pareja explains his duties. The passage has been annotated to show some of the types of adjectives and adverbs covered in this unit.

Literature Model

from I, Juan de Pareja
by Elizabeth Borton de Treviño

One by one, he taught me my duties. First, I had to learn to grind the colors. There were many mortars for this work, and pestles in varying sizes. I soon learned •———— **Demonstrative adjective**
that the lumps of earth and metallic compounds had to be softly and continuously worked until there remained •———— **Adverb**
a powder as fine as the ground rice ladies used on their cheeks and foreheads. It took hours, and sometimes when I was sure the stuff was as fine as satin, Master would pinch and move it between his sensitive fingers •———— **Adjective**
and shake his head, and then I had to grind some more. Later the ground powder had to be incorporated into •———— **Article**
the oils, and well-mixed, and much later still, I arranged Master's palette for him, the little mounds of color each in its fixed place, and he had his preferences about how •———— **Past participle used as an adjective**
much of any one should be set out. And, of course, brushes were to be washed daily, in plenty of good Castile soap and water. Master's brushes all had to be •———— **Proper adjective**
clean and fresh every morning when he began to work.

Grammar Review

Review: Exercise 1 Identifying Adjectives

Write each adjective. Then write in parentheses the noun or pronoun it modifies. Do not include articles *a, an,* and *the.*

1. Velázquez painted in a large room on the second floor of the house.
2. A huge window let in a pure light from the north.
3. Juan learned to stretch the cotton canvas for the painter.
4. The artist never wrote down the secret formulas for preparing the canvas.
5. He called them professional secrets, and Juan had to memorize them.
6. Juan was a trustworthy assistant.
7. Velázquez liked the early light and would paint until late afternoon.
8. The painter's wife was a merry person and a thrifty housekeeper.
9. Juan had to arrange colorful backgrounds for Velázquez.
10. Juan always wore a gold earring.

Review: Exercise 2 Using Comparative and Superlative Adjectives

Write the correct comparative or superlative form of the adjective in parentheses.

SAMPLE De Pareja was (young) than Velázquez.
ANSWER younger

1. Juan de Pareja ground the colors into the (fine) powder.
2. The artist's fingers were (sensitive) than Juan's.
3. He used the mounds of color on his palette to create some of the (beautiful) paintings of all.
4. Every day Juan de Pareja made sure the artist's brushes were (clean) and (fresh) than Velázquez had left them.
5. Velázquez used the (good) materials he could.
6. The painter often sat staring at his subject for the (long) time.
7. When asked why, the artist explained that this was the (good) way to feel the object's shape.
8. The (exciting) moment came when the king asked Velázquez to paint his portrait.
9. That meant the family would move in the (high) circles of society.
10. The king turned out to be (tall) and (pale) than Juan had expected.

Review: Exercise 3   Identifying Adverbs

Write each sentence. Underline each adverb, and draw an arrow to the word it modifies.

1. The compounds had to be worked continuously.
2. Sometimes the painter would ask for more grinding.
3. Brushes had to be washed daily in soap and water.
4. Juan worked clumsily with his carpentry.
5. He could soon cut and fit the pieces.
6. Occasionally he posed so that the painter could draw or paint him.
7. The painter usually started work early in the morning.
8. Velázquez drew silently, making many drawings.
9. Juan earnestly asked the artist if he could learn to paint.
10. But Velázquez answered simply, "I cannot teach you."

Review: Exercise 4   Using Comparative and Superlative Adverbs

Write the correct comparative or superlative form of the adverb in parentheses.

SAMPLE   He painted (boldly) than before.
ANSWER   more boldly

1. Velázquez represented his subjects (realistically) than had many earlier artists.
2. Of all the techniques, the artist's use of rich colors, light, and shadow (clearly) characterized his style.
3. Velázquez painted portraits (frequently) of all.
4. Although many artists have imitated his style, Velázquez (heavily) influenced modern painters.
5. He traveled (far) than many other artists of his day to study the art of ancient Rome.
6. Velázquez faced an upcoming trip to Italy (calmly) than did his family.
7. His wife stayed behind in Spain the (reluctantly) of all.
8. Velázquez found that the light shone (softly) in Italy than in Spain.
9. Juan moved around (freely) in Italy than in Spain.
10. He could buy paint supplies (easily) in Italy, too.

Grammar Review

Review: Exercise 5   Using Comparatives and Superlatives

Write the correct comparative or superlative form of the adverb or adjective in parentheses.

1. Fictional biography presents (interesting) problems than even straight fiction does.
2. Events must be evaluated (deliberately) than in straight fiction.
3. Biographers are (dependent) on written records than are writers of straight fiction.
4. Suppose that the main figure was one of the (famous) painters who ever lived.
5. Painters write (few) letters and diaries than do authors.
6. Velázquez wrote only a handful of letters, which makes things even (hard).
7. What is (difficult) than imagining conversations he might have had?
8. The (helpful) clues are in the artist's paintings.
9. The subjects of the paintings and how they are presented offer the (good) clues to the artist's interests and attitudes.
10. For de Pareja the clues are even (available) because he was less well known than his teacher.

Review: Exercise 6   Distinguishing Between Adjectives and Adverbs

Write the correct adjective or adverb in parentheses.

1. Velázquez and de Pareja became (good, well) friends.
2. Velázquez recognized his assistant's (real, really) love for art.
3. The two worked (easy, easily) together.
4. Velázquez was never (harsh, harshly) with his assistant.
5. Juan was (frank, frankly) about his admiration of Velázquez.
6. He worked (eager, eagerly) to further Velázquez's career.
7. The portrait of de Pareja shows how (high, highly) he was regarded by Velázquez.
8. De Pareja had a (sure, surely) talent for painting.
9. Juan de Pareja served Velázquez (loyal, loyally) until the artist died.
10. De Pareja became a (true, truly) artist himself.

Review: Exercise 7

Proofreading

The following passage is about Spanish artist Diego Velázquez, whose work appears on the next page. Rewrite the passage, correcting the errors in spelling, capitalization, grammar, and usage. Add any missing punctuation. There are ten errors.

Diego Rodriguez de Silva y Velázquez

¹Diego Rodriguez de Silva y Velázquez (1599–1660) was born in the Spain city of Seville. ²He studied a italian artist Caravaggio, whose realistic figures were painted in contrasting light and dark tones. ³Velázquez become the official painter for Spain's King Philip IV in 1623. ⁴However, the artist's portraits of the royal family looked most like pictures from a personal album than paintings advertising the greatly power of Spain.

⁵Velázquez skillful captures the personalities of his subjects. ⁶When he painted his friend, Juan de Pareja, Velázquez omit neither his intelligence nor his dignity.

Review: Exercise 8

Mixed Review

On your paper, write the twenty adjectives and adverbs that appear in the following paragraph. Do not include articles. Identify each word as an *adjective* or *adverb*.

Portraits

¹Why do many painters do portraits? ²There are commissioned portraits and noncommissioned portraits. ³When an artist does a commissioned portrait, he or she has been asked directly to do so by someone who will pay for the finished work. ⁴Sometimes it is the patrons, or buyers, who will sit for the portrait. ⁵Other times they want a painted record of someone dear to them. ⁶Or it may be an official portrait of an important person. ⁷If artists do a noncommissioned portrait, it is usually because they have seen a face that they feel they have to capture. ⁸That kind of portrait has a distinct advantage to sincere artists. ⁹They can paint exactly what they see and do it honestly. ¹⁰When artists are paid, the patron may be concerned with appearances rather than honesty.

Adjectives and Adverbs

Adjectives and Adverbs

Diego Velázquez, *Juan de Pareja*, 1650

Writing Application

TIME

For more about the writing process, see **TIME Facing the Blank Page**, pp. 97-107.

Adjectives and Adverbs in Writing

In this passage from "On Summer," Lorraine Hansberry uses adjectives and adverbs to convey the mood of summer nights in Chicago. As you read the passage, notice the italicized adjectives and adverbs.

Evenings were spent *mainly* on the *back* porches where screen doors slammed in the darkness with *those really very special summertime* sounds. And, *sometimes*, when *Chicago* nights got too *steamy*, the *whole* family got into the car and went to the park and slept out in the open on blankets. Those were, of course, the *best* times of all because the grownups were *invariably* reminded of having been children in *rural* parts of the country and told the *best* stories then.

Techniques with Adjectives and Adverbs

Try to apply some of Lorraine Hansberry's writing techniques when you write and revise your own work.

1 Add detail and interest to your descriptions by combining several adjectives and adverbs in a group of descriptive words. Compare the following:

GENERAL DESCRIPTION special sounds

HANSBERRY'S VERSION *those really very special summertime* sounds

2 When appropriate, use a proper adjective to make your descriptions more precise.

GENERAL DESCRIPTION when nights in *our city*

HANSBERRY'S VERSION when *Chicago* nights

Practice Practice these techniques as you revise the following passage on a separate piece of paper. Experiment with adding one or more adjectives and adverbs in the blanks provided.

Every morning Jason _____ crossed off a day on his _____ calendar. _____ five more until his _____ trip to Gona's house. Gona was _____ special,_____ for a grown-up! Jason could reveal his _____ worries, and she'd understand them _____. She never laughed or teased. Plus, just _____ to Gona's_____ house was the world's _____ restaurant. After his mom's _____ sausage, Jason was _____ for hot _____ food.

UNIT
13

Prepositions, Conjunctions, and Interjections

13.1 Prepositions and Prepositional Phrases

■ A **preposition** is a word that relates a noun or a pronoun to some other word in a sentence.

The boy **by** the window is French.

The word *by* in the sentence above is a preposition. *By* shows relationship of the word *boy* to the noun *window*.

Commonly Used Prepositions				
about	before	during	off	to
above	behind	for	on	toward
across	below	from	onto	under
after	beneath	in	out	until
against	beside	inside	outside	up
along	between	into	over	upon
among	beyond	like	since	with
around	by	near	through	within
at	down	of	throughout	without

A preposition can consist of more than one word.

Yasmin will visit Trinidad **instead of** Jamaica.

Compound Prepositions			
according to	aside from	in front of	instead of
across from	because of	in place of	on account of
along with	far from	in spite of	on top of

■ A **prepositional phrase** is a group of words that begins with a preposition and ends with a noun or pronoun, which is called the **object of the preposition.** The sentence below has two prepositional phrases.

The painting **near you** is **by a Brazilian artist.**

| Exercise 1 | **Identifying Prepositional Phrases and Objects of Prepositions** |

Write each prepositional phrase. Draw a line under the preposition, and circle the object of the preposition.

1. The Louvre is a famous museum in Paris.
2. Do you know the history of this stately building?
3. The Louvre was once a residence for royalty.
4. Then the royal family moved to Versailles.
5. The galleries throughout the Louvre contain paintings and sculpture.
6. Paris, the French capital, is in northern France.
7. Vineyards stretch across the French countryside.
8. Picturesque old churches are scattered about the landscape.
9. Many harbors lie along the Mediterranean coast.
10. The largest French port, Marseilles, is on the Mediterranean Sea.
11. The high-speed Train à Grande Vitesse travels throughout France very quickly.
12. Ferries travel across the English Channel.
13. Cars and trains can also use a tunnel under the Channel.
14. The English held Calais for more than two centuries.
15. Many people enjoy winter sports in the French Alps.
16. Several resort cities cluster along the southern coast.
17. Most of the French kings were crowned at the cathedral in Reims.
18. Travelers to Europe will find many museums in Paris.
19. Each of these museums offers opportunity.
20. Visitors can also view many spacious and elegant gardens in European cities.

| Exercise 2 | **Identifying Compound Prepositions** |

Write each prepositional phrase, and circle any compound prepositions.

1. According to our history book, a major change recently impacted Germany.
2. In place of two nations, West Germany and East Germany, Germany became one unified nation.
3. In spite of the challenges, most Germans celebrated becoming one nation again.
4. Visitors in front of the Brandenburg Gate can imagine the wall that once divided the city.
5. In eastern Berlin, visitors will find old buildings instead of the modern additions of the western city.

13.2 Pronouns as Objects of Prepositions

When the object of a preposition is a pronoun, it should be an object pronoun and not a subject pronoun.

> Dan handed the tickets to Natalie.
> Dan handed the tickets to **her.**

In the example above, the object pronoun *her* is the object of the preposition *to.*

Sometimes a preposition will have a compound object: two nouns or a noun and a pronoun. The pronoun in a compound object must be an object pronoun.

> I borrowed the suitcase from **Ivan and Vera.**
> I borrowed the suitcase from **Ivan and her.**

> Natalie traveled with **Ivan and me.**

In the second sentence above, *Ivan and her* is the compound object of the preposition *from.* In the third sentence, *Ivan and me* is the compound object of the preposition *with.*

If you are unsure about whether to use a subject pronoun or an object pronoun, try saying the sentence aloud with only the object pronoun.

> I borrowed the suitcase from **her.**
> Natalie traveled with **me.**

The pronoun *whom* is an object pronoun. *Who* is never an object.

> The man of **whom** I spoke is from Colombia.
> To **whom** did you lend the guidebook?

Write the correct form of the pronoun in parentheses. Be sure each pronoun you choose makes sense in the sentence.

1. Carmen's aunt in Spain sent a postcard to David and (her, she).
2. This is the aunt about (who, whom) Carmen and David have told.
3. According to Carmen and (he, him), Spain is a great place to visit.
4. Carmen showed photographs of the Costa del Sol to Hector and (him, he).
5. There was one of David and (her, she) in front of the Alhambra in Granada.
6. The castle's magnificent gardens can be seen behind (them, they).
7. It was hard to distinguish between Carmen's cousin and (he, him); they look alike.
8. Because they look so much alike, Carmen's aunt could be mother to either of (them, they).
9. Aside from David, Carmen, and (he, him), no one in our class has been to Spain.
10. The Moors, who occupied Spain for eight hundred years, left architecture that impressed all of (us, we).
11. The description of the Alcázar given by Carmen and (her, she) was impressive.
12. Most of (us, we) thought the Alcázar was the Moors' best gift to Spain.
13. The Spanish lived alongside (them, they) for centuries.
14. The strong North African influences were described by David and (she, her).
15. Since only eight miles separate Spain from Africa at the narrowest point, this influence made perfect sense to (us, we).
16. Carmen explained to (me, I) that the Strait of Gibraltar is very narrow.
17. David showed the class how the Atlantic Ocean waters flow far beneath the surface while Mediterranean waters flow above (they, them).
18. Then Sheila asked why there were no pictures of (him, he) next to the water.
19. David pointed out to (her, she) that he had spent most of his trip inland.
20. Referring to the class map above (him, he), David located Barcelona.
21. Reaching across (I, me), Carmen gave Sheila a picture of a cathedral designed by Antonio Gaudí.
22. Carmen is standing between David and (him, he) in the first photograph.
23. The cathedral absolutely towers above (them, they) as they smile and point.
24. We were amazed to hear the history recounted by David and (her, she) of this never-finished wonder.
25. Some of (us, we) thought Gaudí's building looked a little like a sand castle.

13.3 Prepositional Phrases as Adjectives and Adverbs

- A prepositional phrase is an **adjective phrase** when it modifies, or describes, a noun or pronoun.

  A temple **of great size** stands here.

  I noticed some men **with heavy suitcases.**

In the first sentence above, the prepositional phrase *of great size* modifies the subject of the sentence, *temple.* In the second sentence, the prepositional phrase *with heavy suitcases* describes a noun in the predicate, *men.*

Notice that, unlike most adjectives, an adjective phrase usually comes after the word it modifies.

- A prepositional phrase is an **adverb phrase** when it modifies, or describes, a verb, an adjective, or another adverb.

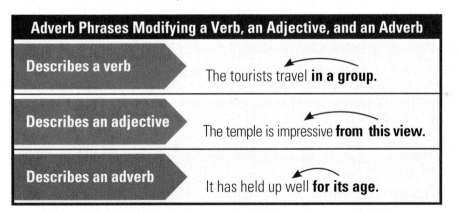

Adverb Phrases Modifying a Verb, an Adjective, and an Adverb	
Describes a verb	The tourists travel **in a group.**
Describes an adjective	The temple is impressive **from this view.**
Describes an adverb	It has held up well **for its age.**

An adverb phrase tells *when, where,* or *how* an action occurs.

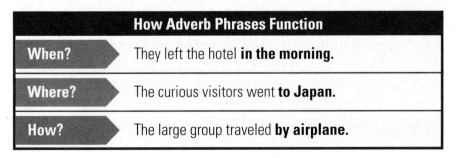

How Adverb Phrases Function	
When?	They left the hotel **in the morning.**
Where?	The curious visitors went **to Japan.**
How?	The large group traveled **by airplane.**

| **Exercise 4** | **Identifying Adjective and Adverb Phrases** |

Write each prepositional phrase, and write whether it is an *adjective phrase* or an *adverb phrase*.

1. Most people in Japan follow the traditional customs of their country.
2. The Japanese traditionally bow on certain occasions.
3. They show great respect for their elders.
4. Throughout their history, the Japanese have also loved beauty.
5. Their gardens are models of grace and delicacy.
6. Japanese gardens are exceptional in their harmony.
7. Artificial and natural elements blend together in their gardens.
8. Soft woven mats cover the floors of many Japanese homes.
9. People customarily wear comfortable slippers inside their homes.
10. The guests of a family receive much kindness and consideration.
11. People sometimes cook on small charcoal stoves.
12. They often prepare bowls of noodles.
13. Diners frequently sit around very low tables.
14. Many Japanese people eat with chopsticks.
15. Hosts serve small cups of fragrant tea.
16. The Japanese tea ceremony has remained popular over the centuries.
17. We can enjoy our memories of Japan more fully with photos.
18. A guide translates the language with care.
19. Many people feel that Japanese is a language of great beauty.
20. When written, its letters are formed with graceful strokes.

| **Exercise 5** | **Writing Sentences with Prepositional Phrases** |

Rewrite each group of sentences, making a single sentence with adjective or adverb phrases.

1. Japan experienced little influence. The influence was from the outside.
2. Japan became an industrial nation. It became an industrial nation within fifty years.
3. We recently visited Nara. A Buddhist temple of historical significance can be seen at Nara.
4. Brightly colored plants dot the hills. The hills are below Kyushu's mountainous slopes.
5. The volcano Mount Aso stands. It stands at the island's highest point.

13.4 Conjunctions

■ A **coordinating conjunction** is a word used to connect parts of a sentence, such as words, clauses, or phrases. *And, but, or, for, so, yet,* and *nor* are coordinating conjunctions.

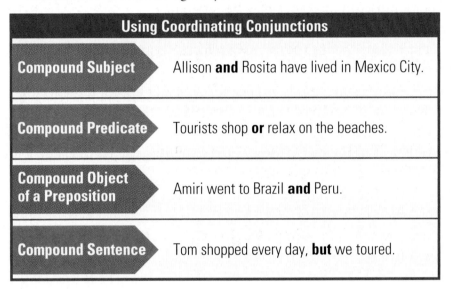

Using Coordinating Conjunctions	
Compound Subject	Allison **and** Rosita have lived in Mexico City.
Compound Predicate	Tourists shop **or** relax on the beaches.
Compound Object of a Preposition	Amiri went to Brazil **and** Peru.
Compound Sentence	Tom shopped every day, **but** we toured.

To make the relationship between words or groups of words especially strong, use a correlative conjunction.

■ **Correlative conjunctions** are pairs of words used to connect words or phrases in a sentence. Correlative conjunctions include *both . . . and, either . . . or, neither . . . nor,* and *not only . . . but also.*

> Examples of great architecture exist in **both** New York **and** Paris. **Neither** Carlo **nor** I have visited those cities.

When a compound subject is joined by the conjunction *and,* it is usually plural. The verb must agree with the plural subject.

When a compound subject is joined by *or* or *nor,* the verb must agree with the nearest part of the subject.

> Winema **and** Tanya **are** in Madrid this week.
> Neither the twins **nor** Ann **is** studying Spanish.

Exercise 6   Identifying Conjunctions

Write each conjunction. Write whether it forms a *compound subject*, a *compound predicate*, a *compound object of a preposition*, or a *compound sentence*.

1. Our teacher traveled to France and toured Paris.
2. The tour took a long time, but it was fascinating.
3. A cathedral or a museum in France may be very old.
4. Visitors spend hours in the bookstores and galleries.
5. After Paris, our teacher went to Normandy, which is between Paris and the English Channel.
6. This picturesque farming region is famous for delicious apples and cheeses.
7. Mr. King told us that he sampled some of the cheeses, but he enjoyed the fresh apple cider the most.
8. The leader and most of the participants voted for seeing the Loire Valley, a region known for its magnificent castles.
9. Our teacher agreed with us, but he requested that the group return to Dunkirk at the end of the tour.
10. Since Mr. King's trip, the tour company offers separate trips to one or the other of these regions.

Exercise 7   Making Compound Subjects and Verbs Agree

Write each sentence, using the correct verb form. Underline each coordinating or correlative conjunction.

1. An auto or a train (is, are) the best transportation for tourists.
2. Neither our teacher nor her companions (speaks, speak) French.
3. Both a subway and a bus system (serves, serve) Paris.
4. Either a taxi or a subway train (is, are) quick.
5. Two buses and a train (goes, go) to the Eiffel Tower.
6. Sometimes musicians and jugglers (performs, perform) in the subway stations in Paris.
7. Neither the Royal Palace nor the Louvre (is, are) open.
8. Still, Parisians and visitors alike (gathers, gather) outside these architectural points of interest.
9. Both the Left and the Right banks of the Seine (is, are) parts of Paris.
10. Either a tour boat or a stroll down the river banks (affords, afford) an intimate view of the city.

13.5 Conjunctive Adverbs

You can use a special kind of adverb instead of a coordinating or correlative conjunction to join the simple sentences in a compound sentence.

> Many Asians use chopsticks, but some use forks.
>
> Many Asians use chopsticks; **however,** some use forks.

Conjunctive adverbs, such as *however* in the sentence above, are usually stronger and more precise than coordinating conjunctions.

Using Conjunctive Adverbs	
To replace and	also, besides, furthermore, moreover
To replace but	however, nevertheless, still
To state a result	consequently, therefore, so, thus
To state equality	equally, likewise, similarly

■ A **conjunctive adverb** may be used to join the simple sentences in a compound sentence.

When two simple sentences are joined with a conjunctive adverb, a semicolon always appears before the second sentence. The conjunctive adverb can appear at the beginning, at the end, or in the middle of the second sentence. When it comes at the beginning or end, it is set off with a comma. When it appears in the middle, one comma precedes it, and one follows it.

> Chinese cooks often stir-fry their food; **therefore**, they must cut it into very small pieces.
>
> Stir-frying should be done quickly; the wok must be very hot, **therefore.**
>
> Vegetables cook more quickly than meat; they must, **therefore,** be added to the wok last.

Exercise 8　　**Identifying Conjunctive Adverbs**

Write each sentence. Underline each conjunctive adverb and add any needed punctuation.

1. People in different lands often have different eating styles moreover they may use different utensils.
2. Many people in India use bread as a scoop some however use a fork.
3. Chinese cooks cut meat into bite-size pieces similarly they chop or slice most vegetables.
4. Food is bite-size thus a knife isn't needed.
5. Soup may be served without spoons it must however be sipped carefully.
6. In the United States, Chinese restaurants may offer diners chopsticks still forks are usually found at each place.
7. Europeans may push their food onto the fork consequently they hold both the knife and the fork while eating.
8. Each of these utensils has its own unique history consequently a complete understanding of the topic requires time and effort.
9. The fork was once used as a fishing tool likewise ancient people took their forks to battle as weapons.
10. The first known table fork in England was made of fragile glass thus it was kept with great care.

Exercise 9　　**Using Conjunctive Adverbs**

Write a conjunctive adverb that makes sense in completing the sentence.

1. Cuisines differ from country to country; _____, they often feature similar dishes.
2. A crepe is a thin pancake around a filling; _____, an enchilada may feature cheese inside a pancake.
3. Each nation has its specialities; _____, these are the best foods to sample.
4. You can enjoy these foods in restaurants; _____, cookbooks offer recipes.
5. You could spend a week trying Asian foods; _____, you could spend a week on other international foods.
6. France is rich in dairy products; _____, French cooks use cream and cheese.
7. Indian food is sometimes vegetarian; _____, it is often spicy.
8. Rice is a staple of Chinese cooking; _____, it is a staple of Japanese cooking.
9. Italian cuisines vary from region to region; _____, each type is delicious.
10. Our school serves international foods; _____, American favorites appear on the menu.

13.6 Interjections

You can express very strong feelings in a short exclamation that may not be a complete sentence. These exclamations are called interjections.

■ An **interjection** is a word or group of words that expresses strong feeling. It has no grammatical connection to any other words in the sentence.

Interjections are used to express emotions, such as surprise or disbelief. They are also used to attract attention.

Any part of speech can be used as an interjection. Some of the more common interjections are listed below.

Common Interjections			
aha	good grief	oh	well
alas	ha	oh no	what
awesome	hey	oops	whoops
come on	hooray	ouch	wow
gee	look	phew	yes

An interjection that expresses very strong feeling may stand alone either before or after a sentence. Such interjections are followed by an exclamation mark.

> We are taking a boat ride around Venice. **Hooray!**

When an interjection expresses a milder feeling, it can appear as part of a sentence. In that case, the interjection is separated from the rest of the sentence by a comma.

> **Wow,** that view of the skyline is spectacular.

You use interjections frequently when you speak. You should use them sparingly, however, when you write. Overusing interjections will spoil their effectiveness.

Identifying Interjections

Write each sentence, adding punctuation where needed. Underline the inter-jection in each sentence.

1. Wow Doesn't Venice, Italy, have a lot of canals!
2. Imagine There are hardly any cars in Venice.
3. The city is built upon nearly 120 islands. Phew.
4. Alas we won't have time to visit every island.
5. There's a candy-striped pole up ahead. Oh, no
6. My goodness that was close.
7. Oops Look out for that gondola on your left.
8. Psst what is that bridge?
9. It is the famous Rialto Bridge. Yippee
10. No kidding Shall we visit it after lunch?
11. Good grief I can't believe I lost my camera.
12. Did you visit the Galleria dell'Accademia? Awesome
13. Come on There's a great outdoor restaurant very near the museum.
14. Hey Did you notice how the narrow, winding streets usually lead to a large, airy plaza?
15. Gee did you realize that the Grand Canal is so long?
16. Is rain in the forecast? Ugh
17. Hey the water is rough in this canal.
18. Eek Don't tip us over.
19. Oh, no Don't stand up in the gondola.
20. Whee Let's spend the whole day on this gondola.

Exercise 11   **Identifying Interjections**

Write an interjection that could complete each sentence. Make sure the sen-tence makes sense. Answers will vary.

1. _____! Our next stop in Italy will be the ancient city of Rome.
2. The city was first built during the great Roman Empire, more than 2,500 years ago. _____!
3. _____! Today's Romans live surrounded by remnants of an entirely differ-ent civilization.
4. _____! The Colosseum isn't one of the stops on today's tour.
5. _____! We are planning instead to lunch on some of Italy's more than two hundred kinds of pasta.

13.7 Finding All the Parts of Speech

Each separate word in a sentence performs a particular job. Each word belongs to a category called a **part of speech.** A word's part of speech depends on the job it performs in the sentence. You have learned all eight parts of speech. The sentence below contains an example of each category.

Gee, Venice is astonishingly beautiful, and it has classic architecture in every quarter.

Parts of Speech		
Word	**Part of Speech**	**Function**
Gee	Interjection	Expresses strong feeling
Venice	Proper noun	Names a specific place
is	Linking verb	Links *Venice* with the adjective *beautiful*
astonishingly	Adverb	Describes the adjective *beautiful*
beautiful	Adjective	Describes the subject, *Venice*
and	Conjunction	Joins two simple sentences
it	Pronoun	Takes the place of a noun
has	Action verb	Names an action
classic	Adjective	Describes the object, *architecture*
architecture	Common noun	Names a thing
in	Preposition	Relates *architecture* and *quarter*
every	Adjective	Describes the noun *quarter*
quarter	Common noun	Names a thing

Prepositions, Conjunctions, and Interjections

Exercise 12   Identifying Parts of Speech

Write each underlined word and its part of speech.

1. Moira often <u>travels</u> to <u>foreign</u> countries.
2. <u>In</u> June <u>she</u> will go to Chile.
3. She <u>is</u> <u>especially</u> fond of Greece.
4. <u>Spain</u> is also close to her <u>heart</u>.
5. Next year she <u>plans</u> to visit Japan <u>and</u> Taiwan.

Exercise 13   Using Parts of Speech

Complete each sentence below by supplying a word whose part of speech is indicated in parentheses. Be sure your finished sentences make sense.

1. Tony (conjunction) Sadie have been to more (common noun) than any other people I know.
2. (Pronoun) visited (proper noun) last year.
3. (Preposition) January they will (action verb) to Israel and Egypt.
4. Tony thought Portugal (linking verb) (adjective).
5. Tony went to (correlative conjunction) Peru (correlative conjunction) Chile.
6. He was (negative adverb) in Asia; Sadie, (conjunctive adverb), went to China.
7. She found (proper noun) amazing, and she (action verb) to go there again.
8. Africa reflects a patchwork of cultures; (conjunctive adverb), its climate varies from desert (preposition) tropical rain forest.
9. (Interjection)! How do so many climates exist in a (adjective) continent?
10. Kyle (adverb) visited Scandinavia, stopping in Norway (conjunction) Sweden.
11. It (linking verb) July, when days are long and the (common noun) is warm.
12. (Pronoun) flew to Lithuania, where he (action verb) this newly open nation.
13. (Correlative conjunction) Kyle (correlative conjunction) Sadie had studied Vilnius in detail.
14. (Interjection), their timetables allowed only two days to see this (adjective) city.
15. Tony, (time adverb), was in Brazil visiting the glorious (conjunction) vanishing rain forest.
16. He (linking verb) amazed by São Paulo, South America's largest (common noun).
17. This (adjective) city's factories produce (indefinite pronoun) from fabrics to electrical equipment.
18. (Preposition) Mexico City, these globe-trotters will (adverb) go home.
19. Good grief! I bet they'll be (adjective) to touch (proper adjective) soil again.
20. (Pronoun) is amazing how often they travel; (conjunctive adverb), they learn.

PREPOSITIONS, CONJUNCTIONS, AND INTERJECTIONS

On a Caribbean island, a young girl discovers Christopher Columbus's boat. The passage is annotated to show some of the parts of speech covered in this unit.

Literature Model

from **Morning Girl**
by Michael Dorris

I forgot I was still **beneath** the surface until I needed air. ● ——— **Preposition**
But when I broke **into the sunlight**, the water sparkling ● ——— **Prepositional phrase (adverb phrase)**
all around me, the noise turned out to be nothing! Only
a canoe! The breathing was the dip of many paddles! It
was only *people* coming to visit, and since I could see they
hadn't painted themselves to appear fierce, they must be
friendly or lost.

I swam closer to get a better look **and** had to stop ● ——— **Coordinating conjunction**
myself from laughing. The strangers had wrapped every
part **of their bodies** with colorful leaves and cotton. ● ——— **Prepositional phrase (adjective phrase)**
Some had decorated their faces with fur and wore shiny
rocks on their heads. Compared to us, they were very
round. Their canoe was short and square, and, **in spite** ● ——— **Compound preposition**
of all their dipping and pulling, it moved so slowly.
What a backward, distant island they must have come
from. But really, to laugh at guests, no matter how odd,
would be impolite, especially since I was the first to meet
them. If I was foolish, they would think they had arrived
at a foolish **place**. ● ——— **Noun as object of preposition**

Grammar Review

Review: Exercise 1 **Identifying Prepositional Phrases and Objects of Prepositions**

Write each prepositional phrase. Draw a line under the preposition, and circle the object.

1. She swam beneath the blue waters.
2. Morning Girl saw an unusual canoe on its way toward her.
3. Its many paddles cut crisply through the clear water.
4. Until this day, Morning Girl had not known people could be so round.
5. The strangers did not look dangerous and wore no paint on their faces.
6. Morning Girl was curious about the new arrivals.
7. The strangers wore fur over their skin.
8. Torn between laughter and courtesy, Morning Girl chose courtesy and greeted the oddly dressed strangers warmly.
9. She wished her mother were beside her.
10. She would help Morning Girl behave correctly and would remind her of island customs.
11. Morning Girl could have called Star Boy from his work.
12. Since the storm, Star Boy had spent many days on his shell collection.
13. Morning Girl could not know how the boat and its occupants would change the lives of the island people.
14. Morning Girl wondered why the strangers were covered by those colorful leaves and cotton.
15. Perhaps they would tell her the meaning of these odd items.
16. The sun shone behind the canoe as the current gently cradled it.
17. Suddenly, Morning Girl saw her island through strangers' eyes.
18. How different the sparkling water and lush trees looked for the first time.
19. Morning Girl waved, as she had seen older people on her island do.
20. One stranger met Morning Girl's wave with a loud shout.
21. She explained who she was and gave her name and the names of her family members.
22. Morning Girl struggled for the correct words and invited the strangers ashore.
23. Although Morning Girl couldn't understand the strangers, she was sure they would all be friends before midday.
24. A meal shared among people usually created friendships.
25. As she turned up the path, Morning Girl observed the strangers in an argument.

Review: Exercise 2   Using Pronouns as Objects of Prepositions

Write the correct form of the pronoun in parentheses. Be sure each pronoun you choose makes sense in the sentence.

1. Morning Girl's visitors brought gifts to Star Boy and (her, she).
2. Morning Girl's story is based on the Native American people about (who, whom) Christopher Columbus wrote.
3. Columbus set sail from Spain in 1492 on a mission long cherished by (him, he).
4. Although Columbus believed in his journey, Queen Isabella was initially skeptical of the voyage planned by (him, he).
5. Columbus convinced the queen that his travels would bring riches and glory to (her, she).
6. Columbus thought that sailing west would bring India and its riches to (he, him).
7. As for the other explorers, most of (they, them) believed that India was to the east.
8. Columbus's men were discouraged, but they believed in (him, he).
9. At last the Caribbean Islands lay before (they, them).
10. The explorers met Native Americans who offered greetings to (they, them).

Review: Exercise 3   Writing Sentences with Pronouns as Objects of Prepositions

Write a pronoun form that would correctly complete the sentence.

1. He thought that these people occupied India, so "Indians" was the name Columbus gave to _____.
2. The Taino is the name they have given to _____.
3. The story could be based on Morning Girl and how change washed around _____ one day.
4. The Taino lived on the bounty of the land and sea around _____.
5. They caught giant turtles from the waters below _____.
6. Some Taino groups made hammocks from twisted cotton and slept in _____.
7. Each village had a chief, and its people looked to _____ for advice.
8. Because the chief was special, a special house was built for _____.
9. Therefore, when meeting Columbus, they gave ready welcome to _____.
10. Columbus started a colony among _____ before he left.

Grammar Review

Review: Exercise 4   **Identifying Adjective and Adverb Phrases**

Write each prepositional phrase, and write *adjective phrase* or *adverb phrase* to tell how it is being used.

SAMPLE   She splashed through the surf.
ANSWER   through the surf (adverb phrase)

1. Morning Girl dove into the water.
2. In the distance, she heard an unfamiliar sound.
3. The strangers were wrapped in leaves and cotton.
4. Some wore shiny rocks on their heads.
5. Morning Girl swam boldly toward the exotic visitors.
6. She hid her laughter and momentarily plunged beneath the waves.
7. Inside her mind, Morning Girl silently addressed the sister she'd named She Listens.
8. She Wins the Race, Morning Girl's mother, had said a new sister would soon add her smiles to the family.
9. Morning Girl had awaited her baby sister with great curiosity.
10. When her mother asked, Morning Girl had a name for the baby sister.
11. Her mother said, "A person isn't real without a name."
12. Morning Girl wondered what was happening when her mother made an unexpected visit to Grandmother's house.
13. She'd known that Father was worried by Mother's absence.
14. Morning Girl was disappointed when only her mother returned from Grandmother's house.
15. Throughout all the months, she had imagined her sister as a companion.
16. There would always be a perfect understanding between them.
17. This sister wouldn't complain about carrying heavy fruit.
18. If Morning Girl misbehaved, her sister would forgive her without hesitation.
19. Surely this friendly sister would always listen to Morning Girl.
20. Morning Girl felt almost as if this sister were really standing beside her.
21. She paused suddenly under the morning sky.
22. She Listens would be the name of her new sister.
23. As Morning Girl approached the strangers, she shared her thoughts with She Listens.
24. She chose her words with great care so she would make no mistakes.
25. Morning Girl kicked through the water.

Review: Exercise 5 **Using Pronouns as Objects of Prepositions**

Write each conjunction, and write *compound subject, compound predicate, compound object of a preposition,* or *compound sentence* to tell what it forms.

SAMPLE Their canoe was square, and it was shorter than any other canoes she had ever seen.
ANSWER and (compound sentence)

1. She wanted to laugh, but she knew that would be impolite.
2. Morning Girl approached the strangers and called out a greeting.
3. The strangers either had come to visit or were lost.
4. In spite of all their dipping and pulling, the canoe moved very slowly.
5. Morning Girl and her brother Star Boy often played together.

Review: Exercise 6 **Making Compound Subjects and Verbs Agree**

Write each sentence, using the correct verb form from the parentheses. Then underline each coordinating or correlative conjunction.

SAMPLE Neither Michael Dorris nor any other anthropologist (know, knows) all about the Taino people.
ANSWER Neither Michael Dorris nor any other anthropologist knows all about the Taino people.

1. Christopher Columbus and the Taino people (was, were) real people.
2. Both Morning Girl and Star Boy (is, are) fictional characters.
3. Michael Dorris's Native American heritage and his anthropology training (give, gives) him strong ties to Morning Girl's story.
4. Neither history teachers nor history books (focus, focuses) often on the people who first met Christopher Columbus.
5. Both Native Americans and their experiences (is, are) overlooked.
6. *Morning Girl* and other works by Michael Dorris (remedy, remedies) this shortage of information.
7. Both Dorris's interests and background (influence, influences) his writing.
8. Sometimes both awards and high sales (greet, greets) Dorris's work.
9. He and Louise Erdrich (were, was) coauthors of *The Crown of Columbus.*
10. Neither the history nor the descriptions (fail, fails) to capture our interest.

Grammar Review

| Review: Exercise 7 | Using Conjunctive Adverbs |

Substitute the conjunctive adverb in parentheses for each of the underlined conjunctions. Then write each compound sentence. Be sure to punctuate the resulting sentences correctly.

SAMPLE Morning Girl swam near the ship, <u>but</u> the crew members didn't see her. (however)

ANSWER Morning Girl swam near the ship; however, the crew didn't see her.

1. She had never seen people dressed as they were, <u>and</u> she didn't know what to make of them. (furthermore)
2. Star Boy collected shells, <u>but</u> he lost them all in a storm. (however)
3. Morning Girl was hot <u>and</u> she swam. (so)
4. The strangers were oddly dressed, <u>and</u> she thought they must have come from a backward island. (therefore)
5. Morning Girl knew it was impolite to laugh at strangers, <u>and</u> Morning Girl didn't want them to think she was foolish. (besides)

| Review: Exercise 8 | Using Interjections |

SAMPLE "_____!" cried Mother and Father when they discovered the neck-laces I had carefully placed in their doorway.

ANSWER Look

1. "_____!" thought Star Boy's mother as she realized the storm was worsening and her son still had not come home.
2. "_____! It's not like Star Boy to disappear like this. Where can he be?" asked She Wins the Race for the hundredth time that day.
3. "_____! I hear footsteps coming up the trail," said the villager who was watching for Star Boy with us.
4. "_____! We found him. We found him," shouted my father when he saw Star Boy stride into the village.
5. "_____!" said Morning Girl to herself, not realizing how worried she had been about her brother.

Review: Exercise 9

Proofreading

The following passage is about the American artist Nereyda García-Ferraz, whose work appears below. Rewrite the passage, correcting the errors in spelling, grammar, and usage. Add any missing punctuation. There are ten errors.

Nereyda García-Ferraz

[1]Nereyda García-Ferraz is born in Havana, Cuba, in 1954. [2]She left Cuba behind she and immigrated to the United States when she was seventeen.

(continued)

Nereyda García-Ferraz, *Without Hearing—Without Seeing*, 1991

³García-Ferraz draws on her experience of living in Cuba for many of her works. ⁴Her images have specific meanings moreover they often tell a story.

⁵García-Ferraz titled this painting *Without Hearing—Without Seeing,* which in spanish is *Sin Oir—Sin Ver.* ⁶The word in the middle of the painting, *nadabas,* refer to swimming. ⁷Words and bright colors is often part of García-Ferraz's work. ⁸Both emotion and intellect is blended by she in her finished works of art.

Review: Exercise 10

Mixed Review

Write a preposition, conjunction, or interjection that would make sense in each sentence. Use the clue in parentheses as a guide in choosing the appropriate word or words.

1. Morning Girl's people called themselves the Taino; _____ , (conjunctive adverb) they are members of a larger group known as the Arawak people.
2. The Arawak lived on islands _____ (preposition) the Caribbean Sea.
3. These islands included three groups now called the Bahama Islands, the Greater Antilles, _____ (coordinating conjunction) the Lesser Antilles.
4. Since Christopher Columbus was searching for India when he sailed among _____ (object pronoun), he named these islands the West Indies.
5. Although Columbus is often considered the first European to reach America, current research suggests that he may have been _____ (compound preposition) the first.
6. Historians believe that Columbus first landed _____ (adverb phrase) in the Bahama Group.
7. Both Watling Island and Samana Cay _____ (present-tense linking verb) among the possible first landing sites.
8. _____! (interjection) There are no longer any Arawaks living in the Caribbean Islands.
9. Many died from European diseases; _____, (conjunctive adverb) the poor living conditions under Spanish enslavement killed many more.
10. The Arawak were primarily a _____ (adjective) people and went to battle only when necessary.

Writing Application

TIME

For more about the writing process, see **TIME Facing the Blank Page,** pp. 97-107.

Conjunctions and Prepositions in Writing

Sometimes the small words make a big difference. Notice how Gary Soto uses conjunctions and prepositions to link his ideas. As you read the passage below from *Living up the Street*, pay particular attention to the italicized words.

> I played *with* my grape knife, stabbing it into the ground, *but* stopped when Mother reminded me that I had better not lose it. I left the knife sticking up like a small, leafless plant. She then talked *about* school, the junior high I would be going to next fall, *and* then about Rick *and* Debra. . . . She stopped talking when she peeked *at* her watch, a bandless one she kept *in* her pocket.

Techniques with Conjunctions and Prepositions

Try to apply some of Gary Soto's writing techniques when you write and revise your own work.

❶ Stress the relationship between ideas or events with appropriate use of conjunctions such as *and*, *but*, and *or*. Study the following:

EVENTS LINKED I played with my grape knife . . . I stopped when Mother reminded me.

SOTO'S VERSION I played with my grape knife, . . . *but* stopped when Mother reminded me.

❷ Use prepositions to add information to a sentence.

BLAND VERSION She talked.

SOTO'S VERSION She talked about school . . . .

Prepositions, Conjunctions, and Interjections

Practice Apply some of Soto's techniques by revising the following passage, using a separate sheet of paper. Add conjunctions or prepositions in the places indicated by carets (∧). Answers will vary.

Ethan suggested the latest horror film, ∧ Doreen said she was sure to get nightmares. They then discussed every film ∧ town until Doreen finally burst out, " ∧ I don't care which film we see. Let's just go!" ∧ the theater, the two friends still couldn't agree on anything. "Come on, Dorrie," insisted Ethan, "I'll sit ∧ the back, ∧ I can't see up close." The disputes began again the minute Doreen ∧ Ethan emerged ∧ the theater. "That was the most awful movie," pronounced Doreen.

UNIT 14

Clauses and Complex Sentences

A **sentence** is a group of words that has a subject and a predicate and expresses a complete thought.

- A **simple sentence** has one complete subject and one complete predicate.

The **complete subject** names whom or what the sentence is about. The **complete predicate** tells what the subject does or has. Sometimes it tells what the subject is or is like.

Complete Subject	Complete Predicate
The Cincinnati Reds	played their first baseball game in 1869.
This Ohio team	was the first professional baseball team.
The American League	played its first games in 1901.

- A **compound sentence** contains two or more simple sentences. Each simple sentence is called a main clause.
- A **main clause** has a subject and a predicate and can stand alone as a sentence.

Main clauses can be connected by a comma plus a conjunction, a semicolon, or a semicolon plus a conjunctive adverb. The conjunctive adverb is followed by a comma. In the compound sentences below, each main clause is in black; the connecting elements are highlighted in red.

Abner Doubleday supposedly invented baseball, **but** some reject this claim. (comma plus coordinating conjunction)

Alexander Joy Cartwright established rules; he was a good organizer. (semicolon)

Cartwright improved the game; **moreover,** many now regard him as the inventor of modern baseball. (semicolon plus conjunctive adverb)

Clauses and Complex Sentences

| **Exercise 1** | **Identifying Simple and Compound Sentences** |

Identify each sentence as *simple* or *compound*.

1. Abner Doubleday or Alexander Cartwright invented baseball.
2. Cartwright wrote rules for the Knickerbocker Baseball Club.
3. The first modern baseball game took place in 1846.
4. One team brought the ball, and the other team provided the field.
5. Pitchers threw underhand, but their pitches were slow.
6. The first team with twenty-one runs would win the game.
7. Both teams played hard; however, only one team could win.
8. The game ended; two men were on third base.
9. The winners were the New York Nines.
10. The first teams were amateur; the players did not earn any money.
11. Baseball players were not paid until the end of the 1860s.
12. Today, North American baseball teams are divided into two leagues.
13. One league is the National League, and the other is the American League.
14. The National League was organized in 1876; it had ten teams at that time.
15. The American League was founded in 1900; its first season began in 1901.
16. The Montreal Expos became the first Canadian team in the National League.
17. Some teams change cities, but they usually keep their names.
18. The Boston Braves moved to Milwaukee and became the Milwaukee Braves.
19. Later, the Braves moved south to Atlanta.
20. The St. Louis Browns moved to Baltimore; they became the Orioles.

| **Exercise 2** | **Punctuating Compound Sentences** |

Write each sentence, and underline each main clause. Add a comma or a semicolon as needed. If it is a simple sentence, write *simple*.

1. There are many theories about baseball's origin but the truth remains a mystery.
2. Ancient people played bat-and-ball games therefore these games could be ancestors of baseball.
3. Did baseball begin as rounders or did it come from cricket?
4. The British played rounders in the early nineteenth century.
5. Baseball resembles cricket however the rules of the game are very different.
6. Cartwright established the rules but Henry Chadwick improved them.
7. Baseball has many serious and devoted fans.
8. Some fans attend baseball games some listen to the games on the radio.
9. You can watch a game on television or you can read about it in the newspaper.
10. More than fifty million fans attend major league baseball games each year.

Complex Sentences

A **main clause** has a subject and a predicate and can stand alone as a sentence.

Sometimes sentences have a main clause and a subordinate clause.

■ A **subordinate clause** is a group of words that has a subject and a predicate but does not express a complete thought and cannot stand alone as a sentence. It is always combined with a main clause.

■ A **complex sentence** has a main clause and one or more subordinate clauses.

In each complex sentence below, the main clause is in light type, and the subordinate clause is in dark type.

> Many basketball fans visit Springfield, Massachusetts, **which was the birthplace of basketball.**
>
> Basketball has increased in popularity **since it began in Springfield.**
>
> Many people know **that basketball is played by men and women.**

Subordinate clauses can function in three ways: as adjectives, as adverbs, or as nouns. In the examples above, the first sentence has an adjective clause that modifies the noun *Springfield,* the second has an adverb clause that modifies the verb *has increased,* and the third has a noun clause that is the direct object of the verb *know.* Such clauses can be used in the same ways that single-word adjectives, adverbs, and nouns are used.

The team waits on the sidelines, **while the substitute warms the bench.**

MAIN CLAUSE **SUBORDINATE CLAUSE**

Identifying Complex Sentences

Identify the main clause in each sentence. Then label each sentence complex or simple.

1. Professional basketball is played during the winter, which was once a dull season for sports.
2. James Naismith developed the game when he saw a need for an indoor sport.
3. He was an instructor for the YMCA in Massachusetts.
4. A soccer ball was the ball that was first used.
5. The first baskets were two half-bushel peach baskets that were hung from balconies.
6. Naismith planned a game with little physical contact because he did not envision basketball as a rough sport.
7. The rules of the game were drafted in 1891.
8. There were thirteen rules that penalized players for rough conduct.
9. Before the first official game was played in 1892, probably no one outside of Naismith's YMCA had heard of basketball.
10. Basketball still follows most of Naismith's original thirteen rules.
11. Although originally nine players were on each team, now each team has five players on the court at one time.
12. In the early 1900s, the first women's teams were formed.
13. Do the rules of the game change when men and women play basketball together?
14. Although the rules for men's and women's basketball are similar, the ball is different.
15. The referee tosses the ball into the air.
16. After the referee tosses the ball, one player from each team jumps within the center circle.
17. Each player tries for the ball.
18. When a team scores, the opposing team takes the ball out of bounds from behind the base line.
19. The team then takes the ball to the basket that is at the other end of the court.
20. A team scores points when it gets the ball into its own basket.
21. The baskets at the top of ten-foot poles are usually called goals.
22. Behind each goal is a backboard, which can guide the ball down into the basket.
23. A special excitement belongs to basketball, which is a fast-moving game.
24. Basketball has won many fans who are dedicated basketball enthusiasts.
25. Many players have fan clubs.

14.3 Adjective Clauses

■ An **adjective clause** is a subordinate clause that modifies, or describes, a noun or pronoun in the main clause of a complex sentence.

> The Aqua-Lung, **which divers strap on,** holds oxygen.
> The divers breathe through a tube **that attaches to the tank.**

Each subordinate clause in dark type in these sentences is an adjective clause. An adjective clause adds information about a noun or pronoun in the main clause.

An adjective clause is usually introduced by a relative pronoun. Relative pronouns signal a subordinate clause, which cannot stand alone.

Relative Pronouns			
that	who	whose	what
which	whom	whoever	

An adjective clause can also begin with *where* or *when.*

> Divers search for reefs **where much sea life exists.**

A relative pronoun that begins an adjective clause can be the subject of the clause.

> Some divers prefer equipment **that is lightweight.**
> Willa is a new diver **who is taking lessons.**

In the first sentence above, *that* is the subject of the adjective clause. In the second sentence, *who* is the subject.

Write each adjective clause and underline each relative pronoun. Write the noun or pronoun that each adjective clause modifies.

1. Scuba equipment, which is used for deep diving, gets its name from the phrase *self-contained underwater breathing apparatus.*
2. Jacques Cousteau, who is famous for underwater exploration, designed the Aqua-Lung.
3. Divers sometimes wear weights that they strap on.
4. Divers often wear wet suits, which are basic diving equipment.
5. Diving methods, which are now advanced, allow close observation of sea life.
6. Alexander the Great, who lived in the fourth century B.C., used a barrel for diving.
7. Leonardo da Vinci, who was a famous artist and inventor, designed a piece of diving equipment.
8. The equipment that da Vinci designed was a leather diving helmet.
9. The helmet, which had spikes on it for protection from monsters, had a long breathing tube.
10. At the end of the tube was a cork that kept the tube afloat.
11. Divers needed an apparatus that would protect them from high water pressure.
12. Diving bells were the earliest containers that were reliable.
13. The diving bells that were used in the 1500s were quite large.
14. Edmund Halley, who was an astronomer and mathematician, designed the first real diving bell in 1716.
15. Halley, whose most famous discovery was Halley's Comet, actually designed two very different diving bells.
16. One bell, which was made of wood, looked like an upside-down bucket.
17. Halley's other diving bell, which stood eight feet tall, could carry several divers.
18. It was the larger one that was made of lead.
19. Halley and four other divers could dive to a depth of ten fathoms, which is equal to sixty feet.
20. The five men, who were very brave, stayed at that depth for over an hour.
21. The only problem that they reported was a pain in their ears.
22. The pain that they felt was due to an increased pressure at that depth.
23. Auguste Piccard designed the bathyscaphe, which is a diving vehicle.
24. Jacques Piccard, who is Auguste's son, wanted to explore the Gulf Stream.
25. The Gulf Stream is a warm undersea current that flows through the Atlantic.

Clauses and Complex Sentences

14.4 Essential and Nonessential Clauses

Read the sentence below. Is the adjective clause in dark type needed to make the meaning of the sentence clear?

The swimmer **who is in lane six** won last time.

The woman **who is near the pool** is a good swimmer.

The adjective clause here is essential, or necessary, to the meaning of the sentence. The clause identifies which woman is a good swimmer.

Our team, **which is undefeated,** is favored to win the championship.

- An **essential clause** is an adjective clause that is necessary to make the meaning of the sentence clear. Do not use commas to set off an essential clause from the rest of the sentence.

Notice, however, the adjective clauses in the sentences below.

Swimmers enjoy the pool, **which is extremely clean.**

The pool, **which is open all week,** is never crowded.

In the sentences above, the adjective clauses are set off by commas. The clauses are nonessential, or not necessary, to identify which pool the writer means. The clauses give only additional information about the noun that they modify.

- A nonessential clause is an adjective clause that is not necessary to make the meaning of the sentence clear. Use commas to set off a nonessential clause from the rest of the sentence.

Did you see the meet **that** our team won yesterday? (essential)

The meet, **which** began late, ended well after dark. (nonessential)

Exercise 5   Identifying Essential and Nonessential Clauses

Write each adjective clause. Identify the adjective clause as *essential* or *nonessential.*

1. The athletes whom I most admire are swimmers.
2. Swimming, which requires strength and stamina, is a challenging sport.
3. A swimmer who wishes to participate in serious swimming competitions must practice constantly.
4. Some swimmers are nervous before competitions, which are usually referred to as swim meets.
5. Our women's team, whose record stands, enters the pool area.
6. The team members, who hope for a win today, listen to the coach's advice.
7. Each race that the team members swim is called a heat.
8. The contestants, who are wearing special racing suits, will swim eight lengths of the pool in the first heat.
9. The racers stand on the starting blocks that are at the far end of the pool.
10. The signal that starts each race is a gunshot.

Exercise 6   Punctuating Essential and Nonessential Clauses

Write each sentence and underline each adjective clause. Identify each as *essential* or *nonessential,* and add commas as needed.

1. In the 1800s, the Australian crawl which replaced the breast stroke in popularity came into use.
2. In the 1920s, Johnny Weissmuller whose other career was acting in movies perfected the front crawl.
3. The skillful athlete who portrayed Tarzan in twelve movies was known to many people as a swimmer rather than an actor.
4. Weissmuller whose swimming ability was quickly recognized began swimming at a young age.
5. He worked hard for the three gold medals that he won at the 1924 Olympics.
6. The two additional gold medals that Weissmuller won at the 1928 Olympic Games probably made all his long hours of practice seem worthwhile.
7. Weissmuller was the athlete who set sixty-five United States and world records.
8. In 1927 he swam to a new record which was 100 yards in 51 seconds.
9. In 1968 Jim Counsilman studied techniques that swimmers were using.
10. Counsilman whose observations were later published became a world-famous coach.

14.5 Adverb Clauses

■ An **adverb clause** is a subordinate clause that often modifies, or describes, the verb in the main clause of a complex sentence.

An adverb clause tells *how, when, where, why,* or *under what conditions* the action occurs.

After she bought safe equipment, Lee explored the undersea world.

Scuba divers wear tanks **because they cannot breathe underwater.**

In the first sentence above, the adverb clause *After she bought safe equipment* modifies the verb explored. The adverb clause tells when Lee explored the undersea world. In the second sentence, the adverb clause *because they cannot breathe underwater* modifies the verb wear. The adverb clause tells why scuba divers wear tanks.

An adverb clause is introduced by a subordinating conjunction. Subordinating conjunctions signal a subordinate clause, which cannot stand alone.

Subordinating Conjunctions			
after	before	though	whenever
although	if	unless	where
as	since	until	whereas
because	than	when	wherever

You usually do not use a comma before an adverb clause that comes at the end of a sentence. However, you do use a comma after an adverb clause that introduces a sentence.

Exercise 7   Identifying Adverb Clauses

Write each sentence. Underline each adverb clause and circle each subordinating conjunction. Draw an arrow to the verb that each adverb clause modifies.

1. Divers wear wet suits and rubber fins when they swim.
2. They wear wet suits because the water might be cold.
3. Divers wear masks since they need them for underwater vision.
4. After you dive for the first time, you will have more confidence.
5. Divers wear weighted belts when they want to stay underwater for a long time.
6. When they return to the surface, divers should rise slowly and carefully.
7. Divers can suffer the bends if they rise to the surface too quickly.
8. Because this condition can occur, divers must learn how to control the ascent.
9. Although they sometimes are in a hurry, divers must rise slowly.
10. Divers should work with partners whenever they dive in unfamiliar waters.
11. Unless she has a buddy with her, a diver should not make a dive.
12. Because it is so mysterious, the deep sea fascinates people.
13. Interest in the deep seas began before Alexander the Great first went diving.
14. He sat inside a glass barrel as sailors lowered it into the sea.
15. Undersea quests progressed after Alexander the Great made his barrel dives.
16. Auguste Piccard flew in a balloon before he invented the bathyscaphe.
17. After he designed this craft, Piccard and his son Jacques descended in it.
18. Jacques used the bathyscaphe when he explored the Gulf of Mexico.
19. Until Jacques Costeau invented the Aqua-Lung, deep-sea diving was difficult.
20. Study of the oceans became much easier after scuba gear was invented.

Exercise 8   Punctuating Adverb Clauses

Write each sentence. Underline each adverb clause, and add a comma as needed.

1. Although it may not seem easy diving is not difficult for most people.
2. Hopeful divers can enroll in diving school when they are ready to learn.
3. Before they learn scuba diving students should learn snorkeling.
4. Trainers teach about the bends since this condition can be life-threatening.
5. The bends can occur when a diver surfaces too quickly.
6. If they surface slowly divers can avoid this problem.
7. After they complete long training and many practice dives divers are certified.
8. Can certified divers dive wherever they like?
9. New divers should dive only 130 feet since deeper dives can be dangerous.
10. If you dive in Belize you will have the ultimate diving experience.

14.6 Noun Clauses

■ A **noun clause** is a subordinate clause used as a noun.

Notice how the noun in dark type in the sentence below can be replaced by a clause.

> **Players** must skate extremely well.
>
> **Whoever plays ice hockey** must skate extremely well.

The clause in dark type, like the noun it replaces, is the subject of the sentence. Since this kind of clause acts as a noun, it is called a noun clause.

You can use a noun clause in the same ways that you can use any noun—as a subject, a direct object, an object of a preposition, or a predicate noun. With most sentences containing noun clauses, you could replace the noun clause with the word it, and the sentence would still make sense.

How Noun Clauses Are Used	
Subject	**What makes ice hockey exciting** is the speed.
Direct Object	Players know **that the game can be dangerous.**
Object of a Preposition	Victory goes to **whoever makes more goals.**
Predicate Noun	This rink is **where the teams will play.**

Following are some words that can introduce noun clauses.

Words That Introduce Noun Clauses		
how, however	where, whether	whom, whomever
that	which, whichever	whose
what, whatever	who, whoever	why, when

Exercise 9   **Identifying Noun Clauses**

Write each noun clause.

1. That ice hockey began in Canada is not surprising.
2. Where the sport began is not easily verified.
3. Three different cities claim that they hosted the first hockey game.
4. Most people believe that the game was played in Jamaica as early as 1830.
5. The fact is that the first recorded game occurred in Montreal around 1875.
6. You could argue that Canadians are still among the best hockey players.
7. There have been some changes in how ice hockey is played.
8. Whoever plays hockey today must wear protective equipment.
9. Do you know which sport is most dangerous?
10. Some people question whether hockey has to be so dangerous.

Exercise 10   **Identifying Noun Clauses and Their Use**

Write each noun clause, and label it *subject, direct object, object of a preposition,* or *predicate noun.*

1. Most people realize that ice hockey is a game of action.
2. Did you know that hockey is the fastest of all team sports?
3. Fast starts, stops, and turns are what the game demands.
4. What the players pursue is the puck.
5. Where they want to put the puck is inside the other team's goal.
6. That the puck often moves over one hundred miles an hour may surprise you.
7. The puck's speed is why hockey players must react so quickly.
8. The goalies know that their role is critical.
9. The goalie is who must block the other team's slap shots.
10. What is important to the team is a goalie's dependability.
11. Chris will demonstrate how a goalie drops to the ice and blocks shots.
12. Whoever stands and blocks shots is called a stand-up goalie.
13. The Vezina Trophy is awarded to whoever is the best goalie of the year.
14. Whoever asks can learn for whom the trophy was named.
15. The answer is that the trophy is awarded in honor of George Vezina.
16. Each year the Stanley Cup Playoffs determine which team is best.
17. That no team won the Stanley Cup in 1919 baffled me.
18. The truth is that a flu epidemic prematurely ended the finals.
19. How players respond can be crucial to the game.
20. Players must respond quickly to whatever happens.

Grammar Review

CLAUSES AND COMPLEX SENTENCES

In this passage, Mickey Mantle tells of his weaknesses in playing the field. The annotations show some of the types of clauses and sentences covered in this unit.

Literature Model

from The Education of a Baseball Player
by Mickey Mantle

My fielding, I knew, was often sorry. I had learned to charge a ground ball well and if I could get an angle on a ball, I could field it cleanly and get off a fast throw. My arm was unusually strong, and my throws would really hum across the diamond. But when a ball came straight at me, I was often undone. Somehow it was almost impossible for me to judge the speed or the bounce of a ground ball like that. I might back off foolishly, letting the ball play me, and then lose it altogether. Or I would turn my head as it reached me, and the ball would skip by or bounce right into my face. I carried around uncounted fat lips in that day from stopping ground balls with my mouth. And the more often I got hit, the more I would shy at such a ball. Even the balls I fielded cleanly did not always mean an out, for I had a habit of rejoicing so in the strength of my arm that I would not take the time to get a sure eye on the target. I would just let fly with my full strength, and often the ball would sail untouched into the stands.

- Main clause
- Complex sentence
- Adverb clause
- Adjective clause
- Compound sentence

Clauses and Complex Sentences

Grammar Review

Review: Exercise 1   Identifying Simple and Compound Sentences

Write whether each sentence is *simple* or *compound*. If it is compound, write it and add commas where needed.

SAMPLE   Mickey Mantle's father loved baseball and he shared this love with his son.

ANSWER   Mickey Mantle's father loved baseball, and he shared this love with his son. (compound)

1. As a young boy, Mantle frequently played ball from morning to night.
2. His father gave him a professional-model baseball glove for Christmas one year and he cared for it devotedly.
3. Mantle considered himself the worst player on his team.
4. His fielding was erratic and other boys hit better than he did.
5. Mantle was known for not only his powerful hitting but also his fast running.
6. Mickey Mantle was a superb base runner but he stole few bases.
7. Base running and base stealing are two different skills.
8. A player may be a good base stealer but he may not be a good base runner.
9. Players like Ty Cobb were good at both.
10. Lou Brock was a great base stealer and he was an excellent base runner.

Review: Exercise 2   Punctuating Simple and Compound Sentences

Write each sentence, and underline each main clause. Add a comma or a semicolon as needed.

SAMPLE   He stole fewer bases than Mantle each season but he was considered an excellent base runner.

ANSWER   <u>He stole fewer bases than Mantle each season</u>, but <u>he was considered an excellent base runner.</u>

1. Joe DiMaggio's father was a fisherman in San Francisco.
2. Joe did not like the smell of fish he chose baseball as a career.
3. His father wasn't thrilled but he wished his son luck.
4. Another DiMaggio son also played baseball.
5. Vince DiMaggio earned his living as a baseball player and he introduced Joe to the game.

Review: Exercise 3 — Distinguishing Between Simple and Complex Sentences

Label each sentence as *simple* or *complex*. If it is complex, write the subordinate clause.

SAMPLE When Willie Mays joined the New York Giants, Mickey Mantle was playing center field for the American League Yankees.
ANSWER (complex) When Willie Mays joined the New York Giants,

1. In the 1950s, the Giants were the National League team from New York.
2. Willie Mays was twenty when he became a Giants player in 1951.
3. Mays played center field, which requires a powerful arm.
4. The arrival of Mays caused a controversy among baseball fans.
5. Fans argued all the time about who was the better player.
6. Some said that Mantle, with his speed and power, was the better of the two.
7. Mays, however, may have been the greatest player of all time.
8. Since Mays was a terrific all-around player, many agree with that opinion.
9. Injuries hindered Mickey Mantle's performance throughout his career.
10. Although he was often in pain, Mantle played well.

Review: Exercise 4 — Distinguishing Between Compound and Complex Sentences

Label each sentence as *compound* or *complex*. If it is complex, write the subordinate clause.

1. New York State has a long baseball history, and it has had many teams.
2. The teams that played for New York include the Yankees, Dodgers, and Giants.
3. When the Dodgers and the Giants moved to California, New York had no National League team.
4. The Mets, which is a National League team, was formed in 1962.
5. Fans agree that some of baseball's best teams have come from New York.
6. Did you know that from 1936 to 1964 the Yankees won sixteen World Series?
7. The Yankees had great teams then, but perhaps the best was the 1961 team.
8. That team had incredibly talented players; Mickey Mantle was one of them.
9. Roger Maris, who came to the Yankees in 1959, also starred on that team.
10. Maris and Mantle both hit more than fifty home runs that season, and they soon became known as the M & M boys.

Clauses and Complex Sentences

Review: Exercise 5   **Identifying Adjective Clauses**

Write each sentence. Underline each adjective clause once and each relative pronoun twice. Circle the noun that each adjective clause modifies.

SAMPLE   In 1955 New York State had another team that is considered one of baseball's best.

ANSWER   In 1955 New York State had another (team) that is considered one of baseball's best.

1. You must mean the 1955 Brooklyn Dodgers, who later moved to Los Angeles.
2. Branch Rickey, whose courage and foresight brought amazing talent to the Dodgers' organization, was the manager of the team then.
3. It was one particularly courageous act that brought fame to Branch Rickey.
4. Branch Rickey signed Jackie Robinson, who was African American.
5. The major league color line, which had restricted African American players to the Negro League, was broken by Jackie Robinson in 1947.
6. Robinson soon proved his worth in the face of the jeers that surrounded him.
7. Insults that came from fans and opposing players surely must have hurt.
8. Jackie responded with the quiet dignity that marked his life and career.
9. Pee Wee Reese, who was a teammate, openly supported Jackie on the field.
10. In 1955 Robinson and the Dodgers won the World Series against the Yankees, whose roster included the young slugger Mickey Mantle.

Review: Exercise 6   **Identifying Essential and Nonessential Clauses**

Write each adjective clause. Label the clause *essential* or *nonessential,* and add commas as needed.

1. Mickey was named after the catcher Mickey Cochrane who made it into the Hall of Fame.
2. Mantle's father who worked in the lead mines had played semi-pro ball.
3. The baseball glove that his father gave him one year cost twenty-two dollars.
4. Mantle who was named the Most Valuable Player three times also played in sixteen All-Star games.
5. Mantle hit 536 home runs during the years that he played with the Yankees.

Review: Exercise 7 — Identifying Adverb Clauses

Write each sentence. Underline the adverb clause, and circle the word that the clause modifies. Add commas where needed.

SAMPLE   When Mantle joined the Yankees Casey Stengel was the manager.
ANSWER   When Mantle joined the Yankees, Casey Stengel (was) the manager.

1. When Mantle was just an infant his father Mutt put baseballs in his crib.
2. Mutt talked baseball to his infant son whenever he got the chance.
3. Mantle considered himself lucky because his father pushed and encouraged him.
4. Mantle was only nineteen years old when the Yankees signed him.
5. Mantle hit poorly because he was confused by major league pitchers.
6. Since he was struggling the Yankees sent him down to the minor leagues.
7. Although he was now a professional Mantle still needed his father's advice.
8. Mantle quickly improved after his father gave him good advice.
9. While he played for the Yankees they were the dominant team in baseball.
10. Mantle was elected to the Hall of Fame as soon as he became eligible.

Review: Exercise 8 — Identifying Noun Clauses

Write each noun clause, and label it *subject, direct object, object of a preposition,* or *predicate noun.*

SAMPLE   Mantle's father knew that baseball could provide a future for his son.
ANSWER   that baseball could provide a future for his son; direct object

1. What made the young Mickey Mantle so extraordinary was his speed.
2. His coaches were amazed at how quickly he sped around the bases.
3. Opposing players knew that Mantle's speed was practically unbeatable.
4. What made Mantle consult a doctor at age fifteen was an injured ankle.
5. Mickey's doctor discovered that Mickey had a serious bone infection.
6. The doctor's conclusion was that Mickey would never play baseball again.
7. Mickey could hardly believe what he had heard.
8. Time and history proved how wrong the doctor was.
9. Whoever knows about Mantle's illustrious career knows the truth.
10. Courage and determination were what kept Mantle's career hopes alive.

Grammar Review

Review: Exercise 9   **Writing Complex Sentences**

Combine each pair of sentences below, using the relative pronoun or subordinating conjunction in parentheses. Put the subordinate clause where it makes sense, and add commas where they are needed.

1. I saw some films about baseball. I was home sick last week. (while)
2. One film was *Eight Men Out*. It was about the 1919 "Black Sox" scandal. (which)
3. Allegedly, eight players took money to lose the World Series. They were members of the Chicago White Sox. (who)
4. The eighth man never admitted guilt in the scheme. The scheme remained a black mark on the history of baseball. (which)
5. The movie was good. I didn't like it as much as others. (although)
6. *Field of Dreams* was my favorite. It starred Kevin Costner. (which)
7. Costner is an Iowa farmer. His character's name is Ray Kinsella. (whose)
8. Ray hears a voice. It says "If you build it, he will come." (that)
9. Ray ponders the mysterious message. He makes a discovery. (as)
10. The "he" in the message refers to Shoeless Joe Jackson. Jackson was one of the eight men in the Chicago "Black Sox" scandal. (who)
11. All the acquitted Chicago players come out of Ray's cornfield. Ray builds the baseball diamond. (when)
12. These men play baseball. These men have been dead for years. (who)
13. Another good film is *A League of Their Own*. You should see it. (that)
14. This story is about a special time in baseball during World War II. Women played professional baseball then. (when)
15. Many of the male players had been drafted into the armed forces. A women's professional baseball league was formed. (because)
16. The All-American Girls Professional Baseball League enlisted top female athletes. It was in existence from 1943 to 1954. (which)
17. Women had played baseball in school and at the amateur level. They had never played professional ball. (although)
18. The film's producer, Penny Marshall, interviewed some of the actual players at a ceremony in Cooperstown. She made the movie. (after)
19. The women must have enjoyed seeing the movie. Their story is also told in a book by Sue Macy titled *A Whole New Ball Game*. (whose)
20. These women put up with taunts and jeers from men. The women loved baseball and were excellent players. (who)

Review: Exercise 10

Proofreading

The following passage is about the American artist Morris Kantor, whose work appears below. Rewrite the passage, correcting the errors in spelling, capitalization, grammar, and usage. Add any missing punctuation. There are ten errors.

Morris Kantor

¹Morris Kantor was an american painter who lived during the early part of this century. ²Although Kantor received formal art training his style seems primitive.

³*Baseball at Night,* which apears below shows a group of people enjoying a game of semiprofessional baseball. ⁴Mutt Mantle, who was Mickey Mantle's father was playing baseball at about the same time and he probably played under similiar conditions.

⁵Mickey Mantle who became an American hero came from the world of small towns and sandlot baseball that Kantor depicts in *Baseball at Night.* ⁶Although Spavinaw, Oklahoma, may not have had night baseball it did produce at least one outstanding major league player.

Morris Kantor, *Baseball at Night,* 1934

Grammar Review

Mixed Review

Write whether each sentence is *simple, compound,* or *complex* If a sentence is complex, write the subordinate clause. Then indicate whether the clause is an *adverb clause,* an *adjective clause,* or a *noun clause.*

¹While three-year-old Mickey Mantle was learning about baseball in Oklahoma, another future baseball star was born. ²He was Roberto Clemente from Carolina, Puerto Rico. ³Roberto, who had six older brothers and sisters, was shy as a young boy. ⁴In spite of this, Roberto eagerly helped others whenever he could. ⁵Roberto also had strong leadership qualities, which helped him enlist the aid of others. ⁶Young Roberto learned about baseball from his older brothers. ⁷They shared with him what they knew about the game. ⁸Roberto had very large hands; he could easily catch a ball. ⁹As his love for baseball grew, his talent also grew. ¹⁰The manager of a softball team for which sixteen-year-old Roberto played recognized this talent. ¹¹The manager believed that Roberto could be a professional. ¹²When major league scouts saw Roberto, they agreed. ¹³The boy had a powerful and accurate throwing arm; he also hit well. ¹⁴Clemente, whose major league career began with the Brooklyn Dodgers, ended up with the Pittsburgh Pirates. ¹⁵He played there until he died on New Year's Eve in 1972. ¹⁶At the time he was thirty-eight. ¹⁷The plane in which he was traveling crashed. ¹⁸He and others were on their way to Nicaragua, where there had been a terrible earthquake. ¹⁹The plane was carrying relief supplies. ²⁰Roberto Clemente had reached out to others all his life; this was true even at the time of his death.

Writing Application

TIME

For more about the writing process, see **TIME Facing the Blank Page**, pp. 97-107.

Clauses in Writing

In *Silent Spring* Rachel Carson uses clauses to expand on her description of the natural world. Examine the passage, focusing on the italicized clauses.

> The countryside was, in fact, famous for the abundance and variety of its bird life, and *when the flood of migrants was pouring through in spring and fall* people traveled from great distances to observe them. Others came to fish the streams, *which flowed clear and cold out of the hills and contained shady pools where trout lay*. So it had been from the days many years ago *when the first settlers raised their houses, sank their wells, and built their barns*.

Techniques with Clauses

Try to apply some of Rachel Carson's writing techniques when you write.

❶ Notice Carson's use of elaboration with the addition of an adjective clause.

WITHOUT EXTRA DETAIL Others came to fish the streams.

CARSON'S VERSION Others came to fish the streams, *which flowed clear and cold out of the hills . . .*

❷ Emphasize the relationship between events and ideas in your writing by combining related sentences into compound sentences. Compare the following:

WEAKER CONNECTION The countryside was, in fact, famous for the abundance . . . and variety of its bird life. People traveled to observe them.

CARSON'S VERSION The countryside was, in fact, famous for the abundance . . . of its bird life, *and when the flood of migrants was pouring through in spring and fall* people traveled . . .

Practice Apply some of these techniques as you revise the following passage, using a separate sheet of paper. Reorganize or reword the sentences, combining clauses as appropriate to show the relationships among your ideas.

> Ben had never used a bank account before. Today he made his first deposit. The Bank It! program was new at Ben's school. The students were learning all about deposits and withdrawals. Ben was eager to learn banking. He hoped to save enough money to buy a new bike. He'd been keeping his savings at home. They were stashed in a shoe box under the bed. The box was getting full. Ben knew that his money would be safer in the school bank.

Clauses and Complex Sentences

LOG ON ▶ **Writing** Online | For more grammar practice, go to **glencoe.com** and enter QuickPass code WC87703p2.

Writing Application **525**

UNIT 15

Verbals

15.1 Participles and Participial Phrases

A present participle is formed by adding *-ing* to the verb. A past participle is usually formed by adding *-ed* to the verb. A participle can act as the main verb in a verb phrase or as an adjective to describe, or modify, nouns or pronouns.

> The player has **kicked** the ball. [main verb in a verb phrase]
>
> The **kicked** ball soared. [adjective modifying *ball*]

Sometimes a participle that is used as an adjective is part of a phrase. This kind of phrase is called a participial phrase.

> **Cheering for the home team,** the fans were on their feet.
>
> The ball **kicked by Donnell** soared into the goal.

■ A **participial phrase** is a group of words that includes a participle and other words that complete its meaning.

A participial phrase that is placed at the beginning of a sentence is always set off with a comma.

> **Running for the ball,** a player slipped in the mud.

The **kicked** ball soared . . .

Other participial phrases may or may not need commas. If the phrase is necessary to identify the modified word, do not set it off with commas. If the phrase simply gives additional information about the modified word, set it off with commas.

. . . into the goal.

> The player **kicking the ball** is Donnell.
>
> Donnell, **kicking the ball,** scored the final point.

A participial phrase can appear before or after the word it describes. Place the phrase as close as possible to the modified word; otherwise, the meaning of the sentence may be unclear.

Exercise 1   Identifying Participles

Write each participle. Write whether it is used as a *verb* or as an *adjective.*

1. Soccer can be a challenging game.
2. Many young people are participating in the sport.
3. The size of the playing field for soccer may vary.
4. Have rules for the sport changed over the years?
5. A player on our team has scored the winning goal.

Exercise 2   Using Participial Phrases

Write each sentence. Underline each participial phrase. Then draw two lines under the word that the phrase describes. Add commas if needed to set off the phrase.

1. Attracting huge crowds soccer is a popular sport.
2. The game consists of two teams competing for goals.
3. Playing within certain areas the goalkeepers can touch the ball with their hands.
4. For other players, the only contact permitted by the rules is with their feet, heads, or bodies.
5. The two teams playing the game kick off.
6. The teams moving almost constantly during play kick the ball back and forth.
7. Varying their formations players move about the field.
8. By the 1800s, English schools playing a similar game had drawn up the first set of rules.
9. Spreading throughout the world soccer became especially popular in Europe and Latin America in the late 1800s.
10. Spectators standing on the sidelines cheered the teams.
11. Representing two rival towns the teams took their places on the field.
12. Last year's champions defending their title played energetically.
13. Blowing a whistle the referee started the game.
14. The team dressed in blue tried to advance the ball toward the goal.
15. Kicking the ball out of bounds the blue team lost its advantage.
16. The team's star player dribbling the ball toward the goal suddenly tripped.
17. An opponent rushing toward the ball prevented a goal.
18. Passing the ball from player to player the team traveled down the field.
19. The goalkeeper jumping as high as possible was unable to catch the ball.
20. Kicking the ball high into the air a player on the blue team finally scored a goal.

15.2 Gerunds and Gerund Phrases

The previous lesson explains that the present participle may be used as a verb or as an adjective. It may also be used as a noun, in which case it is called a *gerund*.

> The **playing** field is one hundred yards long. [adjective]
> **Playing** is our favorite activity. [gerund]

■ A **gerund** is a verb form that ends in *-ing* and is used as a noun.

Like other nouns a gerund can serve as the simple subject of a sentence. It can also be a direct object or the object of a preposition.

> **Blocking** requires strength. [subject]
> The athletes enjoy **exercising.** [direct object]
> They maintain endurance by **running.** [object of a preposition]

■ A **gerund phrase** is a group of words that includes a gerund and other words that complete its meaning.

> **Kicking the ball** takes skill.
> A team tries **scoring a touchdown.**
> A touchdown results from **moving the ball across the goal.**

You can identify the three functions of *-ing* verb forms if you remember that a present participle can serve as a verb, as an adjective, or as a noun, in which case it is called a gerund.

> The Giants are **winning** the game. [main verb]
> The **winning** team scores the most points. [adjective]
> **Winning** is always exciting. [gerund]

Exercise 3   Identifying Verbals

Copy each underlined word, and write *main verb, adjective,* or *gerund* to show how it is used in the sentence.

1. The coach or the captain chooses <u>playing</u> strategies.
2. The quarterback does not like <u>guessing</u> the next play.
3. The team members are <u>hoping</u> for a victory.
4. <u>Scoring</u> in football can occur in four different ways.
5. A team earns six points by <u>crossing</u> the opponent's goal line.

Exercise 4   Identifying Gerunds

Write each gerund or gerund phrase. Then write *subject, direct object,* or *object of a preposition* to show how it is used in the sentence.

1. A win requires earning more points than the opponent.
2. Kicking earns points in two different ways in this sport.
3. A team earns three points by kicking a field goal.
4. Teams also try converting for one point after a touchdown.
5. Defending the team's own goal is crucial.
6. A team's defense features tackling.
7. Blocking is another important element of a good defense.
8. Passing makes football exciting.
9. Testing your skills is an important part of football.
10. Skilled players increase spectators' enjoyment by adding dramatic action to the game.
11. Watching football on television is a favorite pastime for many people.
12. The defense tries to keep its opponents from scoring a touchdown.
13. Enforcing the rules is the referee's job.
14. The home team advanced by passing the ball toward the goal line.
15. Playing well involves speed and teamwork.
16. Shoes with cleats prevent slipping.
17. Players can improve their skills with good coaching.
18. A coach's work involves deciding which positions team members will play and what plays will be used.
19. After preparing the game plan, a coach sometimes discusses ideas with the team's quarterback.
20. Kicking off is decided by flipping a coin.

15.3 | Infinitives and Infinitive Phrases

Another verb form that may function as a noun is an infinitive.

To referee requires training.

Trainees learn **to referee.**

■ An infinitive is formed from the word *to* together with the base form of a verb. It is often used as a noun in a sentence.

How can you tell whether the word *to* is a preposition or part of an infinitive? If the word *to* comes immediately before a verb, it is part of the infinitive.

Those young players want <u>**to win.**</u> [infinitive]

The coach is pointing <u>**to the pitcher.**</u> [prepositional phrase]

INFINITIVE

The player starts **to run.**

She runs
to home base.

PREPOSITIONAL
PHRASE

In the first sentence, the words in dark type work together as a noun to name what the players want. In the second sentence, the words in dark type are a prepositional phrase used as an adverb that tells *where* the coach is pointing.

Since infinitives function as nouns, they can be subjects and direct objects.

To referee demands patience. [subject]

Athletes often try **to argue.** [direct object]

■ An **infinitive phrase** is a group of words that includes an infinitive and other words that complete its meaning.

A player may try **to influence the call.**

To go to every game of the season is my dream.

Exercise 5　　Identifying Infinitives

Write each underlined group of words and label it *infinitive* or *prepositional phrase.*

1. <u>To win</u> is the dream of every World Series player.
2. The top team in each division goes <u>to the play-offs</u>.
3. The two winners are invited <u>to the World Series</u>.
4. <u>To excel</u> is each team's goal at these games.
5. Millions of people plan <u>to watch</u> the World Series on television.
6. We went <u>to a baseball game</u> last Saturday.
7. Would you like <u>to become</u> a professional player?
8. <u>To begin</u> by playing Little League is good.
9. As players improve, they move from the rookie <u>to the minor leagues.</u>
10. <u>To sponsor</u> Little League teams, local organizations pay for uniforms.

Exercise 6　　Identifying Infinitive Phrases

Write each infinitive or infinitive phrase. Label it *subject* or *direct object.*

1. To play in the American or National League is an accomplishment.
2. Most players prefer to play home games.
3. To leave means losing the support of all the home town fans.
4. To understand baseball requires knowledge of the structure of the game.
5. The players want to improve their strategies.
6. We've decided to root for the American League team in the World Series.
7. To attend a World Series game is one of my goals.
8. I want to go to Dodger Stadium.
9. Have you learned to pitch a fastball?
10. People began to play baseball in the 1800s.
11. Players learn to hit the ball.
12. To catch the ball is also very difficult.
13. The catcher needs to wear a mask, a chest protector, and shin guards.
14. To throw a variety of pitches is the goal of every pitcher.
15. Players need to check the batting order.
16. When the ball is hit, the player tries to run.
17. When the bases are loaded, the runner hopes to advance.
18. Try to tag the base!
19. To reach home plate is a wonderful feeling.
20. Would you like to join our team?

Grammar Review

VERBALS

In 1960 Wilma Rudolph became the first American woman to win three gold medals in track and field at the Olympic games. Shortly before she competed in her first Olympics, however, Rudolph was defeated at a regional high school track meet in Tuskegee, Alabama. In the following passage from "Wilma," an autobiographical essay, Rudolph describes how the defeat at Tuskegee motivated her to win in the future. The passage has been annotated to show some of the types of verbals covered in this unit.

Literature Model

from **Wilma**
by Wilma Rudolph

I ran and ran and ran every day, and I acquired this sense of determination, this sense of spirit that I would never, never give up, no matter what else happened. That day at Tuskegee had a tremendous effect on me inside. That's all I ever thought about. Some days I just wanted to go out and die. I just moped around and felt sorry for myself. Other days I'd go out to the track with fire in my eyes and imagine myself back at Tuskegee, beating them all. Losing as badly as I did had an impact on my personality. Winning all the time in track had given me confidence; I felt like a winner. But I didn't feel like a winner any more after Tuskegee. My confidence was shattered, and I was thinking the only way I could put it all together was to get back the next year and wipe them all out.

> **Participial phrase used as adjective**

> **Gerund phrase used as subject**

> **Infinitive phrase**

Grammar Review

Review: Exercise 1   Identifying Participial Phrases

Write each sentence. Underline each participial phrase. Then draw two lines under the word that the phrase describes. Add commas as needed.

SAMPLE   The runner refusing to let her defeat stop her continued to train.
ANSWER   The <u>runner,</u> <u>refusing to let her defeat stop her</u>, continued to train.

1. Rudolph having won two gold medals tried for a third in the 400-meter relay.
2. Crouched at the starting line the runners waited for the signal to start.
3. Leading the field the first runner streaked over the track.
4. Taking the baton the second runner raced away.
5. One runner reaching for the baton nearly let it drop.
6. The spectators watched Rudolph pulling ahead.
7. The runner taking one final stride lunged through the tape.
8. Trying to break a record the runner felt exhilarated.
9. Roaring wildly the crowd rose from their seats.
10. Gasping for breath she knew she could win.

Review: Exercise 2   Using Participles and Participial Phrases

Rewrite each sentence, inserting the participle or participial phrase in parentheses. Use commas as needed.

SAMPLE   Rudolph gained confidence. (running hard)
ANSWER   Running hard, Rudolph gained confidence.

1. The track meet at Tuskegee shocked the runner. (defeated)
2. Rudolph felt like quitting. (shattered by her defeat)
3. She briefly thought she might give up the sport. (discouraged at her failure)
4. She dreamed of winning the meet. (imagining herself back at Tuskegee)
5. The athlete never gave up. (fiercely determined)
6. She realized that a champion can try again, even after a defeat. (crushing)
7. Rudolph helped the 1956 Olympic relay team win a bronze medal. (having trained for just a year)
8. The young woman gained the respect of her coaches. (a talented athlete)
9. Rudolph won a trophy. (honoring her achievements)
10. Rudolph was pursued by reporters. (hoping for an interview)

Review: Exercise 3   Identifying Gerund Phrases

Write each gerund phrase. Then write *subject, direct object,* or *object of a preposition* to tell how it is being used.

1. Having polio when she was young left Rudolph unable to walk without a special shoe.
2. Rudolph proved her determination by learning to walk after her illness.
3. Her Olympic running seemed like a miracle.
4. She had also tried playing basketball.
5. Before setting a world record at the Olympics, Rudolph ran many practice races.
6. After winning her third gold medal in the 1960 Olympics, Rudolph returned home a hero.
7. She anticipated helping other women become runners.
8. Winning a gold medal is not all that matters in the Olympics.
9. Taking part is a great honor.
10. Participating in the Olympics is the high point of an athlete's career.

Review: Exercise 4   Using Gerunds and Gerund Phrases

Write a sentence that answers each question, using the word or words in parentheses.

SAMPLE   What is Wilma Rudolph best known for? (winning three gold medals at the Olympics)

ANSWER   Wilma Rudolph is best known for winning three gold medals at the Olympics.

1. By what means did Rudolph first achieve fame? (competing in the 1956 Olympic games)
2. What is another of Rudolph's achievements? (setting world records in the 100-meter and 200-meter races)
3. What might have prevented Rudolph from pursuing a career in track? (having polio as a young girl)
4. By what means did Rudolph strengthen her muscles after her illness? (running)
5. What was Rudolph's most recent challenge? (working with young people in sports and educational programs)

Grammar Review

Review: Exercise 5   **Identifying Infinitive Phrases**

Write each infinitive phrase. Then write *subject* or *direct object* to tell how it is being used.

1. To run a marathon tests the endurance and courage of even the most dedicated runners.
2. In the high jump, an athlete needs to leap over a high bar.
3. Jumpers learn to kick their legs out at the end of their jump.
4. Pole vaulters need to thrust themselves into the air with a pole.
5. As the pole straightens, they try to twist their bodies.
6. Some athletes prefer to jump over hurdles.
7. To win a hurdle race requires speed, strength, and skill.
8. Broad jumpers like to land in a soft sand pit.
9. To throw the discus requires tremendous strength.
10. To measure jumps and throws accurately demands the skill of experienced and well-trained judges.

Review: Exercise 6   **Using Infinitives and Infinitive Phrases**

Write a sentence that answers each question, using the infinitive phrase in parentheses. Use the phrase as the part of speech indicated.

SAMPLE   What must a race walker learn?
(to maintain proper technique—direct object)

ANSWER   A race walker must learn to maintain proper technique.

1. What is the purpose of the hurdle race?
(to run and jump over obstacles placed on the track—subject)
2. What must relay racers learn?
(to pass the baton smoothly and quickly—direct object)
3. What does a high jumper attempt to do?
(to leap over an upraised bar—direct object)
4. What is an important skill in throwing events?
(to propel an object as far as possible—subject)
5. What requires years of training?
(to throw a discus—subject)

Review: Exercise 7

Proofreading

The following passage is about Jacob Lawrence, an African American artist whose work appears on the next page. Rewrite the passage, correcting the errors in spelling, grammar, and usage. Add any missing punctuation. There are ten errors.

Jacob Lawrence

¹Jacob Lawrence was born in New Jersey in 1917 but growed up in Harlem. ²Studying art in after-school programs he acheived success at an early age. ³Gaining popularity in his twenties Lawrence becomed the first African American artist to have a one-person show at the Museum of Modern Art in New York. ⁴Vivid primary colors and highly stylized figures make Lawrences' work unique. ⁵In the poster shown on the next page, for example, the relay racers visibly strains to cross the finish line. ⁶Imitating Wilma Rudolph's determination each runner wants to win. ⁷The artist using gestures and facial expressions, conveys his figure's emotions.

Review: Exercise 8

Mixed Review

Write *participial phrase, gerund phrase,* or *infinitive phrase* to tell how each underlined phrase is used.

The Olympics, <u>held first in Olympia, Greece</u>, began 3,500 years ago. Greek competitors underwent <u>training for the Games</u>. <u>Reviving the Games</u> was the idea of Pierre de Coubertin. In 1896 thirteen nations decided <u>to send athletes</u>. Each country <u>desiring participation</u> needs <u>to organize a committee</u>. The city <u>holding the Games</u> spends years preparing. As the Games begin, spectators love <u>watching a runner with the Olympic flame</u>. The athletes, <u>carrying their national flag</u>, enter the stadium. <u>Dressed in their uniforms</u>, they watch the release of pigeons. As the birds begin <u>to fly away</u>, the Games

(continued)

Verbals

officially open. In summertime athletes, <u>running around the track</u>, demonstrate great speed. <u>Diving off a high board</u> is another event. In winter people like <u>to watch skiers</u>. Athletes <u>talented in their sport</u> want <u>to bring home a medal</u>, but few expect <u>to win the gold</u>. Even fewer are like Wilma Rudolph, <u>receiving three gold medals</u>. <u>Participating in the Games</u> is a dream come true.

Jacob Lawrence, *Study for the Munich Olympic Games Poster,* 1971

Verbals

Writing Application

TIME

For more about the writing process, see **TIME Facing the Blank Page**, pp. 97-107.

Verbals in Writing

Brent Ashabranner uses participles and gerunds to bring a sense of action to his essay about the Vietnam War Memorial. As you read this passage from *Always to Remember*, pay special attention to the italicized verbals.

> The answer, they decided, was to hold a national design competition open to all Americans. The *winning* design would receive a prize of $20,000, but the real prize would be the winner's knowledge that the memorial would become a part of American history on the Mall in Washington, D.C. Although fund *raising* was only well started at this point, the *choosing* of a memorial design could not be delayed if the memorial was to be built by Veteran's Day, 1982.

Techniques with Verbals

Try to apply some of Brent Ashabranner's writing techniques when you write and revise your work.

❶ Use participle verb forms as adjectives to make your descriptions more lively and engaging. Compare the following:

FLAT VERSION The design *that won* would receive a prize.

ASHABRANNER'S VERSION The *winning* design would receive a prize. . . .

❷ When appropriate, add a sense of action to your sentences by using gerunds.

LESS ACTIVE WORDS They had only just started to raise funds.

ASHABRANNER'S VERSION Although fund *raising* was only well started. . . .

Verbals

Practice Revise the following passage on a separate sheet of paper. Focusing on the underlined words, add gerunds and participles to make it more active.

"It will be a real challenge to work on my science project without electricity," said Sam to his teacher. "I know," Ms. Clayton replied. "The extra effort will expand what you learn from the experience." She flashed Sam a grin that tried to encourage him. "Oh well," he thought. "It's not my style to quit. It's of interest to invent new methods." He started to gather what he needed to mix chemicals and headed for home.

LOG ON ▶ **Writing** Online For more grammar practice, go to **glencoe.com** and enter QuickPass code WC87703p2.

Writing Application **539**

UNIT 16

Subject-Verb Agreement

16.1 Making Subjects and Verbs Agree

The basic idea of subject-verb agreement is a simple one—a singular noun subject calls for a singular form of the verb, and a plural noun calls for a plural form of the verb. The subject and its verb are said to *agree in number.* Read the sentences below. You can see that the subjects and verbs agree.

Note that in the present tense, the singular form of the verb usually ends in *-s* or *-es.*

The **frogs leap.**
PLURAL SUBJECT   PLURAL VERB

A **frog leaps.**
SINGULAR   SINGULAR
SUBJECT   VERB

Subject and Verb Agreement	
Singular Subject	**Plural Subject**
An **ecologist studies** nature.	**Ecologists study** nature.
The **boy learns** about ecology.	The **boys learn** about ecology.
Judy plants seedlings.	**Judy** and **Kim plant** seedlings.

The verb must also agree with a subject pronoun. Look at the chart below. Notice how the verb changes. In the present tense, the *-s* ending is used with the subject pronouns *it, he,* and *she.*

Subject Pronoun and Verb Agreement	
Singular	**Plural**
I **hike**.	We **hike**.
You **hike**.	You **hike**.
He, she, *or* it **hikes**.	They **hike**.

The irregular verbs *be, do,* and *have* can be main verbs or helping verbs. They must agree with the subject, regardless of whether they are main verbs or helping verbs.

I **am** a ranger. They **are** tagging a bear. He **is** digging.
She **does** well. She **does** climb cliffs. They **do** garden.
He **has** gear. He **has** saved birds. They **have** traveled.

Exercise 1   Making Subjects and Verbs Agree

Rewrite each sentence, changing singular subjects to plural and plural subjects to singular. Make the verbs agree with the subjects. Remember that other parts of the sentences might have to change when the subject changes.

1. The student plans a hike to the bog.
2. Bogs contain an interesting variety of organisms.
3. The state park is fun for everyone.
4. A leaflet explains the plants and animals in the park.
5. We are interested in learning more about the park's plants.
6. A ranger speaks to visitors every day at noon.
7. She identifies the various plants growing in the bog.
8. Guidebooks provide good information about the types of plants.
9. A bog offers opportunities for people hunting for fossils.
10. Bogs develop in former glacial lakes.

Exercise 2   Using Correct Subject and Verb Agreement

Write the correct form of the verb in parentheses.

1. The day (is, are) perfect for a visit to the bog.
2. The students always (enjoy, enjoys) field trips.
3. Bogs (contain, contains) acidic soil and many mosses.
4. Swamps (is, are) similar to bogs in many ways.
5. The acidity (tell, tells) you about the type of bog.
6. A bog (is, are) usually smaller than a swamp.
7. Ecosystems (is, are) communities of living and nonliving factors.
8. An ecosystem (include, includes) the surrounding air.
9. An ecosystem (has, have) distinct cycles.
10. Water (is, are) an important part of all ecosystems.
11. An ecologist (do, does) a great deal of fieldwork.
12. Bogs often (provide, provides) interesting ecosystems.
13. This bog (have, has) supported a rare ecosystem.
14. A unique fungus (grow, grows) in this bog.
15. Many creatures (live, lives) in bogs.
16. Ecosystems (consist, consists) of many different plants and animals.
17. Our survival (do, does) depend upon the painstaking work of the ecologists.
18. Their research often (have, has) a great impact on our view of our planet.
19. We (rely, relies) on the research of ecologists.
20. They (has, have) changed our understanding of our planet.

16.2 Problems with Locating the Subject

Making a subject and its verb agree is easy when the verb directly follows the subject. Sometimes, however, a phrase containing another noun comes between the subject and the verb.

In the sentence below, the phrase *except in the polar regions* contains a plural noun. The verb *becomes* must agree with the singular subject of the sentence, *desert,* not with the plural noun *regions,* which is the object of the preposition in the phrase.

The **desert,** except in the polar regions, **becomes** very hot.

In inverted sentences, the subject follows the verb. Inverted sentences often begin with a prepositional phrase. Do not mistake the object of the preposition for the subject of the sentence.

In the desert **roam herds** of camels.

In inverted sentences beginning with *Here* or *There,* look for the subject after the verb. *Here* or *there* is never the subject.

There is a high **mountain** near the desert.
Here at the top **are** many damp **rocks.**

By rearranging each sentence so that the subject comes first, you see the subject and verb in their usual order.

A high **mountain** there **is** near the desert.
Many damp **rocks are** here at the top.

In some interrogative sentences, an auxiliary verb comes before the subject. Look for the subject between the auxiliary verb and the main verb.

Do any **deserts contain** large animals?

Exercise 3   Making Subjects and Verbs Agree

Write each sentence. Underline the simple subject once and its verb twice. If they agree, write *correct*. If they do not agree, correct the verb.

1. The savanna, with its waving grasses, lie next to the desert.
2. It is on the margin of the trade-wind belts.
3. In the savanna lives many large animals.
4. The savanna, except in its rainy summers, are dry.
5. In Africa are the largest savannas.
6. Do savannas exist everywhere in the world?
7. There is many giraffes in the grassland.
8. Names for a savanna includes prairie, scrub, and veld.
9. Do much rain fall each year in a savanna?
10. The balance between grasses and woody plants is delicate.

Exercise 4   Using the Correct Verb Form

Write the correct form of the verb in parentheses.

1. The plains near the North Pole (is, are) very cold.
2. The temperature in these zones (is, are) usually below zero.
3. In this area (live, lives) many animals.
4. During the brief summers (grow, grows) a rare moss.
5. In the moss (nest, nests) many birds.
6. There (is, are) little rainfall during the summer.
7. (Does, Do) snow provide the needed moisture?
8. Some areas of the Arctic (is, are) drier than the world's deserts.
9. There (is, are) several hundred species of plants in the Arctic.
10. Summer melting of icy areas (create, creates) nesting sites for birds.
11. Smog (accumulate, accumulates) over some Arctic areas.
12. Fish, such as cod and salmon, (live, lives) under the ice cap.
13. There (is, are) a reason for the white color of many Arctic animals.
14. (Does, Do) the absence of reptiles affect the ecosystem?
15. Along a well-traveled route (roam, roams) herds of caribou.
16. Here the threat to their habitat (is, are) from oil pipeline construction.
17. The dense, woolly coat of musk oxen (is, are) called *quivet*.
18. There (is, are) many uses for quivet, a valuable raw fiber.
19. In summer (appear, appears) many types of grasses.
20. (Does, Do) lichens help create new soil?

16.3 Collective Nouns and Other Special Subjects

It is sometimes difficult to tell whether certain special subjects are singular or plural. For example, collective nouns follow special agreement rules. A **collective noun** names a group. The noun has a singular meaning when it names a group that acts as a single unit. The noun has a plural meaning when it refers to each member of the group acting as individuals. The meaning of the noun determines whether you use the singular or plural form of the verb.

> The **team agrees** to save papers. [one unit, singular]
>
> The **team agree** to store them in their homes. [individuals, plural]

Certain nouns, such as *mathematics* and *news,* end in *-s* but take a singular verb. Other nouns that end in *-s* and name one thing, such as *trousers* and *pliers,* take a plural verb.

> **Mumps is** a disease that is spread through the air. [singular]
>
> **Scissors are** not practical for shredding paper. [plural]

When the subject refers to an amount as a single unit, it is singular. When it refers to a number of individual units, it is plural.

> **Ten years seems** a long time. [single unit]
>
> **Ten years have passed** since you left. [individual units]
>
> **Five cents is** the deposit on one bottle. [single unit]
>
> **Five cents are** in my hand. [individual units]

A title of a book or work of art is considered singular even if a noun within the title is plural.

> ***Recycling Successes* is** now a best-selling book. [one book]

The team . . .

. . . **collect** cans and bottles at the shore.

The team . . .

. . . **collects** cans and bottles for recycling.

Exercise 5 Identifying Verbs for Collective Nouns

Write each sentence. Underline the collective noun subject once and the verb twice. If they agree, write *correct*. If they do not agree, correct the verb.

1. *Recycling Tips* are a pamphlet of helpful ideas on ways to recycle.
2. Fifteen is the average number of refillings for a returnable bottle.
3. News about the town's recycling efforts are hopeful.
4. After lunch, the class empty their trays in the recycling bins.
5. Each week, the committee award a prize for the best recycling tip.
6. Two tons were the weight of last month's scrap metal collection.
7. Simple mathematics show the value of turning old paper into newsprint.
8. The cafeteria staff show their support by helping students recycle.
9. Scissors is in the desk drawer.
10. The parents' group have donated more recycling bins.

Exercise 6 Using the Correct Verb Form with Collective Nouns

Write the correct form of the verb in parentheses.

1. The committee (decide, decides) to recycle paper.
2. The committee (decide, decides) among themselves.
3. The audience (leave, leaves) when they are bored.
4. The audience (applaud, applauds) in unison.
5. News (is, are) being made at this town meeting.
6. Even eyeglasses (is, are) recyclable.
7. *Seven Ways to Recycle Newspapers* (is, are) the book we need.
8. The class (discuss, discusses) their different opinions about pollutants.
9. The group (discuss, discusses) the problem of landfills.
10. The herd of goats (graze, grazes) at the landfill.
11. The herd (is, are) all healthy.
12. One million gallons (is, are) a large amount of pollutants.
13. *Energy Alternatives* (is, are) an important book.
14. Five hundred dollars (is, are) available for a recycling program.
15. *Fragile Lands* (do, does) seem a significant film.
16. The class (is, are) working on a group project.
17. The group (see, sees) a movie about landfills.
18. Two years (seem, seems) a long time for recovery.
19. Trousers (is, are) recycled with other forms of clothing.
20. The class (draws, draw) posters showing their household recycling efforts.

16.4 Indefinite Pronouns as Subjects

■ An **indefinite pronoun** is a pronoun that does not refer to a specific person, place, or thing.

Some indefinite pronouns are singular. Others are plural. When an indefinite pronoun is used as a subject, the verb must agree in number. Study the indefinite pronouns in the chart below.

Indefinite Pronouns			
Singular			**Plural**
another	everybody	no one	both
anybody	everyone	nothing	few
anyone	everything	one	many
anything	much	somebody	others
each	neither	someone	several
either	nobody	something	

A few indefinite pronouns take a singular or plural verb, depending on the phrase that follows. These pronouns include *all, any, most, none,* and *some.*

Notice how these indefinite pronouns are used below.

Most of the forest **lies** to the east. [singular]

Most of those scientists **study** the process of respiration. [plural]

Some of her lawn **is** brown. [singular]

Some of the ferns **are** large. [plural]

The prepositional phrases include nouns that are singular or plural. To determine whether the verb should be singular or plural, look at the object of the preposition. For example, in the third sentence above, *some* refers to *lawn.* Because *lawn* is singular, the verb is singular. In the fourth sentence, *some* refers to *ferns.* Because *ferns* is plural, the verb is plural.

Exercise 7   Identifying Indefinite Pronouns

Write the indefinite pronoun from each sentence. Then write *singular* or *plural* to tell what verb form it takes.

1. All of the students are working in the science laboratory.
2. All of the needed information is printed in the lab manual.
3. Most of the steps are easy to carry out.
4. None of the laboratory equipment is dangerous to use.
5. Some of the results need to be explained to the class.
6. Most of the experiment concerns respiration.
7. Any of the lab stations have the needed equipment.
8. Some of the underlying theory is written on the chalkboard.
9. None of the lab reports have been written yet.
10. All of the oxygen is used up as the candle burns.

Exercise 8   Using the Correct Verb Form with Indefinite Pronouns

Write the correct form of the verb in parentheses.

1. Much of the process of respiration (is, are) complex.
2. Few completely (understand, understands) it.
3. Many (study, studies) the two types of oxygen exchange.
4. Much (happen, happens) during the two processes.
5. Someone (explain, explains) the respiratory system.
6. Another of our problems (is, are) water pollution.
7. One (need, needs) understanding of the solutions.
8. Some of them (improve, improves) the water supply immediately.
9. Many (provide, provides) sensible approaches.
10. Either of the processes (clean, cleans) the water equally well.
11. Both of them (call, calls) for further study.
12. Neither (is, are) apparently preferable.
13. Most of the higher animals (have, has) lungs.
14. All of the oxygen exchange (occur, occurs) there.
15. Most of the processes (is, are) clearly written.
16. Nobody (deny, denies) the value of the project.
17. Many of the volunteers (work, works) diligently.
18. Any of the projects (need, needs) extra volunteers.
19. Most of the people (support, supports) conservation.
20. Several of the volunteers (suggest, suggests) ideas.

Subject-Verb Agreement

16.5 Agreement with Compound Subjects

A compound subject contains two or more simple subjects for the same verb. Compound subjects take either a singular or a plural verb, depending on how the parts of the subject are joined. When the simple subjects are joined by the coordinating conjunction *and* or by the correlative conjunction *both . . . and,* the verb is plural.

In all of the sentences below, the reference is to more than one place, thing, or idea.

> New York, Denver, **and** London **have** smog.
> **Both** automobiles **and** factories **create** smog.
> Air inversion **and** the absence of wind **aid** the conditions.

Occasionally *and* is used to join two words that are part of one unit or refer to a single person or thing. In these cases, the subject is considered to be singular. In the sentence below, notice that *captain* and *leader* refer to the same person. Therefore, the singular form of the verb is used.

> The captain **and** leader of the air-testing team **is** Joan.

When two or more subjects are joined by the conjunctions *or* or *nor, either . . . or,* or *neither . . . nor,* the verb agrees with the subject that is closer to it.

> The counties **or** the state **responds** to pollution complaints.
> **Either** smoke **or** gases **cause** the smog.

In the first sentence, *responds* agrees with *state,* which is the subject noun closer to the verb. The verb is singular because the subject is singular. In the second sentence, *cause* agrees with *gases,* which is closer. The verb is plural because *gases* is plural.

Exercise 9   Using the Correct Verb Form with Compound Subjects

Write the correct form of the verb in parentheses.

1. A savanna and a desert (is, are) next to each other.
2. Rain forests and deserts (make, makes) good study sites.
3. Jungles, forests, and bogs (has, have) different characteristics.
4. Both Caldwell and the girls (want, wants) to study swamps.
5. The researcher and author (is, are) the opening speaker at the conference.
6. Food, water, and air (is, are) essential to life.
7. Both food and oxygen (come, comes) from plants.
8. Plants and animals in a community (is, are) interdependent.
9. Both days and seasons (change, changes) natural systems.
10. The wind, the sun, and the tides (is, are) sources of energy.
11. Oil and natural gas (forms, form) today's major energy supply.
12. The group's teacher and leader (is, are) an expert on ecological issues.
13. Too much rain and snow (do, does) affect the area.
14. States, cities, and towns (have, has) responsibilities.
15. Air pollution and water pollution (responds, respond) to clean-up actions.
16. The engineer and head of the hiking club (is, are) the pollution inspector.
17. Trout and salmon (need, needs) clean water to survive.
18. Both temperature and acidity (is, are) measured every day.
19. Environmental club members and their leader (helps, help) measure temperature.
20. Both club members and their families (participates, participate) in the program.

Exercise 10   Identifying Compound Subjects

Write the compound subjects for each sentence. Then write *singular* or *plural* to tell what verb form they take.

1. Neither rain nor snow is predicted for the weekend's weather.
2. Television bulletins or radio announcements warn people to evacuate.
3. Either high winds or heavy rains pose a danger of flooding.
4. The town or the state assists in the evacuation efforts.
5. Either a fire fighter or a rescue worker knocks on each resident's door.
6. Either a state helicopter or local boats are used to rescue the stranded.
7. The school gym or the town hall offers a refuge from the storm.
8. Hot chocolate or coffee warms those chilled by the weather.
9. Either soup or sandwiches are provided for the rescue workers.
10. Neither levees nor a dam has been built for flood control.

Grammar Review

SUBJECT-VERB AGREEMENT

To learn about bats, journalist Diane Ackerman accompanied a world authority on the subject to a cave in Texas. In the following excerpt from her essay "Bats," the writer observes an emergence of Mexican free-tailed bats. The passage has been annotated to show some examples of subject-verb agreement covered in this unit.

Literature Model

from Bats

by Diane Ackerman

In the early evening, I take my seat in a natural amphitheater of limestone boulders, in the Texas hill country; at the bottom of the slope is a wide, dark cave mouth. Nothing stirs yet in its depths. But I have been promised one of the wonders of our age. Deep inside the cavern, twenty million Mexican free-tailed bats are hanging up by their toes. They are the largest known concentration of warm-blooded animals in the world. Soon, at dusk, all twenty million of them will fly out to feed, in a living volcano that scientists call an "emergence. . . ."

A hawk appears, swoops, grabs a stray bat out of the sky, and disappears with it. In a moment, the hawk returns, but hearing his wings coming, the bats in the column all shift sidewise to confuse him, and he misses. As wave upon wave of bats pours out of the cave, their collective wings begin to sound like drizzle on autumn leaves.

> Agreement between a singular subject and verb in an inverted sentence

> Agreement between a plural pronoun subject and a plural verb

> Agreement between a plural subject and a verb that have a prepositional phrase between them

---

Grammar Review

Review: Exercise 1   Making Verbs Agree with Noun and Pronoun Subjects

Write the correct form of the verb in parentheses.

1. Snakes (prowls, prowl) by the cave mouth, hunting for fallen bats.
2. A researcher (puts, put) on protective clothing before entering the cave.
3. Free-tailed bats (cruises, cruise) at thirty-five miles an hour.
4. The cave (stretches, stretch) 1,000 feet into the limestone hill.
5. It (averages, average) sixty feet in diameter.
6. Many researchers (comes, come) to see the emergence of the bats.
7. They (finds, find) the sight of the bats awe-inspiring.
8. A hawk (grabs, grab) a stray bat out of the sky.
9. The bats' wings (sounds, sound) like drizzle on autumn leaves.
10. Diane Ackerman (compares, compare) the emergence to a volcano.

Review: Exercise 2   Making Forms of *Be, Do,* and *Have* Agree with Subjects

SAMPLE   Diane Ackerman (is, are) interested in the behavior of bats.
ANSWER   is

1. Bats (is, are) warm-blooded animals.
2. Ackerman (does, do) seem interested in the study of bats.
3. This cave (is, are) a nursery full of mothers and their babies.
4. The cave mouth (is, are) at the bottom of the slope.
5. The spectators (has, have) a splendid view of the emerging bats.
6. Researchers (has, have) carried out many studies of this bat population.
7. Bats (does, do) sleep upside down.
8. A bat (is, are) the only mammal with the ability to fly.
9. A bat (do, does) have a good sense of smell.
10. Some people (has, have) a fear of bats.

Review: Exercise 3 **Locating Subjects and Making Verbs Agree**

Write each sentence, choosing the correct form of the verb in parentheses. Underline the simple subject once and the verb twice.

SAMPLE The bats inside the dark cave (hangs, hang) upside down.
ANSWER The <u>bats</u> inside the dark cave <u>hang</u> upside down.

1. In the cave (is, are) twenty million bats.
2. The hawk, a predator with keen eyes, (swoop, swoops) down upon a bat.
3. Here (is, are) a vivid example of a predator-prey relationship.
4. The bats, reacting to the hawk, (shifts, shift) their position sidewise.
5. (Does, Do) the bats rely on echolocation to know the hawk's position?
6. The scientific name for bats (is, are) *Chiroptera*, meaning "hand wing."
7. There (is, are) forty different kinds of bats in North America.
8. (Is, Are) there a law protecting colonies of bats?
9. The reproductive rate of bats (is, are) quite low.
10. Here (is, are) an important reason to protect bat colonies.

Review: Exercise 4 **Making Verbs Agree with Collective Nouns and Other Special Subjects**

Write the correct form of the verb in parentheses.

1. Binoculars (gives, give) the researchers a clear view of the bats.
2. The research team (takes, take) their seats on the boulders.
3. The bat colony (raises, raise) the temperature inside the cave.
4. Twenty million (is, are) an estimate of the cave's bat population.
5. For those watching the bats, the hours (passes, pass) quickly.
6. "Bats" (is, are) an entertaining and informative essay.
7. The colony (clings, cling) to their roosts on the cave ceiling.
8. *National Geographic* (has, have) published several good articles on bats.
9. News (travels, travel) quickly among the individuals in a bat colony.
10. This colony (represents, represent) the world's largest concentration of warm-blooded animals.

Grammar Review

Subject-Verb Agreement

Review: Exercise 5   Making Verbs Agree with Indefinite Pronoun Subjects

Write the correct form of the verb in parentheses.

1. Everyone (has, have) an opinion about bats.
2. Many (fears, fear) the animals.
3. Few (knows, know) very much about them.
4. Most of the folklore (is, are) untrue.
5. Few (lives, live) in belfries.
6. Everyone (thinks, think) that bats get in people's hair.
7. Nobody (recognizes, recognize) how helpful bats are.
8. Much (remains, remain) to be learned about bats.
9. Some of the species (uses, use) high-frequency sounds to navigate in the dark.
10. Most of these sounds (extends, extend) beyond the range of human hearing.

Review: Exercise 6   Making Verbs Agree with Compound Subjects

Write the correct form of the verb in parentheses.

1. Both snakes and hawks (preys, prey) on bats.
2. Neither the flying fox nor the vampire bat (hibernates, hibernate) in winter.
3. Fruit or insects (provides, provide) food for bats.
4. Either fear or ignorance (accounts, account) for the way many people react to seeing bats.
5. Caves and hollow trees (provides, provide) roosts for bats.
6. Both migration and hibernation (is, are) ways of coping with cold winter weather.
7. Either migration or hibernation (protects, protect) bats from the cold.
8. Both the sense of sight and the sense of smell (is, are) well developed in bats.
9. Either plant nectar or plant pollen (is, are) consumed by some bats.
10. The head scientist and leader of the bat research team (is, are) Dr. Tuttle.

Review: Exercise 7

Proofreading

This passage is about the artist Leonard Koscianski, whose work appears on the following page. Rewrite the passage, correcting the errors in spelling, capitalization, grammar, and usage. Add any missing punctuation. There are ten errors.

Leonard Koscianski

[1]Many of Leonard Koscianski's paintings reflects his concern with issues affecting the earth's future, such as environmental pollution. [2]The painter believes that human society impose an artificial order on the world, the result of such interference are a disruption of the balance of nature.

[3]In *Forest Spirit*, for example, the artist represents the natural order in the forest, where a hawk swoops down to attack hiden prey. [4]Like the mexican free-tailed bats in "Bats," the prey is seized and killed. [5]Koscianski suggest that such activities are neccesary to maintain the natural balance. [6]Besides, many animals fights back. [7]Most of the bats in Ackerman's essay is able to protect themselves and escape.

Review: Exercise 8

Mixed Review

Write the correct verbs in parentheses.

Diane Ackerman, the author of "Bats," [1](has, have) also written essays about other animals. "White Lanterns" [2](is, are) the title of her essay about young penguins being raised at Sea World in California. Scientists and volunteers [3](care, cares) for the young animals by feeding and holding them.

A baby penguin exhibits thigmotaxis, the drive to press up hard against a parent. In the wild, either the mother or the father [4](respond, responds) to the youngster. A colony of penguins [5](is, are) filled with

(continued)

Subject-Verb Agreement

the whistles of the young birds. Parents, in the midst of this noise,
[6](distinguish, distinguishes) the whistles of their own offspring.
Everybody [7](identify, identifies) with penguins. Why [8](does, do) we have this
reaction? There [9](is, are) many possible explanations. Most of these explanations [10](revolve, revolves) around the similarities between penguins and
people. As Ackerman says, we see penguins "as little humanoids."

Leonard Koscianski, *Forest Spirit*, 1991

Subject-Verb Agreement

Writing Application

TIME

For more about the writing process, see **TIME Facing the Blank Page,** pp. 97-107.

Subject-Verb Agreement in Writing

Lack of subject-verb agreement will distract readers from the information you wish to convey. Examine the passage below from *Always to Remember,* noting how Brent Ashabranner keeps his subjects and verbs in agreement. Focus especially on the italicized words.

Maya Lin, reporters soon discovered, was a Chinese-American girl who had been born and raised in the small midwestern city of Athens, Ohio. Her *father,* Henry Huan Lin, was a ceramicist of considerable reputation and dean of fine arts at Ohio University in Athens. *Her mother,* Julia C. Lin, was a poet and professor of Oriental and English literature. Maya Lin's parents were born to culturally prominent families in China.

Techniques with Subject-Verb Agreement

Check carefully for agreement when you write your work.

❶ When checking for subject-verb agreement, remember to bypass phrases that come between a subject and its verb. Compare the following:

HARDER TO CHECK *Maya Lin,* reporters soon discovered, *was* a Chinese American girl.

EASIER TO CHECK *Maya Lin was* a Chinese American girl.

❷ Be careful about suject-verb agreement when subjects include more than one word. Identify the most important words before checking for agreement:

INCORRECT AGREEMENT Maya Lin's parents *was* born to . . .

CORRECT AGREEMENT Maya Lin's *parents were* born to . . .

Practice Complete the following passage on a separate sheet of paper. In each blank, write a present-tense verb that agrees with the subject noun or pronoun.

My family _____ local sports. Both my parents _____ most of the football, baseball, and soccer games that _____ played here. My brother Ken and I sometimes even _____ with the team to road games. Citizens, especially those whose children participate in sports, _____ their support most effectively by being present. Burnsville's athletes _____ better when their friends and family _____ around them. We, the cheering squad for your local sports teams, _____ you to join us at the next game!

Glossary of Special Usage Problems

17.1 Using Troublesome Words I

Like all languages, English contains a number of confusing expressions. The following glossary will help you understand some of the more troublesome ones.

Word	Meaning	Example
accept **except**	"to receive" "other than"	We do not readily **accept** new ideas. Few **except** scientists understand them.
all ready **already**	"completely prepared" "before" or "by this time"	They are **all ready** for new ideas. Ideas have **already** changed.
all together	"in a group"	The planets **all together** weigh less than the Sun.
altogether	"completely"	Most stars are **altogether** too distant to study.
a lot	"very much" *A lot* is two words. Its meaning is vague; avoid using it.	**A lot** of stars can't be seen. [vague] Thousands of stars can't be seen. [more precise]
beside **besides**	"next to" "in addition to"	In May the moon appeared **beside** Mars. **Besides** Saturn, Jupiter and Uranus have rings.
between **among**	Use *between* for two people or things. Use *among* when talking about groups of three or more.	Mercury is **between** Venus and the Sun. Meteor trails are seen **among** the stars.
bring **take**	"to carry from a distant place to a closer one" "to carry from a nearby place to a more distant one"	Astronomers **bring** exhibits to schools. Students will **take** the model planets home.
can **may**	indicates ability expresses permission or possibility	We **can** see Pluto with a telescope. **May** we see the charts?
choose **chose**	"to select" "selected"	**Choose** a planet to study. Last year we **chose** Mars.

Exercise 1   Choosing the Correct Word

For each sentence, write the correct word or words in parentheses.

1. Our galaxy is one (among, between) many.
2. There may be more galaxies (beside, besides) the ones we know.
3. Many people (accept, except) the idea that space is endless.
4. (Can, May) we use that telescope?
5. (Bring, Take) a compass to the lab when you go.
6. Galaxies are (all together, altogether) too numerous.
7. The students were outdoors (all ready, already) to study the night sky.
8. The instructor (choose, chose) a hill away from the glare of city lights.
9. "Stand (beside, besides) me," he told the class.
10. We stood (all together, altogether), looking at the stars.

Exercise 2   Using the Correct Word

For each sentence, write the correct word or words from the lesson. Use the clues in parentheses to help you.

1. We _____ see Pluto through this telescope. (have the ability)
2. Before today we'd observed every planet _____ Pluto. (other than)
3. Scientists have _____ learned a great deal about comets. (by this time)
4. They will _____ our class a meteorite. (carry to a closer place)
5. We will _____ the meteorite home. (carry to a farther place)
6. The instructor told us to _____ a partner. (select)
7. I _____ Marjorie Hall for my partner. (selected)
8. The partners were to share observations _____ themselves. (two people)
9. If you look over there, you _____ see the Big Dipper. (are able to)
10. There was a murmur of agreement _____ the students. (three or more people)
11. We learned the ancient Greeks named forty-eight constellations _____. (in all)
12. We _____ knew that the constellations have Latin names. (by this time)
13. The Big Dipper stars are _____ those of Ursa Major. (three or more things)
14. The instructor said, "You _____ use my telescope." (expresses permission)
15. I will gladly _____ his offer. (receive)
16. _____ the Big Dipper is the Little Dipper. (Next to)
17. There are two ways you might _____ to locate the North Star. (select)
18. Follow a line _____ the stars in the front of the Big Dipper's cup. (two things)
19. You _____ also see it as the end of the Little Dipper's handle. (are able to)
20. The students will _____ many ideas away with them. (carry to a farther place)

Word	Meaning	Example
fewer	Use in comparisons with nouns that can be counted.	There are **fewer** sunspots this year than last year.
less	Use in comparisons with nouns that cannot be counted.	Mars has **less** gravitational force than Earth.
formally	the adverb form of *formal*	A sun is **formally** a star.
formerly	"in times past"	Pluto was **formerly** thought to be a moon of another planet.
in	"inside"	Our Sun is **in** the Milky Way.
into	indicates movement from outside to a point within	Meteorites fall **into** the atmosphere.
its	the possessive form of *it*	A comet wobbles in **its** orbit.
it's	the contraction of *it is*	**It's** difficult to see Neptune.
lay	"to put" or "to place"	**Lay** the charts on the table.
lie	"to recline" or "to be positioned"	Layers of dust **lie** on the moon.
learn	"to receive knowledge"	Astronauts **learn** astronomy as part of their training.
teach	"to give knowledge"	Many astronomers **teach** at colleges.
leave	"to go away"	We will **leave** after the eclipse.
let	"to allow"	The school **let** us use the telescope.
loose	"not firmly attached"	Scientists gather **loose** particles in space and bring them back to study.
lose	"to misplace" or "to fail to win"	Comets **lose** particles.
many	Use with nouns that can be counted.	We know the weight of **many** stars.
much	Use with nouns that cannot be counted.	**Much** of the weight is gas.
precede	"to go or come before"	Typewriters **preceded** computers.
proceed	"to continue"	*Voyager 2* will **proceed** to Neptune.

Glossary of Special Usage Problems

Exercise 3   **Choosing the Correct Word**

For each sentence, write the correct word in parentheses.

1. There are (many, much) kinds of telescopes.
2. Astronomers were (formally, formerly) limited by crude optics.
3. *Voyager 2* is traveling deep (in, into) space.
4. A telescope's power is determined by the size of (its, it's) lens.
5. Our astronomy club is (formally, formerly) organized.
6. Our astronomy club has (fewer, less) than five telescopes.
7. I write my astronomy notes (in, into) a notebook.
8. I (lay, lie) the notebook on the ground beside me while I use a telescope.
9. My young brother wants me to (learn, teach) him about the stars.
10. Tonight I will (precede, proceed) to give him his first lesson.

Exercise 4   **Using the Correct Word**

For each sentence, write the correct word from the lesson. Use the clues in parentheses to help you.

1. Volcanoes _____ erupted on the moon. (in times past)
2. I can _____ on the ground for hours, looking at the sky. (recline)
3. _____ that telescope stay where it is! (allow)
4. A _____ lens will make a telescope inoperable. (not firmly attached)
5. Astronomers _____ from space probes. (receive knowledge)
6. Astronomy involves _____ study. (amount that cannot be counted)
7. That study must _____ the field work. (go before)
8. Those not willing to study should _____ the class. (go away from)
9. More observation and _____ memory is needed. (amount that cannot be counted)
10. Like the stars, Earth was _____ a glowing sphere. (in times past)
11. Some planets have _____ moons. (amount that can be counted)
12. Our Sun can be _____ defined as a giant ball of hot gases. (in a formal manner)
13. Planets are dark, solid bodies _____ space. (inside)
14. _____ than three are closer than Earth to the Sun. (countable comparison)
15. Over time, stars _____ their heat and light. (misplace)
16. At night stars and planets look _____ alike. (amount that cannot be counted)
17. I can _____ you how to tell a star from a planet. (give knowledge)
18. A planet may glow, but _____ light is not like a star's. (possessive of *it*)
19. Relative to stars, planets do not always _____ in the same place. (be positioned)
20. You will _____ that our galaxy has 100 billion stars. (receive knowledge)

Word	Meaning	Example
quiet	"silent" or "motionless"	It is very **quiet** in outer space.
quite	"completely" or "entirely"	It is **quite** dark in outer space.
raise	"to cause to move upward"	**Raise** heavy binoculars with a tripod.
rise	"to move upward"	The stars **rise** into view.
set	"to place" or "to put"	She **set** the camera down carefully.
sit	"to place oneself in a seated position"	Let's **sit** and watch the sky.
than	introduces the second part of a comparison	The sun is denser **than** the earth.
then	"at that time"	Choose a planet, and **then** locate it.
their	the possessive form of *they*	Ask **their** advice about lenses.
they're	the contraction of *they are*	**They're** using special night lenses.
theirs	"that or those belonging to them"	**Theirs** is a reflecting telescope.
there's	the contraction of *there is*	**There's** also a refracting telescope in our observatory.
to	"in the direction of"	Let's go **to** the observatory.
too	"also" or "excessively"	Why don't you come **too**?
two	the number after one	We have only **two** telescopes in our observatory.
where at	Do not use *at* after *where* to indicate what place.	**Where** is the Milky Way? [not *Where is the Milky Way at?*]
who's	the contraction of *who is*	**Who's** a famous astronomer?
whose	the possessive form of *who*	**Whose** discoveries are the most significant?
your	the possessive form of *you*	I liked **your** essay about Mars.
you're	the contraction of *you are*	**You're** looking at the North Star.

Glossary of Special Usage Problems

Exercise 5   Choosing the Correct Word

For each sentence, write the correct word in parentheses.

1. Jupiter's moons look stationary, but (they're, their) always in orbit.
2. Pluto is smaller (than, then) the other planets.
3. (Who's, Whose) bringing the camera to the site?
4. (Set, Sit) the tripod over there.
5. Each of the planets is (quite, quiet) different in color.
6. (Your, You're) sure to see Venus tonight.
7. (Who's, Whose) count of Saturn's rings is correct?
8. Most observers (sit, set) in deck chairs.
9. (Theirs, There's) Venus now!
10. You can see it if you look (to, too, two) your right.

Exercise 6   Using the Correct Word

For each sentence, write the correct word from the lesson. Use the clues in parentheses to help you.

1. Our friends will bring _____ compass and camera. (possessive form of *they*)
2. The telescope is _____. (that belonging to them)
3. The observation site is on a _____ hill. (calm)
4. The night sky can be _____ stunning. (completely)
5. Venus will _____ soon. (move upward)
6. We will _____ our eyes and our spirits. (cause to move upward)
7. _____ our watch will begin. (at that time)
8. I hope it's not _____ cold. (excessively)
9. Mercury and Venus are _____ planets between Earth and the Sun. (a number)
10. I wonder _____ turn it is to use the new telescope. (possessive of *who*)
11. You must _____ your telescope a few degrees to see Mars. (move upward)
12. It is very _____ here, away from the noise of the city. (silent)
13. Find the closest planets, and _____ find the farthest ones. (at that time)
14. _____ going to make a model of the inner planets? (contraction of *who is*)
15. Outer planets are hard to model because _____ distant. (contraction of *they are*)
16. Which planets are _____ far away to see without a telescope? (excessively)
17. It looks as though _____ a white streak in the sky. (contraction of *there is*)
18. I think _____ referring to the Milky Way galaxy. (contraction of *you are*)
19. That's the galaxy _____ we live. (in what place)
20. It's bigger _____ it looks and contains billions of stars. (part of a comparison)

Grammar Review

GLOSSARY OF SPECIAL USAGE PROBLEMS

In her essay "Star Fever," Judith Herbst discusses people's age-old fascination with stars. In the following passage, Herbst considers the worlds that may lie beyond our vision. She also explains the usefulness of the stars. The passage has been annotated to show some troublesome words covered in this unit.

Literature Model

from Star Fever
by Judith Herbst

I love the stars. Sometimes I lie awake at night and think about them. I imagine that they all have planets with strange forms of life. I see red, rugged landscapes bathed in the glare of two suns, one swollen and scarlet, the other a cold steel blue. I see steamy tropical planets covered with silver vines that snake in and out of silver trees. I see planets with methane oceans and iron mountains. It's not so crazy. They could be out there, you know. . . .

The stars not only mark the seasons, they also tell you where north, south, east, and west are. Stars "rise" in the east and "set" in the west, so all you have to do is look for the appearance of a new constellation. If you see one that wasn't there an hour before, you're facing east. Once you know east it's a snap to find the other three directions. Just look behind you for west, to the right side for south, and to the left for north.

As you can imagine, without the compass the early sailors absolutely relied on the stars to find their way around. There are no landmarks on the high seas.

> Lie, meaning "to recline"

> It's, contraction of *it is*

> Rise, meaning "to move upward"

> You're, contraction of you are

Grammar Review

For each sentence write the correct word in parentheses.

SAMPLE   (Beside, Besides) marking the seasons, stars can also be used to tell directions.
ANSWER   Besides

1. The stars (can, may) be used as a means to navigate only when the sky is clear.
2. On an overcast night, (fewer, less) stars are visible in the sky.
3. Chinese navigators were (all ready, already) using magnetic compasses to guide their ships by the 1100s.
4. Some of the objects we see (between, among) the stars are planets.
5. Do you (accept, except) the idea that there may be life on other planets?
6. (Many, Much) stars formed more than ten billion years ago.
7. The color of a star's light depends on (its, it's) surface temperature.
8. As a star dies, it slowly begins to (loose, lose) material and shrink.
9. About one hundred ball-like clusters of stars (lay, lie) around the center of the Milky Way galaxy.
10. People can (learn, teach) about stars at a planetarium.
11. The Sun is nearer to Earth (than, then) any other star is.
12. Scientists have learned (quiet, quite) a bit about other stars by studying the Sun.
13. (Theirs, There's) a solar telescope in Tucson, Arizona, that helps astronomers study the Sun's light.
14. (Who's, Whose) studies in the early 1500s challenged earlier scientists' findings?
15. Polish astronomer Nicolaus Copernicus challenged (their, they're) beliefs about the Sun.
16. Today, scientists continue to (raise, rise) questions about the Sun and its impact on people.
17. There are more than 200 billion billion stars (altogether, all together) in the universe.
18. A powerful telescope can (take, bring) distant stars close enough to view.
19. Stars eventually run out of hydrogen gas and (than, then) stop shining.
20. New stars form from (loose, lose) masses of gas and dust in space.

Proofreading

The following passage is about Fernand Léger, whose work appears below. Rewrite the passage, correcting the errors in spelling, grammar, and usage. Add any missing punctuation. There are ten errors.

Fernand Léger

[1]Fernand Léger a French painter born in 1881, used an abstract stile of art. [2]An artist using this style choses many fragmented aspects of an object and combines them within a single picture. [3]Léger frequently chose cubes and other forms too create mechanical figures that represented the new machines developed in the early 1900s. [4]The artist used his talent two explore the relationship among a person and the industrial world.

[5]Léger present his vision of a world produced by machines in *The Creation of the World*. [6]As it lays beneath a moon and a handful of stars, Léger's world recalls the planets that Judith Herbst imagined in "Star Fever." [7]Perhaps much of the strange images in the painting all ready exist under some distant star.

Fernand Léger, *The Creation of the World*, c. 1925

Grammar Review

Mixed Review

For each sentence, write the correct word or words in parentheses.

1. Migration is an important concept (between, among) the world's creatures.
2. Migration, (formally, formerly) defined, is movement from place to place.
3. Migration (in, into) the past was a way for people and animals to find better living conditions.
4. Today (a lot, millions) of people still migrate.
5. Animals also migrate so that they (can, may) find better living conditions.
6. (Many, Much) different kinds of animals migrate, including birds, whales, fish, frogs, and toads.
7. In the autumn, many birds gather in flocks (all ready, already) to migrate to warmer climates.
8. Although they may enjoy warm weather, (its, it's) plentiful food they seek.
9. Seasonal migrations of animals take place (to, too, two) times a year.
10. The distance that animals migrate (between, among) two habitats varies.
11. Some animals migrate (fewer, less) than a mile.
12. On the other hand, Arctic terns travel up to 22,000 miles each year between (their, they're) summer and winter residences.
13. Salmon migrate from small streams (to, too, two) the vast ocean.
14. They stay where (theirs, there's) a plentiful supply of food.
15. (Than, Then) they reverse the process and return to their home stream.
16. There the female will (lay, lie) her eggs, and the male will fertilize them.
17. The adult salmon may die after spawning, but their offspring (precede, proceed) to develop within the eggs.
18. Without parents to (learn, teach) them, the young salmon repeat the pattern.
19. We must (accept, except) the mystery of animal migration.
20. What sense (brings, takes) animals away to another home?
21. What sense (brings, takes) them back to the exact spot where they once lived?
22. Humans can (choose, chose) the instruments that guide them.
23. They can (leave, let) the stars or a compass be their guide.
24. Electronic equipment will pinpoint (where at, where) they are sailing or flying.
25. Although humans have a great deal of knowledge, we still have much to (learn, teach) about animal migrations.

Writing Application

Usage in Writing

Katherine Paterson chose her words carefully for this passage from *Lyddie* that uses troublesome words correctly. Read the passage, focusing especially on the italicized words.

> Her stomach rumbled, but she ignored it. There would be no breakfast until seven, and that was *two* and a half hours away. By five the girls had crowded through the main gate, jostled their way up the outside staircase on the far end of the mill, cleaned their machines, and stood waiting for the workday *to* begin.
>
> "Not *too* tired this morning?" Diana asked by way of greeting.

Techniques with Usage

Try to apply some of Katherine Paterson's writing techniques when you write and revise your own work.

❶ Remember that some word pairs have related meanings, although their spellings and usages differ. Check each word against its context carefully before making your final choice:

INCORRECT USAGE that was *too* and a half hours

PATERSON'S VERSION that was *two* and a half hours

❷ Homophones, or words with the same sound but different spellings and meanings, are easily confused. Be sure to choose the correct word and spelling for your intended meaning.

INCORRECT USAGE Not *to* tired this morning?

PATERSON'S VERSION Not *too* tired this morning?

TIME

For more about the writing process, see **TIME Facing the Blank Page,** pp. 97-107.

Glossary of Special Usage Problems

Practice Try out these techniques on the following passage, revising it on a separate sheet of paper. Pay particular attention to the underlined words.

"Edna and Tamara asked me to come to <u>they're</u> house to help paint their treehouse. <u>Can</u> I go, Dad?" asked Mari.

"If you <u>may</u> finish <u>you're</u> chores before lunch, <u>its</u> fine with me," replied her father. "The only question is, <u>whose</u> going to bring you home?"

"<u>Among</u> Edna's mom and Tamara's dad, I'm sure someone <u>may</u> do it. They asked me to bring a paintbrush. Will you help me <u>chose</u> one? We have so <u>much</u>," said Mari.

"No problem. Let's get started," answered her father.

LOG ON **Writing** Online For more grammar practice, go to **glencoe.com** and enter QuickPass code WC87703p2.

Writing Application **569**

UNIT 18 Diagraming Sentences

18.1 Diagraming Simple Subjects and Simple Predicates

The basic parts of a sentence are the subject and the predicate. To diagram a sentence, first draw a horizontal line called a baseline. Then draw a vertical line that crosses and extends below the baseline.

To the left of the vertical line, write the simple subject. To the right of the vertical line, write the simple predicate. Capitalize any words that are capitalized in the sentence. Do not include punctuation, however.

People are working.

People	are working

The positions of the subject and the predicate in a diagram always remain the same.

Operators sat by the machines.

Operators	sat

By the machines **sat operators.**

operators	sat

| Exercise 1 | Diagraming Simple Subjects and Simple Predicates |

Diagram each simple subject and simple predicate.

1. People arrived early.
2. They started the machines.
3. Other people were standing around.
4. Four women have arrived late.
5. Most factories are busy.
6. Finally lunchtime arrived.
7. The workers ate lunch.
8. Men took walks.
9. People are watching a show.
10. People played games.
11. Then the workers returned.
12. They restarted the machines.
13. They liked their tasks.
14. The supervisor praises them.
15. The workers show loyalty.
16. They have worked for decades.
17. The factory resembles a home.
18. People care about one another.
19. They work together.
20. The workers help one another.

18.2 Diagraming the Four Kinds of Sentences

The simple subject and the simple predicate of the four kinds of sentences are diagramed below. Recall that in an interrogative sentence, the subject often comes between the two parts of a verb phrase. In an imperative sentence, the word *you* is understood to be the simple subject.

Note that the positions of the simple subject and the simple predicate in a sentence diagram are always the same, regardless of their positions in the original sentence.

DECLARATIVE

People use many machines.

People	use

INTERROGATIVE

Do people use many machines?

people	Do use

IMPERATIVE

Use this machine.

(you)	Use

EXCLAMATORY

What a loud noise **it makes!**

it	makes

Exercise 2   Diagraming Simple Subjects and Predicates

Diagram the simple subject and the simple predicate of each sentence.

1. Where do people use machines?
2. Machines exist in homes, office buildings, and hospitals.
3. What amazing things machines can do!
4. Listen to the radio.
5. Some machines perform several tasks.
6. Do you use a computer?
7. Try this program.
8. What a fast printer you have!
9. How long does it take?
10. This printer works beautifully.

18.3 Diagraming Direct and Indirect Objects

A direct object is part of the predicate. In a sentence diagram, place the direct object to the right of the verb. The vertical line between the verb and the direct object should not extend below the baseline.

Computers solve **problems.**

| Computers | solve | problems |

Computers process **data.**

| Computers | process | data |

An indirect object is also part of the predicate. It usually tells to whom or for whom the action of a verb is done. An indirect object always comes before a direct object in a sentence. In a sentence diagram, place the indirect object on a line below and to the right of the verb. Then join it to the verb with a slanted line.

Operators feed **computers** data.

| Operators | feed | data |
            \ computers

Exercise 3   Diagraming Direct and Indirect Objects

Diagram the simple subject, the simple predicate, and the direct object of each sentence. Diagram any indirect objects as well.

1. People solve problems every day.
2. A computer will provide answers.
3. An idea enters your mind.
4. You collect the information.
5. The method gives you the answer.
6. You offer someone the results.
7. The operator gives the computer a problem.
8. The computer gives you an answer.
9. You may check it again.
10. The computer saves us time.

18.4 Diagraming Adjectives, Adverbs, and Prepositional Phrases

In a diagram, place adjectives and adverbs on slanted lines beneath the words they modify.

Efficient software sells.

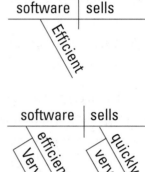

Very efficient software sells **very quickly.**

A prepositional phrase can function as either an adjective or an adverb. In the sentence below, the prepositional phrase *by the hundreds* modifies the verb *appear*. Study the diagram.

Programs appear **by the hundreds.**

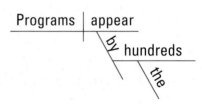

Exercise 4   Diagraming Sentences

Diagram each sentence.

1. Many people use computers regularly.
2. An extremely efficient computer works very quickly.
3. Businesses of all kinds need computers constantly.
4. Computers have changed our way of life.
5. People often play complicated games on personal computers.

Diagraming Predicate Nouns and Predicate Adjectives

You have learned that in a sentence diagram the direct object is placed after the action verb.

People use telephones.

People	use	telephones

To diagram a sentence with a predicate noun, place the predicate noun after the linking verb. Use a slanted line to separate the predicate noun from the verb.

Telephones are useful **instruments.**

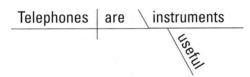

Diagram a predicate adjective in the same way.

Telephones are **useful.**

Telephones	are \	useful

Exercise 5 **Diagraming Sentences**

Diagram each sentence.

1. The telephone is a recent invention.
2. Alexander Graham Bell was the inventor.
3. Telephones have become common.
4. Many calls are international.
5. Early telephones looked odd.
6. The first big change was the dial.
7. A much later improvement was the undersea cable.
8. The cable was a real benefit.
9. The world grew much smaller.
10. Some modern telephones look sleek.

18.6 Diagraming Compound Sentence Parts

Coordinating conjunctions such as *and, but,* and *or* are used to join compound parts: words, phrases, or sentences. To diagram sentences with compound parts, place the second part of the compound below the first. Write the coordinating conjunction on a dotted line connecting the two parts.

COMPOUND SUBJECT

Wood and coal heat homes.

COMPOUND PREDICATE

Fuels **ignite and burn.**

COMPOUND DIRECT OBJECT

Fuel provides **heat or electricity.**

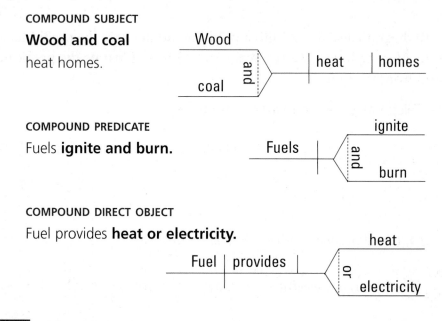

Exercise 6   Diagraming Sentences

Diagram each sentence.

1. Oil or electricity heats most buildings.
2. Prices for fuels rise and fall.
3. Some families use windmills or solar energy.
4. Stoves and furnaces provide heat.
5. Heated air or heated water circulates through the house.

Diagraming Compound Sentences

To diagram compound sentences, diagram each clause separately. If the main clauses are connected by a semicolon, use a vertical dotted line to connect the verbs of each clause. If the main clauses are connected by a conjunction such as *and, but,* or *or,* write the conjunction on a solid horizontal line and connect it to the verbs of each clause by dotted lines.

An electric typewriter once was the essential office tool, **but** today it has been replaced by the desktop computer.

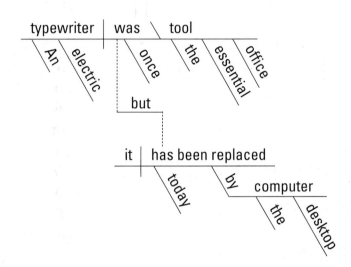

Diagraming Sentences

Diagram each sentence.

1. C. L. Sholes experimented with typewriters in 1867, and he patented a typewriter in 1868.
2. E. Remington marketed the machine in 1874, and soon other firms manufactured typewriters.
3. Businesses used the larger typewriters, but students definitely preferred portables.
4. Word processors have extensive capabilities, but most have rather small display screens.
5. Word processors are efficient, but computers can perform more tasks.

Diagraming Sentences

18.8 Diagraming Complex Sentences with Adjective and Adverb Clauses

To diagram a sentence with an adjective clause, diagram the main clause in one diagram and the adjective clause beneath it in another diagram. Draw a dotted line between the adjective clause and the word it modifies in the main clause. In the adjective clause, diagram the relative pronoun according to its function in its own clause. In the sentence below, *who* is the subject of the verb *cooked*.

ADJECTIVE CLAUSE

People **who cooked** used enormous stoves.

To diagram a sentence with an adverb clause, follow the same process. Then write the subordinating conjunction on the dotted line connecting the verb of each clause.

ADVERB CLAUSE

When people cooked, they used enormous stoves.

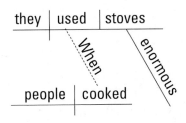

Exercise 8   **Diagraming Sentences**

Diagram each sentence.

1. People once used only stoves that burned wood.
2. Such stoves required attention while they were hot.
3. People who cooked on those stoves worked hard.
4. Families inserted the wood that these stoves required.
5. As the wood burned, ashes and dirt accumulated.

18.9 Diagraming Noun Clauses

Noun clauses can be used in sentences as subjects, direct objects, objects of prepositions, or predicate nouns. In the sentence below, the noun clause is a direct object.

I know **what a refrigerator costs.**

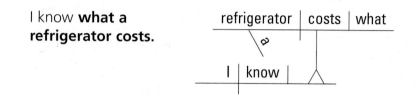

Notice that the clause is placed above the baseline on a "stilt" where the direct object usually appears. The word that introduces a noun clause is diagramed according to its function within the clause. In the noun clause above, the word *what* is the direct object. If the word that introduces the noun clause is not part of either the noun clause or the main clause, place the word on its own line above the verb of the clause it introduces.

You know **that refrigerators are beneficial.**

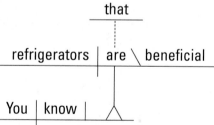

Exercise 9   **Diagraming Sentences**

Diagram each sentence.

1. Whoever uses a refrigerator should be appreciative.
2. That iceboxes were helpful is undeniable.
3. People eagerly awaited what the ice wagon delivered.
4. When refrigeration began may surprise you.
5. People in the last century knew how it worked.

Diagraming Sentences

18.10 Diagraming Verbals I

When diagraming a participle or a participial phrase, make a line that descends diagonally from the word the participle modifies and then extends to the right horizontally. Write the participle along that angled line, as shown below.

The machine, **humming loudly,** cooled the air rapidly.

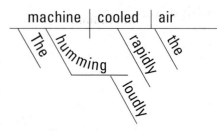

When diagraming a gerund or a gerund phrase, make a "stilt" located according to the role of the gerund. (A gerund can be a subject, an object of a verb or a preposition, or an appositive.) Then write the gerund on a "step" above the stilt.

Cleaning the air is another job of the machine.

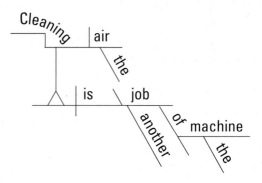

Exercise 10   **Diagraming Sentences**

Diagram each sentence.

1. Cooling the air was the subject of much research.
2. The machines cool the heated air.
3. Controlling the temperature is not an easy task.
4. The circulating air cools everyone.
5. Working people appreciate this modern invention.

Diagraming Verbals II

When diagraming an infinitive or an infinitive phrase that is used as either an adjective or an adverb, diagram it like a prepositional phrase.

The microscope **to choose** depends upon your needs.

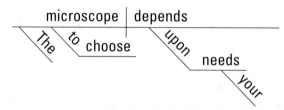

When diagraming an infinitive or an infinitive phrase that is used as a noun, make a "stilt" in the subject or complement position. Then diagram the phrase as you would a prepositional phrase.

The function of the microscope is **to magnify objects.**

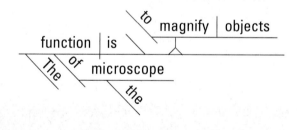

Exercise 11 **Diagraming Sentences**

Diagram each sentence.

1. The Romans may have used glass crystal to magnify objects.
2. To invent the compound microscope was Janssen's mission.
3. It is important to use microscopes carefully.
4. Sloan's job is to prepare the microscope for use.
5. The work to do governs the preparation.

UNIT 19 Capitalization

19.1 Capitalizing Sentences, Quotations, and Salutations

A capital letter appears at the beginning of a sentence. A capital letter also marks the beginning of a direct quotation and the salutation and closing of a letter.

RULE 1: Capitalize the first word of every sentence.

Many people helped our country gain independence.
Among them were George Washington, Thomas Jefferson, and Benjamin Franklin.

RULE 2: Capitalize the first word of a direct quotation that is a complete sentence. A direct quotation gives a speaker's exact words.

Travis said, "**A**nother one of those people was Paul Revere."

RULE 3: When a quoted sentence is interrupted by explanatory words, such as *she said*, do not begin the second part of the sentence with a capital letter.

"I read a famous poem," said Kim, "about Paul Revere."

When the second part of a quotation is a new sentence, put a period after the explanatory words, and begin the second part of the quotation with a capital letter.

"I know that poem," said Sarah. "**M**y class read it last week."

RULE 4: Do not capitalize an indirect quotation. Because an indirect quotation does not repeat a person's exact words, it does not appear in quotation marks. It is often preceded by the word *that*.

The teacher said **the** poem was written by Longfellow.
Travis said **that** another man rode with Paul Revere.

RULE 5: Capitalize the first word in the salutation and closing of a letter. Capitalize the title and name of the person addressed.

Dear **M**rs. **A**dams,   **Y**ours truly,

Write each word that needs to be capitalized. If a sentence contains no error, write correct.

1. our class was learning about heroes of the American Revolution.
2. we wanted to learn more about Paul Revere.
3. he came from Boston and lived in a house that is now open to the public.
4. "let's go to the library," said Lisa, "and see what we can find."
5. one book about Paul Revere says, "he designed the first issue of Continental money."
6. Hasan said that Paul Revere was a silversmith and an engraver.
7. "my aunt," said Hasan, "visited a Boston museum that had a Revere teapot."
8. "he designed the colonies' first official seal," said Hasan. "then he engraved it."
9. "did you know that he took part in the Boston Tea Party?" asked Lisa.
10. about fifty other American patriots went to the harbor in December 1773.
11. "he is best known," said Hasan, "for warning the people that the British were coming."
12. on April 18, 1775, he rode through Lexington toward Concord shouting, "the British are coming! the British are coming!"
13. lanterns were used as signals in the steeple of the Old North Church.
14. we read that on his famous ride Paul Revere was assisted by William Dawes.
15. "isn't it funny," said Hasan, "that Dawes is not known for this deed?"
16. "yes, it is," Lisa agreed. "the famous poem about the ride mentions only Paul Revere."
17. "did you know," asked Hasan, "that the poem was written by Henry Wadsworth Longfellow, who lived in Cambridge?"
18. we also learned that the poem was written more than eighty years after that important ride happened.
19. "because of Paul Revere's ride," said Lisa, "the Minutemen were prepared."
20. we thought we had discovered many interesting facts about this famous hero.
21. we decided to submit our report to a magazine.
22. Hasan began the letter, "dear sir or madam."
23. "we have written a report on Paul Revere," he wrote. "we would like to submit it to you."
24. a few weeks later we received a reply from the magazine.
25. they said that they would publish it.

19.2 Capitalizing Names and Titles of People

A common noun is the general name of a person, place, or thing. A common noun is not capitalized. A proper noun names a particular person, place, or thing and is capitalized.

RULE 1: Capitalize the names of people and the initials that stand for their names.

Lucretia **M**ott   **E. C. S**tanton

RULE 2: Capitalize a title or an abbreviation of a title when it comes before a person's name or when it is used in direct address.

In 1918 **P**resident Wilson planned the League of Nations.
"Has peace been declared, **G**eneral?"

Do not capitalize a title that follows or is a substitute for a person's name.

Dwight D. Eisenhower was a general during World War II.

RULE 3: Capitalize the names and abbreviations of academic degrees that follow a person's name. Capitalize *Jr.* and *Sr.*

Martin Greer, **Ph.D.**   Eve Tanaka, **M.D.**   Carl Healy **S**r.

RULE 4: Capitalize words that show family relationships when used as titles or as substitutes for a person's name.

We have pictures of **A**unt Meg marching for women's rights.
In 1902 **G**randmother was a suffragist.

Do not capitalize words that show family relationships when they follow a possessive noun or pronoun.

Maria's **c**ousin wrote about women's suffrage.
My **a**unt has told me about the women's movement.

RULE 5: Always capitalize the pronoun *I*.

History is the subject **I** like best.

Exercise 2 — Capitalizing Proper Names and Titles

Write each item, using capital letters where needed.

1. miss lucy stone
2. benjamin davis jr.
3. sonia fox, d.d.s.
4. edward r. murrow
5. beth parker, ph.d.
6. peter ashike, m.a.
7. dr. michael thomas
8. general robert e. lee
9. sir walter raleigh
10. j. p. slaughter
11. aunt martha
12. ben casey, m.d.
13. mayor riley
14. private bailey
15. gerald r. ford
16. uncle dexter
17. hillary r. clinton
18. pablo cruz sr.
19. mr. ted dover
20. king george

Exercise 3 — Using Capital Letters for Names, Titles, and Abbreviations

Write each item from the following sentences that needs a capital letter. If a sentence is correct, write correct.

1. Without susan b. anthony, women might not have the vote today.
2. Unfortunately, miss anthony died before women were allowed to vote.
3. With elizabeth cady stanton and m. j. gage, anthony wrote *History of Woman Suffrage.*
4. miss anthony met elizabeth cady stanton in New York.
5. esther p. newton, my great-grandmother, was a suffragist.
6. My great-grandmother once met miss anthony.
7. At the time, most people knew about miss anthony.
8. Later she met president wilson.
9. "Should women vote, mr. wilson?" she asked.
10. A shy man, woodrow wilson did not care to comment.
11. warren g. harding was the first president elected after women could vote.
12. Because harding died in office, calvin coolidge became president in 1923.
13. My great-grandmother knew the importance of the right to vote.
14. My grandmother, beverly newton walsh, says that her mother always voted.
15. She served in the army under general dwight d. eisenhower.
16. A colonel in the army, aunt helen owes a debt of gratitude to the women's movement.
17. In the army, she also met charles lindbergh and general george c. patton.
18. aunt helen smiled and replied, "Yes, sir!"
19. My uncle and i often tease, "Do you think women belong in the military?"
20. I'm sure esther p. newton would have been proud of aunt helen.

Capitalizing Names of Places

The names of specific places are proper nouns and are capitalized. Do not capitalize articles and prepositions that are part of geographical names, however.

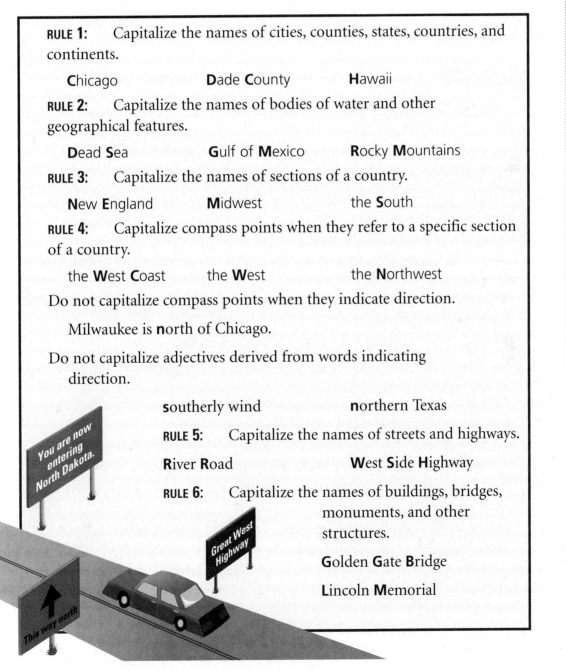

RULE 1:   Capitalize the names of cities, counties, states, countries, and continents.

    Chicago   Dade County   Hawaii

RULE 2:   Capitalize the names of bodies of water and other geographical features.

    Dead Sea   Gulf of Mexico   Rocky Mountains

RULE 3:   Capitalize the names of sections of a country.

    New England   Midwest   the South

RULE 4:   Capitalize compass points when they refer to a specific section of a country.

    the West Coast   the West   the Northwest

Do not capitalize compass points when they indicate direction.

    Milwaukee is north of Chicago.

Do not capitalize adjectives derived from words indicating direction.

          southerly wind   northern Texas

RULE 5:   Capitalize the names of streets and highways.

River Road   West Side Highway

RULE 6:   Capitalize the names of buildings, bridges, monuments, and other structures.

    Golden Gate Bridge

    Lincoln Memorial

You are now entering North Dakota.

Great West Highway

This way north

Capitalization

Exercise 4 **Capitalizing Place Names**

Write each item, using capital letters where needed.

1. northern illinois
2. world trade center
3. spain
4. arabian desert
5. northern california
6. front street
7. national boulevard
8. carlsbad caverns
9. nebraska
10. atlantic ocean
11. yellowstone river
12. yankee stadium
13. fifth avenue
14. mediterranean sea
15. ford's theater
16. bryce canyon
17. caspian sea
18. dallas
19. great britain
20. lake erie

Exercise 5 **Using Capital Letters for Place Names**

Write each geographical name, using capital letters where needed. Write *correct* if none are needed.

1. The louisiana purchase covered 827,987 square miles.
2. The united states bought the land from france.
3. At that time, Napoleon Bonaparte was the leader of france, and Thomas Jefferson was our president.
4. It extended from canada to mexico.
5. Some of the states that were once part of this territory are arkansas, kansas, nebraska, and oklahoma.
6. The land was bordered by the mississippi river on the east and by the rocky mountains on the west.
7. The platte river and the missouri river are also in this region.
8. new orleans was an important city.
9. It is located on the gulf of mexico.
10. The purchase of the land doubled the size of the united states of america.
11. It also ended French control of the mississippi valley.
12. spain still owned parts of florida and texas.
13. General Andrew Jackson defeated the British in new orleans in 1815.
14. The United States had wanted only a small piece of land that allowed access to the west.
15. Leaving from st. louis, missouri, Lewis and Clark explored this region.
16. They traveled to what is now bismarck, north dakota.
17. Meanwhile, people in washington, d.c., were thinking of these men.
18. Lewis and Clark reached the pacific ocean by traveling down the columbia river.
19. Now Americans could move farther westward.
20. Someday the country might extend to the west coast.

19.4 Capitalizing Other Proper Nouns and Adjectives

Many nouns besides the names of people and places are proper nouns. Adjectives that are formed from proper nouns are called proper adjectives. For example, the proper adjective *Cuban* is formed from the proper noun *Cuba*.

RULE 1: Capitalize the names of clubs, organizations, businesses, institutions, government bodies, and political parties.

American Bar Association   Farragut Middle School   the Senate

RULE 2: Capitalize brand names but not the nouns following them.

Smoothies lotion   Neato sneakers

RULE 3: Capitalize the names of important historical events, periods of time, and documents.

Vietnam War   Renaissance   Gettysburg Address

RULE 4: Capitalize the names of days of the week, months of the year, and holidays. Do not capitalize names of the seasons.

Friday   July   Thanksgiving Day   winter

RULE 5: Capitalize the first word, the last word, and all important words in the title of a book, play, short story, poem, essay, article, film, television series, song, magazine, newspaper, and chapter of a book.

Profiles in Courage   "The Necklace"   *Newsweek*

RULE 6: Capitalize the names of ethnic groups, nationalities, and languages.

Vietnamese   Chilean   German

RULE 7: Capitalize proper adjectives that are formed from the names of ethnic groups and nationalities.

Chinese cooking   Japanese flag

RULE 8: Capitalize names of courses.

Algebra II   World History I

Capitalization

Exercise 6 — Capitalizing Proper Nouns and Adjectives

Write the following items, using capital letters where needed.

1. sunnyvale school
2. *reader's digest*
3. english
4. magna carta
5. "yankee doodle"
6. egyptian history
7. american red cross
8. girl scouts
9. wheatola cereal
10. *boston globe*
11. boston tea party
12. memorial day
13. general motors corp.
14. lipton tea
15. mexican food
16. *the red pony*
17. world war II
18. colby college
19. treaty of paris
20. russian literature
21. geometry 101

Exercise 7 — Using Capital Letters

Write each proper noun and adjective needing capitalization. Write *correct* if the sentence has no errors.

1. The emancipation proclamation ended slavery in the South.
2. President Abraham Lincoln wrote this document in the summer of 1862.
3. Lincoln issued it during the civil war.
4. It became official in the winter of 1863.
5. It is as well known as the declaration of independence and the bill of rights.
6. These three writings are vital documents of american history.
7. Lincoln is also famous for the gettysburg address, a short speech he delivered in november 1863.
8. The french, the english, and other peoples around the world have read them.
9. In march 1861 the russians freed their serfs.
10. The Thirteenth Amendment, ratified in december 1865, ended slavery in the United States.
11. *uncle tom's cabin,* a book by Harriet Beecher Stowe, helped end slavery.
12. She wrote the novel while her husband taught at bowdoin college.
13. The book was printed in *national era,* a popular magazine before the civil war.
14. The book was an american best seller.
15. The Fourteenth Amendment to the constitution was also ratified soon after the war.
16. Before each amendment became law, congress had to pass it.
17. The *new york times* printed articles about these amendments.
18. The fourteenth amendment gave african americans the right to vote.
19. The civil war was well documented in *harper's weekly.*
20. Today we can read about the civil war in books like *the blue and the gray.*
21. The civil war is usually covered in american history 1.

Grammar Review

CAPITALIZATION

Morning Star, Black Sun by Brent Ashabranner details the efforts of the Northern Cheyenne to preserve their cherished homeland. In the following passage from the book, Joe Little Coyote, a young Northern Cheyenne man, relates the story of how his people had obtained their reservation. The passage has been annotated to show some of the rules of capitalization covered in this unit.

Literature Model

from Morning Star, Black Sun
by Brent Ashabranner

"When General Miles—the Indians called him Bear Coat—decided to help my ancestors get a reservation," Joe Little Coyote said, "he picked a group of Cheyenne under Chief Two Moons and a troop of soldiers and told them to ride through the country until they found good land for a reservation. The Cheyenne rode straight to the Tongue River, and they said that was the land they wanted. The soldiers wanted them to look further, to be sure they had found the best place. They were afraid General Miles might think they hadn't done their job right. But the Cheyenne said, 'No. This will be our land.'"

Then Joe Little Coyote said, "Our spiritual history is here, in this land, and in Bear Butte where Sweet Medicine received the Sacred Arrows. This is more than a reservation. This is our homeland." And he added, "You don't sell your homeland."

Annotations:
- Title coming before a person's name
- Name of a person
- Name of a body of water
- First word of a direct quotation that is a complete sentence
- Place name

Grammar Review

Review: Exercise 1 **Capitalizing Sentences and Quotations**

Write each sentence, correcting any errors in capitalization.

SAMPLE Joe Little Coyote said, "our spiritual history is in this land."
ANSWER Joe Little Coyote said, "Our spiritual history is in this land."

1. "My ancestors got the reservation," he explained, "With the help of General Miles."
2. general Miles said that we should look for reservation land.
3. "soon a group of Cheyenne headed for a good place to live," Joe said.
4. Chief Two Moons said That they wanted the land along the Tongue River.
5. the Cheyenne were interested in living on this land.
6. the soldiers asked the Cheyenne, "do you want to look further?"
7. "my ancestors were afraid they hadn't looked carefully enough," said Joe.
8. the Cheyenne said that the land near the Tongue River would be their home.
9. "our spiritual history is here," said Joe. "the land is sacred to us."
10. Joe Little Coyote said, "you don't sell your homeland."

Review: Exercise 2 **Capitalizing Direct Quotations**

Write each sentence, correcting any errors in capitalization.

1. Brendan said, "many Navajo who live in places like Monument Valley and Canyon de Chelly still live as their ancestors did."
2. "some make jewelry," said Jason. "they use silver, turquoise, and coral."
3. "did you know," asked Jennifer, "that they are also weavers?"
4. "yes," said Brendan. "they raise their own sheep and spin the wool."
5. "when they weave," said Jason, "their designs are based on ancient patterns."
6. Jennifer said, "once I saw a sand painting that was made by a Navajo."
7. "did you know," she added, "that there are more than five hundred designs?"
8. "no, I didn't," said Brendan. "how big are they?"
9. "some are small and take only an hour or two to make," said Jennifer. "others are so large that several people work for hours."
10. "these pictures are not made from paint at all," added Jason.

Review: Exercise 3   Capitalizing Names and Titles of People

Write only names and titles of people, using capital letters as needed.

SAMPLE   sitting bull isn't the only famous Native American.
ANSWER   Sitting Bull

1. According to howard w. hill, ph.d., pocahontas was always well known.
2. Legend says that she saved the life of captain john smith.
3. Later, she married john rolfe and was baptized under the name rebecca.
4. She is the main character in an old play by j. n. barker and is also the star of the walt disney animated movie called *pocahontas*.
5. squanto, who helped the Pilgrims, was captured by sir ferdinando gorges.
6. william bradford was surprised to find that squanto spoke English.
7. He helped settlers like captain miles standish and governor john carver.
8. Much later, sacajawea helped meriwether lewis and william clark.
9. president thomas jefferson wanted them to find a way to the Pacific Ocean.
10. Artist john white depicted scenes of Native American life.

Review: Exercise 4   Capitalizing Names of Places

Write any place names that need capital letters.

SAMPLE   People first came to north america by crossing over from asia.
ANSWER   North America; Asia

1. During the Ice Age, there was a land bridge between russia and alaska.
2. People settled in the southwest, the east, and other areas of the united states.
3. The first people to see the columbia river were Native Americans.
4. At plymouth rock, the Wampanoag greeted the Pilgrims.
5. narragansett bay, a Native American name, is part of the atlantic ocean.
6. In those days, there was no route 6 winding through cape cod.
7. Many years later, the colonists in boston built Faneuil hall.
8. Soon settlers headed west, traveling along the santa fe trail.
9. Monument valley in utah and arizona was sacred to the Native Americans.
10. Other Native American nations include the cree and the sioux.

Grammar Review

Review: Exercise 5   **Capitalizing Other Proper Nouns**

Write each item, using capital letters where needed.

SAMPLE   girl scouts of america
ANSWER   Girl Scouts of America

1. speed king sneakers
2. monday, september 6
3. *reader's digest*
4. korean war
5. memorial day
6. american medical association
7. general motors
8. "the open window"
9. *the red badge of courage*
10. middle ages
11. kennedy middle school
12. treaty of paris
13. irish
14. republicans and democrats
15. *the lion king*
16. victorian age
17. cadillac sedan
18. fourth of july
19. new york historical society
20. declaration of independence

Review: Exercise 6   **Capitalizing Proper Adjectives**

Write the proper noun from each item correctly. Then write each group of words, changing the proper noun to a proper adjective.

SAMPLE   the language of spain
ANSWER   Spain, the Spanish language

1. a poodle from france
2. the capital of egypt
3. music of germany
4. cars from japan
5. clothes from india
6. antiques from england
7. a bank in korea
8. a lantern from china
9. wood from south america
10. elephants from africa
11. food from brazil
12. the language of norway
13. a beach in hawaii
14. a glacier in alaska
15. a boomerang from australia
16. the mountains of switzerland
17. a doll from russia
18. a song from greece
19. a book from nigeria
20. a palm tree in samoa

Review: Exercise 7

Proofreading

The following passage is about artist Robert Henri, whose work appears on the next page. Rewrite the passage, correcting the errors in spelling, capitalization, grammar, and usage. Add any missing punctuation. There are ten errors.

Robert Henri

¹Robert Henri (1865–1929) was an american portrait and cityscape painter whose subjects sparkle with life. ²The Artist painted ordinary and exotic people rather than the rich and famous. ³His paintings of urban life helped portray a newer, more modern Era.

⁴Henri's aim in painting were to capture feeling sensation, and character. ⁵*Portrait of Po Tse (Water Eagle)* conveys this spirit thru the subject's expressive, dignified face. ⁶The subject who is dressed in traditional clothes, shows pride in his Native American heritage. ⁷like joe Little Coyote in *morning Star, Black Sun,* the subject in the portrait cherishes his homeland.

Review: Exercise 8

Mixed Review

Write each sentence, correcting any errors in capitalization.

SAMPLE   there have been many famous native americans in our history

ANSWER   There; Native Americans

1. massasoit signed a treaty in 1621 with governor john carver of plymouth colony.
2. crazy horse defeated lt. col. george a. custer in the battle of little bighorn on june 25, 1876.
3. geronimo, an apache, once fled to the sierra madre in mexico.
4. He later returned to the united states.
5. he lived on the san carlos indian reservation.
6. sitting bull, a sioux, was born near the grand river in south dakota.
7. "jim thorpe won gold medals in the 1912 olympic games," said jill.
8. he played baseball for the cincinnati reds, a national league baseball team.

(continued)

Capitalization

9. an excellent football player, too, he is enshrined in the football hall of fame in canton, ohio.

10. william cody presented "buffalo bill's wild west show" in the east.

Robert Henri, *Portrait of Po Tse (Water Eagle)*, c. 1916–1925

Capitalization

Writing Application

TIME

For more about the writing process, see **TIME Facing the Blank Page,** pp. 97-107.

Capitalization in Writing

Examine the following passage from *So Far from the Bamboo Grove*, noting how Yoko Kawashima Watkins uses capitalization to identify characters. Pay particular attention to the italicized words.

"Most of my classmates have enlisted," said *Hideyo,* serious for once. "*I* have decided to go to help our country."

"*You* cannot go, *Hideyo*!" *Mother* told him. "*You* must talk with *Father. You* just cannot make such a decision alone."

"*Mother,* I have already sent in my application," said *Hideyo.* "*I* will take the written and physical examinations!"

"How could *you*?" *Mother* moaned. "Why didn't *you* tell me?"

"*I* am eighteen. Big enough to make my own decision."

Capitalization Techniques

Try to apply some of Yoko Kwashima Watkins's writing techniques when you write and revise your own work.

❶ Capitalize people's names, and names describing family relationships when they replace a name:

INCORRECT "How could you?" *his Mother* moaned.

WATKINS'S VERSION "How could you?" *Mother* moaned.

❷ Always capitalize the pronoun *I.* Capitalize other pronouns only when they begin a sentence:

INCORRECT "Why didn't *You* tell me?" "*i* am eighteen."

WATKINS'S VERSION "Why didn't you tell me?" "*I* am eighteen."

Capitalization *(side tab)*

Practice Practice these capitalization techniques as you revise the following passage, using a separate sheet of paper. Focus especially on the underlined words.

"<u>i</u> have never been to New Haven," said <u>eve</u>.

"Of course <u>You</u> have," replied <u>aunt petra</u>. "Don't <u>You</u> remember the cranes we saw while crossing the bridge?"

"<u>father</u> told me about them, but <u>i</u> can't recall what they look like," insisted <u>eve.</u> "How about <u>You, marty</u>? Can <u>You</u> describe them?" asked <u>eve</u>, turning toward her <u>Cousin marty</u>.

"Yes," said <u>marty</u>. "<u>i</u> think they were painted bright red. <u>you</u> always said they looked like giant grasshopper legs, only red."

"Oh, yeah!" exploded <u>eve</u>. "Now <u>i</u> remember."

Writing Online For more grammar practice, go to glencoe.com and enter QuickPass code WC87703p2.

Writing Application **597**

UNIT 20 Punctuation

Using the Period and Other End Marks

Three punctuation marks signal the end of sentences. The period is used for declarative and mild imperative sentences. The question mark is used for interrogative sentences. The exclamation point is used for exclamatory sentences, strong imperatives, and interjections.

RULE 1:   Use a period at the end of a declarative sentence. A declarative sentence makes a statement.

> Tractors perform many jobs on a farm**.**
> I worked on a farm last summer**.**

RULE 2:   Use a period at the end of an imperative sentence that does not express strong feeling. An imperative sentence gives a command or makes a request.

> Turn the key**.** [command]
> Please start the motor**.** [request]

RULE 3:   Use a question mark at the end of an interrogative sentence. An interrogative sentence asks a question.

> When was the first tractor built**?**
> Were you aware of that**?**
> Do modern tractors have both speed and power**?**

RULE 4:   Use an exclamation point at the end of an exclamatory sentence or a strong imperative. An exclamatory sentence expresses strong feeling.

> What a powerful tractor that is**!**
> Get out of the way**!**

RULE 5:   Use an exclamation point at the end of an interjection. An interjection is a word or group of words that expresses strong emotion.

> Wow**!**   My goodness**!**   Hi**!**   Hey**!**
> Hooray**!**   Oh, boy**!**   Oops**!**   Phew**!**

Write the last word of each sentence, and add the correct end mark. Then write whether each sentence is *declarative, imperative, interrogative,* or *exclamatory.*

1. Please tell me about the history of tractors
2. Read about tractors in your book
3. The first tractor was used in the 1870s
4. This tractor was driven by steam and required a licensed steam engineer to operate and repair it
5. Was this machine very large
6. Could it haul and pull heavy loads
7. Can you believe that this tractor could pull as many as forty plows at one time
8. What an amazing sight it must have been
9. Internal combustion tractors were built in the 1890s but did not become practical until about 1920
10. Both early tractors and tractors today are used to move or operate other equipment, such as combines, threshers, or posthole diggers
11. Do some research to find out what else these kinds of equipment do
12. Please tell me about the early days of farming
13. Open your history book
14. Read about the fascinating techniques used by ancient farmers
15. Did you know that the first cultivated crops were probably grasses grown from wild seed
16. The early Egyptians developed the first large-scale irrigation system, which allowed them to distribute water efficiently over a large area
17. What a tremendous advancement this was
18. Each year the Nile River overflowed its banks
19. Farmers discovered they could grow crops by using this water
20. Did farmers prosper when the Nile overflowed
21. In 3000 B.C., Egyptian farmers invented the ox-drawn plow
22. This plow helped Egyptian farmers produce a great deal of food
23. Did your history teacher tell you that they not only fed their own people but also exported huge quantities to other countries
24. Can you imagine the work involved to grow, harvest, and ship twenty million bushels of grain to Rome each year
25. Look at the stylized pictures on Egyptian pottery to see how they raised poultry and cared for their sheep

20.2 Using Commas I

Commas signal a pause between parts of a sentence.

and clog city streets.

RULE 1: Use commas to separate three or more items in a series.

Cars, buses, and trucks clog city streets.

RULE 2: Use commas to show a pause after an introductory word and to set off names used in direct address.

Yes, most cities have few parking garages.

Tony, are you going downtown?

RULE 3: Use a comma after two or more introductory prepositional phrases, when the prepositional phrase is very long, or when the comma is needed to make the meaning clear. A comma is not needed after a single, short prepositional phrase, but it is acceptable to use one.

In the fall of 1991, Frank M. Jordan was elected mayor.

RULE 4: Use a comma after an introductory participle and an introductory participial phrase.

Plagued by deficits, many cities need state aid.

RULE 5: Use commas to set off words that interrupt the flow of thought in a sentence.

A large city, as you can see, employs many police officers.

RULE 6: Use a comma after conjunctive adverbs such as *however, moreover, furthermore, nevertheless,* and *therefore*.

The city is growing; therefore, the city payroll must grow.

RULE 7: Use commas to set off an appositive if it is not essential to the meaning of a sentence.

Alpine Inc., this city's oldest company, joined a large cartel.

Write each sentence, adding a comma or commas where needed. If the sentence needs no changes, write *correct*.

1. Yes cities offer many different places to live.
2. People can live in apartment buildings private homes town houses residential hotels or rooming houses.
3. In the middle of the city you can see skyscrapers.
4. Some buildings are neat clean and attractive.
5. Other buildings are dirty and neglected.
6. The city has a large population.
7. In the tiny yards behind some city buildings the residents have created charming "pocket gardens."
8. Yolanda did you know that San Diego is one of the nation's fastest-growing cities?
9. A big city in my opinion is the best place to live.
10. No I do not mind the crowding; the hustle and bustle in my opinion are part of a city's appeal.
11. Norm do you prefer the city or the country?
12. Does Jo your new friend enjoy living in the city?
13. Pausing a moment to consider my answer I responded that she likes the city.
14. Moreover she has never lived in the country.
15. Eva dislikes the city; nevertheless she refuses to move.
16. Traveling away from the center of the city you can find less crowded living conditions.
17. Country houses you might imagine have more land.
18. I hope Maya that you can find a big house in the country.
19. The suburbs I suppose would be a good alternative Maya.
20. The town of Ridgemont a northern suburb offers some of the advantages of both city and country.
21. From the top of the ridge in the town cemetery you can see the lights and towers of the city.
22. The center of town the commercial district offers convenient services.
23. Around the square at the very center you can find a drug store a bakery a restaurant a hardware store a clothing shop and a shoe store.
24. In most areas outside the city's center grass and trees dominate the landscape.
25. The residents are inspired by this landscape; consequently many take up gardening as a hobby.

20.3 Using Commas II

Commas clarify meaning in sentences with more than one clause. A clause is a group of words that has a subject and a predicate and is used as part of a sentence.

RULE 8: Use a comma before *and*, *or*, or *but* when it joins main clauses.

Farming is a business, and farmers need to make a profit.
Farmers must sell their crops, or they cannot afford to replant.
Farming can be rewarding, but it is hard work.

RULE 9 Use a comma after an introductory adverb clause. Adverb clauses begin with subordinating conjunctions, such as *after, although, as, because, before, considering (that), if, in order that, since, so that, though, unless, until, when, whenever, where, wherever, whether,* or *while.*

When the weather is too dry, farmers have problems.
If there is no rain, crops can be ruined.

In most cases, do not use a comma with an adverb clause that comes at the end of a sentence.

Farmers have problems when the weather is too dry.
Crops can be ruined if there is no rain.

RULE 10: Use a comma or a pair of commas to set off an adjective clause that is not essential to the meaning of a sentence. This means that the clause merely gives additional information. Adjective clauses often begin with the relative pronouns *who, whom, whose, which,* or *that.*

Dairy cows, which are common on farms, are raised for their milk.

Do not use a comma or pair of commas to set off an essential clause from the rest of the sentence. An adjective clause is essential when it is necessary to the meaning of the sentence.

An animal that is raised for milk is the dairy cow.

Exercise 3   Using Commas with Main Clauses

Write each sentence. Find the main clauses and the conjunction. Add commas where necessary. If the sentence needs no commas, write *correct*.

1. Farmers prepare the soil and then they plant crops in the fields.
2. Sometimes they plant a cover crop and plow it into the soil in spring.
3. They sometimes add organic material, which helps build the soil.
4. They maintain a compost pile from which they add finished compost to the soil.
5. Some seeds are planted directly in the ground but others are started indoors.
6. Some seeds are started in a greenhouse and they are planted outdoors when it's warm.
7. The farmers can buy the seeds fresh or they can save them from a previous crop.
8. Even when the plants are in the ground, the farmers' work is not done.
9. Weeds of all kinds suddenly appear and the farmers must act quickly.
10. They must remove the weeds carefully or they will disturb the young plants.

Exercise 4   Using Commas with Subordinate Clauses

Write the subordinate clause in each sentence, adding commas where needed.

1. Whenever farmers grow crops insects move in for the feast.
2. IPM which stands for Integrated Pest Management helps control insects.
3. Because insects flourish in debris farmers try to keep their fields clean.
4. They make sure that seedlings are insect-free before they plant them.
5. They rotate crops so that soil insects don't have a chance to multiply.
6. They choose varieties that can hold their own against insects.
7. Breeders whose job it is to develop such varieties watch for resistant plants.
8. They isolate these plants which are then used to produce seed.
9. When insects are large another effective control is handpicking them.
10. Physical barriers that keep insects away are also helpful.
11. An example is a row cover which discourages maggots and beetles.
12. If an insect responds to visual or chemical cues it can be caught in a trap.
13. A bright red plastic apple lures apple maggots which stick to its surface.
14. Electronic lures that zap bugs are not very effective.
15. Strong pesticides are avoided because they kill beneficial insects.
16. These insects which include lady bugs and praying mantises eat other insects.
17. Although many people fear wasps some wasps help control harmful insects.
18. If all else fails farmers must rely on pesticides.
19. When they do they limit application to the exact problem area.
20. The safest kind is insecticidal soap which doesn't linger in the soil.

20.4 Using Commas III

Several rules for using commas—among those the rules for punctuating dates and addresses—are a matter of standard usage.

RULE 11: Use commas before and after the year when it is used with both the month and the day. If only the month and the year are given, do not use a comma.

> The antipollution project began on May 25, 1992, and lasted a year.
> The first meeting was held in July 1992 and made headlines.

RULE 12: Use commas before and after the name of a state or a country when it is used with the name of a city. Do not use a comma after the state if it is used with a ZIP code.

> Speakers came from Palo Alto, California, to speak at the meeting.
> The address on the envelope was as follows: 123 Ridge Road, Orange, CT 06477.

RULE 13: Use a comma or pair of commas to set off an abbreviated title or degree following a person's name.

> One expert on pollution and health is Jay Carr, M.D.
> Peter Fujita, Ph.D., wrote a book on pollution.

RULE 14: Use a comma or commas to set off *too* in the middle of a sentence, when *too* means "also."

> Air pollution, too, creates problems. The courts, too, are involved.

RULE 15: Use a comma or commas to set off a direct quotation.

> Dr. Flores said, "Pollution causes serious problems in our cities."
> "We will try," said Joan, "to fight pollution."

RULE 16: Use a comma after the salutation of a friendly letter and after the closing of both a friendly and a business letter.

> Dear Sharon,   Your friend,   Yours truly,

RULE 17: Use a comma for clarity in reading a sentence.

> Instead of three, four panelists discussed pollution.

Exercise 5	Using Commas with Names, Titles, Dates, and Quotations

Write each sentence below, adding commas where necessary, or write *correct* if the sentence needs no changes.

1. Larry said "Our conference on pollution is sure to be successful."
2. A letter from Austin Texas arrived today.
3. It said that Jean Loubet Ph.D. will be attending.
4. "Is Dr. Jean Loubet" asked Evan "a physician?"
5. His most famous book appeared in June 1995.
6. His letter told us that dozens of boxes of materials will be sent ahead by train.
7. We must prepare them for distribution at the conference.
8. Dr. Loubet will arrive at the conference on November 5 2001 and depart a week later.
9. He and Sarah McInerney M.D. will be our featured speakers.
10. Dr. McInerney too has written many books and articles.
11. She does research in Ann Arbor Michigan at the university.
12. Dr. McInerney asked "Should I send materials ahead too?"
13. She doesn't have a Ph.D. but is as famous as Dr. Loubet.
14. Larry told both speakers "We're delighted to have you here."
15. Both Dr. McInerney and Jean Loubet, Ph.D. agreed to attend the 2002 conference to deliver speeches.

Exercise 6	Using Commas in Letters

Write each numbered item below, adding commas where necessary.

[1]109 National Boulevard

[2]Los Angeles California 90034

[3]September 30 2001

[4]Dear Aunt Patricia

[5]Last week my teacher said "We can all do more to stop pollution." [6]I think that students too can help. [7]I said to Yoko "Let's make posters for the Stop Pollution Fair." [8]The fair will be like the one that was held on January 5 2000 in Denver Colorado. [9]Alex Gafar M.A. will speak on recycling.

[10]Much love

Antonia

20.5 Using Semicolons and Colons

RULE 1: Use a semicolon to join the parts of a compound sentence when a coordinating conjunction, such as *and, or, nor,* or *but,* is not used.

Many people in Africa farm small pieces of land; these farmers raise food for their families.

RULE 2: Use a semicolon to join parts of a compound sentence when the main clauses are long and are subdivided by commas. Use a semicolon even if these clauses are already joined by a coordinating conjunction.

Herding is an important job for the Dinka, Masai, and Turkana; but plowing, planting, and harvesting are also crucial tasks.

RULE 3: Use a semicolon to separate main clauses joined by a conjunctive adverb, such as *consequently, furthermore, however, moreover, nevertheless,* or *therefore.* Be sure to use a comma after a conjunctive adverb.

Many African farmers grow crops on family-owned farms; however, in some areas, farmers work on land owned by the government.

RULE 4: Use a colon to introduce a list of items that ends a sentence. Use a phrase such as *these, the following,* or *as follows* to signal that a list is coming.

African farmers grow the following: corn, millet, and sorghum.

Do not use a colon immediately after a verb or a preposition.

Some farmers work with hoes, knives, and digging sticks.

RULE 5: Use a colon to separate the hour and the minute when you write the time of day.

Many farmers start working at 5:15 in the morning.

RULE 6: Use a colon after the salutation of a business letter.

Dear Sir or Madam: Dear Ms. Ngai:

Punctuation

Exercise 7   Using Semicolons and Colons

Write each sentence. Add a semicolon or a colon where needed. Remember to use a comma after a conjunctive adverb.

1. I was bored at 330 in the afternoon then the mail arrived.
2. It included these items two bills, three ads, and a letter from my cousin.
3. Jill wrote about her work in Africa she is teaching English in Tanzania.
4. Africa contains these regions deserts, jungles, grasslands, and farmlands.
5. The equator cuts through Africa however most land lies north of it.
6. Some areas are not very hospitable nevertheless most are inhabited.
7. There is fertile land in North Africa however the desert predominates.
8. The southern edge of the desert merges into grassland further south the grassland merges into a tropical rain forest.
9. Southern Africa lies in the temperate zone snow falls there occasionally.
10. Africa is rich in resources thus it supports a variety of life styles.
11. Rubber trees flourish in the rain forest olive trees grow near the sea.
12. In the grasslands, farmers grow wheat and barley they also raise sheep.
13. South Africa is a major wool producer its main crops are corn and sugar.
14. Spectacular rivers flowing through Africa include the following the mighty Nile in the east, the Congo in Central Africa, and the Niger in the west.
15. Agriculture dominates the economy mining is another important activity.
16. Jill mentioned the following Tanzanian products cotton, coffee, and sugar.
17. Some areas are quite poor consequently farmers must struggle to survive.
18. Subsistence farmers depend on corn they may also raise cattle or goats.
19. Jill finds life in Africa fascinating nevertheless she misses home.
20. Now at 345 I am no longer bored Jill's letter has sparked my imagination.

Exercise 8   Using Semicolons and Colons in Letters

Write the numbered items, adding a semicolon or a colon where needed.

¹Dear Mr. Bishop

²I am buying a farm for my venture, I will need farming equipment. ³I will have to buy plows, tractors, and spreaders. ⁴In the near future, I will also need the following seed, fertilizer, and more machinery. ⁵I am currently pricing equipment therefore, please send me a list of your prices.

Sincerely yours,

Eleni Ruiz

Punctuation

20.6 Using Quotation Marks and Italics

Quotation marks enclose a person's exact words, as well as the titles of some works. Italic type—a special slanted type that is used in printing—identifies titles of other works. In handwriting, use underlining to show italic type.

RULE 1: Use quotation marks before and after a direct quotation.

"A nomad is a person who wanders," May said.

RULE 2: Use quotation marks with both parts of a divided quotation.

"Most nomads," said Ali, "travel by animal or on foot."

RULE 3: Use a comma or commas to separate a phrase such as *he said* from the quotation itself. Place the comma inside closing quotation marks.

"Most nomads," Betsy explained, "raise animals."

RULE 4: Place a period inside closing quotation marks.

José said, "Some nomads move their animals through deserts."

RULE 5: Place a question mark or an exclamation point inside the quotation marks when it is part of the quotation.

Bo asked, "Do nomads travel to find water for their herds?"

RULE 6: Place a question mark or an exclamation point outside the quotation marks when it is part of the entire sentence.

Did Ms. McCall say, "Write an essay on nomads"?

RULE 7: Use quotation marks for the title of a short story, essay, short poem, song, magazine or newspaper article, or book chapter.

"Dusk" [short story]   "Mending Wall" [poem]   "Skylark" [song]

RULE 8: Use italics (underlining) for the title of a book, play, long poem, film, television series, magazine, newspaper, or work of art.

The Sea Wolf [book]   *Julius Caesar* [play]   *Newsweek* [magazine]

Exercise 9   **Punctuating Titles**

Write each item below, adding quotation marks or underlining for italics where needed.

1. Nanook of the North (film)
2. New York Times (newspaper)
3. The Eternal Nomad (short poem)
4. The Old Man and the Sea (book)
5. Dream-Children (essay)
6. Star Trek (television series)
7. The Skin of Our Teeth (play)
8. Scientific American (magazine)
9. The Coldest Land (magazine article)
10. To Build a Fire (short story)

Exercise 10   **Using Quotation Marks and Italics**

Write the following sentences, adding quotation marks and other punctuation marks and underlining for italics where needed.

1. Frieda asked Have you read the assignment in our textbook
2. Bonnie shouted What an interesting article on nomads that was
3. I didn't know said Barry that some nomads live in northern Europe
4. Yes said Ms. Ito Lapland lies in Russia, Finland, Sweden, and Norway
5. Did Ms. Ito say The people of Lapland are called Lapps
6. Barry asked Have you read the article on Lapps in National Geographic
7. No I answered but I read about them in another magazine
8. The Lapps have two seasons said Frieda day and night
9. Does the night season really last nine months asked Barry
10. The book The Far North says Lapland has only six weeks of warm weather a year
11. Did the book say Only mosses and a few trees grow in Lapland
12. Why are the Lapps considered nomads asked George
13. Bonnie answered The people live by hunting and fishing
14. During the summer season I said they lay in supplies for the winter
15. Reindeer and dogs added Frieda are their only domestic animals
16. Do the people follow the reindeer all summer asked George
17. Bonnie replied The herds must keep moving to find enough to eat
18. Tim asked What do the Lapps do with the reindeer
19. The article The Land of the Lapps says they use the milk, meat, and hides
20. Did you know asked Ms. Ito that both male and female reindeer have antlers

Unit 20 Punctuation

20.7 Using Apostrophes

An apostrophe shows possession as well as the missing letters in a contraction. It can also signal the plural of letters, numbers, or words.

RULE 1:   Use an apostrophe and an *s* (*'s*) to form the possessive of a singular noun.

 girl + **'s** = girl**'s** Francis + **'s** = Francis**'s**

RULE 2:   Use an apostrophe and an *s* (*'s*) to form the possessive of a plural noun that does not end in *s*.

 women + **'s** = women**'s** mice + **'s** = mice**'s**

RULE 3:   Use an apostrophe alone to form the possessive of a plural noun that ends in *s*.

 girls + **'** = girl**s'** Johnsons + **'** = Johnson**s'**

RULE 4:   Use an apostrophe and an *s* (*'s*) to form the possessive of an indefinite pronoun.

 anyone + **'s** = anyone**'s** somebody + **'s** = somebody**'s**

Do not use an apostrophe in a possessive pronoun.

 That map is **theirs**.   Is this mark **mine**?
 The books on the table are **hers**. The bird flapped **its** wings.

RULE 5:   Use an apostrophe to replace letters that have been omitted in a contraction.

 it + is = it**'s**   you + are = you**'re**
 there + is = there**'s** did + not = didn**'t**

RULE 6:   Use an apostrophe to form the plural of letters, figures, and words when they are used as themselves.

 three *t* **'s** five *6* **'s** no *and* **'s,** *if* **'s,** or *but* **'s**

RULE 7:   Use an apostrophe to show missing numbers in a date.

 the class of **'**87

Punctuation

You · are

You · re

a

You · re

Exercise 11   Using Apostrophes in Possessives

Write the possessive form of each of the words below.

1. cities
2. nation
3. everybody
4. children
5. Mr. Schultz
6. dogs
7. man
8. Sharice

9. woman
10. geese
11. classes
12. teacher
13. Alex
14. someone
15. oxen
16. Jim

17. the Gilsons
18. landowners
19. managers
20. people
21. rooster
22. family
23. nobody
24. Ms. Tremon
25. clowns

Exercise 12   Using Apostrophes

Write each plural, possessive, or contraction. Use apostrophes where needed. Write *correct* if the sentence needs no changes.

1. This citys outlook is uncertain.
2. Ours is an uncertain future.
3. Today cities arent built beneath the earth.
4. Its strange to think of underground cities.
5. Perhaps well see cities floating on the water.
6. Many city planners ideas are unusual.
7. Their reports usually are filled with too many *if*s.
8. Tomorrows cities are a mystery to us.
9. No city can plan its future exactly.
10. All of our visions are full of *maybe*s.
11. What will actually happen to cities is anybodys guess.
12. These authors new book predicts the end of cities.
13. The Murrays idea is that we wont need cities.
14. In their view, computers will let us live anywhere.
15. I can do my job at my house, you can do yours at your house, and other people can work out of their houses too.
16. Ill believe that when I see it.
17. Other peoples dreams take them to space.
18. One of Arthur C. Clarkes books is about a city in a space station.
19. The residents lives would be very different from ours.
20. Someone elses book predicts that cities will expand outward.

20.8 Using Hyphens, Dashes, and Parentheses

RULE 1   Use a hyphen to show the division of a word at the end of a line. Always divide the word between its syllables.

Forests and their products are of the greatest importance to people.

RULE 2   Use a hyphen in compound numbers.

eighty-seven   thirty-nine

RULE 3   Use a hyphen in a fraction that is spelled out.

Forest rangers receive **one-half** pay upon retirement. [modifier]

One-half of all tree diseases are caused by fungi. [noun]

RULE 4   Use a hyphen or hyphens in certain compound nouns.

great-grandfather   brother-in-law   attorney-at-law

RULE 5   Hyphenate a compound modifier only when it precedes the word it modifies.

It's a **well-maintained** park.   It is **well maintained.**

RULE 6   Use a hyphen after the prefixes *all-*, *ex-*, and *self-*. Use a hyphen to separate any prefix from a word that begins with a capital letter.

all-powerful   ex-wife   self-educated   pre-Columbian

RULE 7   Use a dash or dashes to show a sudden break or change in thought or speech.

Mrs. Poulos—she lives nearby—helps the park attendants.

RULE 8   Use parentheses to set off words that define or helpfully explain a word in the sentence.

In tropical rain forests, dozens of species of plants may grow in one square mile (2.6 square kilometers) of land.

Exercise 13 Using Hyphens

Write each item. Use a hyphen where needed. Write *correct* if the item needs no hyphens.

1. two thirds majority
2. one-half of the pie
3. exchampion
4. self knowledge
5. well loved author
6. all inclusive
7. Great aunt Katie
8. sixty five
9. mid American
10. postwar
11. one quarter finished
12. father in law
13. well known author
14. seventy three
15. pro Irish

Exercise 14 Using Hyphens, Dashes, and Parentheses

Write the following sentences, adding any needed hyphens, dashes, or parentheses. Write *correct* if the sentence needs no changes.

1. Before people began to clear the forest for farms and cities, forests covered about one half of the earth.
2. Dr. Orzeck he is an expert on ecology spoke about deforestation.
3. His presentation was well documented.
4. People have used wood products since the beginning of time but more about that later.
5. One tree may have as many as forty two uses.
6. In pre Columbian America vast all pine forests were common.
7. Some pines were huge, up to 240 feet tall and 2 feet in diameter.
8. British law see text on page 311 reserved these huge trees for the Crown.
9. The super straight trunks were perfect for the masts of sailing ships.
10. In 1947 a month long fire in a Maine forest provided a forest laboratory.
11. At first sun loving flowers and shrubs grew up to fill the new clearings.
12. Now, evergreen trees that don't shed their leaves are shading out the birches.
13. These shade tolerant trees will again dominate the forest.
14. About 748 species of trees are native in the continental United States.
15. The National Register of Big Trees page 221 lists champion trees.
16. A sequoia truly a giant at eighty-three feet in circumference is the largest tree.
17. Some sequoias in California have been growing for three thousand years.
18. Others want to protect the remaining old growth forests in the country.
19. Forests grow only where there is at least fifteen inches thirty-eight centimeters of rainfall per year.
20. Forests also require a frost free growing period of at least three months.

20.9 Using Abbreviations

RULE 1: Abbreviate the titles *Mr.*, *Mrs.*, *Ms.*, and *Dr.* before a person's name. Also abbreviate any professional or academic degree that follows a name, along with the titles *Jr.* and *Sr.*

Mr. Roy Sims **Jr**.   Rita Mendez, **M.D.**   Hugo Allen **Sr.**

RULE 2: Use capital letters and no periods with abbreviations that are pronounced letter by letter or as words. Exceptions are *U.S.* and *Washington, D.C.*, which do use periods.

WHO World Health Organization   **JV** junior varsity

ROTC Reserve Officers' Training Corps

RULE 3: With exact times, use A.M. (*ante meridiem*, "before noon") and P.M. (*post meridiem*, "after noon"). For years use B.C. (before Christ) and, sometimes, A.D. (*anno Domini*, "in the year of the Lord," after Christ).

7:15 **A.M.**   9:30 **P.M.**   40 **B.C.**   **A.D.** 476

RULE 4: Abbreviate days and months only in charts and lists.

Sun.   Tues.   Wed.   Feb.   Jul.   Aug.   Sept.

RULE 5: In scientific writing abbreviate units of measure. Use periods with English units but not with metric units.

inch(es) **in.**   pound(s) **lb.**   gallon(s) **gal.**

kilometer(s) **km**   liter(s) **l**   milliliter(s) **ml**

RULE 6: On envelopes only, abbreviate street names and state names. In general text, spell out street names and state names.

Street **St.**   Avenue **Ave.**   Road **Rd.**   Drive **Dr.**
Boulevard **Blvd.**   Parkway **Pkwy.**   Place **Pl.**
Arizona **AZ**   Colorado **CO**   Hawaii **HI**   Oklahoma **OK**
Kentucky **KY**   Utah **UT**   Virginia **VA**   Missouri **MO**

[on an envelope]   Mrs. Emily Anderson
                     3117 Chelsea **Ave.**
                     Norfolk, **VA** 23503

but   We still live on Chelsea **Avenue** in Norfolk, **Virginia.**

National
Aeronautics and
Space
Administration

Punctuation

Exercise 15   **Using Abbreviations**

Write the correct abbreviation for each underlined item.

1. *anno Domini* 2000
2. David Parker <u>Junior</u>
3. 153 <u>kilometers</u>
4. <u>February</u> 23
5. <u>Wednesday</u>
6. 1066 <u>before Christ</u>
7. <u>Young Women's Christian Association</u>
8. <u>Mister</u> Al Moreno
9. ninety-eight <u>pounds</u>
10. Saratoga <u>Road</u>
11. 67 Ryer <u>Avenue</u>
12. Sam Blie <u>Senior</u>
13. Phoenix, <u>Arizona</u>
14. Lewis Wright, <u>Medical Doctor</u>
15. <u>Students Against Driving Drunk</u>
16. *post meridiem*
17. Ann Carey, <u>Doctor of Philosophy</u>
18. Cato <u>Boulevard</u>
19. Denver, <u>Colorado</u>
20. <u>Columbia Broadcasting System</u>

Exercise 16   **Using Abbreviations in Sentences**

Write the correct abbreviation for each underlined item in the following sentences. Write *correct* if there are no changes.

1. The address on the envelope read 48 Bolton <u>Street</u>, Madison, <u>Wisconsin</u>.
2. It contained information from <u>Doctor</u> Rita Tapahonso.
3. <u>Mister</u> Ed Jones is teaching ecology.
4. Last year, classes met from 9:30 <u>in the morning</u> until 3:30 <u>in the afternoon</u>.
5. Scheduled speakers included <u>Doctor</u> Robin Oren.
6. Also present will be a representative of the <u>Environmental Protection Agency.</u>
7. Classes begin in <u>September.</u>
8. My adviser will see me on <u>Tuesday</u>.
9. Do you know the purpose of most <u>United Nations</u> agencies?
10. I know <u>United Nations International Children's Emergency Fund</u> helps children and mothers in developing nations.
11. Also, the <u>International Labor Organization</u> promotes employment and fair labor conditions.
12. The President lives at 1600 Pennsylvania <u>Avenue</u>, Washington, <u>District of Columbia.</u>
13. I was born on <u>February</u> 29, 1980, at 6:50 *ante meridiem.*
14. Madeline Jefferson, <u>Master of Arts</u>, is our English teacher.
15. Mix 3 <u>gallons</u> of Substance A with 2 <u>pounds</u> of Substance B.
16. Salt Lake City, <u>Utah</u>, and Tulsa, <u>Oklahoma</u>, are often compared.
17. Kim Yang, <u>Doctor of Dental Surgery</u>, has been my dentist for three years.
18. His office address is 412 Mullins <u>Road</u>, Kalamazoo, <u>Michigan</u>.
19. Mexico, <u>Missouri</u>, and Paris, <u>Kentucky</u>, are both <u>United States</u> cities.
20. What is the sum of 12 <u>liters</u> and 48 <u>milliliters</u>?

20.10 Writing Numbers

In charts and tables, numbers are always written as figures. However, in an ordinary sentence some numbers are spelled out and others are written as numerals.

RULE 1: Spell out all numbers up to ninety-nine.

My dad had not visited his hometown for **twenty-five** years.

RULE 2: Use numerals for numbers of more than two words.

Approximately **250** people used to live in his hometown.

RULE 3: Spell out any number that begins a sentence, or reword the sentence so that it does not begin with a number.

Nine thousand two hundred people now live in Dad's hometown.

RULE 4: Write very large numbers as a numeral followed by the word *million* or *billion.*

The population of the United States is about **263 million.**

RULE 5: If related numbers appear in the same sentence, use all numerals.

Of the **435** graduates, **30** have received a scholarship to college.

RULE 6: Spell out ordinal numbers (*first, second,* and so forth).

Jan is the **sixth** person to use the new library.

RULE 7: Use words to express the time of day unless you are writing the exact time or using the abbreviation A.M. or P.M.

Classes begin at **nine o'clock.**
They end at **2:45 P.M.**

RULE 8: Use numerals to express dates, house and street numbers, apartment and room numbers, telephone numbers, page numbers, amounts of money of more than two words, and percentages. Write out the word *percent.*

May **24, 1887**   **62** Oak Drive   Room **307**   **98** percent

---

Exercise 17   Writing Numbers

Write the sentences below, using the correct form for writing numbers. Write *correct* if a sentence needs no changes.

1. My father graduated from Red Bank Regional High School with the class of nineteen hundred sixty-one.
2. His class recently had a reunion after thirty years.
3. The reunion was scheduled for April ninth.
4. The party began at seven-thirty P.M.
5. Dad was the 13th person to arrive that evening.
6. The reunion was held in room forty-two, the old cafeteria.
7. 220 people came to the reunion.
8. Of these, 180 guests were graduates and forty were spouses.
9. More than 50% of the graduates attended.
10. There were three hundred thirty-four students in his graduating class.
11. Dad was happy to see his old best friend, whom he had not seen in 27 years.
12. He learned that Mr. Elton has moved back to town, to One Eighteen Jay Road.
13. Dad, Mr. Elton, and 2 other old friends agreed to get together in the coming year.
14. They figure three hundred sixty-five days gives them enough time to plan something.
15. Each alumnus contributed twenty dollars.
16. The committee collected 4 thousand 4 hundred dollars.
17. The party lasted until one o'clock.
18. My father graduated 5th in his class.
19. 75% of the class went on to college.
20. Of these students, 41 did not complete college.

Exercise 18   Writing Numbers

In the following paragraph, use the correct form for writing numbers.

[1]In two thousand seven the population of the United States was approximately 300 million. [2]The estimated population of North America was five hundred fifteen million. [3]North America has the 3rd largest population of the world's continents. [4]Asia has the largest, with fifty-nine percent. [5]More than three billion people live in Asia. [6]Africa ranks 2nd in the world's population. [7]Close to nine hundred million people live there. [8]Australia and New Zealand account for only 20,000,000 people. [9]Antarctica has no permanent population, and fewer than 1,000 scientists stay the winter. [10]Overall, more than six point seven billion people are believed to inhabit the earth.

Grammar Review

PUNCTUATION

Tourists see a place differently from the way local inhabitants do. In *A Small Place,* Jamaica Kincaid writes about her homeland, the small Caribbean island of Antigua. In the following passage from the book, Kincaid looks at the island through the eyes of a tourist. She describes the island's beauty and discusses its history. She also expresses her hopes for the future of Antigua. The passage has been annotated to show some of the rules of punctuation covered in this unit.

Literature Model

from A Small Place
by Jamaica Kincaid

Oh, but by now you are tired of all this looking, and you want to reach your destination—your hotel, your room. You long to refresh yourself; you long to eat some nice lobster, some nice local food. You take a bath, you brush your teeth. You get dressed again; as you get dressed, you look out the window. That water—have you ever seen anything like it? Far out, to the horizon, the color of the water is navy-blue; nearer, the water is the color of the North American sky. From there to the shore, the water is pale, silvery, clear, so clear that you can see its pinkish-white sand bottom. Oh, what beauty! Oh, what beauty! You have never seen anything like this. You are so excited. You breathe shallow. You breathe deep.

Comma before *and* **used to join main clauses**

Semicolon to join parts of a compound sentence without a conjunction

Dash to show an interrupted thought

Comma after two introductory prepositional phrases

Grammar Review

Review: Exercise 1   **Using Commas**

Write each sentence, adding commas where needed.

1. Tourists come for the white sand beaches colorful reefs and balmy climate.
2. Antigua unlike other islands of the Lesser Antilles is not mountainous.
3. Most of the island is flat; however there are hills in the Southwest.
4. These hills the remnants of ancient volcanoes bear patches of rain forest.
5. Did you know Catherine that Antigua was once covered by rain forest?
6. It was deforested by its original inhabitants British planters and modern developers.
7. Antigua does not have much rainfall; therefore rain seldom interferes with tourists' plans.
8. Mangroves tidal flats salt ponds and freshwater pools are found near the shore.
9. These watery habitats as you can imagine host a great variety of wildlife.
10. Magnificent frigate birds black seabirds with long wings soar the cliffs.

Review: Exercise 2   **Using Commas with Introductory Words and Phrases**

Write each sentence, adding commas where needed.

SAMPLE   Lying among the Leeward Islands Antigua is a Caribbean jewel.
ANSWER   Lying among the Leeward Islands, Antigua is a Caribbean jewel.

1. Blessed with low humidity and year-round trade winds Antigua has an ideal climate for tourists.
2. Fringed by coral reefs the island is a snorkeler's paradise.
3. With its miles of undulating coastline it appeals to beach lovers from all over the world.
4. Shimmering in the tropical sun the turquoise waters are very inviting.
5. Indeed all kinds of water sports are popular with both natives and tourists.
6. In the sheltered water of English Harbor sailboats find safe haven.
7. From old military installations on Shirley Heights Antiguans and visitors can view fabulous sunsets.
8. No the capital is not at English Harbor.
9. Situated on the northwest coast St. John's Harbor welcomes cruise ships.
10. Yes that irregular coastline also provides many smaller bays for swimming.

Review: Exercise 3   Using Commas with Adverb Clauses

Write each sentence, adding commas where needed. Write *correct* if the sentence is correct.

SAMPLE   If you want to see mahogany trees stroll through Walling Woodlands.
ANSWER   If you want to see mahogany trees, stroll through Walling Woodlands.

1. Because McKinnon's Salt Pond is very shallow it appeals to sandpipers.
2. Where Indian Creek flows into the sea brown pelicans dive for tarpon.
3. You won't find a tropical rain forest unless you drive up Boggy Peak.
4. Before you drive back down you should look for scarlet tanagers.
5. Visit the lovely beaches of Carlisle Bay after you leave Boggy Peak.
6. Since Farley Bay is accessible only by foot or by water it is very peaceful.
7. Look for unusual shells when you go to Rendezvous Bay.
8. Although blue herons are everywhere Potswork Reservoir attracts the most.
9. If you want to see a mature stand of evergreens visit Weatheralls Hill.
10. In hotel gardens, you will see hummingbirds because they want the nectar in the resort's tropical flowers and fruit trees.

Review: Exercise 4   Using Commas with Adjective Clauses

Write each sentence, adding commas where needed. Write *correct* if the sentence is correct.

SAMPLE   Christopher Columbus who arrived in 1943 named Antigua.
ANSWER   Christopher Columbus, who arrived in 1493, named Antigua.

1. Tourists who like to explore have many options on Antigua.
2. Paradise Reef which offers a mile of coral is popular with snorkelers.
3. Glass-bottomed boats which let nonswimmers see the reef are also popular.
4. You may see the hawksbill whose shell is used for tortoiseshell jewelry.
5. The hawksbill which is named for its beaky upper jawbone is a sea turtle.
6. On Green Castle Hill are rock formations that may date to ancient times.
7. Fig Tree Drive which is named for the Antiguan fig is lush with trees.
8. Devil's Bridge is a natural formation that was created by pounding waves.
9. Captain Horatio Nelson who later became a famous British admiral served for a time in Antigua and gave his name to Nelson's Dockyard.
10. A strenuous hike leads to Monk Hill which overlooks two harbors.

Grammar Review

Review: Exercise 5   Using Commas

Write each sentence, adding commas where needed.

1. Leona's home is at 1147 Schyler Street Gary Indiana.
2. Her aunt Jo lives in Falmouth Antigua.
3. Josephine Susannah Hardy M.D. is her aunt's full name.
4. Leona arrived for a visit on July 15 2000.
5. Leona's brother Conrad came too.
6. "It's great to be here" said Leona "because I love to swim."
7. "You'll have lots of beaches to choose from" said Aunt Jo.
8. Among these three are especially recommended.
9. Leona and Conrad swam every day and studied Antiguan birdlife too.
10. On August 2 2000 they regretfully waved goodbye to Antigua.

Review: Exercise 6   Using Commas, Semicolons, and Colons

Write each sentence, adding commas, semicolons, and colons where needed.

SAMPLE   Old towns can be revived the story of English Harbor proves it.
ANSWER   Old towns can be revived; the story of English Harbor proves it.

1. English Harbor bustled for two centuries but then its glory faded.
2. The English navy sailed for home and traders found different ports.
3. Nelson's Dockyard itself was badly decayed old buildings had fallen in.
4. In 1951 the governor founded the Society of the Friends of English Harbor its purpose was to restore the harbor.
5. The group unearthed original plans consequently their restoration is historically accurate.
6. They tried to get these details right hand-hewn beams, pegged wood, and old glass.
7. Interest among natives, sailors, and business people grew and soon old-timers, visitors, and new residents made the streets bustle again.
8. Now Nelson's Dockyard is full of shops the Galley, the Saw Pit, the Cooper and Lumber Store, and more.
9. Tourists flock to these shops therefore the economy has steadily grown.
10. Charter boats and private boats crowd the harbor it once again welcomes travelers from the sea.

Punctuation

Review: Exercise 7 — Using Commas and End Marks in Direct Quotations

Write each sentence, adding commas and end marks where needed.

SAMPLE "Let's visit an Arawak dig" suggested Ann.
ANSWER "Let's visit an Arawak dig," suggested Ann.

1. "The Caribbean Islands are just like stepping stones from Venezuela to Florida" said Ron
2. Keisha added "Most of the first inhabitants came from South America"
3. "Among those who settled Antigua" said Mr. Hays "were the Arawaks"
4. Did you say "The Arawaks lived in wooden houses"
5. "Yes" said Mr. Hays "the houses were wood with thatched roofs"
6. "Didn't the Arawaks play an early kind of soccer" asked Ron
7. "The object of the game" said Keisha "was to keep the ball in the air"
8. "And you couldn't use your hands" exclaimed Ann
9. Ron asked "How were the points scored"
10. "If you let the ball touch ground, the other side scored a point" said Ann

Review: Exercise 8 — Punctuating Direct Quotations

Write each sentence, adding quotation marks and underlining for italics, commas, and end marks where needed.

SAMPLE Who were the first people on Antigua asked Tony.
ANSWER "Who were the first people on Antigua?" asked Tony.

1. I have been reading about the Arawaks and Caribs in a beautiful book called Lost Empires
2. In it there is a chapter about the Caribbean called Crossroads Cultures
3. I told the class The Arawaks used sophisticated farming methods
4. They knew how to control erosion and irrigate their fields explained Tim
5. Manioc was their chief crop I said but they also grew other foods
6. Tony asked What's manioc
7. It's a starchy, edible root like cassava answered Mr. Hays
8. The sea I said provided the Arawaks with fish and turtles
9. Tim asked Weren't the Arawaks eventually conquered by the Caribs
10. The Caribs were cannibals I exclaimed

Grammar Review

Review: Exercise 9 **Using Apostrophes, Hyphens, Dashes, and Parentheses**

Write each sentence, inserting apostrophes, hyphens, dashes, and parentheses where needed.

SAMPLE Antigua has a well developed educational system.
ANSWER Antigua has a well-developed educational system.

1. The country of Antigua and Barbuda has a total land area of 171 square miles 442 square kilometers.
2. Barbuda is a game preserve, and its anyones guess how many species of birds live there.
3. Redonda an uninhabited island is also part of the island country.
4. The country has been a self governing nation since 1981.
5. The three islands terrain is mostly flat.
6. Most of the countrys population live on the island of Antigua.
7. The majority of the people descendants of Africans speak English.
8. The peoples main foods include beans, fish, lobsters, and sweet potatoes.
9. On their jobs, theyre bankers, shopkeepers, hotel workers, taxi drivers, farmers, and manufacturers.
10. Drought often harms farmers crops of sugar cane and cotton.

Review: Exercise 10 **Using Abbreviations and Numbers**

Write each sentence, correcting the errors in abbreviations and numbers.

1. Mister Vere Cornwall was the prime minister of Antigua and Barbuda.
2. About two percent of the people live on Barbuda, the smaller island.
3. The islands receive about 45 in. of rain annually.
4. 2 deaths and 80 million dollars in property damage resulted when Hurricane Hugo struck in 1989.
5. The island's hospitals need qualified Drs.
6. Slavery was abolished on Antigua in eighteen thirty-four.
7. Forests cover 15.9% of Antigua, and 59.1% of the land is agricultural.
8. When it's 2 o'clock in VA, it's 3 o'clock in Antigua.
9. Tourists can choose from among three hundred sixty-five beaches on Antigua.
10. Summer Carnival is celebrated in late Jul. and early Aug.

Punctuation

Review: Exercise 11

Proofreading

Rewrite the following passage, correcting the errors in spelling, grammar, and usage. Add any missing punctuation. There are ten errors.

Interior at Nice

¹The young woman in the picture on the next page sit in front of a window on a hotel balcony in France. ²With her back to the sea she gazes at the observer. ³The sun reflects off the sea and bathe the room in silvery light. ⁴Intense pinks blues, and grays help convey the atmosphere of warmth.

⁵Like Jamaica Kincaid in the passage from *A Small Place* Henri Matisse has captured a momant by the sea. ⁶The picture on the hotel wall—a picture within the picture duplicate the figure of the woman on the balcony. ⁷The observer's attention is drawed to the woman. ⁸What differences can you find between *A Small Place* and *Interior at Nice*

Review: Exercise 12

Mixed Review

Write each sentence, correcting all errors in punctuation, quotation marks, italics, and numbers.

¹Born on May 25, 1949 young Jamaica Kincaid loved to read, one of her favorite books was Jane Eyre. ²Although she had a happy childhood Kincaid realized that her family her mother father and three brothers underestimated her abilities she also felt stifled by the island. ³By 16 she was a very self directed young woman and she left Antigua for a job in New York. ⁴She attended several colleges but she never earned a degree. ⁵After she had written articles for teenagers magazines she became a staff writer for The New Yorker magazine. ⁶She wrote gardening articles however now her interest in fiction motivated her to write Girl, a short story. ⁷Most of the 10 stories in At the Bottom of the River, which was published in 1983 deal with mothers and daughters. ⁸Among the stories are the following Girl My Mother and In the Night. ⁹Kincaid's 2nd book

(continued)

Annie John, is about a young Antiguan girl who grows from childhood to adolescence. [10] Kincaid also wrote A Small Place which criticizes British colonialism and the government of Antigua.

Henri Matisse, *Interior at Nice,* 1921

Writing Application

TIME

For more about the writing process, see **TIME Facing the Blank Page,** pp. 97-107.

Apostrophes in Writing

David Weitzman uses apostrophes in this passage from *Thrashin' Time* to make his farming characters' dialogue sound realistic. Study the passage, paying close attention to the italicized words.

> "What do you think about all this, Peter, steam power instead of horse power?"
>
> I *wasn't* sure. "If the engine took the place of the horses, I think I'd miss Annie and Lulu and Quinn. *Wouldn't* you, Pa?"
>
> "I would, but, you know, horse-power *thrashin'* is awful hard on them, son. Sure, I'd miss them, but we work them hard all year *plowin'* and *diskin'*, and *seedin'* and *mowin'*. Then just when *they're* so tuckered out, about to drop and *needin'* a good rest, we put them to *thrashin'*."

Techniques with Apostrophes

Try to apply some of David Weitzman's writing techniques when you write.

❶ Use apostrophes to create contractions and help your writing flow more smoothly.

AWKWARD VERSION I *was not* sure.

WEITZMAN'S VERSION I *wasn't* sure.

❷ Dialogue conveys information about a character. Replacing missing letters with apostrophes shows a character's natural speech patterns. The first version, although correct, is not how Pa really speaks.

LESS INFORMATION we work them hard all year *plowing* and *disking*, and *seeding* and *mowing*

WEITZMAN'S VERSION we work them hard all year *plowin'* and *diskin'*, and *seedin'* and *mowin'*

Punctuation

Practice Rewrite the following passage, adding apostrophes to the underlined words to make the dialogue sound more natural.

"<u>Nothing doing</u>, Fred," said Mr. Felters. "I <u>cannot</u> accept this wood. <u>It is</u> not cut short enough."

"Come on, Felters, <u>we have</u> been <u>working</u> together for <u>going</u> on ten years. Trust me. <u>I will</u> come tomorrow and cut it shorter for you," implored Fred.

"Nope! <u>Before</u> I take it, <u>it has</u> got to be right. Cut <u>them</u> down to two-foot lengths and <u>I will</u> be a happy man," insisted Mr. Felters.

"If I must," sighed Fred, "I guess I may as well get <u>going</u> on it."

 **Writing** Online   For more grammar practice, go to **glencoe.com** and enter QuickPass code WC87703p2.

Writing Application   **627**

UNIT 21

Sentence Combining

21.1 Prepositional Phrases

Prepositional phrases are effective tools for sentence combining. They describe nouns and verbs, just as single-word adjectives and adverbs do. Furthermore, because they show relationships between words, prepositional phrases can express complicated ideas.

> **EXAMPLE**   **a.** The landscape has undergone a change.
>
>   **b.** This change is **for the worse.**
>
>   **c.** This is **according to Rachel Carson.**
>
> **According to Rachel Carson,** the landscape has undergone a change **for the worse.**

The new information from sentences *b* and *c* is added to sentence *a* in the form of prepositional phrases. In the new sentence, the prepositional phrase *According to Rachel Carson* modifies the verb *has undergone,* and the prepositional phrase *for the worse* modifies the noun *change.* Prepositional phrases follow the nouns they modify. Prepositional phrases that modify verbs can precede or follow the verbs they modify. (For a list of common prepositions, see page 481.)

■ A **prepositional phrase** is a group of words that begins with a preposition and ends with a noun or pronoun. Prepositional phrases modify nouns, verbs, and pronouns.

Exercise 1   Combining Sentences with Prepositional Phrases

The following sentences are based on an excerpt from *Silent Spring* by Rachel Carson, which you can find on pages 302–305. Combine each group of sentences so that the new information is turned into a prepositional phrase. In the first few items the new information is in dark type.

1. **a.** Carson describes a mythical town.
   b. The town was one **of great natural beauty.**
2. **a.** Prosperous farms surrounded the town.
   b. The farms were dotted **with rich productive fields.**
3. **a.** Birds filled the trees and bushes.
   b. The birds were **of many different kinds.**

(continued)

4. **a.** People visited this town.
   b. They came from miles away.
   c. They came on account of the romantic beauty of this special place.
5. **a.** A blight covered the land.
   b. The blight was one of unknown origin.
6. **a.** A powdery chemical snow fell.
   b. It fell on buildings and land alike.
7. **a.** Strange sicknesses were in the human and animal communities.
   b. Doctors studied the strange sicknesses.
   c. The doctors studied with the latest medical tools.
8. **a.** The vegetation was dead or dying.
   b. The dying vegetation was beside the roads.
   c. The dying vegetation was in the orchards.
9. **a.** Silence now reigned in the springtime.
   b. It reigned after the disappearance of the birds.
10. **a.** The countryside changed dramatically.
   b. It turned into a scene of mysterious mourning.

Exercise 2   Combining Sentences

Rewrite the following paragraphs. Use prepositional phrases to combine sentences. Make any other changes in wording that you feel are necessary.

Rachel Carson describes some tragedies caused by people. She describes them in her book *Silent Spring.* These tragedies were not caused by any alien or mysterious agent. Her mythical town faced a bright and hopeful future. Then people destroyed the land. They destroyed it with their thoughtless actions. Now the land was dying. Everything on it was dying. There were no new young plants and animals to replace those that had died. Therefore, the only prospect was despair.

No one place has suffered all the tragedies described by Carson. However, each blight has occurred somewhere. The blights are upon the environment. Each one might have occurred in this country, or it might have been in other parts of the world. Many communities have undergone several of these misfortunes. This fact is without exaggeration. Carson writes of a "grim specter." This specter is upon our landscape. Carson writes in her book *Silent Spring.* The tragedy might become a reality. The tragedy is that of the mythical town. The reality is for all of us. This is according to Rachel Carson.

21.2 Appositives

Appositives allow you to combine sentences in a compact and informative way. Appositives and appositive phrases identify or reveal something new about a noun or pronoun.

EXAMPLE   **a.** Maya Lin designed the Vietnam Veterans Memorial.

       b. Maya Lin was **an architecture student.**

Maya Lin, **an architecture student,** designed the Vietnam Veterans Memorial.

The appositive phrase *an architecture student* tells us more about *Maya Lin.* The appositive is set off with commas because it gives additional information. If an appositive supplies essential information, it is not set off with commas. (For more information about appositives, see pages 391–392.)

■ An **appositive** is a noun placed next to another noun to identify it or give additional information about it. An **appositive phrase** includes an appositive and other words that describe it.

Exercise 3   Combining Sentences with Appositives

The following sentences are based on "Always to Remember" by Brent Ashabranner, which you can find on pages 250–257. Combine each group of sentences so that the new information is turned into an appositive or appositive phrase. In the first few items, the new information is in dark type. Add commas when necessary to your new sentences.

1. **a.** Congress had authorized the Vietnam Veterans Memorial.
   b. The memorial was to be **a monument to the war's dead and missing soldiers.**
2. **a.** Over one thousand contestants submitted plans.
   b. This number of contestants was **a record number for a design competition.**
3. **a.** The winner was Maya Lin.
   b. She was **the daughter of the dean of fine arts at Ohio University.**
   c. The dean was **Henry Huan Lin.**
4. **a.** She was the child of cultured and educated parents.
   b. Maya Lin felt that art and literature were always beside her.
   c. Art and literature were her childhood friends.

(continued)

5. **a.** Maya Lin studied architecture at Yale University.
   b. She was valedictorian in high school.
6. **a.** Lin was a student in Europe.
   b. There she became interested in the architecture of cemeteries.
   c. Cemeteries are also called "cities of the dead."
7. **a.** In France she was impressed by a memorial.
   b. The memorial was the work of the architect.
   c. The architect was Sir Edwin Lutyens.
8. **a.** Maya learned of the Memorial Competition from Andrus Burr.
   b. She was a Yale student.
   c. He was a professor of funerary (burial) architecture.
9. **a.** During a visit to the site, Maya Lin envisioned the winning design.
   b. The site was in Constitution Gardens.
   c. Maya Lin was an architecture student.
10. **a.** The winner described her feelings to a *Washington Post* writer.
    b. Maya Lin was the winner.
    c. The writer was Phil McCombs.

Exercise 4　　Combining Sentences

Rewrite the paragraph below. Use appositives and appositive phrases to combine sentences. Make any changes in wording you feel necessary.

Before making her design, Maya Lin visited the monument's proposed site. The site was Constitution Gardens in Washington, D.C. During her visit, the park was being enjoyed by many people. These people were Washington, D.C., residents and tourists. Lin did not want to destroy a living, beautiful park with a grim monument. That monument would be a structure out of harmony with its surroundings. Upon returning to Yale, Lin made a clay model of her vision. The vision she had in Constitution Gardens. Professor Burr had been the catalyst to Lin's involvement. He liked her ideas. She plunged onward, and finally her design was ready to submit. It took her six weeks of work to complete. Lin's design fits in with the park's landscape. Her final design was a long wall of polished black stone.

21.3 Adjective Clauses

Adjective clauses are useful in combining sentences. When two sentences share information, one of them can be made into an adjective clause that modifies a word or phrase in the other.

EXAMPLE **a.** Lyddie began her working day long before breakfast.

b. Lyddie **labored in a cloth factory.**
[, who . . . ,]

Lyddie, **who labored in a cloth factory,** began her working day long before breakfast.

The new information from sentence *b*, *labored in a cloth factory,* becomes an adjective clause modifying *Lyddie* in sentence *a*. The pronoun *who* now connects the clauses. Notice the commas in the new sentence. Adjective clauses that add nonessential information require commas. Adjective clauses that add essential information do not require commas. (For more information about adjective clauses, see pages 509–510.)

■ An **adjective clause** is a subordinate clause that modifies a noun or pronoun in the main clause. The relative pronouns *who, whom, whose, which, that,* and *what* tie the adjective clause to the main clause.

Exercise 5   Combining Sentences with Adjective Clauses

The following sentences are based on an excerpt from *Lyddie* by Katherine Paterson, which you can find on pages 188–193. Combine each group of sentences so that the new information is turned into an adjective clause. In the first three items, the new information is in dark type. The information in brackets indicates the relative pronoun to use and whether a comma or commas are needed.

1. **a.** The girls began their working day long before breakfast.
    b. The girls **labored in the cloth factory. [who]**
2. **a.** Lyddie found a job in a cloth factory.
    b. Lyddie **had come from the country. [, who . . . ,]**
3. **a.** The overseer pulled the cord to the leather belt.
    b. The belt **set the factory machinery into motion. [that]**

(continued)

4. **a.** The girls had to rush back at seven-thirty.

   b. The girls were released at seven for breakfast.

5. **a.** Lyddie examined her boots.

   b. Her boots had knotted laces.

6. **a.** Lyddie ran to the window for a breath of fresh air.

   b. Lyddie's eyes were filled with tears.

   c. She needed the breath of fresh air so desperately.

7. **a.** The window was nailed shut.

   b. It was the window Lyddie reached first.

8. **a.** Diana gently guided Lyddie back to the loom.

   b. Diana had already been a great friend to Lyddie.

9. **a.** The day now seemed an endless nightmare.

   b. The day had begun with so much hope.

10. **a.** By the end of the day, Lyddie was too tired to think about the regulations.

    b. These were the rules that all the girls had to learn.

Exercise 6   Combining Sentences

Rewrite the paragraphs below, using adjective clauses to combine sentences. Make any other changes in wording or punctuation you think necessary.

The bountiful supper table made Lyddie nauseated tonight. It might otherwise appeal to Lyddie. Finally, after sitting listlessly through the meal, Lyddie reached her bed. There she began to undress. She struggled with her clothes. She had donned the clothes so quickly and deftly just that morning. The boots were now a sore burden to her. The boots had been her special pride. Triphena's old boots sat on the floor near Lyddie's bed. She had left them there the night before. Maybe these old boots would give Lyddie's swollen feet some breathing space. These boots were stiff and awkward.

Betsy felt Lyddie's pain. She was a fellow sufferer. She remembered the horrors of her own first day. Maybe reading would make Lyddie feel better as well. It always helped Betsy to escape. With this thought in mind, Betsy picked up a book. She hoped Lyddie would enjoy this book.

Betsy read out loud from the novel *Oliver Twist*. *Oliver Twist* was written by Charles Dickens. The novel tells the story of a hungry boy. The boy is punished for asking for more food at a poorhouse. Lyddie heard the description of Oliver's punishment. The man reminded her of the factory overseer. The man scolded Oliver. The overseer had frightened her that very day. Lyddie now wanted to hear the whole story of Oliver. Lyddie had before been too tired to speak. Betsy read on until the curfew bell. Betsy's voice grew hoarse with fatigue.

Adverb Clauses

Adverb clauses are a frequently used and highly effective way to combine sentences. Adverb clauses help you establish clear relationships between two or more ideas or actions. For example, you can use adverb clauses to show that one action causes another or results from another.

EXAMPLE
    a. Mr. Reese drilled the team thoroughly.

    b. They would soon be playing for the championship. **[since]**

Mr. Reese drilled the team thoroughly **since they would soon be playing for the championship.**

In the new sentence, the adverb clause *since they would soon be playing for the championship* explains why Mr. Reese drilled the team so thoroughly. Note that the subordinating conjunction *since* makes the cause-effect relationship very clear. An adverb clause can occupy several positions within a sentence. If it begins the sentence, it is followed by a comma. (For more information about adverb clauses, see pages 513–514.)

■ An **adverb clause** is a subordinate clause that often modifies or describes the verb in the main clause. Adverb clauses are introduced by subordinating conjunctions such as *after, although, as, before, if, since, when, whenever, wherever,* and *while.*

Exercise 7   **Combining Sentences with Adverb Clauses**

The following sentences are based on "The Game" by Walter Dean Myers, which you can find on pages 90–94. Use adverb clauses to combine each group of sentences. In the first few items, the information in brackets signals the subordinating conjunction and the punctuation you should use.

1. **a.** The narrator's team was warming up for the championship game. **[As ... ,]**
   b. They tried not to look at their opponents at the other end of the court.
2. **a.** The other team dominated the game's opening minutes.
   b. They passed and shot the ball extremely well. **[because]**
3. **a.** The narrator's team made a few mistakes. **[When ... ,]**
   b. Mr. Reese, the coach, called timeout to give the players a rest.

(continued)

4. **a.** Mr. Reese seemed as calm and reassuring as he usually was.

   b. His team was not playing well. [**although**]

5. **a.** The team returned to the floor [**When . . . ,**]

   b. They began to play much better.

6. **a.** The other team took the ball and immediately tried a slick move.

   b. The narrator's team was ready and handily outmaneuvered them.

7. **a.** The narrator was in the right place at just the right time.

   b. He made his first basket.

8. **a.** Mr. Reese urged the team to stay cool.

   b. They were losing by seven points.

9. **a.** A basketball player is fouled in the process of making a shot.

   b. He gets two foul shots, not one.

10. **a.** The narrator's teammates were happy and proud.

    b. They had beaten a very rough team.

Exercise 8   Combining Sentences

Rewrite the following paragraphs. Use adverb clauses to combine sentences. Make any other changes in punctuation or wording that you feel are necessary to improve the flow of the paragraph.

The opposing side was tricked by the "Foul him!" strategy. The narrator's team got the ball. The score was tied. The narrator did not realize it at the time. There were just four minutes left in the game. Sam and Chalky, two good players, came back in. They outscored the other team by four points. The narrator's team won the championship.

   The narrator's teammates were given their first-place trophies. They began to jump up and down and slap each other on the back. They had an extra trophy. They gave it to their cheerleaders. The coach shook each player's hand. Then he invited the players' parents and the cheerleaders into the locker room. Mr. Reese made a little speech to the group. He said he was proud of the team. They had worked so hard to win. Mr. Reese finished speaking. The parents and cheerleaders gave the team a round of applause. The narrator started to cry. He often did this. However, this time he was not embarrassed. Leon was crying even more. For the next few days, the narrator and his friends were walking on air. They saw someone in the street. They would just "walk up and be happy."

Mixed Review

The following sentences are based on *Living up the Street* by Gary Soto, which you can find on pages 32–37. Combine each group of sentences using a phrase or clause, as indicated in brackets. The bracketed directions also indicate any pronouns or punctuation that is needed.

1. **a.** Gary Soto describes the experience.
   b. The experience is that of his first day picking grapes. [**prepositional phrase**]
   c. This information appears in his autobiography. [**prepositional phrase; +,**]
2. **a.** Gary had trouble keeping up.
   b. It is with his mother that he had this trouble. [**prepositional phrase**]
   c. She is the person with whom he was picking. [**prepositional phrase; ,+,**]
3. **a.** Mother worried that Gary would get tired.
   b. She is an experienced picker. [**appositive phrase; ,+,**]
   c. He may feel that way before the day is over. [**prepositional phrase**]
4. **a.** Gary ate the sandwich.
   b. He had brought the sandwich for lunch. [**adjective clause; that . . .**]
5. **a.** Mother remembered long ago days.
   b. Those days she worked in the fields. [**adverb clause; when . . .**]
   c. These were the fields of Texas and Michigan. [**prepositional phrase**]
6. **a.** Gary played with his knife.
   b. It was the tool necessary to his job. [**adverb clause; because . . .**]
   c. He was careful not to lose it. [**adjective clause; which . . .**]
7. **a.** Gary thought longingly of the swimming pool.
   b. It was the swimming pool at the YMCA. [**appositive**]
   c. He felt the hot sun. [**adverb clause; when . . .**]
8. **a.** Mother glanced gratefully at Gary.
   b. It was his singing that entertained them. [**adjective clause; , whose . . .**]
   c. They worked at this time. [**adverb clause; as . . .**]
9. **a.** Gary saw the new jeans.
   b. He saw them whenever he closed his eyes. [**adverb clause; Whenever . . . ,**]
   c. These were the jeans that his earnings would buy. [**adjective clause; that . . .**]
10. **a.** He and Scott made several shopping trips. [**adverb clause; After . . . ,**]
    b. Gary finally chose a pair.
    c. It was a pair of pants. [**prepositional phrase**]

Fernand Léger, Woman in an Interior, 1922

"*Herald what your mother said*
Read the books your father read
Try to solve the puzzle in your own sweet time."

—Des'ree and A. Ingram,
"You Gotta Be"

PART 3

Resources and Skills

UNIT 22

Library and Reference Resources

 LOG ON ▶ **Writing** Online For research tools and additional skills practice, go to **glencoe.com** and enter QuickPass code WC87703p3.

22.1 The Sections of a Library

Learning how a library is organized can help you unlock a wealth of information. Although no two libraries are exactly alike, all libraries group like things together. Books for adults are in one section. Children's books are in another. Novels and stories are usually separate from information books. Magazines and newspapers have their own section. So does audiovisual material. Look at the photo below. What familiar parts of a library do you recognize? Turn the page to see how a typical library is organized.

No two libraries are alike, but most of them share the same characteristics and have similar resources.

Librarian A librarian can be the most important resource of all. He or she can help you use the library wisely by directing you to different resources, showing you how to use them, and giving you advice when needed. You might want to prepare your questions for the librarian ahead of time. Librarians are prepared to help their patrons and will be glad to answer questions.

Young Adult and Children's Section Young readers can find books written for them in a separate area of the library. Sometimes reference materials for students are also shelved here, along with periodicals and audiovisual materials.

Stacks The stacks are the bookshelves that hold most of the library's books. Stacks for fiction books are usually in an area separate from the nonfiction stacks.

Circulation At the circulation desk, you can use your library card to check out materials you want to take home.

Reference   The reference area holds dictionaries, encyclopedias, atlases, and other reference works. Usually, you are not allowed to check out these materials. They are kept in the library so everyone has access to them. Computer databases are also part of the reference area. These systems allow you to search for facts or articles from periodicals. For example, *InfoTrac* provides complete articles and article summaries from over one thousand newspapers and magazines. Some computer databases allow you to search for particular types of information, such as history or art. Computers in the reference section, or in a media center, provide access to the Internet.

Periodicals   You can find current issues of periodicals—newspapers, magazines, and journals—in a general reading area. Periodicals are arranged alphabetically and by date. Older issues may be available in the stacks or on microfilm or microfiche. Use the computer catalog to locate them or ask a librarian to help you.

Audio Visual Materials   Compact discs (CDs), videotapes, digital videotapes (DVDs), and computer software are in the audiovisual section. In this section, you can check out a movie, a CD of your favorite music, or an audiobook. Some libraries have listening and viewing areas to allow you to review the materials while at the library.

Catalog   The catalog lists, describes, and locates items in the collection. Most libraries use computer catalogs.

Exercise 1

In which section of the library might you find these items?

1. A compact disc of the musical *Cats*
2. The magazine *American Heritage*
3. *To Kill a Mockingbird* (a novel)
4. The *Dictionary of American Biography*
5. The video of *The Call of the Wild*

Call Number Systems

In a library, are labeled with numbers and letters. These numbers and letters are part of the system the library uses to organize its collection.

Many libraries use the Dewey decimal system. Under this system, a library uses numbers to group books into ten categories of knowledge. Other libraries use the Library of Congress system. This system uses letters, then numbers, to group books.

Ask your librarian which system your library uses. It's best, however, to know how each system works. You also should know where your library has posted the chart that identifies and explains the system it uses. Both systems are shown in the chart below. When doing library research, you will have to begin by deciding which major category or categories your topic falls into.

Library Classification Systems			
Dewey Decimal System		**Library of Congress System**	
Numbers	**Major Categories**	**Letters**	**Major Categories**
000–099	Computers, information, and general reference	A, Z	General works
100–199	Philosophy and psychology	B	Philosophy, religion
200–299	Religion		
300–399	Social sciences	H, J, K, L	Social sciences, political science, law, education
400–499	Language	P	Language
500–599	Science	Q	Science
600–699	Technology	R, S, T, U, V	Medicine, agriculture, technology, military and naval sciences
700–799	Arts and recreation	M, N	Music, fine arts
800–899	Literature	P	Literature
900–999	History and geography	C–G	History, geography, recreation

Each general category contains subcategories. The first number or letter always indicates the main category and will be followed by other numbers or letters. The diagram below shows how each system works.

How the Two Systems Work		
Dewey Decimal	**Description**	**Library of Congress**
700	A book about art	N
750	A book about painting (a subcategory of art)	ND
759	A book about Spanish painting (a subcategory of painting)	ND800
759.609	*The Story of Spanish Painting*	ND804

Exercise 2

1. Suppose a library used the Dewey decimal system. What number (in the hundreds) would it use to show the category of each of the following books?

   a. *A History of Colonial America*
   b. *Science for the Nonscientist*
   c. *Language Made Easy*
   d. *World Religions*
   e. *The Novels of Charles Dickens*

2. At your school or neighborhood library, find an interesting book in each section listed below. Write down the book's title, topic, and full Dewey decimal or Library of Congress call number.

   a. 200–299 or B   c. 400–499 or P   e. 900–999 or C
   b. 300–399 or H   d. 500–599 or Q

22.3 Library Catalogs

So many books, so little time! Maybe you've had this thought since you began your research at the library. The library catalog makes searching for books easier and saves you time.

Using a Computer Catalog

The computer catalog lists all the books, periodicals, and audiovisual materials in the library. You can search for these materials by title, author, subject, or keyword. A *keyword* is a word or phrase that describes your topic. If you type an author's name, you can view a list of all the books written by that author. By typing a subject, you can view all the books about that particular topic. The computer catalog tells you the title, author, and call number of each book, and whether it is available for check out.

For example, suppose you are looking for books by the writer Milton Meltzer. Your computer search might proceed as follows:

1. Type in the author's name, *Meltzer, Milton.*
2. The computer will show a list of all the books in the library by this author. Each item will have a call number.
3. Type the call number of the book you are interested in to get more information about it.
4. Information about the book will appear, including the book's location and availability.

The way the computer catalog works may differ slightly from library to library. Follow the on-screen directions to use any computer catalog. If you have trouble with your search, ask a librarian for help.

```
1. Title:      All Times, All Peoples: A
               World History of Slavery
   Author:     Meltzer, Milton
   Published:  1980
   Media:      Book    Call No: 326 M528a

2. Title:      American Politics: How It
               Really Works
   Author:     Meltzer, Milton
   Published:  1989
   Media:      Book    Call No: 320.473
M528a
```

```
3. Title:      American Politics: How It
               Really Works
   Author:     Berger, Melvin
   Published:  1989
   Media:      Book
               Call No: 320.473 M528a

The Library owns 2 copies of this book. It
is shown as available at:
   Main Branch        Juvenile
   East Branch        Juvenile
```

```
To search enter one of the following
commands:

A/Author-name  to find items by author
name
T/Title             to find items by title
S/Subject                    to find items by
subject
KW                  to find items by WORD or
                    NAME or to COMBINE
                    WORDS
AY                  to see your reserves/
                    checkouts/fines
```

Using a Card Catalog

Some libraries use an older method of organizing books called a card catalog. A card catalog is a cabinet of long narrow drawers that holds cards arranged alphabetically. Each card contains the description of a book and has that book's call number in the upper left-hand corner. Fiction books have an author card and a title card. Nonfiction books have subject cards as well. Because each book has two or three or more cards, a book can be found by searching under its title, its author, or sometimes its subject.

Finding a Book

When you have located a book you want in the catalog, write down the call number shown on the card or computer screen. Note the area in the library where the book is shelved. You will use this information to locate the book.

In the stacks, signs on the shelves tell which call numbers are included in each row. Books with the same call number are alphabetized by the author's last name or by the first author's last name when there is more than one author.

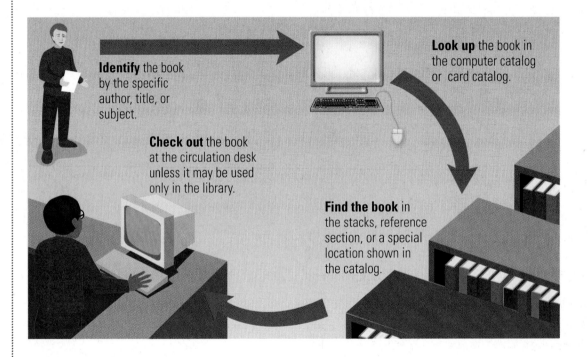

Identify the book by the specific author, title, or subject.

Look up the book in the computer catalog or card catalog.

Check out the book at the circulation desk unless it may be used only in the library.

Find the book in the stacks, reference section, or a special location shown in the catalog.

Exercise 3

Use the card catalog or computer catalog to find a book about any five of the following topics. List the author, title, and call number of each book you find.

1. The brain
2. The development of television
3. Poetry by X. J. Kennedy
4. Marsupials
5. The Spanish language
6. Professional football
7. Mountains
8. The mind

22.4 Types of Reference Works

When you look up the answer to a question or read a book to find information for social studies class, you are doing research. When you check with friends who know more than you do about your bike, you are doing research. For research you need experts. You'll find the opinions and discoveries of many experts in the reference materials in your library.

Reference works are designed to help you locate specific information quickly. You may be doing research for a class project, looking for a single fact, or just feeling curious about a topic. Whatever your purpose, the reference area offers many interesting resources.

The chart below describes some general types of reference sources found in most libraries. Find out where each of these kinds of references is kept in your public library. Locate those references that are available in your school library or classroom as well. You can also access many reference sources by using a computer to go online.

Using General Reference Works to Answer Questions		
Questions	**Where to Look for an Answer**	**Examples of Sources**
When did Henry Ford introduce the Model T?	**Encyclopedias** include general information on a variety of topics.	• *World Book Encyclopedia* • *Grolier Online* • *Encyclopaedia Britannica*
What major cities are on the Ohio River?	**Atlases** are collections of maps. They often include special maps on climate, population, and other topics.	• *Hammond World Atlas* • *The Rand McNally World Atlas*
Who received the Nobel Peace Prize in 2004?	**Almanacs** provide lists, statistics, and other information on recent and historical topics.	• *Information Please Almanac* • *Guinness Book of World Records*
Where was Mark Twain born?	**Biographical reference works** include biographies of notable persons, both past and present.	• *Dictionary of American Biography* • *Webster's Biographical Dictionary*

Encyclopedias

You will find one-volume encyclopedias and sets made up of many volumes. Encyclopedias may be either general or specialized. General encyclopedias contain articles about all branches of knowledge. Specialized encyclopedias present articles in a specific area of knowledge, such as history, science, or the arts. Two examples of specialized encyclopedias are the *McGraw-Hill Encyclopedia of Science and Technology* and *The Focal Encyclopedia of Photography*.

Most encyclopedias are organized alphabetically. To find all of the articles with information on your topic, look up the topic in the index. The index is usually the last volume of a multi-volume encyclopedia. It contains an alphabetical listing of topics. After each topic, you will find the subjects related to the topic you are investigating. The index tells you the volume and page number of the article where you will find the information. Sometimes the index refers you to a different topic heading for a list of articles.

Many encyclopedia entries end with a list of books that contain additional information. These books may be available at your library. The entry may also list other related articles in the encyclopedia.

Atlases

Atlases are collections of maps. General atlases contain maps of all parts of the world. In a general atlas, you can find map information about population, industry, farming, and other topics for all parts of the world. These atlases may also contain graphs, charts, and pictures. For example, the *National Geographic Atlas of the World* includes satellite images of the earth's major regions.

Some atlases are specialized. They may cover one part of the world, such as a single country. Others have maps on a special topic, such as population, the environment, or animals. Travelers often rely on atlases that show highways, national parks, and places of interest to tourists. Historical atlases contain maps for different periods in history and various parts of the world.

Almanacs and Yearbooks

If you're looking for very current information or statistics, consult almanacs and yearbooks. These references contain the most recent available information on a variety of topics. A new edition is published every year.

Two widely used almanacs are the *Time Almanac with Information Please* and the *World Almanac and Book of Facts*. Both cover a wide range of information, from baseball statistics to the latest scientific discoveries. Much of the information is presented in the form of lists or tables.

A yearbook is a book issued each year by some encyclopedia publishers to update their regular encyclopedia volumes. It contains articles about events and developments of that year. The yearbooks for an encyclopedia generally follow the *Z* volume or the Index volume on the reference shelf.

Biographical Dictionaries

Biographical dictionaries contain information on important people. Some of these dictionaries include living persons as well as persons from history. These references may have many volumes or may be contained in a single book.

In the larger, multivolume dictionaries, such as the *Dictionary of American Biography*, entries are lengthy and give a detailed life history. An example of a shorter reference is *Webster's Biographical Dictionary*. In this work, the entries are much briefer, sometimes only a few lines long. An example is shown below. Biographical dictionaries are useful when you need information about particular people.

> **Cassatt** (kə satˊ), Mary Stevenson. 1844–1926. American painter, b. Allegheny City, Pa. To Paris (1866); first exhibited at Salon (1872); associated with Impressionists, esp. Degas and Courbet; exhibited with Impressionists (1879, 1880, 1881, 1886); first solo exhibit (1891); produced oils, pastels, prints, etchings; known esp. for figure studies and portrayals of mothers and children.

Exercise 4

1. Name the type of reference work in which you would expect to find answers to the following:

   a. Who was the Olympic champion in the women's long jump in in 2004?
   b. Of what country is Jakarta the capital?
   c. What occupations did Samuel Clemens follow before becoming a writer?
   d. In what state is the Painted Desert located?
   e. What was *Sputnik*, and why was it important?

2. Use a library reference to write the answers to any two of the above questions.

22.5 Searching for Periodicals

Until the early 1990s, most periodical searches were done with printed indexes, which then led the searcher to periodicals or microforms (copies of magazines and newspapers stored on film). Today, you can search periodicals electronically on the Internet and on various databases. A database is a collection of electronic files that are easily retrieved by a computer. Most libraries have magazine and newspaper databases, such as *InfoTrac,* that contain full articles or article summaries from hundreds of magazines and newspapers.

If you are searching for older materials, however, such as a magazine from around 1980 or before, you still need to search the old way. Scan for your topic in a bound copy of the *Readers' Guide to Periodical Literature* and then follow your citation to the correct issue of the magazine in the periodical section.

However, often you will search online. Most libraries provide two types of electronic databases for periodicals: general databases and databases specific to a subject. *eLibrary,* which searches newspapers, general magazines, maps, and TV and radio transcripts, is an example of a multimedia database. *Social Issues Resource Series (SIRS)* is an example of a database that is focused on one main subject area, sociology and current social problems.

All databases share common features. Most offer the option to do a basic search or a more advanced search. Each has a query screen. On it you key in your search term(s)—either one word or a search phrase. Many databases allow you to use natural language. In other words, you ask the question the way you would ask a friend.

Sample Periodical Search

This search was done on the database called *eLibrary,* which searches current magazines and newspapers. The student was investigating some ideas for a term paper on roller coasters. The following are some of the references that appeared.

Click on a <u>TITLE</u> to view a full text document.

Relevancy: 100; <u>Variations on a Theme Park</u>; The Washington Post

Date: 06-18-1999   *Alexa Steele;* 06-18-1999 Size: 23K

Reading Level: 6.

	Relevancy: 100; Date: 07-04-1996 Reading Level: 7.	RUNAWAY FAVORITES: Coaster to coaster, Americans love life on the fast tracks; The Dallas Morning News *Ellen Sweets/Staff Writer of The* *Dallas Morning News;* 07-04-1996 Size: 11K
	Relevancy: 100; Date: 07-14-1997 Reading Level: 8.	On a roll; Minneapolis Star Tribune *Paul Levy;* *Staff Writer;* 07-14-1997 Size: 10K
	Relevancy: 100; Date: 05-07-1999 Reading Level: 8.	Rock on wood Busch Garden's dual coaster will have rider shaking, shimmying and rolling; The Tampa Tribune *PHILIP MORGAN of* *The Tampa Tribune;* 05-07-1999 Size: 8K
	Relevancy: 100; Date: 08-30-1999 Reading Level: 8.	WHAT WENT WRONG AT WILD WONDER?; The Record (Bergen County, NJ) *SEAMUS* *McGRAW, Staff Writer;* 08-30-1999 Size: 10K
	Relevancy: 100; Date: 08-31-1999 Reading Level: 8.	INDUSTRY MEASURES SUCCESS IN SCARES; The Record (Bergen County, NJ) *DOUG MOST,* *Staff Writer;* 08-31-1999 Size: 9K
	Relevancy: 100; Date: 07-30-1998 Reading Level: 11.	ROLLER COASTERS ARE AS OLD AS THE HILLS; St. Louis Post-Dispatch *Gary A. Warner; 1998,* *The Orange County Register;* 07-30-1998 Size: 4K
	Relevancy: 100; Date: 04-29-1999 Reading Level: 11.	Countdown for Opening Of Transformed Six Flags; Theme Park's Coasters Almost Ready to Roll; The Washington Post *Jackie Spinner* *Washington Post Staff Writer;* 04-29-1999 Size: 5K

Look over your display results carefully. The display screen gives you important information about each article. It includes the title, the author, the source, and the date of the article. It also provides the article's reading level and *relevancy*—an estimate of how closely this article is related to your search item.

Exercise 5

Look at the sample screen and answer these questions.

1. Which of these articles might be difficult reading for an eighth grader?
2. Which are the two most current articles?
3. In your opinion, what term paper topics about roller coasters might these articles suggest?
4. What do you need to do to read the full text of one of these articles?

22.6 Using the Internet and Other Media

Libraries offer several kinds of media. The word *media* (singular *medium*) means methods of communication, such as newspapers, magazines, movies, and television. During the 1990s, a new medium rose to prominence—the Internet.

The Internet

Computers at your public library will also provide access to the Internet, a valuable source of information. The World Wide Web is the part of the Internet that provides information in various formats, including print, sound, graphics, and video.

Because there are so many Internet sites, the best way to find worthwhile information on the Net is by using a *search engine.* If you do not get any useful results with one search engine, try several others. They each search the Internet differently.

All Internet sources are not equally reliable, however. Always check any site for accuracy and timeliness. Check to see when it was last updated. Check for errors and omissions. Check to see what agency sponsors the site. Many libraries now provide a collection of recommended Web sites.

Online or Virtual Libraries   Online or virtual libraries on the Internet are important reference sources. You can connect from home if you have access to a computer and a modem. Examples of excellent online reference sites include: *The Internet Public Library,* hosted by Drexel University's College of Information Science and Technology and the Virtual Reference Shelf, a site with selected Web resources compiled by the Library of Congress.

Some Additional Internet Search Terms	
Term	**Definition**
Abstract	a summary of an article or information source.
Discussion Groups	a virtual place where you can discuss problems and current events.
Hit	a successful result after you have searched online.
Full Text	term indicating that all of an article is present online. However, sometimes full-text articles do not include charts and graphics.
Search Engine	computer software that browses the Internet for places where your search words appear. Examples are Google, MSN, Ask, and Yahoo! Search.
URL	stands for Universal Resource Locator. This is an address for a Web site.

Nonprint Media

Most libraries and media centers offer digital video discs (DVDs) and videotapes of movies, travelogues, and instructional (how-to) films. Compact discs (CDs) and older audiocassettes contain sound recordings of music, drama, language lessons and readings of literature. Microforms are used to store past issues of newspapers, magazines, and other archival materials.

Using Nonprint Media		
Type of Media	**Information Available**	**Equipment Needed**
Microforms	Back issues of newspapers and magazines	Microform viewer or viewer/printer (at the library)
Videotapes	Movies, documentaries, travel and instructional films	VCR and television set
Digital Video Discs	Movies, documentaries, travel and instructional films	DVD player and television set
Audiotapes	Music, readings, dramas, language lessons	Audiocassette player
Compact discs	Same as audiotapes Information sources	CD player and stereo system CD-ROM drive and computer

Exercise 6

In which medium would you expect to find each of the following items? More than one answer may be appropriate in some cases.

1. An article describing a new type of computer
2. Recorded Russian lessons for travelers
3. A documentary about the canal era in Ohio
4. An article about a student from your school who just won a national award
5. A newspaper from 1854?

22.7 | The Dictionary

You can enrich your knowledge of English by frequent use of the dictionary—an essential tool for a writer. A dictionary is an alphabetical listing of words with definitions and often with word origins and other information. Today you can find dictionaries in print, on CD-ROM, and on the Internet. Most dictionaries fall into one of several categories.

Types of Dictionaries

Dictionaries differ according to their purposes. Some have more entries than others and provide detailed word histories. The three main categories are described below.

Type	Characteristics	Examples
Unabridged Dictionaries	• 250,000 or more entries • Detailed word histories • Detailed definitions • Found mostly in libraries	• *Random House Webster's Unabridged Dictionary* • *Webster's Third New International Dictionary*
College Dictionaries	• About 150,000 entries • Detailed enough to answer most questions on spelling or definitions • Widely used in schools, homes, and businesses	• *Random House Webster's College Dictionary* • *American Heritage Dictionary of the English Language* • *Merriam-Webster's New World Dictionary*
School Dictionaries	• 100,000 or fewer entries • Definitions suitable for students' abilities • Emphasizes common words	• *The Scribner's Dictionary* • *Merriam-Webster's School Dictionary*

The illustrations show how to use two helpful dictionary features. Guide words help you locate words quickly. The pronunciation key can help you sound out a word.

Guide words show the first and last entry on the page. Use them to zero in on the word you are seeking.

foot soldier / fore-and-aft

foot soldier, a soldier trained or equipped to fight on foot; infantryman.
foot·sore (foot´sôr´) *adj.* having sore or tired feet, as from much walking.
foot·step (foot´step´) *n.* **1.** a step or tread of the foot: *a baby's first awkward footsteps.* **2.** the sound made by this: *I heard his footsteps in the hall.* **3.** the distance covered in a step.
    to follow in someone's footsteps. to imitate or follow the same course as someone: *Dan followed in his father's footsteps and became a teacher.*

for·bid·ding (fər bid´ing) *adj.* looking unfriendly or dangerous; frightening; grim: *The old house was dark and forbidding.* —**for·bid´ding·ly,** *adv.*
for·bore (fôr bôr´) the past tense of **forbear** .
for·borne (fôr bôrn´) the past participle of **forbear** .
force (fôrs) *n.* **1.** power, strength, or energy: *The batter struck the ball with great force. The force of the explosion broke windows in the nearby buildings.* **2.** the use of such power, strength, or energy; violence: *The sheriff dragged the outlaw off by force.* **3.** the power to convince, or control: *The force of her argument won*

The pronunciation key uses well-known words to interpret the pronunciation symbols.

oneself from (doing something): refrain from: *Tom could not forbear smiling at his embarrassed friend.* [Old English *forberan* to hold back.]
for·bear² (fôr´ber) another spelling of **forebear.**
for·bear·ance (fôr ber´əns) *n.* **1.** the act of forbearing. **2.** self-control or patience: *Jim showed great forbearance during his long illness.*
for·bid (fər bid´) *v.t.,* **for·bade** or **for·bad, for·bid·den** or *(archaic)* **for·bid, for·bid·ding.** to order not to do something; refuse to allow; prohibit: *I forbid you to go out. The school forbids eating in the classrooms.*

fore-and-aft (fôr´en aft´) *adj.* from bow to stern of a ship: *a fore-and-aft sail.*

at; āpe; cär; end; mē; it; īce; hot; ōld; fôrk; wood; fōōl; oil; out; up; tûrn; sing; thin; this; hw in white; zh in treasure. The symbol ə stands for the sound of a in about, e in taken, i in pencil, o in lemon, and u in circus.

Other useful features are located in the front and back pages of the dictionary. In the front, you can find a complete pronunciation key, a list of abbreviations used in entries, and information about punctuation and capitalization. Some dictionaries include a short history of the English language. In the back of the dictionary you may find sections with biographical and geographical entries. Some dictionaries include such information with the regular word listings.

Entry Word

A dictionary entry packs a great deal of information into a small space. By becoming familiar with the basic elements of an entry, you'll find it easier to explore new words.

The entry word is the first element in each entry. It is printed in bold type, which makes it easy to find the beginning of an entry. The entry word shows how to divide a word of more than one syllable. Notice how *flourish* is divided by the dot. Not every dictionary entry is a single word. Some entries are two words, such as *cuckoo clock,* and some, such as *T-shirt,* are hyphenated.

flour (flour, flou´ər) *n.* **1.** soft, powdery substance obtained by grinding and sifting grain, esp. wheat, used chiefly as a basic ingredient in baked goods and other foods. **2.** any soft powdery substance. —*v.t.* to cover or sprinkle with flour. [Form of FLOWER in the sense of "finest part" (of the grain).]

flour·ish (flur´ish) *v.i.* **1.** to grow or develop vigorously or prosperously; thrive: *Crops flourish in rich soil. His business is flourishing.* **2.** to reach or be at the peak of development or achievement: *a civilization that flourished thousands of years ago.* —*v.t.* **1.** to wave about with bold or sweeping gestures; brandish: *to flourish a sword; to flourish a baton.* **2.** to display ostentatiously; flaunt. —*n.* **1.** a brandishing: *He bowed to her with a flourish of his hat.* **2.** ostentatious or dramatic display or gesture: *She entered the room with a flourish.* **3.** decorative stroke or embellishment in writing. **4.** elaborate, ornamental passage or series of notes, as a trill or fanfare, added to a musical work. [Old French *floriss-*, a stem of *florir* to flower, bloom, going back to Latin *flōrēre* to flower, bloom] —**Syn.** *v.i.* see **prosper.**

Labels (right margin): Entry word · Definition · Pronunciation · Part of speech · Word origin

Synonym reference. You can find a list of synonyms for *flourish* in the entry for *prosper*.

Pronunciation

The pronunciation of a word follows the entry word. It is written in special symbols that allow you to sound out the word. If you are not sure how to pronounce a syllable, check the pronunciation key, which is usually at the bottom of the page. The simple words in the key show the sounds of the most common symbols. To see a complete pronunciation key, turn to the front pages of the dictionary. Some words have more than one pronunciation; the most common is generally shown first. Online and CD-ROM dictionaries also usually offer audio pronunciations.

Part of Speech

Every dictionary entry indicates a word's part or parts of speech. For example, in the entry for *flourish*, *v.i.* stands for *intransitive verb* and *v.t.* for *transitive verb*. The letter *n.* stands for noun. What would you expect the abbreviations for adjective and adverb to be? A list of the abbreviations is located in the front of the dictionary.

Definition

The definition, or meaning, of the word is the heart of the entry. Many words have more than one meaning. These meanings are usually numbered from most common to least common. Some unabridged and college dictionaries, however, use a different method. They give definitions from the earliest-known meaning to the most recent meaning. Look at the sample entries on page 659 to see how the definitions of *flourish* are numbered.

Word Origins

The word origin is a brief account of how the word entered the English language. Many words, like *flourish,* were used in more than one language before entering English. For example, look at the *flourish* entry. The source of the word is Latin. The word then moved into Old French. English speakers borrowed it from Old French. Many dictionaries use abbreviations for the language from which a word comes, such as *L.* for Latin. A list of these abbreviations is located at the front of the dictionary.

Exercise 7

Use the dictionary entries in this lesson to answer the following questions:

1. How many definitions does this dictionary include for the verb form of the word f*lourish?*
2. Which meaning of *flourish* is implied in the following sentence? *The students flourished their hand-made signs at the rally.*
3. Does the first syllable of *flourish* rhyme with the first syllable of *flower, flurry,* or *Florence?*
4. Which of the meanings shown for *flour* do you find in the following sentence? *I floured the chicken before putting it into the oven.*
5. What was the meaning of the Latin word that was the original source of *flourish?*

The Thesaurus

More than 150 years ago a British doctor, Peter Mark Roget [rō zhā´], developed a thesaurus. A thesaurus is a dictionary of synonyms—words with similar meanings. Since that time, the thesaurus has grown and changed. Print, CD-ROM, and on-line thesauruses are all available today. In fact, if you do word processing on your computer, you probably have a thesaurus as part of your software.

Using a Thesaurus

Roget organized his thesaurus by categories. Then he listed the categories in an index. When you use this type of thesaurus, you find the category you want in the index. The index will refer you to the lists of synonyms you want.

The excerpt below is from another kind of thesaurus, one in which the words are arranged like those in a dictionary. In a dictionary-style thesaurus the word entries are in alphabetical order.

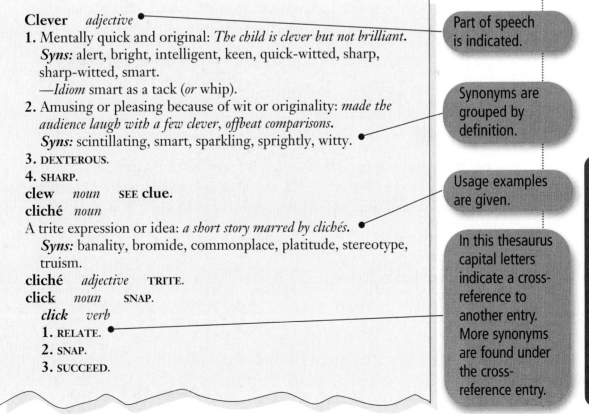

Clever *adjective*
1. Mentally quick and original: *The child is clever but not brilliant.*
   Syns: alert, bright, intelligent, keen, quick-witted, sharp, sharp-witted, smart.
   —*Idiom* smart as a tack (*or* whip).
2. Amusing or pleasing because of wit or originality: *made the audience laugh with a few clever, offbeat comparisons.*
   Syns: scintillating, smart, sparkling, sprightly, witty.
3. DEXTEROUS.
4. SHARP.
clew *noun* SEE **clue.**
cliché *noun*
A trite expression or idea: *a short story marred by clichés.*
   Syns: banality, bromide, commonplace, platitude, stereotype, truism.
cliché *adjective* TRITE.
click *noun* SNAP.
   click *verb*
   1. RELATE.
   2. SNAP.
   3. SUCCEED.

Part of speech is indicated.

Synonyms are grouped by definition.

Usage examples are given.

In this thesaurus capital letters indicate a cross-reference to another entry. More synonyms are found under the cross-reference entry.

Library and Reference Resources

Finding Synonyms

Knowing how the thesaurus is arranged can help you find the exact word you need. You can see from the samples on the previous page that each definition is followed by several synonyms or by a cross-reference to another entry. Synonyms, you recall, are words that have *similar* meanings. The thesaurus can help you distinguish among many synonyms to find the most exact one.

The words in capital letters lead you to further synonyms. If you look up a word shown in capital letters, you will find a definition and many additional synonyms. *Dexterous,* for example, means *clever,* but in a specific way: exhibiting or possessing skill or ease in performance. Your expert handling of a bike might be called dexterous. Conversation on a talk show may be clever, but it is not necessarily dexterous.

Most libraries will have more than one type of thesaurus available. A similar resource, a dictionary of synonyms, is also available to help you locate the most precise word. One example is *Merriam-Webster's Collegiate Thesaurus.*

Many thesauruses list antonyms—words with opposite meanings—as well as synonyms. Your library may have *Webster's Collegiate Thesaurus,* which includes antonyms. For more information on synonyms and antonyms, see pages 676–678.

Exercise 8

Use a thesaurus to find two synonyms for each word below. Then write an original sentence to illustrate the meaning of each synonym. Check the exact meaning of each word in a dictionary before you use it in a sentence.

1. speak (verb)
2. run (verb)
3. thin (adjective)
4. foam (noun)
5. shiny (adjective)

Vocabulary and Spelling

 **Writing** Online   For research tools and additional skills practice, go to **glencoe.com** and enter QuickPass code WC87703p3.

663

23.1 Words from American English

People all over the world use the word *okay*. It began, however, as an American-English word. How did *okay* become so widespread? Citizens of many nations borrowed this word from American travelers. Speakers of one language will often borrow words from speakers of another language. As contact between peoples around the world increases, so will borrowed words.

Kayak

Words from Native Americans

English colonists began settling in North America in the early 1600s. They often borrowed Native American words to name foods, plants, and animals new to them. Some examples are the words *pecan, hickory, squash, moose, chipmunk,* and *skunk*.

Europeans also borrowed Native American words to name natural features and places. The Mississippi River's name, for example, comes from Algonquian words meaning "great water." More than half the states and many cities and counties in the United States have names with Native American origins. Hawaii's name came from its original Polynesian settlers.

Raccoon

States with Native American Names		
Alabama	Kansas	Ohio
Alaska	Kentucky	Oklahoma
Arizona	Massachusetts	Oregon
Arkansas	Michigan	South Dakota
Connecticut	Minnesota	Tennessee
Idaho	Mississippi	Texas
Illinois	Missouri	Utah
Indiana	Nebraska	Wisconsin
Iowa	North Dakota	Wyoming

Other Early Borrowed Words

Europeans from France and Spain were in America even before the English. English speakers had already borrowed many words from the French in Europe. As American English developed, its speakers borrowed more French words in North America. Other new English words came from the Spanish and from Spanish-speaking Mexicans in the Southwest. Some examples of these words of French and Spanish origin are included in the chart below.

Some American-English Borrowed Words	
Sources	**Words**
French	toboggan, pumpkin, bayou, prairie, dime, chowder
Spanish	mustang, ranch, rodeo, stampede, cafeteria, canyon
Dutch	sleigh, cole slaw, Santa Claus, cookie, boss, waffle
African	gumbo, voodoo, juke, jazz, tote
German	hamburger, noodle, pretzel, kindergarten, semester
Yiddish	kosher, bagel, klutz, kibitzer, schmaltz
Italian	macaroni, spaghetti, pizza, ravioli

Americans are often called Yankees or Yanks. The word came from Dutch colonists in America in the 1600s. The Dutch called New Englanders Yankees. (The name was considered an insult at the time.) The Dutch colony of New Netherland and its port city, New Amsterdam, were taken over by the British. The British renamed the colony and the city New York. The Dutch lost their American colony, but they left a number of their words in American English.

Rodeo

Most of the Africans in colonial America were brought here as slaves. Their contribution to the English language included such words as *gumbo, voodoo,* and *juke* (as in *jukebox*). The origin of the word *jazz* is uncertain, but it, too, may have come from an African language. These and some other words that became part of American English are shown in the chart above.

Words from Immigrants

Over the centuries millions of immigrants—Italians, Poles, Czechs, Greeks, Chinese, Filipinos, Haitians, Cubans, and many more—came to America. They passed on some of their customs and some of their words to Americans. These words became part of American English. Often the use of the words spread from the United States throughout the English-speaking world. Some examples are included in the chart on the previous page.

Words Made in America

Americans have also contributed new words that did not originate in another language. *Okay* is an example of a word that was "made in the U.S.A." Inventions and customs that started in America often led to new words. Some examples are *refrigerator, telephone, jeep, inner city, flow chart, zipper, laser,* and *airline.* Like *okay,* these words are now used throughout the world. Can you think of any other words that were probably made in America?

Jukebox

Exercise 1

Work with a small group. Develop a list of more English words that originated in America. The words can have come from Native American languages or from the languages of immigrants to America. They might be words invented by Americans.

Begin by looking at the place names in your area. Where did the names of mountains, rivers, counties, or cities come from? Look in your library for books or articles on the origins of place names. Think about the names of foods you eat that originated in other countries. If family members or friends are recent immigrants, ask them if they know of any American English words that came from their language. Use your dictionary to check the origins of words on your list.

WORDWORKS

TECHNO-TALK

What do the words *nylon*, *silo*, and *gearshift* have in common? All these words—and countless others—entered the English language as a result of developing technology. New machines, products, and processes required a new vocabulary.

Technical words enter the language by different routes. Some words are coined. A coined word is simply created—none of its parts have any meaning by themselves. For instance, in 1938 scientists developed synthetic fiber, and the word *nylon* was coined as a name for it.

Another route into English is through borrowing. The word *silo* was borrowed into English in 1881 as a name for an airtight container for fodder, or food for livestock. The word is Spanish in origin and carries the same meaning in that language.

Another way languages gain new technical words is by compounding. The word parts *gear* and *shift* have existed in English for a long time. It was only because of developing technology that they were combined to name a part of an automobile transmission. Other examples of combining include *transmission* (from Latin word parts) and *telephone* (from Greek word parts). Some words for new inventions originated as names of people; *Ferris wheel* is an example.

Tele— far off or distant
television
telephone
telescope
telecast
telephoto

Challenge

What new technology uses the word silo*? Think of another technology that named a product a* tweeter*. How do the original meanings of these words fit the new ways in which they are used?*

ACTIVITY

Name That Invention

Create several names for the imaginary inventions listed below. Use any of the sources for word formation.

1. a car for air, water, and all surfaces
2. a thermal container that will biodegrade within twelve hours
3. earphones that don't "leak" noise and that allow for loud music without damage to hearing

Vocabulary and Spelling

23.2 Context Clues

Do you check your dictionary every time you read or hear a new word? Probably not—most people don't. The best way to build your vocabulary is to be an avid reader and an active listener. You also can learn the meaning of a new word by looking for context clues. The words and sentences around the word are its context.

Using Specific Context Clues

Context clues help you unlock the meaning of an unfamiliar word. Sometimes the context actually tells you what the word means. The following chart shows three types of specific context clues. It also gives examples of words that help you identify the type of context clue.

Using Specific Context Clues		
Type of Context Clue	**Clue Words**	**Example**
Comparison The thing or idea named by the unfamiliar word is compared with something more familiar.	also same likewise similarly identical	A *rampant* growth of weeds and vines surrounded the old house. The barn was <u>likewise</u> covered with uncontrolled and wild growth.
Contrast The thing or idea named by the unfamiliar word is contrasted with something more familiar.	but on the other hand on the contrary unlike however	Thank goodness Martin didn't *bungle* the arrangements for the party; <u>on the contrary</u>, he handled everything very smoothly and efficiently.
Cause and effect The unfamiliar word is explained as a part of a cause-and-effect relationship.	because since therefore as a result	<u>Because</u> this rubber raft is so *buoyant*, it will float easily, and we won't have to worry about its sinking.

Using the General Context

How do you figure out an unfamiliar word if there are no specific context clues? With a little extra detective work you often can find general clues in the context. Look at the two sentences below. What context clues help you understand the meaning of the word *liaison*?

Joel is a liaison from one group (the students) to another (the faculty).

Joel was chosen student <u>liaison</u> to the faculty. Everyone hoped his appointment would improve communication between the students and the teachers.

Note that the word *communication* helps you figure out that being a liaison means acting as a line of communication between two groups.

Exercise 2

Divide the words below between you and a partner. Use a dictionary if necessary to find the meanings of your words. Then write a sentence using each one. Your sentences should contain context clues to help a reader figure out the meanings of the words. Try to use different types of context clues in the sentences.

Next, exchange papers with your partner and read his or her sentences. Try to use your partner's context clues to understand the words from the list. Discuss how your context clues helped you and your partner understand the meanings of each other's words.

1. depreciate
2. collaborate
3. fathom (noun)
4. adobe
5. crucial

6. olfactory
7. refulgence
8. fathom (verb)
9. omnipotent
10. brinkmanship

WORDWORKS

AS STALE AS DAY-OLD BREAD

If you listen to a CD over and over, most likely you'll get tired of listening to it. Hearing a cliché is something like listening to that CD.

Clichés are expressions you have heard many times before. All clichés, though, were once fresh and original. Some clichés have been in use for centuries. For example, the phrase *I'm all ears* originated in 1634. That's when John Milton (1608–1674) wrote in *Comus,* "I was all ear."

As you can see, sometimes clichés develop through alteration of the writer's or speaker's original words. If you've ever told someone a secret, you may have said, "This is between you and me." That expression comes from a novel by Charles Dickens (1812–1870) called *Nicholas Nickleby* (1838). Dickens's phrase in the book, however, was "between you, me, and the lamp-post." This form of the cliché is still in use, although it is much less popular now than in previous generations. Another cliché, *cool as a cucumber,* can be traced to the playwrights Francis Beaumont and John Fletcher. Their phrase in the seventeenth-century play *Cupid's Revenge* was "cold as cucumbers."

Challenge

Rewrite the following without the clichés:

Beyond a shadow of a doubt, too many clichés will put you in hot water. Sad but true, a cliché sticks out like a sore thumb. Avoid clichés like the plague.

ACTIVITY — Do these Clichés Ring a Bell?

Look up the following clichés in *Bartlett's Familiar Quotations* or another reference book, and record the sources.

1. as old as the hills
2. vanish into thin air
3. busy as a bee

4. few and far between
5. Variety is the spice of life.

23.3 Prefixes and Suffixes

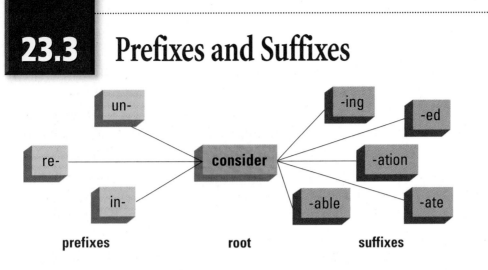

prefixes   root   suffixes

The illustration above shows how word parts can be put together to form many different words. These word parts are called roots, prefixes, and suffixes.

Roots

The **root** of a word carries the main meaning. Some roots (like the word *consider* above) can stand alone. Others (like *lect*, shown in the chart below) make little or no sense without a prefix or suffix. Knowing the meanings of roots can help you figure out the meanings of unfamiliar words.

Word Roots		
Roots	**Words**	**Meanings**
bio means "life"	biography	the story of a person's life
	biosphere	part of the atmosphere where living things exist
dent means "tooth"	dentist	person who treats diseases of the teeth
	trident	spear with three prongs, or teeth
flex or *flec* means "to bend"	flexible	easily bent
	reflect	to bend back (light)
lect means "speech"	lecture	a speech
	dialect	form of a language spoken in a certain region
tele means "distant"	television	device for receiving pictures from a distance
	telescope	device for viewing distant things

Prefixes

A **prefix** is a syllable used in front of a word root. Adding a prefix can change, or even reverse, the meaning of a root (for example, *belief—disbelief*). In English, a number of prefixes have the same, or nearly the same, meaning. For example, *dis-, un-,* and *in-* all can mean "not" or "the opposite of." On the other hand, some prefixes have more than one meaning. The prefix *in-* can also mean "into," as in the word *incise* ("to cut into").

The chart below shows some common prefixes and their meanings. Notice in the example words how the prefixes change the word root's meanings. Learning these prefixes can help you figure out unfamiliar words.

Prefixes			
Categories	**Prefixes**	**Words**	**Meanings**
Prefixes that reverse meaning	*un-* means "not" or "the opposite of"	unnatural unhappy	not natural not happy
	in- means "not" or "the opposite of"	inconsiderate intolerant	not considerate not tolerant
	il- means "not" or "the opposite of"	illegal illogical	not legal not logical
	im- means "not" or "the opposite of"	immoderate imbalance	not moderate lacking balance
	ir- means "not" or "the opposite of"	irregular irreplaceable	not regular not able to be replaced
Prefixes that show relations	*pre-* means "before"	prepay prearrange	to pay in advance to arrange beforehand
	post- means "after"	postdate postpone	to assign a later date to delay until a later time
	sub- means "below" or "beneath"	submarine subway	an underwater boat an underground way or passage
	co- means "with" or "partner"	copilot cooperate	relief or second pilot to work with others

Suffixes

Suffixes are syllables added to the end of a word root. Like prefixes, suffixes change the meanings of roots. Like prefixes, they can have more than one meaning. They can have the same meaning as one or more other suffixes. Unlike prefixes, however, suffixes can also change the part of speech of a word root. For example, adding the suffix *-ness* to *quick* (an adjective) makes it into *quickness* (a noun). Adding *-ly* to *quick* makes *quickly* (an adverb).

Learning suffixes and how they change a root can help build your vocabulary. The following chart shows a sample of common suffixes. As you look at it, try to think of other words to which each suffix might be added.

Suffixes			
Categories	**Suffixes**	**Words**	**Meanings**
Suffixes that mean "one who does [something]"	*-er, -or*	worker sailor	one who works one who sails
	-ee, -eer	employee profiteer	one who is employed one who profits
	-ist	pianist chemist	one who plays the piano one who works at chemistry
	-ian	physician	one who practices medicine (once called "physic")
Suffixes that mean "full of"	*-ful*	joyful wonderful	full of joy full of wonder
	-ous	furious courageous	full of fury (anger) full of courage
Suffixes that mean "in the manner of" or "having to do with"	*-ly*	happily secretly	in the manner of being happy in the manner of a secret
	-y	windy icy	having to do with wind having to do with ice
	-al	musical formal	having to do with music having to do with form

When suffixes are added to words, the spelling of the word may change. For example, when *-ous* is added to *fury*, the *y* in *fury* is changed to *i* to make the word *furious*. See pages 684–686 to learn more about the spelling of words that have suffixes added to them.

Exercise 3

Write a word containing each root listed below. Try to use a word that is not used in the word roots chart. Then write a definition of each word. Check your dictionary if necessary.

1. bio
2. dent
3. flec or flex
4. tele

Exercise 4

Write a word to fit each of the definitions below. Each word should have a prefix or a suffix or both. Underline the suffixes and prefixes in the words. Use the charts in this lesson and a dictionary for help.

1. full of beauty
2. to behave badly
3. to fail to function correctly
4. below the earth
5. one who is a specialist in mathematics
6. a note written at the end of a letter, after the main part of the letter is complete (often abbreviated)
7. not able to be measured
8. in the manner of being not perfect
9. to live or exist together at the same time and in the same place
10. in the manner of being not happy

WORDWORKS

WEIRD OLD WORDS

If someone called you a popinjay, would you be pleased? Do you like to show off a little when you know you look good? A popinjay is a vain, strutting person. The word is old-fashioned and not used much today, but the type of personality it describes isn't old-fashioned at all.

Words come and go in any language. If a word has disappeared from use, some dictionaries label it obsolete. An example of an obsolete word is an older definition of *popinjay*: a "parrot." No one today uses *popinjay* instead of *parrot*. So this meaning for the word is obsolete.

Many words have disappeared from English. Some vanish completely: *egal* once meant "equal," and a *prest* was money one person was forced to lend another. Neither word is used now. Other obsolete words leave traces. For example, a horse that could be hired out for riding was called a hackney or hack. This meaning of *hack* is now obsolete, but modern English does have a related word. Taxis are sometimes called hacks. It's easy to trace this connection, since people hire taxis today, not riding horses, when they want to get around town.

The next time you pick up your dictionary, keep in mind that it's a work in progress.

> ### Challenge
>
> *Words vanish, and one reason may be that they aren't really needed to do the job. List a synonym for each of these obsolete words:* joyance, impressure, argument *(meaning an outward sign).*

(ACTIVITY) Gone but Not Forgotten

Think of a modern word related to each of the old words below. The definitions in parentheses should give you a clue or two. A college dictionary will also help.

1. grue (to shiver) **3.** lorn (forsaken, abandoned)
2. gruel (to exhaust) **4.** yelk (yellow)

23.4 Synonyms and Antonyms

You want your writing to be as clear as you can make it. How can you be sure you have written just the right word to express exactly what you mean? Becoming familiar with synonyms and antonyms—and knowing how to locate them—can help you in your writing. At the same time, you can increase your vocabulary.

Synonyms

Partly because of the borrowings from other languages, English speakers can choose from many words to express the same idea. These words that have the same, or nearly the same, meanings are called **synonyms.**

fast
rapid
quick
fleet
speedy
swift

The important thing to remember is that synonyms rarely mean *exactly* the same thing. When searching for just the right word, the best place to find synonyms is in a thesaurus. (See pages 661–662 for information on how to use a thesaurus.) To use the right word, not *almost* the right word, check your dictionary for the definitions of synonyms, and notice the usage examples given, or refer to a book of usage.

For example, suppose you're writing about someone who spoke before a group. You look up synonyms for the word *speech* and find *address* and *oration*. *Speech* is a more general choice than *address* and *oration*. A speech may or may not be formal. An address is a prepared formal speech. An oration is even more formal and is always given at a special occasion. For example, you may have read Abraham Lincoln's Gettysburg Address. Before Lincoln gave that famous address, another speaker gave a two-hour oration.

Knowing synonyms also helps make your writing more interesting. Writing that uses tired, colorless clichés—no matter how precise—is almost always boring. Use your knowledge of synonyms to substitute lively verbs and adjectives for lifeless, dried-out words.

Antonyms

Antonyms are words with opposite or nearly opposite meanings. The easiest way to form antonyms is by adding a prefix meaning "not." *Un-, il-, dis-, in-*, and *non-* are all prefixes that reverse the meaning of a root. They form antonyms, such as *untrue*, *illegible*, *disbelief*, *insufficient*, and *nonfat*. Sometimes an antonym can be made by changing the suffix. For example, *cheerful* and *cheerless* are antonyms.

fast

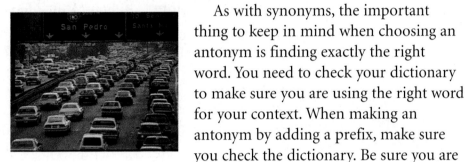

slow

As with synonyms, the important thing to keep in mind when choosing an antonym is finding exactly the right word. You need to check your dictionary to make sure you are using the right word for your context. When making an antonym by adding a prefix, make sure you check the dictionary. Be sure you are using the right prefix.

Exercise 5

For each of the following words, write two synonyms. Then write a sentence using one of the synonyms in each group. Use your dictionary and thesaurus as needed.

1. difficulty
2. nice
3. confusion
4. idea
5. slow (adjective)

Exercise 6

Replace the underlined word or words in each of the following sentences with an antonym. Use a thesaurus and a dictionary if you wish.

1. Jeremy's <u>good health</u> seems to be changing.
2. Andrea looks especially <u>pale</u> tonight.
3. That was the <u>most difficult</u> test I've ever taken.
4. Jake <u>closed</u> his eyes and saw the man who had been chasing him for so many days.
5. This fruit is so <u>dried out</u> I can't eat it.

WORDWORKS

EATING YOUR WORDS—A GREAT DIET?

Can you ever gain weight from eating your words? As a matter of fact, people don't generally sit down to a meal of their words. That's because they know that the expression *eat your words* really means "to take back something you've said." It's an idiom.

Let's look at some idioms and pull them apart. If you have decided *to put up with* something, where do you put it? If you *go back on* a promise, where have you gone? The point is, you can't understand an idiom just by putting together the meanings of the parts.

Idioms are a pretty big part of everybody's vocabulary. Some idioms are so ordinary that we hardly give them a thought—such as *to put over (a trick* or a *joke),* or *to come down with (a sickness).* Others add color to language. For example, you might keep a secret *up your sleeve* or *under your hat.*

Idioms arise in various ways. Some are translations from other languages. Many more probably started out having a word-for-word meaning. Later, people changed the meaning to include other situations. For example, at one time *to break the ice* only meant "to cut through river ice in the winter to make a path for ships and boats." Later the phrase's meaning extended to the process of starting a conversation.

Challenge

English has many idioms that contain the names of animals. How many idioms can you think of that use the names of the following animals?

cat duck crow bird

ACTIVITY   Idio-Matic

How many idioms do you know? Test your idiom vocabulary. Match the following idioms with their meanings.

1. in the pink
2. draw the line
3. in the dumps
4. a good egg
5. hit the ceiling

a. gloomy
b. get angry
c. healthy
d. set a limit
e. nice person

23.5 Homographs and Homophones

If you're like most people, you may have to think for a minute about whether to write *principal* or *principle* when you're talking about the head of your school. Or you might write *there* in your essay when you mean *their*. When someone points out your mistake, you think, "I knew that!" Some words sound alike but are spelled differently. Others are spelled the same but have different meanings.

Homographs

Words that are spelled alike but have different meanings and sometimes different pronunciations are called homographs. The root *homo* means "same," and *graph* means "write" or "writing." *Homograph*, therefore, means "written the same" (in other words, spelled alike).

Fly and *fly* are homographs. You can swat a fly or fly a plane. Although the two words are spelled alike, they have different meanings. The following chart shows some common homographs used in sample sentences. See if you can tell how the homographs in each group differ in meaning.

Homographs
Ed finished the test with one *minute* left before the bell.
To build very small model airplanes, one must enjoy *minute* details.
It's difficult to *row* a canoe upstream.
We sat in the third *row* of seats in the balcony.
We had a terrific *row* yesterday, but today we're getting along fine.
I hope I pick the winning *number*.
This snow is making my feet *number* by the minute.
Abby tried to *console* her little sister when their cat died.
The television *console* has speakers built into it.
Don't let that *wound* on your arm get infected.
Jim *wound* the rope around the tree branch.

Homophones

Homophones are words that sound alike but are spelled differently and have different meanings. *Write* and *right* are homophones. The chart below shows some common homophones with their spellings and meanings.

Homophones			
Words	**Meanings**	**Words**	**Meanings**
sight site cite	act of seeing or ability to see a location to quote an authority	scent cent sent	an odor one one-hundredth of a dollar past tense of *send*
read reed	the act of reading the stalk of a tall grass	bore boar	to tire out with dullness a male pig
four fore	the number following three located at the front	main mane	most important long hair on an animal's neck
mail male	items delivered by lettercarrier the sex opposite the female	blue blew	the color of a clear sky past tense of *blow*
real reel	actual, not artificial spool on which something is wound	would wood	past tense of *will* hard material that makes up a tree

Exercise 7

Write the homophone from the parentheses that best completes each of the following sentences. Use a dictionary for help if necessary.

1. Jackie tried to (real, reel) in the fish.
2. The lion is the (main, mane) attraction at the zoo.
3. Chiyo thought that the speech was a (boar, bore).
4. This is the (cite, sight, site) on which the museum will be built.
5. What is that strange (scent, cent, sent) in the air?
6. A wild (bore, boar) can be dangerous if it attacks.
7. Sol (sighted, sited, cited) a thesaurus as his source.
8. I (scent, cent, sent) the letter on Tuesday.

WORDWORKS

WHEN IS A NOUN NOT A NOUN?

The labels on the figure below are nouns that name body parts. English lets you put these same words into action as verbs. Here's how—from head to toe.

You can *head* a committee, *eye* a bargain, or *nose* a car into a parking space. You can *shoulder* a burden, *elbow* your way through a crowd, *hand* over the key, *knuckle* down to work, *thumb* a ride, *back* into a room, *foot* the bill, and *toe* the mark.

For hundreds of years, speakers of English have used these nouns and many others as verbs. Some words shifted in the other direction, from verb to noun. Today you can *walk* on a *walk, park* in a *park,* and *pitch* a wild *pitch.* Some shifts involve pronunciation. Notice which syllable you accent:

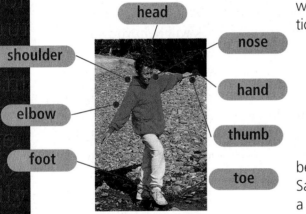

head
nose
shoulder
hand
elbow
thumb
foot
toe

Will you *perMIT* me to drive?
Yes, when you get a *PERmit.*

Does your garden *proDUCE* carrots?
No, I buy *PROduce* at the market.

Still another shift involves nouns that became adjectives, as in the following: Sara unlocked the *steel* door. Tom wore a *straw* hat. Marty made *onion* soup.

So, when is a noun not a noun?

When it's used as a verb or an adjective. The only way to identify a word's part of speech is to see it in a sentence.

Double Duty

Use these clues to identify some words that have two functions.

1. *noun:* a very young person
   verb: to pamper
2. *verb:* to walk with regular steps
   noun: music with a steady beat
3. *verb:* throw pictures onto a screen
   noun: special work in science class

Challenge

Suppose you got this written message: Ship sails today. *What does it mean? Put* the *before* ship; *then put* the *before* sails. *Why can this sentence have two different meanings?*

Vocabulary and Spelling

23.6 Spelling Rules

You may not know it, but you may have something in common with Noah Webster (of dictionary fame). He wanted to simplify the spelling of American English. He convinced people that the British *gaol* should be spelled *jail* in American English. He also got rid of the *k* in the British *musick* and *publick*. Webster especially disliked silent letters. He tried to get people to accept *frend* (*friend*), *hed* (*head*), and *bilt* (*built*), among other spellings.

However, most people didn't like Webster's spelling reforms, so today we have a system of spelling filled with rules and exceptions and words spelled nothing like the way they are pronounced. Using a dictionary to check spelling is the best way to avoid mistakes.

Common Spelling Rules

You won't always have a dictionary handy to check your spelling. Memorizing some of the following spelling rules will help you spell most words correctly even when you don't have a dictionary.

Spelling *ie* and *ei*   The letter combinations *ie* and *ei* are found in many English words, and they often cause confusion in spelling. The problem is that two words might have the same vowel sound— long *e*— but one word might be spelled *ie* while the other is spelled *ei*. You can master the spelling of these words by memorizing the rhyme below.

Rule	Examples
Put *i* before *e*	achieve, retrieve, grieve
except after *c*	deceive, receipt, ceiling
or when sounded like *a*, as in *neighbor* and *weigh*.	eighty, veil, freight
Exceptions: species, weird, either, neither, seize, leisure, protein, height	

Spelling Unstressed Vowels   The unstressed vowel sound in many English words can cause spelling problems. Dictionary pronunciation guides represent this unstressed vowel sound by a special symbol called a schwa (ə). Listen to the unstressed vowel sound in the word *about*. This vowel sound can be spelled in more than a dozen ways—with any vowel letter and with several combinations of vowel letters—but it always sounds the same. Here are a few examples. Pronounce each word, and listen for the sound represented by the underlined letter or letters:

canv<u>a</u>s, ang<u>e</u>l, penc<u>i</u>l, rid<u>i</u>cule, cart<u>o</u>n, medi<u>u</u>m, enorm<u>ou</u>s, anci<u>e</u>nt, pig<u>eo</u>n, courag<u>eou</u>s.

Notice that you hear the schwa sound only in unstressed syllables.

As always, the best way to make sure of your spelling is to check a dictionary. When you can't use a dictionary, you might be able to figure out the spelling of the unstressed vowel sound. Think of a related word in which the vowel is stressed. The word *informative*, for example, has an unstressed vowel, which happens to be spelled *a*. If you don't know that, you might think of the related word *information*, in which the vowel is stressed and sounds like an *a*. The chart below shows some additional examples of how to use this strategy.

Spelling Unstressed Vowels		
Unknown Word	**Related Word**	**Word Spelled Correctly**
popul_rize	popul**a**rity	popularize
plur_l	plur**a**lity	plural
aut_mation	aut**o**	automation
influ_nce	influ**e**ntial	influence
not_ble	not**a**tion	notable
form_l	form**a**lity	formal
practic_l	practic**a**lity	practical
pol_r	pol**a**rity	polar
inhabit_nt	habit**a**tion	inhabitant
hospit_l	hospit**a**lity	hospital

Adding Prefixes   Adding prefixes to words usually doesn't present any spelling problems. Keep the spelling of the word, and attach the prefix. If the prefix ends in the same letter as the first letter of the word, keep both letters. Some common examples include the following:

co- + pilot = copilot   dis- + service = disservice

il- + legal = illegal   co- + operate = cooperate

Suffixes and the Final *y*   Adding suffixes to words that end in *y* can often cause spelling problems. The following rules will help you:

- When a word ends in a consonant + *y*, change the *y* to *i*.

imply + -es = implies   reply + -ed = replied

pry + -ed = pried   apply + -es = applies

- If the suffix begins with an *i*, keep the *y*.

supply + -ing = supplying   fly + -ing = flying

- When a word ends in a vowel + *y*, keep the *y*.

toy + -ing = toying   stay + -ing = staying

delay + -ed = delayed   prey + -ed = preyed

Doubling the Final Consonant   When adding suffixes to words that end in a consonant, you sometimes double the final consonant. In other cases you simply add the suffix without doubling the consonant.

Double the final consonant when a word ends in a single consonant following one vowel and

- the word is one syllable

strip + -ed = stripped   sad + -er = sadder

shop + -ing = shopping   ship + -ed = shipped

war + -ing = warring   tap + -ed = tapped

- the word has an accent on the last syllable, and the accent remains there after the suffix is added

occur + -ence = occurrence   repel + -ing = repelling

forget + -able = forgettable   commit + -ed = committed

upset + -ing = upsetting   refer + -ed = referred

Do not double the final consonant when
- the accent is not on the last syllable

   flavor + -ing = flavoring

   envelop + -ment = envelopment

   remember + -ing = remembering

- the accent moves when the suffix is added

   refer + -ence = reference

   fatal + -ity = fatality

- two vowels come before the final consonant

   remain + -ed = remained   floor + -ing = flooring

   lead + -ing = leading   train + -ed = trained

- the suffix begins with a consonant

   master + -ful = masterful   dark + -ness = darkness

   tear + -less = tearless   leader + -ship = leadership

   loyal + -ty = loyalty   flat + -ly = flatly

   great + -ness = greatness

- the word ends in two consonants

   bring + -ing = bringing   stick + -ing = sticking

   inspect + -or = inspector   hunt + -ed = hunted

   attach + -ment = attachment

SPECIAL CASE: When a word ends in *ll*, and the
suffix *-ly* is added, drop one *l*.

   dull + -ly = dully   full + -ly = fully

Suffixes and the Silent e   Noah Webster did his best to get rid
of the silent letter *e* in American-English spelling. He succeeded in
changing *axe* to *ax*. However, he lost the battle to change *give* to *giv*,
and *medicine* to *medicin*. He also failed to change the spellings of
other words ending in silent *e*. The public was not willing to give up
spellings with which they were familiar.

   The silent *e* can still cause spelling problems, especially when you
add a suffix to a word that ends in a silent *e*. Sometimes the silent *e* is
dropped when adding a suffix, and sometimes it is kept. The following
chart shows the rules for adding suffixes to words that end in silent *e*.

Adding Suffixes to Words That End in Silent *e*	
Rule	**Examples**
When adding a suffix that begins with a consonant to a word that ends in silent *e*, keep the *e*.	state + -ment = statement complete + -ly = completely
Common exceptions	awe + -ful = awful judge + -ment = judgment
When adding -*ly* to a word that ends in *l* plus a silent *e*, always drop the *e*.	able + -ly = ably sensible + -ly = sensibly remarkable + -ly = remarkably
When adding *y* or a suffix that begins with a vowel to a word that ends in a silent *e*, usually drop the *e*.	state + -ing = stating nose + -y = nosy
Common exceptions	lime + -ade = limeade mile + -age = mileage
When adding a suffix that begins with *a* or *o* to a word that ends in *ce* or *ge*, keep the *e* so the word will retain the soft *c* or *g* sound.	exchange + -able = exchangeable courage + -ous = courageous
When adding a suffix that begins with a vowel to a word that ends in *ee* or *oe*, keep the *e*.	disagree + -able = disagreeable shoe + -ing = shoeing flee + -ing = fleeing

Forming Compound Words The rule for spelling compound words is very simple. In most cases, just put the two words together. Seeing two consonants together, such as *hh, kk,* or *kb,* may seem odd. The English language does not have many words with these combinations. However, the rule is to keep the original spelling of both words, no matter how the words begin or end.

foot + lights = footlights   fish + hook = fishhook
busy + body = busybody   book + keeper = bookkeeper
book + bag = bookbag   light + house = lighthouse

Some compound words, such as *hand-me-down* and *forty-niners,* are hyphenated. Others, like *honey bear* (but not *honeybee*), are spelled as two words. Use a dictionary when in doubt.

Forming Plurals The way plurals are formed in English is generally simple, and the rules are fairly easy to remember. The most common way to form plurals is to add -*s* or -*es*. The following chart shows the basic rules, their exceptions, and example words.

Rules for Plurals		
If the Noun Ends in	**Then Generally**	**Examples**
ch, *s,* *sh,* *x,* or *z*	add -*es*	witch → witches toss → tosses flash → flashes ax → axes buzz → buzzes
a consonant + *y*	change *y* to *i* and add -*es*	story → stories folly → follies
a vowel + *y*	add -*s*	play → plays jockey → jockeys
a vowel + *o*	add -*s*	studio → studios rodeo → rodeos
a consonant + *o*	generally add -*s* **Common exceptions** but sometimes add -*es*	piano → pianos photo → photos hero → heroes veto → vetoes echo → echoes
f or *ff*	add -*s* **Common exceptions** change *f* to *v* and add -*es*	staff → staffs chief → chiefs thief → thieves leaf → leaves
lf	change *f* to *v* and add -*es*	self → selves half → halves
fe	change *f* to *v* and add -*s*	life → lives knife → knives

A few nouns form plurals in a special way. Most of these special cases should not give you any problems in spelling. If you do not already know the irregular forms, such as *goose—geese*, you can memorize them. The following chart lists the special rules for plurals and gives some examples.

Special Rules for Plurals	
Special Case	**Examples**
To form the plural of proper names, add either *-s* or *-es*, following the general rules for plurals.	Smith → Smiths Jones → Joneses Perez → Perezes
To form the plural of one-word compound nouns, follow the general rules for plurals.	homemaker → homemakers blackberry → blackberries latchkey → latchkeys
To form the plural of hyphenated compound nouns or compound nouns of more than one word, generally make the most important word plural.	father-in-law → fathers-in-law lunch box → lunch boxes chief of state → chiefs of state
Some nouns have irregular plural forms and do not follow any rules.	goose → geese mouse → mice tooth → teeth child → children
Some nouns have the same singular and plural forms.	deer → deer sheep → sheep fish → fish

Improving Spelling Skills

Learning spelling rules will help you spell new words correctly. You can further improve your spelling skills by developing a method for learning these words.

Keep a notebook of unfamiliar words or words that are hard to spell. When you write, take note of any words you have trouble spelling, and add them to your notebook. As you come across new words, add them to your list. When you master the spelling of a word, cross the word off your list. Follow the steps on the next page to learn to spell those difficult words.

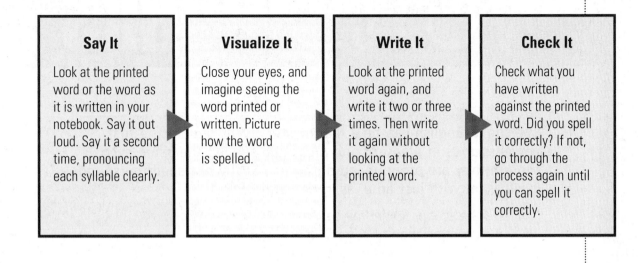

Say It	**Visualize It**	**Write It**	**Check It**
Look at the printed word or the word as it is written in your notebook. Say it out loud. Say it a second time, pronouncing each syllable clearly.	Close your eyes, and imagine seeing the word printed or written. Picture how the word is spelled.	Look at the printed word again, and write it two or three times. Then write it again without looking at the printed word.	Check what you have written against the printed word. Did you spell it correctly? If not, go through the process again until you can spell it correctly.

Exercise 8

Find the misspelled word in each sentence and write its correct spelling.

1. Mr. Harrison, the bookkeeper, has applyed for a government grant to buy new computers.
2. The book describes the lifes of famous artists.
3. Hector is fullly aware that we have to proceed with the polar expedition.
4. Stefanie spends her leisure time with the Walshs.
5. Kevin should be in the barnyard shoeing one of the remainning horses.
6. The zookeeper believes he will succeed in transfering the monkeys from the old cages without any problems.
7. The librarian has suggested two referrence books that should contain photos of wolves.
8. The summer weather has been so changeable that everyone is completly convinced we will have an unusually bad winter.
9. The puffs of clouds in the springtime sky reminded me of sheeps in a meadow.
10. The recent recurrence of fighting between the two warring nations is upseting to everyone who hopes for a peaceful settlement.

WORDWORKS

VOWEL SWITCH

Spelling in English can be a real mystery. Why should the first vowel sounds in *pleasant* and *please* be spelled the same even though they are pronounced differently? Why not spell the sound in *pleasant* with just an *e,* as in *pen* and *red*?

Here's the scoop: Sometime between 1400 and 1600 the pronunciation of certain vowels underwent a change. The vowel in *please* was pronounced like the e in *pen,* only it was longer. This sound gradually shifted to a long *a* sound as in *pane.* Meanwhile, the long *a* had begun to take on the e sound as in *feed,* while the long vowel *e* had begun to take on the long *i* sound as in *ride.* Similar changes occurred in the other long vowels. These pronunciation changes are called the Great Vowel Shift.

Meanwhile, the short vowels (as in *pleasant*) did not change. Because spelling didn't always keep up with pronunciation changes, the words *please* and *pleasant* were still spelled with the same vowel even though *please* was now pronounced like *plays.* Later, some words like *please* changed again. By about 1700 most people pronounced *please* the way you pronounce it today.

So the next time you're puzzled by English spelling, remember that the way a word is spelled sometimes holds a clue to its history.

Challenge

Some spellings have changed to reflect pronunciation changes. One example appears several times on this page. Can you find it?

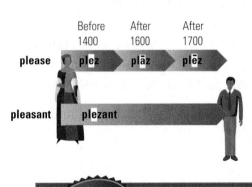

	Before 1400	After 1600	After 1700
please	plez	plāz	plēz
pleasant	plezant		

Shifty Vowels

ACTIVITY

Which of the following word pairs demonstrate the Great Vowel Shift?

1. crime, criminal
2. mouse, mice
3. breathe, breath
4. serene, serenity
5. die, death

23.7 Becoming a Better Speller

Spelling the *really* difficult words—such as *pusillanimous* (meaning "cowardly")—is usually not too much of a problem. The reason is that when you use such words (which is not often), you will probably look them up in the dictionary.

What about the less difficult but more common words that you use often? Following is a list of such words. See if any of them are words you have had trouble spelling. What words would you add to the list?

Words Often Misspelled			
absence	curiosity	incidentally	pneumonia
accidentally	develop	incredibly	privilege
accommodate	definite	jewelry	pronunciation
achievement	descend	laboratory	receipt
adviser	discipline	leisure	recognize
alcohol	disease	library	recommend
all right	dissatisfied	license	restaurant
analyze	eligible	maintenance	rhythm
answer	embarrass	mischievous	ridiculous
attendant	environment	misspell	schedule
ballet	essential	molasses	separate
beautiful	February	muscle	sincerely
beginning	fulfill	necessary	souvenir
beneficial	foreign	neighborhood	succeed
business	forty	niece	technology
cafeteria	funeral	noticeable	theory
canceled	genius	nuisance	tomorrow
canoe	government	occasion	traffic
cemetery	grammar	original	truly
changeable	guarantee	pageant	unanimous
choir	height	parallel	usually
colonel	humorous	permanent	vacuum
commercial	hygiene	physical	variety
convenient	imaginary	physician	various
courageous	immediate	picnic	Wednesday

Spelling and Misspelling

Do you have trouble remembering the spellings of common words? How many *c*'s and *m*'s are in *recommend* and *accommodate*? Is it *separate* or *seperate*? Words like these cause many people problems. The following techniques will help you learn to spell troublesome words.

- Use rhymes (such as "*i* before *e* except after *c*...") and memory tricks (such as "an *r* separates two *a*'s").
- Pay special attention to words likely to be confused with other words. Below are some examples. You can find more in the list of homophones on page 680.

Words Often Confused	
accept except	Marianne will not *accept* the nomination for class president. All the students *except* Barry were on time.
affect effect	This cold weather can *affect* my sinuses. The space program could have an *effect* on future generations.
formally formerly	The new president was *formally* introduced to the student body. Ananda *formerly* lived in southern California.
its it's	Since *its* walls collapsed, the mine entrance has been closed. *It's* been a long time since I saw Winston so happy.
stationary stationery	The radio transmitting station is mobile, not *stationary*. Her *stationery* is decorated with tiny blue flowers.
thorough through	They completed a *thorough* revision of the student handbook. *Through* the window we could see them coming up the path.
than then	The final draft of my story is much better *than* the first draft. What happened *then*?
their there they're	What was the outcome of *their* first game? The address you are looking for is over *there*. The team members say *they're* happy with the new gym.
weather whether	I hope the *weather* stays nice for the picnic. I'm not sure *whether* it was luck or skill, but I made the team.

Exercise 9

Work with one or two other students. Choose three words from the list of Words Often Misspelled on page 691 of this lesson. Develop a memory aid that will help you spell each word. Share your completed memory aids with the class.

Exercise 10

Write the word in the parentheses that correctly completes each sentence.

1. The school decided to change the name of (its, it's) football team.
2. One of the test questions asked for an (effect, affect) of the Civil War.
3. Pete (formerly, formally) played on a soccer team at his old school.
4. If you leave your books (their, there, they're), they may get lost.
5. The cat pushed (its, it's) way through the swinging door.
6. Use your best (stationery, stationary) for the thank-you notes.
7. Have you decided what dress (your, you're) going to wear to the party?
8. The detective was very (thorough, through) in his investigation of the crime.
9. We would like to know (whether, weather) it will rain or be sunny on the day of our field trip.
10. The two dogs need to have (their, there, they're) coats brushed after being out all day.
11. I've never been (formerly, formally) introduced to the new counselor.
12. The three girls said that (their, there, they're) going to go swimming.

UNIT 24 Study Skills

LOG ON ▶ **Writing** Online For research tools and additional skills practice, go to **glencoe.com** and enter QuickPass code WC87703p3.

24.1 Using Book Features

Imagine you're writing a research paper on the Civil War. You've narrowed your topic to the Battle of Gettysburg, focusing on Pickett's Charge, a key event in the three-day battle. You find that the library has many books on the Battle of Gettysburg—but you certainly can't read them all.

How do you decide which books will be the most useful? Looking at certain pages in the front or back of a book will help you narrow your choice.

You can use the pages shown below—title page, table of contents, and index—to help you find the information you need. The title page and table of contents appear in the front, before the main text of the book. You'll find the index in the back.

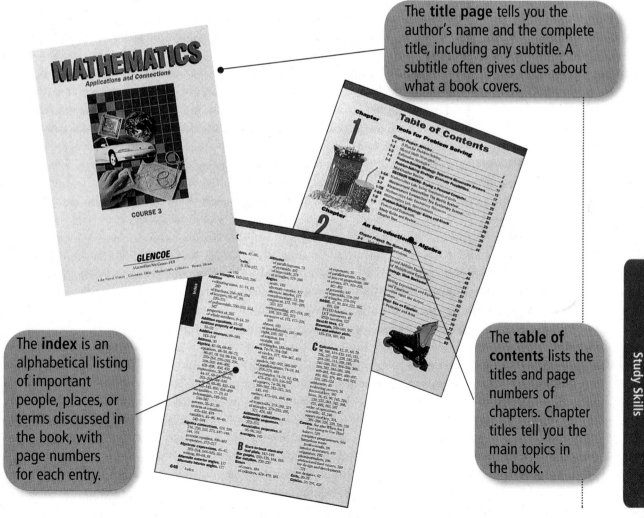

The **title page** tells you the author's name and the complete title, including any subtitle. A subtitle often gives clues about what a book covers.

The **index** is an alphabetical listing of important people, places, or terms discussed in the book, with page numbers for each entry.

The **table of contents** lists the titles and page numbers of chapters. Chapter titles tell you the main topics in the book.

Many books include other informative sections separate from the main text. The copyright page follows the title page. It tells you the year in which the book was published. Also in the front of a book, you may find a foreword, a preface, or an introduction. In the back of some books are glossaries for definitions and pronunciations of unusual words. The chart below shows you how to use some of these parts of a book.

Using a Book Effectively	
Questions	**Where to Look for the Answer**
Who is the author of this book?	The title page contains the author's name and the complete title.
Will this book contain information about my topic?	The table of contents identifies the main topics.
Will this book contain recent information about my topic?	The copyright page tells when a book was published or updated.
Will I find the people, places, and events I'm researching in this book?	The index is an alphabetical listing of people, places, events, and other topics covered in the book.

Exercise 1

Use this textbook to answer all but the first of the following questions:

1. Suppose you were studying how the human heart functions and wanted to find a definition of *atrium*. In what part of a science book would you look?
2. On what page or pages of this book are synonyms discussed?
3. In what year was this book published?
4. What is the title of Unit 10?
5. Does this book discuss homographs and, if so, on what page(s)?

24.2 Skimming, Scanning, and Careful Reading

What if you needed information about the structure of the human heart? You would probably read a book about your topic. You can use a number of strategies as you read for information. Using the right reading strategy for a particular purpose can save valuable time.

Skimming

When you want to know if a book covers the information you need, skimming is a good technique. Skimming can be very helpful in your research or when previewing or reviewing texts. To skim a text, you glance over the text to find the main ideas. You look at the chapter titles, words in italic or boldface type, and at the topic sentence of each paragraph. Without taking too much time, you can grasp the most important ideas in a given chapter. For instance, the notes below were made while a reader was skimming a detailed chapter on the makeup of the human heart.

Heart has four chambers—right and left atria, right and
  left ventricles.
Right ventricle pumps blood from body through lungs.
Left ventricle pumps blood from lungs through body.
Blood from the body enters right *atrium*, through two
  veins, called *superior vena cava* and *inferior vena cava*.
Blood carrying oxygen flows from lungs to left *atrium*
  through *pulmonary veins*.

Scanning

When you are searching for specific information, you can use a strategy called scanning. Scanning is glancing from point to point quickly but thoroughly. While scanning, you move your eyes over a page, looking for key words. When you locate the information you want, you read carefully for specific details.

Careful Reading

Careful reading allows you to understand material thoroughly and to monitor your comprehension. When you use this technique, you read the text slowly. You pay close attention to all details to make sure you clearly understand the information presented. Read carefully when learning material for the first time, such as when studying a new chapter in a science textbook. Pay attention to how well you have understood what you've read. Reread, if a passage is unclear, and jot down questions or comments for later review.

You also practice careful reading when preparing to explain material to someone else. Suppose you were going to present an oral report on the human circulatory system. Any book you find explaining the circulatory system would probably include medical information unfamiliar to you. The only way to fully understand the content is to read slowly and carefully. Read a passage several times until you fully understand it. If you understand what you will be speaking or writing about, you will be able to explain it better to your audience. Keep a dictionary nearby so that you can look up any unfamiliar words.

Exercise 2

Decide which reading strategy—skimming, scanning, or careful reading—should be used in each of the following situations. Explain each decision.

1. You find a library book on a topic that interests you. You wonder whether the book is worth reading.
2. You've been asked to read the first half of a chapter in your science textbook before tomorrow's class.
3. You need information about the causes of the American Revolution for a report you are writing. You need to decide which of the ten books on the American Revolution you've found would best fit your needs.

Study Skills

24.3 Summarizing

Explaining the main ideas of something in your own words is called summarizing. Every time you tell a friend about a movie you saw or a book you read, you are summarizing. You might summarize yesterday's science lesson to a friend who was sick that day. You also might find that explaining or summarizing something for someone else helps you understand it better.

When to Summarize

Though you often make informal summaries, there are also times when you need to make formal ones. When researching material for a report, for instance, you need to summarize important ideas. You also might summarize information you hear in a lecture, speech, or film presented in class. After you take notes on what you read or hear, you can summarize the main ideas for reference or review.

You can also use summarizing as a study tool when reading or reviewing material in your text. Writing passages from a textbook in your own words can help you better understand and remember the material. The following chart shows when and why you might summarize material.

When to Summarize	
Situation	**Purpose**
Preparing a written or oral research report	To include important ideas from your reading in your report
Reading textbook material	To better understand and remember ideas from the textbook
Listening to lectures or speeches	To write a report or prepare for a test on ideas from the lecture or speech
Viewing a film or video documentary	To write a report or prepare for a test on ideas from the film

How to Summarize

When you write a summary, put the ideas in your own words. Concentrate on the main ideas, leaving out examples and supporting details. Look below at the example of an original text and one student's summary of it. Notice what details are left out and how the student's language differs from the original.

Abraham Lincoln (1809–1865), considered one of our greatest presidents, preserved the Union at a time of unrest during the Civil War. With the United States facing disintegration, he showed that a democratic form of government can endure.

One of Lincoln's most important qualities was his understanding. Lincoln realized that the Union and democracy had to be preserved. Lincoln was also a remarkable communicator, able to clearly and persuasively express ideas and beliefs in speech and writing. His most famous speech was the brief but powerful Gettysburg Address. His first and second inaugural addresses were also very significant.

Abraham Lincoln, one of our greatest presidents, is remembered for holding the Union together through the Civil War. He is noted for his understanding and his ability to communicate effectively and persuasively

Exercise 3

With a partner, choose a film or television documentary, a lesson or chapter from a book, or an encyclopedia article about a subject that interests you. Read or discuss the material, and then work together to write a summary. Identify the main ideas, and put them in your own words. Decide whether to use any direct quotes. Share your completed summary with the class.

24.4 Making Study Plans

If you think about ways to study effectively and then take some time to learn good study skills, you can improve your school performance and increase your free time. Think about studying well, not just about spending time studying.

Setting Goals

A good study plan begins with goal setting. Review your assignments, and then set your goals for each class. Break down your assignments into short-term and long-term goals. Short-term goals can be completed in one study session; long-term goals, of course, will take more time. Break down your long-term goals into smaller tasks. Be realistic about what you can get done in each study session.

The chart below shows some short-term and long-term goals and how long-term goals can be broken down.

Setting Goals	
Short-Term Goals	1. learning a short list of spelling or vocabulary words 2. reading several pages in your textbook 3. completing a math exercise for homework
Long-Term Goals	1. completing a research report *short-term tasks* • find library materials • do prewriting • write rough draft • revise draft • prepare final report 2. preparing for a unit test *short-term tasks* • read Chapter 22 • read Chapter 23 • review key terms

Effective Study Time

Once you've determined your goals, set a reasonable deadline for reaching each goal. Write the deadline in a study-plan calendar that includes your regular activities and assignments. When you schedule your study time, keep your deadlines and your other activities in mind. Don't schedule too many deadlines for the same day. Look at the following studying tips. What other tips could you add?

Tips on Studying

1. Study at the same time and in the same place each day. Also, keep your study tools, such as pencils, pens, notepads, and dictionaries, in the same place.

2. Take a short break after reaching each goal.

3. Begin study time with your most difficult assignment.

4. Focus on one assignment at a time.

5. Try a variety of study methods, such as reading, summarizing what you have read, developing your own graphic aids (like clusters), or discussing material with a study partner.

Exercise 4

Keep a "study log" for two weeks. Record the beginning and ending time of each study session, even if it's only fifteen minutes at lunch. Write down what you study each day, and comment on how effective your studying is. You may want to include observations on circumstances that affect your ability to study on a particular day. (For example: It was raining, so I was glad to be inside studying; I had a headache, so I had trouble concentrating.) At the end of the two weeks, take a good look at your study log. Identify the factors that contributed to your most effective use of study time.

24.5 The SQ3R Method

The SQ3R method can help make your study time more productive. SQ3R is an effective method for improving your ability to read and remember written information. SQ3R stands for the steps in the process: **s**urvey, **q**uestion, **r**ead, **r**ecord, and **r**eview. Using this method can help you study more efficiently and remember more of what you read. The diagram shows how the SQ3R method works.

Survey	Question	Read	Record	Review
Preview the material by skimming. Read heads, highlighted terms, and the first sentence of each paragraph. Look at all pictures and graphs.	Ask questions about the material. Your questions might begin with *who, what, when, where, why,* and *how.*	Read the selection carefully. Identify the main idea of each section. Take notes and add questions to your list.	Write answers to your questions without looking at the text. Make brief notes about additional main ideas and facts.	Check your answers in the text. Continue to study the text until you can answer all questions correctly.

The SQ3R method works with any subject. Practice the method, and make it a habit. Once you thoroughly learn the SQ3R method and use it regularly, you will

- remember more of what you read,
- better understand the material by developing specific questions about it, and
- be better prepared to participate in class.

Survey

The purpose of surveying, or previewing, written material is to get a general idea of what it is about. The main ideas are sometimes contained in section headings or subheadings. Read each heading and subheading, and skim all the material. (See page 697 for hints on skimming.) If the material does not include headings, skim each paragraph to find its topic sentence. It will often be the first sentence of the paragraph.

Sometimes important ideas in the text are shown in bold or italic print. Make sure you take note of these ideas. When previewing, also take note of all pictures, charts, graphs, and maps. Examine them to see how the graphic aids fit in with the text. Read the title and caption for each one.

Question

After you survey and before you read, prepare a list of questions you want to be able to answer after reading the material. Having a list of questions before you begin helps you focus on the important ideas. Use questions that begin with *who, what, when, where, why,* and *how.* For example, suppose you're reading a chapter on the Battle of Gettysburg for your history class. You might write questions such as these: Who were the opposing generals in the battle? When did the battle take place? What was the outcome? You might also look at any review questions at the end of each chapter or lesson and add those to your list.

Read

Once you have prepared your list of questions, you are ready to read the material carefully. (See page 698 for tips on careful reading.) As you read, look for answers to the questions on your list. Take brief notes about the main ideas. (See pages 706–707 for more information on taking notes.) For example, your notes might include "Battle of Gettysburg fought July 1–3, 1863. Confederate General Robert E. Lee; Union General George G. Meade. Turning point of Civil War." Add more questions to your list as they arise during your reading. Make sure you thoroughly understand all the ideas. If the ideas are complicated and you are having difficulty, reread the material slowly to help clarify your understanding of important vocabulary concepts.

Record

When you complete your reading, write the answers to your questions without looking at the book or article. If there is a large amount of material, you may wish to stop and answer your questions after you finish reading each section. Answering the questions from your memory will test whether you have thoroughly learned the material. If you have difficulty answering the questions, reread the material. Then try to answer the questions again without looking at the text. Make sure your questions apply to the material. If the material you're studying does not thoroughly answer the questions, revise your questions to fit the text.

Review

Check the answers to your questions against the material you've read. Did you answer them all correctly? If not, review the material to find the answers. Try rewriting some of the questions you missed, or write several new questions that cover the same material. Review the material again, and then answer the new questions. Check your answers against the material. If you miss some of these questions, go through the process again, rewriting questions and reviewing the material until you are able to correctly answer all questions. Save your review questions and answers. You can use them later to study or review for tests.

Exercise 5

Work with a small group of classmates. Each member should choose an event from American history, then find an encyclopedia article or a passage from a book about that event. Study your material using the SQ3R method. Allow each member to give a brief oral report to the group on the material studied. Group members may evaluate one another's reports and discuss how the SQ3R method helped them.

Gathering and Organizing Information

Can you remember the important ideas from a discussion you heard two weeks ago? Unless you took notes, you've probably forgotten what was said. Taking notes and organizing them helps clarify what you hear or read. It also helps you remember information. Well-written notes also come in handy when you're studying for a test or writing a report.

Taking Notes

Taking notes can be challenging, whether you are working from a lecture, a film or video shown in class, or from research material. You may find you are either trying to write down too much or not enough. Taking notes requires special skill.

The notes you take while listening are important for your later review. They'll help you understand and remember what you hear. The notes you take while reading will allow you to review the important ideas from a source. With good notes, you may not have to go back to a source to reread it.

Tips for Taking Notes

While Listening
1. Take down only main ideas and key details.
2. Listen for transitions and signal words.
3. Use numerals, abbreviations, and symbols for speed, making sure that later you can understand what you have written.

While Doing Research
1. Take notes only on material that applies directly to your topic.
2. Use a card for each piece of information, and record the source of the information at the top of the card.
3. Summarize as much as possible.
4. Use direct quotations only for colorful language or something that's particularly well-phrased.

April 25, Science
Gorillas
☆Physical structure
male—weighs about 450 lbs.; 6 ft. tall
female—weighs about 200 lb.; much shorter
than male; fierce-looking; huge shoulders
broad chest, long arms, heavy brow ridge;
all but face, palms an
with black or brown h
and on knuckles of
☆Behavior
Will not attack u
in groups of 2-3
makes decisions
☆Sounds—male
chest to frighte
wimper; adult
when content
☆ Habitats for
Mountain gorillas—eastern part
Zaire and western Uganda in Africa at

The Wonders of Yellowstone, Geri
Hollander, pp. 17–24

The History of Yellowstone
National Park, Jack Brenner, pp.
10–17
John Corter—one of the first non—
Native Americans to find and
explore Yellowstone area (1800s).

Outlining

Once you complete your research, put your note cards in order and prepare an outline. The order you use depends on the kind of paper you are writing. If you're writing a paper on historical events, you might use chronological order, or the order in which events happen. A science paper might be ordered by cause and effect.

Group together your note cards that cover similar topics. Each group will become a main topic. Within each group put similar cards into subgroups. These will become your subtopics.

As your outline develops, you may find that you need to do more research. You may also find that you do not need all the notes you have taken. Set aside any note cards that don't apply to your outline. Examine the sample outline below.

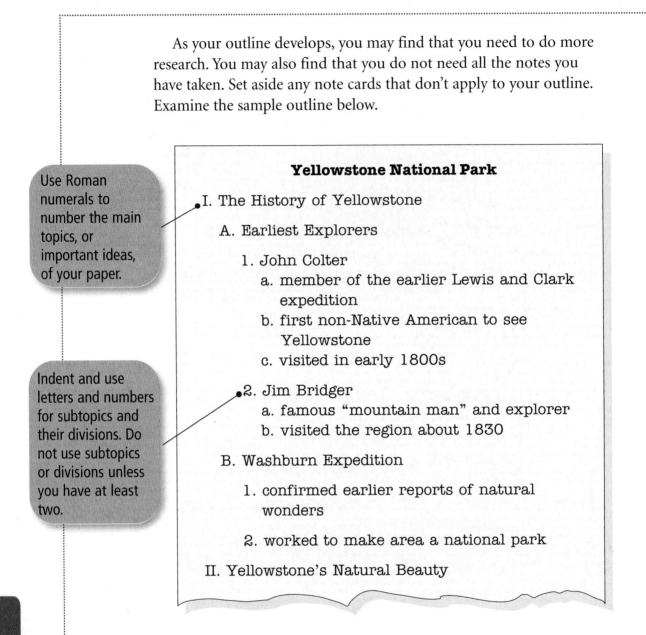

Use Roman numerals to number the main topics, or important ideas, of your paper.

Indent and use letters and numbers for subtopics and their divisions. Do not use subtopics or divisions unless you have at least two.

Yellowstone National Park

I. The History of Yellowstone

   A. Earliest Explorers

      1. John Colter

         a. member of the earlier Lewis and Clark expedition

         b. first non-Native American to see Yellowstone

         c. visited in early 1800s

      2. Jim Bridger

         a. famous "mountain man" and explorer

         b. visited the region about 1830

   B. Washburn Expedition

      1. confirmed earlier reports of natural wonders

      2. worked to make area a national park

II. Yellowstone's Natural Beauty

Exercise 6

Working with a small group of classmates, look through a number of educational magazines. Choose an article that interests all of you. Have each member of the group read the article, take notes on it, and write a detailed outline. Then compare notes and outlines, discussing the differences.

24.7 Graphic Information

Imagine trying to use words alone to explain how a car engine works. A simple written description of a process may seem confusing or incomplete. However, a picture or diagram can make it much easier for people to understand how something works.

Tables and Graphs

Many books use graphic aids such as tables and graphs to present figures or other data that are hard to explain with words alone. Tables and graphs organize information and make it more understandable.

Tables   Tables allow you to group facts or numbers into categories so that you can compare information easily. The left-hand column of a table lists a set of related items. Across the top of the table are column headings that describe the items in each column. With this arrangement, you can read a table horizontally or vertically, and you don't have to read all the information to find the piece you need. For example, in the table below, you can easily find the population growth of the five largest U.S. cities. Looking across the rows, you can see how a particular city's population increased or decreased over the years. Looking down the columns, you can compare the populations in the different years listed.

Population of Largest U.S. Cities							
Rank	**City**	**1950**	**1960**	**1970**	**1980**	**1990**	**2005**
1	New York City	7,891,984	7,781,984	7,895,563	7,071,639	7,322,564	8,143,197
2	Los Angeles	1,970,358	2,479,015	2,811,801	2,966,850	3,485,537	3,844,829
3	Chicago	3,620,962	3,550,404	3,369,357	3,005,072	2,783,726	2,842,518
4	Houston	596,163	938,219	1,233,535	1,595,138	1,654,348	2,016,582
5	Philadelphia	2,071,605	2,002,512	1,949,996	1,688,210	1,585,577	1,463,281

Source: U.S. Bureau of the Census

Study Skills

Bar Graphs In bar graphs, each quantity is shown as a bar. The length of the bar indicates the amount, or percentage, making it easy to visually compare the amounts. Bar graphs can have horizontal bars or vertical bars. Double bar graphs, such as the one below, compare two sets of data. Use the graph to compare how often American adults communicated with a parent in 1989 and 2005.

The frequency of contact with a parent is shown by the colored bars. The height bar shows the percentage of people who chose a particular response.

By comparing the height of the bars, you see that in 1989 and in 2005 most people reported having frequent contact with parents.

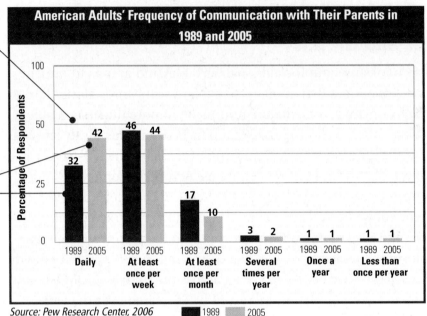

Source: Pew Research Center, 2006   ■ 1989   ▨ 2005

Line Graphs Line graphs help the reader see at a glance changes in numbers or statistics. They also show the period of time in which these changes occur. This line graph shows Americans' saving habits from 1980 to 2004. The graph charts the percentage of available income that people saved. That percentage—the "personal savings rate"—is shown at the left-hand side, or vertical axis. The years are shown at the bottom, or horizontal axis. The line shows that Americans saved a smaller portion of their income over the time period.

Americans' personal savings rates appear along the vertical axis. Horizontal lines make it easy to locate the amount for a given year.

Years are shown along the horizontal axis. Vertical lines on the graph make it easy to see where the year intersects the graph line.

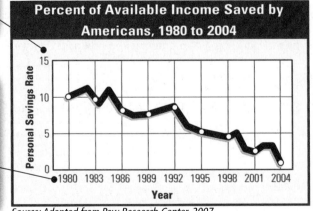

Source: Adapted from Pew Research Center, 2007

Study Skills

Circle Graphs   Circle graphs, or pie charts, begin with a circle representing the whole of something. The parts are shown as slices of a pie, with each slice representing part of the whole. Because a circle graph shows parts of a whole, information is often presented as percentages. For instance, instead of representing the population of North America in numbers of people, a circle graph might show it as a percentage of the total world population.

The circle graph on this page uses the 2005 data from the bar graph on the opposite page. The whole circle represents all the people surveyed in 2005. The graph is then divided proportionally by the different responses. The sizes of the slices allow you to easily compare the percentage of people who chose each response.

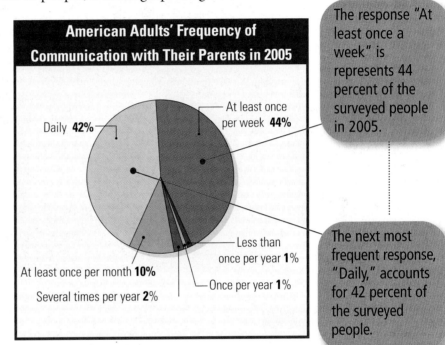

The response "At least once a week" is represents 44 percent of the surveyed people in 2005.

The next most frequent response, "Daily," accounts for 42 percent of the surveyed people.

Diagrams

Diagrams may illustrate the steps in a process or show how the parts of an object work together. You might find it difficult to learn about a complex process by reading about it or by listening to someone give an explanation. You might not be able to follow all the stages or understand all the parts without the help of a diagram.

In a diagram, each part of the object or process is labeled, sometimes with an explanation of its function. The diagram on the next page, for example, shows how heat energy is turned into electricity. Notice how each important part is labeled. Note also how the arrows show the movement of water and energy.

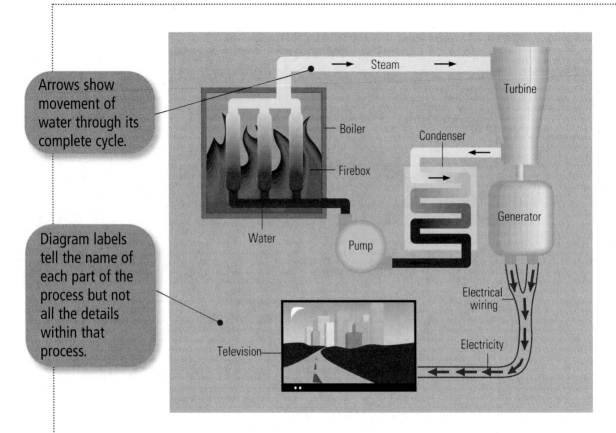

Arrows show movement of water through its complete cycle.

Diagram labels tell the name of each part of the process but not all the details within that process.

Steam
Turbine
Boiler
Condenser
Firebox
Generator
Water
Pump
Electrical wiring
Electricity
Television

Exercise 7

Work with a classmate on one of the following projects. Display your completed project in class.

1. Find out the high temperature in a chosen city for each day of a particular week. Draw the appropriate graph showing the week's temperatures. Then write a brief paragraph explaining the graph.

2. Find the total number of games won by five competing athletic teams this season. Develop an appropriate graphic showing the number of games won by each of the five teams. Then write a brief paragraph explaining your graphic.

Study Skills

24.8 Memorizing

Do you ever call your best friend on the phone? Of course you do. Do you look up your friend's number in the phone book every time you call? You don't if you have it memorized. Memorizing phone numbers is easy, but what about things you need to know in school? What you memorize for school can be as helpful as learning a friend's phone number.

How to Memorize

Different people have different learning styles. A system may work for one person but not for someone else. The following are two techniques for memorizing. Try them and see which works better for you.

The most common technique for memorizing is repetition. If you combine writing with rereading, you may memorize important information even more quickly. If you learn better by hearing, tape record as you read aloud. Play back the tape as many times as necessary until you have memorized what you need to remember.

Visualizing is another method of memorizing. Use it to memorize small pieces of information, such as phone numbers, formulas, or the spelling of words. Look at the information. Then close your eyes and "see" the number or word in your mind. Visualize it in an interesting or humorous way. If you can get a unique picture in your mind, you're more likely to be able to visualize it again.

Tricks for Memorizing

Using memory games or tricks is another way to remember information. There are many different tricks or games you can use. Try making a sentence out of words that start with the first letter of each item in a list you want to memorize. Or make up a name using those same letters. You could also try writing a rhyme. Look at the chart on page 714. When you need to memorize something, try some of these memory tricks.

Study Skills

Tricks for Remembering	
Purpose	**Memory Aid**
To remember the number of days in each month of the year	Thirty days has September, April, June, and November. All the rest have thirty-one, Except February alone, Which has twenty-eight. In leap year, coming once in four, February then has one day more.
To remember the year Columbus sailed to the Americas	In fourteen hundred and ninety-two, Columbus sailed the ocean blue.
To remember the order of the planets from the sun: **M**ercury, **V**enus, **E**arth, **M**ars, **J**upiter, **S**aturn, **U**ranus, **N**eptune	**M**y **v**ery **e**xcellent **m**other **j**ust **s**erved **u**s **n**ectarines!
To remember that the person who runs a school is a *principal*, not a *principle*	The princi<u>pal</u> is my <u>pal</u>.

Exercise 8

Develop a memory trick to remember the parts of the sun: core, photo-sphere, chromosphere, corona. Work on your own or with a classmate or two.

Exercise 9

With a partner choose at least two words from the list of Words Often Confused on page 692 in Lesson 23.7. Develop ways to memorize each word.

UNIT 25

Taking Tests

 LOG ON · **Writing** Online   For research tools and additional skills practice, go to
glencoe.com and enter QuickPass code WC87703p3.

715

25.1 Strategies

Think of a skilled athlete, an accomplished musician, or an inspiring public speaker. Each of these people prepares thoroughly to ensure the success of his or her performance. Being prepared and knowing good test-taking strategies will help you be relaxed and more confident in a test-taking situation.

Preparing for a Test

Preparing for a test begins well before the day of the test. Before you study, try to find out what information will be on the test. Then make a study schedule. Include time for reviewing your class notes, homework, quizzes, and textbook. As you review, jot down questions that you think might be on the test. Try to answer these questions as you go through material. If some questions are difficult to answer, spend some extra time looking up the answers.

When you think you know the material, work with another student or a group of students. Test these students with your study questions. Explaining the answers to someone else will help you learn the information. In addition, ask the students in your group to test you with questions they wrote. They may have come up with some you hadn't thought of yourself.

Taking a Test

You need to make careful use of your time during a test. First, make sure you understand all the test directions. Then estimate how much time each test section will take. Begin with the sections that will take less time, and don't spend too much time on one section. Planning your test time wisely may help you answer all of the questions. The chart on the following page offers suggestions for budgeting your time.

Tips for Budgeting Time During a Test

1. Read the directions carefully. Be sure you understand them before you begin the test.

2. Begin with the section of the test that will take the least amount of time.

3. Answer easier items first. Skip the ones you can't answer.

4. Return to the more difficult items when you have answered everything else.

5. Use any time left over to check your answers. Check the numbers to be sure you didn't write an answer in the wrong place.

Exercise 1

Write the letter of the response that best answers each of these questions.

1. Which of these strategies is a good way to prepare for a test?
   a. Save all studying until the night before you take the test.
   b. Allow plenty of time to review the material.
   c. Sleep with your book under your pillow.
   d. none of the above
2. Which items should you answer first on a test?
   a. the last ones
   b. the first ones
   c. the easy ones
   d. the difficult ones
3. Which of these is *not* a good test-taking strategy?
   a. Skip the items you know.
   b. Read the directions carefully.
   c. Begin with a section that won't take much time.
   d. Check your answers.

25.2   Classroom Tests

You have just found out that your upcoming exam in science will include true-false, multiple-choice, matching, fill-in, short-answer, and essay questions. You can feel confident about taking your exam by learning a few simple strategies for answering these types of questions.

True-False Items

True-false items can be tricky. A single item may include both true and untrue information. You must read the whole statement carefully before answering. If any part of the statement is not true, the answer to the item should be false. Look at the statement below.

> California does have more people than any other state. However, Alaska is the largest state in area. The statement is false.

●California has more people and more land than
   any other state in the United States.

Multiple-Choice Items

Multiple-choice items include either an incomplete sentence or a question and three or four responses. You need to pick the response that best completes the sentence or answers the question. Read the tips below for answering multiple-choice items. Then answer the question that follows.

- Read each item carefully to know what information you are looking for.
- Read all responses before answering. Sometimes an answer may seem correct, but a response that follows it may be better.
- Eliminate answers you know are incorrect.
- Be careful about choosing responses that contain absolute words, such as *always, never, all,* or *none.* Since most statements have exceptions, absolute statements are often incorrect.

Who was the first woman nominated by a major political party to be vice president of the United States?

a. Sandra Day O'Connor

b. Shirley Chisholm

c. Geraldine Ferraro ●———

d. Barbara Jordan

> All these women were first in some way. Geraldine Ferraro, however, was the first woman nominated for vice president by a major party.

Matching Items

To complete a matching item, you must match items found in one group to items in another. For example, you might have to match terms with definitions, cities with countries, or causes with effects. Compare the groups. Do they contain the same number of items? Will every item be used only once? Complete easier items first.

> The number of items in each column is not the same. One item in column 2 will not be used.

If each item will be used only once and if you are allowed to write on your test copy, cross out each item after you use it. When you get to the harder items, you will have fewer choices left.

Read the following example. Match the events or documents in the first column with the dates in the second. Use each date only once.

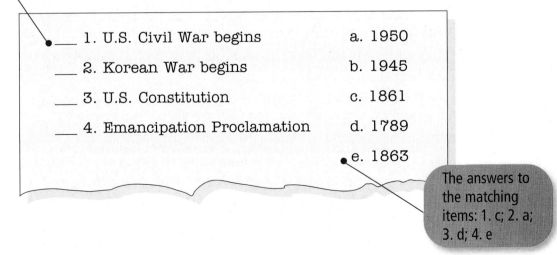

___ 1. U.S. Civil War begins	a. 1950
___ 2. Korean War begins	b. 1945
___ 3. U.S. Constitution	c. 1861
___ 4. Emancipation Proclamation	d. 1789
	● e. 1863

> The answers to the matching items: 1. c; 2. a; 3. d; 4. e

Fill-in Items

To complete a fill-in item, you need to fill in one or more blanks in a sentence. Your answer must make the sentence true as well as grammatically correct. Rereading the sentence with your answer included will help you determine whether you have made the correct choice. Look at the fill-in test item below.

1. A cold-blooded vertebrate that has gills early in life and then develops lungs later in life is an _____.

2. The three states in which matter exists are _____, _____, and _____.

Short-Answer Items

In responding to short-answer items, you must provide specific information. Your answer should be clearly and simply stated and should be written in complete sentences. For example, look at the question and answer below.

Why are the first ten amendments to the United States Constitution known as the Bill of Rights?

The first ten amendments are called the Bill of Rights because they preserve and protect specific rights of the people.

Essay Questions

Essay questions usually require an answer that is at least one paragraph long. To answer an essay question, take time to think about your main idea and the details that will support it. Also allow yourself time to write and revise your answer.

Exercise 2

Read the passage below, and answer the questions that follow.

Most of the paper we use today comes from trees. After the bark has been removed, the wood is ground up and mixed with water. This mixture is called wood pulp. The wet pulp is pressed into layers by machines, which dry the pulp on a series of screens and large rollers. The dried paper is then wound onto rolls.

Different types of paper are made from a variety of materials that are mixed with the pulp. These include wax, plastic, rags, and wastepaper. Making wastepaper into usable paper products is called recycling. Recycling is an important way to save trees.

1. Is the following statement true or false?
   Paper comes from paper plants.

2. Which of the following is not normally used in the making of paper?
   a. wax   **b.** plastic   **c.** wood pulp   **d.** bark

3. Fill in the correct response: Before paper is made, the _____ of a tree must be removed.

4. Correctly match the items in the first column with those in the second.
   1. wood pulp   **a.** added to wood pulp
   2. screens   **b.** saves trees
   3. wax, plastic, rags   **c** ground wood plus water
                               d. what the pulp is dried on

5. What is an important reason you should use recycled paper?

Taking Tests

Standardized Tests

Standardized tests are exams given to groups of students around the country. Educators evaluate scores in order to arrive at a certain national "yardstick" for measuring student performance. Knowing what kinds of questions might be on the tests can help you relax and concentrate on doing well.

Reading Comprehension

Reading-comprehension items measure how well you understand what you read. Each reading-comprehension section includes a written passage and questions about the passage. Some questions will ask you to identify the main idea. Others will ask you to draw conclusions from information in the passage. Practice your skills by reading the passage below and answering the questions.

The paragraph focuses on describing a sushi bar. The best title is *b.*

If you reread the paragraph's second sentence carefully, you will see that *d* is the correct choice.

> If you have ever been to a sushi bar, you have had an experience that is new to most Americans. Sushi is a Japanese delicacy created from raw fish, seasoned rice, pickles, seaweed, and horseradish. At a sushi bar customers sit at long counters and watch expert chefs prepare sushi by hand. The chefs shape some pieces one at a time. They slice other pieces from a long roll of rice, fish, and seaweed.
>
> 1. What is the best title for this paragraph?
>   a. Japanese Traditions
>   b. What Is a Sushi Bar?
>   c. Raw Fish Is Good for You
>   d. Japanese Cooking
>
> 2. What is sushi made of?
>   a. horseradish
>   b. raw fish and rice
>   c. seaweed and pickles
>   d. all of the above

Vocabulary

Vocabulary items are usually multiple-choice. Some items ask you to choose the correct meaning of a word used in a sentence. Others may ask you to choose the word that best completes a sentence or a definition. If you are unfamiliar with the word, look for context clues to help you with the meaning. Also, look for prefixes, suffixes, and roots that may be familiar. For example, you may not know what the word *dentifrice* means. If you recognize the root *dent*, you might guess that it is related to *denture* and *dentist*. If you were asked to choose *boardwalk, can opener, toothpaste,* or *sherbet,* which definition would you choose?

Now try these sample test items.

> The correct answer would be *toothpaste.*

Choose the letter of the correct definition of or the synonym for each underlined word.

1. Jeremy could not make up his mind whether to go to the circus or to the baseball game. He was <u>ambivalent.</u>

   a. carefree
   b. feeling angry
   c. having two conflicting wishes
   d. having no energy

> Context clues can help you guess the meaning of *ambivalent.* Jeremy can't decide between two things. The answer is *c.*

2. "Please be <u>rational!</u>" insisted Mae Ling. It annoyed her when her brother made no sense at all.

   a. sensible   b. confused   c. eager   d. polite

> Note that Mae Ling wants her brother to make sense. *Rational* probably means "sensible." Choice *a* is correct.

3. Samuel planned to perform tricks with his <u>biplane</u> in the county fair competition.

   a. a plane with three sets of wings
   b. a plane with two sets of wings
   c. a glider
   d. a car with two sets of wheels

> The word *biplane* contains two parts: the prefix *bi-*, meaning "two," and the word root. Choice *b* makes the most sense.

Analogies

Analogy items test your understanding of the relationships between things or ideas. On a standardized test you may see an analogy written as *animal* : *whale* :: *tool* : *hammer*. The single colon stands for "is to"; the double colon reads "as." The relationship between the words in the example above is that the category *animal* includes the whale and the category *tool* includes the hammer.

This chart shows some word relationships you might find in analogy tests.

Word Relationships in Analogy Tests		
Type	**Definition**	**Example**
Synonyms	Two words have the same general meaning.	vivid : bright :: dark : dim
Antonyms	Two words have opposite meanings.	night : day :: tall : short
Use	Words name a user and something used.	writer : pen :: chef : spoon
Cause and Effect	Words name a cause and its effect.	heat : boil :: cold : freeze
Category	Words name a category and an item in it.	fruit : pear :: flower : rose
Description	Words name an item and a characteristic of it.	baby : young :: sky : blue

Identify the relationship. A violin is a part of an orchestra. A clown is a part of a ___. The correct answer is *circus*, or *d*.

Although *a* may seem like the right choice, it is not a feeling, as is *sadness*. The correct answer is *b*.

Try to complete these sample analogies.

1. violin : orchestra :: clown : ___
   a. saxophone   b. juggler   c. make-up   d. circus

2. weeping : sadness :: laughter : ___
   a. comedian   b. joy   c. yelling   d. discomfort

Grammar, Usage, and Mechanics

Standardized tests measure your understanding of correct grammar, usage, and mechanics by asking you to identify errors. You may be given a sentence with portions underlined and lettered; or you may be given a sentence with numbered sections. In either case, you will be asked to identify the section that contains an error. Most tests include one choice to indicate that the sentence has no errors.

Before you complete the sample items, study this list of common errors included in standardized grammar tests:

- errors in grammar
- incorrect use of pronouns
- subject-verb agreement
- wrong verb tenses
- misspelled words
- incorrect capitalization
- punctuation mistakes

Now choose the section in each item that contains an error.

In section *c* the preposition *on* is incorrect.

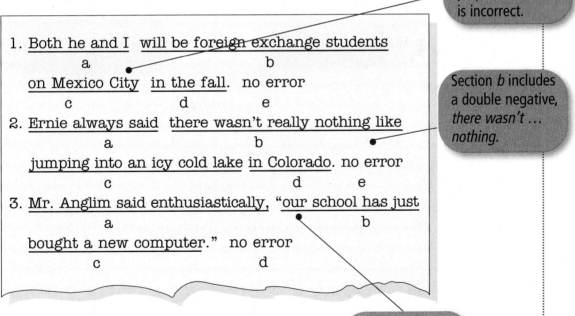

1. Both he and I   will be foreign exchange students
         a   b
   on Mexico City   in the fall.   no error
        c   d   e

2. Ernie always said   there wasn't really nothing like
         a   b
   jumping into an icy cold lake   in Colorado. no error
              c   d   e

3. Mr. Anglim said enthusiastically, "our school has just
              a   b
   bought a new computer."   no error
        c   d

Section *b* includes a double negative, *there wasn't … nothing.*

The first word of a quoted sentence is always capitalized. Section *b* contains the error.

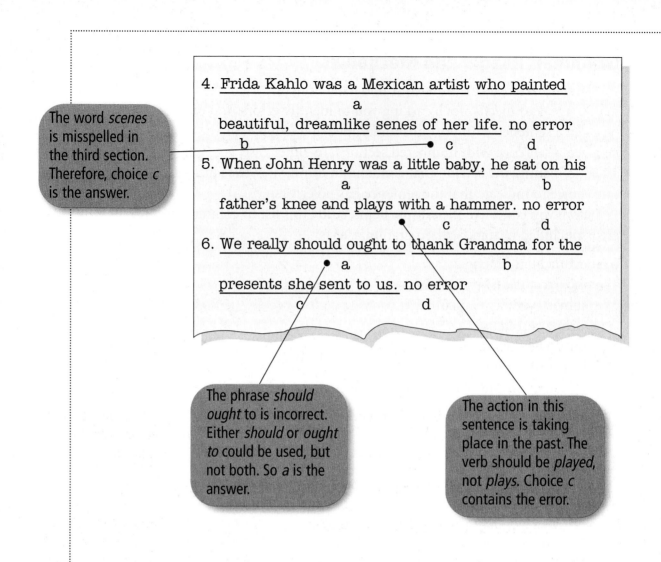

The word *scenes* is misspelled in the third section. Therefore, choice *c* is the answer.

4. Frida Kahlo was a Mexican artist who painted
   a
   beautiful, dreamlike senes of her life. no error
   b   c   d

5. When John Henry was a little baby, he sat on his
   a   b
   father's knee and plays with a hammer. no error
                     c   d

6. We really should ought to thank Grandma for the
                a   b
   presents she sent to us. no error
           c   d

The phrase *should ought* to is incorrect. Either *should* or *ought to* could be used, but not both. So *a* is the answer.

The action in this sentence is taking place in the past. The verb should be *played*, not *plays*. Choice *c* contains the error.

Taking Tests

Taking a Standardized Test

Standardized tests are different from classroom tests. Instead of writing your answers on the test itself, you will be provided with a separate answer sheet. Since answer sheets are usually graded electronically, you should be careful to avoid stray marks that might be misread.

Some standardized tests do not subtract points for incorrect answers. If this is true for the test you are taking, try to give an answer for every item. You might improve your test score by guessing correctly. But don't just guess wildly. Eliminate options that you know are wrong before making a guess.

If you can't answer a question, don't waste time thinking about it. Go on to the next item. You can come back to any unanswered items, if time permits.

Exercise 3

Reading-Comprehension Items   Read the passage below and answer the questions that follow it.

> Medical Research Secretary. Two years' experience in related field required. Must type 50 words per minute. Please send résumé and salary requirements to Tulane University.

1. Where would you most likely find the above paragraph?
   a. the help-wanted page of a newspaper
   b. a teen diary
   c. a science textbook
   d. the front page of a newspaper

2. What experience would be most acceptable?
   a. a typist in a bank
   b. a chemist at a laboratory
   c. a cashier at a supermarket
   d. all of the above

(continued)

Taking Tests

(continued)

Vocabulary Item   Find the best synonym for the under-lined word.

3. We have to make a <u>unified</u> effort, or we will never win the election.
   a. shared   **b.** difficult   **c.** untried   **d.** mighty

Analogy Item   Complete the analogy.

4. flock : geese :: _____ : wolves
   a. herd   **b.** pack   **c.** collection   **d.** sheep

Grammar, Usage, and Mechanics Item   Identify the section that contains an error.

5. <u>The entire side of the mountain</u> <u>exploded into the</u>
                  a   b
   <u>air</u> <u>when Mt. St. Helens was erupted.</u> no error
           c   d

INTRODUCTION

The following pages of exercises have been designed to familiarize you with the standardized writing tests that you may take during the school year. These exercises are very similar to the actual tests in how they look and what they ask you to do. Completing these exercises will not only provide you with practice, but also will make you aware of areas you might need to work on.

These writing exercises—just like the actual standardized writing tests—are divided into three sections.

Sentence Structure In this section, pages 730 to 737, you will be given a short passage in which some of the sentences are underlined. Each underlined sentence is numbered. After you finish reading the passage, you will be asked questions about the underlined sections. The underlined sections will be either incomplete sentences, run-on sentences, correctly written sentences that should be combined, or correctly written sentences that do not need to be rewritten. You will need to select which is best from the four choices provided.

Usage In this section, pages 738 to 745, you will also be asked to read a short passage. However, in these exercises, a word or words in the passage will be omitted and a numbered blank space will be in their place. After reading the passage, you will need to determine which of the four provided words or groups of words best belongs in each numbered space.

Mechanics Finally, in the third section, pages 746 to 753, the short passages will have parts that are underlined. You will need to determine if, in the underlined sections, there is a spelling error, capitalization error, punctuation error, or no error at all.

Writing well is a skill that you will use the rest of your life. You will be able to write more accurate letters to your friends and family, better papers in school, and more interesting stories. You will be able to express yourself and your ideas more clearly and in a way that is interesting and engaging. These exercises should help to improve your writing and to make you comfortable with the format and types of questions you will see on standardized writing tests.

Standardized Test Practice

Read each passage. Some sections are underlined. The underlined sections may be one of the following:

- Incomplete sentences
- Run-on sentences
- Correctly written sentences that should be combined
- Correctly written sentences that do not need to be rewritten

Choose the best way to write each underlined section and mark the letter for your answer. If the underlined section needs no change, mark the choice "Correct as is" on your paper.

A company that supplies lunches to schools has started providing organic lunch options in select elementary schools. <u>Some people consider organic foods to be healthier than non-organic foods. Organic foods are not sprayed with pesticides or herbicides during farming.</u> (1) It is best to wash organic foods thoroughly because of the way that they are grown.

<u>Apart from the usual options of macaroni and cheese and hamburgers. Kids can make their own salads from a salad bar or order a veggie burger from among the hot entrees.</u> (2) The company buys their produce from local farmers.

1 A Some people consider organic foods to be healthier than non-organic produce when organic foods are not sprayed with pesticides or herbicides during farming.

B Some people consider organic foods to be healthier than non-organic foods organic foods are not sprayed. With pesticides or herbicides during farming.

C Some people, who consider organic foods to be healthier than non-organic produce, are not sprayed with pesticides or herbicides during farming.

D Some people consider organic foods to be healthier than non-organic produce because organic foods are not sprayed with pesticides or herbicides during farming.

2 F Apart the usual options of macaroni and cheese and hamburgers, then kids can make their own salads from a salad bar or order a veggie burger from among the hot entrees.

G Apart from the usual options of macaroni and cheese and hamburgers, kids can make their own salads from a salad bar or order a veggie burger from among the hot entrees.

H Apart from the usual options of macaroni and cheese and hamburgers are the usual options but they can make their own salads from a salad bar or order a veggie burger from among the hot entrees.

J Correct as is

Go on

The sea horse is one of the strangest looking creatures in nature. <u>The sea horse swims very poorly it</u>
<u>seems to be going in the wrong direction.</u> It would be much more streamlined if it did not swim belly-
(1)

forward. <u>It moves very slowly. It waves a fin on its back.</u> Perhaps the most unusual thing about sea horses,
(2)

however, is the way that they give birth. <u>The female deposits her eggs. In a special pouch on the male's belly.</u>
(3)

After one to two weeks, the eggs hatch and the males "give birth" to the young.

1 **A** The sea horse swims very poorly and seems to be going in the wrong direction.

   B The sea horse swims very poorly. And it seems to be going in the wrong direction.

   C The sea horse very poorly. It seems to be going in the wrong direction.

   D Correct as is

2 **F** It moves and waves a fin on its back very slowly.

   G It moves very slowly, and it moves by waving a fin on its back.

   H It moves very slowly by waving a fin on its back.

   J It moves very slowly that waves a fin on its back to move.

3 **A** The female deposits her eggs in a special pouch being on the male's belly.

   B The female depositing her eggs it is a special pouch on the male's belly.

   C The female deposits her eggs in a special pouch on the male's belly.

   D Correct as is

Standardized Test Practice

Read each passage. Some sections are underlined. The underlined sections may be one of the following:

- Incomplete sentences
- Run-on sentences
- Correctly written sentences that should be combined
- Correctly written sentences that do not need to be rewritten

Choose the best way to write each underlined section and mark the letter for your answer. If the underlined section needs no change, mark the choice "Correct as is" on your paper.

Donna adored science fiction books. <u>She would take them with her. When she went anywhere.</u> Donna
(1)
had packed a large bag full of science fiction books to take with her on vacation to a lake house. Summer
was a perfect time to read numerous books. <u>When Donna and her parents arrived at the lake house. Donna
(2)
realized that she had forgotten the bag of books at home.</u> Fortunately, there was a library in the town that
had a large selection of science fiction books. <u>Every other day Donna biked to the library she borrowed a
(3)
new book.</u>

---

1 A She was taking them with her when she went anywhere.
   B She would take them with her and she went anywhere.
   C She would take them with her when she went anywhere.
   D Correct as is

2 F When Donna and her parents arrived. At the lake house Donna realized that she had forgotten the bag of books at home.
   G When Donna and her parents arrived at the lake house, Donna realized that she had forgotten the bag of books at home.
   H When Donna and her parents arrived at the lake house and Donna realized that she had forgotten the bag of books at home.
   J Correct as is

3 A Every other day Donna biked to the library and borrowed a new book.
   B Every other day Donna biked to the library. And borrowed a new book.
   C Biking to the library every other day. She borrowed a new book.
   D Correct as is

We all know Thomas Edison. He was the inventor of the light bulb. It seems Edison was a person who
took many risks. When he was a boy, Edison saved a man's life by pulling him off the train tracks. After the
train had passed and the man was safe, the stationmaster came over to him. The stationmaster thought
Edison had done something wrong, he firmly boxed his ears. Because of this, Thomas Edison was almost
entirely deaf in one ear for the rest of his life.

1 A We all know Thomas Edison as the inventor of the light bulb.
   B We all know Thomas Edison when it was the inventor of the light bulb.
   C We all know Thomas Edison, and we know he was the inventor of the light bulb.
   D We all know the inventor of the light bulb and it was Thomas Edison.

2 F When he was a boy, Edison saving a man's life by pulling him off the train tracks.
   G When he was a boy. Edison saved a man's life by pulling him off the train tracks.
   H When he was a boy, it is Edison saved a man's life by pulling him off the train tracks.
   J Correct as is

3 A The stationmaster, thinking Edison had done something wrong. He firmly boxed his ears.
   B The stationmaster thought Edison had done something wrong. And firmly boxed his ears.
   C The stationmaster thought Edison had done something wrong and firmly boxed his ears.
   D Correct as is

Standardized Test Practice

Read each passage. Some sections are underlined. The underlined sections may be one of the following:

- Incomplete sentences
- Run-on sentences
- Correctly written sentences that should be combined
- Correctly written sentences that do not need to be rewritten

Choose the best way to write each underlined section and mark the letter for your answer. If the underlined section needs no change, mark the choice "Correct as is" on your paper.

Jose was teaching Spanish at a high school in Connecticut. Where he lived in an old Victorian house. At
                                                                (1)
night, he heard the sound of flapping wings and high-pitched chirping over his head. Jose thought he was

just imagining the noises. Because he was so tired. Then, he realized that there was something flying around
                                    (2)
in the attic. One night, Jose went up to the attic and saw a big bat flying around. Since the bat wasn't hurt-
                        (3)
ing anything, Jose decided to leave him alone. He did buy earplugs though to keep out the noise at night!

---

1 A Jose teaching Spanish at a high school in Connecticut and living in an old Victorian house.
   B Jose was teaching Spanish at a high school in Connecticut, where he lived in an old Victorian house.
   C Jose was teaching Spanish at a high school in Connecticut, then he lived in an old Victorian house.
   D Correct as is

2 F Jose thought he was just imagining the noises because he was so tired.
   G Jose thought he was just imagining the noises this is because he was so tired.
   H Jose being so tired, and just imagining the noises.
   J Correct as is

3 A One night, Jose went up to the attic and sees a big bat flying around.
   B One night, Jose went up to the attic. And saw a big bat flying around.
   C One night, Jose went up to the attic, saw a big bat flying around.
   D Correct as is

Celia was born in Odessa. <u>Celia had lived in New York for more than five years. She took the citizenship exam.</u> The interviewer asked her many questions. For example, he asked her, "Who was the first President of the United States?" and "When did the American Revolution take place?" <u>By correctly answering these questions, Celia proved a sufficient knowledge of the English language. She also proved a sufficient knowledge of American history.</u> The interviewer complimented her on her good work. <u>Celia was happy it was because she passed the test.</u> She was proud to be an American citizen.

1 A Celia had lived in New York for more than five years, and she took the citizenship exam.

B Celia had lived in New York for more than five years when it was she took the citizenship exam.

C Celia had lived in New York and she took the citizenship exam and it was more than five years.

D Celia had lived in New York for more than five years before she took the citizenship exam.

2 F By answering these questions correctly, which proved a sufficient knowledge of American history, Celia proved a sufficient knowledge of the English language.

G By answering these questions correctly, Celia proved a sufficient knowledge of the English language and American history.

H By answering these questions correctly, Celia proved a sufficient knowledge of the English language and she also proved a sufficient knowledge of American history.

J By answering these questions correctly, Celia proved a sufficient knowledge of the English language and American history, sufficiently.

3 A Celia was happy. Because she passed the test.

B Celia being happy. She passed the test.

C Celia was happy because she passed the test.

D Correct as is

Standardized Test Practice

Read each passage. Some sections are underlined. The underlined sections may be one of the following:

- Incomplete sentences
- Run-on sentences
- Correctly written sentences that should be combined
- Correctly written sentences that do not need to be rewritten

Choose the best way to write each underlined section and mark the letter for your answer. If the underlined section needs no change, mark the choice "Correct as is" on your paper.

<u>Mrs. Carlos took her class on a field trip to the Hartsfield Atlanta International Airport she took them to</u>
<u>see the arrival of two giant pandas from China.</u> **(1)** Everyone was excited to witness the welcoming ceremony for the two-year-old pandas who had traveled seventeen hours from Beijing.

<u>It was in the early afternoon. Mrs. Carlos's class and many other interested people waited.</u> Mrs. Carlos
(2)
told her students to watch for the plane that would be arriving shortly. "The pandas traveled from China in special crates," she said.

<u>Moments after she said this, the plane landed. Carrying the two new visitors to the United States.</u> Mrs.
(3)
Carlos promised her class that the next field trip they would make would be to the zoo to see the pandas in their new home.

---

1 **A** Mrs. Carlos. She took her class on a field trip to the Hartsfield Atlanta International Airport to see the arrival of two giant pandas from China.

  B Mrs. Carlos took her class on a field trip to the Hartsfield Atlanta International Airport. To see the arrival of two giant pandas from China.

  C Mrs. Carlos took her class on a field trip to the Hartsfield Atlanta International Airport to see the arrival of two giant pandas from China.

  D Correct as is

2 **F** It was in the early afternoon therefore Mrs. Carlos's class and many other interested people waited.

  G In the early afternoon Mrs. Carlos's class waited many other interested people.

  H It was in the early afternoon, and Mrs. Carlos's class waited and many other interested people waited.

  J In the early afternoon, Mrs. Carlos's class and many other interested people waited.

3 **A** Moments after she said this, the plane landed carrying the two new visitors to the United States.

  B Moments after she said this, the plane landed it was carrying the two new visitors to the United States.

  C Moments after she said this, the plane landed carrying the two new visitors. To the United States.

  D Correct as is

NASA, the United States' space program, created a spacecraft called the Mars Orbiter. <u>It was launched into space in January 1999. It was on a mission to study the atmosphere of Mars.</u> **(1)** About 9 months later, the spacecraft reached its destination. <u>The Orbiter, however, came too close to the Martian atmosphere, it burned up.</u> **(2)** Scientists on Earth were puzzled over why this happened. Later, they realized that the accident had been caused by a simple miscommunication. <u>One team of scientists used the English system of inches and feet. The other team used the metric system for their calculations.</u> **(3)** This mistake caused the Orbiter to stray from its course.

1 A It was launched into space in January 1999, and it was on a mission to study the atmosphere of Mars.

B It was launched into space in January 1999 on a mission to study the atmosphere of Mars.

C It was launched into space in January 1999 when it was on a mission to study the atmosphere of Mars.

D It was launched on a mission to study the atmosphere of Mars into space in January 1999.

2 F The Orbiter, however, too close to the Martian atmosphere. It burned up.

G The Orbiter, however, came too close to the Martian atmosphere, causing it to burn up.

H The Orbiter, however, came too close to the Martian atmosphere. Causing it to burn up.

J Correct as is

3 A One team of scientists used the English system of inches and feet, while the other team used the metric system for their calculations.

B One team of scientists used the English system of inches and feet, or the other team used the metric system for their calculations.

C One team of scientists used the English system of inches and feet since the other team of scientists used the metric system for their calculations.

D For their calculations, one team of scientists used the English system of inches and feet and the other team used the metric system for their calculations.

Standardized Test Practice

Read each passage and choose the word or group of words that belongs in each space. Mark the letter for your answer on your paper.

> Mei had a conference with Mr. Cellan, her junior high school advisor, about _____(1)_____ to a specialized summer camp. "What are your favorite hobbies?" asked Mr. Cellan.
>
> "I _____(2)_____," said Mei. "Except sleeping."
>
> "Sleeping? Is that all? There must be something else you enjoy doing outside of school," Mr. Cellan _____(3)_____.
>
> "After I sleep," Mei explained, "I transcribe my dreams and then I draw pictures of _____(4)_____."
>
> "That's intriguing," commented Mr. Cellan. He suggested that Mei might enjoy converting her hobby into an actual career path.
>
> Now Mei is applying to several art camps. That is, after she takes a nap, of course.

1 **A** apply
   B application
   C applying
   D applied

2 **F** have never hardly any
   G have never any
   H have barely any
   J have not none

3 **A** persisting
   B persist
   C persistence
   D persisted

4 **F** their
   G them
   H they
   J theirs

Go on

When Marisol was eighteen years old, her father _____(1)_____ a new car and gave her his old station wagon. Marisol drove the car to a garage to get it _____(2)_____. The mechanic said the car was fine and put a new inspection sticker on the windshield.

On the way home, Marisol heard a strange sound and _____(3)_____ pulled into the breakdown lane. She had a flat tire! Luckily, her father _____(4)_____ her how to change a tire and there was a spare in the trunk.

1 **A** is buying
   B bought
   C has bought
   D was bought

2 **F** inspect
   G inspected
   H inspection
   J inspecting

3 **A** slow
   B more slow
   C more slowly
   D slowly

4 **F** was teaching
   G had taught
   H teach
   J is teaching

Standardized Test Practice

Read each passage and choose the word or group of words that belongs in each space. Mark the letter for your answer on your paper.

There are two photographers living in big cities on opposite sides of the world. Marta lives in New York and Wei lives in Hong Kong. Both of _____(1)_____ have personal Web sites where they display their photographs of the cities they live in. Last year, Marta found Wei's Web site. She was very inspired by what she _____(2)_____. She wrote Wei an e-mail message asking if he would like to _____(3)_____ .

"Yes," Wei wrote back.

Now Marta takes photos of New York and sends her rolls of film to Wei in Hong Kong. Wei puts Marta's roll of film into his camera and _____(4)_____ photos of Hong Kong. The double exposures they get merge the two cities into one.

1 **A** us
   B it
   C you
   D them

2 **F** had seen
   G see
   H is seeing
   J saw

3 **A** collaboration
   B collaborate
   C collaborated
   D collaborating

4 **F** was taking
   G took
   H has taken
   J takes

Go on

Max knows trains well: He is a train conductor. He works on the Vermonter train which runs from Grand Central Station in New York City to Montpellier, Vermont. Max lives in Middletown, Connecticut, which is just about the middle of the train's route. It _____(1)_____ Max a long time to get to New York, so the train picks him up in Connecticut.

On the train, Max collects tickets and punches holes in the _____(2)_____ spaces. He _____(3)_____ as a conductor on this train for many years. With time and experience, Max has come to know the route like the back of his hand. He even knows many of the regular travelers by name. On the long stretches between stations, Max likes to converse with the customers about where they _____(4)_____ and where they came from.

1 **A** will have taken
   B will take
   C would take
   D took

2 **F** most rightly
   G rightness
   H right
   J more right

3 **A** has worked
   B will be working
   C works
   D was working

4 **F** is going
   G goes
   H are going
   J was gone

Standardized Test Practice

Read each passage and choose the word or group of words that belongs in each space. Mark the letter for your answer on your paper.

Bonsai trees are miniature trees that _____(1)_____ and pruned into a particular shape. These dwarf trees _____(2)_____ resemble old and gnarled trees.

Bonsai means "tray-planted" in Japanese and _____(3)_____ to the small trays or pots that are most often used for planting bonsai trees. The tradition of making bonsai originated in China but _____(4)_____ a trademark of Japanese culture. A bonsai tree can live a hundred years or more, but the art of bonsai has been around for roughly a thousand years.

1 **A** has been cut
   B is cut
   C are cut
   D were cut

2 **F** close
   G closely
   H more closer
   J closest

3 **A** is referring
   B refers
   C referred
   D has been referring

4 **F** will become
   G has become
   H was becoming
   J have become

Go on

It seems that everybody _____(1)_____ pizza. The Neapolitans first created pizza out of the ingredients _____(2)_____. Because pizza was relatively easy to make and could be baked quickly, it became popular throughout Italy. Each region added its own _____(3)_____ touch. Many other cultures have their own versions of the pizza idea. In Greece and the Middle East, for example, they make a spicy pizza without tomato sauce.

The first pizzeria in America opened in 1905, in New York City. The pizza industry skyrocketed after World War II, when American soldiers came back from Italy. The soldiers missed the taste of _____(4)_____ favorite Italian specialty. Now there are scarcely any towns in America without a pizzeria.

1 A eat
   B ate
   C have eaten
   D has eaten

2 F most available
   G availabler
   H more available
   J availablest

3 A specialty
   B specialist
   C specialness
   D special

4 F its
   G their
   H his
   J your

Standardized Test Practice

Read each passage and choose the word or group of words that belongs in each space. Mark the letter for your answer on your paper.

In 1963, Duke Ellington _____(1)_____ his band on a tour of the Middle East, India, and Ceylon. The journey was a musical discovery for both the band and their audiences. The musicians _____(2)_____ by music lovers in every city they visited. When they returned home, Ellington and his co-writer, Billy Strayhorn, were inspired to write a series of musical compositions called the *Far East Suite.*

Throughout their travels, Ellington's band had encountered many different musical traditions that influenced the *Far East Suite.* One of the compositions, called *The Bluebird of Delhi,* was particularly influenced by the songs of the exotic birds in India, the likes of which the band _____(3)_____ before. In _____(4)_____ you can hear the clarinet playing the part of the bird's sweet song.

---

1 A took
   B taken
   C is taking
   D has taken

2 F was welcomed
   G is welcomed
   H were welcomed
   J has been welcomed

3 A hadn't hardly witnessed
   B had never witnessed
   C hadn't never witnessed
   D had barely never witnessed

4 F them
   G you
   H it
   J him

Mr. Calder taught an introduction to architecture class at the high school. On the first day of class, he entered with an immense stack of newspapers. He told the students that he would _____(1)_____ for an hour while they each built something out of the newspaper.

An hour later he returned to find intricate newspaper castles, airplanes, sailing ships, and many creative objects made from newspaper. The students watched him expectantly, waiting for their teacher to praise the _____(2)_____ work.

Mr. Calder picked up a piece of newspaper folded in two like a little triangular tent.

"This," he said, "is a great work of architecture." The students were _____(3)_____. The architect explained, "Paper is light and fragile. It is not good for airplanes, boats, and castle walls, but it is easy to fold and _____(4)_____ thin edges can bear weight. Therefore, the 'tent' is the perfect object for this particular building material—newspaper."

1   **A**   have left
     B   leave
     C   leaving
     D   left

2   **F**   best
     G   most best
     H   bestest
     J   more best

3   **A**   confuse
     B   confusing
     C   confused
     D   confusion

4   **F**   their
     G   our
     H   its
     J   your

Standardized Test Practice

Read each passage and decide which type of error, if any, appears in each underlined section. Mark the letter for your answer on the paper.

It's hard to imagine, but, movies have been around now for a hundred years. In the beginning, they were
(1)
very different from what we see at the theaters today. Two frenchmen, Louis and Auguste Lumiere, invented
(2)
the "cinematographe" in 1895. This machine could record and project moving images from film.

The first nickelodeon, or old-fashioned movie theater, was built in Philadelphia in 1896, the year after
(3)
the invention of the cinematographe. Nowadays, cinemas can have up to twenty diffrent theaters with
(4)
twenty different movies playing at the same time.

Today some filmakers make their movies on video cameras and computers are used for editing.
(5)
Although you can watch movies at home on videotape or even on your computer people still enjoy going to
(6)
the movies and seeing films projected from something very much like the first cinematographe.

1 A Spelling error
   B Capitalization error
   C Punctuation error
   D No error

2 F Spelling error
   G Capitalization error
   H Punctuation error
   J No error

3 A Spelling error
   B Capitalization error
   C Punctuation error
   D No error

4 F Spelling error
   G Capitalization error
   H Punctuation error
   J No error

5 A Spelling error
   B Capitalization error
   C Punctuation error
   D No error

6 F Spelling error
   G Capitalization error
   H Punctuation error
   J No error

Go on

Maine is called <u>"vacationland" for a good reeson. Nature lovers visit Maine</u> because there are many
(1)
national and state forests and parks. The Appalachian Trail, which runs <u>from Maine to Georgia, begins at</u>
(2)
<u>Mount katahdin.</u> Maine is also home for much wildlife, including bears, moose and beautiful water birds.

<u>There are many senic towns along Maine's seacoast</u> and all of them have a rich history. Wiscasset is con-
(3)
sidered Maine's prettiest village. It is located on <u>the Sheepscot river, in the southwestern region</u> of the state.
(4)
Wiscasset used to be Maine's most important port city in the 18th century.

<u>Like many things in Maine, that has changed.</u> Now it is a tourist attraction. People also come <u>to see Fort</u>
(5)
<u>Edgecombe, a wooden fort</u> built in preparation for the War of 1812 between America and England.
(6)

1 A Spelling error
   B Capitalization error
   C Punctuation error
   D No error

2 F Spelling error
   G Capitalization error
   H Punctuation error
   J No error

3 A Spelling error
   B Capitalization error
   C Punctuation error
   D No error

4 F Spelling error
   G Capitalization error
   H Punctuation error
   J No error

5 A Spelling error
   B Capitalization error
   C Punctuation error
   D No error

6 F Spelling error
   G Capitalization error
   H Punctuation error
   J No error

Standardized Test Practice

Read each passage and decide which type of error, if any, appears in each underlined section. Mark the letter for your answer on your paper.

Alfred Nobel is the <u>Swedish chemist who invented dynamite.</u> Nobel's discoveries made him a very rich
                    (1)
man. <u>Alfred Nobel had many intrests outside of chemistry.</u> When he died in 1896, he left behind a substan-
       (2)
tial fortune that was to be used for annual prizes for achievements in physics, chemistry, medicine, literature, and peace.

When Alfred Nobel was a <u>young man, he had a fondness for english literature.</u> Throughout his busy life
                         (3)
as a scientist, Nobel also wrote his own poetry and drama. Although he did not achieve fame as a writer, the
Nobel Prize for Literature <u>has become the worlds most prestigious literary award.</u>
                           (4)
The last Nobel Prize for Literature of the <u>20th century went to Günter Grass, a famous German Writer.</u>
                                           (5)
Günter Grass became well known for <u>his novel *The Tin Drum* which is about a boy who decides not to grow up.</u>
                                   (6)

---

1 **A** Spelling error
   B Capitalization error
   C Punctuation error
   D No error

2 **F** Spelling error
   G Capitalization error
   H Punctuation error
   J No error

3 **A** Spelling error
   B Capitalization error
   C Punctuation error
   D No error

4 **F** Spelling error
   G Capitalization error
   H Punctuation error
   J No error

5 **A** Spelling error
   B Capitalization error
   C Punctuation error
   D No error

6 **F** Spelling error
   G Capitalization error
   H Punctuation error
   J No error

Go on

Chantal asked her father if he could help her with her math homework. <u>"Of course," he said. Let's get to work."</u> (1) Chantal showed her father <u>the asignment, which involved calculating averages.</u> (2)

<u>After studying the math lesson Chantal's father</u> (3) said he had an idea. He took a stack of papers from a drawer. <u>"Let's calculate the avarage we spent per month</u> (4) on electricity this year," said <u>her father. Chantal was ambivalent about</u> (5) the project. <u>However, once they started working, she could see the value in applying the Knowledge she learned in math class</u> (6) to a situation in real life.

1 A Spelling error
   B Capitalization error
   C Punctuation error
   D No error

2 F Spelling error
   G Capitalization error
   H Punctuation error
   J No error

3 A Spelling error
   B Capitalization error
   C Punctuation error
   D No error

4 F Spelling error
   G Capitalization error
   H Punctuation error
   J No error

5 A Spelling error
   B Capitalization error
   C Punctuation error
   D No error

6 F Spelling error
   G Capitalization error
   H Punctuation error
   J No error

STOP

Standardized Test Practice

Read each passage and decide which type of error, if any, appears in each underlined section. Mark the letter for your answer on your paper.

Scientists have had <u>a hard time studying the sloth, a reclusive, tree-dwelling mammel.</u> Sloths are found (1)

<u>in tropical south and central America. It is hard to</u> photograph sloths because they are mostly active at night (2)

and get scared by the light from camera flashes.

One way to get <u>around this is to use a special infrared film which does not require</u> artificial lighting. The (3)

infrared film <u>picks up heat signal's from the</u> moving animals. Sometimes <u>the photographs are blury because</u> (4)   (5)

<u>of</u> the movement of the tree sloths. <u>Still, these pictures reveal that the sloth hangs upside down most of the</u> (6)

<u>time: nearly three-fifths of each day!</u>

1 A Spelling error
B Capitalization error
C Punctuation error
D No error

2 F Spelling error
G Capitalization error
H Punctuation error
J No error

3 A Spelling error
B Capitalization error
C Punctuation error
D No error

4 F Spelling error
G Capitalization error
H Punctuation error
J No error

5 A Spelling error
B Capitalization error
C Punctuation error
D No error

6 F Spelling error
G Capitalization error
H Punctuation error
J No error

Go on

Michael is a <u>screenwriter living in Ottawa Canada. Every year</u> he writes a screenplay that is turned into a
(1)
two-hour movie. <u>His agent in Los Angeles, Sam,</u> represents Michael at the film studios and keeps contact
(2)
with producers and directors <u>who might be interested in buying Michaels scripts.</u>
(3)

Last year, <u>Michael struck his bigest deal. He wrote a script about a gangster</u> who figures out that he is a
(4)
character in the movies and wants to get out into real life. Sam sold the idea <u>to Paramount pictures for half</u>
(5)
<u>a million</u> dollars.

The film did very well at the box office, so now Michael is taking a break from screenwriting to do a
documentary film. The film is about his hometown and the <u>stories of Greek imigrant families, like his own,</u>
(6)
who came to live there.

---

1 **A** Spelling error
   B Capitalization error
   C Punctuation error
   D No error

2 **F** Spelling error
   G Capitalization error
   H Punctuation error
   J No error

3 **A** Spelling error
   B Capitalization error
   C Punctuation error
   D No error

4 **F** Spelling error
   G Capitalization error
   H Punctuation error
   J No error

5 **A** Spelling error
   B Capitalization error
   C Punctuation error
   D No error

6 **F** Spelling error
   G Capitalization error
   H Punctuation error
   J No error

Standardized Test Practice

Read each passage and decide which type of error, if any, appears in each underlined section. Mark the letter for your answer on your paper.

Wolfgang Amadeus Mozart was a child prodigy. <u>At an early age he impresed everyone with his</u> amazing
(1)
talent for playing the piano. <u>He was even able to impress the austrian queen</u>.
(2)
Legend has it <u>that on a visit to the palace the young Mozart played</u> a piece of music perfectly that he had
(3)
just heard performed for the first time by the royal court pianist. The Queen challenged him <u>to play the</u>
<u>piece again, this time with a long piece of felt</u> over the <u>keys. Mozart accomplished the task beautifully</u>.
(4)   (5)
This child prodigy would go on to write some of the most cherished classical <u>music in the world, includ-</u>
<u>ing operas such as *The Magic Flute, Figaro* and *Don Giovanni.*</u>
(6)

1 **A** Spelling error
   B Capitalization error
   C Punctuation error
   D No error

2 **F** Spelling error
   G Capitalization error
   H Punctuation error
   J No error

3 **A** Spelling error
   B Capitalization error
   C Punctuation error
   D No error

4 **F** Spelling error
   G Capitalization error
   H Punctuation error
   J No error

5 **A** Spelling error
   B Capitalization error
   C Punctuation error
   D No error

6 **F** Spelling error
   G Capitalization error
   H Punctuation error
   J No error

Go on

We all know that the cavity is the healthy <u>tooth's greatest enemy, but where do cavities come from?</u> The
(1)
enamel coating of your teeth <u>is very strong. Certain foods, however create an acidity level</u> in your mouth
(2)
that deteriorates the tooth's surface. <u>Then bacteria from food can get into the little holes, and that is how</u>
(3)
<u>cavities begin.</u>

The average number of cavities per person has increased. Hundreds of years ago, people did not have
<u>toothbrushes, but they also did not eat candy bars and drink Soda.</u> The modern sugary diet <u>greatly increeses</u>
(4)
<u>the likelihood of cavities. That is why</u> fluoride is added to the public water supply in many cities. Fluoride
(5)
helps to strengthen the teeth and can even stop small cavities from growing bigger.

Most dentists recommend brushing <u>your teeth three times a day. Chosing the right</u> foods can also help
(6)
guard against cavities.

1 A Spelling error
  B Capitalization error
  C Punctuation error
  D No error

2 F Spelling error
  G Capitalization error
  H Punctuation error
  J No error

3 A Spelling error
  B Capitalization error
  C Punctuation error
  D No error

4 F Spelling error
  G Capitalization error
  H Punctuation error
  J No error

5 A Spelling error
  B Capitalization error
  C Punctuation error
  D No error

6 F Spelling error
  G Capitalization error
  H Punctuation error
  J No error

UNIT 26
Listening and Speaking

Writing Online   For research tools and additional skills practice, go to **glencoe.com** and enter QuickPass code WC87703p3.

26.1 Effective Listening

It is often hard to listen when external distractions, such as movement and noise, attract your attention or drown out what you are trying to hear. Internal distractions, such as personal biases and conflicting demands on your time, can also keep you from listening effectively. But by learning how to tune out distractions and improve your listening skills, you can increase your ability to understand what you hear.

Listening in Class

What happens when you don't understand how to do your homework assignment? It's difficult to do a good job when you don't understand what's expected of you. Learning how to listen better will make tasks that depend on understanding directions much simpler. The following tips will help you improve your listening skills to better understand what you hear.

Tips for Effective Listening

1. First, eliminate any distractions that may make it difficult to concentrate; turn off the phone, the TV, or the radio.

2. Determine the type of information you are hearing. Are you listening to a story, or is someone giving you directions? Knowing what you are listening for makes understanding easier.

3. Take notes. Identify the main ideas as you hear them, and write them in your own words.

4. Take a note if you hear a statement that tells when you will need the information you are listening to.

5. If you don't understand something, ask a question. Asking questions right away helps avoid confusion later on.

6. Review your notes as soon as possible after the listening experience. Reviewing them soon afterward will allow you to fill in any gaps in your notes.

Listening to Persuasive Speech

What type of argument most easily persuades you? Is it one that includes facts and logical conclusions or one that appeals to your emotions? Speakers who want to persuade you may concentrate on emotional appeals. They may even use faulty thinking to persuade you to accept their opinions.

Faulty Thinking   Faulty thinking may be intentional or unintentional. That is, the speaker may be trying to deceive you or simply may not be thinking clearly. It's up to you, the listener, to analyze the speaker's statements and arguments. Are they well thought out, or are they flawed? Following are some examples of statements you might hear from a political candidate. However, you can find examples of faulty thinking in other kinds of persuasive speeches as well.

Questioning What You Hear	
Statements	**Questions**
Every child in America will have food on the table if I'm elected.	This is a broad statement. Do you think any one candidate can keep such a promise?
Don't vote for my opponent. His brother was investigated by the IRS two years ago.	What was the nature of the investigation? What were its results? Should a candidate be judged by someone else's activities?
I have the support of the great governor of our state in my campaign for senator.	Does the support of the governor prove a person is qualified to be senator? Is the governor a political ally of the candidate?
Voters in three states claim health care is important. I listen to America.	Might voters in some other states have different needs?

Speaker's Bias   Speakers may try to persuade audiences to agree with them by presenting only one side of an issue. Such speeches are biased, or slanted, in favor of one opinion. Always listen with a questioning attitude. Ask yourself if the speaker is dealing with all sides of the issue. Maybe the speaker is giving only the facts that support one opinion.

Be alert for speeches that show bias, such as the first example below. The other example is more objective. As you read, notice the facts each speaker uses.

BIASED SPEAKER: You should vote in favor of the proposed tax increase on gasoline. This tax will give the government enough revenue to rebuild the nation's crumbling highway system. It will provide many thousands of new jobs in the construction industry. It also will help us reduce the national debt. Our country needs this tax increase.

UNBIASED SPEAKER: This tax increase has faults as well as benefits. True, it will help rebuild highways and provide more jobs in highway construction. But it will also place a burden on those who must drive to make a living. The added cost of gas may drive many independent truckers and drivers out of work. People who take buses may find themselves paying higher fares.

The biased speaker gives only arguments in favor of the tax increase. The unbiased speaker admits that the arguments of the biased speaker are valid. However, this speaker points out that the increase will also have some negative effects.

Listening to Radio and Television News

Do you ask questions when you listen to the news? You might be surprised at how much there is to question. It's important to sort out facts from opinions in print, radio, and television news coverage. Doing so will help you evaluate the news coverage for truthfulness and accuracy. It will help you form your own unbiased opinion about what's being said.

Journalists are supposed to be objective. This means that they should not let their own opinions affect what they report and how they report it. This is sometimes a difficult thing to do. For example, a news commentator may call someone an "influential senator." Is the senator really influential, or is the commentator only expressing an opinion? The answer will help you evaluate anything the senator says. It will also help you evaluate what the commentator says about the senator.

Journalists are taught to provide sources for their information. Often it's important to know where the information in a news item came from. For example, suppose you heard the following two items on a newscast. Which would you be more likely to believe?

- Certain unnamed sources reported today that the President would not seek a second term of office.
- The President's chief of staff announced this afternoon that the President plans to seek a second term.

Journalists also try to present information that is complete. In their reports they usually try to answer the questions *what, who, when, where, how,* and *why.* If you carefully read or listen to almost any news story, you will see that it answers questions such as these:

- *What* happened?
- *Who* was involved?
- *When* did it happen?
- *Where* did it happen?
- *How* did it happen?
- *Why* did it happen? (or *Why* is it important?)

The questions may not always follow the above order, but they will all be answered. They'll usually be answered in the first paragraph of a newspaper story or the first minute or so of a radio or television newscast.

When you listen to a news broadcast, you can evaluate the quality of the reporting. Ask yourself some questions, such as the following:

- Was the report complete?
- Is all the information provable, or are some statements only opinions?
- Is any of the report based on faulty thinking?
- If an opinion is expressed, does the reporter tell whose opinion it is?
- Did the reporter identify the sources of the information?

Following are some other examples of how asking questions will help you evaluate a news broadcast.

Evaluating News Statements

Sample Statements	Questions to Ask
The candidate has a liberal voting record on defense spending.	What is a liberal voting record? Who defines *liberal?* Does the candidate's record match the definition?
A reliable source stated that the company has been dumping toxic waste into the river.	Who is the source? How reliable is he or she? Did the source actually see the dumping?
One eyewitness stated that the defendant fired three shots.	Who is this witness? Where was the witness at the time? Does the witness know the defendant?
An expert claims we are in a recession.	Who is the expert? In what field is he or she an expert? Was any proof provided? Do other experts agree?
The tobacco company denies any proven relationship between smoking and illness.	Doesn't the company have an interest in denying the relationship? On what facts does the company base its statement?
Last winter's frost is driving the price of fruit upward.	Is there a proven relationship between the frost and rising fruit costs? Are there other possible reasons for the rising costs?

Exercise 1

Divide into small groups. Each group will form a news broadcast team. Select one person to be the news anchor. Other members of the group can be reporters on special assignments.

Decide which current events in your school or neighborhood to cover. Assign a story to each person. Students should research their stories and write short reports to deliver during a news broadcast of no more than ten minutes. Rehearse your newscast within the group, then present it to the class. Other members of the class should evaluate each broadcast according to criteria the class has generated.

26.2 Interviewing Skills

If you wanted answers to three or four questions on the topic of fly fishing, what would be an efficient way to get them? Would you read about the topic in an encyclopedia or interview a neighbor who is a fly fisher? In an encyclopedia you'd have to sift through much information to get to the facts you want. In an interview your questions could be answered directly as you asked them. An interview with an expert can often provide you with exactly the right amount of information on exactly the right topic.

Whom to Interview

Who is an expert? An expert usually is someone who has very precise, in-depth, and up-to-date information. More importantly, the expert probably has first-hand knowledge about a topic. Look at the topics and the list of people in the chart. People like these might have interesting information you could use in an oral report.

People to Interview	
Topic	**Source**
Local government	mayor, city council member, governor, state legislator
Scuba diving	local diving expert or instructor, equipment shop owner
Automobile engines	auto mechanic, auto designer, school shop teacher
The circulatory system	doctor, nurse, medical student, science teacher
Portrait photography	fashion photographer, portrait studio photographer
Caring for infants	parent, day-care worker, nurse, pediatrician

When you have determined that interviewing an expert will add to your report, you must decide on the kind of interview you want to set up. If the person lives far from you, you might arrange a telephone, letter, or e-mail interview. If the subject is nearby, consider an in-person interview. Whichever form you choose, be sure to keep the following things in mind during the early contacts with your subject.

Listening and Speaking

Setting Up the Interview
1. Make sure you clearly state who you are and why you are seeking the interview.
2. Tell the person if you have a deadline, but respect the fact that your interviewee may be very busy.
3. Ask the subject to suggest times for an interview.
4. Give the person the option of an in-person, letter, telephone, or e-mail interview. You can state your preference, but leave the decision to the subject of the interview.

Preparing to Interview

Before you meet with your subject, research your topic thoroughly. Try to learn all you can about the topic before the interview. This preparation will help you to think on your feet during the questioning. You will be able to ask more intelligent questions if you are familiar with the topic. You also will be able to take advantage of interesting information that your subject might reveal. If you know how a new fact fits into the whole picture, you'll be better able to use it or to discard it as irrelevant.

Also try to learn as much as you can about the person you will interview. If the person is a public figure or is in business, you might ask his or her office for biographical information. Or you might request it from the person before the interview. You should know about the person to whom you are talking. This information will help you formulate good questions. It also saves you the trouble of asking questions that can be answered in a biographical handout.

Before you conduct the interview, write out the questions you plan to ask. It helps if you have a purpose for listening in mind. Are you trying to gather specific or general information about a topic? Are you trying to solve a problem? Regardless of your purpose, try to make your questions open-ended. Don't ask questions that have a yes or no answer. Instead, encourage your subject to talk freely. A *Why?* may bring out important and interesting information. Look at these questions you might ask a marathon runner:

1. How many marathons have you run? Where did you place?
2. How do you prepare for a marathon?
3. What is your weekly running schedule?
4. What types of terrain do you run on when you are in training?
5. What kind of special equipment do you wear?
6. What kind of diet do you eat?
7. What are the three most important aspects of your training?

Conducting the Interview

Your manner during an interview should be serious and respectful, but relaxed. You will put the person you are interviewing at ease if you appear comfortable and confident. This attitude will make the interview flow smoothly. It's much more pleasant to talk in a relaxed atmosphere.

Study the journalist's questions covered in the last lesson. Remember how you used them to evaluate how well a reporter covered a story? See how many *what, who, when, where, how,* and *why* questions you can use in your interview. You'll find that *how* and *why* questions are particularly good for probing deeply into a topic.

Sometimes a person being interviewed will get side-tracked onto something that really doesn't apply to your topic. In this case, it's your job to politely but firmly lead the discussion back to the topic at hand.

Talk as little as possible yourself. Your job as an interviewer is to ask questions clearly and briefly. Then listen to the response and take notes. If the interviewee mentions something interesting that you hadn't thought about, ask some follow-up questions. You might bring out an unexpected piece of information—something that might not have been revealed otherwise. That's when an interview can get exciting.

During the interview you have two jobs to perform. You need to keep track of the questions you've prepared, so you don't forget something important. At the same time, you need to listen carefully to what the person is telling you. Be open to new information you didn't think about and that may raise new questions. You can develop this "thinking on your feet" skill by following some tips.

Tips for Interviewing

1. State your topic and the general scope of the discussion you'd like to have. This will give the person you are interviewing an idea of the boundaries that can be expected during the questioning.

2. Look at the person you're interviewing. Nothing cuts the connection between reporter and subject more quickly than the loss of eye contact. If you're conducting a telephone interview, comment briefly after each point the subject makes.

3. Be courteous at all times, even if your subject wanders away from the topic.

4. If you are unclear about anything the person says, ask a question right away. Then you can build on information you understand.

5. Follow up interesting statements quickly by asking another question. Don't wait, or you might forget the importance of the statement.

6. *Take notes.* At the end of the interview, glance over them. *If something is unclear, ask a question.*

7. Thank the person for the interview. Ask if you can call back if you have a follow-up question or if something is not clear. Review your notes thoroughly when you are alone. If you need to call the person back, do so as soon as you can.

Exercise 2

Work in pairs, and take turns playing the roles of expert and interviewer. Each interviewer should choose a topic. The interviewer's job is to ask good questions and to lead the expert back gently and politely if he or she wanders from the topic. Use one of the following topics or one of your own choosing:

- Why it's important to do well in mathematics
- How to have a great vacation in your own backyard
- The most important person in your life

26.3 Informal Speech

Someone stops you on the street and asks directions to the nearest grocery store. You talk with your friends on the way to school. You respond to a question the teacher asks in class. All of these situations call for informal speech. They are spontaneous and unrehearsed. They are among the most common speech situations.

There are other kinds of informal speech—discussions and announcements, for example. Four types of informal speech are included on the chart below. The chart describes each type and includes some hints that will help you be an effective participant in that type of speaking.

Tips on Informal Speaking		
Type	**Description**	**Hint**
Conversations	Conversations can occur at almost any time and in almost any place. Each person involved contributes and responds to the others.	Be courteous to the person speaking. Taking turns enables everyone to air his or her thoughts.
Discussions	Discussions can occur in many settings, including classrooms. Usually one person leads the discussion, and all are asked to share their thoughts in an orderly manner.	Stick closely to the topic and follow the directions of the discussion leader. Following these rules will ensure an interesting and productive discussion.
Announcements	Announcements summarize the most important information about an activity or event.	List the information you want to include before you make your announcement. Double-check it for accuracy and completeness.
Demonstrations	Demonstrations explain and show a process—how something works, for example. They are useful in many settings, including classrooms.	Number the steps in the process you will demonstrate to make sure the sequence is clear.

The purpose of all speech should be to communicate clearly. To take part in a discussion, you must be prepared and familiar with the topic the group is going to discuss. For example, to answer a question, you must have the information being asked for. In a conversation, on the other hand, you do not need to prepare in advance. You may cover many topics. Your answer to a question may very well be, "I don't know."

Another factor is attitude. Which of the following words describes how you feel when you talk to friends, family, and teachers?

shy   enthusiastic   confident   eager   uninterested

Once you've identified your attitude, you can build on your strengths. You can change whatever gets in the way of good communication. It may take practice, but it will benefit you in the end.

Making Introductions

Everyone is a newcomer at one time or another. Entering into a new situation is much easier if someone in the group knows how to make correct introductions. With practice, that someone can be you.

Keep the following points in mind when introducing two people: First, be sure you look at each person. Don't let either party feel left out. You may be introducing one person to a group of people. In this case, make eye contact with the new person and with members of the group. Also, gesture from one person to another as you make the introduction. This will help point out which person you are referring to.

State each person's full name. You might say, "Evan, I'd like to introduce you to Miguel Hernandez. Miguel, this is Evan Schmit." If there are several people in the group, you might mention first names only for people your own age. First and last names are more appropriate when introducing adults. First and last names are also best used when introducing an adult and a younger person.

Tell each person something interesting about the other. If they have something in common, share that. It will become a natural conversation starter.

Participating in a Discussion

Rules of the game exist for discussions as well. A discussion usually has a leader, whose job it is to guide the discussion and keep it on track. The leader may be appointed for the group or chosen by it. A formal discussion before an audience is a panel discussion. The panel, or group selected to participate, discusses a topic of public interest.

As a discussion becomes lively and members of the discussion group get excited about what they are saying, the discussion becomes more difficult for the leader to organize. It is important that your comments contribute to the topic.

Discussions can focus on any topic. The idea is to come together in an organized group to share ideas and draw conclusions about the subject. A discussion depends totally on the comments of those involved. Before you enter a discussion, be sure you have a thorough knowledge of your subject. That way you can be a valuable participant. Below are a few more tips on how to act responsibly in a discussion.

Tips for Taking Part in a Discussion

1. Come prepared. Review important information, and bring visual aids or research you can use to illustrate the points you want to make.

2. Be polite. Take turns speaking and listening. You're there to learn as well as to contribute.

3. Go into the discussion willing to modify your opinion. That's the best way to learn.

4. Let the discussion leader take the lead. Concentrate on your part in the discussion—expressing yourself and listening to others.

5. Make your comments brief and concise. People will pay attention to your ideas if they are well thought out and clearly presented.

6. When you state your opinions, back them up with reasons or examples. You'll be much more convincing if you do this.

7. If a member of the group says something you don't understand, ask about it. It's likely that you aren't the only one confused.

8. Use standard American English when you speak in the discussion. Standard American English should always be used in the classroom or in a formal speaking situation.

Explaining a Process

If you want to explain how to bake a cake, you must do several things. First, you should tell the type of cake the recipe is for. Next, you need to list the ingredients. Then you'll explain the steps to follow.

An explanation of almost any process has the same parts: materials needed, steps to follow, and the result. If the process is long or complicated, you may need to number the steps. Or you might simply use words such as *before, next,* and *finally* to make the sequence of steps clear.

Correct order is all-important. For example, if the steps for building a model airplane are out of sequence, the plane may be incorrectly assembled. To be sure you don't leave out a part of the process, take time to prepare well. Write your explanation in the proper order. Review your instructions to make sure you haven't left out a step or put one in the wrong place.

Making Announcements

When you're asked to make an announcement, think first about what information your listeners need. If you're planning an announcement for an activity, the important facts include the date, the time, the place, and the price of a ticket.

Next, try to determine the briefest way to deliver your information. Announcements should always be short and to-the-point. They are no-fuss pieces of information. You'll want to include just enough information to interest the audience and convey the important facts.

Below are two examples of how the same information might be conveyed. Which is the better announcement?

Example 1

Tryouts for cheerleaders are coming soon. Get in shape now! Don't miss this once-in-a-school-year opportunity!

Example 2

Tryouts for cheerleaders will be this Wednesday afternoon in the gym right after school. Wear loose clothing and plan to stay a few hours. No need to sign up—just show up Wednesday for this once-in-a-school-year opportunity!

Finally, don't forget your audience! Speak so everyone can understand you. That means you must think about who is listening. You might word an announcement one way for preschoolers and another way for their parents.

Exercise 3

Divide into small groups. Let each member of the group select one of the events listed below. Jot down information about the event, including the date, time, and place. Fold the papers and mix them together. Each group member will select a topic at random, then write a short announcement based on the information on the paper. If you need additional pieces of information, invent them. Read your announcements to the group. Discuss how helpful and effective each announcement is.

- Band tryouts
- Countries of the World Festival
- Square-dancing lessons
- Debate Club meeting

26.4   Oral Reports

What image comes to mind when you think about giving an oral report? For some students the image might be exciting; for others, a little scary. However you feel, you can make the experience more enjoyable by preparing well.

You can prepare to give an oral report in three ways. First, you must prepare the content of your report. Make sure you understand everything you will be saying about your topic. Second, you need to prepare your presentation. Practice is the key here. Finally, you need to prepare yourself mentally so that you feel good about your presentation.

Preparing the Report

Think for a few moments about the purpose of your report. Is it to inform, persuade, explain, narrate, or entertain? Perhaps you have more than one purpose. An oral report can inform, persuade, and entertain, but one purpose should be the main one.

Another important consideration is your audience. To whom will you be speaking? Students your own age? Younger people? Older people? A mixed audience? What is the best way to reach your particular audience?

When you've thought about your purpose and audience, think a little further about your topic. Is it sufficiently narrowed down? If not, can you narrow it further? A precisely defined topic is easier to research than one that is unfocused. It is also easier to write about.

Now begin your research. Read articles in newspapers, magazines, encyclopedias, and other sources. You may also want to interview an expert in the field. Take notes. Develop an outline. Check the relationship of your main ideas and supporting details.

When you feel comfortable with the amount of information you've gathered, prepare your notes for the report. You may want to write out the entire report as you'd like to deliver it. Or you may write the key ideas and phrases on note cards. You might want to note the transitions you'll use to get from one main idea to the next. The transitions will jog your memory as you speak and help you move through your report smoothly.

Practicing the Report

Practicing your report is important. Practice will help you understand and remember your main ideas and supporting details. In addition, practice will give you confidence about your presentation. You will know how you want to speak the words, make the gestures, and display any visual materials you've decided to use.

Begin practicing alone. Speak in front of a mirror. Use the voice and gestures you would use if you were in front of a live audience. Time your report as you practice so that you can adjust the length if necessary.

The more you practice, the more natural the report will sound. Practice glancing from your note cards to the audience. You don't want to read your report word for word, but you'll probably want to memorize parts of it.

When you feel comfortable with your report, ask a friend or family member to listen to your delivery. Then try giving it before more than one person.

Ask your practice audience to listen *and* watch you. You'll want feedback about both the content of the report and your presentation. If the audience thinks the content or delivery needs work, make the changes you think are necessary. Then begin your practice sessions over again. If you need work on the delivery of your report, try using the following tips.

Tips on Delivering an Oral Report

1. Make eye contact with the audience. This helps people feel involved in what you are saying.

2. Use your voice to emphasize main points. You can raise or lower it, depending upon the effect you want to achieve.

3. Use standard American English in this formal classroom speaking situation.

4. Stop a moment after you have made an important point. This stresses the point and allows people to think about what you've said.

5. Use gestures if you have practiced them.

6. If they relate to your topic, use visual aids to help your audience understand your ideas.

Presenting the Report

When it's time to deliver your report, relax. (You'll find some tips for relaxing on page 774.) Deliver your report just as you've practiced it. Speak in a clear, natural voice, and use gestures when they are appropriate.

As you speak, show that you find your information interesting. Be enthusiastic. Think of your audience as people who are there because they're interested in what you have to say. Speak to them as if they were friends. They'll respond to your positive attitude.

When you conclude your report, ask for questions. Remain in front of the audience until you have answered everyone's questions.

Exercise 4

Select a topic from the following list, or use one of your own choosing. Write how you would narrow the topic. Then write your ideas for researching it.

Share the ideas you've developed with a partner. Ask for comments and suggestions. Then look at your partner's work, and make constructive comments about how he or she narrowed the topic and planned to research it.

- The migration of the monarch butterfly
- How our Constitution provides for the election of a president
- How to navigate by compass
- Kente cloth from Ghana

26.5   Formal Speeches

Delivering a formal speech in front of a live audience is the last stage of a five-stage process. You can think of it as the reward for successfully completing the earlier steps in the process. Once you've prepared thoroughly, delivering the speech can be fun and rewarding.

> **TIME**
>
> For more about the writing process, see **TIME Facing the Blank Page,** pp. 97-107.

Preparing a Speech

You are familiar with the stages of writing a report: prewriting, drafting, revising, editing, and presenting. Formal speaking depends on a similar five-stage process. In preparing a speech, however, the editing stage becomes practicing. In effect, you edit your speech as you practice giving it. You are preparing for an audience of listeners rather than of readers.

Each step builds on the work done in the previous step. However, you may find it necessary to move back and forth during the drafting, revising, and practicing stages. For example, you might find during the practicing stage that your speech is too short or too long. To shorten it, you can back up to the revising stage or even the drafting stage to prepare a shorter version. The chart shows the process in detail.

Before you move to the practicing stage you'll want to have a speech you feel confident about. Word it in a way that will be easy to deliver.

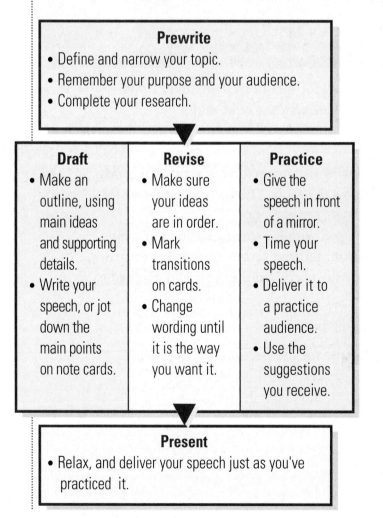

Prewrite
- Define and narrow your topic.
- Remember your purpose and your audience.
- Complete your research.

Draft
- Make an outline, using main ideas and supporting details.
- Write your speech, or jot down the main points on note cards.

Revise
- Make sure your ideas are in order.
- Mark transitions on cards.
- Change wording until it is the way you want it.

Practice
- Give the speech in front of a mirror.
- Time your speech.
- Deliver it to a practice audience.
- Use the suggestions you receive.

Present
- Relax, and deliver your speech just as you've practiced it.

Listening and Speaking

You don't want words you'll stumble over or phrases that sound awkward. If you aren't sure how to pronounce a term, look it up. If you still aren't comfortable with it, find another term that means the same thing.

Practicing a Speech

Practicing also involves several steps. When you practice your speech out loud, you want to make sure it sounds natural. The first time you practice it, just listen to the words as you speak. Listening to yourself on a tape recorder can be helpful. The rhythm of the speech should feel comfortable to you. If you don't like a phrase, rework it out loud until you come up with another way to express the idea.

The next time through, try looking in a mirror and using a few hand gestures to emphasize main points. Don't force the gestures. Try to think about what you're saying, and let your gestures develop spontaneously. Once you see where you need emphasis, make a point of practicing the gestures while speaking until they feel comfortable to you.

Finally, ask friends or relatives to listen to your delivery. Use their responses to fine-tune your speech. Below are a few more tips for practicing your speech.

Tips for Practicing a Speech

1. Each time you deliver your speech in practice, act just as if you were giving it before a live audience. Try to imagine the audience in front of you. This will help cut down on nervousness when you actually present the speech before a real audience.

2. Use standard American English as you practice your speech. This will make it easier for you to use standard American English when you actually give your speech.

3. Practice making eye contact with your imaginary audience. Let your eyes sweep slowly across the room from one side to the other, making contact with each member of the audience. Focus on talking to them, rather than on practicing your speech.

4. Make sure your gestures feel comfortable and fit with the points in the speech. Emphasize main points, or direct attention to visual aids, using gestures that are natural to you.

Listening and Speaking

Delivering a Speech

Formal speaking is like conversation. Although you are the only one talking, your audience is communicating with you. Your success depends in part on how well you can interpret and use the signals they are sending you.

Keep your mind on your speech, and read the audience's response at the same time. A good speaker does both. The best speakers add a third element: They can change what they're doing to accommodate the needs of the audience.

Tips for Relaxing
1. Take a few deep, slow breaths before you begin speaking. When you pause at important points in your speech, you can repeat the process to keep yourself relaxed.
2. When you deliver your speech, talk to people in the audience as individuals rather than to the group as a whole. This will help personalize your message and make you feel comfortable. Some speakers like to pick out and concentrate on a few friendly faces in the audience.
3. Speak in a tone that is normal for you. Speak loudly enough to be heard throughout the room, but don't shout.
4. Let your voice rise and fall naturally at key points in your speech. The idea is to sound comfortable and natural.
5. Keep alert. Don't let your thoughts wander. Focus on the content of your speech and on sharing it with your audience.

Focusing on the audience can help you feel less nervous. The charts on this page can give you some help. The one above contains some tips for relaxing. The chart below offers some suggestions for communicating with your audience.

Communicating with Your Audience	
Audience Signals	**Speaker Response**
People are yawning, stretching, or moving restlessly. They seem not to be paying attention to you.	You may have lost the attention of your audience. Try adding some enthusiasm to what you are saying.
People look confused or seem to want to ask a question.	You may have confused your audience. Try asking if there are questions.
People are sitting forward in their chairs, trying to hear you.	People may be having trouble hearing you. Speak more loudly, and note whether or not that eliminates this audience response.
People look pleased with what you are saying. They nod in agreement.	You are doing a great job. Finish your speech in the same manner.

Exercise 5

With a small group, brainstorm ways to become better listeners and create a list of common listening problems. Then agree on one or two hours of television or radio programming that all of you will watch or listen to in the next few days. Include several types of programming.

Listen to the programs your group selected. After each program write comments telling why you found the listening easy or difficult. When you meet again as a group, compare notes, and discuss kinds of programming that are easy to listen to and those that are more challenging. Discuss distractions and ways to eliminate them in order to listen more carefully to programming with which you had difficulties.

Exercise 6

1. Prepare a two-minute speech on a topic of your choice. Go through each of the steps outlined in this lesson. Then take turns delivering your speeches within small groups. Discuss and evaluate each speech. Share ideas you can all use to improve the presentation and content of your speeches. Then make revisions, and deliver the revised speeches to the class.
2. Exchange copies of speeches with someone in your group. If you have notes instead of a complete written speech, exchange note cards. Alter the speech to suit your manner of speaking, but keep the content the same. Practice delivering the new speech. Join your group, and take turns delivering your new speeches. Discuss how and why they differ from the originals.

26.6 Storytelling

For thousands of years, people from many different cultures have used storytelling as a way to pass on their history, to teach their young, to explain why things happen in nature, and to entertain. Alex Haley, a U.S. novelist and journalist, said, "I acknowledge immense debt to the griots [tribal poets] of Africa—where today it is rightly said that when a griot dies, it is as if a library has burned to the ground."

Today, in the United States, storytelling has become an art and is mostly used to entertain and delight audiences of all ages. Good story-tellers rely on their voices and words to create pictures in the minds of their listeners. Use the guidelines that follow to help you better understand the art of storytelling and then prepare a story to tell to your own audience.

Choose a story that you like and feel comfortable with. Obviously, it would be difficult to do a good job telling a story you don't like. If you choose a story that is from a culture different from your own, you should do some research about that culture to get a feeling for the people in the story. Try to find a story that is short but still interesting—one that will capture the audience's imagination.

Get to know the story. After first reading the story for pleasure, read it over and over again to familiarize yourself with the story's sentence structure, unusual phrases, action, setting, beginning and ending, and other elements. Study the story's characters. Note the way in which each one talks, acts, and thinks. Think about what particular aspect of this story you responded to and how you can relate this aspect to your readers. For example, did the story's humor appeal to you? Did a certain character touch you? Was there a particular lesson taught that is important to you?

Commit the story to memory. You don't have to memorize the whole story word for word. Rather, study the story until you think you can tell it to someone else, using some of your own words. Be sure to preserve the spirit of the story. Memorize exact words and phrases that are central to the story's meaning and that help the audience create a mental picture and put themselves in the place of the story's characters.

Practice, practice, practice. Practice telling your story to anyone who will listen. Use the following tips to help you as you practice your story.

Tips for Practicing Storytelling

❶ Adapt your story to your audience. If you know that you will be telling your story mainly to young children, make sure you adapt the vocabulary you use. You might also wish to introduce the story to an audience that is unfamiliar with it, explaining the story's origin and its relevance to your own culture today.

❷ Correct pacing of the story is very important. Some stories are meant to be told at a brisk pace, whereas others should be told in a slow, leisurely drawl. In many stories, the pace changes throughout. The story's action, sentence structure, and style of writing will give you clues to how to pace your story. In general, action sequences should be told fairly quickly, while poetic, creative passages should be told more slowly.

❸ Practice using your voice to make your story as entertaining as possible. For example, when a girl pushes open the door to an old, abandoned house, you might pause to add suspense before you continue. You might also lower the volume of your voice to a whisper and slow the pace. Decide on an appropriate voice for each character and use the same voice for each one consistently.

❹ Stay connected with the audience. To keep your listeners involved in your story, make eye contact with them frequently.

❺ Use gestures and facial expressions that you would use in everyday conversation. Don't try to dramatize every scene. Remember that you are *telling* a story, not acting it out.

Keep distractions to a minimum.   For your listeners to get the most out of your story, neither they nor you should be bothered by distractions. Close the door, turn off the radio, and close the windows so that you have the undivided attention of your listeners.

Exercise 7

Use the guidelines in this section to help you select a story and prepare to tell it. Once you think you are ready to tell the story, find a partner and tell the story to him or her. Ask your partner to evaluate your storytelling and to make suggestions for improvement. Incorporate your partner's suggestions as you rehearse again. Then tell the story to someone else and ask for feedback. Continue this process until you are confident that you are telling your story well. Once you are able to enjoy telling the story, offer to share it with your class or a younger class in your school. If your efforts are successful, you may consider telling your story to a group less familiar to you, such as listeners at your neighborhood library's storytelling hour.

UNIT 27

Viewing and Representing

 Writing Online For research tools and additional skills practice, go to **glencoe.com** and enter QuickPass code WC87703p3.

779

27.1　Interpreting Visual Messages

A recent report by the American Academy of Pediatrics stated that most young people in the United States spend more of their non-school time watching television than performing any other activity except sleeping. A study by the United States Department of Education shows that students who watch television more than ten hours a week generally get lower grades than those who watch less television.

Mass Media　Young people, far more than their parents and grandparents, are greatly influenced by **mass media**, a term that means "a form of communication that is widely available to many people." Along with television, mass media includes newspapers, magazines, radio, movies, videos, and the Internet.

Most forms of mass media contain advertisements or commercials—messages that have one purpose: to persuade people to buy a certain product. By the time of high school graduation, the typical student will have probably seen an estimated 360,000 television commercials.

The various forms of mass media will have a great influence on your life. Some forms of the media will have positive influences, enabling you to learn new skills and explore new ideas and opportunities or allowing you to relax and enjoy inspiring dramas and music. However, some forms of the media can have negative effects. If you are not careful, the media can mislead you, confuse you, and even endanger you.

As you face such challenges, the best solution is to learn how to make responsible, educated decisions about which media messages are valuable, uplifting, and truthful and which messages are harmful, unfair, or just plain silly. This unit will help you learn how to interpret, analyze, and evaluate the various forms of mass media. With these skills comes the power to enjoy the media's benefits and to protect yourself against possible negative influences.

Media and Values　All media productions—text, pictures, and even music—contain points of view about the world. No media product is neutral or value-free. Each is designed carefully to attract and appeal to a particular audience and to create specific reactions. Every form of media except radio contains visual art. Like all forms of media, each piece of visual art, whether it is a photograph, painting, cartoon, drawing, advertisement, or computer graphic, is created carefully to send a distinct visual message. If you understand how artists and photographers craft visual art to send messages, you will be able to "read" each message and evaluate its value and truthfulness.

Understanding Visual Design

The use of colors, shapes, and various types of lines makes up the *visual design* of a piece of art. The arrangement of such visual elements is called *composition*. The chart on page 782 lists some basic elements in the visual design and composition of a picture and describes how the artist or photographer might manipulate these elements to send different visual messages.

Study the photograph above. Note that the mountain is positioned at the top and is emphasized by sunlight. The viewer's eye is immediately drawn to this dominant feature. Then the eye is attracted to the curved, bright line of the waterfall, which flows into the darkened forest. The visual message of this photograph is the power of the wilderness, as represented by the dominant rocky mountain and the rushing stream.

Exercise 1

Choose a photograph in this textbook other than the two on this page. Use the Elements of Visual Design and Composition chart on the next page to interpret the visual message that is contained in the photograph you chose. Explain how positioning—as well as colors, light, and shadows—and the use of straight and curved lines work together to send the message.

Elements of Visual Design and Composition	
Element	**Possible Significance**
Lines	
Heavy, thick lines	Emphasize an object, person, or space; can suggest boldness or power
Thin lines	Can give a sense of sharpness; create a feeling of lightness and grace
Straight lines	Point in a direction or lead the eye to something else
Curved lines	Suggest motion
Gentle, wavy lines	Create calming, soothing effect
Sharp, zigzag lines	Suggest tension or energy
Vertical lines	Suggest power, status
Horizontal lines	Suggest peace, stillness
Diagonal lines	Suggest tension, action, energy
Repeating lines	Create patterns
Light	
Brightly lit areas	Draw the eye to a specific area; create a cheerful mood
Dimly lit areas or shadows	Give a sense of mystery or sadness; show a lack of emphasis
Colors	
Cool colors (blue, green, gray)	Convey a sense of calm and coolness
Warm colors (orange, yellow, red)	Convey a sense of energy and vibrancy
Bright Colors	Create a sense of warmth and joyfulness
Subdued or pastel colors	Suggest innocence or softness
Repetition of color	Can suggest a pattern or assign a value to what is portrayed
Position of subjects	
Center of picture	Suggests strength, dominance; draws attention to the subject
Top of picture	Suggests power, importance
Bottom of picture	Suggests weakness; adds contrast to images positioned in the middle or top of the picture
Space	
Large space around object	Draws attention to subject; can suggest loneliness, vastness
Small amount of space around subject	Makes subject seem very powerful

Reading a Political Cartoon

Tom Toles, the *Buffalo News* political cartoonist, drew this cartoon in 1999 as a comment on the growing world population. Note Toles's use of position and size—"Phone Booth Earth" surely dominates the page, and the curved lines emphasize that the phone booth is about to burst. What message might Toles have wanted to send by making the inside of the phone booth the most brightly lit part of the cartoon? Then note the dialogue, both in the bubble and at the bottom of the cartoon. What message might Toles have wanted to send with those words? What thoughts and feelings do the jam-packed phone booth bring to your mind? What do you think the cartoonist suggests might happen to an overcrowded planet Earth?

Exercise 2

Study the cartoon below by the *Boston Globe* political cartoonist Paul Szep, entitled "Happy New Year." Identify the visual message that he intends the cartoon to send. Then explain how his use of lines, position, repetition, space, and facial expressions extend or emphasize that message.

Understanding Film Techniques

Like a short story or novel, every motion picture and television drama or comedy tells a story. Also like written literature, films use dialogue to tell much of the story. However, films also use a variety of other narrative elements that go beyond what can be done on the written page. Directors of movies and television shows employ many of the techniques listed in the Elements of Visual Design and Composition chart on page 782 to extend or emphasize the mood or message of the film. Additionally, filmmakers can employ the following special visual techniques.

In many of his early films, movie actor Humphrey Bogart played a tough, savvy, wise-guy villain. Directors generally thought that he was neither tall enough nor handsome enough to be cast as a leading

man. The public disagreed. Therefore, as Bogart's stardom increased, directors began to cast him as a tough, savvy, wise-guy *hero*. Some of his most famous roles included Sam Spade, a private detective, and Rick, the lonely but gallant hero of *Casablanca*.

Study the movie still to the left. It is from the 1942 movie *Across the Pacific,* in which Bogart plays a clever detective who must track down enemy spies. In this scene, director John Huston has Bogart use his characteristic tough stance as he protects the character played by Mary Astor.

Note that the camera angle is low, shooting up at Bogart from the ground. Why might director John Huston have chosen this angle? Note also that Bogart is shown with full, head-on light, making him seem strong and dominant. However, his eyes are shaded by his hat, giving him a mysterious, sly look. Note which elements from the Elements of Visual Design and Composition chart are used by Huston. He has probably instructed Bogart to stand as straight as possible so that the vertical line of that stance would emphasize the character's power. Note the pattern Huston creates with lines. Contrast the parallel lines of the gun and the line painted on the ship with the suggested diagonal lines of vision of both actors. Why might Huston have carefully set up such a diagonal pattern?

What dialogue might the characters be speaking in this shot? How does Huston's visual image extend or emphasize that message? If you were on the creative staff of this movie, what type of background music would you choose for this scene in order to manipulate the audience's emotional response?

Film Techniques for Sending Visual Messages

Technique	Possible Significance
Camera angle	
High (looking down on subjects)	Often makes subject seem smaller, less important, or more at risk
Low (looking up on subjects)	Emphasizes the subject's importance or power
Straight-on (eye level)	Puts viewer on equal level with subject; can make viewer identify with subject
Camera shots	
Close-up (picture of subject's face)	Emphasizes character's facial expressions; leads viewer to identify with him or her
Long shot (wide view, showing character within larger setting)	Shows relationship between character and setting
Lighting	
High, bright lighting	Creates cheerful, optimistic tone
Low, shadowy lighting	Creates gloomy, mysterious tone
Light from above	Makes subject seem to glow with power or strength
Light from below	Increases audience tension
Editing	
Quick transitions between frames	Quickens pace; increases suspense or excitement
Slow dissolve or fade out	Indicates change in perspective or time; may introduce a flashback or dream sequence
Special effects	
Slow motion	Emphasizes movement and heightens drama
Blurred motion	Suggests speed, confusion, or a dream-like state
Background music	Manipulates audience's emotional response

Exercise 3

Study the color still, or movie photo, on page 784. Identify the visual message that the filmmakers intend to send to viewers. Then, using the Elements of Visual Design and Composition chart on page 782 and the Film Techniques for Sending Visual Messages chart on this page, explain what techniques the filmmakers use to extend and emphasize the message.

27.2 Analyzing Media Messages

Photographs, movies, and television programs often seem realistic; they show scenes, characters, actions, and conflicts that could easily happen in real life. Some media presentations *are* realistic. However, all media messages are constructed carefully, to emphasize a particular point of view. Even a factual film documentary or a public service message on a topic such as health care or environmental protection uses carefully chosen colors, lines, and camera angles to persuade the viewer to accept and agree with a certain point of view.

The artist, photographer, or director makes many decisions about what pictures and information to include, what camera angles will prove most effective, and what information should *not* be included. Follow three steps to unravel the sometimes confusing messages sent by the media.

1. Identify the visual message that an artist, photographer, cartoonist, or film director is sending.
2. Spot the techniques of design, composition, and film that were used to extend and emphasize that message.
3. Decide whether you agree or disagree with that message.

Key Questions for Analyzing Media

To analyze a media message, ask yourself these Key Questions:

- What message is this photo (or drawing, cartoon, movie, television show, music video) trying to send me?

- How did the artist or photographer use elements of visual design and composition and/or film techniques to emphasize the message and to persuade the audience to accept and agree with the message?

- What do I already know about this subject?

- How can I use what I already know to judge whether this message is

  ❏ fair or unfair
  ❏ based on reality or fantasy
  ❏ based on facts or opinions

- What sources might I use to find other viewpoints on this subject that I can trust?

  ❏ parent, teacher, or other trusted adult
  ❏ reliable books or other reference sources
  ❏ other _____.

Then, on the basis of your answers to the questions and other trusted viewpoints, make a decision about the visual message. Make sure that in your own mind you can support that decision with well-thought-out reasons.

  ❏ I agree with the visual message because _____.
  ❏ I disagree with the visual message because _____.

Exercise 4

Practice the Key Questions by analyzing one of the political cartoons shown on page 783. Write answers to the questions. Compare your findings, and your ultimate decision, with those of your teacher and classmates.

Exercise 5

Watch carefully as your teacher plays a scene or two from a popular movie or television show and then shows a popular music video. Use the Key Questions for Analyzing Media to have a class discussion analyzing and evaluating the visual messages you received from each segment or video you saw.

Exercise 6

Choose a favorite movie, television show, or music video. Use the Key Questions to analyze and evaluate the visual messages. Write a brief report on your findings and conclusions.

Analyzing Advertisements and Commercials

You can also use the Key Questions to analyze and evaluate the media messages contained in advertisements appearing in newspapers, magazines, and Web sites, as well as on television commercials.

More than any other form of media, advertisements and commercials have one goal: *to persuade the viewer to buy the product or service being advertised.* To accomplish that goal, advertisers often use techniques listed in the Elements of Visual Design and Composition chart on page 782, and the Film Techniques for Sending Visual Messages chart on page 785. Additionally, they often use one or more of the following advertising techniques.

Common Advertising Techniques

Element	Description	Example
"Jump on the **bandwagon** and join in the fun!"	using visual images or carefully chosen words to show that "all popular, attractive, well-liked people" use this product	An advertisement for a certain brand of clothing shows attractive, smiling people enjoying each other's company as they wear that brand of clothing.
"Be like your favorite **celebrity!**"	showing a popular star of movies or television, a famous athlete, or a leading musical performer using the product	An advertisement for a certain shampoo or other cosmetic shows a popular television or movie star who claims that he or she uses that product.
"Use this for **incredible results!**"	using oils, dyes, special lighting, or other "tricks" to make the product results "too good to be true"	An advertisement for jeans uses make-up, special lighting, air-brush photography, or other special effects to make a model look excessively slim and gorgeous while wearing that brand of jeans.
"**Leading experts** are convinced that you should use this product."	using actors to pretend that they are doctors, dentists, and other experts	In an advertisement for a headache medicine, an actor portrays a doctor who recommends using the product.
"**Feel guilty or foolish** if you don't buy this important product."	manipulating scientific terms, statistics, or other data to convince viewers that using another product would be foolish or wasteful	An advertisement for a certain brand of computer suggests that using any other brand will make you less efficient and successful.
Be smart, rich, and successful!	using persuasive language and visual images to make people feel that the "elite" (rich, powerful, and successful people) already use this product	An advertisement for a certain car shows stylish, successful people driving to an exclusive restaurant or golf club.
Enjoy romance!	using persuasive language and visual images to make people feel that using this product will bring them excitement or romance	A fragrance advertisement shows two people looking fondly at each other.

Although commercials and advertisements often contain a few convincing facts, those facts are surrounded by persuasive words and often unrealistic claims. Don't be fooled by the glossy images and exuberant proclamations of advertisements. Use a version of the Key Questions to "cut through" the glitter and make informed, wise decisions about which products to buy. As an example, examine the model of an advertisement on this page.

In time, he may forget whether it rained or not that magic night. In time, he may forget what song the band was playing when he caught your eye. What he'll never forget will be the dazzle in your eyes, the lightness in your step.

Dazzle.
Shine.
Be unforgettable.
Choose clothes by L'Essence.

Exercise 7

Use the Key Questions for Analyzing Media to analyze and evaluate the above advertisement. Discuss your findings with classmates.

Exercise 8

Work with a group to make a collage of advertisements that appear in popular magazines. Use labels and captions to point out the "tricks" that the advertisers used to persuade people to buy the products. Display your poster in class. Discuss your findings with classmates.

Exercise 9

Watch carefully as your teacher plays a video clip of one or more television commercials. Then work as a class to use the Key Questions for Analyzing Media Messages to identify, analyze, and evaluate the message or messages you have just seen.

Another way to increase your understanding of media messages is to produce your own media messages, applying the techniques that artists, filmmakers, and advertisers use. This section will help you to create two types of media messages: a political cartoon and a scene from a television program.

Creating a Political Cartoon

Political cartoonists often use one or more of the following techniques to send a visual message about a current issue or event. Although political cartoons use humor to get their points across, there is virtually always a serious issue behind the cartoon.

Elements of Humor Often Used by Cartoonists

- **Exaggeration:** Drawing something bigger or greater than it would normally be, causing it to have larger-than-life effects on other objects or people

  Example: Tom Toles shows an enormous "Phone Booth Earth" filled with very tiny people.

- **Irony:** Providing an outcome that is completely unexpected or unusual

  Example: Instead of continuing the celebration, Paul Szep's New Year's celebrant went right back to his dull, disinterested pose as soon as midnight passed.

- **Satire:** Poking fun at a person, event, or situation

  Example: A cartoon about a politician who voted against an environmental proposal might show the politician snarling as he frantically chops down a forest of trees.

Satire is perhaps the most common humorous element in political cartoons. Each day political cartoonists poke fun at politicians, news events, or situations that they find amusing. This type of cartoon often carries the strongest visual message because the purpose is not only to create humor but to send a message of criticism about a person, event, or situation.

Tips for Creating a Cartoon

❶ **Brainstorm.** Think about issues, events, and situations at school and in the local and national news, as well as global issues such as the environment or world peace. Concentrate on topics that you would enjoy poking fun at through exaggeration, irony, and satire. You might select a rule or a law that you disagree with, a politician or other public figure whose opinions are contrary to your own, or a serious issue or situation on which you'd like to make a strong statement. Jot down several ideas and then pick one idea to develop into a political cartoon.

❷ **Identify your purpose and message.** What underlying message do you want your cartoon to express? What point of view do you intend to get across through humor? Summarize your point of view in a sentence or two. Keep your point of view in mind as you draw.

❸ **Identify your audience.** To what specific group do you want to focus your message—classmates, all students at your school, members of a particular team or club, neighbors, or family members? Think about what your specific audience already knows and thinks about your topic. What other information might your audience need to know in order to understand your humorous message? Make sure that you somehow include that information in your cartoon.

❹ **Decide whether to use words.** Often the best cartoons use the picture to show, rather than words to tell, the message to the viewer. Will your message be clear from your picture alone, or do you need a caption to make your message precisely clear? Should the characters be labeled so that their identity is clear? Should they speak through speech balloons in order to make the meaning clear? Experiment using words and omitting words until you are satisfied that your message is clear.

❺ **Make layout sketches.** On scrap paper, draw several versions of the cartoon. Refer to the Elements of Visual Design and Composition chart on page 782 for ideas about such elements as lines, colors, positions, and space.

(continued)

Viewing and Representing

❻ Make your final copy. When you are satisfied with your sketches and your decision of whether to include words in your cartoon, make a final copy. If possible, use black felt markers of various thicknesses to give your political cartoon a professional, crisp "newspaper" look.

❼ Publish your cartoon. Share your cartoon with your selected audience. You might publish it in the school newspaper or display it where it will catch the attention of your intended audience. Ask for feedback. Find out if your viewers understood and agreed with your message.

Exercise 10

Use the Tips for Creating a Cartoon to send an effective, humorous media message by creating a political cartoon.

Creating a Scene from a Television Drama

The production of a television program requires the skills and cooperation of a group of people. Group members take on one or more roles, based on their skills and interests. By pooling talents, group members can create a production that one member of the team could not manage alone. Follow these tips to create an effective scene from a television drama. On film, your scene should run for about ten minutes.

Tips for Creating a Television Drama

❶ Build a production team. Have each member of your group commit to one or more of the following roles:

- **Director** – leads the group, overseeing the work of all team members and supervising the filming

- **Source Advisor** – works with the scriptwriter to adapt a published book or short story into a television format

- **Scriptwriter** – writes and revises the script on the basis of input and suggestions from the Source Advisor and Director

- **Organizer and layout expert** – creates a "storyboard," a series of simple sketches that shows each step in the scene. The storyboard outlines the format of the scene from beginning to end. The director, actors, camera operator, and music arranger follow this plan during the filming

- **Set and Props Captain** – works with the director, scriptwriter, and layout expert to gather or make all elements of the scenery and props; has all sets and props in place prior to the filming

- **Actors** – follow the director's guidance to speak the dialogue and act out the scene

- **Lighting expert** – follows the director's plan for creating the proper lighting during the filming

- **Video operator** – videotapes the show

- **Music arranger** – works with the director to choose any background music that may be used; follows the director's cue to start the music at the appropriate time during the filming

❷ **Find your source.** Work together with your group to discuss books and short stories that might provide the source for your television scene. Keep in mind your time limitations. You have only ten minutes of film in which to portray one scene. Keep in mind your set limitations. Avoid scenes that will require extensive scenery or props—or extensive imagination on the part of your viewers!

❸ **Work cooperatively to plan the scene.** Hold a team meeting to begin the planning process. Make suggestions to the director regarding the elements of visual design and film techniques he or she might use. Then work independently to plan and prepare your assigned part of the production. Come together to go over and revise ideas until everyone is satisfied.

❹ **Rehearse.** Do several run-throughs of the scene before actually taping it. At this point, the director should be in charge, planning the camera shots and angles, the lighting, the movements and positions of the actors, and the voice and music cues.

(continued)

❺ Shoot! Tape the scene, following the plan that you perfected during rehearsals. Don't get upset if mistakes occur—they happen in real television and movie studios too! Reshoot if necessary.

❻ Present your scene. Hold a film festival at which your group joins other groups in presenting your films. After each performance, pause for feedback and discussion. Which camera angles, lighting, dialogue, and visual details seemed most effective in sending media messages? Why?

Exercise 11

With a group, use the Tips for Creating a Television Drama to create a dramatic television scene.

UNIT 28 Electronic Resources

28.1 Computers and the Internet

For students whose schools boast computer labs or classroom computers, or for those whose families compete for time on a personal computer at home, the beginnings of the computer age may seem like ancient history. It wasn't all that long ago, and we've come a long way since then. The first operational computers—named Eniac and Univac—were developed in the 1940s and occupied enormous amounts of space. Eniac was more than six feet high and twenty-six yards long! Users required training in a special computer language to access the databases of these machines.

Today's computers are so compact that they are portable and so simple to operate that they can be used by young children. Even computers that respond to the sound of the human voice are now on the market. One of the most helpful resources made available through computers is the Internet. The **Internet** is an electronic connection to a huge fund of information and general data. It uses telephone lines, cable lines, and satellites to link computers all over the world. Among the computer terms that have become a part of our vocabulary are *cyberspace, surfing the Web, googling* and *browsing.*

What we generally refer to as the "Internet" is the part of the Internet called the **World Wide Web**. The World Wide Web is one of the best ways to explore the Internet. The Web, as it is often called, was designed to make it easy to allow millions of computers to exchange data that include text, video, graphics, animation, and sound. You can consult experts in specialized fields, find information in a variety of encyclopedias, listen to radio programs, and find late-breaking news from all over the world on the Web. You can use the Web to communicate with students in other cities, other states, and even other countries. If you don't own a computer, you can access the Internet at a school computer lab or a public library. Many public libraries now have Internet terminals available to their patrons.

Exercise 1

Working in a small group, list the different ways in which you and your family use computers. Then predict how you will use the Internet in your daily life in the next year and what uses the Internet will have in ten years. Finally, predict how your children will use the Internet when they are your age. Compare your predictions with those of others in your class.

28.2   Getting on the Internet

The three basic things you need to access the Internet are a computer, a modem, and an Internet service provider. A **modem** is a device that allows a computer to communicate and share information with other computers over telephone or cable lines. An **Internet service provider**, or ISP, provides a service (for a fee) that allows your computer to connect to the Internet. You can also access the Internet by using an online service, such as America Online (AOL), Earthlink, Microsoft Network (MSN), or NetZero. Such a service lets you access the Internet as well as its own private services. For example, America Online users can use private chat rooms and other exclusive features.

Browsers

To display the contents of a Web site, your computer must have a browser. A **browser** is a software program that displays Web pages as text, graphics, pictures, and video on your computer. Some of the best-known browsers are Microsoft Internet Explorer, Mozilla Firefox, Safari, Opera, and Netscape Navigator. If your computer does not already have a browser installed, your service provider should be able to provide you with one.

Once you have a browser, software programs called plug-ins will allow you to use your browser to play sounds or display movies from a Web site. Examples of plug-ins include RealAudio, which allows you to listen to recorded music and radio broadcasts, and RealVideo, Quicktime, and Flash, which show movies.

Internet Addresses

The World Wide Web is made up of millions of Web sites. A **Web site** is a page, or collection of pages, that have been put together by a person, a company, or an organization such as a university. A Web site may include photos, artwork, sound, and movies in addition to text. A **Webmaster** is the person in charge of building and maintaining a Web site.

To get to a particular Web site, you need to know its address. Every Web site on the Internet has a unique address, or **URL**. URL stands for Uniform Resource Locator. No two Web sites can have the same URL.

As an Internet user, you may want to keep track of some Web sites that you visit. URLs can often be long and difficult to remember. You can keep a record of them by making a bookmark of them or by naming the sites as "favorites." This function lets you keep a list of the URLs of your favorite sites so that you don't have to remember them. To access a site, just pull down the bookmark or favorites menu and click on the site's name.

As you add to your list of bookmarks/favorites, you may want to organize them into folders for categories such as search engines, reference sources, and news.

Hyperlinks

You may notice as you begin to investigate various Web sites that some words or phrases are underlined or are in a different color from the rest of the text. These words are called hypertext links, or hyperlinks. A **hyperlink** is text or a graphic that, when clicked on, takes you to a related Web site or a new page in the site you are on. Sometimes it may be difficult to find a hyperlink on a Web page, especially if it is a photo. If you are not sure whether the text or graphic is a hyperlink, drag the arrow over it. If the arrow changes to a pointing finger, you've found a hyperlink.

Using a Search Engine

One way to find information on the Web is to type in the URL for a specific site. But often you do not know exactly where on the Web you might find the information. How do you find Web sites that will give you the specific information you are looking for? The fastest way is to start with a search engine. A **search engine** lets you look for information on the Web by searching for keywords. A **keyword** is a word or phrase that describes your topic. For example, if you wanted information about the early years of the National Football League, you might try *NFL* and *history* as keywords.

Choosing keywords carefully can help you get better results. Use phrases in quotation marks and combine terms (using a + sign) to narrow your search. If your keyword is too general, try adding additional terms that will help find the information you are looking for. For example, if the keyword *dog* is too general, try searching for *dog* + *"golden retriever"* + *training* to help you find information about training a golden retriever.

Using the commands AND, OR, and NOT can also help narrow your searches. These three words are the basis of **Boolean logic**. If you are searching for Web pages that contain information about three types of birds—cardinals, blue jays, and parrots—you would use the Boolean command AND to link those keywords (cardinals AND "blue jays" AND parrots). The search engine will then suggest only sites that use all three terms. Note the use of quotation marks around the two-word name.

When searching for terms with different spellings, like *theater* and *theatre*, link them with the Boolean command OR (theater OR theatre). Using OR between the words will lead you to Web sites with either spelling. To find Web sites that feature information about dogs other than golden retrievers, you would use NOT in combination with AND to narrow the search (dogs AND NOT "golden retriever").

Metasearch engines, such as Dogpile and Metacrawler, allow you to submit a keyword to several search engines at the same time. You will not get as many results as you would if you were using a specific search engine. However, you are likely to get the most relevant and useful information from each engine that the metasearch engine searches—provided your keywords were well chosen.

If you haven't narrowed your search to a specific topic, you can start with a subject directory. A **subject directory** lists general topics, such as arts and humanities, science, education, entertainment, sports, and health. After you select a broad topic, the directory will offer a list of possible subtopics from which to choose. Click on a subtopic and you'll get a group of more specific topics. Most subject directories also offer a search function.

As you use search engines, remember that you should always "surf the Web" with a purpose. Spending time exploring search engines and Web sites will give you an idea of the kinds of things available on the Internet. When you find something that could be of value later, print a page from the Web site as a reminder of what is there. File the sheet in a binder that you can refer back to or share with other students when you are looking for specific information.

The chart that follows lists some search engines and subject directories that will help you get around the Internet more quickly and efficiently.

Search Engines and Subject Directories		
Name	**Type**	**URL**
Alta Vista	search engine	http://www.altavista.com
Ask	search engine	http://www.ask.com
Excite	search engine	http://www.excite.com
Go	search engine	http://www.go.com
HotBot	search engine	http://www.hotbot.com
Lycos	search engine	http://www.lycos.com
The Mining Company	subject directory	http://www.miningco.com
Yahoo!	subject directory	http://www.yahoo.com

Exercise 2

Using a search engine or a subject directory to locate appropriate Web sites, find the answers to the following questions.

1. Where is Richard Nixon's dog, Checkers, buried?
2. What role did actress Suzy Amis play in the movie *Titanic*?
3. What year was the Beatles' album *Abbey Road* released?
4. Where is the National Inventors Hall of Fame located?
5. How many people attended the first World Series game in 1903?
6. What was Lewis Carroll's given name?
7. Where was Jesse Hilton Stuart born?
8. Name two books written by Japanese author Yoko Kawashima Watkins.
9. What is the Statue of Liberty's complete name?
10. What is the medical name for Lou Gehrig's disease?

Exercise 3

Search for a subject with a single search engine. Then search for the same subject on a metasearch engine. Which engine provided the most results? Which provided the most helpful links?

Exercise 4

As a class, create five subject folders under the bookmark or favorites option of your browser. Bookmark at least five sites in each of the folders. Then create a directory for the classroom that lists the subject headings and the Web site addresses that provide useful information for those headings.

28.3 Evaluating Internet Sources

As you search the Internet and discover new Web sites, remember that anyone can create a Web site. What that means is that you cannot always be sure that the Web site information is correct. Newspapers, magazines, and books are reviewed by editors, but the Internet is a free-for-all. People and organizations who post information on the Internet are not required to follow any specific guidelines or rules. Therefore, it is your responsibility to determine what information is useful to you, whether that information is accurate, and how current the information is.

You'll want to make sure the sources you use in a presentation or research paper are reliable. How can you be sure? One way is to find out who owns the Web site or who created it. For instance, if you are looking for the batting average of a baseball player on the New York Yankees, you could probably rely on the official Yankees Web site to be accurate. However, if you find the data on a personal Web site created by a baseball fan, you may want to find a second source to back up the information.

When evaluating a Web site, ask these questions:

- What person, organization, or company is responsible for the Web site?
- When was the site last updated?
- Can the information presented there be verified?
- Does the site refer to other reliable sources for similar or related information?
- Does the site's text contain spelling mistakes, incorrect grammar, and typographical errors that make you suspicious about the reliability of the information?

Electronic Resources

Citing Sources

Just as you are expected to document the print sources you use when writing a report or giving a presentation, you are also expected to document information from the Internet. Sometimes Web sites disappear or change location, so if you do pull information from the Internet, you should always provide the URL, the title, and information about the author. You should also include the date that the material was available at that Web site and provide a printout of the information.

Works Cited

"Olympic and Titanic: Maiden Voyage Mysteries." <u>Encyclopedia Titanica</u>. 29 April 2007

<http://www.encyclopedia-titanica.orgmaiden_voyage_mysteries.html>.

"Titanic." <u>Encyclopaedia</u> <u>Britannica</u> <u>Online</u>. 20 August 2007

<http://www.search.eb.com/eb/article-9072642>.

Exercise 5

Working with a small group of classmates, create a checklist to use for evaluating Web sites. Include the basic information in your checklist (name of site, URL, etc.).

- Develop a scale by which to rank Web sites.

- Make copies of your checklist to pass out to other students in the class.

- Choose five different Web sites, and ask students to use your checklist to evaluate each of them.

- Use the results to present a brief summary of the five Web sites.

Troubleshooting Guide

As you work on the Web, you may need help in dealing with possible problems.

Here are some error messages that you might see as you spend time on the Web. They are followed by their possible causes and some suggestions for eliminating the errors.

Message:　Unable to connect to server. The server may be down. Try connecting again later.

Possible Causes:　The server is having technical problems. The site is being updated or is not communicating properly with your browser.

Suggestion:　It usually helps if you try again in a few minutes; however, it could be a few days before the server is working properly.

Message:　Unable to locate the server: www.server.com. The server does not have a DNS (Domain Name System) entry. Check the server name in the URL and try again.

Possible Causes:　You have typed in the URL incorrectly, or the site no longer exists.

Suggestion:　Be sure you have entered the URL correctly—check for proper capitalization and punctuation. If you have entered it correctly, try using a search engine to find the site. Keep in mind, though, the possibility that the site may have been abandoned.

Message:　File Not Found: The requested URL was not found on this server.

Possible Causes:　You have reached the server, but that particular file no longer exists or you have entered the path or filename incorrectly.

Suggestion:　Check the URL again. If you have entered it correctly, try searching for the page from the server's home page.

Message: Network connection refused by the server. There was no response.

Possible Causes: You have reached the server, but it is too busy (too many other people are trying to access it) or temporarily shut down.

Suggestion: Try to access the site later.

Message: Connection timed out.

Possible Causes: Your browser attempted to contact the host, but the host took too long to reply.

Suggestion: Try to access the site later.

Message: Access denied. You do not have permission to open this item.

Possible Causes: The URL has moved, the Webmaster no longer allows public access to the site, or you have been denied access to the site.

Suggestion: Contact the Webmaster to verify the URL or try the site again in a few days. Sometimes there is nothing you can do if access has been denied. Many colleges, for example, allow access to parts of their sites only to faculty and registered students.

Message: You do not have the proper plug-in installed to view this content.

Possible Causes: You have attempted to access content that your Web browser is not equipped to view.

Suggestion: A Web site that requires the plug-in will usually provide instructions for downloading and installing the plug-in. Before you download and install the plug-in, evaluate the reliability of these instructions. Some of the popular plug-ins are Flash player, Quicktime, RealPlayer, and Windows Media Player.

28.4 | Using Other Internet Features: E-mail

A popular feature of the Internet is electronic mail, or **e-mail.** E-mail programs allow you to receive, send, and forward e-mail messages. Millions of Americans send or receive e-mail every day. With the click of a button, you can send a message to anyone in the world. A feature called attachments, available with most e-mail software, lets you attach other files to the e-mail. You can send someone pictures of yourself, send a sound clip of a piece of music to a friend, or send a story you have written to a Web site that accepts and publishes submissions from young writers.

To send e-mail, you need an e-mail address. Like Web site addresses, e-mail addresses are unique. No two people can have the same e-mail address. Your Internet service provider will provide you with an e-mail address. You can also use another service, such as Gmail (Google) and Yahoo!, to provide you with an e-mail account.

On many e-mail programs, you can store frequently used e-mail addresses in an address book. Then, when you want to send a message to a person whose address is in your address book, all you have to do is begin typing his or her name and the application "autofills" the individual's address. You can also store additional information, such as the person's street address, birthday, and phone number, in your address book.

Just as you can send an e-mail message to anyone in the world, anyone in the world can send an e-mail message to you. Sometimes you will receive junk e-mail, or **spam.** It is similar to the junk mail your family receives at home. Advertisements are the main form of spam, and sometimes this kind of e-mail can be offensive. E-mail can contain software viruses in the form of attachments that can be harmful to your computer. If you receive an e-mail from someone whose e-mail address you do not recognize, show it to an adult and do not write back unless the adult gives you permission. Some people send links to Web sites through e-mail. If you receive a message with a link to a Web site, show it to an adult before clicking on the link.

E-mail Etiquette

When sending e-mail, follow the rules of e-mail etiquette.

- Use the subject line wisely. Be as brief as you can, but let the recipient know what your message is about.
- Use appropriate capitalization. Using all capital letters is considered SHOUTING.
- Avoid sending unfriendly e-mail. Sending an unfriendly e-mail message is called "flaming."
- Check your message for correct spelling.
- Consider including your name and contact information at the end of your message. This is typically referred to as a signature.
- Be careful when using humor or sarcasm. It can be difficult to indicate emotion in print. Use emoticons if you want to show emotion. The term "emoticons" ismade up of the words *emotion* and *icons*. They are little faces made by the characters on a keyboard—for example:

:-) (a smile)	;-) (a wink)
:-((a frown)	:-D (laughing)

- Keep messages short and to the point.
- Remember that good behavior on the Internet is no different from good behavior in face-to-face situations. Treat others as you would like them to treat you.

Viruses and Security

A **virus** is a computer program that invades your computer by means of a normal program or message and may damage your system. A virus may be spread by e-mail, but more often it occurs when you download a software program and run it on your computer. All computers that are connected to the Internet should have virus-protection software. You can obtain such software from your service provider or your local computer store, or you can even download utility programs from the Internet.

A **hacker** is a computer criminal who may steal valuable data from your computer. A hacker may "tap" into your computer from another location and read through all of your program files. That is why it is important to choose your password carefully. A password for e-mail or other accounts should be random and meaningless, yet easy to remember. Don't tell anyone your password. If you must write it down to remember it, don't leave it near a computer. Most programs that require a password will allow you to change your password if you think somebody might know it. If you do think somebody has your password, let an adult know.

Message Boards and Mailing Lists

A **message board**, also known as a bulletin board, is a place on a Web site where people with similar interests can post and read messages on a specific topic. Message boards are found on certain Web sites and commercial online services, such as America Online. Anyone can post messages on a message board, but the Web site generally asks a user to register first with a full name and an e-mail address. As you surf the Web, look for Web sites that have message boards. If you have a comment or question about a Web site, post your message on its message board. You can use message boards on certain Web sites to post reviews of books, CDs, and movies.

If there is a particular subject that you need to research, you might want to consider subscribing to a **mailing list** concerned with your topic. A mailing list is like a bulletin board on which you exchange information through e-mail. Type "mailing list" into a search engine along with your topic of interest, such as "hockey" or "astronomy." Choose a search result that interests you. You may want to be specific when choosing a topic. For example, instead of typing "hockey," you could type "Chicago Blackhawks." Once you have found a mailing list that interests you, follow the directions to subscribe to the list. You can cancel your subscription to a mailing list at any time.

Exercise 6

Find a Web site that allows you to post reviews of books, movies, or CDs. Choose a book, movie, or CD that you have a strong opinion about and review it. Print the Web page that lists your review and share it with the rest of the class.

Exercise 7

With the help of your teacher, select a class at an elementary school to trade e-mail with. Ask the younger students to send you any questions they might have about the Internet or e-mail. Work together, doing research if necessary, to answer the questions and send them back to the students. As a class, discuss the responses to the questions.

In your search for information, you may use other sources of electronic information besides the Internet. A computer can help you access a wide variety of information from CDs, DVDs, CD-Rs, and CD-RWs. CD-R stands for "compact disc recordable," and CD-RW stands for "compact disc rewritable."

CDs

CD recordables and CD rewriteables (CD-R and CD-RW) look like audio compact discs, but they store more than just audio information. Once data has been written onto a CD, it cannot be removed or changed; it can be read only by the computer. CDs can store text, graphics, and video files.

Because CDs can store large amounts of information, many dictionaries, encyclopedias, and other reference works are stored on them. You can use CDs to read text and look at pictures. You can also use them to view video and audio files of historic events. To use a CD, your computer must have a CD drive. Such drives are standard on most computers.

DVDs

A **DVD**, or digital video disc, can store up to six times the data of a CD on the same surface area. Dual-layer DVDs record on both sides of the disc, thus doubling the storage capacity of a standard DVD. Similar in size and shape to a CD, a DVD can hold enough information for a full-length movie. Like a VCR, a DVD player can be used to watch movies, and like a CD, a DVD requires a special drive on the computer. Some computers now come equipped with DVD drives. Although a DVD drive can play CDs, a CD drive cannot play DVDs.

Removable Storage

Your computer uses a built-in hard drive that stores information. All computers also include a drive for removable discs that can increase your storage capacity. You can insert a removable disc into another computer and transfer files to it. These removable discs can also be used to send information to someone else or to store files as a backup in case your hard drive crashes and you lose the information there.

The average computer user uses CDs or flash drives to store information, although most software is now being distributed on CDs or DVDs. As more people get more involved in multimedia, they need storage devices that can hold the larger multimedia files. Flash drives are removable, rewritable devices. Small and lightweight, most are about the size of a pack of gum. They are also convenient and portable and can be carried in your pocket, on a key fob, or on a lanyard around your neck. These devices are popular with those who use more than one PC and need to move personal data or work files from one place to the other. Many of these devices can hold more than a CD.

External writable CD and DVD drives, also called burners, make it possible to record music or data from a computer or other CD or DVD. These drives are standard equipment with new PCs. Because of the widespread practice of burning CDs and DVDs, laws against illegal copying of music and movies are being enforced.

Exercise 8

A CD incorporates many different elements (text, audio, graphics, video). Work in a small group to select a subject that could be presented on a CD. Use a library, the Internet, or other resources to find information that you could include on your CD.

For the audio portion of your CD, find audiocassettes or CDs that could provide music or spoken word segments. For the visual portion, make drawings of what you would include. If possible, use a video camera to record images to illustrate your subject. After you have compiled all the elements, prepare an audio and visual presentation similar to one that you would find on a CD and present it to the class.

WRITING AND LANGUAGE GLOSSARY

This glossary will help you quickly find definitions used in writing and grammar.

A

Adjective. A word that modifies, or describes, a noun or a pronoun. An adjective may tell *what kind, which one, how many, or how much.*

> The **comparative degree** of an adjective compares two people, places, things, or ideas. (*worse, sadder*)
> The **superlative degree** of an adjective compares more than two people, places, things, or ideas. (*worst, saddest*)
> A **possessive adjective** is a possessive noun or pronoun used before a noun. (*John's, my*)
> A **predicate adjective** always follows a linking verb. It modifies the subject of the sentence.
> A **proper adjective** is formed from a proper noun. It always begins with a capital letter.
> A **demonstrative adjective** is the word *this, that, these,* or *those* used before a noun.

Adjective clause. A dependent clause that modifies a noun or pronoun.

Adverb. A word that modifies a verb, an adjective, or another adverb. Adverbs may tell *how, when, where, in what manner,* and *how often.*

> Some adverbs have different forms to indicate **comparative** and **superlative degrees.** (*loud, louder, loudest; sweetly, more sweetly, most sweetly*)

Adverb clause. A dependent clause that modifies a verb, an adjective, or an adverb.

Allusion. A reference in a piece of writing to a well-known character, place, or situation from a work of literature, music, or art or from history.

Analysis. The act of breaking down a subject into separate parts to determine its meaning.

Anecdote. A short story or incident usually presented as part of a longer narrative.

Antecedent. *See* Pronoun.

Appositive. A noun placed next to another noun to identify it or add information about it. (My basketball coach, *Ms. Lopes,* called for a time out.)

Argument. A statement, reason, or fact for or against a point; a piece of writing intended to persuade.

Article. The adjectives *a, an,* and *the. A* and *an* are **indefinite articles.** They refer to any one item of a group. *The* is a **definite article.** It indicates that the noun it precedes is a specific person, place, or thing.

Audience. The person(s) who reads or listens to what the writer or speaker says.

B

Base form. *See* Verb tense.

Bias. A tendency to think a certain way. Bias may affect the way a writer or speaker presents his or her ideas.

Bibliography. A list of the books, articles, and other sources used as reference sources in a research paper.

Body. The central part of a composition that communicates and explains the main idea identified in the introduction.

Bookmarks/favorites. The feature on many Web browsers that allows the user to save addresses of Internet sites so that the sites can be accessed quickly.

Brainstorming. A group activity in which people generate as many ideas as possible without stopping to judge them.

C

Case. The form of a noun or pronoun that is determined by its use in a sentence. A noun or pronoun is in the **nominative case** when it is used as a subject, in the **objective case** when it is used as an object, and in the **possessive case** when it is used to show possession.

Cause-and-effect chain. A series of events in which one cause leads to an effect that in turn leads to another effect, and so on.

Characterization. The methods a writer uses to develop the personality of the character. A writer may make direct statements about a character's personality or reveal it through the character's words and actions or through what other characters think and say about the character.

Chronological order. The arrangement of details according to when events or actions take place.

Clarity. The quality of a piece of writing that makes it easy to understand.

Clause. A group of words that has a subject and a predicate and that is used as part of a sentence.

> An **independent clause,** also called a **main clause,** has a subject and a predicate and can stand alone as a sentence.

> A **dependent clause,** also called a **subordinate clause,** has a subject and a predicate, but it makes sense only when attached to a main clause.

Cliché. An overused expression. (*white as snow*)

Clustering. The grouping together of related items as a way of organizing information.

Coherence. A quality of logical connection between the parts of a paragraph or composition.

Cohesive writing. A type of writing in which sentences and paragraphs are logically connected to one another.

Collaboration. The process of working with others on writing or other projects.

Colloquialism. A casual, colorful expression used in everyday conversation.

Comparative degree. *See* Adjective; Adverb.

Comparison-and-contrast organization. A way of organizing ideas by illustrating their similarities and differences.

Complement. A word or phrase that completes the meaning of a verb. Three kinds of complements are **direct objects, indirect objects,** and **subject complements.**

Conceptual map. A graphic device that develops a central concept by surrounding it with examples or related ideas in a weblike arrangement.

Conclusion. A restatement or summing up of the ideas in a composition that brings it to a definite close.

Conflict. The struggle between two opposing forces that lies at the center of the plot in a story or drama.

Conjunction. A word that joins single words or groups of words.

> A **coordinating conjunction** (*and, but, or, nor, for, yet*) joins words or groups of words

that are equal in grammatical importance. **Correlative conjunctions** (*both . . . and, just as. . . so, not only. . . but also, either. . . or, neither. . . nor*) are pairs of words used to connect words or phrases in a sentence.

Connotation. The thoughts and feelings associated with a word, rather than its dictionary definition.

Constructive criticism. Comments on another person's writing made with the intention of helping the writer improve a particular draft.

Context. The words and sentences that come before and after a specific word and help to explain its meaning.

Conventions. Correct spelling, grammar, usage, and mechanics.

Coordinating conjunction. *See* Conjunction.

Correlative conjunction. *See* Conjunction.

Credibility. The quality of a speaker or writer that makes that person's words believable.

D

Declarative sentence. A sentence that makes a statement.

Deductive reasoning. A way of thinking or explaining that begins with a general statement or principle and applies that principle to specific instances.

Definite article. *See* Article.

Demonstrative adjective. *See* Adjective.

Denotation. The dictionary definition of a word.

Dependent clause. *See* Clause.

Descriptive writing. Writing that uses sensory detail to convey a dominant impression of, for example, a setting, a person, or an animal.

Desktop publishing. The use of computer programs to format and produce a document that may include written text, graphics, and/or images.

Dialect. A variation of a language spoken by a particular group of people. A dialect may be regional (based on location) or ethnic (based on cultural heritage).

Dialogue. The conversation between characters.

Diction. A writer's choice of words and the arrangement of those words in phrases, sentences, or lines of a poem.

Direct object. *See* Complement.

Documentation. Identification of the sources used in writing research or other informative papers; usually in the form of endnotes or footnotes, or using parenthetical documentation.

Drafting. One of the steps in the writing process; the transforming of thoughts, words, and phrases into sentences and paragraphs.

E–F

Editing. One of the steps in the writing process in which a revised draft is checked for standard usage, varied sentence structure, and appropriate word choice.

Editorial. An article in a newspaper or other form of media that expresses an opinion about a topic of general interest.

Elaboration. The support or development of a main idea with facts, statistics, sensory details, incidents, anecdotes, examples, or quotations.

Ellipsis. A mark of punctuation, consisting of three spaced periods, that shows the omission of a word or words.

E-mail. Short for electronic mail. Messages, usually text, sent from one person to another by way of computer.

Evaluating. Making a judgment about the strengths and weaknesses of a draft in content, organization, and style.

Evidence. Facts or examples from reliable sources that can be used to support statements made in speaking or writing.

Exclamatory sentence. A sentence that expresses strong or sudden emotion.

Explanatory writing. *See* Expository writing.

Expository writing. A kind of writing that aims at informing and explaining. Examples of expository writing are news articles, how-to instructions, and research papers.

Expressive writing. Writing that emphasizes and conveys the writer's feelings.

Fact. A piece of information that can be verified.

Feedback. The response a listener or reader gives to a speaker or writer about his or her work.

Figurative language. Words used for descriptive effect that express some truth beyond the literal level. Figures of speech such as similes, metaphors, or personification are examples of figurative language.

Formal language. Language that uses correct grammar and omits slang expressions and contractions. It is especially common in non-fiction writing that is not personal.

Fragment. An incomplete sentence punctuated as if it were complete.

Freewriting. A way of finding ideas by writing freely, without stopping or limiting the flow of ideas, often for a specific length of time.

Future tense. *See* Verb tense.

G–H

Generalization. A statement that presents a conclusion about a subject without going into details or specifics.

Genre. A division of literature. The main literary genres are prose, poetry, and drama. Each of these is further divided into subgenres.

Gerund. A verb form ending in *–ing* that is used as a noun.

Graphic organizer. A visual way of organizing information; types of graphic organizers are charts, graphs, clusters, and idea trees.

Home page. The location on a Web site by which a user normally enters the site. A typical home page may explain the site, summarize the content, and provide links to other sites.

Hyperlink. Highlighted or underlined phrases or words on a Web page that, when clicked, move the user to another part of the page or to another Web page.

Hypertext. Links in some electronic text that take the user to another document or to a different section in the same document.

I

Ideas. In writing, the message or theme and the details that elaborate upon that message or theme.

Idiom. A word or phrase that has a special meaning different from its standard or dictionary meaning. (*Burning the midnight oil* is an idiom that means "staying up late.")

Imagery. Language that emphasizes sensory impressions that can help the reader of a literary work to see, hear, feel, smell, and taste the scenes described in the work.

Imperative sentence. A sentence that makes a request or gives a command.

Indefinite article. *See* Article.

Indefinite pronoun. *See* Pronoun.

Independent clause. *See* Clause.

Inductive reasoning. A way of thinking or explaining that uses a series of examples to arrive at a general statement.

Infinitive. A verbal made up of the word *to* and the base form of a word. An infinitive often functions as a noun in a sentence.

Informative writing. A kind of writing that explains something, such as a process or an idea. *See also* Expository writing.

Intensifier. An adverb that emphasizes an adjective or another adverb. (*very* important; *quite* easily)

Interjection. A word or phrase that expresses strong feeling and that has no grammatical connection to other words in the sentence.

Internet. A worldwide computer network that allows users to link to any computer on the network electronically for social, commercial, research, and other purposes.

Interpretation. An explanation of the meaning of a piece of writing, a visual representation, or any other type of communication.

Interview. A question-and-answer dialogue that has the specific purpose of gathering up-to-date or expert information.

Intransitive verb. *See* Verb.

Introduction. The beginning part of a piece of writing, in which a writer identifies the subject and gives a general idea of what the body of the composition will contain.

Inverted order. The placement of a predicate *before* the subject in a sentence.

Irregular verb. *See* Verb tense.

J

Jargon. Special words and phrases used by a particular trade, profession, or other group of people.

Journal. A personal notebook in which a person can freewrite, collect ideas, and record thoughts and experiences.

L–M

Learning log. A journal used for clarifying ideas about concepts covered in various classes.

Lexicon. A wordbook or dictionary.

Listing. A technique for finding ideas for writing.

Literary analysis. The act of examining the different elements of a piece of literature in order to evaluate it.

Logical fallacy. An error in reasoning often found in advertising or persuasive writing. Either-or reasoning and glittering generalities are types of logical fallacies.

Main clause. *See* Clause.

Main idea. *See* Thesis statement.

Main verb. The most important word in a verb phrase.

Media. The forms of communication used to reach an audience; forms such as newspapers, radio, TV, and the Internet reach large audiences and so are known as mass media.

Memoir. A type of narrative nonfiction that presents an account of an event or period in history, emphasizing the narrator's personal experience.

Metaphor. A figure of speech that compares seemingly unlike things without using words such as *like* or *as*. (*He is a rock.*)

Mood. The feeling or atmosphere of a piece of writing.

Multimedia presentation. The use of a variety of media, such as video, sound, written text, and visual art to present ideas or information.

N

Narrative writing. A type of writing that tells about events or actions as they change over a period of time and often includes story elements such as character, setting, and plot.

Nonfiction. Prose writing about real people, places, and events.

Noun. A word that names a person, a place, a thing, an idea, a quality, or a characteristic.

Noun clause. A dependent clause used as a noun.

Number. The form of a noun, pronoun, or verb that indicates whether it refers to one (**singular**) or more than one (**plural**).

O

Object. *See* Complement.

Onomatopoeia. The use of a word or phrase that imitates or suggests the sound of what it describes. (*rattle, boom*)

Opinion. A belief or attitude that cannot be proven true or false.

Oral tradition. Literature that passes by word of mouth from one generation to the next and reflects the cultural values of the people.

Order of importance. A way of arranging details in a paragraph or other piece of writing according to their importance.

Organization. The arrangement of main points and supporting details.

Outline. A systematic arrangement of main and supporting ideas, using Roman numerals, letters, and numbers, for a written or an oral presentation.

P

Paragraph. A unit of writing that consists of related sentences.

Parallel construction. The use of a series of words, phrases, or sentences that have similar grammatical form.

Paraphrase. A restatement of someone's ideas in words that are different from the original passage but retain its ideas, tone, and general length.

Parenthetical documentation. A specific reference to the source of a piece of information, placed in parenthesis directly after the information appears in a piece of writing.

Participle. A verb form that can function as an adjective. Present participles always end in *-ing*. Although past participles often end in *-ed*, they can take other forms as well.

Peer response. The suggestions and comments provided by peers, or classmates, about a piece of writing or another type of presentation.

Personal pronoun. *See* Pronoun.

Personal writing. Writing that expresses the writer's own thoughts and feelings.

Personification. A figure of speech that gives human qualities to an animal, object, or idea.

Perspective. *See* Point of view.

Persuasion. A type of writing that aims at convincing people to think or act in a certain way.

Phrase. A group of words that acts in a sentence as a single part of speech.
A **prepositional phrase** begins with a preposition and ends with a noun or

a pronoun. A **verb phrase** consists of one or more auxiliary verbs followed by a main verb.

Plagiarism. The dishonest presentation of another's words or ideas as one's own.

Plot. The series of events that follow one another in a story, novel, or play.

Plural. *See* Number.

Poetry. A form of literary expression that emphasizes the line as the unit of composition. Traditional poetry contains emotional, imaginative language and a regular rhythm.

Point of view. The perspective, from which a story is told, such as first- or third-person.

Portfolio. A collection of various pieces of writing, which may include finished pieces and works in progress.

Predicate. The verb or verb phrase and any of its modifiers that make an essential statement about the subject of a sentence.

Predicate adjective. *See* Adjective.

Preposition. A word that shows the relationship of a noun or pronoun to some other word in the sentence.

Prepositional phrase. *See* Phrase.

Presentation. The way words and design elements look on the page.

Presenting/Publishing. The last step in the writing process; involves sharing the final writing product with others in some way.

Present tense. *See* Verb tense.

Prewriting. The first stage in the writing process; includes deciding what to write about, collecting ideas and details, and making an outline or a plan. Prewriting strategies include brainstorming and using graphic organizers, notes, and logs.

Prior knowledge. The facts, ideas, and experiences that a person brings to a new activity.

Progressive form. *See* Verb tense.

Pronoun. A word that takes the place of a noun, a group of words acting as a noun, or another pronoun. The word or group of words that a pronoun refers to is called its **antecedent.**
   A **personal pronoun** refers to a specific person or thing.

Pronoun case. *See* Case.

Proofreading. The final part of the editing process that involves checking work to discover typographical and other errors.

Propaganda. Information aimed at influencing thoughts and actions; it is usually of a political nature and may contain distortions of truth.

Proper adjective. *See* Adjective.

Prose. Writing that is similar to everyday speech and written language, as opposed to poetry and drama.

Publishing. The preparation of a finished piece of writing often involving available technology, so that it can be presented to a larger audience.

Purpose. The aim of writing, which may be to express, discover, record, develop, reflect on ideas, problem solve, entertain, influence, inform, or describe.

R

Regular verb. *See* Verb tense.

Representation. A way in which information or ideas are presented to an audience.

Research. The search for information on a topic.

Review. The analysis and interpretation of a subject, often presented through the mass media.

Revising. The stage of the writing process in which a writer goes over a draft, making changes in its content, organization, and style in order to improve it. Revision techniques include adding, elaborating, deleting, combining, and rearranging text.

Root. The part of a word that carries the main meaning.

Run-on sentence. Two or more sentences or clauses run together without appropriate punctuation.

S

Sensory details. Language that appeals to the senses; sensory details are important elements of descriptive writing, especially of poetry.

Sentence. A group of words expressing a complete thought. Every sentence has a **subject** and a **predicate**. *See also* Subject; Predicate; Clause.

>   A **simple sentence** has only one main clause and no subordinate clauses.
>   A **compound sentence** has two or more main clauses. Each main clause of a compound sentence has its own subject and predicate. These main clauses are usually joined by a comma and a coordinating conjunction, but a semicolon can also be used to join them.
>   A **complex sentence** has one main clause and one or more subordinate clauses.

Sentence fluency. The smooth rhythm and flow of sentences that vary in length and style.

Sentence variety. The use of different types of sentences to add interest to writing.

Setting. The time and place in which the events of a story, novel, or play takes place.

Simile. A figure of speech that compares two unlike things, using *like* or *as.*

Simple sentence. *See* Sentence.

Spatial order. A way of presenting the details of a setting according to their location—for example, from left to right or top to bottom.

Standard English. The most widely used and accepted form of the English language

Style. The writer's choice and arrangement of words and sentences.

Subject. The noun or pronoun that tells who or what the sentence is about.

Subordinate clause. *See* Clause.

Summary. A brief statement of the main idea of a composition.

Supporting evidence. *See* Evidence.

Suspense. A literary device that creates growing interest and excitement leading up to the climax and resolution of a story. A writer creates suspense by providing clues to the resolution without revealing too much information.

Symbol. An object, a person, a place, or an experience that represents something else, usually something abstract.

T

Tense. *See* Verb tense.

Theme. The main idea or message of a piece of writing.

Thesis statement. A one- or two-sentence statement of the main idea or purpose of a piece of writing.

Time order. The arrangement of details in a piece of writing based on when they occurred.

Tone. A reflection of a writer's or speaker's attitude toward a subject.

Topic sentence. A sentence that expresses the main idea of a paragraph.

Transition. A connecting word or phrase that clarifies relationships between details, sentences, or paragraphs.

U–V

Unity. A quality of oneness in a paragraph or composition that exists when all the sentences or paragraphs work together to express or support one main idea.

URL. The standard form of an Internet address; stands for Uniform Resource Locator.

Venn diagram. A graphic organizer consisting of two overlapping circles; used to compare two items that have both similar and different traits.

Verb. A word that expresses an action or a state of being and is necessary to make a statement.

Verbal. A verb form that functions in a sentence as a noun, an adjective, or an adverb. The three kinds of verbals are participles, gerunds, and infinitives. *See also* Gerund; Infinitive; Participle.

Verb phrase. *See* Phrase.

Verb tense. The form a verb takes to show when an action takes place. The **present tense** names an action that happens regularly. The **past tense** names an action that has happened, and the **future tense** names an action that will take place in the future. All the verb tenses are formed from the four principal parts of a verb: a **base form** (*freeze*), a **present participle** (*freezing*), a **simple past form** (*froze*) and a **past participle** (*frozen*). A **regular verb** forms its simple past and past participle by adding -*ed* to the base form. Verbs that form their past and past participle in some other way are called **irregular verbs**.

In addition to present, past, and future tense, there are three perfect tenses—present perfect, past perfect, and future perfect. Each of the six tenses has a **progressive form** that expresses a continuing action.

Voice. A writer's unique way of using tone and style to communicate with the audience.

W

Web site. A location on the World Wide Web that can be reached through links or by accessing a Web address, or URL. *See* URL.

Word choice. The vocabulary a writer chooses to convey meaning.

Word processing. The use of a computer for the writing and editing of written text.

World Wide Web. A global system that uses the Internet and allows users to create, link, and access fields of information. *See* Internet.

Writing process. The series of stages or steps that a writer goes through to develop ideas and to communicate them.

GLOSARIO
DE ESCRITURA Y LENGUAJE

Este glosario permite encontrar fácilmente definiciones de gramática inglesa y términos que usan los escritores.

A

Adjective/Adjetivo. Palabra que modifica, o describe, un nombre (*noun*) o pronombre (*pronoun*). Un adjetivo *indica qué tipo, cuál, cuántos o cuánto.*

> **Comparative degree/Grado comparativo.** Adjetivo que compara a dos personas, lugares, cosas o ideas (*worse, sadder;* en español: *peor, más triste*).

> **Superlative degree/Grado superlativo.** Adjetivo que compara más de dos personas, lugares, cosas o ideas (*worst, saddest;* en español: *el peor, la más triste*).

> **Possessive adjective/Adjetivo posesivo.** Pronombre posesivo que va antes del nombre.

> **Predicative adjective/Adjetivo predicativo.** Siempre va después de un verbo copulativo y modifica al sujeto de la oración.

> **Proper adjective/Adjetivo propio*.** Adjetivo que se deriva de un nombre propio; en inglés siempre se escribe con mayúscula.

> **Demonstrative adjective/Adjetivo demostrativo.** Se usa antes del nombre: *this, that, these, those* (*este, ese, aquel, estos, esos, aquellos*).

Adjective clause/Proposición adjetiva. Proposición dependiente que modifica un nombre o un pronombre.

Adverb/Adverbio. Palabra que modifica a un verbo, adjetivo u otro adverbio. Los adverbios indican *cómo, cuándo, dónde, de qué manera* y *qué tan seguido* sucede algo. Algunos adverbios tienen diferentes formas para indicar los grados **comparativo** (*comparative*) y **superlativo** (*superlative*) (*loud, louder, loudest; sweetly, more sweetly, most sweetly;* en español: *fuerte, más fuerte, lo más fuerte; dulcemente, más dulcemente, lo más dulcemente*).

Adverb clause/Proposición adverbial. Proposición dependiente que modifica un verbo, un adjetivo o un adverbio.

Allusion/Alusión. Referencia en un texto escrito a un personaje, lugar o situación muy conocidos de una obra literaria, musical, artística o histórica.

Analysis/Análisis. Acción de descomponer un tema o escrito en distintas partes para encontrar su significado.

Anecdote/Anécdota. Narración breve o incidente que se presenta como parte de una narrativa más larga.

Antecedent/Antecedente. *Ver* Pronoun.

Appositive/Apositivo. Nombre colocado junto a otro para identificarlo o agregar información sobre él. (Mi entrenadora de baloncesto, *Ms. Lopes*, pidió tiempo fuera.)

Argument/Argumento. Afirmación, razón o hecho en favor o en contra de algún comentario; texto escrito que trata de persuadir.

Article/Artículo. Nombre dado a las palabras *a, an* y *the* (en español: *un, uno/a, el, la*). *A* y *an* son **artículos indefinidos** (*indefinite articles*), que se refieren a cualquier cosa de un grupo. *The* es un **artículo definido** (*definite article*); indica que el nombre al que precede es una persona, lugar o cosa específicos.

Audience/Público. Persona (o personas) que lee o escucha lo que dicen un escritor o un hablante.

B

Base form/Base derivativa. *Ver* Verb tense.

Bias/Tendencia. Inclinación a pensar de cierta manera. La tendencia influye en la manera en que un escritor o hablante presenta sus ideas.

Bibliography/Bibliografía. Lista de los libros, artículos y otras fuentes que se utilizan como referencia en una investigación.

Body/Cuerpo. Parte central de una composición que comunica la idea principal identificada en la introducción.

Bookmarks/favorites/Marcadores/favoritos. Característica de muchos buscadores de red que permiten guardar direcciones de Internet para entrar a ellas rápidamente.

Brainstorming/Lluvia de ideas. Actividad de grupo en que se generan tantas ideas como sea posible sin detenerse a analizarlas.

C

Case/Caso. Forma de un nombre o pronombre que está determinado por su uso en la oración. El nombre o pronombre está en **caso nominativo** (*nominative case*) cuando se utiliza como sujeto; en **caso acusativo** y **dativo** (*objective case*) cuando recibe la acción del verbo, y en **caso posesivo*** (*possessive case*) cuando se utiliza para indicar posesión o propiedad.

Cause-and-effect chain/Cadena de causa y efecto. Serie de acontecimientos en que una causa lleva a un efecto que, a su vez, lleva a otro efecto, y así sucesivamente.

Characterization/Caracterización. Métodos que utiliza un escritor para crear sus personajes. Puede ser describiendo directamente su personalidad, o revelándola con sus palabras y acciones, o bien a partir de lo que otros personajes piensan y dicen de él.

Chronological order/Orden cronológico. Organización de detalles de acuerdo con el tiempo en que sucedieron los acontecimientos o acciones.

Clarity/Claridad. Cualidad de un escrito que lo hace fácil de entender.

Clause/Proposición. Grupo de palabras que consta de sujeto y predicado, y que se usa como parte de una oración compuesta.

> **Independent clause/Proposición independiente.** También llamada **proposición principal** (*main clause*); tiene sujeto y predicado y hace sentido por sí misma.
> **Dependent clause/Proposición dependiente.** También llamada **proposición subordinada** (*subordinate clause*); tiene sujeto y predicado pero depende de la proposición principal.

Cliché/Cliché. Expresión usada con demasiada frecuencia *(blanco como la nieve)*.

Clustering/Agrupamiento. Reunión de temas relacionados para organizar la información.

Coherence/Coherencia. Relación lógica entre las partes de un párrafo o composición.

Cohesive writing/Escritura coherente. Tipo de escritura en que las oraciones y párrafos están lógicamente relacionados entre sí.

Collaboration/Colaboración. Proceso de trabajar en equipo para escribir un texto o realizar un proyecto.

Colloquialism/Expresión coloquial. Expresión informal y pintoresca que se utiliza en la conversación diaria.

Comparative degree/Grado comparativo. *Ver* Adjective; Adverb.

Comparison-and-contrast/Comparación y contraste. Manera de organizar ideas, señalando sus similitudes y diferencias.

Complement/Complemento (u objeto). Palabra o frase que complementa el significado de un verbo. Tres complementos son: **directo** (*direct object*), **indirecto** (*indirect object*) y **predicativo (atributo)** (*subject complement*).

Conceptual map/Mapa conceptual. Recurso gráfico que desarrolla un concepto central rodeándolo con ejemplos o ideas relacionadas a manera de red.

Conclusion/Conclusión. Afirmación que resume las ideas de una composición, antes de ponerle punto final.

Conflict/Conflicto. Lucha entre dos fuerzas opuestas que constituye el elemento central de la trama en un cuento u obra de teatro.

Conjunction/Conjunción. Palabra que une palabras o grupos de palabras.

> **Coordinating conjunction/Conjunción coordinante.** Las palabras *and, but, or, nor, for, yet* (*y, pero, o, no, para, aun*) unen palabras o grupos de palabras que tienen igual importancia gramatical.
>
> **Correlative conjunction/Conjunción correlativa*.** Las palabras *both . . . and, just as . . . so, not only . . . but also, either . . . or, neither . . . nor* (*tanto . . . como, así como, no sólo . . . sino, o . . . o*) son palabras en pares que vinculan palabras o frases en una oración.

Connotation/Connotación. Pensamientos y sentimientos relacionados con una palabra, más que con su definición de diccionario.

Constructive criticism/Crítica constructiva. Comentario sobre lo que escribe otra persona, con la intención de ayudar a que mejore el borrador.

Context/Contexto. Palabras y oraciones que vienen antes y después de una palabra y ayudan a explicar su significado.

Conventions/Reglas de escritura. Normas que regulan la ortografía, la gramática, el uso y la puntuación de un escrito.

Coordinating conjunction/Conjunción coordinante. *Ver* Conjunction.

Correlative conjunction/Conjunción correlativa*. *Ver* Conjunction.

Credibility/Credibilidad. Cualidad de un hablante o escritor que hace creer sus palabras.

D

Declarative sentence/Oración afirmativa. Oración que declara algo.

Deductive reasoning/Razonamiento deductivo. Pensamiento o explicación que parte de una afirmación o principio generales y los aplica a casos específicos.

Definite article/Artículo definido. *Ver* Article.

Demonstrative adjective/Adjetivo demostrativo. *Ver* Adjective.

Denotation/Denotación. Definición de una palabra que da el diccionario.

Dependent clause/Proposición dependiente. *Ver* Clause.

Descriptive writing/Escritura descriptiva. Tipo de escritura que ofrece detalles sensoriales para comunicar la impresión de un escenario, persona, animal, etcétera.

Desktop publishing/Edición por computadora.
Uso de programas de computadora para formar un documento con texto escrito, gráficas y/o imágenes.

Dialect/Dialecto. Variedad de lenguaje hablado que usa un grupo particular, regional (de un lugar) o étnico (de un grupo cultural).

Dialogue/Diálogo. Conversación entre personajes.

Diction/Dicción. Palabras que escoge un escritor y cómo las utiliza en frases, oraciones o versos.

Direct object/Complemento directo. *Ver* Complement.

Documentation/Documentación. Identificación de las fuentes que se emplean para escribir un artículo u otros textos informativos; generalmente se ponen como notas al pie, al final del texto o entre paréntesis.

Drafting/Borrador. Paso del proceso de escritura; transformación de ideas, palabras y frases a oraciones y párrafos.

E

Editing/Edición. Paso del proceso de escritura en que se revisa que el borrador corregido tenga un lenguaje estándar, una estructura sintáctica variada y la elección adecuada de palabras.

Editorial/Editorial. Artículo en un periódico u otro medio que expresa una opinión sobre un tema de interés general.

Elaboration/Elaboración. Sustento o desarrollo de una idea principal con hechos, estadísticas, detalles sensoriales, incidentes, anécdotas, ejemplos o citas.

Ellipsis/Puntos suspensivos. Signo de puntuación que consiste en dejar tres puntos para indicar que se están suprimiendo una o varias palabras.

E-mail/Correo electrónico. Mensajes, generalmente textos, que se envían por computadora.

Evaluating/Evaluación. Juicio sobre las fallas y aciertos de un borrador en cuanto a contenido, organización y estilo.

Evidence/Evidencia. Datos o ejemplos de fuentes confiables que sirven para sustentar afirmaciones escritas o habladas.

Exclamatory sentence/Oración exclamativa. Oración que expresa una emoción fuerte o repentina.

Explanatory writing/Texto explicativo. *Ver* Descriptive text.

Expository writing/Texto descriptivo. Tipo de escritura que informa o explica, como artículos periodísticos, instrucciones y artículos de investigación.

Expressive writing/Texto expresivo. Texto que realza y transmite los sentimientos del escritor.

F

Fact/Hecho. Información que puede comprobarse.

Feedback/Retroalimentación. Respuesta del escucha o lector al mensaje de un hablante o escritor.

Figurative language/Lenguaje figurado. Palabras usadas con un efecto descriptivo que expresa una verdad más allá del nivel literal. Los tropos, como el símil, la metáfora y la personificación, son ejemplos de lenguaje figurado.

Formal language/Lenguaje formal. Lenguaje que utiliza una gramática correcta y omite contracciones y expresiones coloquiales. Es común en textos de no ficción, que no son de carácter personal.

Fragment/Fragmento. Oración incompleta con puntuación de oración completa.

Freewriting/Escritura libre. Búsqueda de ideas escribiendo durante un tiempo determinado, sin detenerse ni limitar el flujo de ideas.

Future tense/Tiempo futuro. *Ver* Verb tense.

G-H

Generalization/Generalización. Afirmación que presenta una conclusión sobre un tema sin dar detalles específicos.

Genre/Género. Clasificación literaria o de otro medio. Los principales géneros literarios son la prosa, la poesía y el drama. Cada uno se divide en subgéneros.

Gerund/Gerundio. Verboide que termina en *–ing* y se usa como nombre (en inglés).

Graphic organizer/Organizador gráfico. Manera visual de organizar la información, como las tablas, las gráficas, las redes y los árboles de ideas.

Home page/Página principal. Página por medio de la cual un usuario entra normalmente a un sitio de Web. Por lo general, explica el sitio, resume el contenido y proporciona vínculos con otros sitios.

Hyperlink/Hipervínculo. Oraciones o palabras sombreadas o subrayadas en una página en red que al activarse con un clic conectan con otra parte de la página o con otra página de la red.

Hypertext/Hipertexto. Vínculos en textos electrónicos que llevan a otro documento o a una sección distinta del mismo documento.

I-J

Ideas/Ideas. En composición, el mensaje o tema y los detalles que lo elaboran.

Idiom/Modismo. Palabra o frase cuyo significado es diferente del significado estándar o de diccionario. (*Se le pegaron las sábanas* es un modismo que significa "se levantó muy tarde").

Imagery/Imaginería. Lenguaje que describe impresiones sensoriales para que el lector de un texto literario pueda ver, oír, sentir, oler y gustar las escenas descritas.

Imperative sentence/Oración imperativa. Oración que exige u ordena algo.

Indefinite article/Artículo indefinido. *Ver* Article.

Indefinite pronoun/Pronombre indefinido. *Ver* Pronoun.

Independent clause/Proposición independiente. *Ver* Clause.

Inductive reasoning/Razonamiento inductivo. Pensamiento o explicación que parte de varios ejemplos para llegar a una afirmación general.

Infinitive/Infinitivo. Verboide que consta de la palabra *to* y la base del verbo (en español terminan en *-ar, -er* o *-ir*). Se usa como sustantivo en la oración.

Informative writing/Texto informativo. Texto que explica un proceso o una idea. *Ver también* Descriptive text.

Intensifier/Intensificador. Adverbio que refuerza un adjetivo u otro adverbio (*very* important, *quite* easily; *muy* importante, *bastante* fácil).

Interjection/Interjección. Palabra o frase que expresa un sentimiento muy fuerte. La interjección no tiene relación gramatical con las demás palabras de la oración.

Internet/Internet. Red mundial computarizada que permite comunicarse electrónicamente con cualquier computadora de la red para buscar información social, comercial, de investigación y de otro tipo.

Interpretation/Interpretación. Explicación del significado de un texto, de una representación visual o de cualquier otro tipo de comunicación.

Interview/Entrevista. Diálogo a base de preguntas y respuestas cuyo propósito es obtener información actualizada o de expertos.

Intransitive Verb/Verbo intransitivo. *Ver Verb.*

Introduction/Introducción. Sección inicial de un texto en la que el escritor identifica el tema y da la idea general de lo que contendrá el cuerpo del mismo.

Inverted order/Orden invertido. Colocación del predicado *antes* del sujeto.

Irregular verb/Verbo irregular. *Ver Verb tense.*

Jargon/Jerga. Palabras y frases que usa un determinado grupo.

Journal/Diario. Libreta personal en la que con toda libertad se anotan ideas, pensamientos y experiencias.

L

Learning log/Registro de aprendizaje. Diario para aclarar ideas sobre conceptos tratados en varias clases.

Lexicon/Léxico. Diccionario.

Listing/Lista. Técnica para generar ideas a partir de las cuales se escribe un texto.

Literary analysis/Análisis literario. Examen de las diferentes partes de una obra literaria a fin de evaluarla.

Logical fallacy/Falacia lógica. Error de razonamiento que se encuentra con frecuencia en publicidad o en escritos persuasivos, como razonamientos con dos alternativas opuestas o generalidades muy llamativas.

M

Main clause/Proposición principal. *Ver* Clause.

Main idea/Idea principal. *Ver* Thesis statement.

Main verb/Verbo principal. La palabra más importante de una frase verbal.

Media/Medios. Formas de comunicación usadas para llegar a un público. Los periódicos, la radio, la televisión y la Internet llegan a públicos muy grandes, por lo que se conocen como medios de comunicación masiva.

Memoir/Memoria. Tipo de narrativa de no ficción que presenta el relato de un hecho o período de la historia, resaltando la experiencia personal del narrador.

Metaphor/Metáfora. Tropo que compara dos cosas aparentemente distintas sin usar las palabra *like* o *as (como)*. (*Él es una roca.*)

Mood/Atmósfera. Sentimiento o ambiente de un texto escrito.

Multimedia presentation/Presentación multimedia. Uso de una variedad de medios como video, sonido, texto escrito y artes visuales para presentar ideas e información.

N

Narrative writing/Narrativa. Tipo de escritura que narra sucesos o acciones que cambian con el paso del tiempo; por lo general tiene personajes, escenario y trama.

Nonfiction/No ficción. Texto en prosa acerca de personas, lugares y sucesos reales.

Noun/Nombre (o sustantivo). Palabra que nombra a una persona, lugar, cosa, o a una idea, cualidad o característica.

Noun clause/Proposición nominal. Proposición dependiente que se usa como nombre.

Number/Número. Forma del nombre, pronombre o verbo que indica si se refiere a uno (**singular**) o a más de uno (**plural**).

O

Object/Objeto. *Ver* Complement.

Onomatopoeia/Onomatopeya. Palabra o frase que imita o sugiere el sonido que describe (*rattle, boom;* en español: *pum, zas*).

Opinion/Opinión. Creencia o actitud; no puede comprobarse si es falsa o verdadera.

Oral tradition/Tradición oral. Literatura que se transmite de boca en boca de una generación a otra. Puede representar los valores culturales de un pueblo.

Order of importance/Orden de importancia. Forma de acomodar los detalles en un párrafo o en otro texto escrito según su importancia.

Organization/Organización. La disposición y el orden de los puntos principales y los detalles de apoyo en un escrito.

Outline/Esquema. Organización sistemática de ideas principales y secundarias con números romanos, letras y números arábigos para una presentación oral o escrita.

P

Paragraph/Párrafo. Una unidad de un texto que consta de oraciones relacionadas.

Parallel construction/Construcción paralela. Serie de palabras, frases y oraciones que tienen una forma gramatical similar.

Paraphrase/Parafrasear. Repetir las ideas de otro con palabras diferentes del original pero conservando las ideas, el tono y la longitud general.

Parenthetical documentation/Documentación parentética. Referencia específica a la fuente de la información que se pone entre paréntesis directamente después de ésta.

Participle/Participio. Verboide que se usa como adjetivo. El participio presente siempre termina en *–ing* y el participio pasado por lo general termina en *–ed.*

Peer response/Respuesta de compañeros. Sugerencias y comentarios que dan los compañeros de clase sobre un texto escrito u otro tipo de presentación.

Personal pronoun/Pronombre personal. *Ver* Pronoun.

Personal writing/Escritura personal. Texto que expresa los pensamientos y sentimientos del autor.

Personification/Personificación. Tropo que da cualidades humanas a un animal, objeto o idea.

Perspective/Perspectiva. *Ver* Point of view.

Persuasion/Persuasión. Tipo de escritura encaminado a convencer a pensar o actuar de cierta manera.

Phrase/Frase. Grupo de palabras que forma una unidad en una oración.

> **Prepositional phrase/Frase preposicional.** Comienza con una preposición y termina con un nombre o un pronombre.
> **Verb phrase/Frase verbal.** Consta de uno o más **verbos auxiliares** (*auxiliary verbs*) seguidos del verbo principal.

Plagiarism/Plagio. Presentación deshonesta de palabras o ideas ajenas como si fueran propias.

Plot/Trama. Serie de sucesos en secuencia en un cuento, novela u obra de teatro.

Plural/Plural. *Ver* Number.

Poetry/Poesía. Forma de expresión literaria compuesta por versos. La poesía tradicional contiene un lenguaje emotivo e imaginativo y un ritmo regular.

Point of view/Punto de vista. Ángulo o perspectiva desde el cual se cuenta una historia; por ejemplo, primera o tercera persona.

Portfolio/Portafolio. Colección de varias obras escritas de un estudiante, que puede tener obras terminadas y otras en proceso.

Predicate/Predicado. Verbo o frase verbal y sus modificadores que hacen una afirmación esencial sobre el sujeto de la oración.

Predicate adjective/Adjetivo predicativo. *Ver* Adjective.

Preposition/Preposición. Palabra que muestra la relación de un nombre o pronombre con otra palabra en la oración.

Prepositional phrase/Frase preposicional. *Ver* Phrase.

Presentation/Presentación. La forma en que se ven en una página las palabras y los elementos de diseño.

Presenting/Publishing Presentación/Publicación. Último paso del proceso de escritura que implica compartir con otros lo que se ha escrito.

Present tense/Tiempo presente. *Ver* Verb tense.

Prewriting/Preescritura. Primer paso del proceso de escritura: decidir sobre qué se va a escribir, reunir ideas y detalles, y elaborar un plan para presentar las ideas; usa estrategias como lluvia de ideas, organizadores gráficos, notas y registros.

Prior knowledge/Conocimiento previo. Hechos, ideas y experiencias que un escritor, lector u observador lleva a una nueva actividad.

Progressive form/Durativo. *Ver* Verb tense.

Pronoun/Pronombre. Palabra que va en lugar del nombre; grupo de palabras que funcionan como un nombre u otro pronombre. La palabra o grupo de palabras a que se refiere un pronombre se llama **antecedente** (*antecedent*).

   Personal pronoun/Pronombre personal. Se refiere a una persona o cosa específica.

Pronoun case/Caso del pronombre. *Ver* Case.

Proofreading/Corrección de pruebas. Último paso del proceso editorial en que se revisa el texto en busca de errores tipográficos y de otra naturaleza.

Propaganda/Propaganda. Información encaminada a influir en los pensamientos o acciones; en general es de naturaleza política y puede distorsionar la verdad.

Proper adjective/Adjetivo propio*. *Ver* Adjective.

Prose/Prosa. Escritura similar al lenguaje cotidiano tanto oral como escrito, a diferencia de la poesía y el teatro.

Publishing/Publicación. Presentación de una obra escrita terminada mediante el uso de la tecnología, para darla a conocer a un público amplio.

Purpose/Finalidad. Objetivo de la escritura: expresar, descubrir, registrar, desarrollar o reflexionar sobre ideas, resolver problemas, entretener, influir, informar o describir.

R

Regular verb/Verbo regular. *Ver* Verb tense.

Representation/Representación. Forma en que se presenta información o ideas al público.

Research/Investigación. Proceso de localizar información sobre un tema.

Review/Reseña. Análisis e interpretación de un tema presentado por lo general a través de los medios de comunicación masiva.

Revising/Revisión. Paso del proceso de escritura en que el autor repasa el borrador, cambia el contenido, la organización y el estilo para mejorar el texto. Las técnicas de revisión son agregar, elaborar, eliminar, combinar y reacomodar el texto.

Root/Raíz. Parte de una palabra que contiene el significado principal.

Run-on sentence/Oración mal puntuada. Dos o más oraciones o proposiciones seguidas, cuyo significado es confuso debido a su inadecuada puntuación.

S

Sensory details/Detalles sensoriales. Lenguaje que apela a los sentidos; los detalles sensoriales son elementos importantes de la escritura descriptiva, sobre todo en la poesía.

Sentence/Oración. Grupo de palabras que expresa un pensamiento completo. Cada oración tiene **sujeto** (*subject*) y **predicado** (*predicate*). *Ver también* Subject; Predicate; Clause.

Simple sentence/Oración simple. Consta de una proposición principal y no tiene proposiciones subordinadas.

Compound sentence/Oración compuesta. Tiene dos o más proposiciones principales, cada una con su propio sujeto y predicado; van unidas por una coma y una conjunción coordinante, o por un punto y coma.

Complex sentence/Oración compleja. Tiene una proposición principal y una o más proposiciones subordinadas.

Sentence fluency/Fluidez oracional. El ritmo suave y suelto de las oraciones que varían en longitud y estilo.

Sentence variety/Variedad de oraciones. Uso de diferentes tipos de oraciones para agregar interés al texto.

Setting/Escenario. Tiempo y lugar en que ocurren los sucesos de un cuento, novela u obra de teatro.

Simile/Símil. Tropo que compara dos cosas esencialmente distintas, usando las palabras *like* o *as* (*como*). (*Su pelo era como hilo de seda.*)

Simple predicate/Predicado simple. *Ver* Predicate; Sentence; Subject.

Simple sentence/Oración simple. *Ver* Sentence.

Spatial order/Orden espacial. Forma de presentar los detalles de un escenario según su ubicación: de izquierda a derecha o de arriba hacia abajo.

Standard English/Inglés estándar. La forma más ampliamente usada y aceptada del idioma inglés.

Style/Estilo. Forma en que un escritor elige y organiza las palabras y oraciones.

Subject/Sujeto. Nombre o pronombre principal que informa sobre quién o sobre qué trata la oración.

Subordinate clause/Proposición subordinada. *Ver* Clause.

Summary/Resumen. Breve explicación de la idea principal de una composición.

Supporting evidence/Sustento. *Ver* Evidence.

Suspense/Suspenso. Recurso literario que genera interés y emoción para llegar al clímax o desenlace de una historia. Un escritor crea suspenso al proporcionar pistas sobre el desenlace pero sin revelar demasiada información.

Symbol/Símbolo. Objeto, persona, lugar o experiencia que representa algo más, por lo general, abstracto.

T

Tense/Tiempo. *Ver* Verb tense.

Theme/Tema. Idea o mensaje principal de una obra escrita.

Thesis statement/Exposición de tesis. Exposición de la **idea principal** o finalidad de una obra en una o dos oraciones.

Time order/Orden temporal. Organización de detalles en un texto escrito según el momento en que ocurrieron.

Tone/Tono. Reflejo de la actitud del escritor o hablante hacia un sujeto.

Topic sentence/Oración temática. Oración que expresa la idea principal de un párrafo.

Transition/Transición. Palabra o frase de enlace que aclara las relaciones entre los detalles, oraciones o párrafos.

U-V

Unity/Unidad. Integridad de un párrafo o composición; coherencia entre todas las oraciones o párrafos para expresar o sustentar una idea principal.

URL/URL. Forma estándar de una dirección de Internet. (Son iniciales de *Uniform Resource Locator*.)

Venn diagram/Diagrama de Venn. Organizador gráfico que consta de dos círculos que se traslapan, usado para comparar dos cosas con características comunes y diferentes.

Verb/Verbo. Palabra que expresa acción o estado y que es necesaria para hacer una afirmación.

Verbal/Verboide. Forma del verbo que funciona como nombre, adjetivo o adverbio en la oración. Los verboides son: participio (*participles*), gerundio (*gerunds*) e infinitivo (*infinitives*).

Verb phrase/Frase verbal. *Ver* Phrase.

Verb tense/Tiempo verbal. El tiempo de un verbo indica cuándo ocurre la acción.

   Present tense/Presente. Indica una acción que sucede regularmente.

   Past tense/Pasado. Indica una acción que ya sucedió.

   Future tense/Futuro. Indica una acción que va a suceder.

   En inglés todos los tiempos verbales están formados por las cuatro partes principales del verbo: **base derivativa** (*base form*) (*freeze, congelar*), **participio presente** (*present participle*) (*freezing, congelando*), **pretérito simple** (*simple past form*) (*froze, congeló*) y **participio pasado** (*past participle*) (*frozen, congelado*).

   Un **verbo regular** (*regular verb*) forma su pretérito simple y su participio pasado agregando la terminación *ed* al infinitivo. Los verbos que forman su pretérito y participio pasado de otra forma se llaman **verbos irregulares** (*irregular verbs*).

   Además de los tiempos presente, pasado y futuro hay tres tiempos perfectos: **presente perfecto** (*present perfect*), **pretérito perfecto** (*past perfect*) y **futuro perfecto** (*future perfect*).

   Cada uno de los seis tiempos tiene una **forma durativa** (*progressive form*) que expresa acción continua.

Voice/Voz. La forma única que tiene un escritor o escritora de usar el tono y el estilo para comunicarse con los lectores.

W

Web site/Sitio web. Sitio de World Wide Web que puede ser alcanzado mediante vínculos o una dirección Web o URL. *Ver también* URL; World Wide Web.

Word choice/Léxico. El vocabulario que selecciona una escritora o escritor para presentar un significado.

Word processing/Procesador de palabras. Programa de computadora para escribir y editar un texto.

World Wide Web/World Wide Web. Sistema global que usa Internet y permite a los usuarios crear, vincularse y entrar a campos de información. *Ver también* Internet.

Writing process/Proceso de escritura. Serie de pasos o etapas por los que atraviesa un escritor para desarrollar sus ideas y comunicarlas.

*Este término o explicación solamente se aplica a la gramática inglesa.

*W*hat are the basic tools for building strong sentences, paragraphs, compositions, and research papers? You'll find them in this handbook—an easy-to-use "tool kit" for writers like you. Check out the helpful explanations, examples, and tips as you complete your writing assignments.

Writing Good Sentences

A sentence is a group of words that expresses a complete thought. Every sentence has a subject and a predicate.

Using Various Types of Sentences

How you craft a sentence—as a statement, question, command, or exclamation—depends on the job you want the sentence to do.

Type	Job It Does	Ways to Use It
Declarative	Makes a statement	Report information *October is National Pizza Month.*
Interrogative	Asks a question	Make your readers curious *Why is pizza so popular?*
Imperative	Gives a command or makes a request	Tell how to do something *Spread the toppings on the pizza dough.*
Exclamatory	Expresses strong feeling	Emphasize a startling fact *Every second, Americans eat about 350 slices of pizza!*

Varying Sentence Structure and Length

Many sentences in a row that look and sound alike can be boring. Vary your sentence openers to make your writing interesting.

- **Start a sentence with an adjective or an adverb.**
  Suddenly the sky turned dark.

- **Start a sentence with a phrase.**
  Like a fireworks show, lightning streaked across the sky.

- **Start a sentence with a clause.**
  As the thunderstorm began, people ran for cover.

Many short sentences in a row make writing sound choppy and dull. To make your writing sound pleasing, vary the sentence length.

Check It Out

For more about how to vary sentence length and structure, review Unit 21, Sentence Combining, pages 628–637.

- **Combine short sentences into longer ones.**

    Tornadoes are also called twisters. They are spinning clouds. The clouds are funnel shaped.

    Tornadoes, also called twisters, are spinning funnel-shaped clouds.

- **Alternate shorter sentences with longer sentences.**

    Tornado winds are powerful. They can hurl cows into the air, tear trees from their roots, and turn cars upside down.

Using Parallelism

Parallelism is the use of a pair or a series of words, phrases, or sentences that have the same grammatical structure. Use parallelism to call attention to the items in the series and to create unity in writing.

Not Parallel Gymnasts are strong, flexible, and move gracefully.
Parallel Gymnasts are strong, flexible, and graceful.

Not Parallel Do warm-up exercises to prevent sports injuries and for stretching your muscles.
Parallel Do warm-up exercises to prevent sports injuries and to stretch your muscles.

Not Parallel Stand on one leg, bend the other leg, and you should pull on your heel.
Parallel Stand on one leg, bend the other leg, and pull your heel.

Revising Wordy Sentences

Revise wordy sentences to make every word count.

- **Cut needless words.**

    Wordy We need to have bike lanes in streets due to the fact that people like to ride their bikes to work and school, and it's not safe otherwise.
    Concise We need bike lanes in streets so that people can safely ride to work and school.

- **Rewrite sentences opening with the word *there*.**

    Wordy There are many kids riding their bikes in the street.
    Concise Many kids ride their bikes in the street.

- **Change verbs in passive voice to active voice.**

    Wordy Bikes are also ridden by grown-ups who want to keep fit.
    Concise Grown-ups who want to keep fit also ride bikes.

Writing Good Paragraphs

A paragraph is a group of sentences that relate to one main idea. A good paragraph develops a single idea and brings that idea into sharp focus. All the sentences flow smoothly from the beginning to the end of the paragraph.

Writing Unified Paragraphs

A paragraph has **unity** when the sentences belong together and center on a single main idea. One way to build a unified paragraph is to state the main idea in a topic sentence and then add related details.

Writing Topic Sentences A **topic sentence** gives your readers the "big picture"—a clear view of the most important idea you want them to know. Many effective expository paragraphs (paragraphs that convey information) start with a topic sentence that tells the key point right away.

Elaborating Topic Sentences Elaboration gives your readers a specific, more detailed picture of the main idea stated in your topic sentence. Elaboration is a technique you can use to include details that develop, support, or explain the main idea. The following chart shows various kinds of elaboration you might try.

> **Revising Tip**
>
> To make a paragraph unified, leave out details that do not relate to the topic sentence.

Topic Sentence: The state of Florida is known for its alligators.	
Descriptions	Alligators look like dinosaurs from millions of years ago.
Facts and statistics	Alligators can weigh as much as six hundred pounds.
Examples	Alligators eat a wide variety of foods, such as fish, insects, turtles, frogs, and small mammals.
Anecdotes (brief stories)	Silvia almost fainted when she came home to find an alligator paddling around in her swimming pool.
Reasons	Face-to-face encounters with alligators are now common because people have built golf courses over the animals' habitat.

Writing Coherent Paragraphs

A paragraph has **coherence** when all the sentences flow smoothly and logically from one to the next. All the sentences in a paragraph *cohere*, or "stick together," in a way that makes sense. To be sure your writing is coherent, choose a pattern of organization that fits your topic and use transition words and phrases to link ideas.

Organizing Paragraphs A few basic patterns of organization are listed below. Choose the pattern that helps you meet your specific writing goal.

- Use **chronological order,** or time order, to tell a story or to explain the steps in a process.
- Use **spatial order** to order your description of places, people, and things. You might describe the details in the order you see them— for example, from top to bottom or from near to far.
- Use **order of importance** to show how you rank opinions, facts, or details from the most to least important or the reverse.

Using Transitions Linking words and phrases, called **transitions,** act like bridges between sentences or between paragraphs. Transitions, such as the ones shown below, can make the organization of your paragraphs stronger by showing how ideas are logically related.

To show time order or sequence
after, at the beginning, finally, first, last year, later, meanwhile, next, now, second, sometimes, soon, yesterday

To show spatial relationships
above, ahead, around, at the top, below, beyond, down, here, inside, near, on top of, opposite, outside, over, there, under, within

To show importance or degree
above all, first, furthermore, in addition, mainly, most important, second

Check It Out

For more about transitions, see page 72.

TRY IT OUT

Copy the following paragraph on your paper. Underline the topic sentence. Cross out the sentence that is unrelated to the topic sentence. Add a transition to make a clear connection between two of the sentences.

A local artist creates weird and funny sculptures from fruits and vegetables. First he uses a sharp knife to carve faces that look like animals, such as bears and pigs. He glues on tiny beans to make eyes. Finally he uses beet juice to paint the mouth. Although the process sounds easy, it requires great imagination. The octopus sculpted from a banana is the silliest work of art I've ever seen.

Writing Good Compositions

A composition is a short paper made up of several paragraphs, with a clear introduction, body, and conclusion. A good composition presents a clear, complete message about a specific topic. Ideas flow logically from one sentence to the next and from one paragraph to the next.

Making a Plan

The suggestions in the chart below can help you shape the information in each part of your composition to suit your writing purpose.

Introductory Paragraph

Your introduction should interest readers in your topic and capture their attention. You may

- give background
- use a quotation
- ask a question
- tell an anecdote, or brief story

Include a **thesis statement,** a sentence or two stating the main idea you will develop in the composition.

Body Paragraphs

Elaborate on your thesis statement in the body paragraphs. You may

- offer proof
- give examples
- explain ideas

Stay focused and keep your body paragraphs on track. Remember to

- develop a single idea in each body paragraph
- arrange the paragraphs in a logical order
- use transitions to link one paragraph to the next

Concluding Paragraph

Your conclusion should bring your composition to a satisfying close. You may

- sum up main points
- tie the ending to the beginning by restating the main idea or thesis in different words
- make a call to action if your goal is to persuade readers

Drafting Tip

You may need two paragraphs to introduce your topic. The first can tell an anecdote; the second can include your thesis statement. See page 847 for an example.

Drafting Tip

A good conclusion follows logically from the rest of the piece of writing and leaves the reader with something to think about. Make sure that you do not introduce new or unrelated material in a conclusion.

Using the 6+1 Trait® Model

What are some basic terms you can use to discuss your writing with your teacher or classmates? What should you focus on as you revise and edit your compositions? Check out the following seven terms, or traits, that describe the qualities of strong writing. Learn the meaning of each trait and find out how using the traits can improve your writing.

Ideas The message or the theme and the details that develop it

Writing is clear when readers can grasp the meaning of your ideas right away. Check to see whether you're getting your message across.

✔ Does the title suggest the theme of the composition?

✔ Does the composition focus on a single narrow topic?

✔ Is the thesis, or main idea, clearly stated?

✔ Do well-chosen details elaborate the main idea?

Organization The arrangement of main points and supporting details

A good plan of organization steers your readers in the right direction and guides them easily through your composition—from start to finish. Find a structure, or order, that best suits your topic and writing purpose. Check to see whether you've ordered your key ideas and details in a way that keeps your readers on track.

✔ Are the beginning, middle, and end clearly linked?

✔ Is the order of ideas easy to follow?

✔ Does the introduction capture your readers' attention?

✔ Do sentences and paragraphs flow from one to the next in a way that makes sense?

✔ Does the conclusion wrap up the composition?

Voice A writer's unique way of using tone and style

Your writing voice comes through when your readers sense that a real person is communicating with them. Readers will respond to the **tone,** or the attitude, that you express toward a topic and to the **style,** the way that you use language and write sentences. Read your work aloud to see whether your writing voice comes through.

✔ Does your writing sound interesting when you read it aloud?

✔ Does your writing show what you think about your topic?

✔ Does your writing sound like you—or does it sound like you're imitating someone else?

Revising Tip

Use the cut-and-paste features of your word processing program to experiment with the structure—the arrangement of sentences or paragraphs. Choose the clearest, most logical order for your final draft.

Word Choice The vocabulary a writer uses to convey meaning

Words work hard. They carry the weight of your meaning, so make sure you choose them carefully. Check to see whether the words you choose are doing their jobs well.

- ✔ Do you use lively verbs to show action?
- ✔ Do you use vivid words to create word pictures in your readers' minds?
- ✔ Do you use precise words to explain your ideas simply and clearly?

Sentence Fluency The smooth rhythm and flow of sentences that vary in length and style

The best writing is made up of sentences that flow smoothly from one sentence to the next. Writing that is graceful also sounds musical—rhythmical rather than choppy. Check for sentence fluency by reading your writing aloud.

- ✔ Do your sentences vary in length and structure?
- ✔ Do transition words and phrases show connections between ideas and sentences?
- ✔ Does parallelism help balance and unify related ideas?

Conventions Correct spelling, grammar, usage, and mechanics

A composition free of errors makes a good impression on your readers. Mistakes can be distracting, and they can blur your message. Try working with a partner to spot errors and correct them. Use this checklist to help you.

- ✔ Are all words spelled correctly?
- ✔ Are all proper nouns—as well as the first word of every sentence— capitalized?
- ✔ Is your composition free of sentence fragments?
- ✔ Is your composition free of run-on sentences?
- ✔ Are punctuation marks—such as apostrophes, commas, and end marks— inserted in the right places?

Presentation The way words and design elements look on a page

Appearance matters, so make your compositions inviting to read. Handwritten papers should be neat and legible. If you're using a word processor, double-space the lines of text and choose a readable font. Other design elements—such as boldfaced headings, bulleted lists, pictures, and charts—can help you present information effectively as well as make your papers look good.

Revising Tip

Listen carefully to the way your sentences sound when someone else reads them aloud. If you don't like what you hear, revise for sentence fluency. You might try adding variety to your sentence openers or combining sentences to make them sound less choppy.

Check It Out

See the Troubleshooter, pages 308–331, for help in correcting common errors in your writing.

Evaluating a Composition Read this sample composition, which has been evaluated using the 6+1 Trait® model.

Organization Attention-getting introduction includes a thesis statement, which clearly expresses the main idea.

Word Choice Scientific terms convey precise information.

Organization Transitions at the start of each body paragraph signal that key points are arranged in order of importance.

Ideas Details, facts, and examples support key points.

Sentence Fluency Variety of sentence types provides smooth and effortless rhythm.

Voice Writer's values and attitude toward the topic shine through.

Conventions The composition is free of errors in spelling, grammar, usage, and mechanics.

The Treasures of the Rain Forest

Do you ever wonder what incredible discoveries might result from exploring other worlds? Are there miraculous cures for healing the sick? Are there delicious foods that could improve our diets? Are there animals too beautiful to imagine? You don't have to travel through outer space to find this promising but unknown world. It's right here on Earth: It's the rain forest—a warm, lush, and soggy region located mostly in countries near the equator. We have only begun to uncover the treasures of the rain forest and to recognize its many benefits.

First, we know that many rain forest plants provide substances helpful in treating illnesses. For example, the bark of a plant found in Latin America contains a chemical used to treat illnesses such as multiple sclerosis and Parkinson's disease. This same chemical has pain-killing qualities, making it a good drug to use during some kinds of surgery. Madagascar's rosy periwinkle contains two important chemicals that slow the growth of tumors. Wild yams from Mexico and Guatemala are used to make a drug for treating certain diseases, including some forms of cancer.

Second, we know that the rain forest is a source of countless foods that either taste great or keep you healthy. The list of foods that would satisfy hungry teenagers seems endless. Favorite snack foods with ingredients that originally came from the rain forest include chocolate, popcorn, peanuts, cashew nuts, colas, and salsa. Fruits from the rain forest include bananas, pineapples, lemons, coconuts, and avocados.

Finally, we know that as many as 50 million different kinds of animals live in various rain forests. Millions of these animals have no names because scientists haven't identified the animals yet. This number includes animals so tiny you can see them only with a microscope. Brilliantly colored butterflies and birds, jaguars, gorillas, and boas are just some of the animals you would see if you explored rain forests around the world.

All treasures are precious, and the treasures of the rain forest are no exception. These treasures bring important benefits that continue to increase as we learn more about this promising but little-known world.

Writing Good Research Papers

A research paper reports facts and ideas gathered from various sources about a specific topic. A good research paper blends information from reliable sources with the writer's original thoughts and ideas. The final draft follows a standard format for presenting information and citing sources.

Exploring a Variety of Sources

Once you've narrowed the topic of your research paper, you'll need to hunt for the best information. You might start by reading an encyclopedia article on your topic to learn some basic information. Then widen your search to include both primary and secondary sources.

- **Primary sources** are records of events by the people who witnessed them. Examples include diaries, letters, speeches, photos, posters, interviews, and radio and TV news broadcasts that include eyewitness interviews.
- **Secondary sources** contain information that is often based on primary sources. The creators of secondary sources conduct original research and then report their findings. Examples include encyclopedias, textbooks, biographies, magazine articles, Web site articles, and educational films.

When you find a secondary source that you can use for your report, check to see whether the author has given credit to his or her sources of information in **footnotes, endnotes,** or a **bibliography.** Tracking down such sources can lead you to more information you can use.

If you're exploring your topic on the Internet, look for Web sites that are sponsored by government institutions, famous museums, and reliable organizations. If you find a helpful site, check to see whether it contains links to other Web sites you can use.

Evaluating Sources

As you conduct your research, do a little detective work and investigate the sources you find. Begin by asking some key questions so you can decide whether you've tracked down reliable resources that are suitable for your purpose. Some important questions to ask about your sources are listed in the box on the next page.

> **Research Tip**
>
> Look for footnotes at the bottom of a page. Look for endnotes at the end of a chapter or a book. Look for a bibliography at the end of a book.

Ask Questions About Your Sources

✔ **Is the information useful?**
Find sources that are closely related to your research topic.

✔ **Is the information easy to understand?**
Look for sources that are geared toward readers your age.

✔ **Is the information new enough?**
Look for sources that were recently published if you need the most current facts and figures.

✔ **Is the information trustworthy and true?**
Check to see whether the author documents the source of facts and supports opinions with reasons and evidence. Also check out the background of the authors. They should be well-known experts on the topic that you're researching.

✔ **Is the information balanced and fair?**
Read with a critical eye. Does the source try to persuade readers with a one-sided presentation of information? Or is the source balanced, approaching a topic from various perspectives? Be on the lookout for **propaganda** and for sources that reflect an author's **bias,** or prejudice. Make sure that you learn about a topic from more than one angle by reviewing several sources of information.

Giving Credit Where Credit Is Due

When you write a research paper, you support your own ideas with information that you've gleaned from your primary and secondary sources. But presenting someone else's ideas as if they were your own is **plagiarism,** a form of cheating. You can avoid plagiarism by citing, or identifying, the sources of your information within the text of your paper. The chart below tells what kinds of information you do and don't need to cite in your paper.

DO credit the source of . . .	DON'T credit the source of . . .
• direct quotations • summaries and paraphrases, or restatements, of someone else's viewpoints, original ideas, and conclusions • photos, art, charts, and other visuals • little-known facts or statistics	• information that can be found in many places—dates, facts, ideas, and concepts that are considered common knowledge • your own unique ideas

Citing Sources Within Your Paper The most common method of crediting sources is with parenthetical documentation within the text. Generally a reference to the source and page number is included in parentheses at the end of each quotation, paraphrase, or summary of information borrowed from a source. An in-text citation points readers to a corresponding entry in your **works-cited list**—a list of all your sources, complete with publication information, that will appear as the final page of your paper. The Modern Language Association (MLA) recommends the following guidelines for crediting sources in text.

- **Put in parentheses the author's last name and the page number where you found the information.**
  Until then, some women had worked in clothing factories (Appleby, Brinkley, and McPherson 308–309).

- **If the author's name is mentioned in the sentence, put only the page number in parentheses.**
  According to Appleby, Brinkley, and McPherson, some women had worked in clothing factories until then (308–309).

- **If no author is listed, put the title or a shortened version of the title in parentheses. Include a page number if you have one.**
  All able-bodied citizens, including women, should go to work in jobs that would help the war effort ("Office").

Check It Out

Study the sample research paper on pages 847–848 to see the relationship between parenthetical documentation and a works-cited list.

Preparing the Final Draft

Ask your teacher how to format the final draft. Most English teachers will ask you to follow the MLA guidelines listed below.

- Put a heading in the upper left-hand corner of the first page with your name, your teacher's name, and the date on separate lines.
- Center the title on the line below the heading.
- Number the pages one-half inch from the top in the right-hand corner. After page one, put your last name before the page number.
- Set one-inch margins on all sides of every page; double-space the lines of text.
- Include an alphabetized, double-spaced works-cited list as the last page of your final draft. All sources noted in parenthetical citations in the paper must be listed.

On the next three pages, you'll find sample style sheets that can help you prepare the list of sources—the final page of the research paper. Use the one your teacher prefers.

MLA Style

MLA style is most often used in English and social studies classes. Center the title *Works Cited* at the top of your list.

Source	Style
Book with one author	Price-Groff, Claire. *The Manatee.* Farmington Hills: Lucent, 1999.
Book with two or three authors	Tennant, Alan, Gerard T. Salmon, and Richard B. King. *Snakes of North America.* Lanham: Lone Star Books, 2003. [If a book has more than three authors, name only the first author and then write "et al." (Latin abbreviation for "and others").]
Book with an editor	Follett, C. B., ed. *Grrrrr: A Collection of Poems About Bears.* Sausalito: Arctos, 2000.
Book with organization or group as author or editor	National Air and Space Museum. *The Official Guide to the Smithsonian Air and Space Museum.* Washington: Smithsonian Institution Press, 2002.
Work from an anthology	Soto, Gary. "To Be a Man." *Hispanic American Literature: An Anthology.* Ed. Rodolfo Cortina. Lincolnwood: NTC, 1998. 340–341.
Introduction in a published book	Weintraub, Stanley. Introduction. *Great Expectations.* By Charles Dickens. New York: Signet, 1998. v–xii.
Encyclopedia article	"Whales." *World Book Encyclopedia.* 2003.
Weekly magazine article	Trillin, Calvin. "Newshound." *New Yorker* 29 Sept. 2003: 70–81.
Monthly magazine article	Knott, Cheryl. "Code Red." *National Geographic* Oct. 2003: 76–81.
Online magazine article	Rauch, Jonathan. "Will Frankenfood Save the Planet?" *Atlantic Online* 292.3 (Oct. 2003). 15 Dec. 2003 <http://www.theatlantic.com/issues/2003/10/rauch.htm>.
Newspaper article	Bertram, Jeffrey. "African Bees: Fact or Myth?" *Orlando Sentinel* 18 Aug. 1999: D2.
Unsigned article	"Party-Line Snoops." *Washington Post* 24 Sept. 2003: A28.
Internet	"Manatees." *SeaWorld/Busch Gardens Animal Information Database.* 2002. Busch Entertainment Corp. 3 Oct. 2003 <http://www.seaworld.org/infobooks/Manatee/home.html>.
Radio or TV program	"Orcas." *Champions of the Wild.* Animal Planet. Discovery Channel. 21 Oct. 2003.
Videotape or DVD	*Living with Tigers.* DVD. Discovery, 2003. [For a videotape (VHS) version, replace "DVD" with "Videocassette."]
Interview	Salinas, Antonia. E-mail interview. 23–24 Oct. 2003. [If an interview takes place in person, replace "E-mail" with "Personal"; if it takes place on the telephone, use "Telephone."]

CMS Style

CMS style was created by the University of Chicago Press to meet its publishing needs. This style, which is detailed in *The Chicago Manual of Style* (CMS), is used in a number of subject areas. Center the title *Bibliography* at the top of your list.

Source	Style
Book with one author	Price-Groff, Claire. *The Manatee.* Farmington Hills, MI: Lucent, 1999.
Book with multiple authors	Tennant, Alan, Gerard T. Salmon, and Richard B. King. *Snakes of North America.* Lanham, TX: Lone Star Books, 2003. [For a book with more than ten authors, name only the first seven authors and then write "et al." (Latin abbreviation for "and others").]
Book with an editor	Follett, C. B., ed. *Grrrrr: A Collection of Poems About Bears.* Sausalito, CA: Arctos, 2000.
Book with organization or group as author or editor	National Air and Space Museum. *The Official Guide to the Smithsonian Air and Space Museum.* Washington, DC: Smithsonian Institution Press, 2002.
Work from an anthology	Soto, Gary. "To Be a Man." *Hispanic American Literature: An Anthology,* edited by Rodolfo Cortina, 340–341. Lincolnwood, IL: NTC, 1998.
Introduction in a published book	Dickens, Charles. *Great Expectations.* New introduction by Stanley Weintraub. New York: Signet, 1998.
Encyclopedia article	[Credit for encyclopedia articles goes in your text, not in your bibliography.]
Weekly magazine article	Trillin, Calvin. "Newshound." *New Yorker,* September 29, 2003, 70–81.
Monthly magazine article	Knott, Cheryl. "Code Red." *National Geographic,* October 2003, 76–81.
Online magazine article	Rauch, Jonathan. "Will Frankenfood Save the Planet?" *Atlantic Online* 292, no. 3 (October 2003). http://www.theatlantic.com/issues/2003/10/rauch.htm.
Newspaper article	[Credit for newspaper articles goes in your text, not in your bibliography.]
Unsigned article	[Credit for unsigned newspaper articles goes in your text, not in your bibliography.]
Internet	Busch Entertainment Corp. "Manatees." *SeaWorld/Busch Gardens Animal Information Database.* http://www.seaworld.org/infobooks/Manatee/home.html.
Radio or TV program	[Credit for radio and TV programs goes in your text, not in your bibliography.]
Videotape or DVD	*Living with Tigers.* Discovery, 2003. DVD. [For a videotape (VHS) version, replace "DVD" with "Videocassette."]
Interview	[Credit for interviews goes in your text, not in your bibliography.]

APA Style

The American Psychological Association (APA) style is commonly used in the sciences. Center the title *References* at the top of your list.

Source	Style
Book with one author	Price-Groff, Claire. (1999). *The manatee.* Farmington Hills, MI: Lucent.
Book with multiple authors	Tennant, A., Salmon, G. T., & King, R. B. (2003). *Snakes of North America.* Lanham, TX: Lone Star Books. [For a book with more than six authors, name only the first six authors and then write "et al." (Latin abbreviation for "and others").]
Book with an editor	Follett, C. B. (Ed.). (2000). *Grrrrr: A collection of poems about bears.* Sausalito, CA: Arctos.
Book with organization or group as author or editor	National Air and Space Museum. (2002). *The official guide to the Smithsonian Air and Space Museum.* Washington, DC: Smithsonian Institution Press.
Work from an anthology	Soto, G. (1998). To be a man. In R. Cortina (Ed.), *Hispanic American literature: An anthology* (pp. 340–341). Lincolnwood, IL: NTC.
Introduction in a published book	[Credit for introductions goes in your text, not in your references.]
Encyclopedia article	Whales. (2003). In *World Book encyclopedia.* Chicago: World Book.
Weekly magazine article	Trillin, C. (2003, September 29). Newshound. *The New Yorker,* 70–81.
Monthly magazine article	Knott, C. (2003, October). Code red. *National Geographic, 204,* 76–81.
Online magazine article	Rauch, J. (2003, October). Will Frankenfood save the planet? *Atlantic Online, 292.* Retrieved from http://www.theatlantic.com/issues/2003/10/rauch.htm
Newspaper article	Bertram, J. (1999, August 18). African bees: Fact or myth? *The Orlando Sentinel,* p. D2.
Unsigned article	Party-line snoops. (2003, September 24). *The Washington Post,* p. A28.
Internet	Busch Entertainment Corp. (2003). Manatees. In *SeaWorld/Busch Gardens animal information database.* Retrieved October 3, 2003, from http://www.seaworld.org/infobooks/Manatee/home.html
Radio or TV program	Orcas. (2003, October 21). *Champions of the wild* [Television series episode]. Animal Planet. Silver Spring, MD: Discovery Channel.
Videotape or DVD	*Living with tigers.* (2003). [DVD]. Discovery. [For a videotape (VHS) version, replace "DVD" with "Videocassette."]
Interview	[Credit for interviews goes in your text, not in your references.]

Evaluating a Research Paper Read this sample research paper, which has been evaluated using the 6+1 Trait® model.

Rosie the Riveter

If you had been alive during World War II, you would have seen posters on the walls of banks, post offices, and other public places of a young American woman wearing overalls and carrying a wrench or a rivet gun in her hand. Who was this woman, and why was her image seen all over town?

Organization The opening paragraph captures readers' attention and makes them curious about the subject.

The woman in the posters was known as Rosie the Riveter. She was one of the most famous women in the United States in the early 1940s. She was a made-up character. But her name—and her image—may have been based on a real woman named Rosie Bonavita, who was part of a two-woman crew that set more than three thousand rivets in a record six hours (*Our Glorious* 218). Even though the Rosie in the posters wasn't a real person, she set a powerful example for women during the war. She called on them to serve their country by doing jobs they had never done before.

Ideas The ideas give important background information. A thesis statement clearly tells the main point or central idea.

During World War II, millions of men left their jobs to fight for their country. While they were away, somebody had to fill their jobs to keep the country running. Who could do peacetime jobs like driving buses? Who could do special wartime jobs like making weapons? The country needed women to go to work, and that's where Rosie and the Office of War Information, or OWI, came in.

Sentence Fluency These two questions are a good example of parallelism.

The OWI was created by the U.S. government in 1942. One of the OWI's many tasks was to run an advertising campaign. They weren't selling a product, though. They were selling an idea: All able-bodied citizens, including women, should go to work in jobs that would help the war effort ("Office"). Until then, some women had worked in clothing factories (Appleby, Brinkley, and McPherson 308–309). But posters of Rosie that were created by the OWI helped convince women that they could play an important part in the war effort here at home. They could do men's work, and they could do it well.

Ideas Carefully chosen details support the paragraph's main idea. The writer uses parenthetical citations (MLA style) to document the sources of information.

The posters featuring Rosie at work were created by famous American painters who were hired by the advertising designers in the OWI. One poster showed a confident and muscular Rosie, eating a sandwich and holding a rivet gun in her lap. Another poster showed a more delicate Rosie holding a wrench and thinking of her husband off fighting the war. Different posters portrayed Rosie in slightly different ways, but they all had the same purpose. They all challenged women to do their patriotic duty. The posters sent the message that women could help the United States win the war by performing jobs that traditionally had been done by men.

Voice The writer's attitude toward the topic shines through.

Sentence Fluency Sentences vary in length and structure, and the writing flows smoothly and easily.

(continued)

Word Choice A direct quotation supports the main idea of the paragraph. It makes the information seem more trustworthy.

Organization The conclusion ties the ending to the beginning. Using different words, it repeats the idea set out in the thesis statement.

Presentation A properly formatted works-cited list is part of every good research report. This one follows MLA style (see page 844). Remember to double-space your entire report and to put your works-cited list on a separate sheet of paper.

Conventions The composition is free of errors in grammar, usage, spelling, and mechanics.

More than six million women met the challenge ("Rosie"). Women learned many new skills, such as welding, hammering, and—of course—riveting. Joining the work force during the war changed many women's lives. One of these women, Jane Ward Mayta, said, "I learned a lot in those years. . . . I learned to look for a job. I learned to get along with and mingle with people from totally different backgrounds. We were all in little pockets before then" (Wise and Wise 12).

In 1945 World War II came to an end. Men who returned from the war expected to return to their old jobs. As a result, many women had to leave their factory jobs. But the example set by Rosie the Riveter would continue to inspire women in the years that followed. Women now had a real choice about whether they would work outside the home. They also had more choices about the kinds of work they would do, since more jobs were open to them. As the Web page for the American Airpower Heritage Museum says, "Lasting social changes were brought about by the fact that women began working outside the home" ("Rosie"). To this day, the symbol of Rosie the Riveter hard at work remains a real inspiration for generations of women.

Works Cited

Appleby, Joyce, Alan Brinkley, and James M. McPherson. *The American Journey.* New York: Glencoe/McGraw-Hill, 2000.

"The Office of War Information Was Created June 13, 1942." *America's Story from America's Library.* Library of Congress. 22 Oct. 2003 <http://www.americaslibrary.gov/cgi-bin/page.cgi/jb/wwii/owi_1>.

Our Glorious Century: Key Events, Pictures, Places, Personalities, Milestones, Memories, Lifestyles, Traditions, Insights. New York: Reader's Digest, 1995.

"Rosie the Riveter: Women Join the Industrial Workforce." *American Airpower Heritage Museum.* 4 Dec. 1999. American Airpower Heritage Museum. 21 Oct. 2003 <http://www.airpowermuseum.org/trrosier.html>.

Wise, Nancy Baker, and Christy Wise. *A Mouthful of Rivets: Women at Work in World War II.* San Francisco: Jossey-Bass, 1994.

INDEX

Commercials, 785–787
Common nouns, 381
Compact discs (CDs), 656
Comparative form
  adjectives, 243, 461
  adverbs, 467
Comparing two creative
  processes, 49
Comparison-and-contrast essay,
  204, 210–213, 244
  drafting, 211
  editing, 243
  organizing, 212, 814
  Venn diagram, 211, 213, 244
Comparison of modifiers
  comparative degree, 243, 461,
    467, 813
  irregular, 461, 467
  positive degree, 461, 467
  superlative degree, 243, 461, 467,
    813
Comparisons
  as context clue, 668
  double, 461
Complement, 814. See also Direct
  object; Indirect objects
Complete predicates, 363, 505
Complete sentence, 361
Complete subjects, 363, 505
Complex sentences, 507, 820
  diagraming, 545
  main clauses, 507
  subordinate clauses, 507
Compound adjectives, hyphens
  with, 613
Compound nouns
  forming plural of, 383
  hyphens in, 613
Compound numbers, hyphens
  in, 613
Compound objects, 403, 405
  diagraming, 576
  pronouns in, 439
Compound predicates, 367
  diagraming, 576
Compound prepositions, 481
Compound sentences, 369, 505, 820
  commas in, 271, 505
  conjunctions in, 487
  diagraming, 577
  semicolons in, 505, 607
Compound subjects, 367, 487
  diagraming, 576
  pronouns in, 439
  and subject-verb agreement, 549
Compound words, 667, 686
Computer catalog, 646

Computer, 796–812. See also Internet; Using Computers; Word
  processing
  catalog, in library, 646
  CD, 811
  DVD, 811
  e-mail, 807–808
  hyperlink, 799
  Internet, 655, 796–810
  removable storage, 811
  search engine, 800–802
  Troubleshooting Guide, 805
  Univac, 796
  viruses, 809
Conceptual map, 814
Conclusion, of a report, 203, 236,
  814, 837
Concrete nouns, 158, 381
Conflict, 814
Conjugation of verbs, 409, 411, 413,
  415, 541
Conjunctions, 814–815
  in compound sentences, 369
  coordinating, 369, 487, 549, 607,
    814–815
  correlative, 369, 487, 549,
    814–815
  and sentence combining, 635
  subordinating, 513, 603, 635
Conjunctive adverbs, 489, 505, 607
  commas after, 601
Connotation, 814
Constructive criticism, 815
Context clues, 668–669, 723, 815
Contexts for writing. See Writing
  prompts
Contractions, 387, 441, 471, 611
  distinguishing from preposition,
    441, 611
  double negatives, 471
Contrast, as context clue, 668
Conventions, 81, 815, 839, 847. See
  also Grammar Link;
  Mechanics; Spelling
Cooperative learning, 57, 61, 69, 85,
  117, 121, 125, 159, 171, 183,
  209, 217, 221, 225, 229, 233,
  237, 241
Coordinating conjunctions, 369,
  487, 549, 814
  diagraming, 576–577
Correlative conjunctions, 487, 549,
  814–815
Creative writing, 125, 163, 167, 171,
  173, 175, 183, 243
Credibility, 274–276, 815
Critical listening, 755–759

Critical thinking
  analyzing cause and effect,
    218–220
  analyzing essay questions,
    222–224, 721
  analyzing tasks, 701–705
  constructing arguments,
    266–267, 270–272, 274–276,
    278–280, 282–284, 290–292
  drawing conclusions, 306
  evaluating arguments, 266,
    274–276, 287–288
  evaluating details, 206–207
  evaluating literature, 294–296
  inferring meaning, 95
  ordering details logically,
    126–128, 132, 160–162,
    203–208, 210–212, 216, 220,
    234–236, 244, 280, 706–712
Cross-curricular writing topics
  art, 19, 73, 117, 129, 225, 245,
    269, 297
  health and physical education, 23,
    213, 273
  history, 11, 159, 163, 175, 183,
  math, 49
  music, 65
  science, 221, 289
  social studies, 133

D

Dates
  apostrophe to show missing
    numbers in, 611
  capitalization of, 589
  commas in, 605
  numerals in, 617
Days, capitalization of, 589
Declarative sentences, 359, 599, 815
  diagraming, 572
Deductive reasoning, 815
Definite articles, 459, 813
Definitions,
  in dictionary, 657–660
  in expository writing, 204
Demonstrative adjectives, 463, 813
Demonstrative pronouns, 447, 463
Denotation, 815
Dependent clauses. See subordinate
  clauses
Descriptive writing, 108, 149, 815
  describing subject of a
    biography, 134–137
  describing things, 130–133
  details in, 111–112, 118–121,
    126–129, 131, 132, 138

ACKNOWLEDGMENTS

Text

UNIT ONE Reprinted by permission of Simon & Schuster, from *The Lost Garden* by Laurence Yep. Copyright © 1991 by Laurence Yep.

"Jukebox Showdown" by Victor Hernandez Cruz. Copyright © 1976 by Victor Hernandez Cruz. Reprinted by permission of Random House, Inc.

"One Last Time" by Gary Soto is from *Living Up the Street* (Laurel Leaf Books, Bantam Doubleday Dell 1992). Copyright © 1985 by Gary Soto. Used by permission of the author.

UNIT TWO "The Game" from *Fast Sam, Cool Clyde, and Stuff* by Walter Dean Myers. Copyright © 1975 by Walter Dean Myers. Reprinted by permission of Viking Penguin, a division of the Penguin Putnam.

UNIT THREE From *How the García Girls Lost Their Accents.* Copyright © 1991 by Julia Alvarez. Published by Plume, an imprint of Dutton Signet, a division of Penguin USA, Inc., and originally in hardcover by Algonquin Books of Chapel Hill. Reprinted by permission of Susan Bergholz Literary Services, New York. All rights reserved.

From *Thrashin' Time* by David Weitzman. Copyright © 1991 by David Weitzman. Reprinted by permission of David R. Godine, Publisher, Inc.

UNIT FOUR From *Lyddie* by Katherine Paterson. Copyright © 1991 by Katherine Paterson. Reprinted by permission of Penguin Putnam, Inc.

UNIT FIVE "Fall" by Sally Andersen from *A New Treasury of Children's Poetry: Old Favorites and New Discoveries* edited by Joanna Cole. Copyright © 1984 by Joanna Cole. Published by Doubleday & Company.

"The Vision of Maya Ying Lin" from *Always to Remember* by Brent Ashabranner. Copyright © 1988. Reprinted by permission of Penguin Putnam.

UNIT SIX From *Silent Spring* by Rachel Carson. Copyright © 1978. Reprinted by permission of Houghton Mifflin Company. All rights reserved.

Photo

Part 1 Ed Meneely/Art Resource, NY; **1** Christie's Images/SuperStock; **2-3** Alloy Photography/Veer; **5 6** Laurence Yep; **8** Inti St Clair/Blend Images/Getty Images; **9 10** Allan Landau; **11** Leonard Von Matt/Buochs Switzerland; **12** Allan Landau; **16** Art Wise; **18** Widstock/Alamy, Ulrich Baumgarten/vario images/Alamy, Denis Scott/CORBIS, DAL/Jupiterimages; **20** CORBIS; **24** Courtesy Ray Vinella; **26** JGI/Blend Images/Alamy; **28** Tony Freeman/PhotoEdit; **32** Agricultural Research Service, USDA; **33** Courtesy Susan Moore; **35** Courtesy Anthony Ortega; **36** Agricultural Research Service, USDA; **40-41** © Frithjof Hirdes/zefa/CORBIS; **43** Courtesy Kurtis Productions, Ltd.; **46** Judith Collins/Alamy; **49** Courtesy Claes Oldenburg Studio; **50** Art Wise; **53** Collection of the Grand Rapids Art Museum; **54** Art Wise; **56** Dorling Kindersley/Getty Images; **58** Peter Dazeley/Getty Images; **62** Jeff Dunn/Stock Boston; **64** Larry Kolvoord/The Image Works; **65** Located in San Francisco at the Pacific Stock Exchange; **66** Art Wise; **70** (l) Barbra Alper/Stock Boston, (r) Charles Fell/Stock Boston; **73** The Jamison Galleries, Santa Fe, NM; **74 78** Art Wise; **82 84** Art Wise; **86** Tom McCarthy/PhotoEdit; **89** Glennon Donohue/Getty Images; **90-91** file photo; **92** Red Grooms/ARS; **108-109** © Norbert Wu/Getty Images; **110** Tad Merrick; **111 112** Ralph J. Brunke; **114** Picnic in Washington Park, Pat Thomas, Milwaukee, WI, Acrylic over oil on masonite. Dated 1975. 20 x 27. Collection of the Museum of American Folk Art, New York City; **115** Robert Frerck/Odyssey Productions, Chicago; **117** Courtesy American Federation of the Arts; **118** St. Louis Art Museum; **119 122** Allan Landau; **123** (l) Cindy Brodie, (r) Alex Murdoch; **126** Erich Lessing/Art Resource, NY; **129** Courtesy Nancy Hoffman Gallery; **130** Allan Landau; **134** Bettmann/CORBIS; **136** Princeton University Library; **138** Bob Daemmrich/The Image Works; **143** From *Thrashin' Time: Harvest Days in the Dakotas* © 1991 by David Weitzman. Reprinted by permission of David R. Godine, Publisher, Inc.; **145** The Metropolitan Museum of Art, George A. Hearn Fund, 1943; **150-151** Corbis Photography/Veer; **152 153 154** Tom Green; **156** Hampton University Museum; **157** CORBIS; **160** Art Wise; **162** Naper Settlement Village Museum; **164** Vernon Merritt/Black Star; **165** © RICK WILKING/Reuters/CORBIS; **168** Robert Miller Gallery, New York; **171** Courtesy Hughie Lee-Smith; **172** Courtesy June Kelly Gallery, New York, photo by Manu Sassoonian; **174** Giraudon/Art Resource, New York; **176** Neal Hamburg; **178** Focus on Sports; **180** (t)CORBIS, (b)Joe Viesti/Viesti and Associates; **182** David Young-Wolff/PhotoEdit; **184** Tom Prettyman/PhotoEdit; **189** Erich Lessing/Art Resource, NY; **191** Manchester City Art Galleries; **196-197** © Brian Stablyk/ Getty Images; **198** Courtesy Gary McLain; **199** Greg Probst/Allstock; **200** (l)Courtesy Cherokee Historical Association,(c) Stephen Trimble,(r) Art Wise; **202** Clark Mischler/Alaska Stock Images; **206** Art Wise; **207** The Museum of Fine Arts, Houston. Museum purchase with funds provided by Panhandle Eastern Corporation; **208** CORBIS; **210 214** Art Wise; **218** Edith G. Haun/Stock Boston; **219** Culver Pictures; **222 224** Jim Pickerell/The Image Works; **226** William Lishman & Associates; **230** Art Wise; **234** CALVIN & HOBBES © 1992 Watterson. Reprinted with permission of Universal Press Syndicate. All rights reserved.; **238** Sharon Hoogstranten; **242** Jack Wilburn/Animals Animals; **249** Tom Wurl/Stock Boston; **251** Bill Barley/SuperStock; **255** David M. Doody/Uniphoto; **260-261** © Robert W. Kelley/Stringer/Getty Images; **262** Art Wise; **263** Courtesy Indira Freitas Johnson; **264** (t)Courtesy Indira Freitas Johnson, (b) Ralph Burke; **266** Historical Pictures/Stock Montage; **268** David Young-Wolff/PhotoEdit; **269** Courtesy Bernice Steinbaum Gallery; **270** (t)Leonard Lee Rue III/Stock Boston, (b) Herb Snitzer/Stock Boston; **276** Art Wise; **278** CALVIN & HOBBES © 1986 Watterson. Reprinted with permission of United Press Syndicate. All Rights Reserved; **279** Art Wise; **282** R. Fukuhara/CORBIS; **286** Courtesy Brookfield Zoo; **288** Art Wise; **289** Faith Ringgold; **290** Art Wise; **291** Mitchell B. Reibel/Sports Photo Masters, Inc.; **292 294** Art Wise; **296** Alain De Garsmeur/Getty Images; **297** US Department of the Interior/Indian Arts and crafts Board/Southern Plains Indian Museum and Crafts Center; **301** Dean Abramson/Stock Boston; **303** Phyllis Kind Gallery, New York/Chicago; **308-309** © Gary S Chapman/Getty Images; **356 357** Bridgeman Art Library; **359** Courtesy Museum of Fine Arts, Boston. Gift of W.G. Russell Allen; **377** Courtesy Nancy Hoffman Gallery, New York; **389** Myrleen Ferguson, PhotoEdit; **397** Henri Matisse, *La Negresse*, Ailsa Mellon Bruce Fund, © 1992 National Gallery of Art,

Washington, 1952. Collage on canvas/paper collage on canvas, 4.539" x 6.233"; **401** Rhonda Sidney/Stock Boston; **431 453** Phyllis Kind Gallery, New York/Chicago; **469** Dennis Stock/Magnum; **478** The Metropolitan Museum of Art, Fletcher Fund, Rogers Fund, and Bequest of Miss Adelaide Milton de Groot (1876-1967) by exchange, supplemented by gifts from friends of the Museum, 1971.; **491** Joan Messerschmidt/Leo De Wys; **493** Julie Houck/ Getty Images; **501** Courtesy of the artist and Deson Saunders Gallery, Chicago; **511** Focus on Sports; **523** National Museum of American Art, Washington D.C./Art Resource, NY; **538** Paul Macapia/Seattle Art Museum; **545** (t) Jon Riley/ Getty Images,(b) David Young-Wolff/PhotoEdit; **556** Phyllis Kind Gallery, New York/Chicago; **567** Giraudon/Art Resource, NY; **596** Robert Henri, *Portrait of Po Tse (Water Eagle)* Oil on Canvas, 40 x 32 inches. Courtesy Gerald Peters Gallery, Santa Fe NM; **626** Henri Matisse, French, 1869-1954,

Interior at Nice, oil on canvas, 1921, 132.1 x 88.9 cm, Charles H. and Mary F.S. Worcester Collection; **638-639** Scala/Art Resource, NY; **641** Charles Maraia; **642** Cathy Ferris; **647** DAL/Jupiterimages; **651** Cathy Ferris; **653** Allan Landau; **664** Frank Oberle/Photo Resource; **665** Bob Daemmrich/Stock Boston; **666** Richard Pasley/Stock Boston; **675** Steve Bentsen/Natural Selection; **676** Lori Adamski Peek/ Getty Images; **677** (t)George Chan/ Getty Images, (b)Pete Seaward/ Getty Images; **681** David Young-Wolff/PhotoEdit; **695** Ralph J. Brunke; **771** Billy E. Barnes/Stock Boston; **778** George Butler; **781** (t) Rosemary Calvery/ Getty Images, (b) Art Wolfe/ Getty Images; **783** Toles © 1999 The Buffalo News. Reprinted with permission of Universal Press Syndicate. All Rights Reserved; **784** Movie Stills Archives; **789** Superstock; **796** file photo, Doug Martin; **799** file photo.

Proofreading Symbols

⊙	Lieut⊙ Brown	Insert a period.
∧	No one came **to** the party.	Insert a letter or a word.
⌃;	The bell rang⌃ the students left for home.	Insert a semicolon.
≡	I enjoyed paris.	Capitalize a letter.
/	The Class ran a bake sale.	Make a capital letter lowercase.
⌒	The campers are home sick.	Close up a space.
⤶	They visited N.Y. ⤶	Spell out.
⋏	Sue⋏ please help.	Insert a comma.
∩	He enjoyed feild day.	Transpose the position of letters or words.
#	all#together	Insert a space.
⸲	We went to to Boston.	Delete letters or words.
⌄ ⌄	She asked⌄ Who's coming?⌄	Insert quotation marks.
/=/	mid/=/January	Insert a hyphen.
¶	"Where?" asked Karl.¶ "Over there," said Ray.	Begin a new paragraph.
⌄	She liked Sarah⌄s glasses.	Insert an apostrophe.